Novels
for Students

Novels
for Students

**Presenting Analysis, Context and Criticism on
Commonly Studied Novels**

Volume 7

Deborah A. Stanley, Editor

Foreword by Anne Devereaux Jordan, Teaching and Learning Literature

GALE GROUP

Detroit
San Francisco
London
Boston
Woodbridge, CT

National Advisory Board

Novels for Students

Staff

Series Editor: Deborah A. Stanley.

Contributing Editors: Sara L. Constantakis, Catherine L. Goldstein, Motoko Fujishiro Huthwaite, Arlene M. Johnson, Erin White.

Editorial Technical Specialist: Karen Uchic.

Managing Editor: Joyce Nakamura.

Research: Victoria B. Cariappa, *Research Team Manager.* Andy Malonis, *Research Specialist.* Tamara C. Nott, Tracie A. Richardson, and Cheryl L. Warnock, *Research Associates.* Jeffrey Daniels, *Research Assistant.*

Permissions: Susan M. Trosky, *Permissions Manager.* Maria L. Franklin, *Permissions Specialist.* Sarah Chesney, *Permissions Associate.*

Production: Mary Beth Trimper, *Production Director.* Evi Seoud, *Assistant Production Manager.* Cindy Range, *Production Assistant.*

Graphic Services: Randy Bassett, *Image Database Supervisor.* Robert Duncan and Michael Logusz, *Imaging Specialists.* Pamela A. Reed, *Photography Coordinator.* Gary Leach, *Macintosh Artist.*

Product Design: Cynthia Baldwin, *Product Design Manager.* Cover Design: Michelle DiMercurio, *Art Director.* Page Design: Pamela A. E. Galbreath, *Senior Art Director.*

Copyright Notice

Table of Contents

The Informed Dialogue: Interacting with Literature

When we pick up a book, we usually do so with the anticipation of pleasure. We hope that by entering the time and place of the novel and sharing the thoughts and actions of the characters, we will find enjoyment. Unfortunately, this is often not the case; we are disappointed. But we should ask, has the author failed us, or have we failed the author?

We establish a dialogue with the author, the book, and with ourselves when we read. Consciously and unconsciously, we ask questions: "Why did the author write this book?" "Why did the author choose that time, place, or character?" "How did the author achieve that effect?" "Why did the character act that way?" "Would I act in the same way?" The answers we receive depend upon how much information about literature in general and about that book specifically we ourselves bring to our reading.

Young children have limited life and literary experiences. Being young, children frequently do not know how to go about exploring a book, nor sometimes, even know the questions to ask of a book. The books they read help them answer questions, the author often coming right out and *telling* young readers the things they are learning or are expected to learn. The perennial classic, *The Little Engine That Could, tells* its readers that, among other things, it is good to help others and bring happiness:

> "Hurray, hurray," cried the funny little clown and all the dolls and toys. "The good little boys and girls in the city will be happy because you helped us, kind, Little Blue Engine."

In picture books, messages are often blatant and simple, the dialogue between the author and reader one-sided. Young children are concerned with the end result of a book—the enjoyment gained, the lesson learned—rather than with how that result was obtained. As we grow older and read further, however, we question more. We come to expect that the world within the book will closely mirror the concerns of our world, and that the author will *show* these through the events, descriptions, and conversations within the story, rather than *telling* of them. We are now expected to do the interpreting, carry on our share of the dialogue with the book and author, and glean not only the author's message, but comprehend how that message and the overall affect of the book were achieved. Sometimes, however, we need help to do these things. *Novels for Students* provides that help.

A novel is made up of many parts interacting to create a coherent whole. In reading a novel, the more obvious features can be easily spotted—theme, characters, plot—but we may overlook the more subtle elements that greatly influence how the novel is perceived by the reader: viewpoint, mood and tone, symbolism, or the use of humor. By focusing on both the obvious and more subtle literary elements within a novel, *Novels for Students* aids readers in both analyzing for message and in determining how and why that message is communicated. In the discussion on Harper Lee's *To*

Kill a Mockingbird (Vol. 2), for example, the mockingbird as a symbol of innocence is dealt with, among other things, as is the importance of Lee's use of humor which "enlivens a serious plot, adds depth to the characterization, and creates a sense of familiarity and universality." The reader comes to understand the internal elements of each novel discussed—as well as the external influences that help shape it.

"The desire to write greatly," Harold Bloom of Yale University says, "is the desire to be elsewhere, in a time and place of one's own, in an originality that must compound with inheritance, with an anxiety of influence." A writer seeks to create a unique world within a story, but although it is unique, it is not disconnected from our own world. It speaks to us *because* of what the writer brings to the writing from our world: how he or she was raised and educated; his or her likes and dislikes; the events occurring in the real world at the time of the writing, and while the author was growing up. When we know what an author has brought to his or her work, we gain a greater insight into both the "originality" (the world of the book), and the things that "compound" it. This insight enables us to question that created world and find answers more readily. By informing ourselves, we are able to establish a more effective dialogue with both book and author.

Novels for Students, in addition to providing a plot summary and descriptive list of characters—to remind readers of what they have read—also explores the external influences that shaped each book. Each entry includes a discussion of the author's background, and the historical context in which the novel was written. It is vital to know, for instance, that when Ray Bradbury was writing *Fahrenheit 451* (Vol. 1), the threat of Nazi domination had recently ended in Europe, and the McCarthy hearings were taking place in Washington, D.C. This information goes far in answering the question, "Why did he write a story of oppressive government control and book burning?" Similarly, it is important to know that Harper Lee, author of *To Kill a Mockingbird,* was born and raised in Mon-

roeville, Alabama, and that her father was a lawyer. Readers can now see why she chose the south as a setting for her novel—it is the place with which she was most familiar—and start to comprehend her characters and their actions.

Novels for Students helps readers find the answers they seek when they establish a dialogue with a particular novel. It also aids in the posing of questions by providing the opinions and interpretations of various critics and reviewers, broadening that dialogue. Some reviewers of *To Kill A Mockingbird,* for example, "faulted the novel's climax as melodramatic." This statement leads readers to ask, "Is it, indeed, melodramatic?" "If not, why did some reviewers see it as such?" "If it is, why did Lee choose to make it melodramatic?" "Is melodrama ever justified?" By being spurred to ask these questions, readers not only learn more about the book and its writer, but about the nature of writing itself.

The literature included for discussion in the *Novels for Students* series has been chosen because it has something vital to say to us. *Of Mice and Men, Catch-22, The Joy Luck Club, My Antonia, A Separate Peace* and the other novels here speak of life and modern sensibility. In addition to their individual, specific messages of prejudice, power, love or hate, living and dying, however, they and all great literature also share a common intent. They force us to *think*—about life, literature, and about others, not just about ourselves. They pry us from the narrow confines of our minds and thrust us outward to confront the world of books and the larger, real world we all share. *Novels for Students* helps us in this confrontation by providing the means of enriching our conversation with literature and the world, by creating an *informed* dialogue, one that brings true pleasure to the personal act of reading.

Sources

Harold Bloom, *The Western Canon, The Books and School of the Ages,* Riverhead Books, 1994.

Watty Piper, *The Little Engine That Could,* Platt & Munk, 1930.

Anne Devereaux Jordan
Senior Editor, *TALL*
(*Teaching and Learning Literature*)

Introduction

Purpose of the Book

The purpose of *Novels for Students* (*NfS*) is to provide readers with a guide to understanding, enjoying, and studying novels by giving them easy access to information about the work. Part of Gale's "For Students" Literature line, *NfS* is specifically designed to meet the curricular needs of high school and undergraduate college students and their teachers, as well as the interests of general readers and researchers considering specific novels. While each volume contains entries on "classic" novels frequently studied in classrooms, there are also entries containing hard-to-find information on contemporary novels, including works by multicultural, international, and women novelists.

The information covered in each entry includes an introduction to the novel and the novel's author; a plot summary, to help readers unravel and understand the events in a novel; descriptions of important characters, including explanation of a given character's role in the novel as well as discussion about that character's relationship to other characters in the novel; analysis of important themes in the novel; and an explanation of important literary techniques and movements as they are demonstrated in the novel.

In addition to this material, which helps the readers analyze the novel itself, students are also provided with important information on the literary and historical background informing each work. This includes a historical context essay, a box comparing the time or place the novel was written to modern Western culture, a critical overview essay, and excerpts from critical essays on the novel. A unique feature of *NfS* is a specially commissioned overview essay on each novel by an academic expert, targeted toward the student reader.

To further aid the student in studying and enjoying each novel, information on media adaptations is provided, as well as reading suggestions for works of fiction and nonfiction on similar themes and topics. Classroom aids include ideas for research papers and lists of critical sources that provide additional material on the novel.

Selection Criteria

The titles for each volume of *NfS* were selected by surveying numerous sources on teaching literature and analyzing course curricula for various school districts. Some of the sources surveyed included: literature anthologies; *Reading Lists for College-Bound Students: The Books Most Recommended by America's Top Colleges;* textbooks on teaching the novel; a College Board survey of novels commonly studied in high schools; a National Council of Teachers of English (NCTE) survey of novels commonly studied in high schools; the NCTE's *Teaching Literature in High School: The Novel;* and the Young Adult Library Services Association (YALSA) list of best books for young adults of the past twenty-five years.

Input was also solicited from our expert advisory board, as well as educators from various areas. From these discussions, it was determined that each volume should have a mix of "classic" novels (those works commonly taught in literature classes) and contemporary novels for which information is often hard to find. Because of the interest in expanding the canon of literature, an emphasis was also placed on including works by international, multicultural, and women authors. Our advisory board members—current high school teachers—helped pare down the list for each volume. If a work was not selected for the present volume, it was often noted as a possibility for a future volume. As always, the editor welcomes suggestions for titles to be included in future volumes.

How Each Entry Is Organized

Each entry, or chapter, in *NfS* focuses on one novel. Each entry heading lists the full name of the novel, the author's name, and the date of the novel's publication. The following elements are contained in each entry:

- Introduction: a brief overview of the novel which provides information about its first appearance, its literary standing, any controversies surrounding the work, and major conflicts or themes within the work.

- Author Biography: this section includes basic facts about the author's life, and focuses on events and times in the author's life that inspired the novel in question.

- Plot Summary: a description of the major events in the novel, with interpretation of how these events help articulate the novel's themes. Lengthy summaries are broken down with subheads.

- Characters: an alphabetical listing of major characters in the novel. Each character name is followed by a brief to an extensive description of the character's role in the novel, as well as discussion of the character's actions, relationships, and possible motivation.

Characters are listed alphabetically by last name. If a character is unnamed—for instance, the narrator in *Invisible Man* the character is listed as "The Narrator" and alphabetized as "Narrator." If a character's first name is the only one given, the name will appear alphabetically by the name. Variant names are also included for each character. Thus, the full name "Jean Louise Finch" would head the listing for the narrator of *To Kill a Mockingbird,* but listed in a separate cross-reference would be the nickname "Scout Finch."

- Themes: a thorough overview of how the major topics, themes, and issues are addressed within the novel. Each theme discussed appears in a separate subhead, and is easily accessed through the boldface entries in the Subject/Theme Index.

- Style: this section addresses important style elements of the novel, such as setting, point of view, and narration; important literary devices used, such as imagery, foreshadowing, symbolism; and, if applicable, genres to which the work might have belonged, such as Gothicism or Romanticism. Literary terms are explained within the entry, but can also be found in the Glossary.

- Historical and Cultural Context: This section outlines the social, political, and cultural climate *in which the author lived and the novel was created.* This section may include descriptions of related historical events, pertinent aspects of daily life in the culture, and the artistic and literary sensibilities of the time in which the work was written. If the novel is a historical work, information regarding the time in which the novel is set is also included. Each section is broken down with helpful subheads.

- Critical Overview: this section provides background on the critical reputation of the novel, including bannings or any other public controversies surrounding the work. For older works, this section includes a history of how novel was first received and how perceptions of it may have changed over the years; for more recent novels, direct quotes from early reviews may also be included.

- Sources: an alphabetical list of critical material quoted in the entry, with full bibliographical information.

- For Further Study: an alphabetical list of other critical sources which may prove useful for the student. Includes full bibliographical information and a brief annotation.

- Criticism: an essay commissioned by *NfS* which specifically deals with the novel and is written specifically for the student audience, as well as excerpts from previously published criticism on the work.

In addition, each entry contains the following highlighted sections, set apart from the main text as sidebars:

- Media Adaptations: a list of important film and television adaptations of the novel, including source information. The list also includes stage adaptations, audio recordings, musical adaptations, etc.

- Compare and Contrast Box: an "at-a-glance" comparison of the cultural and historical differences between the author's time and culture and late twentieth-century Western culture. This box includes pertinent parallels between the major scientific, political, and cultural movements of the time or place the novel was written, the time or place the novel was set (if a historical work), and modern Western culture. Works written after the mid-1970s may not have this box.

- What Do I Read Next?: a list of works that might complement the featured novel or serve as a contrast to it. This includes works by the same author and others, works of fiction and nonfiction, and works from various genres, cultures, and eras.

• Study Questions: a list of potential study questions or research topics dealing with the novel. This section includes questions related to other disciplines the student may be studying, such as American history, world history, science, math, government, business, geography, economics, psychology, etc.

Other Features

NfS includes "The Informed Dialogue: Interacting with Literature," a foreword by Anne Devereaux Jordan, Senior Editor for *Teaching and Learning Literature* (*TALL*), and a founder of the Children's Literature Association. This essay provides an enlightening look at how readers interact with literature and how *Novels for Students* can help teachers show students how to enrich their own reading experiences.

A Cumulative Author/Title Index lists the authors and titles covered in each volume of the *NfS* series.

A Cumulative Nationality/Ethnicity Index breaks down the authors and titles covered in each volume of the *NfS* series by nationality and ethnicity.

A Subject/Theme Index, specific to each volume, provides easy reference for users who may be studying a particular subject or theme rather than a single work. Significant subjects from events to broad themes are included, and the entries pointing to the specific theme discussions in each entry are indicated in **boldface**.

Each entry has several illustrations, including photos of the author, stills from film adaptations (when available), maps, and/or photos of key historical events.

Citing Novels for Students

When writing papers, students who quote directly from any volume of *Novels for Students* may use the following general forms. These examples are based on MLA style; teachers may request that students adhere to a different style, so the following examples may be adapted as needed.

When citing text from *NfS* that is not attributed to a particular author (i.e., the Themes, Style,

Historical Context sections, etc.), the following format should be used in the bibliography section:

"Night." *Novels for Students.* Eds. Sheryl Ciccarelli and Marie Rose Napierkowski. Vol. 5. Detroit: Gale, 1998. 34–5.

When quoting the specially commissioned essay from *NfS* (usually the first piece under the "Criticism" subhead), the following format should be used:

Miller, Tyrus. Essay on "Winesburg, Ohio." *Novels for Students.* Eds. Sheryl Ciccarelli and Marie Rose Napierkowski. Vol. 5. Detroit: Gale, 1997. 218–9.

When quoting a journal or newspaper essay that is reprinted in a volume of *NfS,* the following form may be used:

Malak, Amin. "Margaret Atwood's The Handmaid's Tale' and the Dystopian Tradition," in *Canadian Literature* , No. 112, Spring, 1987, 9–16; excerpted and reprinted in *Novels for Students,* Vol. 5, eds. Sheryl Ciccarelli and Marie Rose Napierkowski (Detroit: Gale, 1998), pp. 61–64.

When quoting material reprinted from a book that appears in a volume of *NfS,* the following form may be used:

Adams, Timothy Dow. "Richard Wright: Wearing the Mask," in *Telling Lies in Modern American Autobiography* (University of North Carolina Press, 1990), 69–83; excerpted and reprinted in *Novels for Students,* Vol. 5, eds. Sheryl Ciccarelli and Marie Napierkowski (Detroit: Gale, 1999), pp. 59–61.

We Welcome Your Suggestions

The editor of *Novels for Students* welcomes your comments and ideas. Readers who wish to suggest novels to appear in future volumes, or who have other suggestions, are cordially invited to contact the editor. You may contact the editor via e-mail at: **CYA@gale.com@galesmtp.** Or write to the editor at:

Editor, *Novels for Students*
The Gale Group
27500 Drake Rd.
Farmington Hills, MI 48331–3535

Literary Chronology

1694: Voltaire, birth name François-Marie Arouet, is born.

1759: Voltaire's satiric novel *Candide* is published.

1778: Voltaire dies.

1819: Herman Melville is born on August 1, 1819.

1832: Lewis Carroll, birth name Charles Lutwidge Dodgson, is born on January 27, 1832, in Daresbury, Cheshire, England.

1851: Herman Melville's *Moby-Dick* is published. The novel had initially been published in three volumes as *The Whale* (1850).

1865: Lewis Carroll's first novel, *Alice's Adventures in Wonderland*, is published.

1882: James Joyce is born on February 2, 1882, in Dublin, Ireland.

1883: Franz Kafka is born on July 3, 1883, in Prague, Bohemia (now the Czech Republic).

1891: Herman Melville dies in September 1891 of heart failure.

1898: Lewis Carroll dies on January 14, 1898, in Guildford, Surrey, England.

1902: John Steinbeck is born on February 27, 1902, in Salinas Valley, California, an area that served as the setting for many of his best novels.

1903: George Orwell, whose legal name was Eric Arthur Blair, is born at Motihari in Bengal, India, on June 25, 1903.

1908: Richard Wright is born on September 4, 1908, near Natchez, Mississippi.

1915: Herman Wouk is born on May 27, 1915, in New York City, to Abraham Isaac and Esther (Levine) Wouk.

1916: James Joyce's first novel, *A Portrait of the Artist as a Young Man*, is published. The novel was first published serially in *The Egoist* from February 2, 1914 to September 1, 1915.

1924: Franz Kafka dies of tuberculosis, June 3, 1924, in Kierling, Klosterneuberg, Austria.

1925: Franz Kafka's novel *Der Prozess* is published in Germany in 1925. The English translation, *The Trial*, is published in 1935.

1933: Ernest Gaines is born January 15, 1933, in Louisiana.

1939: *The Grapes of Wrath*, published in April, 1939, reaches the top of the best-seller list within two months and remains there throughout the rest of the year.

1940: Richard Wright's first novel, *Native Son*, is published and quickly becomes an influential work in African-American literature.

1941: Anne Tyler is born on October 25, 1941, in Minneapolis, Minnesota.

1941: James Joyce dies following surgery for a perforated ulcer, January 13, 1941, in Zurich, Switzerland.

1944: Fannie Flagg, birth name Patricia Neal, is born on September 21, 1944, in Birmingham, Alabama.

1949: George Orwell's *1984* is published on June 5, 1949, and in its first year sells 45,000 copies in England and over 170,000 copies in the U.S.

1950: Gloria Naylor is born on January 25, 1950, in New York City.

1950: George Orwell dies of tuberculosis on January 21, 1950, at the University of London Hospital, just six months after the publication of his novel *1984*.

1951: Herman Wouk's third novel, *The Caine Mutiny*, is published and quickly becomes a best-seller.

1952: Douglas Adams is born on March 11, 1952, in Cambridge, England.

1952: Herman Wouk receives the Pulitzer Prize in Literature for *The Caine Mutiny*.

1960: Richard Wright dies of a heart attack on November 28, 1960, in Paris, France, and is buried in Paris' Pere Lachaise.

1964: Mohoko "Banana" Yoshimoto is born in July, 1964, in Tokyo, Japan.

1968: On December 20, 1968, John Steinbeck dies of a heart attack in New York City at the age of 66; his ashes are later buried in Salinas, California.

1979: Douglas Adams's first novel, *The Hitchhiker's Guide to the Galaxy*, based on his successful British radio series of the same name, is published.

1985: Anne Tyler's tenth novel, *The Accidental Tourist*, is published.

1985: Anne Tyler's *Accidental Tourist* receives the National Book Critics Circle Award for Fiction.

1987: Fannie Flagg's *Fried Green Tomatoes at the Whistle Stop Café* is published.

1988: Banana Yoshimoto's first novel, *Kitchen*, is published in Japan. The English translation is published in the U.S. in 1992.

1988: Gloria Naylor's third novel, *Mama Day*, is published.

1993: Ernest Gaines's novel *A Lesson Before Dying* is published.

Acknowledgments

The editors wish to thank the copyright holders of the excerpted criticism included in this volume and the permissions managers of many book and magazine publishing companies for assisting us in securing reproduction rights. We are also grateful to the staffs of the Detroit Public Library, the Library of Congress, the University of Detroit Mercy Library, Wayne State University Purdy/ Kresge Library Complex, and the University of Michigan Libraries for making their resources available to us. Following is a list of the copyright holders who have granted us permission to reproduce material in this volume of *NfS*. Every effort has been made to trace copyright, but if omissions have been made, please let us know.

COPYRIGHTED EXCERPTS IN *NFS*, VOLUME 7, WERE REPRODUCED FROM THE FOLLOWING PERIODICALS:

Ariel: A Review of International English Literature, v. 4, April, 1973, for "Sanity, Madness and Alice" by Neilson Graham. Copyright © 1973 The Board of Governors, The University of Calgary. Reproduced by permission of the publisher.—*Book World—The Washington Post,* August 25, 1985. © 1985, Washington Post Book World Service/Washington Post Writers Group. Reproduced by permission of the author.—*The CEA Critic,* v. 54, Winter, 1992. Copyright © 1992 by the College English Association, Inc. Reproduced by permission.—*Chicago Tribune Books,* May 9, 1993, for "End as a Man" by Charles R. Larson. © copyrighted 1993, Chicago Tribune Company.

All rights reserved. Reproduced by permission of the author.—*The Cimarron Review,* v. 102, January, 1993. Copyright © 1993 by the Board of Regents for Oklahoma State University. Reproduced by permission.—*English Studies, Netherlands,* v. XLIX, February, 1968 by Swets & Zeitlinger B. V. Reproduced by permission.—*Enlightenment Essays,* v. IV, Spring, 1973 for "Companionship in Voltaire's *Candide*" by Patrick H. Hutton. Reproduced by permission of the author.—*The Listener,* v. 104, December 18 & 25, 1980 for "Wise-Guy-Sci-Fi" by Peter Kemp. © British Broadcasting Corp. 1980. Reprinted by permission of the author.—*The Midwest Quarterly,* v. XXV, Spring, 1994. Copyright 1994 by The Midwest Quarterly, Pittsburgh State University. Reproduced by permission.—*The New England Quarterly,* v. 52, June, 1979, for "Melville's Vision of Death in *Moby-Dick:* Stepping Away from the Snug Sofa" by James P. Grove. Copyright 1979 by The New England Quarterly. Reproduced by permission of the publisher.—*The New York Times,* January 17, 1993. Copyright © 1993 by The New York Times Company. Reproduced by permission.—*The New York Times Book Review,* September 8, 1985; February 10, 1988; February 21, 1988; August 8, 1993; October 6, 1996. Copyright © 1985, 1988, 1993, 1996 by The New York Times Company. All reproduced by permission.—*The New Yorker,* v. LXVIII, January 25, 1993, for "Day-O" by Deborah Garrison. Reproduced by permission of the author.—*South Atlantic Quarterly,* v. LXVI, Autumn, 1967. Copyright © 1967 by Duke University Press, Durham, NC. Reproduced by permission.—*Southern Quarterly,* v. 30, Winter-Spring, 1992. Copyright © 1992 by the University of Southern Mississippi. Reproduced by permission.—*Studies in Short Fiction,* v. 30, Fall, 1993. Copyright 1993 by Newberry College. Reproduced by permission.—*The Times Literary Supplement,* September 24, 1982. © The Times Supplements Limited 1982. Reproduced from *The Times Literary Supplement* by permission.—*The Virginia Quarterly Review,* v. 49, Winter, 1973. Copyright 1973 by The Virginia Quarterly Review, The University of Virginia. Reproduced by permission.—*Twentieth Century Literature,* v. 40, Fall, 1994. Copyright 1994, Hofstra University Press. Reproduced by permission.—*Victorian Studies,* v. XVII, September, 1973, for "Alice and Wonderland: A Curious Child" by Nina Auerbach. Reproduced by permission of the Trustees of Indiana University and the author.

COPYRIGHTED EXCERPTS IN *NFS*, VOLUME 7, WERE REPRODUCED FROM THE FOLLOWING BOOKS:

Burress, Lee. From "*The Grapes of Wrath*: Preserving Its Place in the Curriculum," in *Censored Books: Critical Viewpoints.* Nicholas J. Karolides, Lee Burress, John M. Kean, eds. The Scarecrow Press, Inc., 1993. Copyright © 1993 by Nicholas J. Karolides, Lee Burress, John M. Kean. Reproduced by permission.—Davis, James E. From "Why *Nineteen Eighty-Four* Should Be Read and Taught," in *Censored Books: Critical Viewpoints.* Nicholas J. Karolides, Lee Burress, John M. Kean, eds. The Scarecrow Press, Inc., 1993. Copyright © 1993 by Nicholas J. Karolides, Lee Burress, John M. Kean. Reproduced by permission.—Levant, Howard. From *The Novels of John Steinbeck: A Critical Study.* University of Missouri Press, 1974. Copyright © 1974 by The Curators of the University of Missouri. All rights reserved. Reproduced by permission.—Quinones, Ricardo J. From *The Changes of Cain: Violence and the Lost Brother in Cain and Abel Literature.* Princeton University Press, 1991. Copyright © 1991 by Princeton University Press. Reproduced by permission.

PHOTOGRAPHS AND ILLUSTRATIONS APPEARING IN *NFS*, VOLUME 7, WERE RECEIVED FROM THE FOLLOWING SOURCES:

Kafka, Franz, photograph. AP/Wide World Photos. Reproduced by permission.—Naylor, Glo-ria, photograph. AP/Wide World Photos. Reproduced by permission.—Steibeck, John, photograph. AP/Wide World Photos. Reproduced by permission.—Wright, Richard, photograph. AP/Wide World Photos. Reproduced by permission.—Adams, Douglas, 1993, photograph by Frank Capri. Archive Photos, Inc. © Frank Capri/SAGA. Reproduced by permission.—Disco dancing, c. 1970s, photograph. © Archive Photos, Inc. Reproduced by permission.—Flagg, Fannie, 1987, photograph. © Archive Photos, Inc. Reproduced by permission.—Home of Colonel Franklin, Kenya, Isle of Lamu, Africa, 1932, photograph. Archive Photos, Inc. Reproduced by permission.—"Hooverville" outside a factory during the Depression, photograph. Archive Photos, Inc./American Stock. Reproduced by permission.—Japanese student (being thrown in air), University of Tokyo, 1996, photograph. Archive Photos, Inc. Reproduced by permission.—Mad Hatter's Tea Party, scene from Disney animated version of "Alice in Wonderland," photograph. Archive Photos/Disney. Reproduced by permission.—Orwell, George, photograph. Archive Photos, Inc. Reproduced by permission.—Sugar cane plantation, Louisiana, photograph. Archive Photos, Inc. Reproduced by permission.—"White Only Store," photograph. Archive Photos, Inc. Reproduced by permission.—Gaines, Ernest J., photograph by Jerry Bauer. Reproduced by permission.—Wouk, Herman, photograph by Jerry Bauer. © Jerry Bauer. Reproduced by permission.—Artist (painting postcards on wall), photograph. Corbis/Bettmann-UPI. Reproduced by permission.—Darwell, Jane, with Henry Fonda and John Carradine in the movie *The Grapes of Wrath*, photograph. Corbis-Bettmann. Reproduced by permission.—Ferney, Voltaire's chateau, photograph. Corbis. Reproduced by permission.—Four army tanks in Tiananmen Square, photograph. Reuters/Corbis-Bettmann. Reproduced by permission.—Male Hitchhiker, (headed to Big Sur), 1972, photograph by Dewitt Jones. Corbis/Dewitt Jones. Reproduced by permission.—Peck, Gregory, as Captain Ahab in the film *Moby Dick*, 1954, photograph. UPI/Corbis-Bettmann. Reproduced by permission.—Radar room on World War II ship, China Sea, 1944, photograph. UPI/Corbis-Bettmann. Reproduced by permission.—Scene from the movie *Alice in Wonderland* (Alice talking with the Mock Turtle), photograph. Corbis-Bettmann. Reproduced by permission.—Women dressed as 18th-century French nobles, (seated in carriage, during parade), Versailles, France, 1989, photograph by Owen Franken. Corbis/Owen

Franken. Reproduced by permission.—Yoshimoto, Banana, photograph. Eiichiro Sakata and Kado-kawa Shoten Publishing Co., Ltd. Reproduced by permission of Grove Press.—Laurence, Margaret, photograph by David Laurence. © David Laurence Photo. Reproduced by permission of the photographer.—Carroll, Lewis, photograph by O. G. Rejlander. Liddell, Alice Pleasance and Liddell, Lorina Charlotte.—Freed slaves waiting for work opportunities, photograph. U.S. Signal Corps, National Archives and Records Administration.—Migrant mother with children, Nipomo, California, 1936, photograph by Dorothea Lange. Farm Security Administration.—Unemployed men lining up outside a depression soup kitchen, opened by Al Capone, Chicago, February 1931, photograph. National Archives and Records Administration.—Voltaire, engraving.—China's first McDonald's, China, photograph by Susan D. Rock. Reproduced by permission.—Young adult smoking, photograph by Bob Daemmrich. stock boston, inc. Reproduced by permission.—Bogart, Humphrey, with Van Johnson and Jose Ferrer, in the movie *The Caine Mutiny*, 1954, photograph.

The Kobal Collection. Reproduced by permission.—Hurt, John, and Richard Burton, in the movie *Nineteen Eighty-Four*, 1984, photograph. The Kobal Collection. Reproduced by permission.—Hurt, William, and Geena Davis, in the movie *The Accidental Tourist*, 1988, photograph. The Kobal Collection. Reproduced by permission.—Love, Victor, and David Rasche in the film *Native Son*, photograph. The Kobal Collection. Reproduced by permission.—Maclachlan, Kyle, and Anthony Hopkins, in the movie *The Trial*, 1993, photograph. The Kobal Collection. Reproduced by permission.—Parker, Mary Louise, and Mary Stuart Masterson, in the movie *Fried Green Tomatoes*, 1991, photograph. The Kobal Collection. Reproduced by permission.—Perkins, Anthony, in the movie *The Trial*, 1963, photograph. The Kobal Collection. Reproduced by permission.—Joyce, James (Ulysses), photograph. The Library of Congress.—Melville, Herman, photograph. The Library of Congress.—Upper-class black family eating dinner, photograph. The Library of Congress.—Tyler, Anne, photograph. Courtesy of Knopf. Reproduced by permission.

Contributors

Anne Boyd: Doctoral candidate in American Studies, Purdue University. Entry on *Mama Day*.

Jane Elizabeth Dougherty: Freelance writer, Medford, MA. Original essay on *Mama Day*.

Darren Felty: Visiting instructor, College of Charleston (SC); Ph.D. in Literature, University of Georgia. Original essay on *Candide*.

Jeremy Hubbell: Freelance writer; M.Litt., University of Aberdeen. Entries on *The Caine Mutiny, Candide, Fried Green Tomatoes at the Whistle Stop Café,* and *The Trial*.

David J. Kelly: Professor of English, College of Lake County (IL). Original essays on *Kitchen* and *A Lesson Before Dying*, and entries on *The Hitchhiker's Guide to the Galaxy* and *Kitchen*.

Nancy C. McClure: Educational consultant and freelance writer, Clarksburg, WV; Ed.D., West Virginia University. Entry on *A Lesson Before Dying*.

Tabitha McIntosh-Byrd: Freelance writer; M.Litt., University of Aberdeen. Original essays on *The Caine Mutiny* and *The Trial*.

Wendy Perkins: Assistant Professor of English, Prince George's Community College, Maryland; Ph.D. in English, University of Delaware. Original essay and entry on *The Accidental Tourist*, and original essay on *Fried Green Tomatoes at the Whistle Stop Café*.

Donna Woodford: Doctoral candidate, Washington University, St. Louis, MO. Original essay on *The Hitchhiker's Guide to the Galaxy*.

The Accidental Tourist

Anne Tyler
1985

When *The Accidental Tourist* was published in 1985, Anne Tyler was already a well-established and successful author. Her tenth novel soon became a best seller and won the National Book Critics Circle Award. Most reviewers consider this to be her best work. The novel has also been made into a successful film starring William Hurt and Kathleen Turner. As in many of her previous works, *The Accidental Tourist* focuses on the complexities of family relationships. In this story, middle-aged travel writer Macon Leary finds himself alone and miserable after his son is murdered and his wife leaves him. As a result, he realizes that he is in danger of becoming "a dried up kernel of a man that nothing real penetrates." During the course of the novel, however, Macon confronts his suffering and carves out a new life for himself with the help of an energetic and eccentric young woman and her son. Tyler's intermingling of comedy and tragedy results in a bittersweet tale of loss and recovery. Critics applaud the novel's lovingly drawn and compelling characters and Tyler's insight into the complex inner workings of the American family.

Author Biography

At fourteen, Tyler discovered a writer who would have a significant impact on her own literary career. While reading Eudora Welty's short story "The Wide Net," Tyler noted that one of the characters reminded her of someone she knew. Pre-

Anne Tyler

viously, Tyler had questioned her desire to become a writer because she thought that to write well one needed to have extraordinary experiences; she thought that her life was too dull. Welty taught her that good literature can also be about ordinary people and events.

Tyler was born on October 25, 1941, to a chemist and a social worker in Minneapolis, Minnesota. She moved frequently with her father, a chemist, and her mother, a social worker, settling at different times in Pennsylvania, Chicago, Duluth, and Raleigh, North Carolina. At one point the family moved to Celo, a commune in the mountains of North Carolina. Tyler has admitted that her writing career began at age three when she used to make up stories to help herself fall asleep at night. By seven, she had written in a notebook her first book, illustrated with drawings. While growing up she toyed with the idea of becoming an artist, but she eventually decided she was a better writer.

At sixteen, Tyler entered Duke University and, three years later, earned her undergraduate degree in Russian language and literature. While at Duke, she had short stories published in the school's literary magazine and won two awards for creative writing. She completed course work for a Ph.D. in Russian at Columbia University but did not finish the degree. After returning to Duke where she ac-

cepted a position as a Russian bibliographer, she married Iranian child psychologist Taghi Mohammed Modaressi and moved with him to Montreal. She now lives in Baltimore. Her first novel, *If Morning Ever Comes,* was published in 1964, shortly before the birth of her two daughters. While raising her family, Tyler maintained a strict writing schedule that enabled her to produce fourteen novels (including *The Accidental Tourist*), over fifty short stories, and numerous book reviews.

Plot Summary

Part I

In *The Accidental Tourist,* Anne Tyler presents an intimate portrait of Macon Leary, a middle-aged man coming to terms with the tragic death of his son. After his wife leaves him, Macon cuts himself off from the rest of the world. Almost against his will, he becomes involved with an unconventional woman who helps him cope with his loss and take control of his life.

On their way back from a vacation at the beach, Macon's wife, Sarah, informs Macon she wants a divorce because he has not been "a comfort" to her since the death of their son Ethan. Initially shocked, he begins to see her departure as a chance "to re-organize" the house. He expresses his penchant for order in a series of guidebooks he writes under the title *The Accidental Tourist* for those people forced to travel on business. Like his readers, Macon hates traveling, and does so only "with his eyes shut and holding his breath and hanging on for dear life." Yet he enjoys "the virtuous delights of organizing a disorganized country" and helping his readers "pretend they had never left home."

As he prepares to leave for a trip to England to update his book, Macon boards his dog Edward at the Meow-Bow Animal Hospital. There he meets Muriel Pritchett, a young woman with "aggressively frizzy" hair. Muriel offers to train Edward, who bit a handler at the last place he boarded. She gives Macon her number and tells him that even if he doesn't want to hire her, he can just call to talk. In London, Macon revisits hotels and restaurants and makes notes for his book.

When he returns, Macon admits he "couldn't think of any period bleaker than this in his life." He feels just as alienated at home as he does while traveling. Since contact with other people depresses him, he shuts himself up in his house, sometimes

Geena Davis and William Hurt in a scene from the 1988 film The Accidental Tourist.

never changing out of his bathrobe. Organizing the house provides him with his only pleasure, because "it gave him the sense of warding off a danger." Reduced to wearing sweat suits every day and eating popcorn he cooks in his bedroom, Macon approaches his breaking point. He recognizes that he is in danger of "turning into one of those pathetic creatures you see on the loose from time to time—unwashed, unshaven, shapeless, talking to themselves, padding along in their institutional garb." Alarmed at the thought, he tries to return to a more normal routine.

Part II

After breaking his leg in a fall down the basement stairs, Macon moves in with his sister Rose and brothers Porter and Charles. He soon finds a sense of contentment with the house's organized household rituals. The Learys "always had to have everything just so ... always clamping down on the world as if they really thought they could keep it in line." Macon enjoys the sense of being "unconnected" at Rose's. He tells nobody about his move, and no one in the family answers the phone. He also enjoys being pampered by Rose, a maternal woman who has taken care of everyone in the family at one time or another, including their grandparents and her brothers, who moved in with her after their marriages failed.

As his leg heals, Macon recalls his childhood in California and his mother, Alicia, a "giddy young war widow" who always seemed to have a new boyfriend. Her spurts of enthusiasm disturbed her children, who thought she went too far with her "violent zigzag of hobbies, friends, boyfriends, and causes." When she remarried, she sent them to live with their grandparents in Baltimore. Macon recalls his childhood as a "glassed-in place with grown-ups rushing past, talking at him, making changes, while he himself stayed mute."

Macon decides to hire Muriel to train Edward, who has been behaving erratically at Rose's. As she teaches Edward how to sit, lie down, and heel, she shares the story of her life with him. When Macon feels that she is treating Edward too harshly, he tells her not to return. Soon after, Sarah calls and asks Macon to meet her for lunch. There she tells him she will not come back to him because she doesn't "have enough time left to waste it holing up in my shell" as he does.

During a trip to New York, Macon experiences an anxiety attack and calls Muriel, who comforts him. When he returns, he begins a relationship with her and eventually moves in with her and her young son, Alexander. Macon admits he doesn't love her but loves "the surprise of her, and also the surprise of himself when he was with her.... He was an entirely different person ... [one] who had never been suspected of narrowness ... of chilliness ... and was anything but orderly." When Charles tells him that Muriel is "not your type of woman" and "you're not yourself these days," Macon replies, "I'm more myself than I've been my whole life long." Yet Macon admits to himself that he does not want to get "involved" in her life.

Part III

Macon develops a relationship with Alexander. He buys clothes for him, shows him how to fix things around the house, and protects him from the jeers of other children. However, when he and Muriel attend Rose's wedding to Julian, he sees Sarah, which rekindles his feelings for her. Macon leaves Muriel and Alexander and moves back in with Sarah, but they soon fall into their old destructive patterns. Sarah tells him, "The trouble with you is that you think people should stay in their own sealed packages. You don't believe in opening up. You don't believe in trading back and forth."

He decides to take a business trip to Paris, hoping it will take his mind off his situation. On the plane, Macon discovers Muriel has booked the same flight. When he asks her why she is following him, she tells him that he needs her. While in Paris, they eat a few meals together, and Macon begins to feel comfortable with her again. The next morning, however, Macon injures his back, and Sarah flies to Paris to take care of him. After Sarah discovers Muriel is staying in the same hotel, she and Macon discuss their relationship. Macon wonders whether he could learn to do things differently, and whether he could learn to make his own decisions. He decides to leave Sarah and go back to Muriel. On his way to the airport, he sees Muriel trying to hail a cab, and he tells his cabdriver to stop and pick her up.

Characters

Garner Bolt

Macon's curious neighbor who comes to Rose's house looking for Macon. He watches Macon's house and reports back to him about Muriel coming over and his water pipes bursting.

Boyd Dugan

Muriel's father. When Macon and Muriel spend Christmas with the Dugans, Boyd stays silent until the talk turns to cars.

Claire Dugan

Muriel's teen-age sister. Claire often stays at Muriel's when she fights with her parents, whom she considers too strict.

Lilian Dugan

Muriel's mother. At Christmas she ignores Alexander and embarrasses Muriel by talking about her past relationships. She embarrasses Macon by asking him what his intentions are toward her daughter. She has apparently always been highly critical of Muriel, who tries to gain her approval.

Julian Edge

Julian publishes Macon's books. Tyler reveals Julian through Macon's point of view, which, based on Julian's interactions with others, seems credible. Macon considers him to be "athletic looking" and "younger ... brashier, [and] breezier" than he is: "Julian's heart was not in the Businessman's Press but out on the Chesapeake Bay someplace." Macon decides Julian is not "entirely real," that "he has never truly grown up" because he has "never had anything happen to him" including having children. Julian "never seem[s] to have a moment's self doubt." He appears to be open-minded when he readily accepts Macon's relationship with Muriel. His one weakness, however, is his fear of being alone, which probably prompts him to become interested in Macon's sister, Rose. After he and Rose marry, Julian begins to have things "happen to him" when Rose decides to move back in with her brothers so she can take care of them. Julian feels vulnerable and turns to Macon for advice.

Edward

Ethan's dog. Macon keeps him when Sarah leaves. Edward figures prominently in Macon's relationship with Muriel. First he causes them to meet at the Meow Bow where Muriel works; then his erratic behavior at Rose's prompts Macon to hire Muriel to train him. Finally after Macon moves in with Muriel, Edward is the first to bond with her son, Alexander.

Alicia Leary

Macon's mother. As a "giddy young war widow," Alicia had little time for her children when they lived with her in California. When she did spend time with them, her enthusiasm disturbed them since it "came in spurts, a violent zigzag of hobbies, friends, boyfriends, causes. She always seemed about to fall over the brink of something. She was always going too far.... The faster she talked and the brighter her eyes grew, the more fixedly her children stared at her, as if willing her to follow their example of steadiness and dependability." After she remarried, she sent her children to live with their grandparents in Baltimore and saw them rarely after that. When she did "dart in and out of their lives," like "some naughty, gleeful fairy," the children considered her too "flashy" and too "vivid."

Charles Leary

Charles is Macon's brother, "a soft sweet-faced man who never seemed to move." He and his brother Porter took over Grandfather Leary's business when he died. Since Charles was "more mechanical," he dealt with the production end of the business. After his marriage failed, he moved in with Rose and fell into the same comforting family routine they practiced as children. While he usually keeps to himself, when Macon moves in with Muriel, Charles interferes. He tells Macon that something must be wrong with him since Muriel is not his "type of woman" and that she is "not worth it."

Ethan Leary

Macon's and Sarah's son who is seen only through their memories of him. He was shot and killed by a teenager at a fast-food restaurant while at summer camp. His loss profoundly affects both of his parents.

Grandfather Leary

Macon's grandfather, seen only through flashbacks. He owned a manufacturing company that he passed down to his grandsons. He and Macon's grandmother were "two thin, severe, distinguished people in dark clothes." He helped raise the children after their mother remarried.

Macon Leary

The novel's main character, a middle-aged man trying to cope with the death of his son and the subsequent shattering of his world. Macon writes a series of guidebooks for business people who, like him, hate to travel. When he is forced to, he does so "with his eyes shut and holding his breath and hanging on for dear life." Yet Macon likes "the virtuous delights of organizing a disorganized country." He also tries to organize his life in an effort to understand and to control it and to "ward off danger." One such effort however, his invention of the Macon Leary Body Bag, comes to symbolize his growing isolation from the outside

Media Adaptations

- *The Accidental Tourist* was adapted as a film released by Warner Brothers in 1988. It starred Kathleen Turner, Geena Davis, and William Hurt.

- The novel was also recorded as a book on tape by Recorded Books in 1991.

---

world. He admits that "gatherings of any sort depressed him. Physical contact with people not related to him … made him draw inward like a snail." As a result, he has become "a fairly chilly man." His wife, Sarah, notes his withdrawal, telling him he has given up on everything—"everything that might touch you or upset you or disrupt you." She observes, "There's something so muffled about the way you experience things…. You're encased. You're like something in a capsule. You're a dried up kernel of a man that nothing real penetrates."

With Muriel's and Alexander's help, however, Macon gains the courage to come out of his protective shell. With her, he becomes "an entirely different person … [one] who had never been suspected of narrowness … of chilliness … and was anything but orderly." By the end of the novel, Macon takes control of his life and makes the decision to become an active participant in the world.

Porter Leary

Macon's brother. Porter was considered the best looking of all the Learys. He was also "the most practical man Macon had ever known…. He gave an impression of vitality and direction that his brothers lacked." Like Macon and Charles, Porter "always had to have everything just so … always clamping down on the world as if [he] really thought [he] could keep it in line."

Rose Leary

Rose is Macon's sister. She lives with and takes care of his two brothers. Rose is as organized as her brothers, as evidenced by her kitchen, which she has completely alphabetized. There seems to be "something vague about her that caused her brothers to act put-upon and needy whenever she chanced to focus on them." When she marries Julian, she appears to be finding a sense of self, but she soon moves back in with her brothers in order to return to her safe, orderly life. She and Julian eventually reunite when she takes over his office and reorganizes it.

Sarah Leary

Sarah, Macon's wife, leaves him because he is not a "comfort" to her after the death of their son, Ethan. Feeling oppressed by Macon's tendency to withdraw from the world, Sarah decides she needs a place of her own. Before Ethan died, she had been a social person, but now she "[doesn't] like crowds anymore." When Macon asks her to come back to him, she explains, "Ever since Ethan died I've had to admit that people are basically bad." She decides to leave him because she knows that he has always believed this. This pessimism, along with the acknowledgment that she too is retreating from the world, scares her and prompts her decision to divorce Macon. She tells him, "I don't have enough time left to waste it holing up in my shell." When she and Macon reconcile, she continually finds fault with the same "little routines and rituals, depressing habits, day after day" that he exhibited before she left him.

Susan Leary

Porter's daughter. Susan accompanies Macon on a trip to Philadelphia and reminisces with him about Ethan.

Alexander Pritchett

Alexander is Muriel's son. When Macon first sees him he appears to be "small, white, [and] sickly ... with a shaved-looking skull." Alexander is a lonely boy, ostracized by his peers, due in part to Muriel's overprotective mothering. She determines that he has allergies to just about everything and so restricts his diet and activities. Macon decides that "school never went very well" for Alexander, since he often comes home "with his face more pinched than ever, his glasses thick with fingerprints." Alexander, however, thrives under Macon's care.

Muriel Pritchett

Macon begins a relationship with Muriel after Sarah leaves him. Tyler presents Muriel through Macon's point of view, which ultimately reveals all aspects of her personality, since his opinion of her continually changes. Muriel detects his fickleness when she tells him, "One minute you like me and the next you don't. One minute you're ashamed to be seen with me and the next you think I'm the best thing that ever happened to you." Muriel has "a voice that wander[s] too far in all directions" and she "talks nonstop." Macon notes her "long, narrow nose, and sallow skin, and two freckled knobs of collarbone that promised an unluxurious body." Muriel has on occasion a "nasty temper, a shrewish tongue, and a tendency to fall into spells of self-disgust from which no one could rouse her for hours." Finally, her parenting skills are inconsistent: "One minute overprotective, the next callous and offhand."

She is obviously intelligent. The quality Macon admires the most is "her fierceness, her spiky, pugnacious fierceness as she fought her way toward the camera with her chin set awry and her eyes bright slits of determination." Muriel fights for everything she wants, including Macon. Unlike Sarah, Muriel does not try to change Macon, yet her openness and acceptance enables him to emerge from his protective shell.

Dominick Saddler

A teenager who lives in Muriel's neighborhood. He fixes her car and baby-sits Alexander. He dies suddenly in an accident while driving Muriel's car.

Themes

Death

Ethan's death triggers the novel's initial conflict. At first it leads to the dissolution of Sarah and Macon's marriage. The past year had been "miserable" for both of them, with "months when everything either of them said was wrong." When Sarah admits, "Now that Ethan's dead I sometimes wonder if there's any point to life," Macon responds, "It never seemed to me there was all that much point to begin with." This pessimism spurs Sarah's decision to leave Macon. She feels he is not grieving as much as she, nor is he providing her with the comfort she requires. Macon looks for someone to blame for Ethan's death, including Sarah and himself.

Order and Disorder

Ethan's death coupled with Sarah's departure throws Macon into a state of disorder that he desperately tries to remedy with an obsessive search for order. This need for organization is a consistent theme in Macon's life, evidenced by the pleasure he takes "organizing a disorganized country" for the readers of his guidebooks. After the death of his son, it provides him with his only pleasure, since it gives him "the sense of warding off a danger." Ultimately, though, his need for order pushes him to the breaking point. In an effort to reorganize the house and thus his life, he invents the Macon Leary Body Bag, which becomes his personal cocoon and allows him to retreat every night from the outside world.

Alienation and Loneliness

Sarah accuses Macon of not being able to maintain a meaningful connection with her or anyone else and cites this as the reason she leaves him. Ethan's death has eventually led him to give up on life, on "everything that might touch [him] or upset [him] or disrupt [him]." Macon cannot dispute Sarah's insistence that "there's something so muffled about the way you experience things.... You're encased. You're like something in a capsule. You're a dried up kernel of a man that nothing real penetrates." He admits that he avoids contact with other people because it "made him draw inward like a snail." As a result, he has become "a fairly chilly man." Sarah fears that she is beginning to adopt Macon's pessimism as well as his desire to alienate himself from the world. Before Ethan died, she had been a social person, but now she, like Macon, avoids contact with others. In order to save herself, Sarah leaves, telling him, "I don't have enough time left to waste it holing up in my shell." The loneliness that results from the loss of his son and his wife submerges Macon into the "bleakest period of his life."

Apathy and Passivity

Macon responds with apathy and passivity in the face of his suffering. At first, he is devastated by Sarah's departure, but he soon comes to accept it. After he breaks his leg, he moves in with Rose, who takes care of all his needs. Ironically his apathy and passivity cause him to enter into a relationship with Muriel, who is fiercely determined to forge a connection with him. When he goes to her apartment, intending to inform her that he cannot have dinner with her because he does not want to explain what has happened to him, he allows her

Topics for Further Study

- Define the term "dysfunctional family" and research the causes and effects of different kinds of dysfunction. Can the families in the novel be considered dysfunctional? If so, how?

- Compare the movie version of *The Accidental Tourist* to the novel. How do the characters compare to the way you imagined them after reading the book?

- Investigate the psychological effects of losing a loved one and compare your findings to Macon's and Sarah's behavior.

- Many critics find southern elements in Tyler's works. Investigate the qualities of a "southern writer" and determine whether or not you find those qualities in the novel.

to change his mind. Muriel gently coaxes him to open up to her and express his grief. Before he realizes it, and almost against his will, Macon begins to reconnect with the world.

Change and Transformation

Macon's relationship with Muriel and Alexander helps transform him from a passive and apathetic man who hides from the world to a man who is strong enough to make his own decisions and to face life's challenges. He realizes that when he was with Sarah, he had been "locked inside the standoffish self he'd assumed when he and she first met. He was frozen there.... Somehow, his role had sunk all the way through to the heart." Muriel allows him to explore his true self, which he acknowledges to Charles when he tells him that with her, "I'm more myself than I've been my whole life long." Muriel and Alexander also help Macon reconnect with the world, even though the process is painful for him. After recognizing his growing attachment to Alexander, Macon admits he feels "a pleasant kind of sorrow sweeping through him. Oh, his life had regained all its old perils. He was forced to worry once again about nuclear war and the future of the planet."

Style

Point of View

Tyler creates an effective narrative structure in the novel by presenting the other characters through Macon's point of view. Although the novel is written in the third person, the narrator limits the perspective as readers observe Macon's interactions with and observations of others. This structure more fully reveals Macon's transformation during the course of the novel. For example, readers understand Macon's confusion over his relationship with Muriel when the narrator reveals his shifting and sometimes contradictory visions of her. Muriel notes this confusion when she tells Macon, "One minute you like me and the next you don't. One minute you're ashamed to be seen with me and the next you think I'm the best thing that ever happened to you." Macon admits "he had never guessed that she read him so clearly."

Symbolism

Tyler employs several symbols to reinforce Macon's sense of isolation and passivity. The first symbols are his logo and the title of his guidebooks. Noting his reluctance to experience life, Sarah tells him, "That traveling armchair isn't just your logo; it's you." Macon not only travels "with his eyes shut and holding his breath and hanging on for dear life," he travels through life in the same manner. Throughout much of the novel, he wanders "in a fog … adrift upon the planet, helpless, praying that just by luck he might stumble across his destination." The cast on Macon's broken leg and his creation of the Macon Leary Body Bag are additional symbolic representations of his alienation. At one point, Macon admits that he wishes his cast would cover him from head to foot. The cast and body bag thus become symbolic of his spiritual death.

Finally, the sleeping pills Sarah gives Macon when he injures his back in Paris become a symbol of Sarah's effect on Macon. After being with Muriel, Macon comes to realize that while he was married to Sarah, he assumed an aloofness and disconnection that had at first attracted Sarah. Now, however, he believes himself to be "locked inside" that self. The powerful sleeping pills thus symbolize the kind of person he becomes in Sarah's presence. When Macon finally rejects the pills, he rejects the self he becomes when he is with her.

Comic Relief

Tyler often employs comic relief after chronicling the suffering experienced by her characters.

Through her presentation of eccentric characters and unconventional developments, Tyler effectively relieves the tensions and heightens the tragic elements of the novel by contrast. These comic elements are an essential and integral part of the whole work. This mixture of comedy and tragedy is often displayed in scenes involving Edward, Macon's dog.

Historical Context

Teenage Homicide Rates

According to the United States Bureau of the Census, the teenage homicide rate soared 169 percent between 1984 and 1993. Studies conducted on this increase conclude that the crack cocaine epidemic and easy access to firearms were to blame. These sobering statistics helped create an atmosphere of fear in the 1980s, when crime became a major concern for the American public. Tyler tapped into this fear through her characterization of Macon Leary, who, at the beginning of the novel, is still grieving the loss of his son, Ethan. As Ethan was eating lunch at a fast-food restaurant, a teenager entered and randomly executed him. After the murder, Macon withdrew from a world he feared.

Divorce Rates in America

The Census Bureau reported that in 1970 there were 4.3 million divorced adults in America; that number rose to 17.4 million in 1994. During that period, the percentage of divorced Americans over eighteen years of age climbed from 3 percent to 9 percent. Many experts determined that the primary cause was no-fault divorce laws, first adopted in California in 1969. Sociologists linked the high divorce rate to what they considered to be the breakdown of the American family. As a result of this perceived breakdown, a new focus on what was termed "the dysfunctional family" emerged.

Dysfunction in a family results from serious crises such as divorce, sexual abuse, alcoholism, or infidelity. Unexpected events like the death of a family member or loss of a job can also trigger a family crisis. As a result, members often assign blame, fail to communicate with each other, experience excessive anger, and shut themselves off from the rest of the family.

The high divorce rate and incidents of dysfunction redefined the American family in the 1980s. As the traditional family unit broke down,

American tourists seeking the security of familiar tastes and sights in China would likely visit a McDonald's restaurant.

new families emerged and a more flexible definition was created. Families now could consist of two parents and their children, a couple who decided to have no children, a single parent and his or her children, a parent and stepparent and their children, or grandparents and their grandchildren. Children and their foster parents were also considered to be a family unit.

In *The Accidental Tourist,* Tyler reflects the changing configurations of the American family as she chronicles the demise of several such traditional families. Yet she also invents some nontraditional ones as a result. After all the Leary men experience failed marriages, they recreate the family of their childhood when they move back in with Rose. Macon and Muriel reconstruct a family unit after both of their marriages end in divorce. Tyler's study of the dynamics of family relationships serves as an apt reflection of the cultural climate of America in the 1980s.

Critical Overview

Anne Tyler's novels have gained mostly favorable reviews, from her first publication, *If*

Morning Ever Comes, in 1964, to her most recent, *A Patchwork Planet,* in 1999. In the 1970s Tyler came to the attention of novelist Gail Godwin, who reviewed her fifth novel, *Celestial Navigation* (1974), and John Updike, who reviewed *Searching for Caleb* (1976). After that, Tyler's books received national and eventually international attention. *The Accidental Tourist,* which won the National Book Critics Circle Award, is considered by many to be her best work. Most critics cite Tyler's astute and compassionate characterizations and clever intermingling of humor and pathos as the reasons for the novel's critical and commercial success.

A *Library Journal* reviewer asserted, "Not a character, including Macon's dog Edward, is untouched by delightful eccentricity in this charming story, full of surprises and wisdom." Larry McMurtry in the *New York Times Book Review* found Muriel Pritchett "as appealing a woman as Miss Tyler has created, and upon the quiet Macon she lavishes the kind of intelligent consideration that he only intermittently gets from his womenfolk." McMurtry added that the novel's themes, "some of which [Tyler] has been sifting for more than twenty years, cohere with high definition in the muted … personality of Macon Leary."

Some reviewers, however, find some of the novel's characters unrealistic. For example, McMurtry admitted, "Two aspects of the novel do not entirely satisfy. One is the unaccountable neglect of Edward, the corgi, in the last third of the book…. The other questionable element is the dead son, Ethan. Despite an effort now and then to bring him into the book in a vignette or a nightmare, Ethan remains mostly a premise." Yet he tempered his criticism when he concluded, "At the level of metaphor … [Tyler] has never been stronger."

Critics also applaud the novel's mixture of comedy and tragedy. Peter Prescott, in his *Newsweek* review of the novel, concluded that Tyler's "comedies," including *The Accidental Tourist,* "are of the very best sort, which is to say that they are always serious, that they combine the humor of a situation with a narrative voice that allows itself moments of wit." Richard Eder, in his article in the *Los Angeles Times Book Review,* noted that the character of Macon Leary "is an oddity of the first water, and yet we grow so close to him that there is not the slightest warp in the lucid, touching and very funny story of an inhibited man moving out into life." McMurtry determined that this quality helps make the novel one of Tyler's best: "Miss Tyler shows, with a fine clarity, the mingling of misery and contentment in the daily lives of her families, reminding us how alike—and yet distinct—happy and unhappy families can be."

Some critics, however, argued that the comedy masks a lack of development in the novel. *Chicago Tribune Book World* critic John Blades wondered whether "Tyler, with her sedative resolutions to life's most grievous and perplexing problems, can be taken seriously as a writer." Elizabeth Mahn Nollen, in her article on the novel in *Family Matters in the British and American Novel,* answered critics like Blades who find the upbeat ending in *The Accidental Tourist* to be "candy coated" with a discussion of the theme of parenting. Nollen claimed that as a result, "the redemption/regeneration of certain characters has not been taken as seriously as it might be." She found the novel to be an effective study of a father who provides "essentially positive, if complicated, examples of parenthood." The ending, she argued, "is the only closure the author could choose to get her message across: that fatherhood matters—that it can be a redemptive and healing force."

Criticism

Wendy Perkins

Perkins is an associate professor of English at Prince George's Community College in Maryland and has published several articles on British and American authors. In the following essay, she examines the traditional and nontraditional roles of the female characters in The Accidental Tourist.

In her article in the *New York Times Book Review,* Katha Pollitt takes an overview of Anne Tyler's work and concludes that her fiction does not reveal a firm sense of time or place. She argues that Tyler's novels "are modern in their fictional techniques, yet utterly unconcerned with the contemporary moment as a subject, so that, with only minor dislocations, her stories could just as well have taken place in the twenties or thirties. The current school of feminist-influenced novels seems to have passed her by completely: her women are strong, often stronger than the men in their lives, but solidly grounded in traditional roles." Other critics have also noted that Tyler's characterizations take precedence over her setting details in her work, including in her tenth novel, *The Accidental Tourist.*

Tyler focuses the narrative in this novel more on Macon's struggles with family life rather than where the families reside. However, she does situate the novel in its historical moment. Through her characterization of Macon, Tyler reflects the paranoia over increasing crime rates in the 1980s, when the novel was written and published. The novel also illustrates the decade's growing concern with the dysfunctional family and its causes and effects. Finally, Tyler explores changing roles for women. All the female characters show their strength in *The Accidental Tourist.* Some exert it as they are firmly entrenched in traditional roles, while others reveal their courageous attempt to adopt more modern attitudes.

All the female characters in the novel are involved or want to be involved in a marital and/or family relationship. This, granted, is considered to be a traditional role for women, but all the characters, male and female, express this desire, which becomes one of the novel's dominant themes. The characters also, however, end up separating themselves from these relationships, as noted by Joseph C. Voelker in *Art and the Accidental in Anne Tyler.* The characters in the novel, he argues, distance themselves from the complex feelings they have for their families. Voelker determines that they experience a "sickness for home (longing, nostalgia) but also sickness of it (the need to escape from the invasiveness of family) and sickness from it (the psychic wounds that human beings inevitably carry as a result of having had to grow up as children in families)."

Rose Leary is the most traditional female character in the novel. She has accepted the role of caretaker for her entire family at one point or another. She cared for her ailing grandparents, and after her brothers' marriages failed, she welcomed them back into the family home and promptly took over the role of nurturer. She reinstated family rituals, like cooking baked potatoes for their evening meal, which used to comfort them as children when left alone by their mother. The narrator notes there was "something vague about her that caused her brothers to act put-upon and needy whenever she chanced to focus on them."

At first Rose appears to be content with the orderly, isolated existence she and her brothers share. However, she soon begins to feel "a sickness of home" as she chafes under her brothers' narrow idea of her role in their lives. When she begins a relationship with Julian, she discovers a new sense of self, and is strong enough to break away from her old ties. Her need to feel useful, though, causes her to return to her traditional role, and eventually she becomes wife and mother when she and Julian move in with Porter and Charles.

Sarah, Macon's wife, also breaks out of a traditional role for a period of time, but instead of moving from one family unit to another, she expresses a desire to live alone. Annoyed by Macon's "little routines and rituals, depressing habits, day after day" and his inability to comfort her, she decides to leave him and establish a place of her own and a more complete sense of self. She admits she has been pulled into Macon's pessimism, and as a result, she too is cutting herself off from the rest of the world. When she leaves, she tells him, "I don't have enough time left to waste it holing up in my shell."

Sarah, however, is unable to assuage the grief she feels over Ethan's death and so moves back in with Macon and returns to her traditional role as wife, because of its familiarity. She admits to Macon, "I think that after a certain age people just don't have a choice.... You're who I'm with. It's too late for me to change. I've used up too much of my life now."

Muriel Pritchett's nonconformity makes her unique among the novel's other female characters. She also wants to enter into a relationship with someone, but if she is unable to accomplish this, she makes it clear that she can take care of herself. She appears to have been left alone virtually all of her life. Her interaction with her mother suggests that Muriel experiences a "sickness from family." She displays what Voelker calls the "psychic wounds that human beings inevitably carry as a result of having had to grow up as children in families." Muriel's wounds emerge in the picture she gives her mother, in which Macon notices that she appears "wary and uncertain, and very much alone." Macon notes that when Lilian Dugan pays attention to her daughter, which happens rarely, she most often criticizes her. Muriel admits that her family considers her to be the "bad one" and her sister the "good one."

Muriel's wounds, though, seem to have helped her develop a strong sense of independence and resilience. When her husband leaves her and her young son, Muriel raises him by herself, aided by her sharp entrepreneurial skills. She also reveals her independent nature when Macon expresses his concern over her quitting one of her jobs. She tells him, "Don't you know [I] can always take care of [myself]? Don't you know [I] could find another

What Do I Read Next?

- *Breathing Lessons,* Anne Tyler's 1988 Pulitzer Prize-winning novel, focuses on family relationships and chronicles a woman's determined efforts to encourage people to connect with each other.

- *Independence Day,* Richard Ford's 1995 novel, reflects the comic and sobering realities of American life in the 1980s as it follows the story of Frank Bascombe, a middle-aged real estate salesman, and his struggles with his career, his ex-wife, his girlfriend, and his children.

- *The Stone Diaries,* the Pulitzer Prize-winning novel written by Carol Shields, presents a fictionalized autobiography of Daisy Goodwill Flett. It recounts her long history as daughter, wife, mother, and widow, and her struggles to finally understand herself and her world.

- In *Dinner at the Homesick Restaurant,* published in 1982, Anne Tyler focuses on family life through the eyes of dying Pearl Tull, who remembers the difficult task of raising three children on her own.

job tomorrow, if [I] wanted?" She can also take care of herself in her dangerous neighborhood. Once while coming back from the supermarket, a teenager emerges out of a shadowy doorway and demands that she give him the contents of her purse. She responds, "Like hell I will," and attacks him. As a result, Macon admits "he felt awed by her, and diminished."

Muriel retains her unconventionality even when acknowledging that it does not always appeal to Macon. She tells Macon that she knows "one minute you like me and the next you don't. One minute you're ashamed to be seen with me and the next you think I'm the best thing that ever happened to you." She does try, briefly, to adopt a more conventional look, when she tries to model herself after Rose, but she soon reverts back to her eccentric but honest self. Finally, "the surprise of her" and her careless enthusiasm for life win Macon over. When Muriel gives Macon a picture of her as a child, he cherishes it, deciding, "she meant, he supposed, to give him the best of her ... her fierceness—her spiky, pugnacious fierceness as she fought her way toward the camera with her chin set awry and her eyes bright slits of determination." Unlike Sarah, Muriel does not try to change Macon, yet her openness and acceptance, and ultimately her independence, enables him to emerge from his protective shell.

Tyler explained in an interview with Marguerite Michaels in *The New York Times Book Review* that "the real heroes to me in my books are first the ones who manage to endure and second the ones who somehow are able to grant other people the privacy of the space around them and yet still produce some warmth." According to her definition then, Muriel, with her independent yet loving spirit, is a real hero.

Source: Wendy Perkins, in an essay for *Novels for Students,* Gale, 1999.

Larry McMurtry

In the following excerpt, McMurtry discusses the way in which Tyler reintroduces her customary themes of sibling bonding and the hapless male protagonist in The Accidental Tourist.

In Anne Tyler's fiction, family is destiny, and (nowadays, at least) destiny clamps down on one in Baltimore. For an archeologist of manners with Miss Tyler's skills, the city is a veritable Troy, and she has been patiently excavating since the early 1970's, when she skipped off the lawn of Southern fiction and first sank her spade in the soil which has nourished such varied talents as Poe, Mencken, Billie Holiday and John Waters, the director of the films *Pink Flamingos* and *Polyester.*

It is without question some of the fustiest soil in America; in the more settled classes, social styles developed in the 19th century withstand, with sporelike tenacity, all that the present century can throw at them. Indeed, in Baltimore *all* classes appear to be settled, if not cemented, in grooves of neighborhood and habit so deep as to render them impervious—as a bright child puts it in *The Accidental Tourist*—to everything except nuclear flash.

From this rich dust of custom, Miss Tyler is steadily raising a body of fiction of major dimensions. One of the persistent concerns of this work is the ambiguity of family happiness and unhappiness. Since coming to Baltimore, Miss Tyler has probed this ambiguity in seven novels of increasing depth and power, working numerous changes on a consistent set of themes.

In *The Accidental Tourist* these themes, some of which she has been sifting for more than 20 years, cohere with high definition in the muted (or, as his wife says, "muffled") personality of Macon Leary....

Like most of Miss Tyler's males, Macon Leary presents a broad target to all of the women (and even a few of the men) with whom he is involved. His mother; his sister, Rose; his wife, Sarah; and, in due course, his girlfriend, Muriel Pritchett—a dog trainer of singular appearance and ability—regularly pepper him on the subject of his shortcomings, the greatest of which is a lack of passion, playfulness, spontaneity or the desire to do one single thing that *they* like to do. This lack is the more maddening because Macon is reasonably competent; if prompted he will do more or less anything that's required of him. What exasperates the women is the necessity for constant prompting.

When attacked, Macon rarely defends himself with much vigor, which only heightens the exasperation. He likes a quiet life, based on method and system. His systems are intricate routines of his own devising, aimed at reducing the likelihood that anything unfamiliar will occur. The unfamiliar is never welcome in Macon's life, and he believes that if left to himself he can block it out or at least neutralize it.

Not long after we meet him, Macon *is* left to himself. Sarah, his wife of 20 years, leaves him. Macon and Sarah have had a tragedy: their 12-year-old son, Ethan, was murdered in a fast-food joint, his death an accidental byproduct of a holdup.

Though Macon is as grieved by this loss as Sarah, he is, as she points out, "not a comfort." When she remarks that since Ethan's death she sometimes wonders if there's any point to life, Macon replies, honestly but unhelpfully, that it never seemed to him there was all that much point to begin with. As if this were not enough, he can never stop himself from correcting improper word choice, even if the incorrect usage occurs in a conversation about the death of a child. These corrections are not made unkindly, but they are invariably made; one does not blame Sarah for taking off.

With the ballast of his marriage removed, Macon immediately tips into serious eccentricity. His little systems multiply, and his remaining companions, a Welsh corgi named Edward and a cat named Helen, fail to adapt to them. Eventually the systems overwhelm Macon himself, causing him to break a leg. Not long after, he finds himself where almost all of Miss Tyler's characters end up sooner or later—back in the grandparental seat. There he is tended to by his sister. His brothers, Porter and Charles, both divorced, are also there, repeating, like Macon, a motion that seems all but inevitable in Anne Tyler's fiction—a return to the sibling unit.

This motion, or tendency, cannot be blamed on Baltimore. In the very first chapter of Miss Tyler's first novel, *If Morning Ever Comes* (1964), a young man named Ben Joe Hawkes leaves Columbia University and hurries home to North Carolina mainly because he can't stand not to know what his sisters are up to. From then on, in book after book, siblings are drawn inexorably back home, as if their parents or (more often) grandparents had planted tiny magnets in them which can be activated once they have seen what the extrafamilial world is like. The lovers and mates in her books, by exerting their utmost strength, can sometimes delay these re-groupings for as long as 20 years, but sooner or later a need to be with people who are *really* familiar—their brothers and sisters—overwhelms them.

Macon's employer, a man named Julian, who manages to marry but not to hold Macon's sister, puts it succinctly once Rose has drifted back to her brothers: "She'd worn herself a groove or something in that house of hers, and she couldn't help swerving back into it." Almost no one in Miss Tyler's books avoids that swerve; the best they can hope for is to make a second escape, as does the resourceful Caleb Peck in *Searching for Caleb* (1976). Brought back after an escape lasting 60 years, Caleb sneaks away again in his 90's....

The Accidental Tourist is one of Anne Tyler's best books, as good as *Morgan's Passing, Searching for Caleb, Dinner at the Homesick Restaurant.* The various domestic worlds we enter—Macon/ Sarah; Macon/the Leary siblings; Macon/Muriel— are delineated with easy skill; now they are poignant, now funny. Miss Tyler shows, with a fine clarity, the mingling of misery and contentment in the daily lives of her families, reminding us how alike—and yet distinct—happy and unhappy families can be. Muriel Pritchett is as appealing a woman as Miss Tyler has created; and upon the quiet Macon she lavishes the kind of intelligent consideration that he only intermittently gets from his own womenfolk.

Two aspects of the novel do not entirely satisfy. One is the unaccountable neglect of Edward,

the corgi, in the last third of the book. Edward is one of the more fully characterized dogs in recent literature; his breakdown is at least as interesting and if anything more delicately handled than Macon's. Yet Edward is allowed to slide out of the picture. Millions of readers who have managed to saddle themselves with neurotic quadrupeds will want to know more about Edward's situation.

The other questionable element is the dead son, Ethan. Despite an effort now and then to bring him into the book in a vignette or a nightmare, Ethan remains mostly a premise, and one not advanced very confidently by the author. She is brilliant at showing how the living press upon one another, but less convincing when she attempts to add the weight of the dead. The reader is invited to feel that it is this tragedy that separates Macon and Sarah. But a little more familiarity with Macon and Sarah, as well as with the marriages in Miss Tyler's other books, leaves one wondering. Macon's methodical approach to life might have driven Sarah off anyway. He would have corrected her word choice once too often, one feels. Miss Tyler is more successful at showing through textures how domestic life is sustained than she is at showing how these textures are ruptured by a death.

At the level of metaphor, however, she has never been stronger. The concept of an accidental tourist captures in a phrase something she has been saying all along, if not about life, at least about men: they are frequently accidental tourists in their own lives. Macon Leary sums up a long line of her males. Jake Simmes in *Earthly Possessions* is an accidental kidnapper. The lovable Morgan Gower of *Morgan's Passing,* an accidental obstetrician in the first scenes, is an accidental husband or lover in the rest of the book. Her men slump around like tired tourists—friendly, likable, but not all that engaged. Their characters, like their professions, seem accidental even though they come equipped with genealogies of Balzacian thoroughness. All of them have to be propelled through life by (at the very least) a brace of sharp, purposeful women— it usually takes not only a wife and a girlfriend but an indignant mother and one or more devoted sisters to keep these sluggish fellows moving. They poke around haphazardly, ever mild and perennially puzzled, in a foreign country called Life. If they see anything worth seeing, it is usually because a determined woman on the order of Muriel Pritchett thrusts it under their noses and demands that they pay some attention. The fates of these families hinge on long struggles between semiattentive males and semiobsessed females. In her patient investigation of such struggles, Miss Tyler has produced a very satisfying body of fiction.

Source: Larry McMurtry, "Life Is a Foreign Country," in *The New York Times Book Review,* September 8, 1985, pp. 1, 36.

Jonathan Yardley

In the following excerpt, Yardley praises The Accidental Tourist *for its many exceptional qualities, describing it as a moving, deeply significant novel.*

With each new novel … it becomes ever more clear that the fiction of Anne Tyler is something both unique and extraordinary in contemporary American literature. Unique, quite literally: there is no other writer whose work sounds like Tyler's, and Tyler sounds like no one except herself. Extraordinary, too: not merely for the quietly dazzling quality of her writing and the abidingly sympathetic nature of her characters, but also for her calm indifference to prevailing literary fashion and her deep conviction that it is the work, not the person who writes it, that matters. Of *The Accidental Tourist* one thing can be said with absolute certainty: it matters.

It is a beautiful, incandescent, heartbreaking, exhilarating book. A strong undercurrent of sorrow runs through it, yet it contains comic scenes—one involving a dog, a cat and a clothes dryer, another a Thanksgiving turkey, yet another a Christmas dinner—that explode with joy. It is preoccupied with questions of family, as indeed all of Tyler's more recent fiction is, but there is not an ounce of sentimentality to be found in what it says about how families stick together or fall apart. There's magic in it, and some of its characters have winning eccentricities, yet more than any of Tyler's previous books it is rooted firmly, securely, insistently in the real world.

That world is of course Baltimore, which in Tyler's fiction, as indeed in actuality, is both a place and a state of mind. By now Baltimore belongs to Tyler in the same way that Asheville belongs to Thomas Wolfe, Chicago to James T. Farrell, Memphis to Peter Taylor, Albany to William Kennedy; like these writers, she at once gives us the city as it really exists and redefines it through the realm of the imagination. When the protagonist of *The Accidental Tourist,* Macon Leary, drives along North Charles Street, he is on the map; when he arrives at Singleton Street, he is in uncharted territory. But there can be no question that Singleton Street, though fictitious, is real….

He was beginning to feel easier here. Singleton Street still unnerved him with its poverty and its ugliness, but it no longer seemed so dangerous. He saw that the hoodlums in front of the Cheery Moments Carry-Out were pathetically young and shabby—their lips chapped, their sparse whiskers ineptly shaved, an uncertain, unformed look around their eyes. He saw that once the men had gone to work, the women emerged full of good intentions and swept their front walks, picked up the beer cans and potato chip bags, even rolled back their coat sleeves and scrubbed their stoops on the coldest days of the year. Children raced past like so many scraps of paper blowing in the wind—mittens mismatched, noses running—and some woman would brace herself on her broom to call, 'You there! I see you! Don't think I don't know you're skipping school!' For this street was always backsliding, Macon saw, always falling behind, but was caught just in time by these women with their carrying voices and their pushy jaws. Singleton Street is not Macon's natural territory. Though by no means wealthy, he belongs to that part of Baltimore north of downtown where houses are detached, have yards, are shaded by trees; this is the world in which he grew up and in which until quite recently he lived all his life. But now, at the age of 43, he is finding that world come apart on him. A year ago something unspeakably awful happened; his 12-year-old son, Ethan, off at summer camp, was murdered in a fast-food restaurant, "one of those deaths that make no sense—the kind where the holdup man has collected his money and is free to go but decides, instead, first to shoot each and every person through the back of the skull." Now he has been left by Sarah, his wife of 20 years, who has been devastated by her son's death and believes that she must start life over because "I don't have enough time left to waste it holing up in my shell," a shell she thinks Macon played a crucial role in constructing.

So there he is, alone in the house with Helen, the cat, and Edward, the rowdy little Welsh Corgi to whom he stubbornly clings because the dog was Ethan's. Macon is a creature of firm if peculiar habit who believes that a system can be devised to meet each of life's difficulties; his stratagems for breakfast, bedclothes and the laundry are nothing if not ingenious, even if they don't exactly work. Change and disruption frighten him, which makes him perfectly suited to be the author of guide-books "for people forced to travel on business," accidental tourists who, like Macon, hate travel and much prefer to be at home:

He covered only the cities in these guides, for people taking business trips flew into cities and out again and didn't see the countryside at all. They didn't see the cities, for that matter. Their concern was how to pretend they had never left home. What hotels in Madrid boasted king-sized Beauty-rest mattresses? What restaurants in Tokyo offered Sweet'n'Low? Did Amsterdam have a McDonald's? Did Mexico

City have a Taco Bell? Did any place in Rome serve Chef Boyardee ravioli? Other travelers hoped to discover distinctive local wines; Macon's readers searched for pasteurized and homogenized milk. It is as Macon heads off on one of his research trips that his life begins to change. The veterinarian who has boarded Edward in the past now refuses to accept him—"Says here he bit an attendant," the girl tells Macon. "Says, 'Bit Barry in the ankle, do not readmit'"—so in desperation Macon pulls into the Meow-Bow Animal Hospital. There Edward is cheerfully admitted by "a thin young woman in a ruffled peasant blouse," with "aggressively frizzy black hair that burgeoned to her shoulders like an Arab headdress." Her name is Muriel Pritchett, and when Macon returns to reclaim Edward she tells him that she is a dog trainer on the side, with a specialty in "dogs that bite." As Edward's bad habits become steadily worse, Macon at last turns to her in desperation. It is the beginning of the end of his old world.

He'd been right on the edge. His grief over Ethan's death and the pain caused by Sarah's desertion had just about done him in, just about turned him into "some hopeless wreck of a man wandering drugged on a downtown street." Enter Muriel—Muriel with her "long, narrow nose, and sallow skin, and two freckled knobs of collarbone that promised an unluxurious body," Muriel babbling away like "a flamenco dancer with galloping consumption," Muriel with her bewildering array of odd jobs and her pathetic young son by a broken marriage and her rundown house on Singleton Street. Love at first sight it is not: "He missed his wife. He missed his son. They were the only people who seemed real to him. There was no point looking for substitutes."

But life deals things out whether you're looking for them or not. Muriel, a fighter all her days, fights her way into Macon's heart: "Then he knew that what mattered was the pattern of her life; that although he did not love her he loved the surprise of her, and also the surprise of himself when he was with her. In the foreign country that was Singleton Street he was an entirely different person. This person had never been suspected of narrowness, never been accused of chilliness; in fact, was mocked for his soft heart. And was anything but orderly." The accidental tourist has become a traveler—"Maybe, he thought, travel was not so bad. Maybe he'd got it all wrong"—whose journeys now are in the heart, whose world has grown larger than he had ever before imagined possible.

Where those journeys at last lead him is Tyler's secret, though it is no indiscretion to say that in the novel's final pages he faces wrenching, painful choices. But those choices are really less important than the change that has already taken place. Macon Leary has been given the gift of life. A man who had seemed fated to spend the rest of his days in a rut—"Here he still was'! The same as ever! *What have I gone and done?* he wondered and he swallowed thickly and looked at his own empty hands"—has been given new connections, with himself and with others.

This is the central theme of Tyler's fiction: how people affect each other, how the lives of others alter our own. As are her previous novels, *The Accidental Tourist* is filled with connections and disconnections, with the exaltation and heartbreak that people bring to each other; she knows that though it is true people need each other, it is equally true "that people could, in fact, be used up—could use each other up, could be of no further help to each other and maybe even do harm to each other." The novel is filled as well with the knowledge that life leaves no one unscarred, that to live is to accept one's scars and make the best of them—and to accept as well the scars that other people bear.

And in *The Accidental Tourist* there are many others: the large and bumptious Leary family, Macon's wonderfully unpredictable boss, the people of Singleton Street, and most certainly Edward, the funniest and most loveable dog within memory. They occupy what indisputably is Tyler's best book, the work of a writer who has reached full maturity and is in unshakable command, who takes the raw material of ordinary life and shapes it into what can only be called art. The magical, slightly fey and otherworldly tone of her previous books is evident here, but more than ever before Tyler has planted her fiction in the hard soil of the world we all know; *The Accidental Tourist* cuts so close to the bone that it leaves one aching with pleasure and pain. Words fail me: one cannot reasonably expect fiction to be much better than this.

Source: Jonathan Yardley, "Anne Tyler's Family Circles," in *Washington Post Book World,* August 25, 1985, p. 3.

Sources

John Blades, in *Chicago Tribune Book World,* July 20, 1986.

Richard Eder, in the *Los Angeles Times Book Review,* September 15, 1985, p. 9.

Library Journal, Vol. 110, September 15, 1985, p. 96.

Larry McMurtry, in *The New York Times Book Review,* September 8, 1985, p. 1.

Elizabeth Mahn Nollen, "Fatherhood Lost and Regained in the Novels of Anne Tyler," in *Family Matters in the British and American Novel,* edited by Andrea O'Reilly Herrera, Elizabeth Mahn Nollen, and Sheila Reitzel Foor, Popular Press, 1997, pp. 217–36.

Peter Prescott, in *Newsweek,* September 9, 1985, p. 92.

Joseph C. Voelker, in *Art and the Accidental in Anne Tyler,* University of Missouri Press, 1989.

> Voelker focuses on family relationships in Tyler's novels. He finds the characters in *The Accidental Tourist* to be in a "utopian emotional state," where they experience "sickness for home (longing, nostalgia) but also sickness of it (the need to escape from the invasiveness of family) and sickness from it (the psychic wounds that human beings inevitably carry as a result of having had to grow up as children in families)."

For Further Study

Paul Binding, "Anne Tyler," in his *Separate Country: A Literary Journey through the American South,* University Press of Mississippi, 1988, pp. 171–81.

> Binding argues that Tyler follows the southern literary tradition, finding echoes of Faulkner, O'Connor, and Welty in her writing.

Laurie L. Brown, "Interviews with Seven Contemporary Writers," *Women Writers of the Contemporary South,* edited by Peggy Whitman Prenshaw, University Press of Mississippi, 1984, pp. 4–22.

> In this interview, Tyler discusses her evolution as a writer and her writing style.

Julie Persing Papadimas, "America Tyler Style: Surrogate Families and Transiency," in *Journal of American Culture,* Vol. 15, No. 3, Fall, 1992, pp. 45–51.

> The author examines family relationships in Tyler's novels and argues that they have a distinctly American sensibility.

Caren J. Town, "Anne Tyler," in *Dictionary of Literary Biography, Vol. 123: American Novelists since World War II, Third Series,* edited by James R. Giles and Wanda H. Giles, Gale Research, 1994, pp. 232–49.

> Town focuses on Macon's search for identity, arguing that he "tries on roles and partners, until he finds ones that fit."

Patricia Rowe Willrich, "Watching through Windows: A Perspective on Anne Tyler," in *The Virginia Quarterly Review,* Vol. 6, No. 3, Summer, 1992, pp. 497–516.

> In this interview, Willrich provides a biography and discussion of Tyler's writing style, focusing on what she calls Tyler's tendency to observe "from a distance."

Alice's Adventures in Wonderland

Lewis Carroll
1865

Lewis Carroll's book *Alice's Adventures in Wonderland* was not originally written for the general public but for a single child: Alice Pleasance Liddell, second daughter of the Dean of Christ Church College, Oxford. The story of its composition, as Carroll recorded it in the prefatory verses to *Alice's Adventures in Wonderland,* goes something like this: On a warm summer afternoon (July 4, 1862, according to Carroll's diary) the author, his friend Reverend Robinson Duckworth, and the three young Liddell sisters (Lorina Charlotte, age thirteen, Alice Pleasance, age ten, and Edith, age eight), daughters of the Dean of Christ Church College, Oxford, made a short trip up the Thames River in a rowboat. "The trip," explains Martin Gardner in his *The Annotated Alice,* "was about three miles, beginning at Folly Bridge, near Oxford, and ending at the village of Godstow. 'We had tea on the bank there,' Carroll recorded in his diary, 'and did not reach Christ Church again till quarter past eight....'" "Seven months later," Gardner continues, "he added to this entry the following note: 'On which occasion I told them the fairy-tale of Alice's adventures underground.'"

According to an account written many years later by Alice Liddell, she pestered Carroll—the pseudonym for mathematician and dean Charles Lutwidge Dodgson—to write the story down for her. "She 'kept going on, going on' at him," explains Morton N. Cohen in his critical biography *Lewis Carroll,* "until he promised to oblige her. For one reason or another, however, it took him two

and a half years to deliver the completed manu-script, illustrated with his own drawings." Between the time that Carroll began work on the manuscript and the time that he completed it, he had lost the friendship of the Liddells. He had also shown the manuscript to his friends Mr. and Mrs. George MacDonald, who read it to their children and urged Carroll to publish the story. Working through friends, Carroll found a publisher—Macmillan of London—and an illustrator, noted cartoonist John Tenniel. The first edition of *Alice's Adventures in Wonderland* was published in June of 1865. How-ever, Tenniel objected to some sloppy reproduction work of his illustrations in the printing, and Car-roll agreed to cancel the entire press run of two thousand copies and to print a new press run of an-other two thousand copies at his own expense. This early, flawed edition of the novel is now consid-ered one of the rarest books in the world and com-mands huge prices among collectors.

"*Alice's Adventures in Wonderland*," writes Cohen, "was widely reviewed and earned almost unconditional praise. Charles's diary lists nineteen notices." Sales were high and many foreign edi-tions were quickly authorized. Inspired by the book's success, Carroll began work on a sequel, *Through the Looking-Glass and What Alice Found There,* published in 1872. The two Alice books re-main in print today, over a century after their pub-lication. They remain, next to the Bible and the works of Shakespeare, among the world's most widely translated works of literature. Translations are available in over seventy languages, including Yiddish and Swahili.

Author Biography

Reverend Charles Lutwidge Dodgson, who wrote under the pseudonym Lewis Carroll, was one of the most creative writers of children's fantasy in the history of literature. His two most famous books, *Alice's Adventures in Wonderland* and *Through the Looking-Glass and What Alice Found There* (1872), are listed among the greatest and most influential books ever written in English. Dodgson is praised as a genius who fused his own love of word-games and logic puzzles with a gen-uine love of and sympathy for children. His two *Alice* books remain popular with both adults and children, and they have been interpreted by critics as guides to a Victorian childhood, as well as so-phisticated treatises on philosophy, logic, and mathematics.

Lewis Carroll

Dodgson was born in Daresbury, Cheshire, England, in 1832. He was the eldest son and third child of Reverend Charles Dodgson, a clergyman in the Church of England, and his wife Francis Jane Lutwidge. He came from a large family, number-ing eleven children, and was often charged with the task of amusing his younger sisters—which may help explain how he developed his love of games and his devotion to little girls. His father educated him at home and at Richmond Grammar School, thus he received a thorough background in litera-ture and mathematics. In 1846, he entered Rugby School, which at the time was not a healthy place for a sensitive young man to be. Dodgson was hazed and bullied unmercifully—perhaps another factor in his adult preference for the company of little girls— but he maintained very high academic standards. In 1851 he entered Christ Church College of Oxford University, and in 1854 he received his undergrad-uate degree. The honors he received there earned him a lifetime fellowship and a residency at Christ Church, provided he became a clergyman of the Church of England and take a vow not to marry.

Up to two years before his death in 1898, Dodgson lived and worked at Oxford University. By 1857, he had begun publishing both mathemat-ical treatises and essays on logic, but even these dry academic writings were marked by his quirky sense of humor, whimsy, and fun. He also developed a passion for photography, which at that time was a very new and very complex process. In 1856, a combination of his interest in photographing little girls and his job at Christ Church brought him into the company of Dean Henry George Liddell, Dean of Christ Church. The Dean's second daughter, Alice Pleasance, was four years old at the time. Dodgson quickly made friends with Alice's sisters Lorina (three years older) and Edith (two years younger). On July 4, 1862, the four of them, in company with Reverend Robinson Duckworth, took a boat trip up the Thames River. As they traveled upstream, Dodgson told the story that would become *Alice's Adventures in Wonderland* to Alice Liddell. She later recorded that she was so enchanted with the story that she demanded he write it down for her. He did so, and on November 26, 1864, he presented a handwritten and self-illustrated copy of the story to her, under the title *Alice's Adventures Under Ground.*

Dodgson published *Alice's Adventures in Wonderland,* an expanded version of the original tale with illustrations by cartoonist John Tenniel, in 1865. It sold so well that in 1872 he published a sequel, *Through the Looking-Glass and What Alice Found There.* These two works, along with his long poem *The Hunting of the Snark: An Agony in Eight Fits* (1876), established his reputation as a writer of nonsense verse and children's fiction. So successful were the sales of the books that Dodgson was able to use the money from them to fund his later publications, including *Sylvie and Bruno* (1889) and *Symbolic Logic* (1895). By the time of his death in 1898, the two *Alice* books had sold over 180,000 copies in England alone, and by 1911 about 700,000 copies were in print worldwide.

Plot Summary

Chapters 1–3: Down the Rabbit Hole

After a short verse prologue, in which he commemorates the day on which he first told his tale, Lewis Carroll begins *Alice's Adventures in Wonderland* with a familiar episode: Alice is sitting by the bank of a stream, bored, when she notices the White Rabbit dressed in a waistcoat scurrying along. The rabbit stops to pull a pocket watch out of its waistcoat pocket, mutters to itself that it will be late for something, then scurries off and disappears down a hole. Alice follows the rabbit down the hole, and suddenly finds herself falling, though

not so fast that she is in any danger of being injured when she lands.

She catches sight of the rabbit after she lands, but soon loses it again, and finds herself in a dark hallway. All of the doors in the hallway, she discovers, are locked; she then comes upon a small table with a tiny key on it, which enables her to open a small door she hadn't seen before, which leads into a garden. She goes back to the table, and this time finds there a bottle labeled "DRINK ME." She does just that, and shrinks to a size where she can fit through the small door. However, she has left the key on the table, and is now too short to reach it. Reduced to tears, she soon collects herself, then sees a small box under the table with a small cake in it labeled "EAT ME." Again, she follows instructions, and is soon nine feet tall. She begins crying again, filling the hallway with a pool of tears several inches deep. The White Rabbit comes and goes again, dropping a fan and pair of gloves. Clutching the fan, Alice eventually shrinks again, but is unable to go into the garden as the door has closed and locked, and the key is once again on the table.

Alice then slips and falls into the pool of tears. She sees the Mouse swimming by, begins talking to it, offends it a couple of times, but manages to coax it back, and soon they swim to the bank of the pool (the hallway having vanished). Joined there by several other creatures, they eventually engage in a "caucus-race" (that is, they simply run around for a while) in order to dry off. Some conversation follows, but it ends abruptly when Alice mentions her cat, and frightens the other creatures away.

Chapters 4–7: Learning the Ropes in Wonderland

The White Rabbit then appears again, and mistaking Alice for his servant, orders her to go fetch him another fan and pair of gloves. Alice obeys, soon finds the rabbit's house, enters it, and going upstairs finds what she is looking for. She also finds a small bottle, drinks half of its contents, and grows until she fills the room. The rabbit returns, and eventually a lizard named Bill is sent down the chimney of the house, presumably to drive Alice out. Alice manages to thrust her foot into the fireplace and kick Bill back up the chimney. The rabbit then determines that the house must be burned down. Alice finds some cakes on the floor of the room, eats enough to shrink herself to the point that she can get out of the house, and then escapes from the white rabbit and the other animals into a forest.

The Mad Hatter, the March Hare, and Alice in a scene from the 1951 animated Disney version of Alice's Adventures in Wonderland.

After an encounter with a giant puppy (Alice again being far smaller than her "normal" size), she comes upon the Caterpillar sitting on a large mushroom smoking a hookah (water pipe). The Caterpillar asks her several questions about her identity that reduce her to confusion; then, as it is leaving, it tells her that by eating opposite sides of the mushroom it was sitting on, she will either grow or shrink. She experiments with pieces from both sides, and soon has more or less mastered the process.

Determined to find the garden again, she instead comes upon a small house. After a confusing conversation with a frog-footman, she enters the house and encounters a chaotic scene: a Duchess is nursing a baby boy, who is crying, and a cook is making soup, and occasionally throwing pots and dishes across the room. Because the cook has put far too much pepper into the soup, the air in the room is full of it, causing Alice and the others to sneeze frequently. The Cheshire Cat makes its first appearance here. Eventually the Duchess gives Alice the baby to nurse, as she has to get ready to play croquet with the Queen. Alice takes the baby out of the house, only to watch it turn into a pig. She then sees the Cheshire Cat perched on the limb of a tree, and goes up to it to ask its advice.

The Cat soon disappears, and Alice comes upon the mad tea party scene from *Alice's Adventures in Wonderland.* After offending some of the creatures she encounters there, it is now her turn to be offended: she receives no tea during her stay there, and eventually receives one insult too many, and leaves in a huff. She then comes again into the hallway she had been in when she first arrived in Wonderland, and from there manages to get into the "beautiful garden."

Chapters 8–10: Alice in the Garden

Alice first encounters a curious spectacle: some playing cards are painting some white roses red. They are doing so, she learns, because red roses were supposed to have been planted there, and if the Queen of Hearts were to discover the mistake, they would have their heads cut off. Just then the Queen and King of Hearts come by, and the Queen does indeed sentence them to be beheaded, though Alice hides them, so that the sentence is never carried out.

The Queen then invites Alice to play croquet. The match is played with flamingos for mallets and hedgehogs for balls, and is predictably chaotic. The Cheshire Cat appears and creates some further confusion. Alice has a brief conversation with the

Duchess whose baby she had watched turn into a pig earlier, then after some more croquet, the Queen recommends to Alice that she meet the Mock Turtle. Alice goes off to meet him in the company of a Gryphon. They talk first about education, then Alice hears the "Lobster Quadrille," and is asked to repeat certain poems she knows, which come out quite differently from the way she expects them to. Soon they hear the cry, "The trial's beginning!" and the Gryphon hurries Alice away.

Chapters 11–12: The Trial and the Return

When they arrive at the courtroom, the trial of the Knave (i.e., Jack) of Hearts, accused of having stolen some tarts made by the Queen, is just beginning. (The episode is based on a familiar nursery rhyme.) The participants in the trial include many of the creatures Alice has already encountered. As with the croquet match, it progresses in a chaotic, absurd fashion. Over the course of the trial, Alice begins to grow again, and with her increased size she grows increasingly bold, and points out more and more frequently the absurdity of the proceedings. Eventually the Queen of Hearts orders that her head be cut off, to which Alice replies that as they are nothing but playing cards, she is not afraid of them. At that point, all the cards fly at her, and she wakes up—her adventures in Wonderland have been a dream.

Alice tells her older sister about her dream, and her sister reflects on how Alice herself will soon grow up. She expresses to herself the wish that Alice might "keep, through all her riper years, the simple and loving heart of her childhood."

Characters

Alice

Alice is in some ways the most complex and the simplest of Carroll's characters. Her character was modeled on that of his young friend Alice Pleasance Liddell, middle daughter of the classics professor and dean of Christ Church College, Oxford. Although John Tenniel's illustrations of Alice look nothing like Alice Liddell—she had short, dark hair cut into bangs, while Tenniel's little girl has long blonde hair—some of the characteristics of Miss Liddell remain in the character of Carroll's Alice. Carroll described his dream-Alice in an article entitled "Alice on the Stage" as loving, courteous, "trustful, ready to accept the wildest impossibilities with all that utter trust that only

dreamers know; and lastly, curious—wildly curious, and with the eager enjoyment of Life that comes only in the happy hours of childhood, when all is new and fair, and when Sin and Sorrow are but names—empty words signifying nothing!"

Carroll's Alice is all of these things and more. She is an ordinary person trying to make sense of a senseless situation and to understand the curious realm into which she has wandered. In Wonderland, Alice is caught in a predicament where none of the rules or logic she has learned does her any good. The creatures of Wonderland behave to her like the Victorian adults of her outside world: they ignore conventional rules in favor of rules of their own that make no sense to anyone but themselves. Alice tries to deal with them logically and fails; the dream only ends for her when she rejects their world in favor of the outside world.

Alice is also a reflection of her own society: in the early chapters of the book she is sometimes arrogant and careless of the feelings of others. Morton N. Cohen writes in his critical biography *Lewis Carroll* that Alice is the means through which Carroll criticizes and compliments Victorian society. "He wove fear, condescension, rejection, and violence into the tales, and the children who read them feel their hearts beat faster and their skin tingle, not so much with excitement as with an uncanny recognition of themselves, of the hurdles they have confronted and had to overcome. Repelled by Alice's encounters, they are also drawn to them because they recognize them as their own. These painful and damaging experiences are the price children pay in all societies in all times when passing through the dark corridors of their young lives." However, in the end, Cohen concludes, Alice overcomes the problems that face her and emerges a stronger person.

Alice's Sister

Alice's sister is unnamed throughout the course of the story. She appears briefly at the beginning—the book she is reading launches Alice on her dream voyage—and in a more lengthy passage at the end of the book, in which she herself dreams about the adventures Alice has just had. Alice's sister offers an adult perspective to the entire Wonderland adventure, interpreting Alice's dream in her own way and then going on to dream about Alice's own future.

Alice Pleasance Liddell, Carroll's model for the character Alice, had in fact two sisters: Lorina Charlotte, three years older than herself, and Edith,

Media Adaptations

- *Alice's Adventures in Wonderland* came to the stage quite early in its history. Carroll himself wrote about an early stage version of his story, written by Henry Savile Clarke and produced in London in November, 1886, in a late article entitled "Alice on the Stage." Later dramatizations produced under the title *Alice in Wonderland,* but usually based on both *Alice's Adventures in Wonderland* and *Through the Looking-Glass and What Alice Found There,* include adaptations by Eva Le Gallienne and Florida Friebus, Samuel French, 1932; by Madge Miller, Children's Theatre Press, 1953; and by Anne Coulter Martens, Dramatic Publishing, 1965.

- *But Never Jam Today,* an African American adaptation for the stage, was written in 1969. Other dramatic adaptations include *Alice and Through the Looking Glass* by Stephen Moore, 1980; *Alice,* by Michael Lancy, 1983; *Alice, a Wonderland Book,* by R. Surrette, 1983; and *Alice* (a ballet) by Glen Tetley, 1986.

- The first movie featuring Alice was *Alice in Wonderland,* produced by Maienthau, 1914, featuring Alice Savoy. Another was produced the following year by Nonpareil. Other versions were released by Pathe Studios in 1927 and by Macmillan Audio Brandon Films. The most famous film versions of *Alice* include: the 1933 Paramount version, featuring Charlotte Henry as Alice and a variety of contemporary Paramount stars (including Gary Cooper as the White Knight, Cary Grant as the Mock Turtle, W. C. Fields as Humpty Dumpty, and Edna May Oliver as the Red Queen); a 1950 satirical version by the French company Souvaine; Walt Disney Production's 1951 animated feature film featuring the voice of Kathryn Beaumont as Alice (available from Walt Disney Home Video); another animated feature by Hanna Barbera in 1965, featuring many of their cartoon stars (including Fred Flintstone and Barney Rubble) in leading roles; *Alice's Adventures in Wonderland,* released by American National in 1972 and featuring Michael Crawford as the White Rabbit, Dudley Moore as the Dormouse,

and Peter Sellers as the March Hare (available from Vestron Video); and *Alice,* a disturbingly surrealistic view of Carroll's universe directed by Jan Svankmajer and released by Film Four in 1988 (available from First Run/Icarus Films).

- Among the numerous recordings featuring Alice and produced under the title *Alice in Wonderland* include one from the 1950s narrated by Cyril Ritchard, Wonderland; one narrated by Christopher Casson, Spoken Arts, 1969; one from the 1970s, narrated by Stanley Holloway with Joan Greenwood as the voice of Alice, Caedmon, 1992; one narrated by Flo Gibson, Recorded Books, 1980; one read by William Rushton, Listen for Pleasure, 1981; one read by Christopher Plummer, Caedmon, 1985; an audio CD read by Sir John Gielgud, Nimbus, 1989; a four-cassette unabridged performance by Cybill Shepherd and Lynn Redgrave, Dove Audio, 1995; and a BBC Radio version with Alan Bennett as narrator, Bantam Books Audio, 1997. A recording of Eva Le Galienne's stage adaptation *Alice in Wonderland,* featuring Bambi Linn as Alice, was released by RCA Victor in the 1940s. Several other records were also released in connection with the Disney film.

- A number of television adaptations of the "Alice" books have also been made. In 1955, NBC television broadcast the Eva Le Gallienne and Florida Friebus stage play on "The Hallmark Hall of Fame." The television version featured Gillian Barber as Alice, Martyn Green as the White Rabbit, puppeteer Burr Tillstrum as the Cheshire Cat, Elsa Lancaster as the Red Queen, and coauthor Le Gallienne as the White Queen. A television special entitled "Alice through the Looking Glass" was broadcast on NBC in 1966; it was a musical and featured Jimmy Durante as Humpty Dumpty, and Tom and Dick Smothers as Tweedledum and Tweedledee. Another all-star television adaptation featured Red Buttons, Ringo Starr, Sammy Davis Jr., Steve Allen, Anthony Newley, Steve Lawrence, and Eydie Gorme. It aired in 1985 and is available on video from Facets Multimedia.

Cary Grant as the Mock Turtle in the 1933 film Alice in Wonderland.

two years younger. Alice's sister apparently is based on neither of the two other Liddells. If there is a historical character that Alice's sister is supposed to represent, it is probably Carroll himself.

Baby

See Pig Baby

Bill the Lizard

Bill is a lizard, one of the White Rabbit's helpers. He is sent down the chimney of the White Rabbit's house to get Alice out of the place.

Canary

Canary is one of the birds that flee Alice's company after she begins to talk about her cat Dinah. The Canary "called out in a trembling voice, to its children, 'Come away, my dears! It's high time you were all in bed!'"

Caterpillar

Alice meets the Caterpillar and spends most of Chapter 5 trying to understand his twisted logic. When she first encounters him, the Caterpillar is sitting on a mushroom and smoking a hookah, a type of water pipe from the Middle East. It is at the Caterpillar's insistence that Alice recites Carroll's "You Are Old, Father William"—a parody of

Robert Southey's poem "The Old Man's Comforts and How He Gained Them." Although he is initially very rude to Alice, the Caterpillar finally tells her that the mushroom will help her control her height.

Cheshire Cat

The Cheshire Cat first appears in the kitchen with the Duchess, the Cook, and the Baby. It has an unusual grin, as well as the strange ability to fade into invisibility—sometimes one part at a time. The Cheshire Cat is one of the few animals in Wonderland that apparently has some sympathy with Alice. He guides her on the next step of her journey (the Mad Tea Party) and is the subject of what may be *Alice's Adventures in Wonderland*'s most quoted line: "'Well! I've often seen a cat without a grin,' thought Alice; 'but a grin without a cat! It's the most curious thing I ever saw in all my life!'" The Cat reappears and provokes an argument between the executioner and The King of Hearts about whether one can decapitate a bodiless character.

The Cheshire Cat's grin is one of the most debated questions about *Alice's Adventures in Wonderland*. Why does the Cheshire Cat grin? There was a common phrase in Carroll's time, "to grin like a Cheshire Cat," but no one really knows how the phrase originated. One theory holds that the grin is based on pictures of grinning lions that a local painter used to paint on the signboards of inns. Another states that Cheshire cheeses were sometimes molded into the shape of grinning cats. Carroll, who was born in the county of Cheshire, could have known both theories. Although he is one of the most popular characters in the Alice stories, the Cheshire Cat does not appear in the original manuscript version, *Alice's Adventures Under Ground.*

Cook

The Cook serves in the Duchess's kitchen. She is primarily noted for two qualities: she throws things (mostly kitchen utensils) at the Duchess and the Baby, and she cooks with an excessive amount of pepper, which causes the Baby and the Duchess to sneeze. She appears again as a witness against the Knave of Hearts.

Crab

See Old Crab

Dinah

Dinah is Alice's cat. She does not appear in person. It is Alice's thoughtless talking about her cat that finally alienates the animals and birds. "Dinah" was also the name of a cat owned by the Liddell girls.

Dodo

The Dodo appears in the drying-off sequence. He suggests the Caucus-Race as a means of drying off and later calls on Alice to provide the prizes for the winners. In the original manuscript, the Dodo makes the suggestion to move the party to a nearby house to dry off.

Like the Mouse and the Duck, the Dodo represents another of the characters who traveled on the "golden afternoon" on which the Alice story was first composed. According to a note in Martin Gardner's *The Annotated Alice,* the Dodo was Carroll himself. "When Carroll stammered he pronounced his name 'Do-Do-Dodgson,' and it is amusing to note that when his biography entered the *Encyclopaedia Britannica* it was inserted just before the entry on the Dodo."

Dormouse

Dormouse is the third character at the Mad Tea Party. The name is actually derived from the Latin verb dormire, which means "to sleep." It looks more like a small squirrel than a mouse. It hibernates during the winter and sleeps during the day, so the name is quite appropriate. Since Alice is touring Wonderland during the day, the Dormouse is very sleepy. Nevertheless, it is able to participate in the tea party and even begins a nonsense tale before falling to sleep again. Martin Gardner reports in *The Annotated Alice* that the Dormouse may have been inspired by the pet wombat of Dante Gabriel Rossetti, a noted literary figure of Carroll's time. Rossetti's wombat "had a habit of sleeping on the table," Gardner writes. "Carroll knew all the Rossettis and occasionally visited them." The Dormouse does not appear at all in Carroll's original manuscript story, *Alice's Adventures Under Ground.*

Duchess

When Alice first encounters the Duchess, she is sitting in the kitchen with the Cook and the Cheshire Cat, and she holds the Baby who will later turn into a Pig. She also sings the Carrollian poem "Speak Roughly to Your Little Boy," a parody of a Victorian verse about manners. She also abuses the Baby by shaking it and tossing it up into the air, and at the end of the poem she throws it at Alice.

John Tenniel's famous big-mouthed illustration of the Duchess from the original edition of the novel is probably based on a portrait of Margaretha Maultasch, a duchess of Carinthia and Tyrol during the fourteenth century. Martin Gardner, in his *The Annotated Alice,* reports that "'Maultasch,' meaning 'pocket-mouth,' was a name given to her because of the shape of her mouth." He also explains that Margaretha "had the reputation of being the ugliest woman in history." Carroll's Duchess appears again, and is now very friendly to Alice. Then it is revealed that the Queen had sentenced her to death, and she leaves quickly.

Duck

The Duck is one of the birds that gets caught in the pool of Alice's tears. The Duck gets into an argument with the Mouse over the interpretation of a pronoun in the "dry" passage of English history that the Mouse reads. The Duck originally represented Reverend Robinson Duckworth, a companion of Carroll and the Liddell sisters on the "golden afternoon" on which Carroll told Alice Liddell the story that became *Alice's Adventures in Wonderland.*

Eaglet

The Eaglet is one of the animals caught in the pool of tears. She demands that the Dodo "speak English" and adds, "I don't know the meaning of half those long words, and, what's more, I don't believe you do either!" The Eaglet represents Alice Liddell's younger sister Edith Liddell.

Father William

Father William is the title character of Carroll's parody poem "You Are Old, Father William," a takeoff of Robert Southey's didactic poem "The Old Man's Comforts and How He Gained Them." Carroll's poem inverts the didactic purpose of Southey's original. While the Old Man in Southey's poem won his comforts through thriftiness, conservative behavior, and religious devotion, Carroll's Father William moves through his old age by refusing to conform to Victorian norms. While Southey's young man seeks to understand his father's good health and good humor, Carroll's young man seeks information only to satisfy his curiosity. Carroll's poem ends with Father William's threat to kick his son downstairs.

Father William's Son

Father William's Son is the other character in Carroll's parody poem "You Are Old, Father William," a take-off of Robert Southey's didactic poem "The Old Man's Comforts and How He Gained Them." While Southey's young man seeks to understand his father's good health and good humor, Carroll's young man seeks information only to satisfy his curiosity. Carroll's poem ends with Father William's threat to kick his son downstairs.

Fish-Footman

The Fish-Footman brings an invitation to the Duchess from the Queen to play croquet.

Five of Spades

Five of Spades is one of the gardeners Alice discovers in the Queen's garden who are painting the white roses red.

Frog-Footman

The doorman at the house of the Duchess, the Frog-Footman goes outside to accept the invitation from the Queen for the Duchess to play croquet that afternoon. He then poses a logical conundrum for Alice: since he can only answer the door from inside the house, how is she to get in? Alice discusses the problem with him for some time before she finally gives up, opens the door to the Duchess's house herself, and goes in.

Griffin

The Gryphon is assigned by the Queen of Hearts to be Alice's guide and takes her to see the Mock Turtle. He is one of the more sympathetic characters in the novel, and he treats Alice better than most of his fellow Wonderland creatures.

Gryphon

See Griffin

Guinea Pigs

Guinea Pigs appear in several different roles in *Alice's Adventures in Wonderland.* A couple of them serve as the White Rabbit's servants and help revive Bill the Lizard after Alice kicks him up the chimney in Chapter IV. Another couple—or perhaps the same ones—serve as jurors in the trial of the Knave of Hearts in Chapters XI and XII.

King of Hearts

The King of Hearts first makes his appearance at the Queen's croquet party, but his most important role is as the conductor of the Knave of Heart's trial. He objects to the Cheshire Cat's rudeness and sentences the animal to lose its head. He is not as forceful as his wife, the Queen of Hearts, but he shares with her and the other Wonderland characters a form of logic that first confuses Alice, then irritates her.

Knave of Hearts

Made of cardboard, the Knave (or Jack) of Hearts makes a brief appearance in Chapter 8. He is later arrested and held for trial on the charge of stealing the Queen's tarts.

Lory

Lory is a type of Australian parrot who gets into an argument with Alice, and "at last turned sulky, and would only say, 'I'm older than you, and must know better.'" Critics agree that the Lory represents Lorinda Liddell, Alice's older sister, who was also a participant on the "golden afternoon" on which the concept of *Alice's Adventures in Wonderland* was composed.

Mad Hatter

The Mad Hatter, like his friend the March Hare, is stuck in an endless tea time. In Carroll's time, hat makers regularly used mercury to treat their hats, and mercury vapor is poisonous. It can cause hallucinations as well. The depiction of the Hatter in the original illustrations by John Tenniel may be based in part on an Oxford furniture dealer named Theophilus Carter. "Carter," says Martin Gardner in his *The Annotated Alice,* "was known in the area as the Mad Hatter, partly because he always wore a top hat and partly because of his eccentric ideas." Carter invented a bed that tossed the sleeper out on the floor when the alarm went off, which "may explain why Carroll's Hatter is so concerned with time as well as with arousing a sleepy dormouse." His poem "Twinkle, Twinkle, Little Bat" parodies Jane Taylor's song "The Star," and he proposes the famous riddle "Why is a raven like a writing-desk?" He appears again as a witness in the trial of the Knave of Hearts. He does not appear at all in Carroll's original manuscript story, *Alice's Adventures Under Ground.*

Magpie

See Old Magpie

March Hare

The March Hare hosts the Mad Tea Party. He is called the March Hare because he is mad. In England March is the breeding season for hares, and they often act strangely during the month. With his friends the Mad Hatter and the Dormouse, he is stuck in a perpetual tea party, in which time never progresses and tea never ends. He is very argumentative and challenges almost all of Alice's remarks by challenging the meanings of specific words. When Alice leaves the tea party, she looks back to see the Hatter and the Hare trying to drown the Dormouse in a teapot. He later appears as a witness in the trial of the Knave of Hearts. He does not appear at all in Carroll's original manuscript story, *Alice's Adventures Under Ground.*

Mary Ann

Mary Ann is the White Rabbit's servant. He mistakes Alice for her in Chapter IV, but she never actually appears in the book.

Mock Turtle

The Mock Turtle is a character who has the front limbs and shell of a turtle and the head and hind limbs of a calf, because "mock turtle soup" is made from veal. In Chapters 9 and 10 he entertains Alice with the story of his education (liberally sprinkled with puns) and the song known as "The Lobster Quadrille"—a parody of a poem by Mary Howitt called "The Spider and the Fly." He also performs "Beautiful Soup," a Carrollian parody of a popular song, "Star of the Evening," that Carroll had heard the Liddell sisters sing on occasion.

Mouse

Mouse is the first creature Alice meets after she falls into the pool of her own tears she had cried while she was nine feet tall. Alice inadvertently offends the Mouse by talking about her cat Dinah, but the Mouse forgives her and tries to help her dry off by reciting a passage from a very dry—in the sense of boring—book of English history. Later the Mouse tells her and the other assembled animals "The Mouse's Tale," perhaps the most famous example in English of "figured" verse, poetry in which the shape of the poem reflects something of the poem's subject matter.

In the original manuscript, the Mouse was held to represent Alice Liddell's governess Miss Prickett. The book with the very dry passage that the Mouse quotes was an actual book of English history that Miss Prickett used to teach the Liddell children.

Old Crab

The Old Crab gives a moral lesson to her daughter: "Let this be a lesson to you never to lose your temper!"

Old Magpie

The Old Magpie is one of the "curious creatures" from the pool of tears. When Alice begins to talk about her cat Dinah, the Old Magpie declares, "I really must be getting home: the night-air doesn't suit my throat!" and leaves.

Pat

Pat is the White Rabbit's manservant. He speaks with an Irish brogue and tries to get Alice out of the White Rabbit's house.

Pig Baby

The Baby first appears in Chapter 6, where he is alternately wailing at the Duchess and sneezing from the Cook's pepper. After Alice rescues him from the Duchess's abuse and the Cook's thrown dishes, he changes into a Pig. Martin Gardner, in his *The Annotated Alice,* suggests that Carroll made the Baby change into a Pig because of his low opinion of little boys.

Pigeon

Alice encounters the Pigeon after the Caterpillar's mushroom has made her grow up over the surrounding trees. The Pigeon mistakes her for a serpent because Alice's neck has grown very long. The Pigeon cannot conceive of anything that long and serpent-like being anything but a serpent and refuses to accept the idea that Alice does not want to eat her eggs.

Puppy

Alice encounters the Puppy toward the end of Chapter 4, after she shrinks to a height of three inches. Because of her smallness the playful puppy poses a serious threat to Alice, and she is forced to run away from it. She compares playing with the Puppy to "having a game of play with a cart-horse, and expecting every moment to be trampled under its feet."

Queen of Hearts

The Queen of Hearts is the driving force behind Wonderland. She constantly orders the execution of her subjects, but her command "off with his head!" is never carried out. It is fear of her anger that motivates the White Rabbit at the beginning of the book, and it is fear of the queen that suppresses the Duchess's behavior. Alice's own anger at the Queen's illogical, reckless behavior makes her overturn the conventions of Wonderland and break out of her dream at the end of the book. In "Alice on the Stage," Carroll wrote, "I pictured to myself the Queen of Hearts as a sort of embodiment of ungovernable passion—a blind and aimless Fury." "Her constant orders for beheadings," explains Martin Gardner in his *The Annotated Alice,* "are shocking to those modern critics of children's literature who feel that juvenile fiction should be free of all violence and especially violence with Freudian overtones."

Seven of Spades

The Seven of Spades is one of the gardeners Alice discovers in the Queen's garden who are painting the white roses red.

Sister

See Alice's Sister

Two of Spades

The Two of Spades is one of the gardeners Alice discovers in the Queen's garden who are painting the white roses red.

William

See Father William

White Rabbit

White Rabbit is the first character that Alice meets in her dream wonderland. He looks much like any other white rabbit, with a white coat and pink eyes, but he wears a waistcoat (vest) and carries a large gold watch. John Tenniel's illustration from the first edition of the novel shows him wearing a jacket and carrying an umbrella. He also speaks English, but to Alice his clothes and watch are his most amazing characteristics. In the second chapter he drops his white kid gloves and a fan, which Alice picks up; it is the fan that causes her to shrink to below her normal size. (In the original manuscript, *Alice's Adventures Under Ground,* the fan was replaced by a nosegay, a small bouquet of flowers.) Later he mistakes Alice for his maidservant Mary Ann.

The White Rabbit, with his preoccupation with time and clothing, is in many ways a representative Victorian adult. Carroll wrote about him in the article "Alice on the Stage": "For her 'youth,' 'audacity,' 'vigour,' and 'swift directness of purpose,' read 'elderly,' 'timid,' 'feeble,' and 'nervously shilly-shallying,' and you will get *something* of what I meant him to be." "I *think* the White Rabbit should wear spectacles," the author continued. "I am sure his voice should quaver, and his knees quiver, and his whole air suggest a total inability to say 'Boo' to a goose!"

Themes

Identity

Lewis Carroll's *Alice's Adventures in Wonderland* has been one of the most analyzed books of all time. Critics have viewed it as a work of philosophy, as a criticism of the Church of England, as full of psychological symbolism, and as an expression of the drug culture of the 1960s. Readers all differ in their interpretations of the book, but there are a few themes that have won general acceptance. One of the clearly identifiable subjects of the story is the identity question. One of the first things that the narrator says about Alice after her arrival in the antechamber to Wonderland is that "this curious child was very fond of pretending to be two people." The physical sign of her loss of identity is the changes in size that take place when she eats or drinks. After she drinks the cordial and eats the cake in Chapter 1, for instance, she loses even more of her sense of self, until at the beginning of Chapter 2 she is reduced to saying, "I wonder if I've been changed in the night? Let me think: was I the same when I got up this morning? I almost think I can remember feeling a little differ-

Topics for Further Study

- Make a chart of the sequence of events in *Alice's Adventures in Wonderland*. Many critics find a definite pattern to Alice's adventures. Do you agree with them? Explain why or why not, and give examples from the text to support your argument.

- One of the chief characteristics of Wonderland is its twisted logic. Read Carroll's books on *Symbolic Logic* and *The Game of Logic* and compare Carroll's concept of logic in these books to that in *Alice's Adventures in Wonderland*.

- Compare *Alice's Adventures in Wonderland* to other Victorian works of fantasy, including John Ruskin's *The King of the Golden River* and Jean Ingelow's *Mopsa the Fairy*. How does Alice compare to these books?

- Research the roles of women and children in Victorian England during the period when *Alice's Adventures in Wonderland* was written. Write a diary of what daily life might have been like for the real Alice, and include what her expectations for the future might have been.

---

ent. But if I'm not the same, the next question is, Who in the world am I?" She begins to cry and to fan herself with the White Rabbit's fan, which causes her to shrink down to almost nothing. After she shrinks, she falls into a pool of her own tears, in which she almost drowns. For Alice, the question of identity is a vital one.

Alice continues to question her identity until the final chapters of the book. When the White Rabbit mistakes her for his servant Mary Ann, she goes along willingly to his house to find his gloves. At the beginning of her encounter with the Caterpillar in Chapter 5, she answers his question "Who are *you?*" with the response "I—I hardly know, Sir, just at present—at least I know who I *was* when I got up this morning, but I think I must have been changed several times since then." At the end of

Chapter 5, she tells the hostile Pigeon who calls her a serpent that she is a little girl; but she says it "rather doubtfully, as she remembered the number of changes she had gone through that day." As late as Chapter 10, she says to the Gryphon, "I could tell you my adventures—beginning from this morning ... but it's no use going back to yesterday, because I was a different person then." As she progresses through Wonderland, however, Alice slowly gains a greater sense of herself and eventually overthrows the Queen of Hearts' cruel court.

Coming of Age

The question of *why* Alice is so confused about her identity has to do with her developing sense of the difference between childhood and adulthood. She is surrounded by adult figures and figures of authority: the Duchess, the Queen, the King. Even the animals she encounters treat her as a Victorian adult might treat a small child. The White Rabbit and the Caterpillar order her about. They also break the rules of politeness that adults have drilled into Alice. The Mad Hatter, the March Hare, and (to a lesser extent) the Dormouse are all rude to her in various degrees. They also break the rules of logic that Alice has been taught to follow. It is not until Alice stops trying to understand the Wonderland residents logically and rejects their world that she "comes of age"—she takes responsibility for her own actions and breaks powerfully out of her dream world.

Alice's Adventures in Wonderland is, on this level, a very affirming book for children. It offers them a path by which they can find their own way into the power of adulthood. "By a magical combination of memory and intuition," writes Morton N. Cohen in his critical biography *Lewis Carroll*, "Charles keenly appreciated what it was like to be a child in a grown-up society, what it meant to be scolded, rejected, ordered about. The *Alice* books are antidotes to the child's degradation.... Charles champions the child in the child's confrontation with the adult world, and in that, too, his book differs from most others. He treats children ... as equals. He has a way of seeing into their minds and hears, and he knows how to train their minds painlessly and move their hearts constructively."

Absurdity

Carroll communicates Alice's confusion about her own identity and her position between childhood and adulthood by contrasting her logical, reasoned behavior with that of the inhabitants of Wonderland. Everything about Wonderland is absurd by Alice's standards. From the moment that she spots the White Rabbit taking his watch from his waist-coat pocket, Alice tries to understand the twisted Wonderland logic. None of the rules she has been taught seem to work here. The inhabitants meet her politeness with rudeness and respond to her questions with answers that make no sense. The Mad Hatter's question "Why is a raven like a writing-desk?" is an example. Alice believes that he is posing a riddle and tries to answer it, believing (logically) that the Hatter would not ask a riddle without knowing the answer. When she is unable to answer the question, the Hatter explains that there is no answer. He does not explain his reasons for asking the riddle; he simply says that he hasn't "the slightest idea" of the answer. When Alice protests that asking riddles with no answers wastes time, the Hatter responds with a lecture on the nature of Time, which he depicts as a person. The connections between the two subjects make no logical sense to Alice.

Alice's encounter with the Gryphon and the Mock Turtle are as equally absurd, although less grating, as the Mad Tea Party. When the two of them call on her to recite, Alice begins another of Carroll's nonsense verses, "'Tis the Voice of the Lobster." At the end, she "sat down with her face in her hands, wondering if anything would *ever* happen in a natural way again." Alice finally rebels during the trial scene when the King requires *All persons more than a mile high to leave the court.* She objects to the absurd nature of the trial, saying finally "Stuff and nonsense!" and "Who cares for *you?*" "You're nothing but a pack of cards!" Her final break precipitates the end of her dream, and she wakes up with her head in her sister's lap.

Style

Parody

Alice's Adventures in Wonderland was originally told to entertain a little girl. One of the devices Lewis Carroll uses to communicate with Alice Liddell is parody, which adopts the style of the serious literary work and applies it to an inappropriate subject for humorous effect. Most of the songs and poems that appear in the book are parodies of well-known Victorian poems, such as Robert Southey's "The Old Man's Comforts and How He Gained Them" ("You Are Old, Father William"), Isaac Watts's "How Doth the Little Busy Bee" ("How Doth the Little Crocodile"), and Mary Howett's "The Spider and the Fly" ("Will You Walk a Little Faster"). Several of the songs

were ones that Carroll had heard the Liddell sisters sing, so he knew that Alice, for whom the story was written, would appreciate them. There are also a number of "inside jokes" that might make sense only to the Liddells or Carroll's closest associates. The Mad Hatter's song, for instance, ("Twinkle, Twinkle, Little Bat") is a parody of Jane Taylor's poem "The Star," but it also contains a reference to the Oxford community. "Bartholomew Price," writes Martin Gardner in his *The Annotated Alice,* "a distinguished professor of mathematics at Oxford and a good friend of Carroll's, was known among his student by the nickname 'The Bat.' His lectures no doubt had a way of soaring high above the heads of his listeners."

What makes Carroll's parodies so special that they have outlived the originals they mock is the fact that they are excellent humorous verses in their own right. They also serve a purpose within the book: they emphasize the underlying senselessness of Wonderland and highlight Alice's own sense of displacement. Many of them Alice recites herself under pressure from another character. "'Tis the Voice of the Lobster" is a parody of the didactic poem "The Sluggard" by Isaac Watts. It is notable that most often Alice is cut off by the same characters that require her to recite in the first place.

Narrator

Alice's Adventures in Wonderland opens with Alice's complaint, "For what is the use of a book ... without pictures or conversations?" So most of the story is told through pictures and dialogue. However, there is another voice besides those of Alice and the characters she encounters. The third-person ("he/she/it") narrator of the story maintains a point of view that is very different from that of the heroine. The narrator steps in to explain Alice's thoughts to the reader. The narrator explains who Dinah is, for instance, and also highlights Alice's own state of mind. He frequently refers to Alice as "poor Alice" or "the poor little thing" whenever she is in a difficult situation.

Point of View

Although the narrator has an impartial voice, the point of view is very strongly connected with Alice. Events are related as they happen to her and are explained as they affect her. As a result, some critics believe that the narrator is not in fact a separate voice, but is a part of Alice's own thought process. They base this interpretation on the statement in Chapter 1 that Alice "was very fond of pretending to be two people." Alice, they suggest, consists of the thoughtless child who carelessly jumps down the rabbit-hole after the White Rabbit, and the well-brought-up, responsible young girl who re-members her manners even when confronted by rude people and animals.

Language

Part of the way Carroll shows Wonderland to be a strange place is the way the inhabitants twist the meaning of words. Carroll plays with language by including many puns and other forms of word play. In Chapter 3, for instance, the Mouse says he can dry everyone who was caught in the pool of tears. He proceeds to recite a bit of history—"the driest thing I know." Here, of course, the Mouse means "dry" as in dull; the Mouse's words have no ability to ease the dampness of the creatures. When Alice meets the Mad Hatter and the March Hare, they play with syn-tax—the order of words—to confuse Alice. When she says "I say what I mean" is the same thing as "I mean what I say," the others immediately contradict her by bringing up totally unrelated examples: " 'Not the same thing a bit!' said the Hatter. 'You might just as well say that "I see what I eat" is the same thing as "I eat what I see"!' " The power of language is also evident in the way Alice continually offends the inhabitants of Wonderland, often quite unintention-ally. For instance, she drives away the creatures at the pool of tears just by mentioning the word "cat." Eventually Alice learns to be careful of what she says, as in Chapter 8 when she changes how she is about to describe the Queen after noticing the woman be-hind her shoulder.

Historical Context

The Victorian Age in England

According to his own account, Lewis Carroll composed the story that became *Alice's Adventures in Wonderland* on a sunny July day in 1862. He created it for the Liddell sisters while on a boating trip up the Thames River. Although the book and its sequel *Through the Looking-Glass and What Alice Found There* have since become timeless classics, they nonetheless clearly reflect their Vic-torian origins in their language, their class-consciousness, and their attitude toward children. The Victorian age, named for the long rule of Britain's Queen Victoria, spanned the years 1837 to 1901.

The early Victorian era marked the emergence of a large middle-class society for the first time in the history of the Western world. With this middle-class population came a spread of so-called "family values": polite society avoided men-tioning sex, sexual passions, bodily functions, and in extreme cases, body parts. They also followed an elaborate code of manners meant to distinguish one class from another. By the 1860s, the result, for most people, was a kind of stiff and gloomy prudery marked by a feeling that freedom and enjoyment of life were sinful and only to be in-dulged in at the risk of immorality. Modern crit-ics have mostly condemned the Victorians for these repressive attitudes.

The tone for the late Victorian age was set by Queen Victoria herself. She had always been a very serious and self-important person from the time she took the throne at the age of eighteen; it is reported that when she became queen, her first resolution was, "I will be good." After the death of her hus-band Albert in 1861, however, Victoria became more and more withdrawn, retreating from public life and entering what became a lifelong period of mourning. Many middle-class Englishmen and women followed her example, seeking to find morally uplifting and mentally stimulating thoughts in their reading and other entertainments.

Victorian Views of Childhood

Many upper-middle-class Victorians had a double view of childhood. Childhood was regarded as the happiest period of a person's life, a simple and uncomplicated time. At the same time, chil-dren were also thought to be "best seen and not heard." Some Victorians also neglected their chil-dren, giving them wholly over into the care of nurses, nannies and other child-care professionals. Boys often went away to boarding school, while girls were usually taught at home by a governess. The emphasis for all children, but particularly girls, was on learning manners and how to fit into soci-ety. "Children learned their catechism, learned to pray, learned to fear sin—and their books were meant to aid and abet the process," states Morton N. Cohen in his critical biography *Lewis Carroll.* "They were often frightened by warnings and threats, their waking hours burdened with homilies. Much of the children's literature ... were purpose-ful and dour. They instilled discipline and compli-ance." Although the end of the century saw a trend toward educating women in subjects taught to men, such as Latin and mathematics, this change affected only a small portion of the population, specifically the upper classes.

This emphasis on manners and good breeding is reflected in Alice's adventures. She is always

Alice Pleasance Liddell, inspiration for the title character of Alice's Adventures in Wonderland, *pictured with her sister, Lorina Charlotte Liddell.*

apologetic when she discovers she has offended someone, and she scolds the March Hare for his rude behavior. Nevertheless, Carroll seems to share the view that childhood was a golden period in a person's life. He refers in his verse preface to the novel to the "golden afternoon" that he shared with the three Miss Liddells. He also concludes the book with the prediction that Alice will someday repeat her dream of Wonderland to her own children and "feel with all their simple sorrows, and find a pleasure in all their simple joys, remembering her own child-life, and the happy summer days." On the other hand, Alice's own experiences suggest that Carroll felt that children's feelings and emotions were fully as complex as any adult emotions. By the end of the novel, she is directly contradicting adults; when she tells the Queen "Stuff and nonsense!" she is acting contrary to Victorian dictates of proper children's behavior.

The Early Development of Children's Literature

"Children's literature" first emerged as a genre of its own in the mid-1700s, when English bookseller John Newbery created some of the first books designed specifically to entertain children. (He is honored today in the United States by the American Library Association, who awards the annual John Newbery Medal to the best children's work of the year.) Prior to that time, works published for children were strictly educational, using stories merely to impart a moral message. If children wished to read for entertainment, they had to turn to "adult" works, such as Daniel Defoe's 1719 classic *Robinson Crusoe*. Despite Newbery's groundbreaking work, few works of entertainment for children appeared over the hundred years.

Most early Victorian fairy-stories and other works for children were intended to promote what contemporaries believed was "good" and "moral" behavior on the part of children. Carroll's "Alice" books take a swipe at this Victorian morality, in part through their uninhibited use of nonsense and wordplay (a favorite Victorian pastime) and in part through direct parody. Alice recalls in Chapter 1 of *Alice's Adventures in Wonderland* that "she had read several nice little histories about children who had got burnt, and eaten up by wild beasts and other unpleasant things, all because they *would* not remember the simple rules their friends had taught them." Most of the verses and poems Carroll included in the story are parodies of popular Victorian (i.e., morally uplifting) songs and ballads, twisted so that their didactic points are lost in the pleasure of wordplay.

Carroll's "Alice" books were part of a flourishing movement throughout the world to write entertaining books for children. English translations of the fairy tale collections of the German brothers Grimm first appeared in the mid-1820s. The tales of Danish writer Hans Christian Andersen appeared in English in 1846. The United States saw Louisa May Alcott's *Little Women* in 1868–69, part of a movement to publish realistic stories for children. In England, many noted authors for adults published works for children, including Charles Dickens and Robert Louis Stevenson, whose 1883 work *Treasure Island* is considered a classic children's adventure story. The ground broken by Carroll and other children's authors of the nineteenth century led the way for today's huge market for children's books, which have their own publishers, critical scholars and journals, and librarians.

Critical Overview

In part because of its popularity with children and in part because of the fascination it has for adults, *Alice's Adventures in Wonderland* has become one of the most widely interpreted pieces of literature ever produced. Victorians praised Lewis Carroll's wordplay and brilliant use of language. Critics after his death found psychological clues to Carroll's own subconscious in the book's curious dream-structure and the strange and often hostile creatures of Wonderland. During the 1960s, many young people read the book as a commentary on the contemporary drug culture. *Alice's Adventures in Wonderland* and its sequel *Through the Looking-Glass and What Alice Found There* still fascinate critics, who continue to find new readings and new meanings in Carroll's stories for children.

Early reviews of the novel on its original release in 1865 concentrated on Carroll's skills at invention and his ability as a molder of words. They mentioned his parodies, his use of language, and his literary style. According to Morton N. Cohen in his critical biography *Lewis Carroll,* the noted poets Christina Rossetti and Dante Gabriel Rossetti both praised the book in private letters to the author. Novelist Henry Kingsley thanked Carroll for his copy, saying "I received it in bed in the morning, and in spite of threats and persuasions, in bed I stayed until I had read every word of it. I could pay you no higher compliment ... than confessing

that I could not stop reading ... till I had finished it. The fancy of the whole thing is delicious.... Your versification is a gift I envy you very much."

"*Alice's Adventures in Wonderland* was widely reviewed," notes Cohen, "and earned almost unconditional praise." Important newspapers and magazines, including the *Reader* and the *Press* commended the story's humor and its style. "The *Publisher's Circular,*" asserts Cohen, " ... selected it as 'the most original and the most charming' of the two hundred books for children sent them that year; the *Bookseller* ... was 'delighted.... A more original fairy tale ... it has not lately been our good fortune to read'; and the *Guardian* ... judged the 'nonsense so graceful and so full of humour that one can hardly help reading it through.' " An anonymous review in the " Children's Books" section of *The Athenaeum* magazine (reprinted in Robert Phillips's *Aspects of Alice*) was an exception to the general praise the work received. The reviewer declared that "Mr. Carroll has labored hard to heap together strange adventures and heterogeneous combinations, and we acknowledge the hard labor..... We fancy that any real child might be more puzzled than enchanted by this stiff, overwrought story."

After Carroll's death in 1898, critics expanded the number and type of their readings of the *Alice* books. They analyzed the stories from many points of view—political, philosophical, metaphysical, and psychoanalytic—often evaluating the tales as products of Dodgson's neuroses and as reactions to Victorian culture. Because of the nightmarish qualities of Alice's adventures and their violent, even sadistic, elements, a few critics have suggested that the books are not really suitable for children. "We have also been bombarded by a horde of wild surmises," declares Cohen, "mostly from the psychological detectives determined to unlock deep motives in the man and to discover hidden meanings in the books. These analysts sometimes seem to be engaged in a contest to win a prize for the most outlandish reading of the texts. One such writer has proved to his satisfaction that *Alice* was written not by Lewis Carroll at all, but by Queen Victoria."

Some of the most well-known interpretations of *Alice's Adventures in Wonderland* are those that try to understand the story in light of Carroll's well-documented preference for the company of young, preteen, girls. Critics who take this approach connect Carroll's apparent inability to form an adult relationship with a woman and his artistic photographs of little girls, and conclude that Carroll was a closet pedophile—although major critics agree that there is absolutely no biographical information to support this theory. Analysts who use the theories of noted psychologist Sigmund Freud, says Cohen, "suggest that the book is about a woman in labor, that falling down the rabbit hole is an expression of Carroll's wish for coitus, that the heroine is variously a father, a mother, a fetus, or that Alice is a phallus (a theory that, at least, provides us with a rhyme)." Other readings interpret the story as about toilet training or about fallen women. "Unfortunately," Cohen concludes, "these eccentric readings, while they may amuse, do not really bring us any closer to understanding Carroll or his work."

To the extent that critics are able to agree about the meaning of the *Alice* books, they conclude that the stories are primarily games, stories invented by a man who loved young children and who loved to invent his own word-games and mind-puzzles. *Alice's Adventures in Wonderland*, they agree, is the work of a lonely and brilliant man who found consolation in the company of children and tried to repay some of the debt he felt.

Criticism

Stan Walker

In the following essay Walker, a doctoral candidate at the University of Texas, explains the background of Charles Dodgson, who wrote Alice's Adventures in Wonderland *under the pseudonym Lewis Carroll. He explores the sources the author used in creating the novel, and examines how its major themes of growing up and finding one's identity are a reflection and product of the Victorian age.*

Alice's Adventures in Wonderland (1865), Lewis Carroll's masterpiece of children's nonsense fiction, has enjoyed a life rivaled by few books from the nineteenth century, or indeed any earlier period. Alice has inspired several screen adaptations, from Disney's well-known 1951 animated feature to more "adult" versions by contemporary Czech surrealist Jan Svankmajer and Playboy. It has been adapted for the stage several times, has served as the basis for countless spin-offs in the realm of fiction, and has inspired at least one well-known pop song (Jefferson Airplane's 1967 hit "White Rabbit"). Episodes from *Alice* and its companion piece, *Through the Looking Glass* (1872), have also frequently been used to illustrate problems in contemporary physics and ethics. On one level, perhaps, the reason for *Alice's* popularity

What Do I Read Next?

- The roughly contemporary fairy tales of the Danish novelist Hans Christian Andersen (available in many editions), which established a Victorian passion for fairy stories.

- John Ruskin's *The King of the Golden River* (1851), a classic Victorian fairy tale that, like *Alice's Adventures in Wonderland,* was originally written for a little girl. Ruskin was at one time an instructor for Alice Liddell.

- The Victorian wordplay of Edward Lear, contained in *A Book of Nonsense* (1846), *Nonsense Songs, Stories, Botany, and Alphabets* (1871), *More Nonsense, Pictures, Rhymes, Botany, Etc.* (1872), *Laughable Lyrics: A Fourth Book of Nonsense Poems, Songs, Botany, Music, Etc.* (1877), and *Nonsense Songs and Stories* (1895).

- George Macdonald's allegorical fairy tale about growing up and coming to sexual maturity, *The Golden Key* (1867).

- Victorian poet Christina Rossetti's famous narrative poem "Goblin Market" (1862), which, like the "Alice" books, is outwardly for children, but nonetheless deals with many adult themes—particularly repressed sexuality.

- The American fairy tales of L. Frank Baum, including *The Wonderful Wizard of Oz* (1900) and its many sequels.

- Gilbert Adair's *Alice through the Needle's Eye* (1984), a modern attempt to add to the "Alice" stories.

needs no explanation: its sheer imaginative force, coupled with its blend of humor, unsentimental sweetness, and a sense of wonder, make the book unique, and likely to endure for some time. As Sir Richard Burton puts it in the "Terminal Essay" to his famous translation of *The Thousand and One Nights* (1886), "Every man at some turn or term of his life has longed for ... a glimpse of Wonderland."

Lewis Carroll was the pen name of the Reverend Charles Lutwidge Dodgson, a professor of mathematics at Christ Church, one of the colleges of Oxford University. Politically, he was conservative, "awed by lords and ladies and inclined to be snobbish toward inferiors," according to Martin Gardner in *The Annotated Alice.* He was also a skillful photographer (when photography was a new technology), a patron of the theater (a pastime generally discouraged by church officials at the time), and a fan of games and magic. And if "he was so shy that he could sit for hours at a social gathering and contribute nothing to the conversation, ... his shyness and stammering 'softly and suddenly vanished away' when he was alone with a child," notes Gardner.

This fondness for children, specifically young girls (he intensely disliked boys), has led to much speculation about Carroll's psychological makeup. There is little to no evidence, however, that his numerous relationships with girls were anything other than purely platonic. These relationships tended to break off after the girls passed through adolescence. A principal exception was his relationship with Alice Liddell, daughter of Henry George Liddell, dean of Christ Church. *Alice in Wonderland* was written at her request, and represents a record (expanded and polished) of a tale he told her one afternoon in July 1862. On this "golden afternoon" of the verse prologue, the two went rowing on the Thames River with Dodgson's friend the Reverend Robinson Duckworth and Alice's two sisters.

Much of the nonsense in *Alice,* as well as many incidental details, are based on things from mid-nineteenth century English life. The majority of the songs in the book are burlesques of poems and songs popular at the time, and familiar to Carroll's child audience. The last of Alice's adventures, the trial, is based on a then-familiar nursery rhyme. Another device Carroll used was creating incident out of common sayings. The character of the Cheshire Cat, for example, is based on the then-common phrase, "Grin like a Cheshire cat," while the episode of "The Mad Tea-Party" is based on two common expressions, "mad as a hatter" and "mad as a March hare." (the "madness" by which hatters were frequently afflicted was caused by prolonged exposure to mercury, used in the curing of felt, while March in England was the mating season of the hare.)

Certain more "exotic" details attest to the successful ventures of the British Empire: the flamingos, for example, pointed to missionary and colonial expansion in Africa. The hookah-smoking Caterpillar was evidence of a very profitable and still encouraged trade in opium with China; Sir Arthur Conan Doyle's fictional detective Sherlock Holmes, for example, was addicted to opium.

Alice's Adventures in Wonderland can be characterized as a funhouse mirror version of a child's "journey" through the "adult" world, specifically the world of upper-class Victorian England. One of the main things that the child must grapple with on such a journey, and one of the principal themes that *Alice* takes up, is the question of his/her identity in that world. "Who are you?" Alice is frequently asked early in her adventures, and it is a question that she at first has a difficult time answering. Her initial erratic changes in size could be said to represent her inability to "fit" herself into this world. Her mastery of this process enables her to begin to be the master of her own destiny—to "fit," by enabling her to walk through the door that leads to the "beautiful garden," which she has wanted to enter since the beginning of her adventures.

This garden is hardly a Garden of Eden, though. Indeed, what Alice is immediately confronted with, the painting of the roses and condemnation to death of the painters by the Queen of Hearts, is an instance of the other principal of *Alice:* the absurdity, even insanity, of the "adult" world from the point of view of the innocent. "We're all mad here," the Cheshire Cat informs her in their famous exchange. This absurdity is frequently little more than a source of amusement to Alice; many times, though, it is a source of grief. Her treatment at the hands of the inhabitants of Wonderland, though brought upon her at times by her childish candor, is often rough, occasionally even cruel, and many times she is reduced to tears. Moreover, her adventures end with an apparent vision of the ultimate injustice of this adult world—the trial—though with her innocent frankness she is able to overcome this injustice, as her body symbolically grows to fill the courtroom.

Yet *Alice* is not political or social satire per se. Carroll may turn the adult world on its head, but there is no sense in the book that he is advocating any substantial changes to things as they are. Moreover, if an absurd, and even at times menacing world, Carroll's England as reflected in Wonderland is a world that can be mastered, suggesting (though some critics have contested this) that it is ultimately a benign world. Despite all the transformations she undergoes, Alice is never harmed, at least in any overt way. Indeed, her self-assured responses to the rough treatment she receives comes from the confidence—fortified by her class position—that "God's in His Heaven, all's right with the world."

Source: Stan Walker, in an essay for *Novels for Students,* Gale, 1999.

Roger B. Henkle

In the following excerpt, Henkle examines Carroll's emphasis on play, including its limitations.

It was just over a hundred years ago that *Through the Looking-Glass,* the second of Lewis Carroll's two Alice books, was published, yet Carroll's fantasy adventures into a little girl's dream worlds have a wider, more responsive audience than they may ever have had. Looking-Glass inversions and Wonderland absurdities give us striking shorthand renditions of the language and behavior of a modern world in which it sometimes seems—to quote the Cheshire Cat—that "I'm mad. You're mad. We're all mad here." André Gregory's recent New York stage version exalted the manic potential of the Alice worlds to black humor proportions. The dry, ingenuous tone and the mix of rebellion and self-indulgence in the Alice books have been made to order for the canny, loose "youth culture" of the last few years; and the psychedelic landscapes that the Jefferson Airplane and others have discovered are stunning enough to cause some people to wonder whether shy, inhibited Charles Lutwidge Dodgson, creator of a hookah-puffing caterpillar and mushrooms that change your size, might not have been surreptitiously in the opiate tradition of Coleridge and DeQuincey.

There is no real evidence that Carroll tripped to hallucinatory worlds, but there are enough indications that Carroll was deliberately probing in the Alice books for a new adult life-style, built around a concept that is close to play, to explain their strong appeal to contemporary readers. *Alice's Adventures in Wonderland* and *Through the Looking-Glass* have always led double lives as adult fantasy literature as well as children's classics—Katherine Anne Porter once observed that she found them, in fact, enjoyable *only* when she read them as an adult—but we have been inclined to look upon them largely as grownup escapes into childhood and not as attempts to define and come to new terms with adult life. William Empson has argued, for instance, that the Alice books reflect the post-Romantic feeling that "there is more in the child than any man has been able to keep." Though Empson adds that Carroll uses Alice to bring out some hard-headed and unsentimental judgments about the foolishness and even puerility of adult behavior, he apparently

does not see any sustained and, one might say, "serious" attempt in the Alice books to explore the possibilities of a freer, richer adult life-style. Such a dimension seems, indeed, almost too much to expect of books that we turn to for the whimsy of talking animals, logic games, and parodies.

Yet within the Alice books are explorations of an adult life that venture as far as Carroll could risk going toward freedom from the duties, responsibilities, and arid self-limitations of modern society—and in this aspect we may discover the immediacy of their appeal to contemporary readers. Furthermore, in Carroll's ambiguous feelings toward the relatively stable middle-class society that oppressed him, and in his anxieties about the self-exposure that his nonsense barely cloaked, we discover something of the reasons why writers probing from within a culture turn predominantly to comedy—as they have done in England for a century and a half and in America for the last decade.

One of the pleasures, surely, of reading *Alice in Wonderland* is to witness the absurd and sometimes devastating ways in which a rather too well-bred little girl learns of the caprices of language and logic and of the alarmingly erratic tracks of her own mind. I am going to concentrate here, however, on what may be an even stronger source of its appeal to adult readers, the covert delight that we take in madcap behavior. Much of our enjoyment of all comedy lies in our realization that we, too, would like to play and carry on, just as the adult creatures of *Wonderland* and *Through the Looking-Glass* do. The creatures Alice meets are clearly grown-ups (with the exception of the Tweedles) and they are engaging in pastimes whose allure would seem to be peculiarly to adults.

What a pleasant change the caucus-race would be from the competition of most "games" and adult occupations: "they began running when they liked and left off when they liked," and at the end of the race "*everybody* has won and *all* must have prizes." How nice it would be to sit, as the Mock Turtle does, on a shingle by the sea, and sentimentally ruminate on one's experiences—to surrender to all the self-indulgence that seems too rarely possible in modern life. It is always tea-time for the Mad Hatter, the March Hare, and the Dormouse, and people they don't like just aren't invited; "No room! No room!" says the Hare. When Humpty Dumpty uses a word it means what *he* chooses it to mean, neither more nor less....

The exuberance of play, however, is often deliberately restrained by an arbitrary order of rules invented by the player, and this was especially important to Carroll . In this quality of personally devised order—the brief moments in the Alice books of creatures rehearsing their individual delights—one captures the pleasure of personal control of one's life, and perhaps achieves the stasis that so many Victorians sought in a rapidly changing world.

Even more important is the relief play brings from the officious moralizing of other people. The "moral" of *Wonderland* is drawn by the Duchess (although she doesn't practice it): "If everybody minded their own business, the world would go round a deal faster than it does." Victorian comic writers from Thackeray to Butler tried to fend off those ponderous forces that were bent on dictating ethical, social, and even psychological conformity. In moments of play, at least, one can operate, as Johan Huizinga has noted, "outside the antithesis of wisdom and folly … of good and evil." In later years, Carroll could rhapsodize about his dream-Alice because she was living in the happy hours "when Sin and Sorrow are but names—empty words signifying nothing!" The homiletic hymns and rhymes that Alice tries to recall in *Wonderland* but cannot—"The Old Man's Comforts," "Against Idleness and Mischief," "The Sluggard," and "Speak Gently"—all share three elements: an injunction to be industrious and responsible, the reminder that we shall all grow old, and an invocation of our religious duties. Significantly, these banished thoughts are those we try to forget in play.

Carroll could not forget them for long, however, and Wonderland's imaginative projection as a possible variant life style was at the same time an opportunity to register and somehow "work out" the very anxieties that gave rise to the search for a new life style. In dreams we are often able to do all these things, and *Wonderland* is such a dream.

True to the dream, most things in Wonderland do not happen in a logical and chronological manner. There is no "plot" to the book; instead, dream thoughts pull seemingly disorganized elements together. Almost immediately the anxieties Carroll recorded so often in his diaries come to the surface in the behavior of the White Rabbit, who's late, who's lost his glove, who'll lose his head if he doesn't get to the Duchess' house on time. The Rabbit will later act for the Crown in the surrealistic trial of the knave at the book's end, thereby explicitly linking such social anxieties with the arbitrary punishment and the dread of fury that persistently flashes along hidden circuits of Wonderland's dreaming brain and periodically seizes Alice

and the creatures. At the end of the innocuous caucus race, the Mouse tells Alice his "tale"; it is about Fury and it prefigures the terrifying dissolution of the Wonderland dream itself. According to the tale, personified Fury, who this morning has "nothing to do," imperiously decides he'll prosecute the Mouse: "'I'll be judge, I'll be jury,' said cunning old Fury; 'I'll try the whole cause and condemn you to death.'"

Time and again the delights of play are cut off suddenly by such arbitrary violence, for we perceive that play by its nature cannot last. No wonder the Mad Hatter curtly changes the subject when Alice reminds him that he will soon run out of places at the tea-table. Too soon he is dragged into court by the Queen to be badgered and intimidated, despite his pathetic protest "I hadn't quite finished my tea when I was sent for." Play can only temporarily remove us from outside reality, as Carroll himself repeatedly discovered, because authority, society (characterized in those adult women—Queens and Duchesses) will interfere and impose its angry will. This is why I believe it is inaccurate to assert, as Hugh Kenner and Elizabeth Sewell have, that Carroll's books are "closed" works of art, literary game structures that are deliberately isolated and fundamentally unrelated to the Victorian social world outside them. They show, on the contrary, Carroll's reluctant conclusion that totally independent life patterns are impossible and even dangerous, and they are Carroll's paradigms of the way social power is achieved and how it operates in Victorian England.

Inherent in the very freedom of play is its weakness. Functioning by personal whim, it is potentially anarchic, thus vulnerable to the strongest, most brutal will. Halfway through the book, Alice unaccountably must enter Wonderland a second time and she finds its tenor radically different. Instead of the pleasantly free caucus race, she is in a croquet game where "the players all played at once, quarrelling all the while." All order has collapsed; hedgehog balls scuttle through the grass, bodiless cats grin in the dusk. And the domineering Queen of Hearts imposes her angry will more and more as she exploits the anarchy of the hapless world of play.

The antics that the mad tea party group, the Caterpillar, and other free souls had been indulging in were, in a word, nonsense. Just as nonsense writing is a form of play activity, play itself—at least as Carroll conceived it—is nonsensical in the context of the "real world"; it has been deliberately deprived of meaning, of any overt social and moral significance. Alice noted at the tea party that "the Hatter's remark seemed to her to have no sort of meaning in it, and yet it was certainly English." At the trial of the knave, however, suddenly there *is* meaning attached to nonsensical actions and statements: it is the meaning that the autocratic Queen wants attached to them, so they can be made to serve her lust for persecution. The most damning piece of evidence, according to the Crown, is a non-sensical letter purportedly written by the defendant. Alice argues, "*I* don't believe there's an atom of meaning in it," but the King of Hearts insists, "I seem to see some meaning in [the words] after all." The individuals who assert power in society, Carroll is suggesting, decide what things shall mean. *Their* whims, prompted and carried out by an irrational fury against people who would be free, dictate our responsibilities, our duties, our guilts, our sins, our punishment.

Here the adult victim's view nicely corresponds to the child's view of grown-up authority. If a child is called to task, told to remember some rule or duty he has forgotten about or never fully realized he was responsible for, he feels like the Mad Hatter, who is told "Don't be nervous, or I'll have you executed on the spot." Justice from a child's perspective often does seem to function like the Queen's: verdict first, guilt later....

The madness in the Alice books is often no more than the "looniness" of children's literature , or a harmless addlepatedness, which Alice usually absorbs with considerable aplomb. But there is a more worrisome dimension to the motif. The hallucinatory qualities of the books, the sudden metamorphoses, the wayward thoughts of cannibalism and dismemberment, the hot flashes of fury, all remind us that in dreams, especially, our minds seem to wander dangerously close to insanity. Throughout his life Carroll displayed a fascination with mental derangement. His long poem, "The Hunting of the Snark," subtitled "An Agony in Eight Fits," takes us imaginatively to the borderline of dissolution: a Baker goes out like a candle at the sight of a boojum snark. An insomniac, Carroll worked off and on at the small book of mathematical "pillow problems" to take the mind, he said, off the "undesired thoughts" that fly into the head in those late-night hours before sleep. And Carroll recorded in his diary the confusion between dream and wakefulness that makes us question our very sanity:

> Query: when we are dreaming and, as often happens, have a dim consciousness of the fact and try to wake, do we not say and do things which in waking life would be insane? May we not then sometimes define

insanity as an inability to distinguish which is the waking and which the sleeping life?

The psychologist Ernst Kris suggests that the venture into comedy itself is "double-edged," often carrying us near to the most unpleasant and terrifying aspects of existence and non-existence. So often do comic writers from Cervantes to the present play with insanity that we can well wonder about the standard of "common sense" prevalent in comedy; it seems at times to be an attempt to hold onto some generally agreed-upon reality.

All this is not to show that Carroll feared he would go mad, but that he was acutely conscious of the distortions of the human mind. He was preoccupied enough with the train of his own uncanny thoughts to have strong doubts about those potentially anarchic individual life styles that he concocted. He was evidently uneasy about deviation from societal norms. For this reason Alice herself acts in *Wonderland* and *Looking-Glass* as a check on the possibly manic behavior of even the "free" adult creatures like the Hatter and the Hare. She retains throughout a nice balance of self-control and imagination, which may be, in part, what made pre-adolescent little girls so attractive to Carroll. Even at her most disoriented, Alice can declare firmly that "I'm I." Though Carroll gently spoofs Alice's literal-minded common sense, she serves to remind us that no matter how appealing some of the creatures' life styles are, any sensible child her age must see it all as silly behavior by grown-ups. When the chaos and foolishness of Wonderland get out of hand at the end of the book, it is Alice who becomes the adult by growing in size and authority, and the imaginary creatures appear to be only errant children. Built into the work which vividly and alluringly explores the free behavior patterns that Carroll was attracted to is a perspective that makes it all seem puerile and pathetic, as if Carroll had doubts in his own mind about the sense (as well as the social wisdom) of that life style.

Source: Roger B. Henkle, "The Mad Hatter's World" in *The Virginia Quarterly Review,* Winter, 1973, pp. 99–117.

Nina Auerbach

In the following excerpt, Auerbach suggests that each character Alice meets in her adventures represents a part of Alice's own personality.

Dinah is a strange figure. She is the only above-ground character whom Alice mentions repeatedly, almost always in terms of her eating some smaller animal. She seems finally to function as a personification of Alice's own subtly cannibalistic hunger, as Fury in the Mouse's tale is personified as a dog. At one point, Alice fantasizes her own identity actually blending into Dinah's:

> "How queer it seems," Alice said to herself, "to be going messages for a rabbit! I suppose Dinah'll be sending me on messages next!" And she began fancying the sort of thing that would happen: "Miss Alice! Come here directly, and get ready for your walk!" "Coming in a minute, nurse! But I've got to watch this mousehole till Dinah comes back, and see that the mouse doesn't get out."

While Dinah is always in a predatory attitude, most of the Wonderland animals are lugubrious victims; together, they encompass the two sides of animal nature that are in Alice as well. But as she falls down the rabbit hole, Alice senses the complicity between eater and eaten, looking-glass versions of each other:

> "Dinah, my dear! I wish you were down here with me! There are no mice in the air, I'm afraid, but you might catch a bat, and that's very like a mouse, you know. But do cats eat bats, I wonder?" And here Alice began to get rather sleepy, and went on saying to herself, in a dreamy sort of way, "Do cats eat bats? Do cats eat bats?" and sometimes, "Do bats eat cats?" for, you see, as she couldn't answer either question, it didn't matter which way she put it.

We are already half-way to the final banquet of *Looking-Glass,* in which the food comes alive and begins to eat the guests.

Even when Dinah is not mentioned, Alice's attitude toward the animals she encounters is often one of casual cruelty. It is a measure of Dodgson's ability to flatten out Carroll's material that the prefatory poem could describe Alice "in friendly chat with bird or beast," or that he would later see Alice as "loving as a dog … gentle as a fawn." She pities Bill the Lizard and kicks him up the chimney, a state of mind that again looks forward to that of the Pecksniffian Walrus in *Looking-Glass.* When she meets the Mock Turtle, the weeping embodiment of a good Victorian dinner, she restrains herself twice when he mentions lobsters, but then distorts Isaac Watt's *Sluggard* into a song about a *baked* lobster surrounded by hungry sharks. In its second stanza, a Panther shares a pie with an Owl who then becomes dessert, as Dodgson's good table manners pass into typical Carrollian cannibalism. The more sinister and Darwinian aspects of animal nature are introduced into Wonderland by the gentle Alice, in part through projections of her hunger onto Dinah and the "nice little dog" (she meets a "dear little puppy" after she has grown small and is afraid he will eat her up) and in part through the semi-cannibalistic appetite her songs express. With the exception of the powerful Cheshire Cat, whom I shall discuss below; most of the Wonderland animals stand in some danger of being exploited or eaten. The Dormouse is their prototype: he is fussy and cantankerous, with the nastiness of a self-aware victim, and he is stuffed into a teapot as the Mock Turtle, sobbing out his own elegy, will be stuffed into a tureen.

Alice's courteously menacing relationship to these animals is more clearly brought out in *Alice's Adventures under Ground,* in which she encounters only animals until she meets the playing cards, who are lightly sketched-in versions of their later counterparts. When expanding the manuscript for publication, Carroll added the Frog Footman, Cook, Duchess, Pig-Baby, Cheshire Cat, Mad Hatter, March Hare, and Dormouse, as well as making the Queen of Hearts a more fully developed character than she was in the manuscript. In other words, all the human or quasi-human characters were added in revision, and all develop aspects of Alice that exist only under the surface of her dialogue. The Duchess' household also turns inside out the domesticated Wordsworthian ideal: with baby and pepper flung about indiscriminately, pastoral tranquillity is inverted into a whirlwind of savage sexuality. The furious Cook embodies the equation between eating and killing that underlies Alice's apparently innocent remarks about Dinah. The violent Duchess' unctuous search for "the moral" of things echoes Alice's own violence and search for "the rules." At the Mad Tea Party, the Hatter extends Alice's "great interest in questions of eating and drinking" into an insane *modus vivendi;* like Alice, the Hatter and the Duchess sing savage songs about eating that embody the underside of Victorian literary treacle. The Queen's croquet game magnifies Alice's own desire to cheat at croquet and to punish herself violently for doing so. Its use of live animals may be a subtler extension of Alice's own desire to twist the animal kingdom to the absurd rules of civilization, which seem to revolve largely around eating and being eaten. Alice is able to appreciate the Queen's savagery so quickly because her size changes have made her increasingly aware of who she, herself, is from the point of view of a Caterpillar, a Mouse, a Pigeon, and, especially, a Cheshire Cat.

The Cheshire Cat, also a late addition to the book, is the only figure other than Alice who encompasses all the others. William Empson [in *Some Versions of Pastoral,* 1950] discusses at length the spiritual kinship between Alice and the Cat, the only creature in Wonderland whom she calls her "friend." Florence Becker Lennon [in *The Life of Lewis Carroll,* 1962], refers to the Cheshire Cat as "Dinah's dream-self" and we have noticed the subtle shift of identities between Alice and Dinah throughout the story. The Cat shares Alice's equivocal placidity: "The Cat only grinned when it saw Alice. It looked good-natured, she thought: still it had *very* long claws and a great many teeth, so she felt it ought to be treated with respect." The Cat is the only creature to make explicit the identification between Alice and the madness of Wonderland: "'... we're all mad here. I'm mad. You're mad.' 'How do you know I'm mad?' said Alice. 'You must be,' said the Cat, 'or you wouldn't have come here.' Alice didn't think that proved it at all...." Although Alice cannot accept it and closes into silence, the Cat's remark may be the answer she has been groping toward in her incessant question, "who am I?" As an alter ego, the Cat is wiser than Alice—and safer—because he is the only character in the book who is aware of his own madness. In his serene acceptance of the fury within and without, his total control over his appearance and disappearance, he almost suggests a post-analytic version of the puzzled Alice.

As Alice dissolves increasingly into Wonderland, so the Cat dissolves into his own head, and finally into his own grinning mouth. The core of Alice's nature, too, seems to lie in her mouth: the eating and drinking that direct her size changes and motivate much of her behavior, the songs and verses that pop out of her inadvertently, are all involved with things entering and leaving her mouth. Alice's first song introduces a sinister image of a grinning mouth. Our memory of the Crocodile's grin hovers over the later description of the Cat's "grin without a Cat," and colors our sense of Alice's infallible good manners:

How cheerfully he seems to grin,
How neatly spreads his claws,
And welcomes little fishes in,
With gently smiling jaws!...

When the Duchess' Cook abruptly barks out "Pig!" Alice thinks the word is meant for her, though it is the baby, another fragment of Alice's own nature, who dissolves into a pig. The Mock Turtle's lament for his future soupy self later blends tellingly into the summons for the trial: the lament of the eaten and the call to judgment melt together. When she arrives at the trial, the unregenerate Alice instantly eyes the tarts: "In the very middle of the court was a table, with a large dish of tarts upon it: they looked so good, that it made Alice quite hungry to look at them—'I wish they'd get the trial done,' she thought, 'and hand round the refreshments!'" Her hunger links her to the hungry Knave who is being sentenced: in typically ambiguous portmanteau fashion, Carroll makes the trial both a pre-Orwellian travesty of justice and an objective correlative of a real sense of sin. Like the dog Fury in the Mouse's tale, Alice takes all the parts. But unlike Fury, she is accused as well as accuser, melting into judge, jury, witness, and defendant; the person who boxes on the ears as well as the person who "cheats." Perhaps the final verdict would tell Alice who she is at last, but if it did, Wonderland would threaten to overwhelm her. Before it comes, she "grows"; the parts of her nature rush back together; combining the voices of victim and accuser, she gives "a little scream, half of fright and half of anger," and wakes up.

Presented from the point of view of her older sister's sentimental pietism, the world to which Alice awakens seems far more dream-like and hazy than the sharp contours of Wonderland. Alice's lesson about her own identity has never been stated explicitly for the stammerer Dodgson was able to talk freely only in his private language of puns and nonsense, but a Wonderland pigeon points us toward it:

"You're a serpent; and there's no use denying it. I suppose you'll be telling me next that you never tasted an egg!"

"I have tasted eggs, certainly," said Alice, who was a very truthful child; "but little girls eat eggs quite as much as serpents do, you know."

"I don't believe it," said the Pigeon; "but if they do, why, then they're a kind of serpent: that's all I can say." This was such a new idea to Alice, that she was quite silent for a minute or two ...

Like so many of her silences throughout the book, Alice's silence here is charged with significance, reminding us again that an important technique in learning to read Carroll is our ability to interpret his private system of symbols and signals and to appreciate the many meanings of silence. In this scene, the golden child herself becomes the serpent in childhood's Eden. The eggs she eats suggest the woman she will become, the unconscious cannibalism involved in the very fact of eating and desire to eat, and finally, the charmed circle of childhood itself. Only in *Alice's Adventures in Wonderland* was Carroll able to fall all the way through the rabbit hole to the point where top and bottom become one, bats and cats melt into each other, and the vessel of innocence and purity is also the source of inescapable corruption.

Source: Nina Auerbach, "Alice and Wonderland: A Curious Child," in *Victorian Studies,* September, 1973, pp. 31–47.

Sources

Morton N. Cohen, *Lewis Carroll: A Biography,* Alfred A. Knopf, 1995.

Martin Gardner, editor and author of notes, *The Annotated Alice: Alice's Adventures in Wonderland and Through the Looking-Glass by Lewis Carroll,* Bramhall House, 1960.

For Further Study

Daniel Binova, "Alice the Child-imperialist and the Games of Wonderland," in *Nineteenth Century Literature,* Vol. 41, No. 2, September 1986, pp. 143-171.
   Reading *Alice* in the context of Victorian imperialism, Binova argues that Alice behaves as an "imperialist" by attempting to force the behavior of the creatures she encounters to fit the "rules" for such behavior as she understands them. He concludes that Carroll is critiquing the ethnocentric attitude that underlies such an attempt.

Kathleen Blake, *Play, Games, and Sport: The Literary Works of Lewis Carroll,* Cornell University Press, 1974.
   Blake's work examines the many ways in which Carroll's works play with the reader.

Kathleen Blake, "Lewis Carroll (Charles Lutwidge Dodgson)," in *Concise Dictionary of British Literary Biography, Volume 4: Victorian Writers, 1832-1890,* Gale, 1991, pp. 111-28.
   A brief biographical and critical survey of Carroll's life and works.

Harold Bloom, editor, *Lewis Carroll,* Modern Critical Views series, Chelsea House, 1987.
   A useful compilation of essays that contains several pieces on the Alice books, including a feminist psychoanalytic reading of the character of Alice by Nina Auerbach and a discussion of Carroll's "philosophy" by Peter Heath.

Lewis Carroll, *Alice's Adventures Under Ground,* Facsimile edition, Dover Publications, 1965.
   A reprint of the author's manuscript, produced by hand (including drawings and other illustrations by Carroll himself) for Alice Liddell. The Dover edition also includes some information from the 1886 facsimile edition of the manuscript.

Lewis Carroll, *Alice in Wonderland: Authoritative Texts of Alice's Adventures in Wonderland, Through the Looking-Glass, The Hunting of the Snark,* edited by Donald J. Gray, Norton, 1971.
   The Norton Critical Edition of Carroll's most famous works presents a text with footnotes, excerpts from Carroll's diaries, appreciations by some of his friends (including Alice Liddell, the model for Alice), and a selection of the most important criticism of the author's work.

Lewis Carroll, "Alice on the Stage," in *The Theatre,* April, 1887.
   In this article, Carroll himself describes the chief characteristics of his "Alice" character.

Charles Frey and John Griffith, "Lewis Carroll: Alice's Adventures in Wonderland," in their *The Literary Heritage of Childhood: An Appraisal of Children's Classics in the Western Tradition,* Greenwood Press, 1987, pp. 15-22.
   In their article Frey and Griffith survey some of the ways critics have chosen to read *Alice's Adventures in Wonderland.*

Jean Gattegno, *Lewis Carroll: Fragments of a Looking-Glass,* translated by Rosemary Sheed, Crowell, 1976.
   This work takes a thematic approach to various aspects of Carroll's life and work.

Edward Guiliano, editor, *Lewis Carroll: A Celebration,* Clarkson N. Potter, 1982.
   A collection of essays compiled for the 150th anniversary of Carroll's birth, several of which focus on Alice. Among them are Terry Otten's discussion of Alice's "innocence," Nina Demurova's consideration of Alice's genre, and Roger Henkle's argument that the Alice books are "forerunners of the modernist novel."

Richard Kelly, *Lewis Carroll,* revised edition, Twayne, 1990.
   Kelly touches the main bases of Carroll's life and works in this survey. His chapter on the Alice books goes through both works episode by episode, offering critical perspectives as he does so.

James R. Kincaid, "Alice's Invasion of Wonderland," in *PMLA (Publications of the Modern Language Association of America),* Vol. 88, No. 1, January 1973, pp. 92-99.
   Kincaid argues that Carroll's own attitudes toward both Alice and the worlds she visits in *Alice* and *Looking Glass* are highly ambivalent.

Florence Becker Lennon, *Victoria through the Looking-Glass: The Life of Lewis Carroll,* Simon & Schuster, 1945.
   Although this biography is more than fifty years old and its biographical details have been superseded by more recent scholarship, it does help place Carroll in the context of his time and provide a survey of earlier criticism.

Robert Phillips, editor, *Aspects of Alice: Lewis Carroll's Dreamchild as Seen through the Critics' Looking-Glasses, 1865-1971,* Vanguard Press, 1971.
   A survey of critical evaluations of Carroll's work, including personal and biographical criticism, comparisons of Carroll with other Victorians and other writers, and philosophical, Freudian, Jungian and other interpretations of *Alice.*

Phyllis Gila Reinstein, *Alice in Context,* Garland Publishing, 1988.
   Reinstein places *Alice* and *Looking-Glass* in the context of Victorian children's literature. She argues that Carroll's books, unlike their predecessors, do not "capitulate at one point or another to the pressures of their society," but instead "consistently offer amusement without intending instruction".

The Caine Mutiny

Herman Wouk
1951

Herman Wouk's best-selling novel *The Caine Mutiny,* subtitled *A Novel of World War II,* remains one of the greatest American novels to come out of World War II. Wouk, himself a WWII veteran who had served aboard minesweepers in the South Pacific, won a Pulitzer Prize in 1952 for this account of a mutiny aboard a fictional minesweeper, the USS *Caine.* Commercially speaking, Wouk is the most successful writer of his generation. In critical terms, his work is sneered at or altogether ignored. At a time when American ideals were questioned and literature was full of rebellious heroes, Wouk championed conservative morals such as valor, chivalry, patriotism, and loyalty. Almost half a century after its publication, Wouk's morally idealistic novel remains popular.

Author Biography

Wouk was born into a wealthy family on May 27, 1915, in New York City. He graduated from Columbia University in 1934. His first job was writing for radio in New York, and then scripts for Fred Allen from 1936 to 1941. When war broke out, he put his writing talents into the service of the U.S. government and became a "dollar-a-year-man," writing the U.S. Treasury Department's radio plays promoting the sale of war bonds.

In 1942, he joined the U.S. Navy and served aboard the USS *Zane* and the USS *Southard,* both minesweepers in the South Pacific. While aboard

Herman Wouk

ship in 1943, Wouk—like the character Tom Keefer—began to write fiction. The experience aboard minesweepers was reflected in *The Caine Mutiny*. The novel was not autobiographical, except for the shared experience of Navy duty. It was, however, a staunch defense of the American ideals Wouk evokes in all of his work: valor, honor, leadership, patriotism, and chivalric heroism. The public loved Wouk's work. *The Caine Mutiny* was a best-seller for weeks and almost single-handedly rescued its financially challenged British publisher. Cape Limited, despite owning the rights to Alan Paton's phenomenally successful *Cry, the Beloved Country,* was saved by Wouk's World War II novel.

Before leaving the Navy, Wouk married Betty Sarah Brown on December 9, 1945. They had three sons: Abraham Isaac, Nathaniel, and Joseph. When he was discharged, Wouk began writing again. His first novel, *Aurora Dawn,* was published in 1947 and was a Book-of-the-Month-Club selection. In 1949, his play, *The Traitor,* had a short run on Broadway. Wouk's nonfictional interests include Judaic scholarship and Zionist studies. After the publication of *The Caine Mutiny,* he was appointed as a visiting professor at Yeshiva University. During the 1960s, he served as a trustee of the College of the Virgin Islands. Returning to the mainland,

he served as a member of the board of directors for the Washington National Symphony (1969–71); scholar-in-residence at Aspen Institute of Humanistic Studies (1973–74) and then at Kennedy Center Productions (1974–75); and a member of an advisory council, Center for U.S.-China Arts Exchange (1981–87).

In addition to these public duties, Wouk wrote a number of other novels including *The Winds of War* and *War and Remembrance.* The latter was adapted for television and aired as a popular miniseries.

Plot Summary

The Caine Mutiny opens with a page torn from the book of Navy regulations outlining the articles that will become critical to the plot: the regulations describing the conditions that must be fulfilled in order for a captain to be relieved of his command.

Willie Keith

In a chapter appropriately titled *Through the Looking Glass,* the novel starts by introducing the reader to the protagonist of the novel, Willie Keith, from whose viewpoint the entire novel is told. Seeking a way to avoid being drafted into the infantry, Willie Keith—an educated, piano-playing dilettante—is joining the U.S. Navy. His days in training are interspersed with a series of flashbacks that introduce us to his former life and to his girlfriend, an Italian-American singer called May Wynn. A rebellious type, Keith immediately gets into trouble, and faces expulsion throughout his training period. He eventually passes, and is assigned to the USS *Caine.*

The Caine

Keith arrives in San Francisco to report to his ship and amuses some military officers with his piano playing. To his horror, the *Caine* is a rusty vessel that seems on the verge of collapse, and Keith feels only contempt for it and his superior officer, Captain de Vriess. Keith hears that discipline on the ship is criminally lax and anticipates that the arrival of a new captain will mark a new order onboard the ship. After failing to decode an important message, Keith is given an unsatisfactory fitness report; his life is changed again when Captain Queeg arrives to take over as commander.

Captain Queeg

Queeg arrives early. His habit of rolling steel ball bearings in his palms contributes to the growing belief of his men that something is not quite right. The first time the *Caine* sets sail, he runs the ship aground and then fails to report the incident. The dangers of his obsessive need for discipline become clear when the ship fails a training exercise and loses expensive Navy equipment because Queeg is lecturing a sailor about his untucked shirt. When the crew is granted shore leave, Queeg browbeats the other officers into giving him their alcohol rations and illegally hoards liquor. Keith finds May and his mother waiting for him in San Francisco and introduces his girlfriend by her given name, Marie Minotti.

Shore Leave

Willie, confused by his feelings after having sex with May for the first time, proposes to her, but she turns him down. He confides his feelings for May to his mother and she suggests he should look for someone of "their sort." Onboard the ship, Maryk is made Executive Officer, and Stilwell, desperate to see his wife, goes AWOL.

The Mutiny

Queeg's behavior grows stranger and even cowardly, and the officers are increasingly disenchanted. Maryk refuses to allow their critical talk whenever he is present. Unknown to everyone else, Maryk records Queeg's aberrant behavior as he believes that Queeg is paranoid and psychotic. Tension escalates when Queeg places a ban on water usage and a container of strawberries is eaten anonymously. Queeg conducts a bizarre search for the culprit. After encouraging Maryk in his concerns about Queeg, Keefer refuses to back him up when Maryk wants to take their concerns to the Admiral.

A typhoon hits. With the ship in bad shape, Maryk decides that the Captain's orders are leading them into certain death, and he takes control of the bridge. He formally relieves Queeg of his authority, supported by Keith and Stilwell, and the section closes with Maryk guiding them all to safety.

The Court-Martial

It is months later, and lawyers for Maryk's defense are being assigned. The only man who will take the case, albeit reluctantly, is Barney Greenwald. After meeting Maryk, Greenwald realizes that Keefer orchestrated the entire situation. The court martial of Maryk begins. Greenwald's strategy is to show that Maryk was justified in his opinion that Queeg had become unfit for duty. To prove this, however, the defense must chronicle Queeg's failures and bizarre behavior in court—a highly controversial strategy. Keefer sells Maryk out a second time, omitting his role in the affair. Against frequent objections from the court, Greenwald brings to light Queeg's illegal acts and wrongheaded decisions, allowing the man to incriminate himself on the stand with a show of his personality collapse under stress. Maryk is acquitted.

A party is thrown to celebrate Keefer's publishing contract and Maryk's acquittal. Greenwald dramatically accuses Keefer of setting the mutiny in motion, tells Maryk that his actions were unjustified, and says that Queeg was in fact the hero—a man who devoted his life to protecting the country and who cracked under the unbearable pressure of the situation.

The Last Captain of the Caine

Onboard the *Caine,* Keefer has been made captain, and Keith is second in command. During a kamikaze attack, Captain Keefer jumps ship while Keith heroically battles to save it. Keefer is forced to admit to himself that he is no better than Queeg. Shaken by his experience, Keith writes to May asking her to marry him. The war ends, and Keefer is demoted, leaving Keith to become the last captain of the *Caine.* He and the crew sail back to America, where he is met again by his mother. He has still not heard from May. He tracks her down and finds that she is going by her real name, has bleached her hair, is involved with another man, and doesn't want him in her life anymore. In the final scene, Keith stands in the drifting confetti of the Navy parade, vowing to himself that he will win her back.

Characters

Everett Harold Black
See Horrible

Captain De Vriess

Captain De Vriess is the first commander of the USS *Caine,* which has seen constant action near the front and, therefore, appears rather bedraggled. His style of command disgusts Keith, who would prefer following Navy regulations, but that is because he is fresh to the war. Still, for all De Vriess' laxness, the crew performs amazing feats of speed

Humphrey Bogart, Jose Ferrer, and Van Johnson, in a scene from The Caine Mutiny *(1954).*

for him. They consistently out-drill all the other minesweepers in the fleet. Keith surprises himself when, late in the novel, he speaks of De Vriess with respect.

Ducely

Ducely is Keith's assistant. Soon, however, his mother arranges for his transfer stateside.

Walter Feather

Walter is May Wynn's new boyfriend. He is a great entertainer and has crafted her reputation as a "bombshell."

Bill Gorton

When Keith arrives on the *Caine,* Bill Gorton is the Chief Executive Officer.

Barney Greenwald

Barney Greenwald is the lawyer who defends Maryk at his court-martial trial. He accepts Maryk's case after meeting him and realizing that Maryk was duped by someone more intelligent: Keefer, the novelist. At Keefer's celebratory dinner, Barney makes a speech when, for the first time, the morality play of the novel is revealed. Barney hopes that his mother will not be a victim of Hitler's "final solution" because of military men like

Queeg, though other relatives already have been. In this light, Barney admits he would rather not have seen Maryk acquitted and took the case only because he felt Keefer ought to have been the man on trial.

Harding

Harding arrives aboard the USS *Caine* at the same time as Keith. At the end of the novel, Harding is Keith's executive officer.

Horrible

Horrible becomes a casualty aboard the ship when he is killed during the kamikaze attack.

Roland Keefer

See Rollo

Tom Keefer

Tom Keefer is intelligent, a writer, and "queer as a three dollar bill" according to Rollo, his half-brother. Keefer reminds Greenwald of his shifty roommate at college. While under the command of De Vriess, Keefer puts minimal effort into his duty but maximum effort into writing his novel. He regards the war as a silly distraction from his literary pursuits. Keefer reveals himself as a coward under pressure: he talks Maryk out of exposing

Queeg; he fails to substantiate Keith's and Maryk's story; and he abandons the ship to Keith when they are hit with a kamikaze attack.

Edwin Keggs

A schoolteacher named Keggs is Keith's roommate at midshipman school. He is assigned duty aboard the USS *Moulton.* His military experience is vastly different from life on the *Caine.*

Dr. Keith

Dr. Keith is Willie's father. In declining health, he keeps this from his son but finally reveals it in a jarring letter that Keith promises to read only after he is aboard the ship. Due to a mishap, Keith reads it at Pearl Harbor but telegraphs home too late—his father is dead. The message of Dr. Keith's letter is that he is proud of Keith and hopes that, whatever else he does, he will not follow his father's path toward an easy, rich life. Instead, he hopes that Keith will pursue his dreams and the love of his choice.

Mrs. Keith

Mrs. Keith is Willie's mother. She seems to be playing a game of appearances. The Keiths are not as wealthy as they appear to be, and it is only through her cunning that they are able to keep up with the house payments and other necessities. Keith does not know about his mother's work. For her sake, he will give up May Wynn because he suspects that she would not approve. But she surprises him with her response when he comes home and he tells her he wants May. "I wouldn't want to be shut out of your life, whatever you do," she says. And then, to reveal that she understands far more than Keith ever thought possible, she says, "I took her at the value you set on her."

Willie Keith

The protagonist of the story is Willie Keith "because the event turned on his personality as the massive door of a vault turns on a small jewel bearing." That personality, at first, is arrogant and overbearing. The trait that sees Keith through the military is his honesty and his growing sense of patriotism. Keith has difficulty accepting subordinate positions to those persons who would not normally be his superiors in terms of economic class, intelligence, or social standing.

By the end of the novel, Keith has been humbled by the turn of events. He has risen to a position of authority and is a responsible and honorable soldier. He is able to reject the bourgeois standards

Media Adaptations

- Using the screenplay by (Seymour) Michael Blankfort, *The Caine Mutiny* was filmed by Columbia Pictures in 1954. Humphrey Bogart stars as Captain Queeg, Charles Nolte is Willis Keith, and May Wynn plays herself. The movie received seven Academy Award nominations including Best Picture, Best Actor, and Best Screenplay.

- Alvin Rakoff adapted Wouk's story for television as "The Caine Mutiny Court Martial," first broadcast by BBC-TV, June, 1958.

- Herman Wouk adapted the novel into a staged version of the court-martial trial. Paul Gregory first produced the play in the Granada Theatre, Santa Barbara, California, on October 12, 1953. Several persons of note were in the production, including Henry Fonda as Lt. Barney Greenwald and Charles Nolte as Lt. Willis Seward Keith. In a later production of the play, James Garner made his acting debut.

of his family and hopes to form a meaningful relationship with May Wynn.

Willis Seward Keith

See Willie Keith

Steve Maryk

A native San Franciscan, Steve Maryk is a fisherman by trade and upbringing. As he tells Keefer, fishing is not bucolic: "It boils down to making a dollar the hardest way there is.... It's a business for dumb foreigners.... I'm dumb too, but I'm not a foreigner." Maryk, therefore, has both the incentives of a second-generation immigrant: to make it rich in America and to be patriotic. While not as educated as Keefer or Keith, Maryk is not dumb; as a result of his seaman's knowledge, Maryk is immediately recognized by his fellow crewmembers—as well as Captain De Vriess—as the best sailor among them. Consequently, he is relied upon to fulfill his natural leadership role. It is due to Maryk's expertise that the crew is able to set drill-time records that no other minesweeper can approach. Maryk tells Keefer, "I know seamanship, and I'd damn rather put in twenty years for the Navy and get a pension than get arthritis and a sprung back hauling fish out of the water."

After Gorton is transferred, Maryk becomes the USS *Caine*'s executive officer. Having decided that Queeg is not an able skipper, Maryk loses faith in him. At first, Maryk is not mutinous and keeps his distance from the crew when they disparage the Captain. Gradually, he is influenced by Keefer's psychological theories. He begins to keep a logbook on the captain's behavior. In the midst of a typhoon, he decides that the captain has lost his ability to command and assumes the role under Navy articles 184-186. He does save the ship.

The result of his mutiny is the end of a brilliant naval career. Maryk's fate is the most troubling of the book and it results from a false belief in intellectual superiority over skill. He is a tragic hero.

Marie Minotti

See May Wynn

Old Yellowstain

See Captain Queeg

Paynter

Paynter is a V-7 engineer acting as a communications officer aboard the ship. It is Paynter who finds Keith. Paynter leaves soon after bringing his replacement aboard.

Captain Queeg

Queeg replaces De Vriess as captain of the USS *Caine*. Queeg is a short man with an inferiority complex. He is not very smart but he winds up as captain of his own vessel. His crew finds many of his actions strange and even cowardly, such as the incident in which he dangerously stays ahead of the Marines he is escorting and then flees before bringing them to the appointed drop-off. The incident earns him the nickname "Old Yellowstain." He also refuses to return fire on behalf of an assaulted fellow vessel. Queeg tells his officers that he will run his ship according to Navy codes and regulations, but he fails to follow procedure when the typhoon hits, putting the ship and its men in danger.

Rabbitt

Rabbitt is the OOD into whose arms Keith jumps when arriving on the USS *Caine*. He manages to get transferred to the USS *Oaks*.

Rollo

Half-brother to Tom Keefer, he shares a room with Keith in midshipman's school. He is assigned to the USS *Montauk,* an aircraft carrier. After the executive officer is killed, Rollo takes command of the fire fighting and conning of the ship. He dies from the effort.

Marty Rubin

Keith dislikes May Wynn's agent, Marty Rubin. Rubin, on the other hand, likes Keith and tries to help the young man. This becomes clear, even to Keith, when Rubin brings him to Wynn though she is trying to keep Keith away.

Stilwell

The best steersman on the boat is Stilwell. Queeg blames him for the cut towline. Soon after this, he is court-martialed for reading a comic on duty. He is acquitted but restricted to the ship for six months. He concocts a scheme in order to see his wife and finds himself in more trouble. Due to Queeg's ensuing persecution, he has no qualms about following Maryk in mutiny.

A year of Queeg's persecution coupled with the dangerous typhoon are possible causes of Stilwell's growing mental illness. He soon begins to complain of headaches. Stilwell is unable to testify on Maryk's behalf because he is receiving shock therapy at a mental hospital.

Urban

Urban has the misfortune of being the only other person besides Keith, Stilwell, and Maryk to witness the Captain's behavior during the typhoon. Urban is too terrified to grasp the ramifications of the situation and is unable to help Maryk's case.

Whittaker

The master of the mess is a black man named Whittaker. He announces mealtime with, "Chadan, suh." As involved as he is with serving the officers, there is no interaction with the black sailor.

May Wynn

May Wynn is Keith's love interest from the moment she hands him an arrangement of *The Marriage of Figaro* for her audition at Club Tahiti where Keith plays the piano. Keith's discovery that she is a poor Italian girl from the Bronx living among other poor immigrants disappoints him. They start working together and dating but Keith attempts to keep a distance. The reason for the distance is that he wants to marry someone from the same class. During the war, they break up. Having matured by the end of the novel, Willie pursues her again.

Themes

Authority

As a moral tract for the 1950s, *The Caine Mutiny* suggests that a strong authority is all-important for safeguarding the nation. Keith, for both his father and himself, turns down his first vocation—a fun, independent life of playing the piano—to fight for his country. This enables him to become a man in his own mind. His training allows him to put aside his own fear and concerns to take command when Keefer places the ship and its men in danger.

The novel centers on Queeg's inability to embody authority or command respect. Queeg begs for it: "There is such a thing as loyalty upward, and such a thing as loyalty downward. I desire and expect to get absolute loyalty upward." Queeg quotes from the regulation book and constantly reminds his men that he is the author of their fitness reports. Further, he will resort to court-martialing them if he has to. Along with fitness reports, he pays too much attention to issues such as missing strawberries and fixing even the smallest assignments. "You never saw a more fearless wielder of a checklist than Old Yellowstain," says Keefer. The reaction of his crew is predictable. They doubt their Captain.

Sex Roles

A subplot of the novel concerns the relationship between Wynn and Keith. Their courtship is wrought with all the societal tensions surrounding the roles of the sexes. One of these tensions is employment. At that time, society determined that women should stay at home to raise children into good citizens. But Wynn was forced to work for financial reasons. On top of this, but not touched on in the novel, women from all economic classes during World War II were encouraged through propaganda to work in the munitions factories. Later in the 1940s, as the men returned from the war, the roles reverted and women were encouraged to stay

Topics for Further Study

- Pick one of the novels referenced by Wouk in the story. Read that novel and compare it to *The Caine Mutiny*. How does the constant referencing of other novels enrich Wouk's work?

- Given the environmental concerns of the late 1990s, reflect on the prescience of the following: "Willie thought it was curious that with the coming of the Americans, the once-charming tropical islands had taken on the look of vacant lots in Los Angeles."

- There is a passing reference to Native American legal battles through the person of Barney Greenwald. Do some research on the legal battles of Indian tribes in America. What possible relevance does this have to the novel's theme of authority?

- Discover what happened to Japanese-American citizens domestically. A good account of this experience is contained in Joy Kogawa's 1981 novel, *Obasan*. Why were the citizens of Japanese descent interred?

home again. Wouk reflects these attitudes when Keith fantasizes about saving Wynn and making her a properly domesticated woman. Keith's resolve to save her gets stronger when he sees her, ill, living in a seedy hotel, and trying hard to make it as "Broadway's Beloved Bombshell."

Wynn is a hardened, independent woman; she has had to be because of her background. She considers men like "hogs" at the trough. Yet she has romantic notions of Keith as a prince who will whisk her away to a suburban castle. However, Keith's "matter-of-fact courtship was no part of love and marriage as she had vaguely imagined it." She knows that his mother does not like her, and she is a proud woman. She tells him, "Let's get one thing straight. If you're starting a little home for fallen women, I'm not interested. I don't want you to marry me because you're sorry for me, or because you want to do the manly thing by me, or anything like that."

Race and Class

Wouk summarizes American economic, racial, and social tensions during WWII. He also foreshadows the future; for example, at one point in the novel the lawyer Barney Greenwald states that Native American tribes are regaining their sovereignty in federal courts. Native Americans, for their part, were heavily involved in World War II. They thought that by fighting for the United States they could gain some respect from white Americans. Therefore, they were willing coding experts in the European theater as well as excellent soldiers. The same is true of African-American soldiers. They enlisted hoping that their contribution to the war effort would lessen racial barriers. Instead, in the novel, African Americans are depicted as the men who eat the last of the strawberries. Finally, Keith's hesitation to commit to May originates in his belief, fostered by his mother, that she is of a lower social and ethnic class than himself. By the end of the novel, he rejects the bourgeois standards of his family and hopes for a reunion with her, no matter the circumstances.

Coming of Age

Willie Keith "had risen from his fumbling, incompetent beginnings as Midshipman Keith to the command of a United States warship." The boy who became Captain of the USS *Caine* is certainly different from the one who played "If you knew what the Gnu knew" and entered the wardroom with an "unfortunate sign of immaturity," sucking his thumb. From his attempt to leave his mother in the opening scene without looking back—"his old identity was hauled away to camphor balls"—to his return (after "a year in the wilderness") to his mother as a full-uniformed captain, the novel is a *bildungsroman:* the story of Keith's education in the ways of man.

Style

Narration

Wouk's narrative technique is perhaps the most interesting yet problematic aspect of the novel. There is evidence of almost every form of narration, although it remains third-person omniscient. It is full of overt fictional references as well as subtle allusions, especially to the classic American novel *Moby-Dick.* The constant reference to other works of fiction and near mimicry of famous tales makes the novel a self-conscious work.

The narration can also be suspected of being unreliable. Most commentators dismiss Barney's spin on events aboard the ship. However, if Barney's speech is accepted, then the entire narration is suspect of duplicity. This possibility makes the work even richer in its thematic import.

Realism

Wouk considered himself a realist, like authors such as Theodore Dreiser and W. D. Howells who attempted objective positions, realistic descriptions, and accurate observation of human behavior. Realist writing is bereft of philosophy, judgment, or propaganda. Such writing by Wouk stands in marked contrast to John Steinbeck's overt socialism, Albert Camus' existentialism, and James Farrell's and Ralph Ellison's cynicism. Given these contemporaries and their rejection of the value system of Wouk's martial characters, it is little wonder that critics dismissed Wouk or that no person of American letters claims to have been influenced by him.

The elements of Wouk's novel that make it realistic cover everything from opening with the articles under which an officer can take over command of a vessel to the exact descriptions of the boat that only an experienced Navy officer could provide—including standing orders, course work, and drawings. The action of the book itself is rather routine—practice drills, sitting around waiting for orders, and the otherwise predictable life aboard a ship. This depiction of everyday life in the Navy is exciting in its minutiae, especially as it is being reflected in Maryk's log.

Irony

Irony, a self-aware moment of incongruity, is an important part of Wouk's technique. Perhaps the greatest irony in the novel concerns the court-martial of an executive officer aboard an old minesweeper while the grandest war ever fought on earth is mere background noise; "It amused Willie to consider, as he struggled to dress in his galloping room, that the issue of the morning had dwindled so quickly from life-or-death to a question of the wardroom's breakfast." In another instance, "There was an unsettling contrast between himself eating ice cream, and marines on Namur a few thousand yards away, being blown up. He was not sufficiently unsettled to stop eating ice cream."

Compare & Contrast

- **WWII:** After Japan's surrender, America occupies Japan.

  1950s: On September 8, 1951, the United States and Japan sign a security pact that permits U.S. troops to remain on Japanese soil while any other nation must have U.S. permission to enter Japan.

  Today: In response to missile tests by North Korea, Japan and the United States invest in the deployment of Strategic Defense Initiatives, also known as Star Wars.

- **WWII:** The United States is the first nation to use a nuclear bomb in war.

  1950s: In 1951, the United States stages the first military maneuvers involving troops and nuclear bombs.

  Today: The United States has been unwilling to deter the spread of nuclear weapons and has made it nearly impossible for Russia to ratify SALT II, a treaty that massively reduces the number of armed nuclear missiles.

- **WWII:** America's productive capacity makes the United States the greatest military power in the world.

  1950s: Truman's 1951 budget contains the largest military expenditure to date.

Today: President Clinton reverses the decline in military spending that began in 1985. Under his tenure, an eighth Nimitz-class carrier joins the fleet, the USS *Harry S Truman*. Also, America commits to deploying Star Wars by 2001.

- **WWII:** At the war's end, America insists on a proactive United Nations where nations can peaceably resolve disputes.

  1950s: America begins a tradition of using the United Nations as a cover for its foreign policies.

  Today: The United States won't pay its United Nations dues. Though it retains its permanent seat on the U.N. Security Council, the United States currently has no speaking rights and risks losing sitting rights in the U.N. General Assembly.

- **WWII:** The United States and the Soviet Union are allies against Germany and Japan.

  1950s: The two superpowers are immersed in a Cold War and support opposing sides in the Korean War.

  Today: The de-militarized zone (DMZ) still exists at the 38th parallel. The United States is still unable to resolve the dispute.

Historical Context

World War II—The South Pacific

On December 7, 1941, the Japanese plan to deliver a declaration of war to President Roosevelt just moments before a pre-dawn raid on America's naval base in Pearl Harbor. Instead, the message is an hour late and the act becomes "the day of infamy" which rouses America into the dominant military and industrial complex it remains today.

The Pacific fleet is not entirely destroyed and Japan hurries to gain advantage before America can build more ships. Along with industrial might, the crucial element of success in the war of the South Pacific is American interception of Japanese communications. The first such interception reveals that Japan is going to attack and remove Australia from the war. Australia and America meet Japan in the Coral Sea in the summer of 1942 at Port Moresby in New Guinea. Militarily, the battle is a draw, but the attack on Australia is checked.

Japan decides to attack Midway, an American base. America again intercepts communications and is ready. Japan overestimates the damage given to U.S. carriers and believes the USS *Yorktown* is out of commission. Japan expects an easy victory in June. Instead, the USS *Yorktown* is the only American carrier lost while Japan loses four of its

Radar room on a World War II Essex Class Carrier (China Sea, 1944).

eight carriers. From this point on, Japan retreats and the ferocious combat to take back each and every island is underway.

Korea

The sudden Japanese surrender that ends World War II leaves Japanese troops in possession of Korea. The Soviet Union allows Japanese troops to leave Korea. Eventually, an American-supported state under Syngman Rhee exists in the south and a Soviet-subsidized state under Kim Sung II exists in the north. Both leaders dream of ruling a united Korea.

In order to ease tensions on the Korean peninsula as well as to focus on Europe, the Soviets and the Americans withdraw their armies. In January 1950, President Truman delivers a speech reassuring all involved that America has no imperial interest in the area or in aiding Chaing Kai Shek. Further, America will only safeguard the perimeter it freed from Japan —a line stretching from the Aleutians, around Japan, and to the Philippines—but no mention is made of Korea. In June, with a green light from the Soviet Union, North Korea attacks the south and pushes U.N. troops into a tiny perimeter at the southern tip of the peninsula, starting what is now known as the Korean War.

Race Relations

The days of Jim Crow are numbered but the brightest of Americans, like James Baldwin and Richard Wright, refuse to wait. They find the atmosphere of America so oppressive that they prefer self-imposed exile in Paris. In Baldwin's case, he is young and still honing his talents. Richard Wright is haunted by his communist past. Meanwhile, the preeminent legal thinker of the day, Thurgood Marshall, brings important cases regarding civil rights before the Supreme Court—a distinguished court that he is soon to join.

While gathering evidence for his civil rights report on racial integration in the military, Marshall interviews General Douglas MacArthur. Marshall asks MacArthur why there is not one "Negro" on his entire headquarters staff or in his personal guard. MacArthur responds that there is not one qualified black man. Marshall tells him about one obvious legendary war hero. Then, Marshall asks why there is not one black in "that big beautiful band playing at the ceremony." And before the General can answer, Marshall says, "Now, General, just between you and me, goddammit, don't you tell me that there is no Negro that can play a horn."

Critical Overview

Despite his status as a Pulitzer Prize winner and best-selling author, most literary critics do not like the work of Herman Wouk. As an anonymous reviewer in *Time* noted, Wouk "spearheads a mutiny against the literary stereotypes of rebellion—against three decades of U.S. fiction dominated by skeptical criticism, sexual emancipation, social protest, and psychoanalytic sermonizing." The Wouk hero is not the outlaw gunslinger of the dime-store novel, the migrant worker of Steinbeck, or the bongo-thumping poets of the gathering Beat Generation. Moreover, Wouk intentionally refuses to give in to pop-psychology, Freudianism, or the fascination with sociopaths. Instead he prefers to tell realistic tales in which the hero is a true patriot upholding American ideals. Such a story was considered anachronistic and derivative at the time.

Frederic I. Carpenter, in "Herman Wouk and the Wisdom of Disillusion," was very specific in his disfavor. Wouk, while engaging, is too moralistic, and the anagnorisis, or moment of character self-realization leading to self-growth, of his characters is too unbelievable. Carpenter says that *The Caine Mutiny* continues the attempt to tell a story in a "straightforward manner" that Wouk had begun in *Marjorie Morningstar.* Both novels used the "traditional techniques of allegorical implication and conversational realism." Both indict the "irresponsible romantic" (the Tom Keefer figure) as being culpable for the brief straying of the young and naive. Further, asserts Carpenter, Wouk's plot device has a continual failing, whether in *The Traitor* or *The Caine Mutiny.* That failing is evinced in Keith's ability to be a responsible captain simply by the assumption of authority, which is very difficult to believe. Still, says Carpenter, *"The Caine Mutiny* remains the best of Wouk's novels because it is the least moralistic."

Summing up the problem more than reflecting on the novel itself, Edmund Fuller wrote it this way in his *Man and Modern Fiction,* 1958: "It seems to me that Mr. Wouk has been the victim of an unusual amount of unfair criticism. I think much of this is due to [*Caine Mutiny*'s] considerable contrast to the view of life and behavior reflected in [Norman Mailer's] *The Naked and the Dead* and *From Here to Eternity,* which have been accepted far too readily as valid or normative views of the behavior and attitudes of man particularly within the framework of the military experience...."

But Fuller is rather exceptional in his charitable defense. In the same year, Maxwell Geismer judges Wouk, in *American Moderns: From Rebellion to Conformity,* saying, "The novels of Herman Wouk lie in a curious realm between art and entertainment." By the early 1960s, however, David Dempsey was able to admit that there was something else troubling people about Wouk. In "It Didn't Pay to Strike It Rich," Dempsey hints that there may be money involved in the negative reviews. Wouk, he says, is the "most commercially successful writer of his generation." Leslie A. Fiedler also noted the monetary connection, saying, in his *Love and Death in the American Novel,* that "writers like Dreiser, ironically enough, made it possible to write ... the pure bourgeois novel." Wouk's realism is a cover for the presentation of one class' moral myth: the rebellious youth who matures through war to want nothing more than a suburban tract house and a beautiful wife.

Although *The Caine Mutiny* remains his best work by critical consensus, Wouk did not fare any better over time. "Like Sinclair, he writes journalese, and he never rises far above that level.... His characters are never living human beings," says Granville Hicks in a 1971 *New York Times Book Review.* In fact, Wouk's continued popularity and his continued use of anachronistic ideals led critics to charge him with pandering to the populace. As Pearl K. Bell states for a 1978 review in *Commentary,* Wouk is "an unembarrassed believer in such 'discredited' forms of commitment as valor, gallantry, leadership, patriotism." Be that as it may, Wouk remained on the bestseller charts with *The Caine Mutiny* and *The Winds of War* even during the Vietnam era.

In 1997, Chris Godat commented on Wouk's staying power in *Contemporary Popular Writers.* He said that Wouk had not sacrificed "his moral integrity. Wouk perceives himself as a realist in the tradition of Cooper, Howells, and Dreiser, and like his predecessors he addresses his fiction to a popular, rather than critical, audience."

Theater critics have been more forgiving and it is fair to notice the reserved praise bestowed on the stage adaptation of the novel. Eric Bentley, for example, in "Captain Bligh's Revenge," appreciates the novelist's "crisp dialogue." Further, says Bentley, Wouk "has an excellent story." That is until one realizes that Wouk's story is not a thriller but a "tract for the times" that says we should "respect authority: mutiny is unjustified." It is not as important to "save a particular ship but to preserve the authority of commanders; for they win wars while we sit reading Proust." Finally, Bentley asks a prescient question for the late 1990s: How mad would a commander have to be before he could be relieved according to Wouk? "The answer seems to be *plumb* crazy, raving, stark, staring mad."

Criticism

Tabitha McIntosh-Byrd

Tabitha McIntosh-Byrd is a doctoral candidate at the University of Pennsylvania. In the following essay, she analyzes Herman Wouk's The Caine Mutiny *as a 'hostile text'—a novel that resists critical and analytic interpretive strategies.*

The Caine Mutiny opens with a textual artifact—a page torn from the book of Navy Regulations which contains the articles relating to relief of a commanding officer. It closes with another—the "torn paper" of parade confetti which "brushed the face of the last captain of the Caine." Between these ripped paper bookends lies a densely intertextual work which is layered with deliberate echoes of a multitude of canonical texts—the most obvious being *The Rime of the Ancient Mariner, Moby-Dick,* and the book of Genesis—and contains scattered references to dozens of others. Though this would seem, at first glance, to mark it as a novel that invites literary interpretation, nothing could be more wrong.

The Caine Mutiny is in fact a novel that is aware of interpretation and resists it—providing obvious entry points for literary critique only to turn them back on the reader and undermine the analytic process. The ways in which the author deflects interpretation and expectation are many. The book proclaims itself to be a novel about World War II, but the action almost exclusively concerns non-combat life. It performs a narrative about-face four-fifths of the way through, forcing an abrupt shift in sympathies for all of the characters involved. It is shot through with morally ambiguous characters who spot the literary and symbolic references just as the reader has begun to, and thus draw us into uneasy complicity with them, making us question the very validity of textual interpretation. In the final analysis, *The Caine Mutiny* is a novel about the ethics of reading, about the moral implications of overlaying reality with literary meaning. The torn paper of the novel's last line is

both a summation of the plot's resolution and an explicit injunction to do likewise—to tear up textual meaning.

From the title of the novel onwards, an analytic reader is predisposed to perform certain kinds of interpretation. Caine, of course, would seem to refer to the Biblical story of Cain and Abel, the mutiny fitting in as an analog for the famous verse, "Cain rose up and slew his brother Abel." Analytic assumptions follow logically from this easy literary clue: that the ship and its crew will be outcasts, the mutiny will be couched in the language of family, honor and sin, and that the novel will conform to an easy series of symbolic devices. Several chapters into *The Caine Mutiny* however, this entire reading is defeated in a masterly sleight of hand. Not for the first or the last time, we as readers have been encouraged to congratulate ourselves on our reading skills, only to find that the narrative is quite aware of the interpretation that we have begun to give it. In a critical discussion during an Officers' meal, Tom Keefer—"the novelist"—tips our hand when he explains to the other officers the symbolic order that we too are using. As he says:

> "This ship is an outcast, manned by outcasts, and named for the greatest outcast of mankind."

Their replies deflate both his reading and our own:

> "That's the literary mind for you. I never thought of the Caine being a symbolic name—" "It seems to me, Mr. Keefer ... that you can twist any ship's name into a symbolic meaning...."

This latter comment is especially significant. As Keith says, Keefer is an "endless treasury of plays on words," and his identification of the *Caine* with Cain is just one instance of his intellectual games and—increasingly—his clear moral relativism. Wouk has deliberately staged his narrative to encourage us to make the exact identifications that Keefer does, and in debunking Keefer he debunks us too.

This way of reading—as a search for literary "clues" that can be made to form a coherent pattern—comes consistently under attack throughout the novel, first encouraged, then identified and finally exploded. To an astute reader on the lookout for such clues, the "rotting hull" of the *Caine* is a clear reference to *The Rime of the Ancient Mariner,* and the water-ban episode reinforces the identification. Almost as if it is anticipating the comments that we are about to write in the margin, the narrative again forestalls us:

What Do I Read Next?

- Herman Melville wrote a brilliantly and symbolically charged novella in 1797. It focuses on the experiences of a family member of Melville's who presided over the court-martial and execution of a sailor. Though written in 1891, *Billy Budd, Foretopman* or *Billy Budd, Sailor* was first published posthumously in 1924. Coincidentally, the English composer Edward Benjamin Britten, aided by E. M. Forster's libretto, made *Billy Budd* into an opera in 1951.

- A romantic novel by Charles Nordhoff describes what has become the archetypal story of mutiny. His 1932 novel, *Mutiny on the Bounty,* is based on the actual mutiny aboard the HMS *Bounty* in 1789 as narrated by Roger Byam.

- In the 1970s, Wouk returned to World War II as a setting for a novel with a two-volume historical novel *The Winds of War* (1971) and *War and Remembrance* (1978). The first novel tells of the heroic Lt. Henry and the plight of Jews in Poland. The second novel is the translations of a Nazis' private papers near the end of the war. Both novels have been praised for their historical accuracy.

- The other great American novel to come out of World War II in 1948 is Norman Mailer's first novel, *The Naked and the Dead.* The novel chronicles the experiences of a platoon on the Japanese-held island of Anopopei in the Pacific.

- After the war was over, most just wanted to forget the horrors of the camps. Elie Wiesel, however, refused to let the experience be swept under the rug. He wrote a 1956 novel called *Night* that described some of his own experiences in concentration camps during World War II. Wiesel then began a lifelong quest to talk about the camps and do whatever he could to prevent them from ever happening again.

"The bodies stirred, and rose, and began to move through chores with leaden limbs, like the crew of *The Rime of the Ancient Mariner.*"

In pointing out the connections we are in the process of making, we are yoked into the viewpoint of characters like Keith and Keefer, who "read" in exactly the same way that we do. Keefer's analysis of Queeg and his steel balls is as predictable as ours—"the man's a Freudian delight. He crawls with clues," while Keith's way of understanding the crew is entrenched in our shared comparative literary methods:

> "They reminded him of incidents in novels about men
> on long sea voyages, and there was a not quite pleas-
> ant amusement in seeing the classic symptoms pop-
> ping out...."

Nor is this all. The novel does not seek only to reflect our reading process back on itself; it also serves as a moral judgment on us. The identification of literary methods with morally ambiguous characters is the first way in which this begins. The "strawberry episode" reinforces it, with Queeg's insane search for clues and his obsessive gathering of keys being a clear analogy for critical analysis. However, it is after the mutiny that this theme becomes openly vicious—when Barney Greenwald, arguably the moral center of the novel, realizes that Tom Keefer's literary games lie at the heart of the whole affair. As he says to Maryk after hearing the narrative of events, "Your sensitive novelist is the villain of this foul-up."

The shared celebration for Maryk's victory and Keefer's literary contract underscore the insistent suggestion that there are two novels for which Keefer must take credit. Not only is his half-finished work *Multitudes, Multitudes* being published, but also his most triumphantly authored work, *The Caine Mutiny* itself. Even as we begin to recognize this parallel, however, Wouk outplays us again, taking the analysis from us and putting it in the mouth of Barney Greenwald. As the lawyer says of Keefer shortly before throwing a drink in his face, "He was the author of the *Caine* mutiny among his other works." Through the drunken speeches of Greenwald, the fundamental truths of the war are elaborated for the first and only time in the novel, and act as a series of narrative about-turns that utterly destabilize the reading of the situation that we have been encouraged to accept. To the shocked party-goers he elaborates that the war is about the Holocaust; that enlisted officers like Queeg have devoted their lives to standing between America and such horrors; that Maryk is indeed guilty of making a mutiny; and that the hero of the piece should have been Captain Queeg himself.

Accepting Greenwald's interpretation leads to a series of uneasy realizations about our own complicity in the case, the chief being that we, like the deluded crew, have accepted the romance of the tale and ignored the reality. Just as Keith "had whispered to himself, "'the *Caine* mutiny, the *Caine* mutiny,' savoring the ring of the phrase," so we have read the mutiny as an adventure tale, ignoring the narrative injunction at the novel's opening:

> "It was not a mutiny in the old-time sense, of course, with flashings of cutlasses, a captain in chains, and desperate sailors turning outlaws."

This is, of course, precisely the way that the Mutiny section has been crafted, and the way in which it is interpreted by the novel's civilians, May Wynn and Keith's mother. The purpose of Wouk's layers of literary reference become clearer—they are there to show us that the reality of war is outside literary craft and that our understanding of it is immorally confused by our reading matter. If we are to disassociate ourselves from Keefer—the critic and coward who is "stained yellow" forever—we must reject criticism and interpretation. By the end of the novel Keefer has himself realized his own nature, and is still unable to extract it from literary conceit. His cowardice is linked in his mind with *Lord Jim* and he tells Willie that he will be "Lord Tom" from this point onwards. It is highly appropriate that he damns himself with reference to a seafaring novel, since he has begun the whole mutiny with his allusion to another. As he said to Maryk early in the escalating tension, "Ever read *Billy Budd,* by Melville? Read it. That's the whole story."

Of course this is *not* the whole story, and Maryk tells him so, relating the actual causes behind Queeg's dislike of Stilwell. He points out the real reasons for the hostility, and comments, "I don't have any theories. I'm a dumb comic-book reader." In fact, "dumb" comic-book reading, in which word and image have a direct and uncomplicated relationship, turns out to be the only kind of reading that doesn't morally incriminate the reader. In a truly shocking moment, the scenes at the celebration party have revealed to us that everything before them has been word-play—a literary game stylistically embodied by Keefer's favorite novel, *Finnegan's Wake.* The version of *The Caine Mutiny* that we have been reading is no more or less than Keefer's novel, wearily assessed by Greenwald as a book which:

> "exposes this war in all its grim futility and waste, and shows up the military men for the stupid, Fascist-minded sadists they are."

If we accept Barney's insistence that this is not true, that it is Queeg who should have been the tragic hero of the tale, then the purpose of the torn page of regulations at the frontispiece comes into retrospective focus. The articles contained therein are the facts—the elements by which we should have judged the action of the novel. It has, in fact, been a trial, and Barney Greenwald is telling us that we too have made a false judgment, and have been found wanting. We are just as gullible as Maryk and, like him, should have stuck to comic books.

Source: Tabitha McIntosh-Byrd, in an essay for *Novels for Students,* Gale, 1999.

Ricardo J. Quinones

In the following excerpt, Quinones argues that The Caine Mutiny *is "deeply flawed," but that this flaw lends literary interest to the work and also invites analysis of the story from a historical perspective.*

Herman Wouk's *The Caine Mutiny* [is] concerned with defining the nature of the American experience, wherein the character of Cain becomes something of a national type....

The Caine Mutiny has been a remarkably successful novel, with close to 250,000 volumes in thirteen printings in the first eight months of its publication. But our interest does not lie in the book's success, but rather in its failure. Deeply flawed, *The Caine Mutiny* is of great interest precisely because of that flaw. The fault line that runs through the work amounts to a recantation of the dynamic of the Sacred Executioner, the pattern of which in many of its variations we have been following. What Wouk has done is to return the story to the same moral sluggishness, the same undifferentiation from which it emerged when Byron first put his hand to the Cain theme. But in so doing he has given us an accurate barometer of the morale of a decade, of a postwar mentality that, although understandable in its causes, denied civilization itself the powers of rejuvenation.

The Caine Mutiny betrays a high degree of literary self-consciousness (and this might explain its later drastic and vengeful turnabout). The character who provides the higher consciousness, the literary *leit-motives,* is Tom Keefer, the author's needed mouthpiece. It is he who serves as double and perhaps even evil genius for Maryk, who himself becomes the Cain of the piece when he relieves Queeg of his command. Keefer first explains why the story is a Cain story:

> "I've given up [putting in for transfer]. This ship is an outcast, manned by outcasts, and named for the greatest outcast of mankind. My destiny is the *Caine.* It's the purgatory for my sins...." The captain regarded Keefer admiringly. "That's the literary mind for you. I never thought of *Caine* being a symbolic name—"
>
> "The extra *e* threw you off, Captain. God always likes to veil his symbols a bit, being, among his other attributes, the perfect literary mind." (p. 90)

This is peculiar officers' mess banter. But the message of the cursed Cain is reinforced with greater ominousness when Maryk finds out that he is named executive officer of the *Caine.* On shore leave with Keefer in San Francisco, Maryk is in unaccountably low spirits. "Ever have one of those days, Tom, when you feel something bad is in the air—something bad's going to happen to you before the evening's out?" (p. 202). When they return to the boat Maryk learns of his new responsibilities, and Keefer learns that no order has come through for his transfer. "God damn the Caine," said Keefer, "and strike everyone aboard it, including me, with a curse." Maryk can only see his earlier premonitions confirmed. "'This is it,' he thought—but he could not have said what he meant by 'it'" (p. 206). Wouk utilizes the post-romantic dimensions of the theme: in place of any insistence on human freedom, he endows his story with grim foreboding and with a sense of cursed destiny.

Obviously, in his reign of neurotic terror, Captain Queeg qualifies as a vindictive Cain, visiting all sorts of retaliatory punishments on the innocent seamen (in this regard, the repeated broadcast of the phrase, "condition Able," is eerie and ironic). But the point of the work, what makes it an extremely revealing document of the times, is the exchange of roles, the evident vindication of Queeg and the immolation of the cowardly intellectual, that is, the transformation—for which we are not unprepared—of the rebellious, malcontented Keefer into the malefactor Cain.

There are no brother murders in this work, but there is a brother death (significantly, the very early death of Willie Keith's father does seem to open the terrain of moral development, that is, leave it open for all the counterinfluences). Tom's brother, Roland (as his name indicates, he will hold heroically and fatally to his post), is an officer aboard the carrier *Montauk.* He sends a blinker message to his brother and their mutual friend, Willie, inviting them to visit him on the carrier. However, permission must first be gained from Captain Queeg. Keefer: "Guess I'll have to pay a visit to Grendel's cave.... Here's hoping he's not in a blood-drinking mood" (pp. 279–80). The request is of course denied. In a moving scene Roland tries to shout his farewells to the two by means of a megaphone: "They could see Roland laugh and nod. He was far ahead of them in a moment. He called back once more but nothing was distinguishable except the word '... brother....'"

In action at Leyte Gulf the carrier *Montauk,* under serious attack, is struck at its bridge by a Japanese suicide plane. Roland, engaged in heroic efforts to save the ship, is fatally burned. Anticipating his own later cowardice in a similar incident (for which he also provides the appropriate literary reference from *Lord Jim*), Tom is unsure how he would behave in similar circumstances, commenting, "Rollo had good instincts." The brothers had never been very close; Keefer confesses, "I'm afraid I thought he was too dumb." But then, in a nagging concession that is crucial for the purposes of the theme, Keefer admits that their father had always preferred Roland. "Maybe he knows something" (p. 286). Clearly preparations are being made for a turn against a complex consciousness on the basis of a defense of a simpler effectiveness.

Keefer is more important as the double—his name does suggest *Lucifer,* where the *c* would naturally have a hard sound. Typical of the double, he provides the guileless Maryk with arcane lore, now from the scientific field of psychology. Captain Queeg suffers from paranoia (of which Maryk admits he has never heard). Keefer further instructs his pupil in the fictionalized Articles 184, 185, and 186 of the Navy Regulations by which the captain may be relieved of his command. Not only does Keefer, as a kind of evil genius, provide the seeds of doubt, he even provides the literary text by which the captain's hatred of natural instincts may be understood. He specifically refers to *Billy Budd* and Claggart's envy of Billy (to which he adds his own sexual connotations):

"Okay. He hates Stilwell for being handsome, healthy, young, competent and naturally popular and attractive—all the things that Queeg is not. Ever read *Billy Budd,* by Melville? Read it. That's the whole story. Stilwell is a symbol of all the captain's frustrations, all the things he would like to smash because he can't have them.... Infantilism is very strong in our captain." (p. 268)

But when the simpler and more forthright Maryk, finally convinced that Keefer is right, wishes to present his log of Queeg's bizarre and pathetic actions to the fleet commander, Admiral Halsey, Keefer backs off at the last moment. Keefer admits that he is scared, but wishes to be credited for his honesty (p. 316). This dishonest honesty causes Maryk to compare Keefer with Queeg, and indeed the exchange of roles is complete.

In the extraordinarily compelling "Typhoon" chapter, Queeg's pathetic incompetence and stubborn pride are fully revealed. In order to save the ship—and the hull of the sunken ship that they pass would seem to indicate the reality of the danger—Maryk relieves the captain of his command. He is the Sacred Executioner, who undertakes a desperate and extraordinary action at a crucial moment. The emotionally paralyzed and incompetent Queeg abdicates, and Maryk assumes the burden of responsibility. In this change of command, in the midst of the defection of authority, an abler leader, a new order of humanity, emerges. The significance of this change is not lost on Willie, who is the first of the young officers to support Maryk's decisive actions. It takes forty minutes for the *Caine* to restore itself, maneuvering by the lost ship and taking an enormous beating from the waves: "Willie was scared each time. But he now knew the difference between honest fright and animal terror. One was bearable, human, not incapacitating; the other was moral castration. He was no longer terrorized, and felt he no longer could be, even if the ship went down, provided Maryk were in the water with him" (p. 342). The passage is undeniably clear: a new order of humankind, not without its doubts and fears, is able to enter into the perils of critical, even revolutionary change and emerge with the restoration of order. Human resourcefulness reasserts itself. Queeg, already associated with Grendel, has, in his own psychic terror, reduced life to the level of the bestial. In the more significant and broader restoration of the human image, an apparent illegitimate act has been legitimized, and humankind has escaped from animalistic undifferentiation.

Given all this—the clear and evident support for Maryk's actions and the slow build-up of evidence that Queeg is an emotional basket case—the conclusion of the book amounts to a recantation. Wouk offers a palinode to the act of legitimate revolution that the novel itself seems to endorse. This surprise reversal is, however, not as strange as the reasons given for it. And here we approach the fault line of the novel. After all, we have already been given ample clues as to Keefer's character, and his failure to support Maryk in the court-martial was not unexpected. He is the Luciferean evil genius who switches places with Queeg and becomes the Cainite fall guy. This is prepared and anticipated. What is unexpected—and, what is more important, unprepared—are the reasons given, the strange argumentative displacement that occurs. Not content with sacrificing Keefer, his own surrogate and artistic mouthpiece, Wouk, in the words of his new moral and legal mouthpiece, Greenwald, must also vindicate Queeg. Authority that had defected must now, in the pact of postwar reconciliation that follows, be restored.

Greenwald's defense of Queeg is so displaced and skewed as to be practically incredible. Rather than the issue being Queeg's base incompetence—for which there is ample evidence—the terms of the argument are shifted to those of regular navy versus wartime enlistees and draftees. Greenwald argues that if it had not been for the regular navy types like Queeg, Hitler would have triumphed and his Jewish mother would have been made into soap to wash Herman Goering's fat behind (pp. 447–48). Leaving aside the fact that Queeg was serving in the Pacific, the argument could more profitably go as follows: if the regular navy had been made up of any more Queegs what would there have been to prevent Goering from occupying Chicago? The argument has shifted from Queeg's evident manic incompetence to Keefer's guilt, and beyond Keefer's guilt to the general guilt of all those who "sat on the sidelines getting rich and pursuing their own careers, while the real grunts of the world were carrying out the necessary chores." The argument is actually that debased. Whenever the terms of the argument shift, or are displaced so radically, one must suspect a psychic fault line. The fault line is guilt (in this case, sadly, not transcended)—not Maryk's, not Keefer's, but Wouk's. Greenwald's argument is this: "See, while I was studying law 'n' old Keefer here was writing his play for the Theatre Guild, and Willie here was on the playing fields of Prinston, all that time these birds we call regulars—these stuffy, stupid Prussians, in the army and the navy—were manning the guns" (p. 446). The restoration of the regular army and navy—the people who hold the world together, Wouk might argue—could be valid but it certainly does not fit the book that Wouk has written up until this point. A different volition has overtaken the novel, an intrusive will that has a point to make against the would-be intellectual—and against himself. Like Keefer, Wouk wishes to have his cake and eat it too, to establish a literate *raisonneur* who will provide the mythic structure and literary resonances with which the work is somewhat encumbered, and then to disestablish him. It is like writing a book about the war in which the character who writes a book about the war is branded. The vindication of Cain in the works of Hesse and of Steinbeck requires some transcendence of guilt; this Wouk was unable to do. Unnaturally, given the circumstances of the work and its own inner coherence, Wouk could not overcome his sense of guilt, or those aspects of himself that he needed to condemn in the character of Keefer.

The importance of the intrusive retraction does not stop there. The hinge of the work, as Wouk describes it in his brief foreword, is the character of Willie Keith. In the absence of his father, Keith is open to the many influences present on the ship, and his developing character becomes something of a touchstone. Thus to Willie is left the final summing-up, a summation that he acknowledges is derived from Greenwald's own accusations in the bitter post-trial "victory" celebration, and that he sends in the form of a letter proposing marriage to May, the night-club singer with whom, he now recognizes, he is in love. In some ways the letter becomes the sad testament of a generation.

The Caine Mutiny is an important book, even a crucial book, and despite Wouk's obvious skills (the depiction of the V12 program at Columbia, the typhoon chapter, and the court-martial), it is more important for what it reveals unconsciously, almost against itself: the preparation of a generation for its descent into simple stagnation and moral sluggishness. Tired of war and trauma, suspicious of intellectuals, of ideology, and of animosities based upon ideas and issues, eager to get on with the business of living, this generation settled down, seeking out common interests, emotional cohesion, and community. In the projection of these idyllic qualities (they are Abelite), it is little wonder that any possibility of a regenerate Cain should be prohibited.

In the letter to May, Willie identifies Keefer as the troublemaker, but then goes on to declare, in the wake of Greenwald's denunciation, "But I don't think Maryk had to relieve the captain." He then reaches a further conclusion: "The idea is, once you get an incompetent ass of a skipper—and it's a chance of war—there's nothing to do but to serve him as though he were the wisest and the best, cover his mistakes, keep the ship going, and bear up" (p. 468). But here again we must demur: obviously Queeg is more than an "incompetent ass"—that phrasing itself is part of the go-along-with-it, nothing-really-is-all-that-important ingratiating message of the letter. Queeg is shown to be dementedly dangerous, an emotional disaster, but his true sickness is covered in the general need for reinstatement. The father, who had been absent in several ways in the regeneration of Cain, is now returned to his former commanding status when Cain is condemned. In this sense, we see how the letter compounds the book's general retreat into the undifferentiated sentiment from which Byron first tried to extricate the Cain-Abel theme.

If the figure of authority is restored, then the virtues of Abel are validated. Queeg, a Cain, is now justified by being an Abel, that is, part of a general mess of undifferentiated feeling and, actually, the victim of a hostile, divisive Cain (Keefer). By jettisoning Keefer-Cain, Wouk demonstrates his own credentials for admission into the common purposes of American life. For comparisons we can think back to our prior discussion of *The Secret Sharer* and anticipate the coming section on *Billy Budd.* (Both works being part of the background of *The Caine Mutiny,* in some ways we can see that Wouk's work is a literary response to and comment not only on them, but on the development of regenerate Cain himself.) Finally, the promotion of Queeg has the moral equivalence of the vindication of the captain of the *Sephora,* and to blame Maryk would be the same as delivering up Leggatt to the authorities. But, even more dangerous, this particular justification of Queeg for his being "regular navy" echoes strangely the sense of things rendered by the naval chronicle relating—from a great distance—the events of Claggart's death and of Billy's punishment in Melville's work. It should be remembered that it is this report, "News from the Mediterranean," that Melville's own "inside narrative" is designed to correct. In fact, what Wouk has done is to discredit the inside narrative that he himself has given us and to reaffirm the public evaluation. In the report, Billy is degraded to a knife-wielding foreigner, whose "crime" is all the more heinous because directed against "a middle-aged man respectable and discreet, belonging to that minor official grade, the petty officers, upon whom, as none know better than the commissioned gentlemen knew, the efficiency of His Majesty's navy so largely depends" (p. 1433). Wouk's vindication of Queeg resorts to the same defense of his general function, and indulges in the same consolatory practice: just as the "commissioned gentlemen" must give the "petty officer" his due, so the hot-shot, successful, and college-educated draftees are made to appreciate the regular Navy as well as the regular values of American democratic life. The generalized process of undifferentiation seems demeaning for all concerned.

In this becalmed world, all possibility of historical change is denied, and the Cain-Abel theme loses its modern meaning. An indication of this loss of the capacity for differentiation is the sloppiness of the letter. Lacking precise care and filled with disarming "I guesses," it suggests that all issues are really petty in nature and of no importance in the face of the larger vision of peace and the need for fusion. In the letter, eager intelligence and moral will are immobilized. When the only intellect conceivable is cowardly, then the modern Cain of consciousness is badly impaired. *The Caine Mutiny* remains one of the notable expressions of the regressive ethos of the 1950s, and of a generation that ratted on its diamond. In seeking to avoid the envy of the gods, in finding acceptance, it became the generation that the gods despised.

Source: Ricardo J. Quinones, "The New American Cain: *East of Eden* and Other Works of Post-World War II America," in his *The Changes of Cain: Violence and the Lost Brother in Cain and Abel Literature,* Princeton University Press, 1991, pp. 135-52.

Robert Bierstedt

In the following excerpt, Bierstedt faults "the conclusions to which the author of The Caine Mutiny *felt constrained to come at the end of his book."*

The Caine Mutiny was published on March 19, 1951. After a somewhat sluggish start it found its way to the best-seller list of the *New York Times* and to the surprise of almost everyone, including a publisher who had rejected the manuscript, it remained there for one hundred twenty-three weeks. Domestic sales in various editions are well over the three million mark. It has been translated into sixteen foreign languages; it has been syndicated in forty-one American newspapers; it has been distributed by no less than four book clubs; and its au-

thor has been awarded a Pulitzer Prize. *The Caine Mutiny Court Martial,* a play prepared by the author himself, opened on Broadway in January of 1954 and is still [November, 1954] playing to capacity audiences. The movie opened at the Capitol Theater in New York on June 24, and by now it is impossible to estimate the number of millions of people who have joined the crew of the *Caine* and who have participated, however vicariously, in one of the best advertized "mutinies" in history.

We have here a phenomenon which has one set of implications for Madison Avenue, however, and quite another for this quiet seminary on Morningside Heights [The Jewish Theological Seminary of America, where the chapter was originally presented as a lecture]. For *The Caine Mutiny,* whatever one thinks of it as a publishing success, is a work of considerable literary merit. It is a book, moreover, which introduces an interesting moral issue. This, of course, is one of the functions of literature, and the greater the literature, as this entire series exemplifies, the more imposing the moral problem. Although the rank of the book as a work of art does not directly concern us, we should be disposed to argue that a moral flaw in its structure, if such it be, is relevant to an esthetic judgment. That the novel does contain a moral flaw is the case I want to propose and this in spite of a personal admiration for Herman Wouk which is both wholehearted and humble. The flaw is one which no amount of admiration can altogether subdue, no casuistry wholly conceal.

The extraordinary popularity of *The Caine Mutiny,* in book and play and movie, renders unnecessary a recapitulation of the plot. As an aid to recollection, however, we may reintroduce the cast of characters so that the problems they severally and individually confront can claim our attention.

The protagonist of the novel is Willie Keith, a Princeton man and sometime singer in night clubs who aspires to a professorship in Romance languages. (It is, we are encouraged to believe, a genteel profession and one well suited to the otherwise idle rich.) In the course of his tour of naval duty Willie greatly matures and as we leave him at the book's end we suspect, with some apprehension, that he may turn out to be a professor after all. In the book, however, Willie serves an important purpose. It is his eyes through which we observe the mutiny on the *Caine* and further, as Wouk says, "the event turned on his personality as the massive door of a vault turns on a small jewel bearing." When, at the height of the storm, the two officers of the *Caine,* the captain and the executive officer, give contradictory orders to the helmsman, the latter, Stilwell, appeals in real fear to Willie, then on duty as Officer of the Deck. It is apparent that if Willie, at this tense moment, had supported the captain instead of the executive officer, the latter's attempt to relieve his skipper would have failed. In this sense, the author is saying, Willie is essential to the plot; this is his *raison d'être*.

The importance of a single individual in the causation of a complex event in human affairs is always open to question, as Tolstoy has so supremely taught us. Given the circumstances, it may be argued that the result was inevitable and that Willie had no more to do with it—and no less—than any other member of the fated company. But historiography and fiction are two different enterprises. The novelist's art requires him to accept a theory which a sociologist is ordinarily tempted to reject, that is, the heroic (or diabolic) theory of history. We may readily concede to Wouk, therefore, that Willie was not only important but essential to the mutiny of the *Caine*. At the same time we ought to note, perhaps, that all of the officers of the *Caine* supported Maryk in his relief of Queeg, and this without further question or controversy.

The second officer to engage our attention is Philip Spencer Queeg, named no doubt after Midshipman Philip Spencer, one of three men actually hanged for mutiny in 1842, the only mutiny recorded in the naval history of the United States, and that, too, incidentally, a dubious one. Lieutenant Commander Queeg is the captain of the *Caine*. He is also "regular Navy" and the Articles for the Government of the Navy are his only Bible and his only Law. He is more than a disciplinarian; he is a martinet. He possesses that combination of qualities which usually makes for success in any bureaucracy and for failure everywhere else. While martinets and myrmidons may be conspicuous in military organizations, they can be found, of course, in all the organizations of society. Wouk need not apologize therefore to the Navy for drawing this kind of portrait of one of its officers, although his compunction to do so is unaccountably clear. The normal curve of probability has ends as well as a middle, and in any group as large as the Navy some persons will find their places at the extremities of the curve.

We learn very early that as a ship's handler Queeg is clumsy and inept. His seamanship is not only faulty; it is often dangerous. At the time of the typhoon it is clear, although Wouk later tries to compromise the picture, that he is doing everything wrong. His refusal to come into the wind, to ballast his tanks, and to turn the depth charges on "Safe" all increase the hazards to his ship. He fails to do what a reasonably prudent and capable seaman would do on the ground that standing orders are still standing and that not even a typhoon justifies the slightest departure, or exercise of initiative.

But Queeg is not, in other circumstances, a "book-officer" at all. He illegally transports back to the States a consignment of liquor for his own personal use and then extorts the cost of it from Willie when, because of his own mistakes, it is lost overboard. On several occasions he submits to his superiors reports which stray rather considerably from the truth in the direction of self-justification, and he offers, in the instance of the "mutiny" itself, to erase and rewrite the rough logs of the ship. This last, for obvious reasons, is an exceedingly serious offense against naval regulations.

The issue of cowardice as affecting Queeg is one which the author treats with insight and skill. The captain never stays on the exposed side of the bridge when the ship is under fire. In one case he fails to return enemy fire when he has an opportunity to do so, and instead moves the *Caine* out of range as rapidly as possible. In escorting assault boats to the beach at Kwajalein he runs far ahead of them, drops a dyemarker indicating the line of departure, and then hastily runs again for safety. This last incident wins him the name "Old Yellowstain" among his subordinate officers, and the "Yellow," of course, stands for more than the color of the dye. For the reader at least, Wouk clearly, steadily, and consistently establishes, beyond any lingering possibility of skepticism, that Queeg is a coward.

Queeg, however, is not on trial, and the charge of cowardice which Willie Keith's testimony so clearly implies has no legal stature. The defense attorney, Greenwald, denies that Queeg is guilty of cowardice, on the ground that no man certified by the Navy as qualified for command could possibly be guilty of so heinous a charge. On the contrary, if Queeg's actions seem to suggest cowardice, they must instead be attributed to a mental affliction. The testimony of three psychiatrists that Queeg's condition is not disabling suffers heavily under cross-examination and particularly when Greenwald maintains that the court is better qualified than a board of medical examiners to estimate the stresses of command.

Finally, of course, Queeg convicts himself by going to pieces on the witness stand, repeating tiresome trivialities over and over to the point of echolalia and clicking his little steel balls together as his case disintegrates. The captain and his creator together have convinced us all that the "mutiny" was justified and that Maryk, the executive officer, is innocent even of the lesser charge of "conduct to the prejudice of good order and discipline." It is a dramatic, colorful, and exciting story, and at the climax, as throughout, only one conclusion is possible.

Lieutenant Stephen Maryk, who relieves Queeg and who thus becomes the defendant in the court-martial action, is not so fully rounded nor so richly detailed as the other officers. A fisherman before the war who now aspires to transfer to the Regular Navy, he is an extraordinarily able seaman. He is more than that. He is a decent, honest, and courageous citizen. As executive officer under Queeg he is caught between the parlous captain and the reluctant crew, and he performs the duties of this trying and essentially ambivalent position with distinction, retaining both the trust of his subordinates and the confidence of the skipper. As the situation is constructed this would seem to be an impossible task, but Maryk somehow manages to accomplish it. He relieves Queeg only after he is convinced that the ship is in its last extremity and that the captain, in panic, has lost touch with the reality of the raging seas.

Maryk is not stupid, however, and to suggest that he is the mere pawn of Keefer, cowed by Keefer's superior intellect and supposedly superior insight into the dark recesses of the human mind, is to do him a disservice. Maryk may not know the technical language of psychoanalysis, but he knows an incompetent mariner when he sees one, and Wouk leaves no doubt that he does see one on the bridge of the *Caine* at the height of the typhoon. Maryk acts throughout—and especially in the action for which he is court-martialed—with vigor and decision. To suggest that he is at any time motivated by disloyalty, is to distort the image of a character which the author has carefully, if briefly, constructed.

Lieutenant Thomas Keefer, of course, is the Cassius of the *Caine.* An intellectual and a writer, Keefer induces Maryk to keep a medical log on the captain and explains the captain's symptoms as they appear. It is Keefer who is always somewhere else when unpleasant decisions have to be made; it is Keefer who displays both moral and physical cowardice; and it is Keefer finally who betrays his friend Maryk on the witness stand. Keefer is conscious of his weaknesses, however, and with a curious candor even confesses to them. At least one critic—Granville Hicks—has regarded Wouk's treatment of Keefer as an assault upon intellectuals and as one more indication of the anti-intellectualism of our time. This is a complaint which we shall consider in the sequel.

We come finally to Lieutenant Barney Greenwald, the only one of the five officers who was not a member of the *Caine*'s company and who serves instead as Maryk's counsel. He appears first as a quiet but arrogant individual who thinks, on the one hand, that Steve Maryk and Willie Keith "deserve to get slugged" and, on the other, that only a "halfway intelligent defense" will suffice to get them off. He hesitates at first to take the case and then expresses himself so dogmatically against his own prospective clients that one might question the wisdom of his superior in permitting him to do so. "I just don't want to defend these *Caine* people," he says. "Captain Queeg obviously is not crazy. The psychiatrist's report proves it. These fools find a paragraph in Navy Regs that gives them ideas, and they gang up on a skipper who's mean and stupid—as a lot of skippers are—and make jackasses of themselves, and put a ship out of action. I'm a damn good lawyer and a very expensive one, and I don't see contributing my services to get them acquitted."

This speech attracts our attention for several reasons. In the first place the reader by this time has thoroughly identified himself with the defendants and like them he is desperately in need of an adequate defense against the recommended charge of mutiny. It comes as a disappointment therefore that the attorney who will serve in this capacity has so enthusiastically prejudged the case. His prejudgment might possibly be excused on the ground that he is talking only to two other lawyers, but, on the other hand, one of them, Challee, is scheduled, as judge advocate, to be his opponent at the trial. But even worse, it is a prejudgment which stems from ignorance. When Greenwald makes this remark he knows nothing whatever about the events which occurred on the *Caine* and has no warrant for assuming that it is merely a case of discontented men "ganging up" on a "mean and stupid skipper."

Greenwald is also wrong in his anticipation of the character of Maryk. The person he expects to see is the college radical of the thirties—thin, dark, sensitive, *intellectual,* antimilitary in general and anti-Navy in particular, possibly even a Communist. Maryk, of course, is none of these things, and so Greenwald receives his first surprise.

Finally we learn—in the book but not in the movie—that Greenwald is a Jew, and we are informed that he therefore has an especial reason to appreciate the United States Navy. In the movie Greenwald is merely a loyal American who supports, as "intellectuals" apparently do not, the importance of the peacetime Navy.

This, then, is the cast of characters. To this cast we may now add Herman Wouk, the man who wrote the book. Wouk sees the action which occurred on the *Caine* as a rebellion against authority, a rebellion he first considers justified and then, inconsistently and unaccountably, unjustified. Mutiny, of course, is rebellion of a high order since it is a challenge to the authority of a captain of a ship at sea. We are prepared to concede that such authority is and must be almost absolute. Indeed, it has been remarked that a captain on his bridge is the closest a civilized society ever comes to an absolute monarch. It is a situation in which only monarchy can work. Obedience to such authority must be instantaneous and unquestioned; it is an authority recognized, protected, and supported both by naval law and by long maritime tradition. The perils of the sea require special vigilance, and special rules, in consequence, have arisen to cope with them.

Now as Wouk tells us himself, there was no genuine mutiny on the *Caine*. We have here no "flashing of cutlasses, no captain in chains," no criminal sailors seizing the ship in order to pursue their own designs. After Maryk relieves the captain the structure of authority remains precisely what it was before. The functions of the crew remain the same and so also does the mission of the ship. Particular individuals no longer occupy the same places in the structure, but the authority itself is both intact and unchallenged.

Nor is it a mutiny in another sense. As Greenwald immediately recognizes, "There's no question of force or violence or disrespect." Maryk even apologizes to Queeg at the moment of relief, using the following formula, "Captain, I'm sorry, sir, you're a sick man. I am temporarily relieving you of command of this ship, under Article 184 of *Navy Regulations*." Article 184 reads as follows:

> It is conceivable that most unusual and extraordinary circumstances may arise in which the relief from duty of a commanding officer by a subordinate becomes necessary, either by placing him under arrest or on the sick list; but such action shall never be taken without the approval of the Navy Department or other ap-

propriate higher authority, except when reference to such higher authority is undoubtedly impracticable because of the delay involved or for other clearly obvious reason. Such reference must set forth all facts in the case, and the reasons for the recommendation, with particular regard to the degree of urgency involved.

Article 185 says in addition, and in part:

> In order that a subordinate officer, acting upon his own initiative, may be vindicated for relieving a commanding officer from duty, the situation must be obvious and clear, and must admit of the single conclusion that the retention of command by such commanding officer will seriously and irretrievably prejudice the public interests.

These passages indicate that the authority to relieve a commanding officer under certain conditions is clearly present in naval law and that Maryk's action is therefore no challenge to authority. Indeed, Maryk invokes the relevant authority at the moment of relief. In all that has preceded, Wouk has demonstrated that the situation is "obvious and clear" and admits of the single conclusion "which a reasonable, prudent, and experienced officer would regard as a necessary consequence from the facts thus determined to exist." The notion that Maryk's action is somehow a rebellion against authority, is one which is susceptible to serious question. The action must, of course, be justified and this is the task to which Greenwald devotes himself, with the unwitting assistance of Queeg himself, in the famous trial scenes. We all rejoice therefore when a sensible verdict is sensibly reached. From the facts which the author has given us, not only in court but during the long cruise of the *Caine* itself, acquittal is the only possible conclusion.

So now the trial is over, the case concluded, the novel finished. Maryk's acquittal in the confusion and tumult of war is itself a potent compliment to the Navy. We can take pride in a military organization in which the exercise of authority is not unaccompanied by compassion. The Navy we see in Wouk's book is no Prussian organization, placing discipline above all other considerations, including the safety of its ships and the lives of its men. Our suspense during the trial is sustained by our suspicion of the Navy; now we discover with relief that the suspicion is unjustified, that the Navy, too, can take account of human frailty and human need. The dinner party to celebrate the verdict and to pay tribute to Greenwald for his defense of Maryk promises to be an anticlimax. For us, the readers, justice has triumphed—as we were afraid it would not—and right has prevailed.

But now something happens which alters the complexion of the book and reverses its thesis. The victory party does not finish the novel but instead destroys the consistency of the plot and mars the moral integrity of the author's achievement. Something happens which we are induced to call the tergiversation of Herman Wouk.

The scene is the victory dinner, called and paid for by Keefer as a double celebration, first for the acquittal and second for the acceptance of his novel by a publishing house. In the midst of the alcoholic gaiety Greenwald stumbles drunkenly into the room and, as the hero of the trial, is called upon to speak. In response he asks first about Keefer's book, a war novel, and then—incredibly—says, "It suddenly seems to me that if I wrote a war novel I'd try to make a hero out of Old Yellowstain." He is quite serious. To explain the reason for making Queeg a hero he invokes his little old Jewish mother. When the "Germans started running out of soap and figured, well it's time to come over and melt down old Mrs. Greenwald—who's gonna stop them? Not her boy Barney. Can't stop a Nazi with a lawbook. So I dropped the lawbooks and ran to learn how to fly. Stout fellow. Meantime, and it took a year and a half before I was any good, who was keeping Mama out of the soap dish? Captain Queeg."

In this maudlin scene we are suddenly asked to believe that Queeg, in contrast to everything we have known of him before, is a hero; that Keefer, who gets the champagne in his face, is a villain; and that Maryk, in relieving the captain, has committed an unforgivable crime. Here is transvaluation with a vengeance! Why has Wouk done this? For many pages we have followed him in good faith, believing that Queeg was indeed afflicted with a mental aberration (remember, for example, the strawberry incident), believing that he was at bottom a coward who preferred not to face the enemy, believing, finally, that he was wholly incapacitated by fear at the height of the typhoon and unable in consequence to save his ship. We believe that Maryk is the savior of the *Caine* and of the lives of the men, because Wouk, with a superior artistry, has convinced us that this is so. We have given him our total attention throughout and now, without warning, he is telling us that he has deceived us, that Maryk and the other officers are guilty, that Queeg is to be praised for having joined the peacetime Navy, and that authority ought to be upheld in any cause however ignoble and in any person however cowardly, crazy, or incompetent. The story for him has become as simple as the as-

sertion in the Book of Luke (7:8), "For I also am a man set under authority, having under me soldiers, and I say unto one, Go, and he goeth; and to another Come, and he cometh."

Wouk is telling us in addition that he is sorry he has written the story the way he has and that he, too, deserves an appropriate punishment. He will now do penance and write the remainder of his book from an opposite point of view. This opposition, amounting to a contradiction, is expressed in the words of the reviewing authority, which disapproves the acquittal of Maryk, which "believes the specification proved beyond a reasonable doubt," and which continues:

> There is in this case a miscarriage of justice whereby an officer escapes punishment for a serious offense and a dangerous precedent has been established. The fact that the ship was in hazard does not mitigate, but rather intensifies the responsibility of the accused. It is at times of hazard most of all that the line of naval discipline should be held rigidly, especially by senior officers on a ship.... A ship can have only one commanding officer, appointed by the government, and to remove him in an irregular manner without referring the matter to the highest available authority is an act exceeding the powers of a second-in-command. This doctrine is emphasized, not weakened, by the description in Articles 184, 185, and 186 of the exceedingly rare circumstances in which exception may be made, and the intentions of the Navy Department to this effect are therein expressed with the utmost clarity and vigor.

Finally, Willie himself accepts the thesis that Maryk was acquitted by legal trickery. In a letter to May Wynn he accuses himself and Maryk of disloyalty and suggests that they transferred to Queeg the hatred they should have felt for Hitler and the Japanese. The reverse rationalization of the letter concludes with the following remarkable recommendation to serve authority with a blind obedience: "The idea is, once you get an incompetent ass of a skipper—and it's a chance of war—there's nothing to do but serve him as though he were the wisest and the best, cover his mistakes, keep the ship going, and bear up." And when he reads the words of the reviewing authority he says, "Well, I concur too. That makes it unanimous."

But Willie is wrong. The verdict is not unanimous. It is for us, the readers, to render judgment and most of us, I suspect, will support the court against the author's belated change of mind. We need no legal trickery, no courtroom prestidigitation, to show that the novelist has now done us—and himself—a disservice, and that his final philosophy of authority requires reexamination and rejection.

A number of reasons weigh in the balance and encourage this conclusion. The first of these is that not even so competent a writer as Herman Wouk is able to refute in roughly fifty pages a point of view he has taken four hundred and fifty pages to advance. What he has done he cannot now undo. Having convinced us at length that Queeg is guilty of both incompetence and cowardice, he cannot now convince us in so short a space that Queeg, on the contrary, is a hero who is motivated throughout only by his own conceptions of what is good for the Navy and that these conceptions are valid. Such a transformation does not square with the yellowstain incident, the extortion for the lost liquor, the case of the missing strawberries, or the captain's paralysis during the storm.

Similarly, Maryk, limned for us throughout as an able and decent citizen, stands now accused of stupidity and of conduct to the prejudice of good order and discipline. After observing him for many, many pages and many, many months at sea it is simply not possible to concur in this opinion. Our author, however, is adamant, and therefore has to punish Maryk. He may be only half-guilty, as Greenwald tells him in the climactic scene, but, on the other hand, he is only half-acquitted, too. His chances of transfer to the Regular Navy are now forfeit and he is in fact demoted to the command of an LCI (Landing Craft, Infantry). Willie, by the way, who is equally guilty, becomes the last captain of the *Caine*. The quick twist, in short, requires Wouk to punish Maryk and to reward Willie for what was roughly the same offense.

But even more serious is what the tergiversation does to Greenwald, whom Wouk has obviously chosen to represent his new point of view. Greenwald now assures us, in his party speech, that he got Maryk off by "phony legal tricks." Taking him at his word, is it proper for an attorney to resort to trickery in order to save a man who is at least "half-guilty" and in the process destroy another man (Queeg) to whom he now says he owes a favor? Instead of a St. George in shining armor we now have an attorney who takes a case in which he does not believe and which he wins through conscious trickery rather than conviction. By his own admission he owes a favor to Queeg but he is nevertheless responsible for consigning Queeg to the oblivion of a naval supply depot in Stuber City, Iowa. Greenwald, whom we were prepared to acclaim not only as the savior of Maryk but also as a servant of justice, now convicts himself of hypocrisy, with only the thin excuse that the wrong man was on trial. His morbid speech robs us of our respect for him. If we still have sympathy it is because we see that he, like Queeg, has symptoms of a mental affliction. The notion that Queeg, because he joined the Navy in peacetime, somehow prevented Goering from making soap out of Greenwald's mother, is about as far out of touch with reality as Queeg's search for the nonexistent key in the strawberry incident. We regretfully conclude that Greenwald has his little steel balls, too, and that they are clicking around in his head as incessantly as Queeg's click in his hand.

Wouk's change of mind involves more than a transformation in his characters. It involves in addition an incomprehensible logic. The movie critic of the *New Yorker,* John McCarten, remarks impatiently about Wouk's "odd notion that it was somehow heroic to have joined the Navy in the nineteen-thirties, as the befuddled captain did, while civilians were out making fortunes on the W.P.A." But Queeg is more than befuddled; he is wholly bereft of ideas. There is no evidence that he has ever made a commitment to a political or philosophical position. It is difficult to see him as a champion of democracy, or of any other political philosophy. It is all very well for Wouk to defend the importance of a peacetime Navy but it is a little extravagant to contend that those who manned it did so because they were opponents of totalitarianism or enemies of antisemitism. Indeed, men like Queeg are wholly innocent of political preferences and predilections. Wouk does not seem to have noticed that Queeg would have served equally well and with equal attention to discipline in the German Navy. His superior might as easily have been Admiral Doenitz as Admiral Halsey. Nothing matters to him except the shirttails of his sailors.

Our next charge against Wouk is that he does the United States Navy a disservice in implying now that it is an organization incapable of handling the extremities of the normal probability curve, that in personnel problems it can see only black and white and none of the shades between, that it is permanently and inflexibly an authoritarian organization. Articles 184, 185, and 186 are to be found in Navy Regulations and we may presume at least, Wouk now to the contrary notwithstanding, that they were put there for a purpose. What that purpose might be, Wouk himself devotes the greater part of his book to explaining. It is again incomprehensible therefore that he should turn his back upon his own explanation and imply that these articles ought not to be used, that it is somehow degrading to the Navy even to suggest that an occasion could arise on which they might properly be invoked. I should hazard the guess that most of us would rather serve in Maryk's Navy than in Greenwald's, in the Navy represented by the officers who acquitted Maryk than in the Navy whose officers disapproved the verdict.

A final question remains. As mentioned earlier, Granville Hicks in *The New Leader* has suggested that Wouk's treatment of Lieutenant Keefer is an assault upon intellectuals and must therefore be regarded as one more sign of the anti-intellectualism of the times. One would like to register a dissent from this view and to defend the author against the indictment. If intellectuals occasionally stray from the canons of a strict morality, this implies merely that they share the defects and imperfections of other men. Wouk may portray Keefer's perfidy, but there is no reason for supposing that it is the perfidy of a class. Nor does Wouk maintain that there is a higher incidence of dishonesty among intellectuals than in other groups. The villains of literature come in all colors and shapes and sizes, represent every nationality, religion, and vocation, and belong to every social group.

Unfortunately, however, Wouk cannot be so easily absolved. Upon further reflection it is clear that he is objecting to Keefer not because Keefer is perfidious but because he is thoughtful. He deprecates Keefer not because of his betrayal of Maryk but because of his inclination to think. There is the clear conclusion now that if no one had done any thinking the "mutiny" would never have occurred and that Keefer, as the leading thinker, is largely to blame for the unfortunate history of the *Caine*. Here is an author telling us that blind obedience to authority is preferable to its rational acceptance. And this, I submit, is dangerous doctrine. An obedience which is blind is an obedience ill-equipped to match the menaces of our century. This kind of obedience is the antithesis of responsible social action and ultimately the denial of an adult morality.

In these remarks I have been critical of the conclusions to which the author of *The Caine Mutiny* felt constrained to come at the end of his book. These criticisms, while relevant to both an esthetic and a moral judgment, do not detract from the esteem in which I hold both the author and his book. Nor do they reduce, in any respect but one, the distinction of Wouk's achievement. Criticism, after all, is easy, creation difficult. If my remarks are co-

gent they imply only that *The Caine Mutiny*, which is a very good book, could have been a much better one. They suggest that consistency is not only a canon of logic and a requirement of literature—it is also a moral virtue. And they assert without equivocation that authority differs from authoritarianism in that it always makes some attempt, however small, to satisfy the criterion of reason.

Source: Robert Bierstedt, "The Tergiversation of Herman Wouk," in *Great Moral Dilemmas in Literature, Past and Present,* edited by R. M. MacIver, Harper & Brothers, 1956, pp. 1-14.

Sources

Pearl K. Bell, in *Commentary,* December, 1978.

Eric Bentley, "Captain Bligh's Revenge," in his *The Dramatic Event: An American Chronicle,* Horizon Press, 1954, pp. 191-94.

Frederic I. Carpenter, "Herman Wouk and the Wisdom of Disillusion," in *English Journal,* Vol. XLV, No. 1, January, 1956, pp. 1–6, 32.

David Dempsey, "It Didn't Pay to Strike It Rich," in *The New York Times Book Review,* May 20, 1962, pp. 1, 38.

Edmund Fuller, in *Man in Modern Fiction: Some Minority Opinions on Contemporary American Writing,* Random House, 1958.

Maxwell Geismar, in *American Moderns: From Rebellion to Conformity,* Hill and Wang, 1958, p. 38.

Chris Godat, *Contemporary Popular Writers,* edited by Dave Mote, St. James Press, 1997.

Granville Hicks, in *New York Times Book Review,* November 14, 1971, pp. 4–5.

Time, April 9, 1951.

Juan Williams, *Thurgood Marshall: American Revolutionary,* Times Books, 1999, 459 p.

For Further Study

Samuel Beckett, *Watt,* Grove Press, 1970.
>   For a stark contrast to Wouk, there is this work of the Irishman who fought for the French resistance when Germany occupied France in World War II, Samuel Beckett. His absurdist novel of 1953 features a protagonist named Watt who wanders around searching for meaning.

Joseph Conrad, *Heart of Darkness,* Everyman's Library, 1993.
>   Recounts Marlow's journey into the Congo to retrieve Mr. Kurtz.

Barbara Ehrenreich, *The Hearts of Men: American Dreams and the Flight from Commitment,* Doubleday, 1983.

Ehrenreich examines some of the reasons and motivations behind a male revolt against reverence for the nineteenth-century cult of motherhood. She draws her evidence from pop cultural developments ranging from the rise of *Playboy* to the gray flannel suit.

Jack Kerouac, *On the Road,* Penguin, 1991.

This novel became the bible of a whole generation of disillusioned beatniks. His philosophy and images provide a vivid contrast to Wouk's.

Matthew Klam, "The Pilot's Tale: At Sea with 90,000 Tons of Diplomacy," in *Harpers,* February, 1999, pp. 33–48.

Describes the nuclear power of today's ships as well as the technical brilliance of their features and their planes.

Herman Melville, *Moby-Dick,* Penguin, 1992.

Wouks' story contains many subtle references to this 1851 American classic. This is the original story of the mad captain and his obsession with the capture of a great white whale.

James A. Michener, *Tales of the South Pacific,* Fawcett Books, 1989.

Another great American novel of World War II, this novel won the Pulitzer Prize in 1948 and became the material for the Rogers and Hammerstein musical. The novel is a romantic story of a Marine who falls in love with a Tonkinese girl.

Candide

Voltaire

1759

François-Marie Arouet, best known under his pen name, Voltaire, is such a historical giant that some scholars, like Ariel and Will Durant, call the eighteenth century the "Age of Voltaire." Voltaire was unrivaled in stature as an author. He criticized everyone and signed his works with "Ecrasez l'infame" or "down with infamy." Though he wrote more than eighty volumes of material, his most popular work remains *Candide; ou L'optimisme, traduit de l'Allemand, de Mr. le Docteur Ralph,* translated in 1759 as *Candide; Or All for the Best.* The reception of the work was controversial; in fact, the Great Council of Geneva immediately denounced it and ordered all copies to be burned.

Candide parodies the philosophy of optimism put forth by Gottfried Wilhelm von Leibnitz. This philosophy states that since God created the world and God is perfect, everything in the world is ultimately perfect. Voltaire had already attacked this philosophy of optimism in his poem on the 1756 Lisbon earthquake. Rousseau answered the poem with a letter, which was leaked to the press, saying it was Voltaire who was mistaken. Voltaire answered back three years later with the tale of Candide. The tale is a fantastic picaresque journey that takes Candide around the world. After he and his friends are killed, they are brought back to life; first rich, then poor; and finally, they wind up on a farm in Turkey.

Author Biography

Voltaire's mother, Marie Marguerite Daumard, was the daughter of a member of Parliament and sister of the comptroller general of the royal guard. She had access to the court of the Sun King, Louis XIV. Daumard married François Aruoet, an affluent attorney, investor, and friend of the poet Nicolas Boileau, dramatist Pierre Corneille, and the courtesan Ninon de Lenclos. The Arouets had five children; the youngest one, born in Paris on November 21, 1694, was Voltaire.

At the age of 10, Voltaire entered the Jesuit College of Louis-le-Grand on the Left Bank of Paris. Voltaire graduated in 1711 with every intention of being a writer. His father, however, wanted him to study law.

In 1713, Voltaire was sent to The Hague as page to the French ambassador. Scandalously, he fell in love with Olympe de Noyer (nicknamed "Pimpete") and was summoned home, disinherited, and threatened with exile to the New World. Voltaire surrendered and studied law. His reputation and covert writing, however, caused him to be blamed for two poems critical of the regent, Phillipe d'Orleans, written by Le Brun. As a result, he was imprisoned in the Bastille from 1717 to 1718. There he wrote *Oedipe,* a tragedy, between the lines of books because he was denied paper. After his release, he began calling himself de Voltaire after a nondescript farm he inherited of that name.

In 1722, his father died and Voltaire was free from his control. In the same year, he met his rival, Rousseau, in Brussels. His growing squadron of enemies, spearheaded by the chevalier de Rohan, managed to have him exiled to England in 1726 where he was delighted to meet Englishmen like Jonathan Swift. In 1729, back in France, he regained favor, published *Lettres philosophiques* in 1734, and became royal historiographer.

Voltaire frequented the court of Frederick the Great from 1750 to 1753. Disillusioned with the powerful Prussian, Voltaire settled permanently in Ferney, near the Swiss border, so that he could easily flee from trouble. There, word of the Lisbon earthquake shook his optimism and he wrote the Lisbon poem of 1756 and *Candide* in 1759. Over the next decade, he and his comrades—the philosophes—joined together to try and topple a few columns holding up "l'infame."

Voltaire had many hobbies. He single-handedly made his town, Ferney, a prosperous watch-

Voltaire

manufacturing center. He was also concerned with injustice—most famously in the case of Jean Calas, whose innocence he helped to restore. With an authorial claim on some 80 total volumes of writings, he died in May 1778 in Paris, months after a successful showing of *Irene.* His ashes were moved to the Pantheon in 1791.

Plot Summary

Voltaire's *Candide* opens by introducing the honest youth, Candide, a servant in Westphalia to Baron Thunder-ten-tronckh, who may be Candide's uncle. Candide loves the Baron's daughter, Cunégonde, and is the avid student of Pangloss, a philosopher who continuously "proves" Leibniz's belief that this is "the best of all possible worlds." Candide is expelled from Westphalia when the Baron catches him in a romantic embrace with Cunégonde.

Two seemingly friendly men rescue the cold, hungry Candide, then force him to become a soldier for the Bulgars. After being caught leaving the army camp, Candide receives two thousand whiplashes. Before his punishers can grant his request to be killed, however, the Bulgar King passes by and pardons him.

The Bulgar army engages in a terrible battle with the Abar army. Candide wanders through burned towns with butchered people to reach Holland, where he is treated rudely until he meets Jacques, an Anabaptist. Jacques kindly cares for Candide, who soon discovers a beggar with a rotted nose. It is Pangloss, who caught syphilis from the Baron's servant, Paquette. Pangloss tells Candide that Cunégonde was ravished by Bulgar soldiers, then killed. Jacques has Pangloss cured and the three men travel by ship to Lisbon.

When the ship is struck by a storm, Jacques helps a sailor back into the tossed ship but is thrown overboard himself. Candide wants to try to save him, but Pangloss dissuades him. Jacques drowns. After surviving the ship's sinking, Candide and Pangloss are in Lisbon when a devastating earthquake strikes.

In order to prevent further earthquakes, Lisbon authorities hold an auto-da-fé, where sacrificial victims are tortured and burned alive. Candide and Pangloss are chosen for sacrifice. Because of rain, Pangloss is hanged. Candide is flogged, but before he is burned, another earthquake strikes and an old woman leads him away.

The old woman tends his wounds and takes him to a wealthy home where he encounters Cunégonde, still alive. After the Bulgar attack, she was sold to a Jew, Don Issachar, in whose house she now lives. She also caught the attention of the Grand Inquisitor, who shares her with Issachar.

Issachar arrives, and, seeing Candide, attacks him. Candide kills him. The Inquisitor then arrives, and Candide kills him as well. The old woman plans their escape to Cadiz, where Candide displays his military skills and is hired to fight the Jesuits of Paraguay.

Aboard ship, the old woman tells them her riches-to-rags life story, which includes slavery, losing one buttock, constant labor, and travel. Despite repeatedly desiring to kill herself, she asserts that she suffers from humankind's "ridiculous weakness": she is "still in love with life."

They arrive in Buenos Ayres and go see the Governor, who lusts after Cunégonde and proposes to her. The old woman suggests Cunégonde accept his offer, especially after they discover that they are being pursued for the Inquisitor's murder. They warn Candide to escape.

Candide's servant, Cacambo, agrees with the warning and suggests they join forces with the Jesuits. They go see the Colonel Father Provincial, who, to Candide's dismay, is Cunégonde's brother.

When Candide tells the Colonel that he plans to marry Cunégonde, however, the formerly friendly Colonel becomes indignant and strikes him. Candide stabs him then laments his action. Cacambo, thinking rationally, disguises Candide as the Colonel and they escape.

While eating, they see two naked girls being chased by two monkeys nibbling at their buttocks. To save the women, Candide shoots the monkeys. The two girls cry over the fallen monkeys, who, Cacambo realizes, were the girls' lovers. Candide and Cacambo run off but are captured by Oreillons, who are planning to cook them and "have Jesuit" for dinner. Cacambo, who knows their language, talks them out of it by telling them about Candide slaying the Jesuit Colonel.

Candide and Cacambo endure many hardships until they find themselves in Eldorado, an isolated country of gold mud, jeweled stones, and peaceful contentment. Candide decides this must be the place "where everything is for the best," the place that Pangloss described and Candide has never encountered. Though they are in paradise, Candide cannot live without Cunégonde and Cacambo has a "restless spirit," so they leave with gifts of vast riches carried by a hundred red sheep.

After one hundred days, only two sheep remain, but they are still quite rich. They encounter a tortured black slave. Overcome by the man's plight, Candide exclaims that he must renounce Pangloss's optimism. Cacambo asks, "What's optimism?" Candide replies, "It is a mania for saying things are well when one is in hell." Candide sends Cacambo to rescue Cunégonde while he sails for Venice. But Candide is double-crossed by Vanderdendur, a merchant ship captain, who steals Candide's treasure. Embittered, Candide decides to hire the most unfortunate man in the province to accompany him to France. He chooses a poor scholar named Martin.

Candide is better off than Martin because he still possesses some jewels and he still longs for Cunégonde, while Martin, a confirmed pessimist, hopes for nothing. They soon witness a sea battle in which one ship sinks. When Candide happily saves a red sheep from the water, they realize that Vanderdendur has been killed and the treasure lost. Candide and Martin debate philosophy all the way to France.

They experience the many corruptions of Paris, then sail to England where they witness an admiral executed for not killing enough enemies. He serves as an example to other admirals.

They reach Venice but cannot find Cacambo, which does not surprise Martin. Candide attempts to refute Martin's cynicism by pointing to a monk and girl walking happily together. They discover, however, that both of them also are miserable. The woman is Paquette, who is now a prostitute. The man, Brother Giroflé, detests his life as a monk.

Candide and Martin visit Count Pococurante, a wealthy Venetian. Because Pococurante thinks for himself and can find little to please his tastes, Candide thinks him a genius.

Candide and Martin dine with six strangers, all of whom are deposed kings. Cacambo is the slave of one king, and he helps Candide and Martin sail to Constantinople, where they will find Cunégonde, who is now a slave. Candide buys Cacambo's freedom. While aboard ship, they discover that two of the galley slaves are Pangloss and Cunégonde's brother. Candide buys their freedom and they join him. Pangloss asserts that he still holds to his optimistic views, but mainly because it would be improper for a philosopher to recant and because Leibniz cannot be wrong.

They find Cunégonde, who has become horribly ugly, though she does not know it. Candide ransoms her and the old woman. He also agrees to keep his word and marry Cunégonde. The Baron stubbornly refuses to allow it, however, because of Candide's genealogy.

Though he no longer wants to marry Cunégonde, Candide is angered by the Baron's arrogance and, without Cunégonde's knowledge, the group ships the Baron to Rome. Candide then buys a small farm where they all live, dissatisfied. They wonder which is worse, their previous tortures or the boredom of the farm. Paquette and Brother Giroflé, both destitute, arrive. After visiting a rude dervish philosopher, who tells them God is indifferent to their troubles, the group encounters a Turkish farmer who treats them kindly. He tells them that his family's work "keeps us from those three great evils, boredom, vice, and poverty." They all agree that this is a sensible approach to life, and each assumes a task on the farm. When Pangloss philosophizes about their adventures and fate, "proving" that all has turned out as it should in this "best of all possible worlds," Candide replies that they "must cultivate our garden."

Characters

Cacambo

Cacambo is "a quarter Spanish, born of a half-Indian father in the Tucuman province of Argentina. He had been a choir boy, a sexton, a sailor, a monk, a commercial agent, a soldier and a servant." He is now Candide's beloved valet and traveling companion. They experience Eldorado together. Towards the end, it is Cacambo who arranges for Candide to find Cunégonde again. Cacambo is also the one who does all the work when they first start farming.

Candide

The fantastically naïve young man who is "driven from his earthly paradise" with hard kicks in his backside is Candide. Like Everyman, from the medieval morality play by that name, Candide experiences as much as a man could experience in order to arrive at a well-deserved conclusion regarding the plight of man. He exemplifies the idea of optimism when he reluctantly enters the world and leaves the household of the Baron's castle in Westphalia behind. Westphalia, so Candide was told, is the best of all possible kingdoms. In retrospect, he sees that it had a few problems.

It is suspected that Candide is the bastard offspring of the Baron's sister and a gentleman of the neighborhood. This ignoble birth is not held over him except when it matters most—marriage to Cunégonde. In the course of his travels he is conscripted, beaten, and robbed. Circumstances make Candide a criminal, "I'm the kindest man in the world, yet I've already killed three men, and two of them were priests!" People take advantage of him especially when they learn about his love for Cunégonde. Consequently, pretenders mislead him and, therefore, he experiences the loss of love many times. During any pause in the excitement, he ponders his predicament and the human condition in terms worthy of the deepest philosopher.

Lady Cunégonde

Cunégonde is Candide's love interest. As a young woman, she sees her family butchered and is passed from man to man. She ends up with Don Issachar, whose advances she is able to adequately handle. He houses her in Lisbon and the Old Woman becomes her maid.

Having caught the eye of the Grand Inquisitor, she is then shared by the two men until rescued by Candide. Cunégonde travels with him to Buenos

Voltaire's chateau in the town of Ferney, in eastern France.

Aires. There she marries Don Fernando de Ibarra until Cacambo pays her ransom. But instead of re-union with Candide, she is taken by pirates and sold into slavery. When Candide pays for her freedom, she is old, ugly, and washing dishes. However, she ends up a very good pastry cook.

Brother Giroflé

Despite appearing to be a happy Theatine monk, Brother Girofé hates monastic life. His family forced him to enter the monastery so that his elder brother could inherit the family's wealth. He hates his family as a result. He fantasizes about setting fire to the monastery and running away to Turkey. Candide gives him some money and loses his bet with Martin. Brother Giroflé soon spends the money and he and Paquette, who has spent her money, run away to Turkey. There they live on Candide's farm.

Jesuit Baron of Thunder-ten-tronckh

Cunégonde's brother also survives the destruction of Westphalia and the brutal slaying of their parents. The very handsome young Baron is taken in by a Reverend Father and is soon sent to the Father General in Rome. He is made a Jesuit because he is not Spanish and sent to Paraguay. There he works his way up to become a Colonel who is fighting the Spanish troops. He refuses to allow Candide to marry Cunégonde, so Candide runs him through with his sword.

After recovering from Candide's assault, the Baron is captured by the Spanish. He asks to be sent back to Rome, and leaves Rome as a chaplain to the French Ambassador at Constantinople. After being found naked with a Mussulman, he is beaten and sent to the galleys. Candide rescues him. He lives with them in Turkey but when he refuses to allow the marriage again, Candide arranges to have him put back in the galleys.

King of Eldorado

The King of Eldorado is the ideal sovereign with an ideal system of government.

Martin

Candide chooses Martin to be his traveling companion. Martin is a scholar who "had been robbed by his wife, beaten by his son and abandoned by his daughter, who had eloped with a Portuguese [and] had just lost the minor post that had been his only means of support." Martin, accordingly, is cynical and not the least bit optimistic. However, he is a pleasant man and willing conversationalist. Candide enjoys him so much that he never parts with him.

The Negro

Although Candide had several encounters with slavery, none is more memorable than the encounter with the Negro. The Negro is wearing only a pair of short blue trousers and is missing his left leg and his right hand. He symbolizes the brutality of the institution of slavery in the Americas. But also, he conjures up the first Spanish expeditions to the New World. The Spanish were so desperate for gold that they slowly butchered the Indians when they did not find it.

Old Woman

See Princess of Palestrina

Dr. Pangloss

Dr. Pangloss tutors the baron's son and Candide in metaphysico-theologo-cosmonigology. Pangloss contracts syphilis from Paquette and loses an ear and a nose. Then he is hanged as part of an "Auto da Fé" ("act of faith"), but not properly. The person who takes his body resuscitates him. He winds up in the galley of a slave ship and is freed by Candide. Up to the end, he still professes a belief in optimism.

Paquette

Paquette is the chambermaid of Cunégonde's mother. She gives Pangloss the syphilis she contracted from a Franciscan friar. Her relations with her priestly confessor are the cause of her expulsion from Westphalia. Since then, she has lived the life of a prostitute. She winds up on Candide's farm, having spent the money he gave her.

Pococurante

Candide and Martin visit a Venetian senator named Pococurante. They have heard that he is a man who has "never known sorrow or trouble." They reckon that Pococurante is a wise man who will be able to help them understand such a troubling world. They expect to find a happy man. Indeed, Candide thinks that he is the happiest man he's ever seen because he is content with nothing and seems to be forever in search of contentment and novelty. Martin disagrees and says that for just those reasons, Pococurante is the most miserable wretch alive. Quoting Plato, Martin says that the best stomach is not the one that rejects all food. There is no "pleasure in having no pleasure." Candide sees his friend's logic and counts himself fortunate, yet again, that he has Cunégonde to look forward to.

Media Adaptations

- *Candide* was adapted to the stage with a great deal of difficulty. The writing of the stage production took several decades. The basis for the play was created in 1953 by Lillian Hellman and Leonard Bernstein as their reaction to the "Washington Witch Trials" being waged by the House Un-American Activities Committee. Poet Richard Wilbur was the lyricist, though Dorothy Parker contributed to "The Venice Gavotte." Tyrone Guthrie directed the first performance of the play, with sets by Oliver Smith and costumes by Irene Sharaff. It opened at the Martin Beck Theater in New York on December 1, 1956, to mixed reviews. The play has been continually rewritten ever since.

Princess of Palestrina

The Princess of Palestrina has the body, when young, of the Venus de Medici. She is betrothed to the prince of Massa-Carra, but he is poisoned and dies. Saddened, she goes to her mother's estate near Gaeta. On the way, Barbury pirates attack them and the Princess is raped. Then she and her mother become slaves. When the pirate ship arrives in Morocco, the fifty sons of Emperor Muley Ismael are at war. The Princess witnesses her mother drawn and quartered by four men. The Captain kills anyone who approaches and she survives. She then meets a castrato who once sang in her mother's chapel. He promises to take her back to Italy but instead sells her into slavery in Algiers where she catches the plague. She is sold several more times. Finally, she is a servant in the house of Don Issachar where she serves Cunégonde. Taking a fancy to the lady, she stays with her.

Themes

Human Condition

The grand theme of the novel is the human condition. Candide wonders, what is the best way to approach life? In the story, Candide has been ed-

Topics for Further Study

- Based on the evidence in *Candide,* what does Voltaire know about the world's climate and geography? Are these physical facts related to human customs? Do the best locations and climates contain the best societies? How do humans interact with the natural world in *Candide?*

- Although he is exaggerating human customs, what does the satire reveal about Voltaire's awareness of other cultures? Or, what does Voltaire think about the New World—both its indigenous populations and its colonizers?

- Voltaire's grasp of scientific knowledge is far above the average person's of the time. Based on the book, surmise the extent of the knowledge of the day of anatomy, physics, and chemistry.

- Voltaire subtly attacks the theory of progress. What is that theory, and do we still believe in it? Is it a good belief?

- Why is satire such an effective method of critique? As critiques, why are satires so often categorized as children's books? In the late twentieth century, why is animation the most appropriate medium for satire?

- Doing a little research into Voltaire's hopes for humans, what do you think would most excite or surprise him if he were alive today? What would depress him?

ucated in the system of optimism. It is all he knows, but if Candide had been a flat enough character to accept optimism, the book would be without hope. Instead, Candide doubts the philosophy of optimism and eventually rejects it.

The quest of Candide centers on whether the doctrine of optimism taught by Dr. Pangloss is true. If it is, optimism must be reconciled with what Candide experiences. The reconciliation is not possible without some absurd postulations. For example, Pangloss says that syphilis "is an indispensable el-

ement in the best of worlds, a necessary ingredient, because if Columbus, on an American island, hadn't caught that disease which poisons the source of generations ... which often prevents generation ... the great goal of nature, we would now have neither chocolate nor cochineal." (Cochineal is a dye made from squishing millions of bodies of a certain insect native to Central and South America. The dye was used, most notoriously, to make the British Army uniforms scarlet red.) The example also shows how the attempt of a philosophical system to explain every single phenomenon leads to ridiculous connections.

Candide doesn't find such incidental and simple explanations for everyday occurrences as interesting or as valid as his big question, "Do you believe that men have always slaughtered each other as they do today, that they've always been liars ... hypocritical and foolish?" To which Martin replies that that is the nature of the human animal. But the point is made that humans have free will, and the discussion moves beyond the realm of optimism. Candide eventually defines optimism as, "a mania for insisting that everything is all right when everything is going wrong."

The only possible defense of optimism is Candide's luck, which is regularly recited as evidence of that philosophy. For example, "if I hadn't been lucky enough to thrust my sword through the body of Lady Cunégonde's brother, I'd surely have been eaten ... instead ... these people showered me with polite kindness as soon as they found out I wasn't a Jesuit." Still, Candide realizes there is no perfection in the world. He realizes this at the end when he finally has everyone he has been looking for together on a farm. By then, his search appears to be in vain.

Religion

The old man in Eldorado expresses the most positive view of religion. The people of Eldorado, who always agree with each other, are all priests who don't pray for anything. Instead, "we constantly thank him." The old man's presentation stands opposite to Candide's experience of religion: "You have no monks who teach, argue, rule, plot, and burn people who don't agree with them?" The old man replies, "we'd be mad if we did." Both in the story, and for Voltaire, religion is something between a man and God—not something that lends itself to power dynamics, priests, churches, and inquisitions.

Happiness

Martin and Candide play a game as part of their debate over optimism. They place bets on whether passersby are happy. Candide always bets that they are, and he always loses. Whenever it appears, happiness is unmasked (usually by Martin) as a cover for anger, grief, and discontent. Happiness, it seems, is the method one uses to get through another day of miserable living.

War

The art of war is not a noble art in the novel. Instead, it is a barbaric system governed by its own rules and using its own reason. Candide's experience of war is as a conscripted soldier. That is, he is arrested and forced to fight. War is revealed as a complete waste of resources. One element of war that is constantly evoked is the idea of acting in "accordance with international law." This is an idea we hear a good deal about today. For Voltaire, through Candide, this meant that soldiers had the right to rape every woman, plunder and pilfer every village. "International law" is the excuse for conducting war. The end of war is always the same, as "the ground was strewn with brains and severed arms and legs."

Style

Setting

Taking seriously the old adage that the entire world is a stage, Voltaire employed that idea in his novel. Much the same way science fiction does today, Voltaire placed ideal societies and backward societies in obscure parts of the world. The rest simply needed to be exaggerated. For example, with a few facts about the unexplored mountains of Peru and the legends of golden cities, Voltaire can create a credible Eldorado. Likewise, the lack of knowledge about tribes in the Amazon jungle allows the tale of the cannibalistic Oreillons.

Another element of Voltaire's use of setting is his invocation of the Eden trope. Many writers since the writer of the biblical book Genesis have used the idea of gardens as paradises (or hells) that one finds oneself in and, for some reason, banished from. Candide journeys through a series of such gardens. Each garden has a geographic location and a lesson to be learned. However, the best garden, like the best bed, turns out to be the one Candide makes himself.

Satire

Voltaire chose satire as a way to challenge the cult of optimism that reigned during that time. While this form of storytelling and literary composition is ancient, its historical form came into being with the Greek author, Aristophanes, and became its own genre with two Roman poets, Horace and Juvenal. Voltaire is a comic satirist. He simply loved humans too much to be tragic. But because he loved them, he tried to help them as much as possible. Through the exposure of man's follies in the insane but fantastic adventure of Candide, his satire is fresh for all time.

Picaresque

The picaresque story originates in Spanish efforts to satirize the chivalric romance. Whereas the romance tells about the ideal knight and his brave adventures, the hero of the picaresque rambles along the highway living by his wits rather than his honest work. Both the knight and the picaresque hero share the motto, "a rolling stone gathers no moss." During the eighteenth century, changing demographics led to a demand for tightly woven, realistic novels. The picaresque became a low form of artistry.

Candide is a picaresque novel. Candide is forced by fate to ramble about the world collecting people and losing them, gaining riches and losing it all. His travels bring him into contact with the workings of the world, but this only makes him more skeptical. Finally, he just stops rambling. So long as he is still and at work—like neither the picaresque hero nor the brave knight—he can find peace of mind.

Historical Context

Lisbon

Lisbon was destroyed by earthquake on the morning of All Saints' Day, November 1, 1755. The six-minute earthquake kills 15,000 people, injures at least that many more, and destroys thirty churches as well as thousands of houses. Despite the sophistication of natural science, the coincidence that Lisbon, a city fervently Catholic, is destroyed on a Catholic feast day—when the pious were at church—gives rise to superstitious speculation.

On November 19, 1500 Pilgrim homes are destroyed by earthquake. Many explanations again explain the disasters in religious terms. Voltaire, out-

Compare & Contrast

- **The Eighteenth Century:** France and Britain are continually fighting to see who will be the number one colonial power. Half of this war effort involves stirring up Indian "allies" to kill each other before the colonists spread into the wilderness.

  Today: With the demise of the Soviet Union, America stands as the sole superpower.

- **The Eighteenth Century:** The first intentional use of biological agents by a military occurs during King Phillip's War. The British intentionally infect blankets en route to the Indians with smallpox.

  Today: The United States enforces economic sanctions against Iraq because of their suspected development and use of biological weapons.

- **The Eighteenth Century:** General George Washington advocates fighting from behind trees and rocks, ambush style, instead of the traditional parade-style formation.

  Today: Though guerilla warfare is now the style when necessary, fighting strategies today rely heavily on airpower and missile bombardment to soften up the enemy before ground troops move in. The style today seeks to minimize casualties.

- **The Eighteenth Century:** Medical technology is crude, often doing more damage than the original problem. The STD syphilis is the most dangerous disease of the time.

  Today: AIDS remains a devastating and deadly virus despite "space age" medical technology.

- **The Eighteenth Century:** Modes of transportation are limited. All entertainment, such as concerts and plays, is live and industrial necessity attracts more and more people into the large cities.

  Today: With cellular phones, computers, and automobiles, people are moving out of the cities and into smaller communities.

---

raged at such stupidity, writes an infamous reaction to the Lisbon earthquake. In response comes a letter from Rousseau, stating that Voltaire is the one who is wrong. Humans are at fault. Had we not left the natural world, or committed the original sins, and lived in cities, the disasters would not have happened. Further, Rousseau argues that Leibnitz is right—in the long run, everything must be for the best in this best of all possible worlds. To believe otherwise is to give into suicidal pessimism.

France

The Enlightenment period in Europe is about to give way to political revolution. Reason, during this period, is held to be the supreme power with which to challenge the old institutions and superstitions. In Britain, where the church had long been relegated to the role of ceremonial trappings, science and industry were the dynamos of progress. France, on the other hand, is still dominated by the Catholic Church. In addition, France is still under the control of a nearly all-powerful King. The bourgeoisie in France is weak and its numbers few. The majority of people belong to the lower classes and are barely literate, burdened by taxes, and underemployed. France is slowly industrializing and cannot compete with British factories. France needs reform desperately.

In government, various reforms are attempted. The finance minister attempts to overhaul the economic framework of government. It is too painful, however, and Etienne de Silhouette succeeded only in giving us a new word: A silhouette is the reduction of a figure to its simplest form.

Seven Years War

France renewed hostilities with England over the issue of control over North America. Two moves by the British in 1759 effectively conclude the question of America. First, well-equipped British forces and their American and Native-

American allies drive the French out of the Lake Champlain region. They even take Duquesne and, consequently, Crown Point Military road is built through Vermont. The second push is more decisive. The British take Niagara. Then, an epic battle occurs upon the Plains of Abraham, just outside the city of Quebec. British General Wolfe beats French General Louis-Joseph Montcalm in a battle that effectively ends the Seven Years War. Both men die as a result of wounds received during the battle.

Critical Overview

The rulers of Geneva expressed their view of *Candide* by burning it. The idea that the authorities in one part of Europe were incensed enough to set the work ablaze was very good publicity. Smugglers, meanwhile, made sure that anyone anywhere in Europe could get a copy of the small work on the black market. In general, that is the history of Voltaire's reception—people either fervently loved him, or they wanted to burn him. Today Voltaire's works are studied as artifacts and for amusement.

Immediate reviews of *Candide* were often defensive. For example, an anonymous review of the work in the *The Gentleman's Magazine and Historical Chronicle,* in May of 1759, defended Leibnitz. The reviewer stated that no less a figure than Alexander Pope, in his *An Essay on Man,* expressed a belief in optimism. Furthermore, wrote the reviewer, it is not possible to disprove this philosophy, for in order to do so, one must intrinsically know every other system. Only then can judgment be passed on our system of civilization. *Candide,* asserted the reviewer, "is an attempt to ridicule the notion that 'all things are for the best,' by representing the calamity of life, artfully aggravated, in a strange light."

In 1791, James Boswell compared *Candide* to Samuel Johnson's *Rasselas.* In his *The Life of Samuel Johnson,* he wrote, "Voltaire I am afraid, meant only by wanton profaneness to obtain victory over religion, and to discredit the belief of a superintending providence … " Whereas, Samuel Johnson used satire to direct man's hope toward the "eternal" rather than to satisfaction on earth.

In the first half of the nineteenth century, "the born minister of literature," as John Morley dubbed Voltaire, was posthumously winning the race against Rousseau. Gustave Lanson, in his *Voltaire* of 1902, covers the publication history of Voltaire

A woman and young girl, dressed as eighteenth-century French nobility, riding in a carriage parade at Versailles.

during the 1800s. During a seven-year period (1817–1824), for example, of the 2,159,500 volumes of anti-clerical and anti-royalist writings in Revolutionary France, 75% were written by Voltaire. "But," Lanson wrote, "where Voltaire's influence was immense, obvious, and still persisted is in the fields of journalism, pamphleteering, and all forms of polemical writing. He was the master of militant irony and murderous ridicule." In terms of total book printings and sales, Voltaire remained the most popular writer.

After 1850, however, as the French Republic established itself and bourgeoisie fervor for the revolution waned, so did Voltaire's influence. Lanson summed up Voltaire's influence: "In general, in countries outside of France, to the extent that historical circumstances moved further away from conditions that obtained in France when Voltaire's work first appeared, his influence is not easily discernible except among certain clear-thinking minds at odds with their social groups or in revolt against its demands and prejudices."

Critic Georg Brandes, wrote about Voltaire against the backdrop of WWI. He suggested that the mood of *Candide* was still relevant. This idea of relevancy remains a strong current in Voltaire criticism. In 1960, in *The Art of Writing,* André Maurois wrote that *Candide* said all that can be said on today's topic—the world is absurd. Therefore, "*Candide* was the high-point of Voltaire's art." Partisanship has disappeared and the focus of criticism now trains on the ideas Voltaire had. A. Owen Aldridge, in *Voltaire and the Century of Light,* wrote that "structural analysis does very little to explain the universal appeal of *Candide.* It ranks as one of the masterpieces of European literature, not primarily because of style but because of its realistic portrayal of the human condition."

That does not mean that structural analysis of Voltaire's work is not being done. In fact, it is being done more and more. William F. Bottiglia undertook an analysis entitled, "Candide's Garden." His close textual analysis of "a literary masterpiece risen out of time to timelessness" discusses the possibility of approaching the novel as internally structured or externally structured. He feels the latter is not possible as "*Candide* encompasses all—there is no outside. Thus, those who claim that *Candide* reflects or comments on the times miss the fact that the times are in the book." He also examines Candide's journey as a series of 12 gardens.

Critics like Roland Barthes and Ira O. Wade have focused on Voltaire's work in context. They often suggest, in the case of *Candide,* that Voltaire was very hypocritical. By critical consensus and in terms of sales, Voltaire will always be cherished and *Candide* will always be read.

Criticism

Darren Felty

Darren Felty is a Visiting Instructor at the College of Charleston. In the following essay, he explores how Voltaire satirizes both extreme optimism and extreme pessimism through his characters' reactions to the world's evils.

Candide is a dazzling display of ridiculously brutal situations that dramatize the many evils of human experience. Voltaire speeds the reader through multiple episodes of extreme cruelty that prove both horrible and vibrantly comic. Nothing seems to escape his satiric treatment, and one is tempted to say that Voltaire's only purpose in the work is to condemn. A closer reading, however, reveals the limitations of this perception. Voltaire's criticisms are tempered by both comic exaggera-

tion and a strong moral sense that wishes to expose wrongs in order to alleviate them. The key targets of Voltaire's satire are totalizing perceptions of the world, whether extreme optimism or extreme pessimism, both of which offer excuses for indifference to human suffering. Voltaire explores this subject through Candide's many misadventures; indeed, understanding Candide's haphazard growth is necessary for understanding the development of the story, which often seems patternless. But one cannot understand Candide without also understanding those around him and the roles that they play in the story. Through his characters' experiences, relationships, and final solution to their many troubles, Voltaire shatters the tenets of "rationally" optimistic and deadeningly pessimistic philosophies, replacing them with a vision, albeit tentative, of practical, communal work.

From the first chapter, Voltaire portrays systematized optimistic philosophies as totally divorced from lived reality. Voltaire's main proponent of this belief system, Doctor Pangloss, is a follower of Gottfried Leibnitz, who attempted to use logic to explain the existence of evil. Leibnitz asserted that laws of "sufficient reason," such as unalterable mathematical relationships, restrain even God's ability to create a perfect universe. Thus, while the world contains evil, it is still the "best of all possible worlds," one of the book's most memorable satiric refrains. Pangloss upholds such beliefs to the point of absurdity, justifying all events through cause-and-effect relationships. For instance, he contends that "things cannot be otherwise than they are, for since everything is made to serve an end, everything necessarily serves the best end. Observe: our noses were made to support spectacles, hence we have spectacles." His "lessons" are rife with such tortured logic, making him the epitome of a learned fool. Voltaire proceeds to bludgeon Pangloss's reductive, self-serving ideals by opposing them with constant examples of human cruelty and natural disasters that apparently defy all explanation, particularly Pangloss's.

Yet Voltaire does not characterize Pangloss's beliefs as simply foolish. They are dangerous. They allow people to justify any inhumanity and prevent them from actively helping to alleviate the suffering of others. If, for instance, one can relate another's miseries to preceding causes, no matter how slight, then one need not act on that person's behalf or even feel sympathy. Voltaire demonstrates the pernicious effects of Pangloss's beliefs in multiple episodes, but none more so than in his response to Jacques the Anabaptist's death. When

Jacques is thrown overboard during a storm, Pangloss prevents Candide from trying to save him by "proving that the bay of Lisbon had been formed expressly for this Anabaptist to drown in." Instead of reacting with compassion, like Candide, or even explaining that Candide will only die in the futile attempt to retrieve his friend, Pangloss resorts to a bold-faced absurdity that excuses his passivity and callousness. Because he can construct the flimsiest of "rational" explanations for this tragedy, he can save his own skin and absolve himself of any culpability in Jacques' death. By presenting many such moments, Voltaire makes the philosophical vindication of rampant injustice and destruction into a caustic joke of seemingly cosmic proportions.

As he does with Pangloss, throughout the book Voltaire employs vivid secondary characters who serve particular functions and represent types of responses to the human condition. By pairing Candide with such emblematic yet compelling figures, Voltaire highlights Candide's reactions to the guidance others provide him. And, because most of these characters remain unchanged in their basic attitudes, the reader can trace Candide's sometimes erratic development. First, of course, Voltaire depicts Candide under Pangloss's influence. The young man naively believes in the world's "rightness" and cannot assimilate the slaughters and injustices he encounters. Voltaire balances Pangloss's influence in the book, however, by contrasting him with men like Martin and the wealthy Pococurante, both of whom reflect the inadequacy of total pessimism, showing it to be as self-defeating as irrational optimism. More pragmatic characters like the old woman, Jacques, and Cacambo expose the limitations of pure practicality, but this approach to life ultimately proves most sympathetic to the characters' final attempt to secure their comfort and security.

Because of his unremitting pessimism and dark wit, many readers have viewed Martin as a voice for Voltaire's own views. Yet, as a passive man who can see the goodness in no one, he differs fundamentally from Voltaire. Martin's assertions are often penetrating and bitingly clever, but they also are essentially empty. Martin feels no outrage at injustice since, as a Manichean, he believes that God and the devil hold equal power in the universe and the devil effectively rules human existence. For him, misery is universal and inevitable; any efforts to curtail it are futile. This philosophy enables him to avoid emotional attachments or commitments to others. For example, even though he stays with Candide and the group on their farm, he does so

What Do I Read Next?

- In reaction to the controversy surrounding the Lisbon earthquake and who was at fault, Voltaire penned "On the Lisbon Disaster" in 1756. The poem attempted to reconcile disaster with Leibnitzian optimism.

- Historical background for *Candide* and Voltaire's work generally can be found in Peter Gay's *Voltaire's Politics: The Poet as Realist.*

- One of Voltaire's models for *Candide* was a work first published in 1726, while he was exiled in Britain, by his new friend, Jonathan Swift. At first titled *Travels into Several Remote Nations of the World,* the work is known today as *Gulliver's Travels.* It is a satire of Europe in the 1720s told through the story of Gulliver's travels to many strange and wonderful lands.

- An English satire of clergymen by Laurence Sterne, entitled *A Political Romance* (and later titled *The History of a Good Warm Watch-Coat*) was published in 1759. Sterne, a clergyman himself, is also the author of the stories about Tristram Shandy.

- A marked contrast to Voltaire can be found in the works and the person of Samuel Johnson. Johnson's *The History of Rasselas, Prince of Abissinia* was published in 1759. It tells how the Prince gathered scientists and philosophers from near and far to discover for him the secrets of a happy life, only to realize he had wasted time he could have spent living.

- The brilliant anti-utopian satire by George Orwell is *Animal Farm.* In this 1945 tale, revolutionary efforts are lampooned when the barn animals revolt against their human masters and establish a commune. The pigs, however, usurp power and impose a dictatorship.

only because "things are just as bad wherever you are" and working without argument is "the only way of rendering life bearable." Like Martin, the rich senator Pococurante is unable to experience joy in anything, and he, too, is often taken as a counterpart to Voltaire, with whom he shares iconoclastic literary tastes. With Pococurante, even wealth proves a burden. Because he can possess anything he desires, little satisfies him. He longs for nothing and is besieged by the malady that haunts Candide and the others in Constantinople: boredom. Though Candide thinks Pococurante a "genius" and "the happiest of all men, for he is superior to everything he possesses," Martin recognizes, as always, the man's true misery. The reader, too, can see that Voltaire satirizes the person who can only reject and not embrace, who refuses to see any beauty in human achievements.

The three characters who appear to garner the lightest of Voltaire's satiric barbs are the characters who rely on practical action instead of paralyzing philosophical indifference. The old woman, Jacques, and Cacambo all suffer considerably throughout the course of the work, but their decisive actions still provide sharp counterpoints to the inertia and ineptitude of the other characters. The old woman, though most often self-serving and even callous, makes a fit tutor for Cunégonde. Both women are victims of rape, violence, and enslavement, but the old woman has learned to survive and not exaggerate her often outlandish injuries. Like Martin, she harbors no romantic delusions; unlike Martin, however, she is not utterly hopeless. She often moves quickly to save herself, Cunégonde, and Candide, such as when she calmly arranges their escape after Candide kills Issachar and the Grand Inquisitor. Indeed, despite her frequent desire to commit suicide, she continues on because she is "still in love with life." With this assertion, she articulates (and exemplifies) one of Voltaire's central themes in the book: humankind's absurd yet unconquerable will to live.

Jacques and Cacambo often act out of more benevolent impulses than the old woman, but they share her commitment to tangible endeavors. Jacques, especially, represents an ideal. He aids both Candide and Pangloss because they are fellow men in need, not because he hopes to exploit them. He is not an idealist, but a virtuous man who values work, believes in humankind's basic goodness, and knowingly acknowledges people's capacity for self-corruption. His presence in the book is brief, however, perhaps because someone of his humane character would tend to blunt the edge of a satire. Voltaire gives Jacques a fitting death for this radically unjust world: he perishes while rescuing a man who has done him ill and who takes no notice of his demise. Like the country of Eldorado, then,

Jacques stands as a testament to what people can achieve if they respond to what is best rather than worst in themselves, which most rarely do. Cacambo, too, reflects the value of maintaining sympathy and loyalty, though he is more of a survivor than Jacques, acting with quick-witted self-interest when the need arises. His most exemplary characteristic is his devotion to Candide, whom he supports simply because Candide is "a very good fellow." He even works to fulfill Candide's plan to rescue Cunégonde from Buenos Ayres, though he could, as Martin believes he has, run off with the jewels from Eldorado and avoids his eventual enslavement by a deposed monarch. Thus, both Jacques and Cacambo counter the predominant exemplars of human malevolence in the book, preventing Voltaire's satire from descending into a misanthropic condemnation of all humanity.

Voltaire's protagonist must negotiate these differing approaches to life, judging them according to his own experiences. Candide, while generally likable because of his genuineness and compassion, is a parodic version of the *bildungsroman* hero, who matures while being subjected to many trials. Candide's gullibility is so extreme, his trials so outrageous, and his reactions so farcically naive that he often appears ridiculous. Through most of the book, he also is driven by lust and a hopelessly idealized perception of Cunégonde. These desires, though, keep Candide moving forward, pursuing a goal, and believing in the possibility of happiness. And, despite his frequent bungling, he does grow throughout the course of the book, finally qualifying his initial optimism, while avoiding outright pessimism. His dreams about Cunégonde may get crushed, which is not unexpected given their blatant romanticism, but he still keeps his word and marries her, thereby remaining true to his own basically honest disposition. He also does not attempt to rationalize his thwarted passions with Pangloss's empty formulations or sink into Martin's passive despair. Desire, though radically tempered, still pushes him forward, looking for ways to live a satisfactory life without exploiting others. In the world of *Candide,* that makes him a fit, if comic, hero.

But what of his closing statement in the book, that he and the others "must cultivate our garden"? This vision has spawned much critical discussion, and readers still disagree over its message. Is it, as many argue, an assertion of the sustaining power of mutual labor, and if so, is it an adequate response to life's injustices and the need to improve the human condition? Some critics, like William F. Bottiglia, contend that Voltaire offers his closing scene as a viable means of finding contentment and limiting social evil. Others, however, particularly Roy S. Wolper, see the close as ironic. Wolper holds that Voltaire satirizes Candide, depicting him as a man who has learned nothing and who, in effect, helps to perpetuate inequality and suffering. The tone of Voltaire's presentation and the fact that Candide remains essentially decent would seem to qualify both of these interpretations, however.

The view that the small garden represents a microcosmic solution to worldwide rapacity and aggression appears overstated. The characters merely wish to find some safety and combat the pernicious effects of boredom. If Voltaire were to take a more hopeful stance than this vision of limited happiness, he would violate the bitingly satiric tone he so carefully maintains. On the other hand, the group's decision works on the practical level. For instance, they effectively banish, through choice, the destructive hierarchies imposed by political, economic, and religious institutions. Their solution may not work on a grand scale or qualify as a philosophy of life, but it does allow them a degree of beneficial autonomy and peace. Also, to say that their decision reflects a cowardly retreat into Candide's petty fiefdom ignores the fragile mutual understanding the characters develop, as well as the process of reaching this understanding. Voltaire, in essence, leaves his characters (and readers) in a precarious situation, tentatively hopeful, yet always aware of the dangers of growing too comfortable in one's righteousness and safety.

Source: Darren Felty, in an essay for *Novels for Students,* Gale, 1999.

Patrick H. Hutton

In the following excerpt, Hutton argues that the fulfillment of Candide's need for companionship is essential to resolving the problem of "how a good man can live in an evil world."

Few literary works of the Enlightenment have enjoyed the enduring acclaim of Voltaire's *Candide*. Scholars consider it to be an expression of what is best and deepest in the thought of the Enlightenment. But efforts to unravel the novel's meaning from the wit and satire in which it is cast have revealed a number of philosophical puzzles which are not easily solved. Despite much sophisticated analysis, critics today seem to be no nearer agreement about the novel's meaning than they were two hundred years ago. There is an apparent consensus that the theodicy question is Voltaire's primary concern in the novel, but critics by no means agree as to how he answered it, or whether he thought it could be answered at all.

Without pressing the analogy too far, it would not be inaccurate to say that recent *Candide* criticism has produced its own schools of optimists and pessimists. The critics who stress the sunnier side of the Voltairian temperament (scholars such as William F. Bottiglia and William H. Barber) interpret *Candide* as a philosophy of hope—an affirmation of the author's faith in the possibility of limited but real social progress. In the novel, Voltaire rejects the coherence of speculative philosophy in favor of the efficacy of empirical reasoning, which provides man with a practical basis for living in and acting upon a world of his own creation. But *Candide,* for these scholars, is not only a profession of faith. It is Voltaire's way of laboring in the garden. In composing *Candide,* Voltaire came to terms with the deeper issue of what the relationship between thought and action ought to be. Hitherto, he had considered moral questions only in formal philosophical essays. The inadequacy of his efforts to deal with the theodicy question in such abstract and disinterested terms drove him to despair. Through his novel, however, Voltaire tied his ethical imperatives to concrete problems of human existence. In the process, his writings acquired a new kind of energy. Thus the novel itself became a weapon in the service of a common-sense morality.

The critics who emphasize the darker recesses of the Voltairian temperament (Ira O. Wade and J. G. Weightman, for example) read *Candide* as a philosophy of despair—an expression of the author's mordant insights into the demonic mysteries of the human predicament. The meaning of *Candide,* these scholars contend, is to be derived from Voltaire's conclusion that man is unable to bridge the gap between his powers of rational thought and his largely instinctual activity. Unable to perceive a viable relationship between thought and action by which to remedy social evil, he chose instead to transpose the problem of theodicy into an imaginary world in which he could creatively defy the chaos of the phenomenal world. What he gained in the process was not the resolution of a philosophical problem, but a deeper aesthetic perception of the process of life itself. Interpreted in this light, *Candide* represents a personal catharsis for the author rather than a message to "enlighten" his age.

Perhaps the inability of the critics to arrive at a consensus about the meaning of *Candide* stems from the limitations of the conceptual framework in which they have so long approached the novel.

If Voltaire was preoccupied with the theodicy question, he considered it in an intellectual milieu more thoroughly secularized than that in which it had been posed by Leibniz a half-century before. The question which *Candide* raises is not the speculative one of the religious apologists of the seventeenth century, i.e., how can man account for evil in a world created by a beneficent deity; but rather the more practical one which the *philosophes* asked in the eighteenth century, i.e., how can good men live in an evil world? Voltaire's moralism has a social rather than a religious orientation. His concern in the novel is not to explain the presence of evil in the world, but to explore its effects upon human relationships. He traces the ways in which evil operates in the world as a framework for considering the preconditions under which trust in human relationships may be conceived. Voltaire's interest is less in theodicy than it is in community. The greatness of *Candide* is related to the intensity of Voltaire's concern about the relationship of man to his fellow man—his sensitive understanding that all men, optimists and pessimists alike, must journey through life by experiencing suffering that is incomprehensible, and that there is far more solace in making that journey in good company than in isolation. From this perspective, *Candide* is a quest for fraternity in the midst of enduring social crisis. Its meaning is less metaphysical than it is existential; less polemical than discerning, less satirical than compassionate.

Hence it is the evil which man fashions for himself that invites Voltaire's special attention in the novel. Natural catastrophes appear in the narrative, but the examples of these are only three (the tempest off the coast of Portugal, the Lisbon earthquake, and the Algerian plague), and they are dwarfed by the welter of man-made horrors which are amassed in comparison. The persistence of evil is poignant precisely because it is largely man's own creation. The dilemma is posed early in the narrative by Jacques the Anabaptist:

> It must be … that men have somewhat corrupted nature, for they were not born wolves, and yet that is what they have become: God gave them neither twenty-four-pound cannon, nor bayonets; yet they have made bayonets and cannons in order to destroy one another.

Nor may social evil be escaped. The world of *Candide* is one of imminent catastrophe. Beauty, wealth, and power are but ephemeral possessions. With or without such assets, no one may consider himself secure. Evil propagates its wrath indiscriminately. Indeed, a confrontation with some form of misery seems to be man's only certainty. All of the leading characters are pariahs, driven from the garden of tranquility into a wider world of perpetual conflict. Whether in the military outposts of Paraguay, or the sophisticated salons of Paris, they are thoroughly trapped in the snares of society's corruption, despite their efforts to cling to the vestiges of their youthful innocence. Even the gentle Candide is caught in situations so violent that two men (and nearly a third) die by his hand.

The manifestations of social evil in the novel may appear baffling in their variety. But just as Voltaire affirmed that there is a moral core to human nature beneath the "manners of men," so in *Candide* he sought to locate the cause of social evil in a single source. The source is man's longing for security, which leads him into illusions about himself and his social relationships. In this sense, man is a myth maker. He fashions conceptions of the world which provide comfort in their coherence, but which are largely fictitious constructs if measured against the realities of the phenomenal world with which they are supposed to correspond. This imaginary world seals off the real world which man is afraid to confront. Hence he is unable to perceive, let alone to sympathize with, the concrete life situations of his fellow man, whom he views only in terms of abstractions. Herein lies the origin of social evil. It is these abstract conceptions of the world which enable man to exploit his fellow man without admitting the evil nature of his actions.

It is for this reason that man is so readily prepared to subscribe to some form of dogma. At the simplest level, this may be the illusion of social pretensions. In a social order built upon legal inequality, it is not surprising that abstract arguments defending the privileges of caste should be prominent. The pompous Governor of Buenos Ayres, the pedantic Parisian critic, and the Jesuit colonel in Paraguay all base their actions upon such illusory convictions. Even the worldly-wise Old Woman sentimentalizes about her illustrious background. More pernicious still are the religious doctrines with which cruelty is justified. The "sermon" at the Portuguese auto-da-fé, the "missionary work" in Paraguay, and the "conversion" of the native laborers in the sugar factories of Surinam are examples of this kind of casuistry. Speculative philosophy merely translates dogma into a metaphysical idiom. Optimism and Manichaeanism are at one in dictating passive resignation to accident and misfortune, as if these were required to preserve the harmony of a moral order over which man has no control.

The propensity to deal with man in terms of abstraction is not a matter of theorizing alone. It permeates a broader fabric of law and custom through which acts of brutality and exploitation find more impersonal expression. The political order in Paraguay and the labor system in Surinam present obvious forms of slavery. But the leading characters must continually contend with institutions which demand behavior hardly less servile and degrading. Cunégonde, the Old Woman, and Paquette are forced into prostitution. Brother Giroflé and the Baron-priest are given to the clergy when still too young to choose that vocation for themselves. The Baron-priest, again, and Doctor Pangloss must serve in the Turkish galleys at the whim of arbitrary judges. Candide, too, is inveigled into the Bulgar army in his first encounter outside the walls of the Baron's castle. Eunuchs, concubines, soldiers, and priests haplessly serve one abstract master or another, and so become enmeshed in the evil mores of the world. It is for the civilized barbarism of war, however, that Voltaire reserves his most biting satire. Its internationally recognized laws may provide the necessary justification for its toll in horror, but, as the Old Woman who has suffered its consequences attests, these can provide no consolation.

While these external manifestations of social evil find prominent expression in the novel, it is the internalization of such evil which is the most insidious. As man's social relationships become more impersonal, his innate sympathies for his fellow man are stifled. Denied the solace of genuine relationships, man in his isolation turns his hostilities inward upon himself. The result is the anguish of alienation. Boredom is a psychological expression of man's capacity for cruelty to himself. Paris is the pleasure garden where this capacity is most fully revealed—with its sycophantic parasites, callous frauds, and viciously pedantic critics. In the apparent intimacy of the Parisian salon, the wit and mirth at the gaming tables are but masks for the most ruthless efforts of men to exploit one another. As the rakes desperately vie to destroy one another, they are nonetheless enslaved to one another in the boredom of this jaded setting. Perhaps nowhere else are men so unhappy.

Boredom, however, is a form of self-retribution, and its sins are venial compared with the evil of indifference. Indifference is the most detestable form of evil because it is a denial of mutual obligations among men. The theme of the disinterested spectator in the arena of human misery is ceaselessly repeated, and no less frightening for the variations upon its setting: the sailor who loots amidst the carnage at Lisbon after the earthquake, the populace who enjoy the auto-da-fé, the crowd which disperses satisfied after the execution of the English admiral, and the passengers aboard Candide's ship who watch the naval duel in comfort. Indeed, the novel strikes its most bitter note in the passage describing the callous indifference of the Dutch judge to Candide's plight, despite the judge's obligation to help him:

> This legal proceeding drove Candide to despair; to tell the truth he had endured misfortunes a thousand times more painful; but the indifference of the judge, and that of the captain who had robbed him, aroused his bile, and threw him into a deep melancholy. The malice of men stood out in his mind in all of its ugliness; he dwelt only upon gloomy thoughts.

The logic of social evil thus works toward its vicious end, and man is left with the icy axiom of the Old Woman, uttered en route from the Old World to the New:

> Just for fun, ask each passenger to tell you his life's tale; and if you find a single one who has not often cursed his lot, who has not often told himself that he is the most miserable of men, toss me into the sea headfirst.

The wanderings of Candide only confirm the observations of the Old Woman. Whether it be the languid setting of the Surinam coast, the gay salons of the Parisian aristocracy, or the peaceful cloisters of Giroflé's monastery, all are but facades for the most excruciating personal anguish. Even the noble Pococurante finds his place in this familiar pattern. For all his learning, wealth, and power, he is desperately unhappy, and surely he will not find that happiness in a larger garden: Herein, Voltairian irony is at its most masterful. For the last instance of insecurity which follows from this process of alienation was in the first instance born of a quest for security.

Does Voltaire in *Candide* offer man any means by which to escape from this process which leads him into isolated misery? Those critics who emphasize the author's pessimism would answer, no. The world of *Candide,* they would argue, is an absurd world from which there is no escape, and in which there is at best the negative solace of ironical laughter. Even suicide is no alternative, as the Old Woman remarks in her reflections at sea, and as Candide demonstrates when he considers that possibility after escaping from Paraguay. The critics who read *Candide* as a philosophy of hope would reply, yes. The world of *Candide* is rational at its foundations. Man must therefore withdraw into isolated communities where, through honest labor, he may rationally refashion the world in microcosm. Through work in this limited sphere, gradual progress toward the improvement of the human condition in the world at large is possible.

There is a partial truth in each of these observations. Man cannot escape from the world and therefore must make some accommodation with it. Until the finale, this is precisely what Candide is unable to do. With the ingenuousness of Rousseau, he "always speaks as his heart dictates," and suffers accordingly. But man must temporize with the world. It is for this reason that the resourcefulness of Cacambo and the Old Woman are to be admired. Invariably, they are able to show the avenues of escape when Candide is confronted with a seeming impasse. Moreover, it is the Old Woman who suggests that the small band of friends use the last of their fast-dwindling resources to purchase a small farm where they may await a more fortunate turn of circumstances.

It is revealing that the mistress of expediency should advise this course of action. The presentation of labor in the garden goes to the heart of Voltaire's conception of the nature of the human predicament. Candide and his companions work in the garden out of necessity, but not with a spirit of condemnation. Work has none of the dirge-like connotations which the pessimistic critics assert. Work banishes the three great evils of boredom, vice, and poverty. Throughout his wanderings, Candide remained passive before experience. His nature was shaped by the ideas and institutions which others imposed upon him. Through labor in the garden, however, he has the opportunity to affirm the potential capacities for goodness which are within him, and hence to define himself against the world. The possibility that the earth may be cultivated is Candide's faith. But it is the quest for that goal, rather than its achievement, in which he finds his consolation. El Dorado may be the utopian ideal toward which man must ultimately strive, but the garden of Candide is a microcosm of the only world in which he may at present labor. Voltaire is not the bourgeois prophet of social progress that some of the optimistic critics would like to make of him. The labor of Candide and his companions in the garden reaps abundant fruits. But, as the narrative reveals throughout, progress of this sort may be stamped out at any moment.

It is more important, therefore, that work anchors Candide in one locale so that he may fulfill his most important existential need—companionship. It is only by satisfying this need that the problem of how a good man can live in an evil world may be resolved. Through work, illusions are dispelled; through common labor, a basis for communication with his fellow man is established.

Candide needs companionship. In the course of the narrative, he is never left in isolation for very long. When he is forced to part with his trusted ally, Cacambo, he immediately seeks a new traveling companion. Martin's talents may be theoretical rather than practical, but Candide soon finds that he can no more dispense with his philosopher than he can with his pragmatic guide, whose return with Cunégonde he anxiously awaits. Candide is sustained throughout his journey by the hope of finding his lover again. This hope is not for a better world, symbolized by the pursuit of Cunégonde, as some critics argue. If it were, he might just as well have remained in El Dorado. Candide is in fact in quest of Cunégonde herself, and he will allow neither the barriers of caste nor the delights of El Dorado to stand in his way.

Is Candide's faith in the possibility of trust in human relationships but another illusion? Both the Old Woman and Martin answer in the affirmative, the former for practical, the latter for philosophical reasons. The Old Woman chides Cunégonde for her fidelity to Candide when such devotion threatens her own security. Likewise, Martin advises Candide to put away his thought of Cacambo and Cunégonde when they fail to keep their appointed rendez-vous at Venice. Martin's words, however, offer Candide no consolation. Martin, it must be remembered, has nothing for which to hope. But Candide has been sustained through the course of his travels by the solace which he has found in genuine communication with his companions. It is important to note how much satisfaction Candide and his companions find in relating the tales of their harsh trials. Compassionate understanding is gained through such commiseration. The hours which Candide and Martin while away at sea in discussions of philosophy serve the same end:

> Meanwhile the French and Spanish vessels continued on their way, and Candide continued his discussions with Martin. They argued for two entire weeks, and at the end of that time they were no further along than they had been the first day. But at least they were conversing, they were exchanging ideas, they were consoling one another.

Philosophy, it seems, is useful chiefly for its aesthetic value. Nothing may be resolved in these discussions, but there is much pleasure derived from a happy exchange of ideas. It is perhaps for this reason that the unfortunate Doctor Pangloss, even as he emerges from the galleys a broken man, may still affirm that he remains a philosopher because "the 'pre-established harmony' is the most beautiful thing in the world."

Candide finds consolation in charity as well. Martin scoffs at such a notion, and believes himself vindicated when Paquette and Brother Giroflé only sink deeper into misery as a consequence of Candide's generosity. Candide's experiences among the Oreillons, and Jacques's death at sea would seem to confirm Martin's view. But Martin misses the point. Charity and evil are incommensurable. Charity's function is not to reform the receiver, but to humanize the donor. Jacques the Anabaptist is not a saint. As "a creature without wings but with two legs and a soul," he practices the religion of humanity.

Most important, Candide finds not only solace, but his only source of joy in the course of his wanderings in companionship itself. The only instances in which Candide expresses happiness are in his reunions with his former companions. There are six such encounters in the course of the narrative: with Dr. Pangloss (ch. IV); Cunégonde (ch. VII); the Baron-priest (ch. XIV); Cacambo (ch. XXVI); the Baron-priest and Dr. Pangloss (ch. XXVII); and Cunégonde and the Old Woman (ch. XXIX). Each one brings Candide as much satisfaction as the last.

Can these ephemeral moments of companionship be transformed into the permanence of community? Herein lies the meaning of the garden episode. Voltaire conceives of the garden not as a solution, but as an experiment in the quest for that ideal. The garden roots this small band in honest labor. It is not clear from the novel's finale that evil has been permanently banished or that progress is bound to follow. But Candide and his fellows can fulfill themselves through work and communicate in trust. Cunégonde is no longer all that Candide had hoped for, nor is the garden a completely ideal setting for any of his band. But the possibility of community can only be tested in a setting without illusions. Such a goal requires neither the eradication of evil, nor the continuation of economic progress, but only a faith that man may end his alienation and find his innate goodness through his trust in, and compassionate understanding of, his fellow man. Voltaire's religion is not of progress, but of humanity.

Voltaire's irony takes strange turns, and in the last analysis, *Candide* is not as cynical as one might expect. In his first encounter outside the castle where he had passed his childhood in innocence, Candide was deceived by recruiters from the Bulgar army. The recruiters thought that they were being ironical when they lured him into the army by posing as his friends:

> Ah, dear sir! Come to the table; not only will we pay your expenses, but we shall never allow a man like you to be without money; men are made only to help one another.

Voltaire's final parody is upon them.

Source: Patrick H. Hutton, "Companionship in Voltaire's *Candide*," in *Enlightenment Essays,* Vol. IV, No. 1, Spring, 1973, pp. 39-45.

Sources

A. Owen Aldridge, in *Voltaire and the Century of Light,* Princeton University Press, 1975.

James Boswell, in *The Life of Samuel Johnson,* J. M. Dent & Sons, Ltd., 1978, pp. 210-11.

William F. Bottiglia, "Candide's Garden," in his *Voltaire: A Collection of Critical Essays,* ed. by W. F. Bottiglia, Prentice-Hall, Inc., 1978, pp. 87-111.

Georg Brandes, in *Voltaire,* Frederick Ungar Publishing Co., 1964.

The Gentleman's Magazine and Historical Chronicle, Vol. XXIX, May, 1759, pp. 233–37.

Nikolai Mikhailovich Karamzin, "A Letter on October 2, 1789," in his *An Account of a Young Russian Gentleman's Tour through Germany, Switzerland, France, and England,* translated by Florence Jonas, Columbia University Press, 1957, pp. 144–50.

Gustave Lanson, in *Voltaire,* John Wiley & Sons, Inc., 1966.

André Maurois, "Voltaire: Novels and Tales" in his *The Art of Writing,* The Bodley Head, 1960, pp. 35–50.

John Morley, in *Voltaire,* Macmillan and Co., 1872.

For Further Study

C. J. Betts, "On the Beginning and Ending of *Candide*," *Modern Language Review,* Vol. 80, 1985, pp. 283–92.

Betts examines the parallels and oppositions between *Candide*'s opening and closing chapter, contending that the end of the story reverses the beginning.

Moishe Black, "The Place of the Human Body in *Candide*," in *Studies on Voltaire and the Eighteenth Century,* Vol. 278, 1990, pp. 173–85.

Black argues that Voltaire employs bodily references throughout *Candide* in order to concretize his treatment of violence, philosophy, and sexuality.

William F. Bottiglia, "Candide's Garden," in *Voltaire: A Collection of Critical Essays,* edited by William F. Bottiglia, Prentice-Hall, 1968, pp. 87–111.

In his assertive and thorough study, Bottiglia holds that the ending of *Candide* affirms that social productivity within one's own limits can lead to both "private contentment and public progress."

Donna Isaacs Dalnekoff, "The Meaning of Eldorado: Utopia and Satire in *Candide,*" in *Studies on Voltaire and the Eighteenth Century,* Vol. 127, 1974, pp. 41–59.

Dalnekoff examines Voltaire's use of Eldorado to further his satire by offering a utopian counterpoint to the corrupt world. Dalnekoff also believes, however, that Voltaire satirizes Eldorado through mockery and ironic detachment.

Will & Ariel Durant, in *The History of Civilization: The Age of Voltaire,* Simon and Schuster, 1965.

This series by the historians Will and Ariel Durant synthesizes the width and breadth of Western European history from the dawn of history to the Napoleanic era. Though their rendition of history emphasizes great ideas and great men, it is surprisingly inclusive. The ninth volume is named for Voltaire and, therefore, the eighteenth century is filled in around him.

Josephine Grieder, "Orthodox and Paradox: The Structure of *Candide,*" in *The French Review,* Vol. 57, No. 4, March, 1984, pp. 485–92.

Grieder places *Candide* in the genre of "paradox" literature and asserts that its paradoxes attack rhetorical, logical, sentimental, and psychological orthodoxies.

Patrick Henry, "Sacred and Profane Gardens in *Candide,*" in *Studies on Voltaire and the Eighteenth Century,* Vol. 176, 1979, pp. 133–52.

Employing a mythical point of view derived from Mircea Eliade, Henry examines three gardens in *Candide,* connecting them to Voltaire's theme of time and to the tension between myth and history in the book.

Patrick Henry, "Time in *Candide,*" in *Studies in Short Fiction,* Vol. 14, 1977, pp. 86–8.

In this short article, Henry contends that only when Candide stops looking to the future for fulfillment does he reconcile himself to his situation and live in the present.

Patrick Henry, "Travel in *Candide:* Moving On but Going Nowhere," in *Papers on Language and Literature,* Vol. 13, 1977, pp. 193–97.

Henry reads the characters' travels in *Candide* as an effort "to attain ultimate permanence in the flux of reality."

Patrick Henry, "War as Play in *Candide,*" in *Essays in Arts and Sciences,* Vol. 5, 1976, pp. 65–72.

Henry analyzes Voltaire's war themes "in light of Johan Huizinga's *Homo Ludens: A Study of the Play Element in Culture.*

Frederick M. Keener, "*Candide:* Structure and Motivation," in *Studies in Eighteenth-Century Culture,* Vol. 9, 1979, pp. 405–27.

Keener closely examines the novel's psychological progression, tracing his self-conscious development and scrutiny of his own character.

Manfred Kusch, "The River and the Garden: Basic Spatial Modes in *Candide* and La Nouvelle Heloise," in *The Past as Prologue: Essays to Celebrate the Twenty-Fifth Anniversary of ASECS,* edited by Carla H. Hay and Sydny M. Conger, AMS, 1995, pp. 79–89.

Kusch analyzes how Voltaire creates a stagnating "closed garden" image of Eldorado by including a river that leads nowhere. He then contrasts this garden with the group's more feasible "open garden" in Constantinople.

James J. Lynch, "Romance Conventions in Voltaire's *Candide,*" in *South Atlantic Review,* Vol. 50, No. 1, January, 1985, pp. 35–46.

Lynch defines Voltaire's "burlesque of the romance tradition by comparing *Candide* to one tradition of seventeenth-century romance, the Heliodoran novel."

Haydn Mason, in *Candide: Optimism Demolished,* Twayne, 1992.

In this thorough study of *Candide,* Mason traces the literary and historical context of the work and offers a reading of Voltaire's treatment of philosophy, character relationships, and form.

Alan R. Pratt, "'People Are Equally Wretched Everywhere': *Candide,* Black Humor and the Existential Absurd," in *Black Humor: Critical Essays,* edited by Alan R. Pratt, Garland, 1993, pp. 181–93.

Pratt connects Voltaire's use of satiric black humor with the works of contemporary black-humor writers who, like Voltaire, use dark comedy to reflect the world's absurdities.

Gloria M. Russo, "Voltaire and Women," in *French Women and the Age of Enlightenment,* edited by Samia I. Spencer, Indiana University Press, 1984, pp. 285–95.

Russo investigates gender issues in the Enlightenment in her book. In the chapter on "Voltaire and Women," she tells about the many important women in Voltaire's life and their curious, though platonic, interaction with him.

Arthur Scherr, "Voltaire's 'Candide': A Tale of Women's Equality," in *The Midwest Quarterly,* Vol. 34, No. 3, Spring, 1993, pp. 261–83.

Scherr contends that *Candide* reveals the equality and mutual dependence between men and women, as shown through Candide's own reliance on women for happiness.

Mary L. Shanley and Peter G. Stillman, "The Eldorado Episode in Voltaire's *Candide,*" in *Eighteenth-Century Life,* Vol. 6, No. 2-3, January-May, 1981, pp. 79–92.

Shanley and Stillman contrast the unattainable ideal of the static Eldorado with the garden image, which represents an appropriate goal for Europeans living in a non-static world.

Renee Waldinger, ed., in *Approaches to Teaching Voltaire's Candide,* Modern Language Association, 1987.

Waldinger's collection contains essays detailing a variety of approaches to *Candide,* including studies of its intellectual ideas, philosophical background, satire, and comedy, among many others.

Fried Green Tomatoes at the Whistle Stop Café

Fannie Flagg

1987

Most often described as folksy, Pulitzer Prize-nominated *Fried Green Tomatoes at the Whistle Stop Café,* written by comedian and actress Fannie Flagg, spent thirty-six weeks at number two on the best-seller charts. At heart a love story about Ruth and Idgie, Flagg's novel is often listed among the great novels written by women. Reviewers often compare the novel to Garrison Keillor's *Lake Wobegone Days* or Alice Walker's *The Color Purple.*

In an interview with Samuel S. Vaughan, Flagg said, "Strangely enough, the first character in *Fried Green Tomatoes* was the café, and the town. I think a place can be as much a character in a novel as the people." The actual writing of the novel, however, began when Flagg received a shoebox full of items once belonging to her Aunt Bess who, like Idgie, owned a café near the railroad tracks. Flagg developed the story through countless hours of interviews with old-timers. The story of the town, composed of news clippings, narration, and Mrs. Threadgoode's reminiscences, is told to Evelyn Couch, a woman having a mid-life identity crisis and awakening to a sense of feminism. Evelyn finds therapeutic help in the stories of Mrs. Threadgoode about life in Whistle Stop during the 1920s, 1930s, and 1940s.

Author Biography

Before *Fried Green Tomatoes at the Whistle Stop Café,* Fannie Flagg was a famous character

Fannie Flagg

actress wishing she had more time to write. This changed when she attended a writer's workshop featuring her favorite author, Eudora Welty. Embarrassed by her lack of education and her dyslexia, Flagg hid in the persona of a twelve-year-old girl in the short story *Daisy Fay and the Miracle Man.* She won the workshop contest and the story became her first novel. With some success as a writer, she turned to a story dear to her heart: *Fried Green Tomatoes at the Whistle Stop Café.*

Flagg was born on September 21, 1944, in Birmingham, Alabama. Her given name was Patricia Neal. Her parents, William (a small business owner and projectionist) and Marion Leona (LeGore) Neal, died when she was young. At the age of five, Flagg began her acting career by writing and starring in a three-act comedy entitled "The Whoopee Girls." She started working in theater at thirteen by writing skits. Her big break came when she sold some material for a revue at "Upstairs at the Downstairs" in New York. The following week, late in 1956, she began her ten-year association with "Candid Camera," on CBS-TV.

Flagg attended the University of Alabama on both the Pittsburgh and Pasadena playhouse scholarships in 1962. She did not finish her studies. Instead, she continued to study acting at the Pittsburgh Playhouse and the Town and Gown Theatre.

After "Candid Camera," she produced the "Morning Show" in Alabama. Since then, she has written, produced, and acted in many popular television shows, including *The New Dick Van Dyke Show,* CBS-TV, 1971-73; *The New, Original Wonder Woman,* ABC-TV, 1975; and the *Love Boat.* She has also appeared in many films, including *Five Easy Pieces* (1970), and she played Nurse Wilkins in *Grease* (1978). In addition to television and film, she acted on Broadway in such productions as *Come Back to the Five and Dime, Jimmy Dean, Jimmy Dean,* 1979; and *The Best Little Whorehouse in Texas,* 1980.

A politically conscious artist who tries to better the world through her stories, Flagg is an active supporter of the Equal Rights Amendment. Flagg has written comedy routines, recorded four comedy albums, and submitted articles to magazines and newspapers, including the *New York Times Book Review.* Her first novel, *Coming Attractions: A Wonderful Novel,* was reissued as *Daisy Fay and the Miracle Man* (1992). She has homes in New York and Santa Barbara, CA, and continues to write and produce. She likes spending time in the Midwest—southern Missouri—because she feels that the Midwest is more representative of the country as a whole.

Plot Summary

Part I

Flagg's *Fried Green Tomatoes at the Whistle Stop Café* weaves together the past and the present in a story of the blossoming friendship between Evelyn Couch, a middle-aged housewife, and Ninny Threadgoode, an elderly woman who lives in a nursing home. Every week Evelyn visits Ninny, who recounts her memories of Whistle Stop, Alabama where her sister-in-law Idgie and her friend Ruth ran a café. These stories, along with Ninny's friendship, enable Evelyn to begin a new, satisfying life.

The novel opens with a 1929 column from *The Weems Weekly,* Whistle Stop, Alabama's weekly newspaper, announcing the opening of the Whistle Stop Café, run by owners Idgie Threadgoode and Ruth Jamison, with cooking done by "two colored women," Onzell and Sipsey, and barbecue by Onzell's husband, Big George. The narrative then jumps to December 1985 when Evelyn arrives at the Rose Terrace Nursing Home in Birmingham, Alabama, with her husband, Ed, to visit Big

Momma, his mother. As Evelyn sits in the visitors' lounge eating candy bars, she meets Ninny, who begins to tell stories about the Threadgoode family. Flagg intersperses descriptions of the past, gained through Ninny's memories and columns from *The Weems Weekly,* with the story of the developing friendship between Ninny and Evelyn. Ninny explains that she grew up next to the Threadgoodes and married Cleo, one of their boys. Most of her stories focus on Idgie, who "used to do all kinds of crazy harebrained things just to get you to laugh."

Ninny tells Evelyn about the untimely death of Buddy, Idgie's popular brother, and Idgie's generosity to hobos, like Smokey Phillips, who often stopped at the café for a hot meal. When Idgie started selling food to blacks who came to the back door, the local sheriff warned her that if she continued, the Klu Klux Klan would come after her. Idgie, however, refused to stop. At home Evelyn recalls her own past, deciding she became "lost along the way.... The world had become a different place, a place she didn't know at all." Her feelings of uselessness and her inability to stop eating fill her with despair and thoughts of suicide.

When, in 1924, twenty-one-year-old Ruth came to Whistle Stop to take charge of activities at the local church, Idgie promptly developed a crush on her. One day while Idgie and Ruth picnicked by a stream, a swarm of bees covered Idgie as she extracted wild honey from a beehive. After they flew off, Ruth collapsed in tears, voicing her fear that Idgie would be harmed. Both then admitted their love for each other, which prompted Ruth's decision to go back home and marry her fiancé, Frank Bennett. Idgie, wild with grief, found comfort with Eva, a woman Buddy had loved. At night, Evelyn imagines herself at Whistle Stop with all the figures from Ninny's past, which helps her forget about her problems for a while and fall sleep.

Part II

Ruth married Frank, a vain man filled with hatred and bitterness after discovering his mother's affair with his uncle. When Idgie heard rumors that Frank was beating Ruth, she threatened his life. In her fourth year of marriage, Ruth sent Idgie a note suggesting that she was ready to leave Frank. Idgie and Big George then returned a pregnant Ruth to Whistle Stop and learned of Frank's brutal treatment of her. A few years later when Frank was reported missing, sheriffs questioned everyone at the café, but no one would admit to knowing or seeing him. One sheriff later returned and let Idgie

know she was heard threatening Frank. He admitted that no one would care if Frank were dead, but whoever did it should cover her tracks.

Evelyn feels "in control" after being on her diet for nine days, but when a boy is rude to her at a supermarket, she crumbles, feeling "old and fat and worthless all over again." In response, she establishes an imaginary self she calls "Towanda the Avenger," who in her fantasies destroys all the mean people in the world. One day two young girls steal a parking spot Evelyn had been waiting for. When the driver won't give up the space, declaring, "I'm younger and faster than you," Evelyn rams her car, explaining, "I'm older than you are and have more insurance." Evelyn admits that she is always angry except when she is with Ninny "and when she would visit Whistle Stop at night in her mind. Towanda was taking over her life ... and she knew she was in sure danger of going over the edge and never coming back." In an effort to find guidance, she goes to church where she finds the churchgoers' joy contagious. As a result "the heavy burden of resentment and hate released itself," and she is able to forgive everyone including herself.

Part III

Ninny concludes stories of some Whistle Stop residents. Willie Peavey, Onzell's and Big George's son, was killed by a black man in a bar, just before he was to come home from serving in World War II. Willie's brother Artis found the man and killed him. Artis was sent to jail after he was seen freeing a dog caught by the dogcatcher, but Idgie and Grady helped get him out. Years later, Artis died in a Birmingham flophouse lobby. After watching Ruth endure excruciating pain from terminal cancer, Onzell, who had not left her side during the entire ordeal, gave her enough morphine to end her suffering.

When Frank's truck was discovered near Whistle Stop about twenty-five years after he was declared missing, Idgie and Big George were accused of his murder. At the trial, Reverend Scroggins, whom Idgie had harassed for years, told the court she and George were at a tent revival the night Frank was reported missing. The reverend lied for Idgie because she had helped get his son out of jail. The judge knew the testimony was a lie, but he closed the case citing lack of evidence. Ninny tells Evelyn that Sipsey killed Frank when he came into the café one night and tried to sneak out with Ruth's baby. Afterwards, Big George cooked Frank's remains in his barbecue and served them to the two detectives who came looking for him.

Mary Louise Parker and Mary Stuart Masterson in a scene from the 1991 film Fried Green Tomatoes.

Ninny's friendship and support help Evelyn develop a new faith in herself. She begins a successful career with Mary Kay Cosmetics, a position suggested by Ninny, and spends time at a "fat farm" in California where she loses weight, makes friends, and gains more confidence. While Evelyn is away, Ninny dies. When she returns, Evelyn visits Whistle Stop, where she meets Ninny's next-door neighbor, Mrs. Hartman, who shows her photos of many of the people she had heard about there. Two years later Evelyn goes to the cemetery where Ninny has been buried to tell her how much happier she is with her life. While there, Evelyn finds a note from the "bee charmer" on Ruth's grave. One month later a family on its way to Florida stops at a roadside inn run by Idgie and her brother Julian. Idgie gives the couple's eight-year-old daughter a free jar of honey.

Characters

Eva Bates

Eva Bates is "just an old redheaded gal that runs a joint over by the river.... A friend of ours." That joint is the Wagon Wheel Fishing Farm and it is where people go to forget their worries—a wa-tering hole out in the woods. Eva doesn't know much about the world, but she knows how to love.

Frank Bennett

Frank Bennett is a man with an Oedipus complex. He adores his mother so much it riles his already abusive father. Everything changes for Frank when he comes home early from school to find his mother having sex with his uncle. Henceforth, he hates everyone. With inheritance and hard work, he prospers, but he also beats up, impregnates, and ruins many women in the area. Frank's left eye is a glass eye and he loves to ask strangers to guess which is the real eye. One bum guesses correctly and later tells the bartender, "The left one was the only one with even a glimmer of human compassion." Frank decides that Ruth is the woman to give him a son to carry on his family name. They marry, and he starts to abuse her regularly.

Ruth Bennett

Considered an example of a lesbian relationship, Ruth and Esther are biblical figures who are heroes to the lesbian community. Ruth, in a twist on her biblical namesake, inspires steadfast loyalty. Ruth falls in love with Idgie the moment Idgie is covered by a swarm of bees. Sadly, she is engaged and must return home. Ruth marries Frank Bennett in order to ensure proper care for her mother, whose dying wish is that Ruth leave Frank. When Frank's abuse becomes too much, Ruth sends Idgie a message. Idgie comes to get her and they return to Whistle Stop. There, the two women run a café and raise Ruth's son, Stump.

Big George

See George Pullman Peavey

Ed Couch

Evelyn's husband, Ed, is a lazy man. Hence his family name, Couch, is allegorical and a shortened form of "couch potato." Ed works, drinks beer, watches the television, visits his mother, and "on Saturdays … would wander around the Home Improvement Center alone, for hours; looking for something, but he didn't know what." This humorous but pointless act is highly symbolic of the way shopping in the 1980s displaces real activity. Ed's view of life is very simple: He is the man, breadwinner, and ruler of his household.

Evelyn Couch

Evelyn Couch is miserable, overweight, depressed, and growing resentful of her husband, Ed. The Couches are symbolic of all middle-class couples struggling to find meaning in the world without getting off the couch. Evelyn has a difficult time handling her dissatisfaction with life. At first, she escapes into a fantasy life wherein she is a superhero—like Wonder Woman—who single-handedly rights the wrongs of the world. Those wrongs mostly involve the mistreatment of women at the hands of men.

Her salvation comes through the dreaded weekly visit to Big Momma at the nursing home. Evelyn goes with Ed to visit Big Momma, but usually ends up sitting by herself eating candy in the lounge. There she becomes caught up in Mrs. Threadgoode's stories. Before she knows it, Evelyn has found a friend in Mrs. Threadgoode. Bonding with another woman and hearing her life story acts as Evelyn's therapy. As a result, she is able to deal with her anxiety and build her self-esteem.

Mrs. Threadgoode shows Evelyn that she is not worthless and, in fact, could be someone who is proactive and can enjoy life. Evelyn takes the encouragement and attends a "fat farm." She loses weight and starts selling Mary Kay products. Evelyn feels better about herself, feels empowered, and is no longer sitting on the couch.

Media Adaptations

- Released by Universal Studios in 1991, *Fried Green Tomatoes* stars Jessica Tandy and Kathy Bates. The scriptwriters were Fannie Flagg and director/producer Joe Avnet. The script received an Academy Award nomination for best screenplay based on material previously produced or published. The film was shot in Juliet, Georgia. It received rave reviews for its actors as well as its ability to portray multiple historic eras with authenticity. Fannie Flagg makes a cameo appearance as a teacher.

- Fannie Flagg narrated the work for an audio edition in 1992. She received a Grammy Award for her recording of *Fried Green Tomatoes at the Whistle Stop Café*.

Peggy Hadley

Peggy is Stump's wife. She has to warn him against telling any "R-rated" versions of the tales of Whistle Stop when her granddaughter, Linda—who is nearly a grown woman—is present.

Grady Kilgore

Local sheriff and head of the local Klan, Grady butts heads with Idgie a few times over her open servicing of blacks at the café. When Grady realizes he jeopardizes his welcome in the café, he puts the café under his protection (both legal and otherwise) and everything goes on as usual. Over the years, Grady and Idgie become fast friends and form the main muscle of the Dill Pickle Club. This club ostensibly gambles and drinks at Eva's place but often sneaks around doing good deeds. One of their favorite pranks is to send a person for liquor to the Reverend's place because he is a prohibitionist. Through such late-night bonding and law enforcement contacts, the outlaw Railroad Bill is able to avoid capture.

Ninny

See Virginia Cleo Threadgoode

Artis O. Peavey

Stump suspects that the cook's son, Artis, is Railroad Bill because he is the same size as the infamous outlaw. Artis, however, has a bigger secret. He is a witness to murder and he helps destroy evidence with his father. Artis is a stereotype of the way circumstantial luck turns decent black men in a racist society into criminals. He takes revenge for Willie Boy's death but is not caught. Ironically, he is sent to prison for "attempting to murder" two black dogcatchers while freeing a friend's dog.

Clarissa Peavey

Jasper's daughter, Clarissa, is light-skinned enough to pass for white. She takes advantage of this and sometimes rides the whites only elevator. While shopping one day, Artis—drunk and disheveled—greets her. She is startled. The saleswoman screams for security and Artis is thrown out.

George Pullman Peavey

Given away by his mother at the train station, Big George is one of the bravest people in the world, according to Idgie. When Idgie is little, she falls into a pen of boars. It is Big George who dives in and fights off the pigs so she can get out. It is also Big George who scoops up Stump and runs him to Doc Hadley's after a train cuts off his arm. Poppa Threadgoode teaches Big George the butchering trade and employs him at the family's store. Later he cooks the café's famous barbecue.

Jasper Peavey

Jasper, son of George and Onzell, is the direct opposite of Artis. He has a family and a career aboard the trains. In order to survive, Jasper swallows his pride in the company of whites and becomes a celebrated porter. Yet he still fights in his own way. For example, when the Klan dynamites his and his neighbors' homes, Jasper refuses to move. His sacrifice enables his children to attend college just as the benefits of the Civil Rights era begin.

Naughty Bird Peavey

Naughty Bird is Big George's daughter. She grows into a pretty beautician who works at Opal's beauty shop. She falls for a man named Le Roy Grooms who works as a cook on one of the trains that passes through town. She has a daughter by him named Almondine. When she learns that he has moved in with a "high yellow octoroon woman in New Orleans" she becomes severely depressed and stops working. She decides that by appearing less black she will regain Grooms' love. She tries various methods of lightening the color of her face and straightening her hair, but to no effect. The problem does not resolve until Naughty Bird learns that Grooms is dead. Then, she recovers her smile and returns to work.

Onzell Peavey

Onzell is married to Big George and works at the Whistle Stop Café. Mrs. Threadgoode says of Onzell, "I never saw anybody more devoted to a person than Onzell was to Ruth." Onzell acts as Ruth's nurse during her bout with cancer. As Ruth declines, Onzell, by being miserly with the morphine, is able to end Ruth's suffering with an overdose. When Dr. Hadley brings the ambulance to take Ruth to the funeral home, Onzell violates every Jim Crow statute in existence by marching past the good doctor and into the "whites only" ambulance. She lays Ruth out in the manner that Ruth would have liked best.

Sipsey Peavey

Sipsey is an employee of Momma Threadgoode, and is described as "a skinny little thing, and funny. She had all those old-timy colored superstitions. Her mother'd been a slave, and she was scared to death of spells…." One of her beliefs is that you must bury the head of the animal you are about to cook or that animal's spirit will make you insane. Consequently, the yard behind the café fills with heads and the garden is always bounteous.

Sipsey loves babies and will baby-sit for anyone who asks. A friend tells her that there is a woman giving her baby away at the train station. Without putting on a coat, Sipsey runs for the station, yelling, "I got to go get me that baby." She returns with the baby, whom she names George Pullman Peavey—"after the man who invented the pullman car."

Willie Boy Peavey

The "first colored soldier in Troutville" to fight in World War II, Willie Boy is the pride of the Peavey family. He survives the war and gains admittance to the Tuskegee Institute with plans to become a lawyer. At a bar in Newark, New Jersey, a soldier named Winston Lewis demeans his father. Although trained not to react to insults, Willie Boy breaks a beer bottle in his face. That night, Winston Lewis cuts Willie Boy's throat while he sleeps and goes AWOL.

Smokey Phillips

Smokey, with his knife, fork, spoon, and can opener in his hatband, represents the many people who are homeless, unemployed, and wandering as a result of the economic downturns in the 1920s and 1930s. The Whistle Stop Café tries to feed the hungry a little something and, as a result, the hobos etch the name of the café on as many boxcars as possible from Whistle Stop to Canada. Smokey is singled out from all the other hobos, because "you could trust him with your life." He is given a home at the café and is staunchly devoted to Idgie while being secretly in love with Ruth.

Smokey Lonesome

See Smokey Phillips

Stump

See Buddy Threadgoode Jr.

Buddy Threadgoode Jr.

Named for Idgie's deceased brother, Stump is the son of Ruth and Frank though he is legally made a Threadgoode. The raising of Stump by Ruth and Idgie is a focal point of the novel. Ruth is more of a disciplinarian while Idgie plays the role of indulgent father. Together, they form Stump into an athletic youth and decent family man.

Idgie Threadgoode

Idgie, with her short blonde hair, is a "tomboy" who falls in love with Ruth. The pressures of normalcy would have squashed the relationship but Idgie's parents supported their obstinate daughter and she develops into her natural self. Idgie is able to relate and communicate freely with everyone, and she tries to treat everyone as human beings. In the segregated society she lives in, those practices may get her in trouble, but she refuses to treat people any differently.

Idgie is the most likely person to pull off the Railroad Bill stunt though she undoubtedly has help from the Dill Pickle Club. From one point of view, Railroad Bill is the ultimate joke on Grady. From another point of view, Railroad Bill presents Idgie as a modern-day Robin Hood. Idgie fails to uphold Jim Crow laws in other ways. She stages a miracle by bringing Miss Fancy to Troutville. She is also intolerant of abuse, especially of those she loves. Thus, without thinking, she publicly confronts Frank immediately after hearing that he beats Ruth regularly.

One of Idgie's most endearing qualities is her love of mischief and her joy for life. Like the rabbit of Uncle Remus' stories, Idgie tells wild tales, has a good heart, and tries to make the world a better place. She teaches by parable and by example, not by lecture.

Virginia Cleo Threadgoode

Ninny is the one who tells Evelyn about Whistle Stop. She grew up in the town and married Idgie's brother Cleo. Her stories and yarns are "threaded good" but seldom involve herself as she has spent most of her life as a spectator. She is a wise old woman who teaches Evelyn what she needs to know to become a full adult and be happier with herself.

Dot Weems

Dot Weems runs the post office in the town of Whistle Stop. She also publishes the town newspaper, *The Weems Weekly*. She represents the thousands of people who served as information conduits for news in small communities before the Internet, television, and radio.

Themes

Race and Racism

Fried Green Tomatoes at the Whistle Stop Café explores the width and depth of race and racism. While the evidence of racism is obvious, discussion of the situation is hushed and never crosses the color line. In fact, the only person who successfully crosses that line is Idgie, who simply doesn't understand the world in those terms.

Mrs. Threadgoode and Evelyn discuss race in terms of fear. "You know, a lot of these people resent having colored nurses out here. One of them said that deep down, all colored people hate white people and if those nurses got a chance, they'd kill us off in our sleep." Evelyn later realizes that her mother raised her to fear blacks. The novel, except to hint that time is the best teacher, provides no solution to racism. If people like Evelyn can realize that, despite their liberal opinions, they are squeamish, then perhaps they can make an effort to at least cease propagating fear to their children.

Gender Roles

A major step in Evelyn's progression toward being a self-possessed adult is being aware of society's prescribed gender coding. She realizes for

Topics for Further Study

- Flagg was a spokesperson for the Equal Rights Amendment (ERA). What is the status of the ERA today? What happened?

- Does Flagg criticize capital punishment in the novel? Is it an effective or just criticism? What is your view of the death penalty? Conversely, does the novel argue in favor of justified homicide?

- Who is the Tommy Thompson to whom Fannie Flagg dedicates her book? How do you think he influenced Fannie Flagg? Who are some of her other southern influences?

- Compare the experiences of the Peavey children. How do they handle the challenges of living in a racist society?

- Try a recipe or two of Sipsey's included with the book. While cooking, consider the allegorical role of food in the novel. For example, consider the significance of the community—from Georgia and Alabama—eating a murdered wife-beater cooked into a black man's barbecue.

- React to the following statement Flagg made in an interview with Samuel S. Vaughan: "I tend to rail against the current fashion in American culture of glamorizing only very young, pretty girls and completely ignoring the most wonderful and sexiest of women, those who are adult. I find there is nothing more attractive than a genuinely adult man or woman."

- What is domestic violence? How has society's view of domestic violence changed since 1929?

---

herself what the feminist movement of the 1970s had been trying to tell her—it's a man's world. She had been terrified of "displeasing men" her whole life. Consequently, she walks on tiptoes, as if in "a cow pasture" in order to avoid the words a man might say to her. One day, by accident, it happens. A boy at the supermarket hurls abuse at her. Bruised but not dead, she realizes she has survived

her worst nightmare and sets about examining it. Her first reaction, and an important step in terms of her growth, is to realize that "Evelyn Couch was angry." The second is to be carried away by her superhero fantasy of Towanda.

In the midst of a Towanda episode, she talks back to Ed when he habitually asks her to bring him a beer. The inadvertent outburst leads to more reflections. She surmises that having "balls" "opens the door to everything." When she realizes how silly these gender roles are, and in this she believes she has Idgie's backing, she finds herself a little more confident about herself.

There are other ways the novel explores gender roles. The physical abuse Evelyn fears has happened to Ruth. However, the reverse happens to Mr. Adcock. He eventually leaves his wife after he has fulfilled his duty to his children. The positive examples come from the old-timers, like the Weems, or from the rebels, like Idgie and Ruth. The message is that love and happiness allow people to make up their own roles.

Wealth

According to the novel, wealth, in the form of money, is not an end in itself. In fact, a happy life, a healthy family, good food, and good friends are more important than savings. Thus, when Cleo complains to Idgie that their father ruined himself by his generosity and that Idgie is bound to do the same, he receives a wise response. "Listen," says Idgie, "money will kill you," and then she tells a parable about a man who is squashed in the mint by hundreds of pounds of coin.

Sex

The discussion of sex, like race, is done in hushed tones. Men don't discuss sex at all except in joking and embarrassed tones (and usually in reference to Eva Bates). Evelyn wonders if her virginal discomfort with sex is unique. To her delight, Mrs. Threadgoode admits to the same position. "But Cleo was so sweet with me, and by and by, I got the hang of it." As with gender roles, sex is a happy thing when the act is not repressed or forced and there is respect for the other person. Helen Claypoole, who is a drunken buffoon used by men, represents the alternative approach. She doesn't respect herself, and no one respects her.

Sex education is a tough topic but Idgie broaches the subject of sex with her son in a straightforward, pragmatic, and enlightened manner. Stump, who dreads being incapacitated by his missing arm during sex, has insulted Peggy rather than face her interest in it. Stump's fears, like Evelyn's, are not unique to him: "I'll fall on her or lose my balance because of my arm and maybe I just won't know how to do it right.... I might hurt her or something...." Idgie takes her son to an easy woman, Eva, for his first time.

Evelyn, on the other hand, is incapable of dealing with her daughter's budding sexuality. On the day she purchases her daughter's diaphragm, she locks herself in her sewing room with a second pint of Baskin-Robbins chocolate ice cream, remembering that she had waited until her wedding night. "She still didn't enjoy sex."

Style

Episodes

An episode is usually a brief segment of action within a larger work that can be separated from that larger work. It is similar to a parenthetical remark. The term comes from the Greek word *epeisodion,* meaning "following upon the entrance." In Greek drama, an episode occurs between choric songs. While the chorus began as an ensemble of fifty or more men, by the time of Christopher Marlowe (*Doctor Faustus,* 1604) the chorus had shrunk to a single man reciting a prologue and epilogue.

In Flagg's novel, there are several choruses and a multitude of episodes narrated by a third-person omniscient narrator. The most objective chorus is composed of news clippings. The other chorus is the exchange between Evelyn and Mrs. Threadgoode, who, in proper choric fashion, comment on the characters' heroic actions. In between the choruses, the stories of the people of Whistle Stop are filled in. Only by taking all three components together can the reader understand the full drama of Whistle Stop.

Comedy

Flagg, a successful comedian, utilizes humor in her writing. She does so in *Fried Green Tomatoes* to lighten the dark and depressing passages. Obvious examples include Idgie's stories or Sipsey's superstitions. However, comedy enables Flagg to cover very dangerous ground and successfully shows both sides of a conflict. The best example of this is the confrontation between Grady and Idgie. He tells her to stop selling to "niggers" and she confesses that she "ought to" just like Grady ought to stop cheating on his wife. This ex- posure of hypocrisy is possible only because it is done with a smile between two friends.

As Flagg told an interviewer: "Oh yes. I suffer from what most humorists do, a deep need to be taken seriously. And I have to grab her by the neck and shake her and say 'Oh, shut up,' just tell the story and stop preaching. But writing humor is very serious and hard. Still, I find a novel without humor is not interesting to me. Life is, after all, very funny. If I did not really believe that I would jump off a building tomorrow."

Characterization

According to E. M. Forster, there are flat and round characters. The difference between them is that flat characters remain uncomplicated while round characters develop depth through the course of a novel. Flagg tells a story full of characters who are round. She is able to describe the development of an impressive array of characters in a very short span of time. For example, only two pages are required to tell the whole tale of the Adcocks and leave readers knowing their entire life. With a comedian's sense, Flagg describes Mrs. Adcock as the president of the "I'm Better Than Anyone Else Club." Unfortunately, the reader doesn't need too much more information to understand this character completely, because everyone knows someone like Mrs. Adcock.

Assisting Flagg in her narration is the running commentary provided by Mrs. Threadgoode. Mrs. Threadgoode is not an alternative narrator. Instead, she is an example of character zone, as formulated by Mikhail Bakhtin. Character zones are created by the encroachment of a character on the author's voice to the extent that she and Flagg filter each other's words. Flagg's story concerns a café, while Mrs. Threadgoode, as her husband points out, is only concerned with Idgie.

Trickster

The trickster is a universal character who behaves in the same manner whether in the context of the Pacific Northwest or in Australia. The trickster has been symbolized as a Loki in Norway, a hare in Sudan, a spider, turtle, or human in Africa, and a coyote or raven in America. Sometimes a supernatural being who can become other shapes, the trickster is a cyclical hero—now creator god, now duplicitous fool, now destroyer. The trickster tale normally involves the trickster, in whatever form, on a picaresque adventure. That is, the trickster is "going along," often in the company of a companion who is either a lackey or a foil, when a circumstance is encountered to which the trickster can respond with wit or stupidity. If the former, victory is achieved, but the latter brings violent death. The most famous example in the American South is Joel Chandler Harris's tales about Brer Rabbit from the mouth of a fictitious Uncle Remus.

In Flagg's novel, the journey is life and the trickster is Idgie. She tells tales, pulls pranks, and laughs. She sets Smokey Lonesome at ease with a ridiculous story and teaches Ruth's son what he needs to know through stories and example. She shape-shifts into Railroad Bill in order to redistribute some wealth. Through cunning and high alcohol tolerance, she brings an elephant to Naughty Bird. She also has the amazing talent of charming bees, or tricking them into giving her honey.

Historical Context

The Great Depression

Flagg's novel refers to several historical eras but primarily to the period after the café's opening, the summer of 1929. "By the way," reports Dot Weems on October 15, 1929, "is it just my imagination or are times getting harder these days? ... Five new hobos showed up at the café last week...." The hard times she refers to are the result of what John Galbraith describes as a "fundamentally unsound" economy. A mere five percent of the American population receives thirty percent of all personal income. The booming economy is the result of an over-productive industrial sector. Two weeks after Dot Weems's report, the stock market crashes on "black Tuesday," October 29. Millions are thrown out of work and soups made of dandelions and catsup pass for a good meal.

In the 1930s, people clog the highways looking for work while overhead new airplanes are tested. The railroad business booms from all the travel. The Great Migration is in full swing as blacks move from the rural South to the factories of the North. Many who take to the road stay transient for a long time. Socialism becomes an acceptable ideology among the majority of people who are profoundly affected by poverty. Franklin Roosevelt is voted into office on the basis of his innovative social programs. The economy starts to hum again but it is World War II, and the boom years of Truman and Eisenhower, that brings prosperity to America and the world again.

Race Relations

In the 1980s, the American Civil Rights era is considered over as a backlash comes from the conservative right. Civil rights leaders are caught off-guard. White middle-class voters express their anxiety that the previous decades of change were too abrupt and elect conservative candidate Ronald Reagan. Disagreeing with the view that Reagan saved the nation, U.S. Supreme Court Justice Thurgood Marshall said that in terms of equal rights for blacks, "Honestly ... I think he's down there with Hoover and that group ... when we really didn't have a chance."

A dark sign of the times is the rise of hate crimes throughout the decade. Neo-Nazi groups and the Ku Klux Klan gain new members after a long decline. There is a race riot in Miami and Vernon Jordan, head of the national Urban League, is shot and wounded in 1980. Between 1985 and 1987, the year in which *Fried Green Tomatoes* is published, the Southern Poverty Law Center reports forty-five cases of arson and cross burnings. From 1986 to 1988, there is a rise in racially motivated incidents on campus to 163 a year. The Reverend Jesse Jackson, considered a successor to Martin Luther King Jr. by some, is a Democratic presidential candidate while David Duke, former grand wizard of the Klan, wins a seat as a Republican representative in the Louisiana legislature.

Religion

In the 1980s, the Christian fundamentalist movement challenges many of the social changes of the 1950s and 1960s. Mainline Protestantism is superseded and high-school science classes are forced, in some states, to present the biblical story of creation as an alternative to evolution. The fundamentalist movement hits a snag, however, in the mid-1980s. Televangelist Jim Bakker, head of PTL Ministries, misuses church funds to pay off his mistress, Fawn Hall. He is replaced by Jimmy Swaggart, who later confesses to adultery and resigns. As a result of the scandals, fundamentalist churches lose nearly five billion dollars. With the fall of the Iron Curtain at the end of the 1980s, Christian broadcasting massively expands its global reach.

Critical Overview

Critical commentary on *Fried Green Tomatoes* has been enduringly positive. The most typical reactions involve comment on Flagg, the comic tele-

Compare & Contrast

- **1930s:** Blacks are treated as second-class citizens. In the South, a legal regime of "separate but equal" enforces this status.

  1980s: Civil Rights legislation and affirmative action have opened up opportunities to blacks and enabled legal recourse for those who suffer the effects of racism.

  Today: Affirmative action has been successfully overturned in some parts of the country. Other legislation is under attack and Congress refuses to pass a federal hate-crimes statute.

- **1930s:** Warren Harding keeps a mistress and illegally transfers naval oil reserves at Teapot Dome, WO, to the Department of the Interior. From there, they are leased to Harry G. Sinclair of Sinclair Oil. A Senate investigation finds that Sinclair and Edward L. Doheny had loaned large sums of money to Albert B. Fall, Secretary of the Interior. In 1927 the Supreme Court restores the oil fields to the U.S. government.

  1980s: The Reagan administration illegally sells drugs and weapons to Iran, through Israel, to fund the Contras in their bid to oust the leftist government of Nicaragua.

  Today: The sexual affair between President Clinton and intern Monica Lewinsky nearly results in the President's impeachment.

- **1930s:** Iraq, no longer under Turkish rule, is a British mandate.

  1980s: The West helps Iraq in its war against Iran.

  Today: The West maintains sanctions on Iraq until it destroys its weapons of mass destruction.

- **1930s:** Roosevelt creates the "welfare state" with the Social Security Act of 1935.

  1980s: Republicans begin to advocate an end to the "welfare state" by disseminating a myth of welfare queens who drive Cadillacs.

  Today: Welfare "as we know it" has been ended but, ironically, no funding was allocated for tracking former welfare recipients. Consequently, nobody is quite sure how successful the end of welfare is, but homeless shelter use is up.

- **1930s:** Apartheid, a system of white rule, is implemented in South Africa.

  1980s: The opposition group, the African National Congress, increases its military assault on the apartheid government.

  Today: Apartheid has ended and Nelson Mandela is the current president.

---

vision personality, writing serious literature. Critics also deem her portrayal of a lesbian relationship as tactful—in case anyone might fear the novel with its mainstreet cover could be steamy and lewd. There are also comparisons between her work and Garrison Keillor's amusing tales.

"What, Fannie Flagg write a novel? That lady with the gorgeous body and the Southern accent who seemed for a while to live her life only on or in the television set, saying kindly, witty, but certainly not very profound or serious things?" comes the question from Carolyn See, in a review for *The Los Angeles Times.* See then presents a summary of Flagg's accomplishment, which she views as a

deft encapsulation of the American South, the Great Depression, and John Steinbeck. Through Flagg's Mrs. Threadgoode, according to See, "this *past,* this *Alabama,* is magically spun ... into vivid myth."

Carolyn Banks, in *The Washington Post,* describes the novel as "funny and macabre." She emphasizes the psychological plight of Evelyn Couch as, at first, a failure to perform "The Ten Steps of Happiness" and be a "Complete Woman." Banks is also impressed by Flagg's style with "the segues and the juxtapositions [that] ... are sometimes amusing, sometimes touching, sometimes sad."

A southerner named Jack Butler, who was prepared to dislike the novel because the title made

Federally subsidized housing began under President Herbert Hoover's administration, at the beginning of the Great Depression. Pictured here is a Depression-era temporary housing community, commonly (and sarcastically) called a "Hooverville."

him "flinch" from "yokel exaggeration," found that this "is a real novel and a good one" with "scores of tossed-off hilarities." In his review for *The New York Times,* Butler finds the characterizations to be true from the portrayal of blacks to "the unusual love affair between Idgie and Ruth, rendered with exactitude and delicacy, and with just the balance of clarity and reticence that would have made it acceptable in that time and place." However, Butler faults Flagg for a prose style that "is serviceable, often good, but sometimes baggy and careless." The mix of medium and narrative voice, however, "are on key and fetching." Finally, Butler finds that at a time in American culture when there is so much that is "merely trendy experimentalism," he must "admire a writer who can end with a genuinely productive innovation" and a great recipe for fried green tomatoes.

Gayle Kidder focuses on Flagg's anxiety over "saying some things I really believe." Kidder reveals that Flagg took a page out of Eudora Welty, "who told [Flagg] you must write what fascinates you. And I think Southern writers, like Jewish writers, have always been fascinated with themselves and their own culture." The portrayal of blacks, like the stereotypical Artis O. Peavey, causes Flagg to

be self-conscious and disconcerted. Flagg is ready to defend herself but unlike the reception of Alice Walker, she has received nothing but praise from white and black reviewers alike with a, "oh, yes, I knew people like this."

At first, Orlando Ramirez thought Flagg's publishers were being too calculating with their folksy attempt to capitalize on the success of Garrison Keillor's *Lake Wobegone Days,* which takes advantage of "big-city boulevard brats" who "love to lap up local yokel yarns." Ramirez then finds that his "cynicism evaporated … by this surprising tale of two lesbians and their family and friends." Flagg's novel, according to Ramirez, does succumb to the "'feel-good' syndrome" but, fortunately, not to "Keillor-style irony." There is depth and intellect that is almost ruined by the "pretentiously unpretentious packaging."

Erica Bauermeister, in *500 Great Books by Women: A Reader's Guide,* asserts that "this gem of a book almost could have been shelved as just another light romantic comedy." Instead, Flagg's novel is a deep story told by several female voices about being a woman. There is a great deal of wisdom here, states Bauermeister: "Fannie Flagg mixes direct and empowering confrontations with racism, sexism, and ageism with the colorful and endearing language of the depression-era South and the café's recipes for grits, collard greens, and, of course, fried green tomatoes."

Criticism

Wendy Perkins

Perkins is an associate professor of English at Prince George's Community College in Maryland and has published several articles on British and American authors. In the following essay, she explores the gift of storytelling and its link to friendship in Fried Green Tomatoes at the Whistle Stop Café.

When an interviewer asked Fannie Flagg about the powerful sense of friendship that often appeared in her novels, she admitted that the theme was an important one to her. She explained, "Being an only child and losing both my parents at an early age, I have found that the friends I have made over the years are the people who help me get through life, good times and bad." In Flagg's *Fried Green Tomatoes at the Whistle Stop Café,* several strong friendships form among the characters. The central relationship, between Evelyn Couch, a middle-aged housewife, and Ninny Threadgoode, an elderly nursing home resident, develops through the art of storytelling. As Ninny narrates the stories of her past, the residents of Whistle Stop, Alabama, come alive for Evelyn, and the process provides comfort and a sense of purpose for both women.

As Evelyn shares her candy with Ninny in the Rose Terrace Nursing Home, Ninny reciprocates with the gift of her stories. Ninny's tales of her hometown provide models of living for Evelyn, who, at the start of the novel, appears crippled by a feeling of uselessness and an inability to take control of her life. The stories that have the most impact on her are the ones centered on Ninny's sister-in-law, Idgie Threadgoode, and Idgie's interactions with others. Evelyn's visualization of these episodes helps her face and eventually overcome the serious obstacles that have impeded her search for a sense of self.

When Evelyn and Ninny begin their relationship, Evelyn is a lonely, lost woman who has turned to food for comfort. Her husband and her grown children have become indifferent toward her, and she experiences a growing sense of hopelessness.

She feels cut off not only from her family but from her time period as well. "She had been a good girl, had always acted like a lady" but now "movie stars were having children out of wedlock" and "the best people were waltzing into the Betty Ford Center" getting help for their addictions. As a result, she decides she got "lost along the way…. The world had become a different place, a place she didn't know at all." She admits that "the quiet hysteria and awful despair had started when she finally began to realize that nothing was ever going to change, that nobody would be coming for her to take her away." When she begins to feel "as if she were at the bottom of a well, screaming, [with] no one to hear," she contemplates suicide as a way out. Ninny's stories, however, soon begin to pull her out of the well of her despair.

One way Ninny's stories accomplish this is through her descriptions of Idgie, who "used to do all kinds of crazy harebrained things just to get you to laugh." Idgie's pranks also make Evelyn laugh. Ninny tells her about how Idgie one day put poker chips in the church's collection basket. Once in April, the menu in the café offered fillet of possom, prime rib of polecat, goat's liver and onions, bullfrog pudding, and turkey buzzard pie a la mode. "An unsuspecting couple, who had come all the way from Gate City for dinner, read the menu and were halfway down the block when Idgie opened the door and yelled April Fool's at them." Idgie's tall tales included stories about the time she found a ten-dollar bill in one of her hen's eggs, and how a flock of ducks got frozen in a nearby lake and "flew off and took the lake with 'em." She used her best tale to help prove her point that "money will kill you." Idgie explained to Ninny that "a man … told me about his uncle, who had a good-paying job working up in Kentucky at the national mint, making money for the government, and everything was going fine until one day he pulled the wrong lever and was crushed to death by seven hundred pounds of dimes." At least she thought it was dimes; it could have been quarters. Ninny's humorous stories of Idgie's pranks and tall tales help to alleviate Evelyn's suffering.

Most of Ninny's memories about Idgie, however, fall into a problem/solution format. They begin with a serious predicament faced by one of Idgie's family or friends and end with Idgie engineering an effective solution through her strength of character and her genuine concern for others. Idgie showed her strength when she confronted Frank with his abusive treatment of Ruth and ultimately removed her from harm when she brought

What Do I Read Next?

- Flagg's latest novel, *Welcome to the World Baby Girl!* (1998), is a long way from Whistle Stop. The novel tells the story of Dena Norstrom who makes it big in New York. On the way, Dena achieves an ulcer, a psychologist, and ethics.

- Flagg's first novel was reissued as *Daisy Fay and the Miracle Man* in 1992. The novel tells about the misadventures of twelve-year-old Daisy Fay in the Mississippi Gulf Coast region of the 1950s.

- The Pulitzer Prize-winning novel *Bastard Out of Carolina,* by Dorothy Allison, tells the tale of another Southern family with experiences very different from the Threadgoodes. The story centers on the coming of age of Ruth "Bone" Boatwright.

- Published in 1982, and winner of the Pulitzer Prize in 1983, Alice Walker's *The Color Purple* tells the story of an abused woman who finally becomes self-empowered. This feminist novel is praised for its character depth and depiction of black vernacular.

- The 1985 novel by radio comedian Garrison Keillor tells the complete story of that special Norwegian utopia. *Lake Wobegone Days* mythologizes Minnesota in a quaint, and ironic, manner. Keillor's audio recording of the novel won a Grammy Award.

- The most famous novel by one of the best contemporary black authors is *The Autobiography of Miss Jane Pittman* by Ernest Gaines. Published in 1971, the novel is purportedly the story of a 110-year-old woman. Her story begins with the reading of the Emancipation Proclamation and ends in the 1960s. Gaines, like Flagg, spent many hours interviewing old-timers for this novel.

---

her back to Whistle Stop. She also stood her ground and risked her own safety when she continued to allow blacks to eat at her restaurant after the Ku Klux Klan threatened her. According to Idgie, "nobody was gonna tell her what she could and could not do." Ninny explains, "As good natured as she was, Idgie turned out to be brave when push came to shove."

Idgie's influence on Evelyn becomes apparent as she thinks about her run-in one day with a teenaged boy in a supermarket. At that point Evelyn had lost some weight and had started to feel "in complete control of her life." However when the boy's abusive and insulting invectives make her feel "old and fat and worthless all over again," she concludes, "I wish Idgie had been with me. She would not have let that boy call her names. I'll bet she would have knocked him down." As a result, Evelyn becomes angry, "a feeling that she had never felt before." She unleashes this emotion through an imaginary self she calls "Towanda the Avenger," who in her fantasies fights the injustices of the world. Yet when Evelyn starts to have visions of attacking her husband, Ed, she recognizes that Towanda is threatening to "take over her life." Evelyn admits that she is always angry except when she is with Ninny and "when she would visit Whistle Stop at night in her mind."

Eventually, though, Ninny's stories of Idgie's compassion, along with the peace Evelyn experiences during a church service, enable Evelyn to temper her righteous indignation and to forgive others and herself for her perceived shortcomings. Ninny recalls how Idgie solved problems by offering her time and support, as when she provided a homeless Smokey Phillips with a place to live and engineered an early release from jail for Big George's son Artis. When Naughty Bird, Big George's youngest child, was once ill with pneumonia, Idgie won the right in an all-night poker game with a trainer to walk his elephant over from a nearby park to lift Naughty Bird's spirits. Igdie also helped Ruth raise her son, Buddy Jr. After Buddy lost his arm in a train accident, Idgie encouraged him to find activities, like sports, he could master. When he became frustrated with his disability, she helped him gain the confidence he lacked. Finally, she risked a prison sentence for murder when she refused to reveal Sipsey's and Big George's involvement in Frank's death.

The giving of food also figures prominently in Ninny's stories about Idgie. During the Depression, Idgie saved lives by giving food from her café to blacks and homeless men. Disguised as the infamous bandit Railroad Bill, she would sneak onto government supply trains at night and throw food and coal onto the ground where people could find them the next day. Her efforts saved half of the poor population of Whistle Stop from freezing and starvation. One November, the local paper reported that when Railroad Bill threw seventeen hams off of the train, "our friends in Troutville had a wonderful Thanksgiving."

Inspired by Ninny's sharing of her stories, Evelyn also gives the gift of food. "Food had become the only thing she looked forward to, and candy, cakes, and pies were the only sweetness in her life." At the beginning of every visit to the nursing home, Evelyn shares that sweetness with her friend Ninny, who is comforted by the food she brings. Sometimes Evelyn brings special meals, prepared like the ones Ninny used to enjoy at the café. Before she leaves for the "fat farm," Evelyn gives money to Ninny's aide at the nursing home to guarantee that her friend "got what ever she wanted to eat and anything else she wanted." Evelyn also supports Ninny by the act of listening. Ninny admits to Evelyn "that's what I'm living on now, honey, dreams, dreams of what I used to do." Ninny's reminiscences of the past and Evelyn's rapt attention to her stories provide Ninny with a sense of satisfaction.

Ninny's friendship and support help Evelyn develop a new faith in herself. Evelyn admits, "After all these months of being with Mrs. Threadgoode each week, things had begun to change. Ninny Threadgoode made her feel young. She began to see herself as a woman with half her life still ahead of her." Her newfound confidence allows her to lose weight, to begin a successful career, and to become closer to her family. When she discovers that Ninny died while she was away, Evelyn misses her terribly, but realizes "because of knowing Mrs. Threadgoode, she was not as scared of getting old or dying as she had once been, and death did not seem all that far away. Even today, it was as if Mrs. Threadgoode was just standing behind a door." All

the residents of Whistle Stop also stand behind a door, ready to comfort Evelyn and to help her retain the confidence she needs to enjoy her new life. Ninny's storytelling had been her greatest gift to her friend.

Source: Wendy Perkins, in an essay for *Novels for Students,* Gale, 1999.

Angeline Godwin Dvorak

In the following excerpt, Dvorak examines the importance of cooking and serving food as a form of nurturing in Fried Green Tomatoes at the Whistle Stop Café.

The table spread with culinary delights easily triggers images of home, hearth and familial companionship. In southern culture, especially, food is nothing less than the social base of most interchanges of human experience and activity. The concept of "southern hospitality" has remained long after the demise of the antebellum era that birthed it. This graciousness surely began as much from logistics as generosity, for plantation and even tenant-farming neighbors, separated by hundreds of acres and miles of dirt roads, gathered at each other's homes for a gala "get together" that ultimately centered around food. Each plantation and homestead boasted its own specialties and secret recipes, which can still be enjoyed in eating establishments across the South. Barbecue, for example, was and certainly is a southern favorite. The role of cooking in southern culture, however, is even more relevant to everyday life in a common kitchen, shared by ordinary people, usually women, often mothers, frequently nurturers, but always southern cooks. It is what preparing food and feeding people mean to a southerner, especially "the cook," that makes "cookin' and eatin'" in the South an "in-culture" experience.

Southern fiction intimately captures the significance of cooking in a culture richly laced with a sense of community and Christian duty as well as a host of social facades and hypocritical masques. For the traditional, middle-class southern mother-woman, preparing food for the nourishment and enjoyment of other people plays a major role in her life. The act of cooking for and feeding someone—be it family, friend or total stranger—goes far beyond physical nurturance. Cooking is not simply a task or a chore; it is a mission that fulfills a sense of belonging as one earns a reputation for being, at least, a caretaker for her family, and at best, a very good cook. It is also a ministry that nurtures people's emotional and spiritual needs as much as their physical ones. Hunger of the soul and spirit drives the force behind the spoon and the skillet with the same intensity as a growling stomach. In southern culture, cooking can be an extension and sometimes a substitution for maternal nurturance, and even a token for martyrdom. Cooking serves the southern cook, likewise, as evidence of self-esteem and social status, moral soundness and spiritual faith, human compassion and community conscience.

Two contemporary southern writers, Clyde Edgerton in *Walking Across Egypt* and Fannie Flagg in *Fried Green Tomatoes at the Whistle Stop Café,* feature characters for whom cooking food and feeding people form the central core of their everyday lives and the culture. Intimate communication and personal bonding accompany the physical as well as emotional and spiritual nurturance of a meal prepared, served and consumed. Ruth and Idgie Threadgoode, proprietors of the Whistle Stop Café, Whistle Stop, Alabama, and Mattie Rigsbee of Listre, North Carolina, dramatize the words heard by almost any troubled, lonely, injured or estranged person who happens to stumble into a southern home—"let me fix you somethin' to eat; it will make you feel better." Whether facing abandonment, marital infidelity, a bout with arthritis, a lost loved one or a spat with the preacher, that "somethin'" becomes the solstice, the balm. That "somethin'" also becomes the impetus of doing something for someone in a situation that makes everyone involved feel helpless, insecure or inadequate….

Fried Green Tomatoes at the Whistle Stop Café is a novel of many stories, set in places from Whistle Stop, Alabama, to Chicago, Illinois, intricately woven into years from 1917 to 1988, told through many voices, including that of an eighty-six-year-old nursing home resident who links the past and present and that of the editor of *The Weems Weekly,* the Whistle Stop weekly newsletter. Characters, connected by time and place, migrate in, and sometimes out, of each other's lives; their individual stories become part of another's and so the links are formed. Mrs. Cleo Threadgoode, "Ninny," reaching into the past which seems much more real and more immediate than the present day, resurrects her family and friends of Whistle Stop. As she pieces together the lives of her husband's family, for she has none of her own, and those around them, these figures from the past become as approachable to the reader as Ninny herself.

One of the strongest narrative streams of the novel recaptures the devotion and love between two women, Idgie (Ninnie's sister-in-law) and Ruth. Idgie, an aggressive but truly brave individual, denounces femininity but retains a powerful, nurturing maternity. After Ruth's marriage to an abusive man, it is Idgie who saves her and makes a secure life—at the Whistle Stop Café—where they can raise Ruth's son.

For the women of Flagg's novel, cooking is the focal point of much of their daily lives. For Ruth and Idgie, as well as the restaurant's cooks Sipsey and Onzell, cooking fundamentally serves them as a means to support themselves and thus to secure their independence. The café is a simple extension of the home where the "kitchen is the hub of social intercourse." Whether selling food or giving it away to the neighboring blacks and boxcar hobos from the back door of the Whistle Stop, both Idgie and Ruth carry on their own isolated yet fervent efforts to combat the injustices of the South in the days before the civil rights movement and after the Depression.

For Idgie, preparing food for her "front door" customers is only the superficial function of the restaurant, not her mission or ministry. A rebellious creature, she has spent most of her life grooming a relentless determination to live out her convictions. As a child of ten or eleven, Idgie simply stood up at the dinner table "and announced, just as loud … 'I'm never gonna wear another dress as long as I live!' And with that … she marched upstairs and put on a pair of Buddy's old pants and a shirt." Years later, she poses as Railroad Bill, thought to be a Negro man, who throws food off the government supply trains for the area's poor people, mostly blacks and hobos.

Ruth and Idgie share with less fortunates, even in economically strained years. With the Ku Klux Klan members paying visits, usually addressing themselves to the frank-talking, brassy Idgie, not the gentle, soft-spoken Ruth, the backdoor business of the cafe undergoes some modifications: "After that day, the only thing that changed was on the menu that hung on the back door; everything was a nickel or a dime cheaper." That humble discount seems more substantial when weighed against the menu prices on the grand opening on 12 June 1929, when for breakfast a customer could get "eggs, grits, biscuits, bacon, sausage, ham and red-eye gravy, and coffee for 25¢ … For lunch and supper you can have: fried chicken; pork chops and gravy; catfish; chicken and dumplings; or a barbecue plate; and your choice of three vegetables, biscuits or cornbread, and your drink and dessert—for 35¢."

Not only do Ruth and Idgie pursue their mission of cooking for people, but so does Sipsey, whose cooking talents brought the local consensus that "there wasn't a better cook in the state of Alabama." Sipsey, in turn, "taught Idgie and Ruth everything they knew about cooking." She makes a living working at the Whistle Stop Café, but more importantly, she spends her entire life nurturing and protecting the same people that she cooks for, including an orphan baby boy that she raises as her son. Sipsey works diligently in the café to feed people but also to support Ruth and Idgie. Sharing Sipsey's loyalty, Onzell nurses Ruth on her deathbed, accepting no one's help or allowing no interference of "Miz" Ruth's care. These four women, over many years and many hot stoves, make a life to sustain themselves as well as nurture other people. Moreover, no color distinctions interrupt or cloud their relationships.

As the novel shifts from the primary narrator, Ninny Threadgoode, to her stories, an intense relationship between two women of different generations unfolds. During her stay at Rose Terrace Nursing Home, Ninny develops a friendship with the middle-aged Evelyn Couch. Food surfaces again and again as a bonding element in their relationship. Evelyn is starving for understanding of herself and meaning in life. Ninny is hungry for home life—"I miss the smell of coffee … and bacon frying in the morning"—and for human companionship. Unhappy with herself as much as with anyone else, Evelyn eats and eats and eats. Ninny talks and talks and talks, comforting Evelyn with "Well, honey, a candy bar's not gonna hurt you." She waits patiently for her surrogate daughter's visit to the nursing home. Evelyn, who dreaded the trips to Rose Terrace before she meets Mrs. Threadgoode and hears her stories, eagerly anticipates returning to the company and the comfort of the old woman.

On Evelyn's last visit before Ninny's death—just prior to leaving for a California "fat farm"—Evelyn prepares Ninny a special lunch:

> When Mrs. Threadgoode saw what she had on her plate, she clapped her hands, as excited as a child on Christmas. There before her was a plate of perfectly fried green tomatoes and fresh cream-white corn, six slices of bacon, with a bowl of baby lima beans on the side, and four huge light and fluffy buttermilk biscuits.

So long the recipient of Ninny's patient and consistent attention, Evelyn is finally capable of nurturing Ninny, whose physical needs at the age of eighty-seven are the most immediate. Ninny leaves Evelyn Sipsey's recipes (which Flagg gives as an addendum to the novel), but in recalling the past, she gives Evelyn a recipe for salvaging her life, for nourishing herself.

When the woman in the kitchen *only* cooks the food and puts it on the table, nurturing does not exist. The literal act of frying chicken and cornbread, creaming potatoes, boiling field peas and butterbeans and baking biscuits does not constitute true southern cooking. The preparation alone is not enough; completing the task of cooking is, in fact, the least significant aspect of its role in southern culture. Rather, what is crucial is the social and emotional intercourse between the preparer and the partaker of the food.…

But why *is* cooking so intimate to southerners and so ostentatious in southern culture? Is it a patriarchally imposed, gender-designated task that southern women have embraced for a sense of purpose, willfully or subconsciously or reluctantly? Or perhaps the "nurturing values provide a counterpoint to patriarchal values"? Or is it, at least for some, a readily available occasion for martyrdom?

Although the "cooks" in the three novels explored here do not set themselves up as martyrs, martyrs they could easily be. They each deal with situations and problems with a means available to them—cooking. The ability to reconcile the circumstances and the possible (and even practical) responses and reactions to them functions to confirm the ingrained determination to "do the best you can." As Bettina Aptheker notes, "[W]e see that many of our mothers [and other maternal figures] sacrificed, worked hard, nurtured, did the best they could to 'make do,' to improve the quality of our daily lives." As Dilsey, in Faulkner's *The Sound and the Fury,* tries to cater to the Compson family with Caroline screaming, Benjy whining and Mrs. Compson complaining, she remains the "vital presence." Dilsey alone is the "keeper of the peace, the protector and constant nourisher." Faulkner captures her ultimate role as the endurer.

The cooks in *Walking Across Egypt, Fried Green Tomatoes at the Whistle Stop Café* and *Dinner at the Homesick Restaurant* all endure.… Although Ruth dies in *Fried Green Tomatoes at the Whistle Stop Café,* she remains alive to those who love her, especially Idgie, her son Stump and the hobo, Smokey Lonesome. Idgie is surely the unnamed keeper of a roadside stand on Highway 90 in Marianna, Florida, an old woman with "snow-white hair and brown weatherbeaten skin" who sustains the same sharp wit, love of fun and open generosity that she did as the owner of the Whistle Stop Café…. Their missions and ministries prevail….

A fear that someone may come to their house hungry drives all of these women always to "have somethin' fixed." Like Mattie, who keeps a running menu of what she can prepare in a moment's notice, they overcook and save and plan. The far-reaching scope of a problematic situation or a troublesome circumstance can be immediately addressed over "a bite to eat," which promises to soothe and heal even though it cannot cure or solve anything. Sometimes, they feel compelled to justify their value in the home and community, just as Sister, in Eudora Welty's "Why I Live at the P.O." "humbly" acknowledges her fate, standing "over the hot stove, trying to stretch two chickens over five people and a completely unexpected child into the bargain, without one moment's notice." Southerners cook for themselves as they prepare food for others; the nurturance is simultaneous, just as filling, just as satisfying, just as essential.

Source: Angeline Godwin Dvorak, "Cooking as Mission and Ministry in Southern Culture," in *Southern Quarterly,* Vol. 30, Nos. 2-3, Winter-Spring, 1992, pp. 90-98.

Sources

Carolyn Banks, "Down-Home News & Blues," in *The Washington Post,* October 5, 1987, p. B10.

Erica Bauermeister, Jesse Larson, and Holly Smith, in *500 Great Books by Women: A Reader's Guide,* Penguin USA, 1995.

Jack Butler, "Love with Reticence and Recipes," in *The New York Times,* October 18, 1987, p. 14.

Gayle Kidder, "Flagg Writes about Real South," in *The San Diego Union-Tribune,* November 12, 1987, p. C-1.

Orlando Ramirez, "Flagg Displays Depth, Intellect in Café," in *The San Diego Union-Tribune,* January 15, 1988, p. C-3.

Carolyn See, "Book Review; Fannie Flagg Offers Tale Full of Nostalgia," in *The Los Angeles Times,* September 28, 1987, p. 4.

Samuel S. Vaughan, in *A Conversation with Fannie Flagg,* Ballantine Reader's Circle, 1998, http://www.random-house.com/BB/readerscircle/flagg/excerptguide.html.

For Further Study

Bruce Bibby, in *Premiere,* February 1992, pp. 33–4.
    In this interview Flagg discusses the female characters in her book.

Rosellen Brown, "Why Audiences Hunger for 'Fried Green Tomatoes,'" *New York Times Current Events Edition,* April 19, 1992, p. 2.
    This article explores the theme of friendship in the novel, praising its depiction of "real women who band together in an unspoken conspiracy of affection."

Jack Butler, in the *New York Times Book Review,* August 20, 1992, p. 14.
    Butler praises Flagg's sensitive portrayal of the love affair between Idgie and Ruth and her accurate depiction of small-town life during the Depression.

Fannie Flagg, *Fannie Flagg's Original Whistle Stop Café Cookbook,* Fawcett, 1993.
    Flagg has issued a complete cookbook of southern café recipes.

Renee Hartman, a review of *Fried Green Tomatoes at the Whistle Stop Café,* in *Belles Lettres,* Vol. 4, No. 1, Fall, 1988, p. 6.
    Hartman focuses on the novel's realism, praising this "chronicle of life in a small town."

R. Kent Rasmussen and Kent Rasmussen, *Farewell to Jim Crow: The Rise and Fall of Segregation in America* (Library of African-American History), Facts on File, Inc., 1997.
    This work examines segregation from its beginnings in colonial Virginia through passage of the Civil Rights Act in 1964. Emphasis is placed on the struggle of African-Americans for equality before the law.

Sybil Steinberg, a review of *Fried Green Tomatoes at the Whistle Stop Café,* in *Publishers Weekly,* August 28, 1987, pp. 64–5.
    Steinberg finds "the book's best character [to be] the town of Whistle Stop itself."

Diane Young, a review of *Fried Green Tomatoes at the Whistle Stop Café,* in *Southern Living,* January, 1995, p. 78.
    Young's positive review finds this "folksy tale" to be written with "heart, humor and insight."

The Grapes of Wrath

John Steinbeck

1939

When *The Grapes of Wrath* was published on March 14, 1939, it created a national sensation for its depiction of the devastating effects of the Great Depression of the 1930s. By the end of April, it was selling 2,500 copies a day—a remarkable number considering the hard economic times. In May, the novel was a number-one best-seller, selling at a rate of 10,000 copies a week. By the end of 1939, close to a half million copies had been sold.

John Steinbeck was shocked by the tremendous response to his novel. Almost overnight, he was transformed from a respected, struggling writer into a public sensation. Yet *The Grapes of Wrath* was bound to cause controversy in a country experiencing a decade of major social upheaval during the Depression. With the novel's publication, Steinbeck found himself immersed in a great national debate over the migrant labor problem. Many people were shocked by the poverty and hopelessness of the story, and others denied that such circumstances could happen in America. Admidst the controversy, people who had never read a book before bought a copy of *The Grapes of Wrath*. At $2.75 per copy, it was affordable and quickly sold out. Libraries had waiting lists for the novel that were months long.

It was perhaps inevitable that such an epic novel would cause a sensation. With the exception of Margaret Mitchell's *Gone with the Wind* (1936), *The Grapes of Wrath* was the publishing event of the decade. Widespread charges of obscenity were brought against the novel, and it was banned and

burned in Buffalo, New York; East Saint Louis, Illinois; and Kern County, California, where much of the novel is set. In fact, the novel remains one of the most frequently banned books in the United States, according to school and library associations. The book was denounced in Congress by Representative Lyle Boren of Oklahoma, who called the novel's depiction of migrant living conditions a vulgar lie. Charges were made that "obscenity" had been included in the book in large part to sell more copies. Eventually, First Lady Eleanor Roosevelt stepped in to praise the book and defend Steinbeck against his critics. In 1940, the novel won the Pulitzer Prize. Yet, at the time, such were the pressures of Steinbeck's celebrity that he described fame as "a pain in the ass."

The popularity of the novel has endured. It is estimated that it has sold fifteen million copies since its publication. For almost sixty years, Steinbeck's novel has been a classic in American literature; it has been translated into several languages, including French, German, and Japanese. *The Grapes of Wrath* has also been an integral part of the school curriculum in America since the end of World War II.

Author Biography

John Ernst Steinbeck was born on February 27, 1902, in Salinas, California. He was the third of four children, and the only son born to John Ernst Sr. and Olive Hamilton Steinbeck. A fourth child, Mary, was born in 1909. Olive Steinbeck had been a teacher in one-room schools in Big Sur, California, before her marriage to John Sr. After their marriage, the Steinbecks moved to Salinas in 1894, where John Sr. became a manager at the Sperry Flour Mill and later served as treasurer of Monterey County.

Salinas is located one hundred miles south of San Francisco, near Monterey Bay. At the time of Steinbeck's birth, it was a town with a population of approximately three thousand. During John's early childhood, the first automobiles could be seen rumbling through town. Family life was apparently secure and happy. Steinbeck's father quickly recognized his son's talents and eventually both parents encouraged Steinbeck in his dream to become a writer.

Steinbeck's best-known works of fiction, including *The Grapes of Wrath* and *Of Mice and Men*

John Steinbeck

(1937), are set in central California, where he grew up. In particular, one of the principal locales in *The Grapes of Wrath* is the San Joaquin Valley, a fertile farming area which lies east of the Gabilan Mountains. Although Steinbeck's family was solidly middle class, he had to earn his own money during high school. He worked on nearby ranches during the summer and he also delivered newspapers on his bike, exploring Salinas's Mexican neighborhood and Chinatown. Later, he would use his boyhood memories of these places in his stories and novels.

As a child, Steinbeck was shy and often a loner. Other children teased him about his large ears, and he responded by withdrawing into books. He was an excellent storyteller, a lifelong trait that found its natural outlet in his writing. In 1915, Steinbeck entered Salinas High School and began writing stories and sending them anonymously to magazines. He was president of his senior class and graduated in a class of twenty-four students. Steinbeck enrolled in Stanford University in 1919, which he would attend on and off for the next six years. He left Stanford in 1925 without a degree.

During the summers and other times he was away from college, Steinbeck worked as a farm laborer, sometimes living with migrants in the farm's bunkhouse. After leaving school for good in 1925,

Steinbeck took a job on a freighter and went to New York City. There he worked in construction and later as a reporter for *The American* for twenty-five dollars a week. But he was fired because his reporting was not "objective" enough. When he failed to find a publisher for his short stories, he returned to California by freighter. In 1930, Steinbeck married Carol Henning and settled in Pacific Grove. While Carol worked at various jobs to support John's career, he continued to write. Finally, in 1935 his first successful novel, *Tortilla Flat,* was published. In 1937, *Of Mice and Men* became an immediate best-seller, and Steinbeck became a respected writer. He adapted this novel into a play, which won the New York Drama Critics Circle Award in 1937.

The stress that came with success and fame hastened the collapse of Steinbeck's marriage, which ended in 1942. A year later, Steinbeck married dancer-singer Gwen Conger, with whom he had two sons—his only children—before their divorce in 1948. By 1950, Steinbeck had married his third wife, Elaine Scott.

After leaving California in the early 1940s, Steinbeck lived the rest of his life in New York City and on Long Island in New York. His final novel, published the year before he was awarded the Nobel Prize for Literature, was *The Winter of Our Discontent.* The story focuses on the decline of the moral climate in America. When he won the Nobel Prize in 1962, only five other Americans had received the award: Sinclair Lewis, Eugene O'Neill, Pearl Buck, William Faulkner, and Ernest Hemingway.

Accepting the Nobel Prize in Sweden, Steinbeck said: "The ancient commission of the writer has not changed. He is charged with exposing our many grievous faults and failures, with dredging up to the light our dark and dangerous dreams for the purpose of improvement. Furthermore, the writer is delegated to declare and to celebrate man's proven capacity for greatness of heart and spirit—for gallantry in defeat—for courage, compassion, and love. In the endless war against weakness and despair, these are the bright rally-flags of hope and of emulation. I hold that a writer who does not passionately believe in the perfectibility of man, has no dedication nor any membership in literature."

Steinbeck wrote no fiction after receiving the Nobel Prize. His reporting on the Vietnam War for *Newsday,* a Long Island newspaper, in 1967 caused many people to label him a hawk and a warmonger. Steinbeck died following a heart attack on December 20, 1968. He was sixty-six years old. His ashes were buried in Salinas, California.

Plot Summary

Chapters 1–11: Leaving Oklahoma

The Grapes of Wrath follows the trials and tribulations of the Joad family as they leave the dust bowl of Oklahoma for a better life in California. The narrative begins as Tom Joad hitchhikes across the Oklahoma panhandle to his parents' forty-acre farm. Tom has just been paroled after serving four years in prison for manslaughter. He meets ex-preacher Jim Casy, who is alone and singing by the side of the road. Casy recounts his own fall, his doubts about the saving grace of religion, and his growing sense of a collective human spirit. When the two men arrive at the Joad farm, they find it abandoned. A neighbor, Muley Graves, explains how the banks have repossessed the family farms, forcing people to leave. The smell of their dinner brings the sheriff and the men have to hide in the fields.

At the house of Tom's Uncle John, Tom and Casy meet up with the Joads: Granma; Grampa; Ma; Pa; Noah, the eldest son, who is slightly crazy; Al, sixteen, who is a "tomcat" and a mechanic; Rose of Sharon who is four months pregnant and married to Connie Rivers; and Ruthie and Winfield, Tom's younger sister and brother. The Joads have seen handbills announcing work in California and are preparing for their departure by selling their possessions, slaughtering their pigs, and loading a secondhand car. Casy asks to go along and is accepted into the family. When the time comes to leave, Grampa refuses to go. He has lived his whole life in Oklahoma and he can't imagine starting over. At Tom's suggestion, they get him drunk and load him on the truck with the rest of the family.

Chapters 12–21: Into California

Once they leave Oklahoma, Tom becomes a fugitive for breaking the terms of his parole. The Joad family meets the Wilsons, another family traveling west. They camp together, and Grampa dies of a stroke in the Wilsons' tent. The Wilsons and Joads drive west on Route 66 until a rod in the Wilsons' car breaks. Ma refuses to let the families split up, so they wait while the young men search for a wrecking yard and a replacement part. At the California border, the families ready themselves for a night crossing of the Mojave desert. A man and his son, heading east, warn the group about the dire conditions facing migrants in California. Upon crossing the Colorado River into California, things take a turn for the worse. Noah vows to stay and wanders off along the river. The Wilsons decide not to go any farther. As the Joads make their night crossing, Granma dies. Ma, who is lying next to her, refuses to say a word for fear that they will stop.

They leave Granma's body with the local coroner and make their way to a Hooverville, a camp where the migrant workers live. The rumors they have heard are true. There is little or no work. The basic necessities are hard to come by and the residents of the state do not want "Okies" around. A contractor drives up looking for produce pickers. It is a trick—a sheriff's deputy is with the contractor and plans to arrest the "Okies" and clean out the camp. In the ensuing altercation, the deputy is knocked unconscious by Tom. Casy takes the blame and tells Tom to escape so he won't be returned to Oklahoma. Upon hearing about Casy's sacrifice, Uncle John gets drunk to drown his feeling of worthlessness. The family hears a rumor that the Hooverville will be burned to the ground by townspeople who are angry at the migrants. Tom leaves a message at the store for Connie, who has suddenly disappeared, abandoning Rose of Sharon for dreams of a three-dollar-a-day job driving corporate tractors in Oklahoma. As they leave, an angry mob warns them not to return. Tom drives the truck south in search of the government camp, with the glow of the Hooverville burning in the night behind them.

Chapters 22–30: The Reality of California

The Joads are lucky to arrive at the government camp just as a site has opened up. In the morning, neighbors share their breakfast with Tom and together they go to work for a small grower who is forced by the Farmers Association and Bank of the West to offer low wages. The grower warns them about a plot to shut down the government camp that Saturday night. Ma enjoys a tour of the facilities given by the camp's governing committee. Rose of Sharon, abandoned and vulnerable, has two frightening encounters with an evangelist. Pa, John, and Al search for work without luck.

That Saturday night, three outsiders try to start a fight at the dance but their attempt is quickly thwarted. At the same moment, the deputies try to enter the camp under the pretext of restoring law and order. They, too, are turned back.

Although the conditions in the government camp are the best the Joads have encountered, they cannot find work. They pack the car and drive north. A man tells them about work picking peaches. When they arrive, they are escorted by the police into the orchard. They soon realize they have been brought in as strikebreakers. That night, Tom slips under the fence surrounding the orchard and discovers Casy leading the strike. They are ambushed by an agent of the growers and Casy is killed. Tom avenges his friend by killing the agent. He sneaks back to camp and has to hide since the cut on his face will give him away.

With Casy's death, the strike is broken and the pickers' pay is cut in half. The Joads drive north, eventually commandeering half of an abandoned boxcar. Tom hides in the marsh. Ruthie gets in a fight and boasts that her brother has killed two men. Ma goes to the marsh to send her son away. When she expresses her concern for his safety, he soothes her with what he has learned from Casy.

The next day, a torrential rain falls and floodwaters rise. Rose of Sharon's sudden labor prevents the Joads from leaving the boxcar for higher ground. Several families stay to help Pa dig a dike. A giant tree topples, spins slowly through the water, and destroys the dike. The waters quickly rise, eliminating any chance for immediate escape. Rose of Sharon delivers a stillborn child. Eventually, the family is able to leave the boxcar. Al stays behind with his new bride-to-be. The family wades through the flood until they find a barn on higher ground. Inside are a boy and his father who is near death. As they settle in, Ma and Rose of Sharon exchange a look, and the novel ends with Rose of Sharon suckling the starving man with her breast milk.

Inserted into this narrative are sixteen chapters of varying prose styles and subjects. Although they do not directly involve members of the Joad family, these chapters introduce topics that are thematically or symbolically relevant to the main narrative. The first and last interchapters, for example, address the weather and climate: the first announcing the dust and its impact on the land, the last speaking to the California rain and floods. The second interchapter follows a turtle as it patiently makes its way over the land. Other chapters critique ownership, capitalism, and consumerism, or address the social impact of technology, cars and tractors. One provides a history of California that highlights how settlers stole the land from the Mexicans. Another explores how the Oklahomans killed the Indians for their land. Several interchapters follow the great westward movement of 200,000 people over Route 66 and chart their social evolution from farmers to migrants and their new relationships to canneries, land owners, and banks.

Characters

Jim Casy

Jim Casy accompanies the Joad family on their journey from Oklahoma to California. He is a former preacher who has given up both Christian fundamentalism and sexuality, and is ready for a new life dedicated to helping people like the Joads. He is honest, compassionate, and courageous. Casy's new "religion" is based on love and a belief in each person's soul as well as an all-inclusive soul, the "Holy Spirit" of humanity. As critics have noted, these non-secular views of humanity can be traced to the transcendentalist philosophy of Walt Whitman and Ralph Waldo Emerson. Casy is a new convert to this transcendentalism.

Casy's initials (J. C.) have been cited as evidence that his character is a symbol of Jesus Christ. Moreover, his words and actions in the novel parallel those of Jesus Christ. For instance, he takes the blame for the deputy's beating at the Hooverville, and is taken to jail instead of Tom. His selfless struggle eventually leads him to become a strike organizer and leader. He is killed for this activism, and his last words recall those of Christ on the cross: "You fellas don' know what you're doin'." Through his actions, he helps Tom Joad to choose the same selfless path. Casy's new personal identity is an expression of a larger self, although such self-realization earns society's disapproval and is responsible for his murder.

Muley Graves

Muley Graves is a classic example of the stubborn man; even his name is a pun on this trait. At the beginning of the novel, he refuses to leave Oklahoma. He is homeless and his isolation drives him somewhat insane. His pessimism and blind violence against "the Bank" and its representatives are rejected by the stronger Joads, whose essential optimism infuses their journey to California.

Al Joad

Al Joad is the third Joad son; he is younger than Noah and Tom, to whom he looks for guidance. Al is fond of cars and girls. He assumes a greater position in the family because of his mechanical knowledge, but he is not always mature enough to deal with the responsibility. He helps drive the family to California. He wants to leave the family and go on his own, but duty and love force him to stay.

Grampa Joad

Grampa Joad is rowdy and vigorous, like a "frantic child." He refuses to leave the family's farm in Oklahoma and has to be drugged so that the family can begin their journey. But Grampa's vigor declines drastically when he leaves the land he has grown up on, and he dies on the first night of the trip. Both Granma and Grampa die because they are incapable of absorbing a new, difficult experience. In addition, Grampa's stroke is probably caused in part by the "medicine" that Ma and Tom give him.

Granma Joad

Granma Joad is deeply religious and energetic; she has thrived in her war of words with Grampa because "she was as mean as her husband." She is unable to adapt to a new way of life and the loss of her husband. She dies as the family crosses the Mojave Desert, and her burial in a pauper's grave violates her wishes. Her death outweighs the achievement of finally reaching California and foreshadows the reality to come.

Ma Joad

Ma Joad is the matriarch and foundation of the Joad family. She is the basis for the family's strength in the face of all their hardships. Ma Joad often behaves heroically for the sake of the family, yet she also expresses her fears. Nonetheless, Ma is brave and intelligent. She is an example of the indestructible woman who at times is ignorant, wary, and suspicious of strangers. She has much family pride and is active and assertive on their behalf.

Ma Joad displays numerous traditionally masculine qualities without losing her femininity or her maternal instinct. She assumes authority to prevent the weakening of the family unit. Once Ma Joad assumes the power as the head of the family, the others do not resist her. She passes her strength and wisdom on to her daughter, Rose of Sharon. Ma's transformation is seen when she finally comes to accept commitments to people beyond her family. As she tells the Hooper store clerk, "I'm learnin' one thing good.... If you're in trouble or hurt or need—go to poor people. They're the only ones that'll help—the only ones."

Jane Darwell, Henry Fonda, and John Carradine (left to right) in the 1940 film The Grapes of Wrath.

Noah Joad

Noah is the eldest Joad child. Slow, deliberate, and never angry, he is often mistaken as mentally challenged. Pa treats him kindly, because of his guilt over Noah's birth; scared by Ma's struggles, Pa tried to help deliver Noah and injured his head. Midway through the journey to California, Noah gives up the struggle to survive the arduous trip.

Pa Joad

Before the Joad family leaves Oklahoma, Pa Joad is considered the head of the clan. As the family travels, however, Pa loses his authority in the family to Ma Joad and his son Al. Ma's enduring faith in the family eventually gives her final say on decisions, while Al's mechanical ability makes him important because the family needs the car for their journey to California. This loss of Pa Joad's authority represents the shift in values within the family. Pa carries the family's burdens, although he is constantly challenged by Ma. Each time Ma asserts her newfound leadership, she meets with Pa's resentment. Nevertheless, he realizes that she has necessarily usurped his authority and does not act out his anger. His powerlessness is somewhat exorcised when he leads the boxcar migrants in a group effort to save their temporary homes from the flood. Throughout the novel, Pa's common sense, dependability, and steadfastness contrast with Uncle John's melancholy and Connie's immaturity.

Ruthie Joad

Twelve years old, Ruthie is the youngest daughter of the Joads. She is a selfish individual who has not learned her correct place in the social group. She learns a hard lesson when she is ostracized by the other children at the government camp for trying to take over their croquet game. In a childish fight, she reveals to another child that Tom has killed a man. This disclosure finally forces Tom to flee the family. Ruthie has a tendency towards cruelty that is aggravated by the family's hard luck. Her childish behavior shows how poverty can make even an innocent person harsh.

Tom Joad

Tom Joad killed a man in self-defense and has just been released from an Oklahoma state prison. Tom is depicted as wary, insensitive, skeptical, matter-of-fact, and confident. He has an ability to adapt and is a shrewd judge of character. At the beginning of the novel, Tom is only concerned with survival and keeping his prison record a secret. He is looking for peace and quiet at his family's farm. He undergoes a transformation in the course of the novel; by the end of the story, he believes in the potential of humanity's perfection and universality of spirit. Tom demonstrates this through social action, for instance, as he organizes the migrant farm laborers in California. Although Tom is emotionally numb from his experience in prison, he is by nature inquisitive: he always asks questions and is always seeking answers in life. Tom is forced to leave his family at the end of the novel.

Tom Joad Sr.

See Pa Joad

Uncle John Joad

John Joad, or Uncle John, is a prisoner of his guilt over his wife's death years before. Uncle John's melancholy balances the family's experiences. His sense of guilt causes him to blame all the family's misfortunes on what he thinks of as his sin: his failure to call a doctor when his wife complained of illness. As a result of this emotional scar, he has become an alcoholic. Uncle John's lifelong sense of guilt is transformed into anger when he sets Rose of Sharon's stillborn baby afloat in a box on the river to remind townspeople that they are starving children by their failure to help the migrants.

William James Joad

See Grampa Joad

Winfield Joad

Ten-year-old Winfield is the youngest child of the Joad family. He is treated cruelly by his sister Ruthie, yet Winfield retains his innocence. Unlike their grandparents, who die when uprooted from Oklahoma, the youngest Joads are "planted" in California and will perhaps take root there, fulfilling Ma's statement that "the people will go on."

Floyd Knowles

When the Joad family meets him outside of Bakersfield, Floyd Knowles tries to warn Al and the other men about the difficulties they will face in California. After Al helps him fix his car, he tells the family of potential work. When a contractor comes to the Hooverville to look for workers, Floyd's questions lead the police to try to arrest him. During the scuffle, Jim Casy kicks the deputy in the head and takes the blame for the fight.

Jim Rawley

A small, friendly man, Jim Rawley is the manager of the government camp. He makes Ma feel comfortable her first day at the camp, and his sim-

Media Adaptations

- *The Grapes of Wrath* was adapted as a film by Twentieth Century Fox in 1940. The film was directed by John Ford and starred Henry Fonda as Tom Joad; Jane Darwell as Ma Joad; Doris Bowdon as Rose of Sharon; and John Carradine as Jim Casy. The screenplay was written by Nunnally Johnson; the cinematography was by Gregg Toland. The film won two Academy Awards: for Best Director (John Ford) and Best Supporting Actress (Jane Darwell). It also won two awards from the New York Film Critics Circle for 1940: Best Director (Ford), and Best Film. Available from Fox Video, Baker & Taylor Video, Home Vision Cinema.

- *The Grapes of Wrath* was also adapted as an audio cassette (58 minutes), Dolby processed, published by Harper Audio in New York City. Read by Henry Fonda, who starred as Tom Joad in the 1940 movie, the sound recording contains excerpts from the novel about the plight of the migrants during the 1930s. Harper Audio, 1994.

- The novel was also adapted as a 58–minute audio cassette by Caedmon Inc. in 1978.

ple kindness almost drives Ma to tears. Even though Pa mistrusts him at first, to Ma he symbolizes the goodness of a community who allows the poor their dignity.

Connie Rivers

Connie is Rose of Sharon's nineteen-year-old husband who is "frightened and bewildered" by the changes his wife's pregnancy has brought upon her. He constantly talks of educating himself by correspondence in order to get a good job, but he is all talk and no action. He often tells Rose of Sharon that he should have stayed behind in Oklahoma and taken a job driving a tractor. Although he is described as "a good hard worker [who] would make a good husband," he eventually deserts Rose of Sharon because he has no faith in the family's struggle to find a better life in California. Connie's values can be connected with those of "the Bank": a focus on acquiring money and learning about technology in order to advance in the world. He also serves as a contrast and warning to Al Joad, whose fondness for the ladies could put him in the same situation. Unlike Connie, Al sticks it out with his family and wife.

Rose of Sharon Joad Rivers

Rose of Sharon is the elder Joad daughter. Still a teen, she is already married and pregnant. Throughout most of the novel, she thinks only of herself and her unborn child. She is depicted as a sheltered and thoughtless teenager. Yet Rose of Sharon undergoes a transformation during her pregnancy, which coincides with the difficult journey to California.

With Ma's guidance, she grows from child to adult. As she prepares to change roles from daughter to mother, she becomes "balanced, careful, wise." She endures much hardship, including the birth of her stillborn child, and by the end of the novel, she is ready to take her place with Ma Joad as a pillar of the family. It is clear that Rose of Sharon will succeed Ma as matriarch; in fact, she becomes something of an extension of Ma. Right until the end of the novel, she is referred to as a girl, but in the final scene, Steinbeck makes clear that Rose of Sharon and Ma are equals. He writes, "and the two women looked deep into each other." When Rose of Sharon feeds the starving man from her breast, she takes her place as the indestructible matriarch who, by her selfless act, comes to signify hope and survival of the people. It is through Rose of Sharon's selfless human gesture that the author symbolizes and emphasizes the most effective method of survival against oppression and exploitation: that people must develop compassion for their fellow human beings.

Rosasharn Joad Rivers

See Rose of Sharon Joad Rivers

Ivy and Sairy Wilson

Ivy and Sairy Wilson are a married couple that the Joads meet on the first night of their journey. They camp next to the Joads, and lend their tent to the sick Grampa, who subsequently dies. The Wilsons split from the Joads at California's Mojave Desert because Sairy Wilson is dying and is in too much pain to continue. That action contrasts with the Joads' choice, which is to turn back in spite of death.

Themes

Hope

The Joads experience many hardships, deprivations, and deaths, and at the end of the novel are barely surviving. Nevertheless, the mood of the novel is optimistic. This positive feeling is derived from the growth of the Joad family as they begin to realize a larger group consciousness at the end of the novel. The development of this theme can be seen particularly in Ma Joad, from her focus on keeping the family together to her recognition of the necessity of identifying with the group. "Use' ta be the fambly was fust. It ain't so now. It's anybody. Worse off we get, the more we got to do," Ma says in the final chapter.

Hope comes from the journey that educates and enlightens some of the Joads, including Ma, Tom, Pa, John, Rose of Sharon, and also Jim Casy. On the surface, the family's long journey is an attempt at the "good life," the American dream. Yet this is not the only motive. In fact, the members of the family who cannot see beyond this materialistic goal leave the family along the way: Noah, Connie, and Al. The Joads travel from their traditional life that offered security, through chaos on the road and on into California. There, they look for a new way of life, and a larger understanding of the world. And whether or not the remaining Joads live or die in California, their journey has been successful. Hope survives, as the people survive, because they want to understand and master their lives in the face of continual discouragement.

Class Conflict

The conflict in the novel between the impoverished migrants and the established, secure business people and Californians serves as a strong criticism of economic injustice. In fact, *The Grapes of Wrath* can be read as a social comment on the economic disasters of the time. The migrants' agrarian way of life has all but disappeared, threatened not only by nature's drought and dust storms, but also by big farms and financial establishments, called "the Bank." At the beginning of the novel, the owners and the banks push the tenants off of their land. Later the arrival of hundreds of thousands of poor people causes conflict in California.

The migrants represent trouble for businessmen in the form of higher taxes, labor unions, and possible government interference. The potential for future conflict is understood by all the business owners: if the migrants ever organize, they will seriously threaten the financial establishment. The Joads' travails dramatize such economic and social conflicts. In California, the conflict between the two sides grows violent as the migrants' desperation increases. The government camps are harassed or even burned down by angry state residents with financial interests.

There are also conflicts within the family that reflect the materialistic concerns of this class conflict. Rose of Sharon is preoccupied with her pregnancy and daydreams of the future. Her husband, Connie, wanted to stay in Oklahoma, and he does little to help the family on the road. Finally he disappears. Uncle John is consumed with worry and frustration. The children, Ruthie and Winfield, are selfish and restless. The hardships of dispossessed families are made personal and individual in the account of the Joads.

Fanaticism

Fanaticism—both as a religious fundamentalism and as a social phenomenon—is condemned in the novel. During Tom's first meeting with Jim Casy, the former preacher talks about his discovery that organized religion denies life, particularly sexuality. He in fact had found a connection between the "Holy Spirit" and sexuality when he was a preacher. Later, in the government camp, Rose of Sharon is frightened by a fanatic religious woman's warning that dancing is sinful and that it means that Rose of Sharon will lose her baby. In addition, the religious fanatic tells Ma that religion approves of an economic class system that incorporates poverty. She tells Ma: "(A preacher) says they's wicketness in that camp. He says, 'The poor is tryin' to be rich.' He says, 'They's dancin' an' huggin' when they should be wailin' an' moanin' in sin.'" This type of religious fanaticism is shown to be a denial of life and is associated with business in its economic deprivation and denial.

One of the most profound lessons from the story of the Joads and their real-life American counterparts is that one of the causes of the crises of the 1930s in California was social fanaticism and prejudice shown to the "Okies." The fear of the migrants, combined with the lack of faith in the government's ability to solve the temporary problems, often caused violence. It also led to such shameful events as starvation, malnutrition, and homelessness. In retrospect, it is obvious that World War II "solved" the migrant problem by absorbing the manpower into the war effort. How much better it would have been if California had developed emergency solutions for this period of great social tran-

Topics for Further Study

- Compare and contrast the current conditions of migrant farm workers in California with those of the migrants of the 1930s. Research current labor laws protecting the rights of these workers today. Have conditions improved in the last sixty years?

- Besides drought, one cause for the tragedy of the Dust Bowl was poor farming practices— including overgrazing by cattle and failure of farmers to rotate their crops—which exhausted the land's resources. How have farming practices changed since the 1930s to protect and manage the land to help ensure it will remain fertile for future generations?

- The mass migration of the Okies to California was caused by drought and economic depression. What other important mass migrations have occurred in U. S. history? Research the reasons behind these migrations and discuss the effects they have had on local economies and societies.

sition that could have served as an historical example.

Individual vs. Society

The novel demonstrates the individual's instinct to organize communities within the groups of migrants in roadside camps. "In the evening a strange thing happened: the twenty families became one family, the children were the children of all. The loss of home became one loss, and the golden time in the West was one dream." The people cooperate because it is beneficial to their welfare in order to survive. Yet Steinbeck develops the concept of the group beyond the political, social, and moral level to include the mystical and transcendental. Jim Casy reflects this when he says: "Maybe all men got one big soul everybody's a part of." The conversion of Tom, Ma, Rose of Sharon, and Casy to a "we" state of mind occurs over the course of the novel. As they gradually undergo suffering, they learn to transcend their own pain and individual needs. At the end, all four are able to recognize the nature and needs of others. The process of transcendence that occurs in these characters illustrates Steinbeck's belief in the capacity of humanity to move from what he calls an "I" to a "We" consciousness.

The Joads are also on an inward journey. For them, suffering and homelessness become the means for spiritual growth and a new consciousness. Ma sums up this new consciousness and what it means to her when she says: "Use' ta be the fambly was fust. It ain't so now. It's anybody." Yet although each of the four characters undergoes a spiritual transformation, each also finds an individual way to help others in the world and to take action. At the end, Tom has decided to become a leader in the militant organizing of the migrants. Ma accepts her commitments to people other than her family. Rose of Sharon loses her baby but comes to understand the "we" of the starving man to whom she blissfully gives life as if he were her child. Casy, who has been jailed, reappears as a strike leader and union organizer, having discovered that he must work to translate his understanding of the holiness of life into social action. Casy dies when vigilantes attack the strikers and kill him first.

Steinbeck makes clear that this potential for transcendental consciousness is what makes human beings different from other creatures in nature. In Chapter 14, Steinbeck describes humanity's willingness to "die for a concept" as the "one quality [that] is the foundation of Manself, and this one quality is man, distinctive in the universe."

Commitment

Steinbeck develops extensively the theme of social commitment. Both Casy and Tom were inspired to make Christ-like sacrifices. When Jim Casy surrenders to the deputies in place of Tom and Floyd, Jim is acting on his commitment to love all people. He later becomes a labor organizer and dies in his efforts. His statement to Tom, "An' sometimes I love 'em fit to bust....," exemplifies his commitment. In Tom, the development of commitment is even more striking. At the beginning of the novel, Tom is determined to avoid involvement with people. After his experiences on the journey and through his friendship with Casy, Tom becomes committed to social justice. His commitment extends to a mystical identification with the people. When Ma worries that Tom may also be killed like Casy, Tom tells her: "Then I'll be

ever'where—wherever you look. Wherever there's a fight so hungry people can eat, I'll be there. Wherever they's a cop beatin' up a guy, I'll be there. If Casy knowed, why, I'll be in the way guys yell when they're mad an' I'll be in the way kids laugh when they're hungry an' they know supper's ready. An' when our folks eat the stuff they raise an' live in the houses they build—why I'll be there."

Style

Point of View

The novel is narrated in the third-person voice ("he"/"she"/"it"). What is particularly significant about this technique is that the point of view varies in tone and method, depending on the author's purpose. The novel's distinctive feature is its sixteen inserted, or intercalary, chapters (usually the odd-numbered chapters) that provide documentary information for the reader. These chapters give social and historical background of the mid-1930s Depression era, especially as it affects migrants like the Joads.

These inserted chapters range from descriptions of the Dust Bowl and agricultural conditions in Oklahoma, to California's history, to descriptions of roads leading west from Oklahoma. In the more restricted chapters that focus on the Joads, the point of view shifts to become close and dramatic. In addition, many of the inserted chapters contain basic symbols of the novel: land, family, and the conflict between the migrants and the people who represent the bank and agribusiness. The turtle in Chapter 3 symbolizes Nature's struggle and the will to survive. It characterizes the will to survive of the Joads and "the people."

Setting

John Steinbeck wrote some of his best fiction about the area where he grew up. The territory that Steinbeck wrote about is an area covering thousands of square miles in central California. He particularly used the Long Valley as a setting in his fiction, which extends south of Salinas, Steinbeck's hometown. The Long Valley, covering more than one hundred miles, lies between the Gabilan Mountains to the east and the Santa Lucia Mountains on the Pacific Coast. The major site of *The Grapes of Wrath* is the San Joaquin Valley, which lies east of the Long Valley and the Gabilan Mountains. The Long Valley is also the general setting for *Of Mice and Men* (1937) and *East of Eden* (1952), two of

Steinbeck's other well-known works. This rich agricultural area is an ironic setting for a novel that examines the economic and social problems affecting people during the Depression. It was no promised land for the Joads and others like them.

One of Steinbeck's major achievements is his remarkable descriptions of the environment and nature's effects on social history. He was also ahead of his time in writing about the circumstances of the migrant workers and small farmers fighting corporate farms and the financial establishment decades before such subjects gained national press coverage in the 1970s.

Symbolism

The major symbol in the novel is the family, which stands for the larger "family" of humanity. The Joads are at the center of the dramatic aspects of the novel, and they illustrate human strengths and weaknesses. Dangers in nature and in society disrupt the family, but they survive economic and natural disasters, just as humanity does. At the end, the Joads themselves recognize they are part of a larger family. The land itself is a symbol that is equated in the novel with a sense of personal identity. What the Joads actually suffer when they lose their Oklahoma farm is a sense of identity, which they struggle to rediscover during their journey and in California. Pa Joad, especially, loses his spirit after the family is "tractored off" their land. He must cede authority in the family to Ma after their loss.

There is also a sequence of Judeo-Christian symbols throughout the novel. The Joads, like the Israelites, are a homeless and persecuted people looking for the promised land. Jim Casy can be viewed as a symbol of Jesus Christ, who began His mission after a period of solitude in the wilderness. Casy is introduced in the novel after a similar period of retreat. And later, when Casy and Tom meet in the strikers' tent, Casy says he has "been a-gin' into the wilderness like Jesus to try to find out sumpin." Also, Jim Casy has the same initials as Jesus Christ. Like Christ, Casy finally offers himself as the sacrifice to save his people. Casy's last words to the man who murders him are significant: "Listen, you fellas don' know what you're doing." And just before he dies, Casy repeats: "You don' know what you're a-doin'." When Jesus Christ was crucified, He said, "Father forgive them; they know not what they do." Tom becomes Casy's disciple after his death. Tom is ready to continue his teacher's work, and it has been noted that two of Jesus's disciples were named Thomas.

Biblical symbols from both Old and New Testament stories occur throughout the novel. Twelve Joads start on their journey from Oklahoma, corresponding to the twelve tribes of Israel or the twelve disciples of Christ (with Jim Casy, the Christ figure) on their way to spiritual enlightenment by a messiah. Like Lot's wife, Grampa is reluctant to leave his homeland, and his refusal to let go of the past brings his death. Later, the narrative emphasizes this symbolism when Tom selects a Scripture verse for Grampa's burial that quotes Lot. The shifts between the Old and New testaments coalesce with Jim Casy, whose ideas about humanity and a new social gospel parallel Christ's new religion two thousand years ago. Biblical myths also inform the final scene through a collection of symbols that demonstrate the existence of a new order in the Joads' world. As the Joads seek refuge from the flood in a dry barn, the narrative offers symbols of the Old Testament deluge (Noah's ark), the New Testament stable where Christ was born (the barn), and the mysterious rite of Communion as Rose of Sharon breast feeds the starving man. With this ending, it is clear that this is a new beginning for the Joads. All the symbols express hope and regeneration despite the continuing desperate circumstances.

Allusion

Allusions, or literary references, to grapes and vineyards are made throughout the novel, carrying Biblical and economic connotations. The title of the novel, from Julia Ward Howe's poem "The Battle Hymn of the Republic," is itself an allusion dating back to the Bible's Old Testament. In Isaiah 63:4–6, a man tramples grapes in his wrath: "For the day of vengeance was in my heart, and the year for my redeeming work had come. I looked, but there was no helper; I stared, but there was no one to sustain me; so my own arm brought me victory, and my wrath sustained me. I trampled down peoples in my anger, I crushed them in my wrath, and I poured out their lifeblood on the earth." Steinbeck's first wife, Carol, suggested the title after hearing the lyrics of the patriotic hymn: "Mine eyes have seen the glory of the coming of the Lord / He is trampling out the vintage where the grapes of wrath are stored." Steinbeck loved the title and wrote to his agent: "I think it is Carol's best title so far. I like it because it is a march and this book is a kind of march—because it is in our own revolutionary tradition and because in reference to this book it has a large meaning. And I like it because people know the 'Battle Hymn' who don't know the 'Star Spangled Banner.'"

Indeed, Steinbeck knew that his unfinished novel was revolutionary and that it would be condemned by many people as Communist propaganda. So the title was especially suitable because it carried an American patriotic stamp that Steinbeck hoped would deflect charges of leftist influence. He decided that he wanted the complete hymn, its words and music, printed on the endpapers at the front and back of the book. He wrote his publisher: "The fascist crowd will try to sabotage this book because it is revolutionary. They will try to give it the communist angle. However, the 'Battle Hymn' is American and intensely so. Further, every American child learns it and then forgets the words. So if both the words and music are there the book is keyed into the American scene from the beginning."

Allegory

An allegory is a story in which characters and events have a symbolic meaning that points to general human truths. The turtle in Chapter 3 is the novel's best-known use of allegory. The patient turtle proceeds along a difficult journey over the dust fields of Oklahoma, often meeting obstacles, but always able to survive. Like the Joads, the turtle is moving southwest, away from the drought. When a trucker swerves to hit the turtle, the creature survives, just as the Joads survive the displacement from their land. Later, Tom finds a turtle and Casy comments: "Nobody can't keep a turtle though. They work at it and work at it, and at last one day they get out and away they go—off somewheres." The turtle is hit by a truck, carried off by Tom, attacked by a cat and a red ant, yet, like the Joads and "the people," he is indomitable with a fierce will to survive. He drags himself through the dust and unknowingly plants a seed for the future.

Historical Context

Troubles for Farmers

The story of the Joads in *The Grapes of Wrath* begins during the Great Depression, but troubles for American farmers had begun years before that. Having enjoyed high crop prices during World War I when supplies of food were short and European markets were disabled, American farmers borrowed heavily from banks to invest in land and equipment. After the war, however, prices for wheat, corn, and other crops plummeted as European farmers returned to their businesses, and American farmers were unable to repay their loans. Thus, in the 1920s, while much of the country was enjoying economic good times, farmers in the United States were in trouble. Banks began to foreclose on loans, often evicting families from their homes. Families who rented acreage from landowners who had defaulted on loans would, like the Joads, be evicted from their homes. The situation, of course, became much worse after the stock market crash of 1929.

The Great Depression and the Dust Bowl

In October, 1929, stock prices dropped precipitously, causing businesses and banks to fail internationally and wiping out the savings of many families. Over the next few years, unemployment rates soared up to twenty-five percent. Although there is much disagreement today about the causes of the stock market crash, many analysts feel that the root of the problem was weaknesses in the coal, textile, and farming industries. Forty percent of the working population in America at the time were farmers. When low crop prices made it difficult or impossible for consumers to buy items such as radios and refrigerators, it had a significant impact on the economy. Goods began to pile up in warehouses with no customers to buy them, leading to the sudden devaluation of company stocks.

The resulting pressure on banks to collect on loans caused them to evict many farmers. However, this wasn't the only problem that plagued farm families. Six years of severe droughts hit the Midwest during the 1930s, causing crops to fail. This, compounded by poor farming practices such as overgrazing and failure to rotate crops, caused the land to wither and dry up. Great dust storms resulted that buried entire communities in sand. More than five million square miles of land from Texas to North Dakota and Arkansas to New Mexico were affected. The Midwest came to be called the Dust Bowl. Although no one escaped the economic pain this caused, small farm families similar to the Joads were the hardest hit. Of these states, Oklahoma was especially hard-pressed. Dispossessed farming families migrated from their state to California by the thousands. These people were called "Okies," although many of the migrant workers were from states other than Oklahoma.

A migrant family in Nipomo, California, 1936.

Migrant Camps and Labor Unions

Upon taking office in 1933, President Franklin D. Roosevelt launched a comprehensive agenda of government programs to combat the Depression. Collectively called the New Deal, these programs included new federal agencies designed to create employment opportunities and to improve the lot of workers and the unemployed. Among the many such agencies, the one that most directly touched the Okies' lives was the Farm Security Administration (FSA). Operating under the authority of the Department of Agriculture, in 1936 the FSA began building camps in California in which the homeless migrants could live. Ten such camps were finished by the following year. Steinbeck visited several in his research for *The Grapes of Wrath.* He had the Joads stay at one—the Arvin Sanitary Camp, also called the Weedpatch Camp, in Kern County. The intention was that the orchard owners would follow this example and build larger, better shelters for their migrant workers. This never came about, however, and many families ended up staying at the uncomfortable federal camps for years.

In an attempt to defend their right to earn living wages, migrant workers tried to organize labor unions. Naturally, this was strongly discouraged by the growers, who had the support of the police, who often used brute force. In Kern County in 1938, for example, a mob led by a local sheriff burned down an Okie camp that had become a center for union activity.

Critical Overview

When the novel was published on March 14, 1939, 50,000 copies were on order, a remarkable number for a Depression-era book. By the end of April, *The Grapes of Wrath* was selling 2,500 copies a day. By May, it was the number-one best-seller and was selling 10,000 copies a week. At the end of the year, close to a half-million copies had been sold. It was the top seller of 1939 and remained a best-seller throughout 1940. Since then, the novel has been continuously in print.

Despite its overwhelming popularity, the novel did not receive only favorable reviews. Journalists who wrote early reviews in the newspapers were not particularly impressed with the book. Steinbeck had broken many of the "rules" of fiction writing with his novel. Several reviewers could not understand the novel's unconventional structure. In *Newsweek,* Burton Roscoe wrote that the book has some "magnificent passages" but that it also contains factual errors (including statements that the Dust Bowl extended into eastern Oklahoma when that region of the state had actually remained fertile) and misleading propaganda. A reviewer in *Time* magazine criticized the chapters that did not describe the Joads' story, saying they were "not a successful fiction experiment." In the *New Yorker,* Clifton Fadiman wrote that the novel "dramatizes so that you cannot forget the terrible facts of a wholesale injustice committed by society," yet he also wrote that the latter half of the book was "too detailed."

Similarly, other critics found fault with the structure of the novel. Louis Kronenberger in the *Nation* and Malcolm Cowley in the *New Republic* criticized the latter half of the book and particularly the ending. Other magazine reviewers, especially those writing for monthlies and literary quarterlies, did not focus entirely on the sociological aspects of the novel and considered its artistic merit. These reviewers, on the whole, recognized that Steinbeck had written a seminal and innovative novel. The editor of the *Atlantic Monthly,* Edward Weeks, wrote that it was a "novel whose hunger, passion, and poetry are in direct answer to the angry stirring of our conscience these past seven years." Weeks found the novel almost "too literal, too unsparing," yet he could "only hope that the brutality dodgers will take my word for it that it is essentially a healthy and disciplined work of art."

In the *North American Review,* Charles Angoff defended the novel: "With his latest novel, Mr. Steinbeck at once joins the company of Hawthorne, Melville, Crane and Norris, and easily leaps to the forefront of all his contemporaries. The book has all the earmarks of something momentous, monumental, and memorable…. The book has the proper faults: robust looseness and lack of narrative definiteness—faults such as can be found in the Bible, *Moby-Dick, Don Quixote,* and *Jude the Obscure.* The greater artists almost never conform to the rules of their art as set down by those who do not practice it."

One early reviewer who summed up the novel's greatness was Joseph Henry Jackson in the *New York Herald Tribune Books.* Jackson was the book editor of the *San Francisco Chronicle* and had followed Steinbeck's career. He wrote in his review of April 16, 1939, that the novel was the finest book that Steinbeck had written. The review stated: "It is easy to grow lyrical about *The Grapes of Wrath,* to become excited about it, to be stirred to the shouting point by it. Perhaps it is too easy to lose balance in the face of such an extraordinarily moving performance. But it is also true that the effect of the book lasts. The author's employment, for example, of occasional chapters in which the undercurrent of the book is announced, spoken as a running accompaniment to the story, with something of the effect of the sound track in Pare Lorentz's *The River*—that lasts also, stays with you, beats rhythmically in your mind long after you have put the book down. No, the reader's instant response is more than quick enthusiasm, more than surface emotionalism. This novel of America's new disinherited is a magnificent book. It is, I think for the first time, the whole Steinbeck, the mature novelist saying something he must say and doing it with the sure touch of the great artist."

Criticism

Richard Henry

In this overview of The Grapes of Wrath, *Henry, a professor at the University of Minnesota, declares that Steinbeck's work still has relevance today, as it addresses the distinct issues of social classes and the importance of community.*

The Grapes of Wrath is arguably John Steinbeck's finest novel and the summation of his California experience. His first two novels received little attention from the critics or the public. His third, *Tortilla Flat* (1935), a novel set in his native Monterey, found a national audience. He followed this success with *In Dubious Battle* (1936) and *Of Mice and Men* (1937), novels that explore the conditions suffered by migrant workers in California. These conditions were made worse by the massive influx of Midwesterners who had fled the drought and the economic depression of the 1930s. *The Grapes of Wrath* (1939) recounts the plight of the underclass in the story of the Joads, a family from Oklahoma, who lose their farm and travel to California, the land of milk and honey, only to find their hopes and expectations dashed. It won the Pulitzer Prize in 1940.

The Grapes of Wrath traces the decline of the family and the rise of the community as the basic unit of social structure in the United States. What precipitated this evolution is a social and economic situation that no longer allowed family farms to provide enough income for a family to survive. With the industrial revolution and the development of tractors, family farms were giving way to factory farming. One of the difficulties Steinbeck faced was how to demonstrate the shared plight of hundreds of thousands of displaced peoples without lapsing into abstractions. On the other hand, were he to tell the story of one person or one family, he would risk obscuring the universal nature of their distress. Steinbeck resolved this problem in several ways. By writing his narrative in the third person and diffusing attention across several characters, he prevents readers from sympathizing too closely with any one individual. To support his universal thesis, Steinbeck intersperses chapters within the Joads' story that move the narrative away from the Joads in order to discuss Judeo-Christian and American sociopolitical traditions that relate to the novel's themes.

Of the novel's thirty chapters, only fourteen tell the story of the Joads. The other sixteen chapters offer thematic or symbolic counterpoints to the story of the Joads. An early chapter, for example, follows a turtle's indomitable progress over the land and across a highway, where it is struck by a passing vehicle. Subsequently, the seeds caught on the turtle's shell are inadvertently planted as they are plowed into the soil. The turtle serves as a sym-

What Do I Read Next?

- *In Dubious Battle,* (1936), is John Steinbeck's first book of a trilogy by the author that looks at the migrant labor problem in the 1930s. The novel focuses on labor organizers and a strike in California's apple fields. The book caused controversy when it was published.

- *Of Mice and Men* (1937) is the second book in Steinbeck's trilogy of migrant farmers. It is about two migrants, one who is mentally handicapped, and how their dreams of a better life can never be realized because of the oppressive social system.

- Emile Zola's *Germinal* (1885) is set in a French mining town. The main character in the novel, Etienne Lantier, witnesses how the families of the working class are destroyed by a social environment that sees people only as disposable resources. It is a fate that Etienne is unable to change.

- *The Octopus* (1901) by Frank Norris, is the first in Norris's "Trilogy of the Wheat." It is set in the San Joaquin Valley of California and addresses the abuses of railroad companies on the local wheat farmers. Norris was concerned with the question of how a Judeo-Christian ethic can exist in a harsh and uncaring world.

- In the nonfiction book *Factories in the Field: The Story of Migratory Farm Labor in California,* (1939) by Carey McWilliams, the author takes a look at the migrant labor problem in his study published the same year as *The Grapes of Wrath.*

- Justin Kaplan's *Lincoln Steffens: A Biography* (1974) is a look at one of the most famous muckrakers of American journalism. Steffens wrote a series of articles in 1902-1903 that exposed corruption in various city governments. He was one of America's renowned social critics and a great voice for reform. As an old man living in Carmel, California, in the 1930s, he and John Steinbeck became friends, and Steffens was the link who provided Steinbeck with his knowledge of migrant labor and contacts with union organizers that eventually led to his assignment to cover the migrants for the *San Francisco Chronicle.* Kaplan's book won the National Book Award and the Pulitzer Prize.

- James N. Gregory's *American Exodus: The Dust Bowl and Okie Culture in California* (1989) is an account of the Dust Bowl in the 1930s and the migration to California depicted in *The Grapes of Wrath.*

---

bol for the Okies, their movement, and their indomitable will, which tie their destiny to the land.

Other chapters, from descriptions of apocalyptic dust and floods, to the presentation of used-car salesmen, the selling of household items, and the flight of 200,000 migrants over Route 66, expand the focus beyond the particular plight of the Joads. Steinbeck augments this movement from the particular to the universal by employing a diversity of narrative styles, thereby giving voice to a nation in transition. For example, in one chapter he uses the cadences of a used-car salesman trying to fast-talk his customers. In other chapters, he employs the diction, phrasing, and sentence structures of the Bible, of the poets Walt Whitman and Carl Sandburg, and of the colloquial speech patterns of the

Okies. Still other chapters follow the conventions of journalism and documentaries.

The novel is divided loosely into thirds, according to the setting of the action. In Oklahoma, the Joads ready themselves for their journey; across Route 66, they flee the Dust Bowl for the promised land; and, in California, they attempt to make a new life for themselves. This division supports a pointed analogy to the Old Testament exodus of the Hebrews from Egypt to Canaan. The Dust Bowl's drought and the banks' persecutions parallel Egypt's plagues and the Pharaoh's oppressions. The journey undertaken by hundreds of thousands of displaced Midwesterners is similar to that of the Hebrews. California is the land of milk and honey, but its citizens are less than welcoming to the migrants.

Similarly, Canaan, the promised land of the Old Testament, resisted the influx of Hebrews. More specific parallels follow from the analogy. For example, the family name of Joad invokes Judah; the slaughtering of pigs just before the Joads depart is similar to the sacrifice of lambs; and the grandparents die on the journey, just as do the elders during the exodus. These and other references to the Old Testament help Steinbeck universalize the Joads, though not without cost. Some critics have found that by the end of the novel, Ma, Tom, Rose of Sharon, and the other characters serve little more than an allegorical or symbolic function. They, therefore, seem to lose some of their human appeal.

The novel also has its parallels to the New Testament in its language, imagery, and the values it conveys. Jim Casy's teachings and his self-sacrifice evoke Jesus Christ's teachings and his sacrifice. From this perspective, parallels emerge between the twelve Joads and the twelve apostles. Connie, for example, is a Judas figure who leaves the family for an alleged three dollars a day. As strong as these references to the Judeo-Christian tradition are, however, *The Grapes of Wrath* is not an exercise in piety. Steinbeck strikes a decidedly anti-religious tone early in the novel, where Casy explains why he has given up his ministry. Moreover, the evangelists who preach sin and damnation in the camps are treated with scorn.

A second major strain of social and political thought comes from nineteenth- and early-twentieth-century America. Casy recalls Ralph Waldo Emerson and his theory of the transcendental oversoul when he says that everyone "jus' got a little piece of a great big soul," an idea that is later picked up by Tom. But Emerson's emphasis on individualism falls by the wayside in Steinbeck's novel. When he shares his string of rabbits with Tom and Casy, Muley Graves gives an early nod to the novel's communal undertones: "I ain't got no choice in the matter," he says, "... if a fella's got somepin to eat an' another fella's hungry—why, the first fella ain't got no choice." From the Wilsons' sharing of their resources with the Joads on the road, to the final scene—Rose of Sharon's giving her breast milk to a starving man—the novel displays the importance of a mass democracy.

Ma recognizes that the power of the people is in their community. She worries Tom will do something foolish after learning that the banks have foreclosed on farms throughout Oklahoma: "Tommy, don't you go fightin' 'em alone. They'll hunt you down like a coyote. Tommy, I got to thinkin' an'

dreamin' an' wonderin'. They say there's a hun'erd thousand of us shoved out. If we was all mad the same way, Tommy—they wouldn't hunt nobody down—." The novel also demonstrates the pragmatism of philosophers William James and John Dewey, who argued that political, social, or economic ideas are only important or relevant in their practical consequences in the world. The world in *The Grapes of Wrath* is a world of action.

Although Steinbeck gave a democratic voice to the migrant workers, the emphasis upon community and the general critique of capitalism and exploitation led to early charges that the novel advocated communist principles. Protests followed, fueled in part by the character Jim Casy's rejection of religion. These protests focused attention not on the novel as a work of literature, but on issues of representation and whether it depicted reality or was merely propaganda. There was little doubt that the social and economic conditions of the migrant workers were as Steinbeck reported. He had toured the Hoovervilles and had worked with the migrants in 1936. Issues of representation, therefore, were not about the specific details of the Hoovervilles and the orchards, but about the entire socioeconomic system, whether or not it was failing, and what to do about it. In this debate, the Joads moved from the world of fiction to impact the real world, much as earlier novels (*Uncle Tom's Cabin,* for example) had forced social change. This debate continues in light of the social, political, and economic changes in the fifty years since the novel's publication. Although the Joads, Jim Casy, and the thousands of migrants are firmly rooted in the circumstances of the 1930s, *The Grapes of Wrath* also rewards interpretations informed by more recent trends in criticism. Thus, the novel is still relevant with regard to questions about the role of children in the novel, the distinct issues of class, and the decided victimization of people of other races or nationalities.

Source: Richard Henry, in an essay for *Novels for Students,* Gale, 1999.

Lee Burress

In the following excerpt, Burress provides an overview of The Grapes of Wrath *and rejects the claims that the novel is sympathetic to atheism and to communism.*

Steinbeck's success in creating a potent or powerful novel may be seen in the characters of the novel, in the complete structure of the novel, in the use of symbols especially the contrast of the animal with the mechanical aspects of life, in the powerful and varying prose styles of the novel and finally in a set of themes that reflect traditional American values. Moreover, in several of these aspects of the novel, Steinbeck drew on Biblical and religious materials that add to the richness and depth of the book.

The novel's ability to catch and keep the reader's interest owes much to its characters, whom Steinbeck has endowed with vitality and thematic significance. Many readers have seen embodiments of basic Christian virtues in such characters as Ma Joad, Tom Joad, Jim Casy, and Rose of Sharon. Tom Joad's growth in insight illustrates one of the important themes in the novel. Whether Tom or Jim Casy best illustrates a Christ figure depends on the reader's interpretation of the novel; each character has seemed to some readers to be illustrative of Christ's self-sacrificial life.

The structure of the novel is based on the Joads' journey westward. The journey gives the novel a mythical quality and achieves emotional power by relating the Joads' journey to that of many previous journeys, including the exodus of the Hebrew people out of Egypt to the promised land as well as westward journeys of the American Western myth. The ironic differences between the promised land found by the Hebrews in Palestine and the tragic plight of the Joads in California is not lost on the reader.

Steinbeck's use of a series of interludes as he tells the story of the Joads is an effective method of relating the particularities of the Joad family to a more universal set of realities. There are sixteen of these interchapters; these do not refer to the Joads, Wilsons, or Wainwrights. Instead, Steinbeck uses these chapters to tell of the larger significance of the situation in which the Joads find themselves. The interchapters draw on the material which Steinbeck had found in his visits to the migrant camps and his observations of the general situation of drought and depression.

Several of the memorable features of the novel appear in these interchapters, the turtle in chapter three, the tractor episode in chapter five in which an old farmhouse is destroyed by an enormous tractor. The farmer stands helplessly by with a rifle. The observation that nature imitates art, that life is often parallel to great works of literature, is illustrated by the tragic event in Minnesota in which a farmer, dispossessed of his farm by the bank that owned the mortgage, shot and killed two officials of the bank, then later killed himself. Would that farmer have committed such a violent and useless act if he had read and thought about *The Grapes of Wrath?*

Chapter eleven describes a vacant house, symbolic of the many vacant houses left across the deserted rural landscape. In other interchapters, Steinbeck discusses land ownership in California, the development of the migratory labor situation, and the accompanying results for society. In the final interchapter Steinbeck describes the rain which sets the scene for the last chapter of the book with its poignant episode of Rose of Sharon feeding the starving old man.

While some readers have felt that scene unrealistic, others have seen in it a poetic, or mythical, or metaphorical effort to realize several themes of the book—especially the traditional Western world theme of the essential oneness of humankind. Rose of Sharon cannot save her own baby, but she can still serve as one who ameliorates suffering and demonstrates the ennobling possibilities for humanity, in even the worst of situations.

The varying prose styles add to the strength of the book. In [*A Case Book on "The Grapes of Wrath"*] Peter Lisca has shown how the prose has a Biblical ring in several places, for example in the passage comparing horses and tractors. Lisca makes this clear by printing the passage in the style of the Psalms:

> The tractor had lights shining,
> For there is no day and night for a tractor
> And the disks turn the earth in the darkness
> And they glitter in the daylight.
> And when a horse stops work and goes in the barn
>
> There is a life and vitality left,
> There is a breathing and a warmth,
> And the feet shift on the straw,
> And the jaws champ on the hay,
> And the ears and eyes are alive.
> There is a warmth of life in the barn,
> And the heat and smell of life.
>
> But when the motor of a tractor stops,
> It is as dead as the ore it came from.
> The heat goes out of it
> Like the living heat that leaves a corpse.

In a different style, Steinbeck describes a folk dance in chapter thirteen; "Look at that Texas boy. Long legs loose, taps four times for every damn step. Never see a boy swing aroun' like that. Look at him swing that Cherokee girl, red in the cheeks and her toe points out." Throughout the novel the prose style varies to fit the subject under consideration. Lisca illustrates this point further by reference to chapter seven in which there is a description of the sale of used cars: "Cadillacs, LaSalles, Buicks, Plymouths, Packards, Chevvies, Fords, Pontiacs. Row on row. Headlight glinting in the afternoon sun. Good Used Cars. Soften 'em up, Joe. Jesus I wisht I had a thousand jalopies. Get 'em ready to deal, and I'll close 'em."

Steinbeck's use of symbols in the novel is another of the ways in which the Joads' predicament is shown to extend their own limited situation. These include the turtle, the vacant houses, the enormous tractor, the worn out automobiles, Rose of Sharon nursing the old starving man, the grapes, both in the title and throughout the novel as a symbol of plenty and as ironic counterpoint of the denial of plenty to the Joads, Rose of Sharon's stillborn child, set adrift to float down the stream, again in ironic counterpoint to the child Moses in the Bible, who became a saviour of his people. The Joads' journey is itself an archetype of mass migration, as Lisca suggests. These symbolic objects or actions are carefully integrated into the action of the novel, contributing to the artistic success of the whole book.

Symbolic contrasts between animals and machines appear frequently in the book. Generally, the animal references stand for life and the references to machinery stand for depersonalized, inanimate ways of dealing with human problems. "I lost my land, a single tractor took my land." The phrase "tractored out" or "tractored off" appears often. Some animal references are derogatory, as when human beings behave like ants, or fight like a couple of cats. But generally, as in the contrast between horses and tractors quoted above, animal references are hopeful and positive; mechanical references suggest the destructive and negative aspects of contemporary life. The turtle, for example, symbolizes the persistence of living beings in spite of danger or hardship. As machines threaten the turtle, so machines threaten the farmer. As the turtle persists, so will the Joads.

The thematic structure of the book is a major source of its continuing power. In the decades since its publication readers have seen a number of traditional American ideas that complement each other in the texture of the book. While some critics have seen tension in the ideas of the book, on the whole most readers have seen artistic integrity in the book's thematic structure.

Frederick Ives Carpenter [in *A Case Book on "The Grapes of Wrath"*] suggested, not long after the book's publication, that a number of the most characteristic American ideas appeared in the book—"the mystical transcendentalism of Emerson," "the earthy democracy of Walt Whitman," the "pragmatic instrumentalism of William James and John Dewey." Other readers have seen in the book the agrarian philosophy of Thomas Jefferson—a faith in the small farm that has strongly influenced our society. It was agrarianism that led to the homestead laws passed by the Republican Party when Abraham Lincoln was president, and that lay back of a variety of twentieth-century efforts to assist farmers and protect the family farm.

No feature of the book is better illustrative of the tendency of the American novel to protest the conflict between American ideals and American practice than the novel's agrarianism. The Joads have as a major motivation their desire to own a piece of land, where they can raise the grapes of plenty, enough so that Pa Joad can squash the grapes across his face and feel the juice run down his chin, a destiny he is not to achieve.

The essential reality of the Joads' predicament is demonstrated by the fact that between 1940 and 1980 the number of American farms declined from 6 million to 2¼ million. Millions of Americans in that period left their farms for life elsewhere, as the Joads left their Oklahoma home. That migration of millions of people from rural areas to the city affected the United States in many ways—increasing crime and welfare on the one hand, and providing a ready force of factory workers on the other. Few people note that, as the novel implies, we pay for our food not only at the grocery store, but also in taxes caused by crime and welfare.

It is an ironic possibility that if all the political and editorial language calling for the preservation of the family farm were printed in a single set of volumes, it might exceed the attacks on *The Grapes of Wrath*. But it is doubtful that any other American novelist has so vigorously upheld the ideal of the American family farm or so artistically protested the failure of our society to make that ideal possible in reality.

The transcendentalism in the book has led to two groundless charges by the critics, first that the book is atheistic, as expressed in the ideas of Jim Casy, and second that the book is collectivist, a code word meaning sympathetic to communism. These misreadings of the book grow out of an ignorance of transcendentalism and a misinterpretation of the call for unified action presented by the book.

The concept of the oversoul, in Emerson and in this book, is an affirmation of the universal presence of deity in all aspects of life. Emerson coined the term "oversoul" to express his understanding of the Christian tradition as he learned it from many Puritan sermons as well as from his reading of Luther, Calvin, Milton, and other theologians, as the literary historian Perry Miller has shown. Though Jim Casy probably had not read any works of theology, he does express the transcendental concept of the oversoul several times in the book in such language as this: "Maybe all men got one big soul ever'body's a part of." Transcendentalism has been criticized for its vagueness, but rightly or wrongly, it is an effort to assert that spiritual values are present in, and ultimately control, the material reality of the visible universe. It is clearly not the intent of Emerson nor of Jim Casy to deny the existence of deity. The charge of atheism is often made by those who say, "If you don't accept my definition of God, you must be an atheist." Neither Emerson nor Jim Casy would have agreed that they were atheists.

In fact the four major characters, Ma Joad, Tom, Jim Casy, and Rose of Sharon represent Steinbeck's effort to dramatize Biblical and Christian values in a realistic way among an unlikely group of poor and deprived persons. Ma Joad is one of the few saints in American literature. The qualities of saintliness—a cheerful and self-sacrificial life, and an understanding and consistent love for others—are realistically embodied in this portrait of a poverty stricken Oklahoma farm wife. Ma Joad's family disintegrates, her few possessions are lost, and she finds herself on the brink of starvation. Yet she does not fall into despair or bitterness but continues to respond in a helpful and life affirming way not only to the members of her own family but also to hungry neighbor children and a starving, unknown man. Ma Joad is a vivid dramatization of the "love that passeth understanding." It is hard to imagine what a truly saintly life would be like in the twentieth century. Steinbeck's imagination has given us a believable picture of a saint from an unlikely source—an Okie, an uneducated, migrant fruit picker, driven from her home to wander the land in search of a place to live.

Tom Joad illustrates the Biblical theme of growth, the Biblical assertion that the good life requires continued rebirth. Furthermore, Tom illustrates the Biblical notion that even the most unpromising persons have the possibility of a new life. Tom comes out of prison an unchanged person, selfishly individualistic, primarily interested in sex and drinking, though he does have a strong love for his family. But the events that follow, and the influence of his mother and of Jim Casy, greatly change him.

As the Joads experience the loss of their land, the breaking up of the family, near starvation, brutal treatment by police and landlords, and the death of Jim Casy, Tom grows in "wisdom and stature" to quote the Biblical phrase. When Ma Joad told Tom, "You're spoke for…" she contributed to his growth. When Jim Casy spoke of the Oversoul, Tom listened and grew out of his selfish concerns with his own satisfactions. He became aware, as his mother made clear to him, that he had to be concerned, not only for his own family's welfare, but for the welfare of all families, that the death of his sister's child was loss to all families, that the birth of a healthy child was cause for celebration by all families. He became quite willing to work for other families, even if it cost him his life, as it had cost the life of Jim Casy.

When Tom told his mother goodbye, as he set out to carry on the mission that he had learned from Jim Casy, she spoke with sorrow, "How'm I gonna know about you? They might kill ya an' I wouldn't know." But Tom tells her it doesn't matter. He explained in terms of the lesson he had learned from Casy of the Oversoul, of which all human beings are a part. Though we appear to be isolated individuals, still there is a transcendental unity that joins us:

> I'll be all aroun' in the dark. I'll be ever'where— wherever you look. Wherever they's a fight so hungry people can eat, I'll be there. Wherever they's a cop beatin' up a guy, I'll be there. If Casy knowed, why, I'll be in the way guys yell when they're mad an'—I'll be in the way kids laugh when they're hungry an' they know supper's ready. An' when our folks eat the stuff they raise an' live in the houses they build—why I'll be there. See?

Though the dialect is lower class Okie, the ideas are derived from the Gospel of John.

Some would-be censors have mistakenly asserted that Steinbeck is sympathetic to communism. Steinbeck was in fact rather conservative; he supported the war in Vietnam, for example. His insistence in several works of fiction on the right of each person to his own piece of land can hardly be reconciled with communist tendencies toward collectivist forms of agriculture. However, Steinbeck's views outside the book are irrelevant to the implications of the symbols and actions in the book. It is clearly wrong to judge a book by the actual or assumed characteristics of the author.

The call for united action which runs through the book is not to be identified with the term "collectivist" as a synonym for communist. There is a tension between the individual and the group in the book, but its reconciliation is in the traditional Western world notion of the oneness of the humankind, as for example in the famous passage from John Donne, "Never send to know for whom the bell tolls, it tolls for thee."

The book calls for unified action that will preserve the right of farmers to their own farms, that will provide food for the hungry, that will subordinate the machine to the needs of the garden and to the needs of the human beings who toil in the garden. The book's call for unified action to meet the disasters of the 1930s is no more collectivist than was the action of the colonists who dumped the tea in Boston Harbor or who took up arms at Concord to fight the redcoats. There are many illustrations in the book of the need and ability of ordinary citizens to work together in solving problems, as for example when the migrants helped each other on the journey, or maintained order in the camp. This aspect of the novel is typical of American pragmatism—not of Marxist ideas.

In the original meaning of the word, a classic is a book taught in the classroom. Steinbeck's book is certainly a classic in this sense of the word. As with a number of other classics, it is likely that many people read this book in high school. This use is appropriate because the book lends itself well to studying many aspects of American literature and life. *The Grapes of Wrath* won a Pulitzer prize in 1940 and is one of the major works of an American novelist who won the Nobel prize in 1962. It is difficult to understand how any American high school or college could forbid the teaching or use of the book while maintaining a claim to act as a proper agency for the education of the young in this democratic republic.

Source: Lee Burress, *"The Grapes of Wrath*: Preserving Its Place in the Curriculum," in *Censored Books: Critical Viewpoints,* edited by Nicholas J. Karolides, Lee Burress, and John M. Kean, Scarecrow Press, 1993, pp. 278–86.

Howard Levant

In the following excerpt, Levant discusses Steinbeck's individual and universal characterizations of the Joads.

[In *The Grapes of Wrath,* function], not mere design, is . . . evident in the use of characterization to support and develop a conflict of opposed ideas—mainly a struggle between law and anarchy. The one idea postulates justice in a moral world of love and work, identified in the past with "the people" and in the present with the government camp and finally with the union movement, since these are the modern, institutional forms the group may take. The opposed idea postulates injustice in an immoral world of hatred and starvation. It is associated with buccaneering capitalism, which, in violent form, includes strikebreaking and related practices that cheapen human labor.

The Joads present special difficulties in characterization. They must be individualized to be credible and universalized to carry out their representative functions. Steinbeck meets these problems by making each of the Joads a specific individual and by specifying that what happens to the Joads is typical of the times. The means he uses to maintain these identities can be shown in some detail. The least important Joads are given highly specific tags—Grandma's religion, Grandpa's vigor, Uncle John's melancholy, and Al's love of cars and girls. The tags are involved in events; they are not inert labels. Grandma's burial violates her religion; Grandpa's vigor ends when he leaves the land; Uncle John's melancholy balances the family's experience; Al helps to drive the family to California and, by marrying, continues the family. Ma, Pa, Rose of Sharon, and Tom carry the narrative, so their individuality is defined by events rather than through events. Ma is the psychological and moral center of the family; Pa carries its burdens; Rose of Sharon means to ensure its physical continuity; and Tom becomes its moral conscience. On the larger scale, there is much evidence that what happens to the family is typical of the times. The interchapters pile up suggestions that "the whole country is moving" or about to move. The Joads meet many of their counterparts or outsiders who are in sympathy with their ordeal; these meetings reenforce the common bond of "the people." Both in the interchapters and the narrative, the universal, immediate issue is survival—a concrete universal.

On the other hand, the individualized credibility of the Joads is itself the source of two difficulties: the Joads are too different, as sharecroppers, to suggest a universal or even a national woe, and they speak an argot that might limit their universal quality. Steinbeck handles these limitations with artistic license. The narrative background contains the Joads' past; their experience as a landless proletariat is highlighted in the narrative foreground. The argot is made to seem a typical language within the novel in three ways: It is the major language; people who are not Okies speak variations of their argot; and that argot is not specialized in its relevance, but is used to communicate the new experiences "the people" have in common as a landless proletariat. However, because these solutions depend on artistic license, any tonal falseness undermines severely the massive artistic truthfulness the language is intended to present. So the overly editorial tone in several of the interchapters has a profoundly false linguistic ring, although the tonal lapse is limited and fairly trivial in itself.

The Joads are characterized further in comparison with four Okie types who refuse to know or are unable to gain the knowledge the family derives from its collective experience. They are the stubborn, the dead, the weak, and the backtrackers; they appear in the novel in that order.

Muley Graves is the stubborn man, as his punning name suggests. He reveals himself to Tom and Casy near the beginning of the novel. His refusal to leave Oklahoma is mere stubbornness; his isolation drives him somewhat mad. He is aware of a loss of reality, of "jus' wanderin' aroun' like a damn ol' graveyard ghos'," and his blind violence is rejected from the beginning by the strongest, who oppose his pessimism with an essential optimism.

Deaths of the aged and the unborn frame the novel. Grandpa and Grandma are torn up by the roots and die, incapable of absorbing a new, terrible experience. Rose of Sharon's baby, born dead at the end of the novel, is an index of the family's ordeal and a somewhat contrived symbol of the necessity to form the group.

The weak include two extremes within the Joad family. Noah Joad gives up the struggle to survive; he finds a private peace. His character is shadowy, and his choice is directed more clearly by Steinbeck than by any substance within him. Connie has plenty of substance. He is married to Rose of Sharon and deserts her because he has no faith in the family's struggle to reach California. His faith is absorbed in the values of "the Bank," in getting on, in money, in any abstract goal. He wishes to learn about technology in order to rise in the world. He does not admire technique for itself, as Al does. He is a sexual performer, but he loves no one. Finally, he wishes that he had stayed behind in Oklahoma and taken a job driving a tractor. In short, with Connie, Steinbeck chooses brilliantly to place a "Bank" viewpoint within the family. By doing so, he precludes a simplification of character and situation, and he endorses the complexity of real people in the real world. (*In Dubious Battle* is similarly free of schematic characterization.) In addition, the family's tough, humanistic values gain in credibility by their contrast with Connie's shallow, destructive modernity. The confused gas station owner and the pathetic one-eyed junkyard helper are embodied variations on Connie's kind of weakness. Al provides an important counterpoint. He wants to leave the family at last, like Connie, but duty and love force him to stay. His hard choice points the moral survival of the family and measures its human expense.

The Joads meet several backtrackers. The Wilsons go back because Mrs. Wilson is dying; the Joads do not stop, in spite of death. The ragged man's experience foreshadows what the Joads find in California; but they keep on. Some members of the Joad family think of leaving but do not, or they leave for specific reasons—a subtle variation on backtracking. Al and Uncle John wish deeply at times to leave, but they stay; Tom leaves (as Casy does) but to serve the larger, universal family of the group. Backtracking is a metaphor, then, a denial of life, but always a fact as well. The factual metaphor is deepened into complexity because the Joads sympathize with the backtrackers' failure to endure the hardships of the road and of California, in balance with where they started from—the wasteland—while knowing they cannot accept that life-denying solution. All of these choices are the fruit of the family's experience.

A fifth group of owners and middle-class people are accorded no sympathetic comprehension, as contrasted with the Joads, and, as in *In Dubious Battle,* their simply and purely monstrous characterization is too abstract to be fully credible. The few exceptions occur in highly individualized scenes or episodes (Chapter XV is an example) in which middle-class "shitheels" are caricatures of the bad guys, limited to a broad contrast with the good guys (the truck drivers, the cook), who are in sympathy with a family of Okies. This limitation has the narrative advantage of highlighting the importance and vitality of the Okies to the extent that they seem by right to belong in the context of epic materials, but the disadvantage of shallow characterization is severe. Steinbeck can provide a convincing detailed background of the conditions of the time; he cannot similarly give a rounded, convincing characterization to an owner or a disagreeable middle-class person.

On the whole, then, fictive strength and conviction are inherent in the materials of *The Grapes of Wrath.* The noticeable flaws are probably irreducible aspects of the time context and of narrative shorthand counterpointed by a complex recognition of human variety in language and behavior.

Source: Howard Levant, *The Novels of John Steinbeck: A Critical Study*, University of Missouri Press, 1974, pp. 104-108.

Sources

Charles Angoff, review of *The Grapes of Wrath,* in *North American Review,* Summer, 1939, p. 387.

Malcolm Cowley, review of *The Grapes of Wrath,* in *New Republic,* May 3, 1939, p. 382.

Clifton Fadiman, review of *The Grapes of Wrath,* in *New Yorker,* April 15, 1939, p. 101.

Joseph Henry Jackson, review of *The Grapes of Wrath,* in *New York Herald Tribune Books,* April 16, 1939, p. 3.

Louis Kronenberger, review of *The Grapes of Wrath,* in *Nation,* April 15, 1939.

Burton Roscoe, "Excuse It, Please," *Newsweek,* May 1, 1939, p. 38.

Edward Weeks, review of *The Grapes of Wrath,* in *Atlantic Monthly,* June, 1939.

For Further Study

Frederick I. Carpenter, "The Philosophical Joads," in *College English,* Vol. 2, January, 1941, pp. 324-25.
    Carpenter describes the origins of Steinbeck's social philosophy in American thought from Ralph Waldo Emerson to William James.

Chester E. Eisinger, "Jeffersonian Agrarianism in *The Grapes of Wrath,*" in *University of Kansas City Review,* Vol. 14, Winter, 1947, pp. 149-54.
    The critic discusses the relationships between people and the land and how these relationships have changed in the twentieth century.

Joseph Eddy Fontenrose, *John Steinbeck: An Introduction and Interpretation,* Barnes & Noble, 1963.
    The critic discusses the novel's biblical references, its relation to myth, and its stylistic devices.

Warren French, editor, *A Companion to* The Grapes of Wrath, Penguin, 1989.
    A selection of criticism and interpretations of the novel.

Howard Levant, *The Novels of John Steinbeck: A Critical Study,* University of Missouri Press, 1974.
    A collection of essays on Steinbeck's novels. Levant examines the role of symbolism and allegory in *The Grapes of Wrath.*

Peter Lisca, *The Wide World of John Steinbeck,* Rutgers University Press, 1958.
    Lisca is an important critic of Steinbeck and is knowledgeable about his life and works. His readings of the novel range from Steinbeck's use of symbols and political thought to his work with the migrants.

Paul McCarthy, *John Steinbeck,* Ungar, 1980.
    Among other things, the critic discusses Steinbeck's biblical references and the styles of discourse he uses in the novel.

Harry Thornton Moore, *The Novels of John Steinbeck: A First Critical Study,* Kennikat Press, 1968.
    Moore discusses how the novel helped the migrant workers and compares this to other works of literature that have had social impact.

Martin Staples Shockly, "The Reception of *The Grapes of Wrath* in Oklahoma," in *American Literature,* Vol. 15, January, 1954, pp. 351-61.
    The critic notes how and why the citizens of Oklahoma were offended by the novel.

John Steinbeck, *Working Days: The Journals of "The Grapes of Wrath,"* edited by Robert DeMott, Penguin, 1989.
    Steinbeck's journal entries recording his thoughts and the physical exhaustion he endured while writing his novel.

David Wyatt, *New Essays on "The Grapes of Wrath,"* Cambridge University Press, 1990.
    Wyatt provides an overview of criticism on the novel from 1940–1989.

The Hitchhiker's Guide to the Galaxy

Douglas Adams
1979

When *The Hitchhiker's Guide to the Galaxy* was first broadcast as a 12-part radio series on the British Broadcasting System in 1978, it was successful. No one could have guessed, though, that it would mushroom into a multimedia phenomenon that would encompass five novels, a television series, a stage production, and, more than twenty years later, dozens of websites created by devotees who could not get enough of its bizarre universe. Douglas Adams's novel based on the series, *The Hitchhiker's Guide to the Galaxy* concerns the exploits of Arthur Dent, an average British citizen who gets caught up in a myriad of space adventures when his house, and then the Earth, is demolished. With no planet to call home, he is left to hitchhike through space with his friend Ford Prefect, whom he thought was an out-of-work actor, but who is really a researcher for the intergalactic guidebook named in the title. Adams's book is one in which literally anything can happen, with the only rule being that what comes next will probably be the last thing the reader would expect and is bound to be amusing.

Author Biography

Douglas Adams was born in 1952, in Cambridge, England. He attended school at John's College in Cambridge, where he began his career writing comedy sketches, and received his master of arts degree. In 1978 he began writing radio scripts for the British Broadcasting System. One of the se-

Douglas Adams

ries he created was *The Hitchhiker's Guide to the Galaxy,* which he produced and wrote. The series ran in twelve installments in 1978. For two years he was a script editor and writer for the world-renowned, long-running *Dr. Who* television show.

Because of the popularity *The Hitchhiker's Guide* had on radio, a publishing house approached Adams to turn the series into a novel—up to that point, he had never even considered writing a novel. The book sold an astounding 100,000 copies in the first month of its publication in 1979. *The Hitchhiker's Guide to the Galaxy* has inspired four sequels—*The Restaurant at the End of the Universe; Life, The Universe and Everything; So Long, and Thanks for All the Fish;* and *Mostly Harmless.* Collectively, more than fourteen million copies of the five books have been sold. Because of the huge popularity of *The Hitchhiker's Guide to the Galaxy,* it has also been adapted to a stage play, a television series, and a computer game, and the scripts from the original radio series have been published.

Douglas Adams has also written another science-fiction series that is similar in style to *The Hitchhiker's Guide* books. In *Dirk Gently's Holistic Detective Agency* (1987) and *The Long Dark Tea-Time of the Soul* (1988), Dirk Gently, a time-hopping detective, encounters a range of humanity

that includes troglodytes, Norse gods, and the ghost of poet Samuel Taylor Coleridge. In spite of his success as a novelist, Adams thinks of himself as a humor writer, but he is serious about environmental concerns: he has donated his talents to a number of charities and has cowritten a book called *Last Chance to See* about places and animals in Indonesia, Zaire, New Zealand, China, and Mauritius that are being destroyed by industrialization.

Plot Summary

Earth

As *The Hitchhiker's Guide to the Galaxy* opens, Arthur Dent wakes to discover bulldozers ready to tear his house down in order to build a freeway bypass. He goes out and lies in front of the bulldozers. The foreman cannot convince Arthur to move. The foreman insists that the plans have been on display for months and that Arthur could have filed a complaint if he wanted to, but Arthur says he knew nothing about the plans until the day before, and when he did learn of them, he found them "displayed" in a locked file cabinet in the dark basement of the local planning office.

Ford Prefect is a friend of Arthur's. Arthur doesn't realize that his friend is an alien who has been stranded on Earth for fifteen years. He is a researcher for *The Hitchhiker's Guide to the Galaxy,* a book explaining how to travel the galaxy on less than thirty Altairian dollars a day. Ford drops by Arthur's house and asks Arthur to join him for a drink. Ford manages to convince the foreman to take Arthur's place lying in the mud so that the house will not be torn down. Once in the bar, Ford explains to the disbelieving Arthur that the world is about to end.

Overhead, huge yellow spacecrafts are hovering, but no one on earth notices, except for Ford Prefect. The ships are Vogon spacecrafts, and the Vogons announce to Earth that they are there to demolish the planet in order to build a hyperspatial express route, as stated in plans that have been on display in the local planning department on Alpha Centauri for fifty years. The Vogons destroy the earth.

The Heart of Gold-*1*

Meanwhile on the opposite spiral arm of the galaxy, Zaphod Beeblebrox, the two-headed President of the Imperial Galactic Government, is attending the unveiling of the *Heart of Gold* ship, a top-secret project that is only today being revealed to the public. Zaphod steals the ship, taking with him Trillian, a girl he recently picked up at a party on Earth.

Hitchhiking

Seconds before Earth is destroyed, Ford hitches a lift on one of the Vogon ships, taking Arthur with him. The Vogons hate hitchhikers, but luckily they employ the Dentrassis people as their caterers, and the Dentrassis love to annoy the Vogons, so they gladly picked up the hitchhikers and hid them in a small cabin in the ship. Ford explains this to Arthur, and hands him *The Hitchhiker's Guide to the Galaxy* so that he can learn more. He also puts a Babel fish in Arthur's ear. The fish allows Arthur to understand any language.

The Vogons discover Ford and Arthur. They torture the hitchhikers by reading them Vogon poetry. Then they throw them off the ship. According to *The Hitchhiker's Guide to the Galaxy,* it is possible to survive in deep space for thirty seconds if you hold your breath, but it is highly improbable that one will be picked up by another ship during those thirty seconds. Twenty-nine seconds after being thrown into deep space, Arthur and Ford are rescued.

The Heart of Gold-*2*

Arthur and Ford are picked up by the *Heart of Gold,* which is powered by the Infinite Improbability Drive. Once the ship is out of improbability drive, Trillian and Zaphod order a depressed robot named Marvin to fetch the hitchhikers and to bring them to the control cabin. Ford already knows Zaphod because they are cousins. Arthur already knows Zaphod and Trillian because he was at the party where Zaphod picked up Trillian, also an earthling, after Arthur had spent the whole night trying to talk to her.

They all retire to separate cabins to sleep and think about the day's events. In the middle of the night, however, they reconvene in the control cabin, where Zaphod reveals that he found the planet Magrathea.

Magrathea

Magrathea was once the home of an industry that built custom-designed planets for the very wealthy. When the wealthy ran out of money, Magrathea disappeared. Ford does not believe that it ever existed. As they approach the planet they hear an answering machine on the planet announce that Magrathea is temporarily closed for business.

Subsequent recordings ask them to leave, and then inform them that two guided missiles are headed towards their ship. They attempt to evade the missiles, and finally Arthur turns on the improbability drive.

The ship continues on as though nothing has happened, except that its interior has been redesigned. The missiles have turned into a bowl of petunias and a whale, both of which fall to the planet below. The ship lands. Zaphod, Ford, Trillian, Arthur, and Marvin (the depressed robot) all exit the ship, Trillian pausing only briefly to bemoan the fact that the white mice she brought with her from earth have escaped. They find the planet barren and desolate, but the whale's impact has opened a crater into the surface, and Zaphod, Ford, and Trillian set off to explore this, leaving Arthur and Marvin on the surface.

While heading down the passageway Zaphod reports that he has discovered that his brains have been tampered with and that the person who did this left the initials "Z. B." burned into the synapses. Before he can say more, a door shuts behind them, and gas begins to pour into the chamber.

Meanwhile on the surface, Arthur encounters a Magrathean named Slartibartfast, who takes Arthur to the factory floor of the planet and shows him that a new earth is being built. The original Earth, he explains, was actually an organic computer commissioned by mice, who ran the planet and used it to conduct experiments on men. Because Arthur looks confused he explains further. Long ago some very intelligent beings had designed a computer to figure out the answer to the big question of life, the universe, and everything. The computer took seven-and-a-half million years to conclude that the answer was forty-two. Unfortunately it was not able to come up with the precise question for which this was an answer. But it designed another computer that could find the question. That computer was Earth, and all the creatures living on it during its ten million-year program were part of the computer, except for the mice, who were the creatures running the computer. Unfortunately, the earth had been destroyed only minutes before it came up with the correct answer, and so the mice needed a new computer.

After Zaphod, Ford, and Trillian wake up and recover from the gas, they discuss Zaphod's brain. Zaphod believes that he altered his own brain, but he does not know why. A man enters and announces that the mice will see them now.

Arthur is also brought to see the mice. He finds his friends sitting at a table along with Trillian's mice. The mice inform him that they want his brain as they think it may have the question encoded in it. They have been asked to appear on a television show to reveal the question. Arthur and his friends try to escape, but the doorway is blocked by armed guards. Just then an alarm sounds and a voice warns that a hostile ship has just landed on the planet. In the confusion Arthur and his friends escape. The mice decide to make up a question.

The intruders, however, turn out to be cops after Zaphod. They fire on Zaphod and the others until suddenly their life support systems fail. Zaphod, Ford, Trillian and Arthur return to their ship, where they find Marvin, who explains that the cops' ship committed suicide when he talked to it. They leave Magrathea, and Ford suggests that they stop at the Restaurant at the End of the Universe for a bite.

Hitchhiking was very common in the 1970s. Pictured here, a hitchhiker headed for Big Sur in 1972.

Characters

Zaphod Beeblebrox

Zaphod is described as having two heads and three arms, the third arm having been attached "to improve his ski-boxing." As the President of the Imperial Galactic Government, Zaphod was presiding over a ceremony unveiling the *Heart of Gold,* which was the first ship to run on Infinite Improbability Drive, when, on impulse, he paralyzed all of the onlookers and stole the ship.

Zaphod is not sure what compels him to do the things he does. For most of the book he assumes that his freewheeling, happy-go-lucky personality drives him to seek danger and allows him to talk his way out of it. "And then whenever I stop to think—why did I want to do something?—how did I work out how to do it?—I get a very strong desire just to stop thinking about it." Thinking about this, he runs a brain scan on himself, to see if someone else has put ideas into his mind: after careful searching, he finds that his brain has been tampered with, and that the culprit signed his initials. They are his own initials, indicating that he was the one who altered his own brain, without knowing it. He is convinced that he had himself made President of the Galaxy just to steal the *Heart of Gold* and travel to Magrathea, but he does not have a clue as to why it was necessary to do that.

Arthur Dent

Arthur was born and raised on Earth, and he is the book's protagonist. When the novel begins, Arthur wakes up to find that bulldozers outside of his house in England are ready to demolish it so that a bypass for the expressway can be built. While he is trying to stop the demolition by lying in the way of the trucks, his friend Ford Prefect comes and convinces him to go to the pub with him. It turns out that a similar event is happening on a much larger scale—that the Vogon race is about the demolish the Earth in order to build a new bypass—and that the beer that Arthur drank at the pub was necessary to prepare his muscles for space travel.

Arthur's main function in the novel is that of an observer. He is the one to ask questions, to bring out facts that the other characters are already familiar with. Throughout the novel, Arthur is referred to derogatorily as "Earthman" and "Monkey Man," the latter because of humans' relationship to their ancestors, the primates.

Eddie

Eddie is the computer on board the *Heart of Gold.* He is as annoyingly cheerful as Marvin is depressed. As the ship plummets toward the surface of Magrathea, for example, the crew is terrified, but Eddie sings a happy song, interrupting itself frequently to tell them how many seconds there are until impact. Later, Zaphod programs it with an "emergency back-up personality," but that personality is whiny and argumentative.

Flook

One of the computer programmers who was responsible for programming Deep Thought, the second greatest computer in the Universe of Time and Space, to solve the ultimate question of life, the universe and everything.

Prostetnic Vogon Jeltz

The commander of the Vogon ship that provides Arthur and Ford an escape from the destruction of Earth. He first tortures the stowaways by reading his awful Vogon poetry to them, then orders them thrown out of the ship into space.

Loonquawl

One of the officials in charge of the ceremony on the Great and Hopefully Enlightening Day, when Deep Thought, after seven and a half million years of computation, is supposed to reveal the Answer.

Lunkwill

One of the two computer programmers who was responsible for programming Deep Thought, the second greatest computer in the Universe of Time and Space, to solve the ultimate question of life, the universe and everything.

Majikthise

The elder philosopher from Cruxwan University. At a ceremony when the computer is ready to give its answer to the question of life, the universe and everything, Vroomfondel and Majikthise are honored as "the Most Truly Interesting Pundits the Universe has ever known."

Marvin

A robot, referred to sometimes as the Paranoid Android, Marvin is a prototype of the Sirius Cybernetics Corporation's new Genuine People Personality feature: unfortunately, the personality he has been given is terminally depressed. He is capable of solving complicated problems when asked, but he is also inclined to complain when asked to do the simplest tasks.

Media Adaptations

- *The Hitchhiker's Guide to the Galaxy.* Videocassette. Six-episode British Broadcasting Corp. (BBC) Television series. BBC Video/CBS Fox, 1981.

- *The Hitchhiker's Guide to the Galaxy.* Audiocassette. Read by Stephen Moore. Ontario: Music for Pleasure Ltd., 1981.

- *The Restaurant at the End of the Universe.* Audiocassette. Read by Stephen Moore. Ontario: Music for Pleasure Ltd., 1983.

- *Life, the Universe and Everything.* Audiocassette. Read by Stephen Moore. Ontario: Music for Pleasure Ltd., 1984.

- *So Long, and Thanks for All the Fish.* Audiocassette. Read by Douglas Adams. Beverly Hills, CA: Dove Audio Books, 1992.

- *Mostly Harmless.* Audiocassette. Read by Douglas Adams. Beverly Hills, CA: Dove Audio Books, 1993.

- *The Hitchhiker's Guide to the Galaxy: The Complete Audio Books.* Set of four compact discs. Beverly Hills, CA: Dove Audio Books, 1998.

Tricia McMillan

See Trillian

Benjy Mouse

The mice of planet Earth are revealed to actually be from the ancient race that commissioned the Magratheans to create the Earth. Slartibartfast explains: "They are merely a protrusion into our dimension of vastly hyperintelligent pandimensional beings." When they find out that Arthur Dent was born on the planet and lived there up until a few minutes before its destruction, they offer to buy his brain in order to read the information imprinted there.

Frankie Mouse

The mice of planet Earth are revealed to actually be from the ancient race that commissioned the Magratheans to create the Earth. When they find out that Arthur Dent was born on the planet and lived there up until a few minutes before its destruction, they offer to buy his brain in order to read the information imprinted there.

The Paranoid Android

See Marvin

Phouchg

One of the officials in charge of the ceremony on the Great and Hopefully Enlightening Day, when Deep Thought is supposed to reveal the Answer.

Ford Prefect

Ford is a researcher for *The Hitchhiker's Guide to the Galaxy*. For years, he traveled from planet to planet by begging free rides, but as the novel starts he has been stranded on Earth for fifteen years. On Earth, he assumed the name Ford Prefect, thinking that it would allow him to blend in (although his cousin, whom he knew in childhood, calls him "Ford" in a later chapter, an inconsistency that is not explained). His disguise on Earth, that of an out-of-work actor, has satisfied the curiosity of people who might otherwise wonder about him. Because he is mostly used to introduce the concept of space travel and of *The Hitchhiker's Guide to the Galaxy* to Arthur, Ford's role in the novel drops off sharply in the book's second half.

L. Prosser

Mr. Prosser is a descendent of Genghis Khan, although he does not know it. He is in charge of the demolition crew sent to destroy Arthur Dent's house.

Slartibartfast

Described as a very old man, Slartibartfast is a resident of Magrathea, the planet where other planets are created. He is a planet designer, specializing in coastlines. He won an award for his work on Norway on the original Earth, and he has designed Africa on the replacement Earth with fjords—"I happen to like them," he explains, "and I'm old-fashioned enough to think that they give a lovely baroque feel to a continent."

Trillian

Trillian is a girl that Zaphod Beeblebrox picked up at a party on Earth, while she was talking to Arthur Dent. She is introduced in the novel as being "slim, darkish, humanoid, with long waves of black hair, an odd little knob of a nose and ridiculously brown eyes." She travels with Zaphod and is with him when he steals the *Heart of Gold*. The odds against picking up Arthur and Ford floating in space as they did are the same as her phone number on Earth.

Vroomfondel

Vroomfondel is the younger philosopher from Cruxwan University. Vroomfondel and Majikthise are honored as "the Most Truly Interesting Pundits the Universe has ever known."

Themes

Absurdity

One of the guiding principles of *The Hitchhiker's Guide to the Galaxy* is that of absurdity, of things happening randomly without cause or meaning. This does not mean that the whole book is a series of events that occur in random order. Most of the extreme examples of meaninglessness, in fact, do have a cause—they are the products of the Infinite Improbability Drive on the *Starship Heart of Gold*. The fairly logical explanation of the Improbability Drive in Chapter 10 allows the novel to introduce its most fantastic oddities and coincidences.

For instance, the *Heart of Gold* picks up Arthur Dent and Ford Prefect when they are dangling in space because it is highly improbable it would happen. The same force makes Arthur's limbs dissolve and turns Ford into a penguin; it redecorates the bridge of the ship with mirrors and potted plants; and it causes a whale to materialize in the skies above Magrathea. All of these events are notable for being shockingly unpredictable. These elements of absurdity would not have nearly as much impact if they occurred in an atmosphere of total absurdity, but the novel highlights them by placing them alongside of a struggle for reason, which makes the lack of reason stand out. Characters are constantly trying to explain the sense of their actions, ignoring the chaos around them.

This pattern is established in the opening chapter, with the demolition crew coming to take down

Arthur Dent's house. While Mr. Prosser is convinced that Arthur was given a fair and sensible warning of the demolition, to Arthur the fact that the plans for destruction were "on display" in a locked filing cabinet in a disused lavatory in the darkened, stairless cellar of the planning office, behind a sign reading "Beware of the Leopard," represents an absurd form of "giving notice." Throughout the book, bureaucratic thinking struggles against the natural absurdity of the universe and often creates its own, even more frustrating, kind of absurdity.

Nature and Its Meaning

Rather than being a source of meaning, as is frequently assumed, humanity is presented in this book as a taker of meaning, acting out the roles that are assigned by the animals around us. This is most evident in the interactions with the laboratory mice: scientists believe that they are manipulating the mice's behaviors in order to learn more about nature, but the mice are actually manipulating the scientists' behaviors to learn more about humans. To these mice, the meaning of the Earth and its ten-million-year history comes down to one particular instant, when, at a pre-programmed date and time, Earth will produce the Question to the Answer.

To the dolphins, the second most intelligent species on the planet (ahead of humanity), human life is worth saving, but when humans misinterpret their warnings of the coming cataclysm—whistling and backward somersaults—for tricks, the dolphins get into the spaceship they have constructed and leave. Even the topography of Earth has a meaning that is vastly different than what is usually ascribed to it by humans. The fjords of Norway, for example, are not a result of glacial development, but they instead have the appearance that they do because they were designed by Slartibartfast, who happens to like making fjords and in fact won several design awards for his work. In this way, the novel tells its readers that all of the things in the natural world do have a particular meaning, just as the greatest thinkers are prone to speculate, but that humans would never to be able to determine these meanings with the limited information at hand.

Permanence

The book begins with what would ordinarily be considered the end of all that we know—the destruction of the Earth—but then it goes on to explain a broader context in which the Earth's existence played only a small part. The Earth came into existence because it was manufactured by the

Topics for Further Study

- Make up a work order for the Magratheans, explaining the kind of world you would like them to build. Be specific about the kinds of geographical features and animals you would like to see, and explain why.

- *The Hitchhiker's Guide to the Galaxy* summarizes the whole Earth with only two words: "mostly harmless." Write up an extended entry for a guidebook that will explain your town in detail to people from other planets.

- Write a poem that you think might have been written by Paula Nancy Millstone Jennings of Greenbridge, Essex, England, whose work is identified in the novel as the worst in the universe. Explain the elements of your poem that you think make it so terrifyingly awful.

- Suppose that the novel is right in saying that humans are not in control of Earth, but wrong in believing that either mice or dolphins are the most intelligent animals on the planet. Which animals do you think might actually be an intelligent species from another world, controlling human behavior wordlessly? Why do you think so?

Magratheans, who would never have done it without being paid for the job. So its destruction, like the demolition of Arthur Dent's house or the crumpling of a piece of paper, is irrelevant to the people who have used it. With this perspective of Earth, and the limitless varieties of life forms that Arthur Dent encounters in his travels, the fact that Earth's existence is not permanent is treated as insignificant.

Culture Clash

In a sense, this novel presents the entire universe as belonging to a different culture that citizens of Earth just do not understand. The non-Earth characters, from Vogsphere, Betelgeuse, and Magrathea, all seem to understand each other, even in cases where they have not been introduced to each other's culture before. For example, both Ford Prefect and Zaphod Beeblebrox believe the planet of Magrathea to be a myth, but soon after they arrive they accept it for what it is with little further conflict. Even Trillian, who was born on Earth but has been traveling the universe for roughly six months more than Arthur Dent, is unshaken by the strange occurrences that she observes.

There are several explanations for the different attitudes displayed. One is that Earth is an insular culture, unfamiliar with the other races existing throughout the universe, and so Earth people are more prone to be surprised by new circumstances and more awkward in their reactions. Another might be that the customs of Earth people are, in general, uptight, and look even more so when placed beside the carefree attitudes of the rest of the occupants of the universe. Strategically, it helps this work as a comedy to have Arthur Dent come from a repressive culture and to have his sensibilities and drive for order offended by the casualness of those he meets. This follows a comic tradition at least as old as Shakespeare that pits sophisticates against the good-natured people with simple common sense.

Style

Parody

The Hitchhiker's Guide to the Galaxy is a parody of traditional science fiction adventure stories. A parody is a work that takes the conventions and rules of one form and uses them for comic effect. It is distinguished from a satire in that satire usually tries to point out human folly and vices in order to reform them, while the subject of parody is the style of writing itself.

Traditional science fiction takes the reader, often through the adventures of a common person like Arthur Dent, into a world where the universal laws of physics as we know them have been stretched beyond current capacities. Space travel is often associated with science fiction because introducing beings from other planets allows writers to account for the fact that they are able to manipulate reality in ways that are currently unheard of; time travel is often an important element for the same reason. Most good science fiction uses the different physical rules it presents to explore constants in behavior, while most bad science fiction introduces bizarre elements for their own sake, just to show off the author's active imagination. This book derives its humor from reversing the usual results that readers have come to expect.

For example, readers might expect the Earth to be destroyed in a war, so its destruction is presented here as a result of petty bureaucracy; the President of the Galaxy is not a fearsome sovereign but a joy-riding party animal; traveling through space, which has been the goal of multi-billion-dollar government programs, is presented as hitchhiking; something usually as insignificant as bad poetry is one of the most terrifying weapons used in the book. Traditional science fiction stories expend much energy explaining how things work under the rules they have created: this story adds preposterous elements at will, and does not insult its readers' intelligence by pretending that they make sense.

Episodic Plot

The story that this book is based on was originally written as a 12-part radio series for the British Broadcasting System. Being presented in installments created certain requirements for its plot structure. The action had to reach a peak every so often, raising the curiosity of listeners who would not be able to simply turn the page to find out what would happen next. At the same time, the individual segments each had to tell an independent story, in case someone heard just one episode in the middle of it all.

When adapting the series to a novel, Douglas Adams rewrote the story so that it would not just read like a string of events but more like a story; still, signs of the original structure are not hard to find. Points of heightened interest, such as when Arthur and Ford are seemingly doomed to drift in space, or Zaphod Beeblebrox's teaser at the end of a chapter that foreshadows description of the most improbable planet that ever existed," show the original strategy meant to hold readers' interest for a week.

Also, instead of following one broad stretch, the plot follows several distinct, sequential arcs: the destruction of Earth; the theft of the *Heart of Gold;* the encounter with Prostetnic Vogon Jeltz; the rescue from space; the approach to Magrathea and escaping its attack; the encounter with Slartibartfast; and the explanation of the ancient race seeking the answer to the Ultimate Question. Any of these episodes could be skipped without doing sustained damage to one's understanding of the whole story.

Compare & Contrast

- **1979:** Iranian leader Mohamed Reza Shah Pahlevi fled the country. Shiite Muslim leader Ayatollah Ruholla Khomeini, returning from fifteen years' exile, took *de facto* control of Iran. In November, workers at the American embassy were taken hostage by terrorists with state backing. Throughout the 444 days they were held, American morale dropped.

  Today: Having played a key role in the 1991 international military action against Iran's neighbor Iraq, the United States government is less hesitant to become involved in international conflicts.

- **1979:** Disco, a musical trend popular in urban areas throughout the mid-seventies, was at its peak. Big hair, big collars, and platform shoes were popular across the country.

  Today: Because of the changing nature of fashion, today's trends are destined to look ridiculous to people twenty years from now.

- **1979:** Comedy was very popular: *Monty Python's Flying Circus,* a British show from the early 1970s, was finishing its first run on American television; the young unknowns who starred on *Saturday Night Live* were making movies; and comedians like Richard Pryor and Steve Martin were playing to capacity crowds at stadiums.

  Today: The proliferation of comedy shows on cable television and of franchised comedy clubs in malls have diluted the impact and popularity of comedy in America.

- **1979:** A partial meltdown at the Three Mile Island nuclear power plant in Harrisburg, Pennsylvania forced an evacuation of thousands of nearby residents and left Americans fearful of radiation poisoning from a larger catastrophe.

  Today: The larger catastrophe that Americans feared in 1979 has not happened in the U.S., but some experts say that it becomes increasingly likely as the nation's nuclear power plants age.

Anthropomorphism

Anthropomorphism is the practice, common in literature, of giving human thoughts, motives and behavior patterns to non-human things, such as animals or inanimate objects. It is most evident here in the thoughts that are ascribed to animals. This does not apply to the mice, because it is explained that they are not really mice but humanoid aliens in disguise. Yet no such explanation is offered to explain why the dolphins would be able or willing to conceive of a warning about the Earth's impending doom, or why the sperm whale that materialized in the air would think of the extended monologue that runs through its mind in Chapter 18.

In addition, the book derives continuous humor from the human-like personalities of the chronically depressed robot, given the common human name Marvin, and from Eddie, the sickeningly cheerful computer that becomes whiny after

Zaphod activates its "back-up personality." Science fiction stories often speculate that advanced civilizations will program computers to interact with humans on human terms, which would mean that they would display some sort of personality—as the book explains, Sirius Cybernetics Corporation had programmed Marvin with a Genuine People Personality. *The Hitchhiker's Guide* takes that assumption to an extreme by giving the machines undesirable personalities.

Historical Context

Space Exploration

By the time *The Hitchhiker's Guide to the Galaxy* was published in 1979, many people had tired of the American and Soviet race for dominance in space. Twenty years earlier, there had been

Disco dancing was one of the biggest trends of the 1970s.

excitement and anticipation in the United States, spurred on by fear that the Soviet Union would be the first country to conquer space.

The first evidence of real progress in the exploration of space was witnessed in 1957, when the citizens of the world woke up one day to find that the Soviets had put an artificial satellite, *Sputnik I,* into orbit. In many parts of the world people could step outside and, looking into the sky, watch the satellite pass by. America, which was the only other country of comparable military might to the Soviet Union, entered into a competition meant to preserve national pride, as well as to prevent the Soviets from gaining superior missile technology.

Through the 1950s the lead in the space race shifted back and forth. The Russians put a living being, a dog, into space in 1957. The U. S. Congress established The National Aeronautics and Space Agency in 1958. The first human to go into space was a Russian, in 1961; the first American went into space the following month. During the 1960s, Russia fell behind and America progressed steadily. The race was finally won on July 20, 1969 when an American was the first human being to walk on the moon. After that, both countries continued to explore space, but public interest dropped off. *Apollo* missions landed on the surface of the moon five more times; the Soviets built a space sta-

tion in 1971; an American space station, *Skylab,* was built in 1973.

Because the missions were generally successful, public interest dwindled until danger or irregularities occurred. In 1979, the most covered story in space exploration was that *Skylab* was due to fall out of orbit. Since nobody could accurately predict where it would land, the world anxiously watched forecasts for months—a far cry from the expectant days when new boundaries were being broken, new challenges being surpassed. When it did come down, it rained debris over western Australia and over the Indian Ocean, but no one was hurt by the falling wreckage.

The Internet

The basic concept of the Internet had started in 1969, when the Defense Department of the United States ordered that information that was crucial to national defense should not be held in one place where it could be vulnerable to a nuclear attack. In response to the order, the University of California at Los Angeles organized a "node," a network that could disperse information to decentralized locations. Soon, other universities linked their databases with UCLA's, as did government research facilities, so that by 1975 there were nearly 100 nodes with international connections.

At the same time, advances were being made that would bring personal computers into homes. By the 1970s, word processors using cathode ray tubes had become available, offering offices ways of handling the flow of written materials economically. In 1976, Wang Laboratories produced computers that could connect terminals within offices, while that same year Apple Computers was formed. In 1977 the Apple II personal computer became the first economically feasible computer for home use—it ran through the screen of the common television and backed up its memory on simple audio tape, but its $1300 price was much lower than anything seen up to then. In 1979, CompuServe Information Systems was launched, making on-line linkups available to people outside of the Defense Department/University system.

Critical Overview

Initially, reviewers praised *The Hitchhiker's Guide to the Galaxy,* pleased to have found a book that attempted to be humorous and was, for the most part, successful. "This hilarious and irrepressibly clever book is one of the best pieces of humor to be produced this year," applauded Rosemary Herbert in *Library Journal.*

Richard Brown, writing in *The Times Literary Supplement,* characterized Douglas Adams's writing as having "a posh-school, wide-eyed, naive manner related, perhaps, to the primitive manner currently in vogue in high-brow poetry circles." The main point of Brown's review, though, was to explore the relationship between the *Hitchhiker* books and the media, television and radio, that Adams was writing for when the books came into existence. Most reviewers categorized this book with science fiction novels and, in that context, found much to appreciate.

Because science fiction is a genre that often takes itself too seriously, critics have tended to take *The Hitchhiker's Guide to the Galaxy* and its sequels as a breath of fresh air. Lisa Tuttle, writing in the *Washington Post,* compared the book's relationship to traditional science fiction novels and concluded that "it's extremely funny—a rare and precious conjunction in a field where what usually passes as humor is a bad pun at the end of a dull story."

Like Tuttle, many reviewers saw this first book in the series as a reaction to the claustrophobic world of science fiction writing. Gerald Jonas, in *The New York Times Book Review,* pointed out that "[h]umorous science fiction novels have notoriously limited audiences; they tend to be full of 'in' jokes understandable only to those who read everything from Jules Verne to Harlan Ellison." Adams's novel, in contrast, was a "delightful exception." *Voice of Youth Advocates* reviewer M.K. Chelton felt that *The Hitchhiker's Guide* was "a bizarre, wildly funny, satiric novel," but did not feel that this made it an exception to mainstream science fiction, explaining that it had "lots of in-jokes SF fans will either love or loathe, and a free-floating irreverence which is irresistible."

As the series of books progressed and came to be known as *The Hitchhiker Trilogy* (even after the publication of the fourth and fifth novels), reviewers found it more and more resistible. They started tiring of the tricks that had won Adams their enthusiasm in the first place. John Clute, who reviewed *The Hitchhiker's Guide* for *The Magazine of Fantasy and Science Fiction,* acknowledged that the book was a joy. He also gave recognition to the less clever elements that it involved: "Given its music-hall premises, the tone of *Hitchhiker* is sometimes damagingly sophomoric, and there is a constant taint of collegiate wit in the naming of silly names and the descriptions of silly alcoholic beverages…." He went on to praise the novel as "one of the genre's rare genuinely funny books," but the elements that he pointed out tended to become more obvious to reviewers as they appeared in one book after the next.

Losing the element of surprise did not stop Adams from producing the series' fourth and fifth installments, and though reviewers, taking the series for granted, did not express further delight, there has been growing respect for Adams's growth as a novelist. While the first book in the series was appreciated for what it was not—a traditional science-fiction comedy—Adams's recent works have been praised for their characterization and plotting.

Criticism

Donna Woodford

Woodford is a doctoral candidate at Washington University. In the following essay she examines the search for the meaning of life in The Hitchhiker's Guide to the Galaxy.

What Do I Read Next?

- This book is just the first in a series about Arthur Dent, Ford Prefect, and the colorful characters that they encounter in their travels through space and time. Fans have followed them through a series of five novels, including this one, *The Restaurant at the End of the Universe* (1980), *Life, the Universe, and Everything* (1982), *So Long and Thanks for All the Fish* (1984), and *Mostly Harmless* (1992).

- For fans who have trouble keeping a handle on the characters and events in the *Hitchhiker* books, Pocket Books published a guide in 1981 that covers the original trilogy, called *Don't Panic: The Official Hitchhiker's Guide to the Galaxy Companion.*

- Mark Leyner's novels have been compared to Adams's for their unpredictability and sense of fun. His most recent, 1997's *The Tetherballs of Bouganville,* bounces through a cultural landscape strewn with markers of our time, such as scholarship awards, lethal injection, screenplay writers, supermodels and videos.

- The fiction of Kurt Vonnegut has always been admired for its ability to present a comically unreal world in a slightly plausible way. One of his early books, *Cat's Cradle* (1963), is a darkly funny story about the end of the world.

- The standard for this type of story, in which a normal person is thrown into a surreal world of tortured logic, was set in 1865, by mathematician Lewis Carroll's fantasy *Alice's Adventures in Wonderland.*

- Douglas Adams's latest achievement is a collaboration with Terry Jones, a member of the Monty Python troupe, *Starship Titanic: A Novel,* published in 1998. Adams wrote the introduction; and the idea behind the book was his—Starship Titanic is first mentioned in *Life, The Universe and Everything,* one of the original *Hitchhiker's Guide* trilogy; and Adams wrote the interactive CD-ROM of the same name. Jones wrote the actual book.

The first thing that readers and critics usually notice about Douglas Adams's novel, *The Hitchhiker's Guide to the Galaxy,* is that the book, written in a sharp and witty style, is remarkably funny. What may seem less obvious to readers, and what has often puzzled critics, is the meaning behind this light, clever exterior. David Leon Higdon has noted that imagining the end of the world has long been a tradition in science fiction, as it has been in myth and theology; and Brian Aldiss has observed the tremendous impact that the invention of bombs, which could conceivably cause the end of the world, have had on science fiction and science fiction writers. But while Adams's book does describe the destruction of the earth, his humorous, irreverent treatment of this subject does not fit neatly into the traditions described by Aldiss and Higdon.

Carl R. Kropf has suggested that the novel should be read as a mock science fiction novel that reverses the expectation readers have of science fic-

tion and "by reversing the usual conventions of the genre … also reverses its entire ideological function." In support of this theory, Kropf notes that while traditional science fiction often suggests a meaning and a purpose for human life and civilization, *The Hitchhiker's Guide to the Galaxy* and the novels which follow it do the exact opposite: "Instead of confirming that the phenomenal universe implies a meaning or purpose, they affirm its meaninglessness." While Kropf is certainly correct in noting that the novel's characters are constantly thwarted in their attempts to find meaning, this does not necessarily imply that the book as a whole affirms the meaninglessness of human life. Rather, the fact that the characters continue to search for meaning in the universe, even when they are repeatedly confronted by an apparent lack of meaning and purpose, suggests the universality of the desire to find a purpose, and ultimately, Adams's novel suggests that the purpose of life is to search for a meaningful purpose to life, and to find humor in the absurdities one encounters in the search for meaning.

It is true that meaning does seem illusive in the novel. The reader and the characters are frequently given hints that meaning exists, but those promises of meaning always prove to be deceptive. These unfulfilled promises first appear in the novel's introduction, in which the narrator describes the problem that the earth faces: "most of the people living on it were unhappy for pretty much of the time." The narrator then goes on to describe how many people suggest solutions to this problem, and how finally one girl thinks of a solution to this problem and tries to phone a friend, only to be prevented by "a terrible, stupid catastrophe." But after this lengthy description of the earth, its problem, and the girl who finally found a solution to the problem, the narrator abruptly shifts focus by saying, "this is not her story" and revealing that the story of this girl and her solution have been merely a digression from the real story. Such abruptly ended digressions are a common trope in the novel. They give the reader the sense that meaning is about to be revealed, but then the door to that meaning is closed before the reader can see through.

The Hitchhiker's Guide to the Galaxy, for which the novel is named, is another example of how meaning is promised and then denied. The fact that there is a guide to the galaxy suggests that the galaxy can be somehow understood and explained. And while *The Guide* does not promise to explain the meaning of "life, the universe, and everything" is does promise to tell you "everything you need to know about anything" and how to "see the marvels of the Universe for less that thirty Altairian dollars a day." But even this amazing guide is disappointing, since it "has many omissions and contains much that is apocryphal, or at least wildly inaccurate" and since it is "a very unevenly edited book and contains many passages that simply seemed to its editors like a good idea at the time." In fact, one of its best points is that it has the words "DON'T PANIC" inscribed on its cover in "large friendly letters," and "don't panic" is probably a good message to keep in mind when one is exploring a seemingly meaningless and incomprehensible galaxy.

Probably the best example of the constantly thwarted quest for meaning is the plight of pan-dimensional beings who build two computers in their attempt to discover the meaning of life, the universe, and everything. The first computer, Deep

Thought, takes seven and a half million years to determine that the answer to the great question is 42, but that another computer will be needed to determine what the precise question is. The second computer, Earth, spends ten-million years running a program to determine the precise question to which 42 is the answer, and minutes before the conclusion of its program Earth is destroyed by the Vogons so that they can build a hyperspatial express route that the invention of the *Heart of Gold* then makes useless and unnecessary. Each computer is built with the hope of finally understanding the meaning of life, the universe, and everything, and each time the pan-dimensional beings eagerly await the results, only to be disappointed. Even Arthur's attempt to find some meaning in this series of accidents is undercut. He suggests to Slartibartfast that:

> All this explains a lot of things. All through my life I've had this strange unaccountable feeling that something was going on in the world, something big, even sinister, and no one would tell me what it was.

But Slartibartfast quickly undercuts Arthur's attempt by telling him, "No... that's just perfectly normal paranoia. Everyone in the Universe has that." And even Arthur's suggestion that if everyone feels that way it must mean something is dismissed by Slartibartfast, who asserts that "the chances of finding out what really is going on are so absurdly remote that the only thing to do is to say hang the sense of it and just keep yourself occupied." And even Slartibartfast's philosophy of happy ignorance is undercut when Arthur asks him if he is happy and he is forced to admit, "No. That's where it all falls down, of course." Nobody in the novel seems to know what the meaning of life really is, and no amount of searching for an answer seems to lead to any revelation. Even after millions of years and two super computers, the hyper-intelligent pan-dimensional beings are no more enlightened than the Vogon guard who continues with the "mindless tedium" of "stamping around, throwing people off spaceships" and shouting, without "even knowing why he's doing it."

These continually frustrated attempts to find meaning would certainly seem to support Kropf's suggestion that the *Hitchhiker* books affirm the meaninglessness of the universe rather than finding meaning in it. But this interpretation is still too dark. In arguing that Adams's novels are actually mock science fiction, Kropf cites as a point of comparison Kurt Vonnegut's *The Sirens of Titan,* which parallels *The Hitchhiker's Guide to the Galaxy* in many ways. At the end of *The Sirens of Titan,* the protagonist, Malachi, realizes that the "purpose of human life, no matter who is controlling it, is to love whoever is around to be loved." Although it is not expressly stated, a somewhat similar purpose for life is suggested in *The Hitchhiker's Guide to the Galaxy.*

While meaning and purpose seem impossible to discover, beings of all sorts continue to search for meaning in the universe, and while no one finds a specific meaning, the only ones who are made to look really foolish are those who give up the search. The Vogon guard, for example, who decides to continue with the mindless tedium of his job so that he "can eventually get promoted to Senior Shouting Officer" seems far more pathetic than any of the people who search for meaning unsuccessfully. And the hyper-intelligent pan-dimensional beings who spend millions of years searching for the meaning of life only seem truly absurd when they decide to simply fake an answer to the question of life, the universe, and everything, because they are tired of searching:

> Well, I mean, yes, idealism, yes the dignity of pure research, yes the pursuit of truth in all its forms, but there comes a point I'm afraid where you begin to suspect that if there's any real truth, it's that the entire multidimensional infinity of the Universe is almost certainly being run by a bunch of maniacs. And if it comes to a choice between spending yet another ten million years finding that out, and on the other hand just taking the money and running, then I for one could do with the exercise.

If searching for meaning seems pointless, the decision not to search seems pathetic. Furthermore, while the meaning of life is elusive, life is not portrayed as worthless. Though Ford worries about the number of things humans don't know, he decides that he likes them, and he saves Arthur when the Earth is destroyed. While Zaphod teases Arthur about his ignorance of the ways of the universe, he does help to save Arthur from the mice. Even Slartibartfast, who does not believe in searching for the meaning of life, affirms the value of life and friendship when he saves the lives of Arthur and his friends by leaving the aircar in which they escape. It may be impossible to discover the meaning of life, but life does have value and is worth preserving. Finally, the irrepressible humor of the novel reveals a purpose for living. Although the novel portrays the destruction of the earth and a universe in which meaning seems impossible to discover, *The Hitchhiker's Guide to the Galaxy* never presents a grim or depressing view of life. Rather Adams depicts a universe full of laughable, amusing creatures and situations. If the point of life in

The Sirens of Titan is to love whoever is around to be loved, then the point of life in *The Hitchhiker's Guide to the Galaxy* is to laugh at whatever is around to be laughed at, or at least to continue searching for a point while enjoying the gifts of friendship, life, and laughter, which even a meaningless universe has to offer.

Source: Donna Woodford, in an essay for *Novels for Students,* Gale, 1999.

Richard Brown

In the following excerpt, Brown suggests that Adams's Hitchhiker's Guide *makes a successful transition from audio to printed format.*

Television and radio announcers have a distinctive but necessarily rather limited critical vocabulary. They use up all their superlatives on "gripping sagas", "action-packed crime-busters" and "uproarious, side-splitting" comedies, and have little left with which to package anything more genuinely youthful, imaginative and funny. It reflects rather badly on everyday programming that Douglas Adams's clever science-fiction comedies *The Hitch-Hiker's Guide to the Galaxy* are unfamiliar enough to be introduced into the domestic arena as "zany" and "madcap", and it is a comment on the mass audience that the enjoyment of such unexceptionable pleasures should be thought of as some kind of cult.

British programmes such as *I'm Sorry I'll Read That Again, Monty Python's Flying Circus* and *Not the Nine O'Clock News* manage to thrive on this special status—on the fact that they are held at a distance from the rest of the evening's offerings. They build up a semi-private language of stock situations, favourite satirical targets and recurring comic triggers, and have established an anarchic, facetious, though also teasingly symbiotic relationship with the fully domesticated mainstream. The good-humour of that relationship shows up clearly in the characteristic play they make with the manners and language of news-readers and announcers themselves.

There is a rich vein of satire here into which Adams's writings fall, suggesting, in general, that some science-fiction takes itself just as appallingly seriously as, and can be exposed as no more imaginative than the reading of the news....

The mini-genre is one which seems to have evolved within the electronic media. *The Hitch-Hiker's Guide,* with its clipped, up-to-date, joke-a-minute style, bristling with gimmickry and microtechnological blobs and bleeps, seemed ideally suited to radio and even more so to television, where its diagrams and print-outs have an appeal somewhere between watching Ceefax and playing Space-Invaders.

As followers will know, the formula has been transferred with some success to the printed page. This latest volume, *Life, the Universe and Everything,* is the third, following on from *The Hitch-Hiker's Guide to the Galaxy* and *The Restaurant at the End of the Universe.* This gives the publishers the opportunity to talk of a "trilogy".

The constant element in Adams's plot is the helpless, semi-clad character of Arthur Dent, last remaining inhabitant of the Earth, which has been demolished to make way for an interstellar by-pass. [In *Life, the Universe, and Everything*], Arthur and his know-all space friend Ford Prefect find themselves caught up in the malevolent plan of the rulers of the planet Krikkit to destroy everything that isn't cricket and to seize the Golden Bail that will give them great power. Meanwhile Arthur hopes to discover the Ultimate Question of Life, knowing already that the Ultimate Answer to the Question is forty-two. The pair come across a number of extra-terrestrial phenomena, such as the planet of Squornshellous Zeta, whose swamps are inhabited by mattresses, and the Campaign for Real Time. This, though, is only the plot. Much of the comedy arises from a variety of pseudo-high-tech mis-information....

The Hitch-Hiker's Guide retains its life on the page because much of this humour is primarily verbal, using mild parody, making the everyday absurd by giving it a strange name or simply by giving it a capital letter. It has an imaginative energy which derives as much from its consistent play with a cosy, familiar world—the suburban English world of cricket, dressing-gowns and by-passes—as from the extravagance of its characters and settings.

Adams's writing has a likeable, posh-school, wide-eyed, naive manner related, perhaps, to the primitive manner currently in vogue in high-brow poetic circles. It would be wrong, though, to claim too much for the books. Print shows up also the extent to which the humour depends on a limited repertoire of gimmicks, and this third volume, though by no means lacking in enthusiastic drive, does little to suggest that the idea could or should be taken much further from here.

Source: Richard Brown, "Posh-School SF," in *The Times Literary Supplement,* No. 4147, September 24, 1982, p. 1032.

Peter Kemp

In the following excerpt, Kemp offers a positive review of The Hitchhiker's Guide to the Galaxy.

Douglas Adams's book, *The Hitch-Hiker's Guide to the Galaxy*—a spin-off from his radio series—shot hilariously away from the gravity that so often weighs down modern science fiction, and proved an appropriately astronomical success. Now, he has launched a follow-up, *The Restaurant at the End of the Universe.*

It contains the same central figures: Arthur and Trillian, who escaped just before the Earth was destroyed to make way for a hyperspatial express route; Ford, who 'was in fact from a small planet somewhere in the vicinity of Betelgeuse and not from Guildford as he usually claimed'; Zaphod, rogue President of the Galaxy, 'recently voted the Worst Dressed Sentient Being in the Known Universe'; and Marvin the Paranoid Android, an oppressively depressive robot with 'this terrible pain in all the diodes down my left side'.

In *The Hitch-Hiker's Guide*—a sardonically funny exercise in galactic globe-trotting—they hurtled through space. Here, they also speed through time—finally reaching Milliways, the fabled 'Restaurant at the End of the Universe', an ultra-chic eatery boasting 'lavatory facilities for all of fifty major lifeforms' and laying on apocalypse as cabaret, since it is situated at the closing moments of the cosmos (for those who want to go to the opposite extreme, there is the Big Bang Burger Bar).

Not that Adams's characters spend much time eating. As usual, they are propelled through a series of interplanetary adventures....

What makes this book, like its predecessor, almost unputdownable is its surreal, comic creativity. Adams's galaxy blazes with spectacular phenomena like binary sunrises, and swarms with highly coloured worlds—like Golgafrincham, a planet 'rich in legend, red, and occasionally green with the blood of those who sought in days gone by to conquer her'.

To fabricate it, he has taken hints from Lewis Carroll and Edward Lear: there are logical extensions of mad premises, grotesque creatures with crazily evocative names, chattering objects, moments of satiric farce, and picturesquely absurd landscapes. The tone, though—this is often wise-guy sci-fi—owes a lot to Raymond Chandler (one of Arthur's big regrets after the Earth's destruction was that all the Bogart movies had been wiped). In the previous book, the chunky Vogon ships 'hung in the sky in much the same way that bricks don't'. Here, there are snappy bouts of repartee: the droning robot is snubbed with the line, 'Stay out of this, Marvin … this is organism talk.'

Finally, the book comes down to earth—or, in any rate, to a replica of it being repopulated by detritus from another planet: ad-men, middle-management consultants and the like. It's not the best of manoeuvres since it means that Adams's weakness—a sporadic tendency to Monty Pythonesque silliness—is given too much scope, while his genially weird inventiveness rather goes into abeyance. But for most of the book, the characters zoom exuberantly through other worlds.

Source: Peter Kemp, "Wise-Guy-Sci-Fi," in *The Listener,* Vol. 104, No. 2692, December 18-25, 1980, p. 866.

Sources

Richard Brown, "Posh-School SF," *The Times Literary Supplement,* No. 4147, September 24, 1982, p. 1032.

M. K. Chelton, in *Voya,* Vol. 3, February, 1981.

John Clute, in *The Magazine of Fantasy and Science Fiction,* Vol. 62, No. 2, February, 1982, pp. 34–5.

Rosemary Herbert, in *Library Journal,* September 15, 1980.

Gerald Jonas, in *The New York Times Book Review,* January 25, 1981, pp. 24–5.

Lisa Tuttle, "As Other Worlds Turn," *Book World—The Washington Post,* November 23, 1980, p. 6.

For Further Study

Douglas Adams, *The Original Hitchhiker Radio Scripts,* edited by Geoffrey Perkins, Harmony Books, 1985.

This book contains the scripts for the original radio show on which the novel was based; an introduction in which Adams talks about his writing; another introduction by the producer of the show, Geoffrey Perkins; and many notes about the script.

Brian W. Aldiss, introduction to *Hell's Cartographers: Some Personal Histories of Science Fiction Writers,* edited by Brian W. Aldiss and Harry Harrison, Weidenfeld and Nicolson, 1975, pp. 1–5.

Aldiss discusses the effect that the dropping of the first atomic bomb on Hiroshima had on science fiction and science fiction writers.

Thomas M. Disch, *The Dreams Our Stuff Is Made of: How Science Fiction Conquered the World,* The Free Press, 1998.

To understand how well *The Hitchhiker's Guide to the Galaxy* parodies the science fiction tradition, and how much it follows the rules that it lays out, it helps to understand what that tradition is. Disch has published in almost all genres, and he is a cult figure in science fiction.

John Griffiths, *Three Tomorrows: American, British and Soviet Science Fiction,* Barnes and Noble Books, 1980.

Although this book gives little consideration to the *Hitchhiker* phenomenon, which was relatively new when it was written, it is helpful for those interested in considering how the ideas of science fiction differ on both sides of the globe.

David Leon Higdon, "'Into the vast unknown': Directions in the Post-Holocaust Novel" in *War and Peace: Perspectives in the Nuclear Age,* edited by Ulrich Goebel and Otto Nelson, Texas Tech UP, 1988, pp. 117–24.

Higdon traces developments in Post-Holocaust fiction.

Carl R. Kropf, "Douglas Adams's 'Hitchhiker' Novels as Mock Science Fiction," *Science-Fiction Studies,* Vol. 15, No. 1, March 1988, pp. 61–70.

Kropf suggests that Adams's books could be seen as Mock Science Fiction, much as Alexander Pope's *The Dunciad* is a mock epic.

Kurt Vonnegut, *The Sirens of Titan,* Dell Publishing, 1970.

A science fiction work which shares many common plot devices and themes with *The Hitchhiker's Guide to the Galaxy.*

Kitchen

Banana Yoshimoto
1988

Kitchen is the title of a novella by Mahoko ("Banana") Yoshimoto, and it is also the name of the book containing that novella along with the novella *Moonlight Shadow.* When the book was published in Japan in 1988, it was an immediate success, propelling its author to a superstar status in the literary world that she has managed to maintain since then, due in part to her tremendous output, averaging a book a year. With the English release of *Kitchen* in 1992, her U.S. publisher gambled a fortune on pre-publication publicity, having posters of the author plastered on walls in major American cities. The book went on to be a major best-seller and "Banana-mania" eventually spread across the globe. Yoshimoto's fans tend to be fanatical in their ardor, exchanging testimonials and gossip about the author on the Internet and anxiously speculating about which novel will be the next one translated into their own language.

In the novella *Kitchen,* the elements of a typical Banana Yoshimoto work can be found. Death, the occult, sexual ambiguity, love, physical beauty, and the trials and tribulations of young adults living in the big city are themes that present themselves, to varying degrees, in most of her works of fiction. It is Yoshimoto's penchant for exploring the same territory time and again, along with her self-professed goal of providing an upbeat ending, that lead to criticism of her work as derivative and saccharine. Yet it is plain to see, from the wide range of her readership and the intensity of their devotion, that Banana Yoshimoto is a writer who has earned respect and serious consideration.

Author Biography

Banana Yoshimoto is a worldwide phenomenon, with millions of fans falling in love with her novels and waiting eagerly for the next one—a circumstance referred to on the many web pages dedicated to her as "Banana-mania." Her rise to fame came quickly and early in her life. She was born Mahoko Yoshimoto in Tokyo in 1964. Her father, Takaaki Yoshimoto, was a famous literary critic, poet, and commentator; his works were extremely influential on Japan's radical youth movement in the 1960s. She majored in arts and literature at Nihon University in Tokyo, graduating in 1987. While there, she won the Izuini Kyoka Prize, which is Nihon's Department of Arts Award, for the novella *Moonlight Shadow,* which has been published in the same volume as *Kitchen.*

In 1987, *Kitchen* was awarded the prestigious Kaien Magazine New Writers' Prize. Upon the book's first publication in 1988, it was an instant hit, selling more than two million copies and earning its author literary awards in Italy and Japan. She was twenty-four, and took the pen name "Banana" because she thought it was cute. For the U.S. edition of *Kitchen* in 1992, her publisher staged a full-out marketing blitz, which turned out to be a great success, landing the book on the best-seller lists. The book has had over sixty printings in Japan since it premiered, and has been adapted into movies twice: the first version in 1989 was quick and cheap, so in 1997 famed Chinese director Yim Ho created an art-house version that moved the story to Hong Kong and made the male lead the narrator.

Yoshimoto has had eleven novels published in Japan so far, and four have been translated into English: *Kitchen, NP, Lizard,* and *Amrita.* Her fans are devoted, but so are her detractors, calling her work slick, superficial, and driven by a standard formula. The author herself denies that her novels follow any set recipe in an attempt to keep up with her early fame. Many of the themes found in her books such as androgyny and psychic phenomena are familiar fixtures in the Japanese literary form known as *magna,* which are graphic novels similar to the comic books published in America. In Japan, *magna* account for a third of all works published. Yoshimoto explains that she does not write for editors or readers, that she does not really have anyone in mind when she writes her novels. Her influences, she says, are literary, including Truman Capote and Isaac Bashevis Singer.

Banana Yoshimoto

Plot Summary

Section 1: Kitchen

The first half of the story starts with Mikage's praise for kitchens of all kinds, clean or dirty, large or small. This becomes a description of her situation: with the death of her grandmother "the other day," Mikage is alone in the world. That situation, however, lasts only briefly, for the first plot twist appears a few pages into the novella, with the appearance of Yuichi Tanabe at her front door. Mikage does not know Yuichi, but she remembers having seen him at her grandmother's funeral, and she later remembers her grandmother having mentioned him as the nice boy who worked in the flower shop she went to every day. "I just stopped by to ask you something," he explains. "I was talking to my mother, and we were thinking that you ought to come to our house for a while." Mikage agrees to come for supper that night, and while she is there she falls in love with their kitchen and becomes fascinated with Yuichi's mother, Eriko, who was his father before having a sex-change operation. "Dumbfounded, I couldn't take my eyes off her," she says of their first meeting, before knowing of Eriko's male past. She finds that she sleeps well on the sofa, which is next to the kitchen, and the next day when Eriko asks her to come and live in the apartment with her and Yuichi, Mikage accepts.

Once, while removing things from her old apartment, she receives a phone call from Sotaro, her old boyfriend. When they meet, he says that he knows she is living with "that Tanabe guy," that everyone knows it at the school she has dropped out of, that Yuichi's girlfriend slapped him during a loud, jealous argument in the cafeteria. Mikage does not think that it is the big deal that the others do, and when she later asks Yuichi if he doesn't think her living there is "a little weird," he assures her it's not.

Mikage has a dream that is recounted in detail, about her and Yuichi cleaning her old apartment as a final step for her leaving it. In the dream, they sing a love song together, and then Yuichi, who "was suddenly revealed to be a prince," says, "After we finish cleaning up here, I really feel like stopping at the ramen noodle stand in the park." Waking from the dream, Mikage goes into the kitchen and runs into Yuichi, who woke in the night with a hunger for ramen noodles. He correctly guesses the color of the floor tile in the kitchen of the old apartment, indicating that they both had the same dream at the same time. The first section ends with Mikage content and happy with living in the Tanabe apartment, just vaguely aware that she will have to move out some day.

Section 2: Full Moon

The second half of the novella opens with Mikage describing the circumstances under which Eriko died: she was stalked by a patron of the nightclub that she owned, and when he found out that she had once been a man, he stabbed her, although she managed to beat him to death with a barbell before she died. After relating these events, Mikage, as narrator, explains that she had not been living at the Tanabe apartment for months at the time of the murder; in fact, she had found her own apartment and was working as an assistant at a cooking school. Yuichi's call to break the news about Eriko's death comes long after her funeral. Mikage races over to be with him that night and finds that since Eriko's death he has withdrawn into himself, much as she had after her grandmother's death in the beginning of the story. They stay up all night talking about Eriko, and the next morning, before he leaves for school, they decide to have a magnificent meal together, "a dinner to end all dinners," that evening. When he brings home the groceries for the meal, they notice the beauty of the nearly-full moon and speculate about how it affects one's cooking in a non-mystical, "human" sense.

After the meal they discuss the possibility of Mikage moving back into the apartment again, but neither of them can decide if it would be as Yuichi's lover or his friend. In the morning, Mikage is wakened by the phone, but the caller hangs up when she answers, and she assumes it is a jealous girl. Yuichi's old girlfriend Okuno visits her at the cooking school where she works to tell her to stay away from Yuichi: "You say you're not his girlfriend, yet you go over there whenever you want, you spend the night, you do what you please, don't you?" she says with angry tears. "That's *worse* than living together." Unsure of her relationship with Yuichi, Mikage arranges to go on a business trip in order to avoid deciding which apartment she will live in.

Before leaving, though, she receives a call from Chika, who was one of Eriko's friends. They meet for lunch, at which Chika expresses amusement that Yuichi and Mikage do not realize that they are in love with each other, even though it is obvious. One night on her trip, Mikage phones Yuichi at an inn in Isehara. They complain to each other about the dull food that they have been served at the inns they are staying at, and when Mikage hangs up the phone, she eats some *katsudon* at the diner she phoned from and finds it delicious. So she gets a take-out order and takes a cab to Isehara, sixty miles away, dropping off the food and then leaving just as mysteriously as she came: "A matter of love, is it?" the cab driver asks, and she responds, "Something along those lines." On the last day of her trip, Yuichi phones Mikage at her hotel. He is over his grief and has returned to Tokyo, and he arranges to pick her up at the train station when she arrives the next day.

Characters

Chika

The head "girl" at Eriko's club, Chika has more masculine features than Eriko because she is a transvestite who has not had her gender changed surgically. The only thing that Eriko does not leave to Yuichi after her death is the nightclub, which she leaves to Chika. Late in the story, Chika calls Mikage to meet her and tell her something urgent. Chika tells her that she knows that Yuichi and Mikage are in love with one another, even though neither one of them admit it.

Like Kitchen*'s main character, Mikage, author Mahoko Yoshimoto studied at a university in Tokyo. The students pictured here are celebrating their recent acceptance to the competitive University of Tokyo.*

Kuri

One of Mikage's colleagues, Kuri's sunny disposition gives her "an appealing cuteness." She is Nori's best friend.

Nori

Nori is described as "a beauty of the 'proper young lady' variety." She works with Mikage as an assistant to the cooking teacher. Mikage admires her open and loving relationship with her mother.

Okuno

Okuno thinks of herself as Yuichi's girlfriend. She claims to have been the one who comforted Yuichi when Eriko died, although Yuichi never mentions any such thing to Mikage. When she finds out that Mikage has spent the night at Yuichi's apartment, Okuno confronts Mikage at work and threatens her, telling her to stay away from him.

Mikage Sakurai

The protagonist and narrator of *Kitchen* is Mikage, a young student in Tokyo. Her parents died when she was young and she was raised by her grandmother, whose death leaves her depressed, listless, and unable to face the world. When Yuichi Tanabe comes to her door and asks her to move in with his mother and him, she is surprised, because she does not know much about them. Despite this fact, she accepts an invitation to dinner.

At the Tanabe house, she finds comfort, and she falls in love with the kitchen "at first sight." She is overwhelmed upon meeting Eriko, and the feelings that she has are expressed in terms that border on romance: "Still, she was stunning. She made me want to be with her again. There was a warm light, like her afterimage, softly glowing in my heart. That must be what they mean by 'charm.'" In spite of this, she is only slightly shaken by the news that Eriko is a transsexual. Mikage discovers that she is able to sleep well on the couch at the Tanabe home, in part because it is next to the kitchen. She moves in with them, partly because of her loneliness over the death of her grandmother, partly because of her enchantment with Eriko, and partly because she recognizes that Yuichi, raised by Eriko alone as she was raised by her grandmother, has much in common with her.

By the end of the novella, Mikage seems to have found the courage to face life again. After Eriko's death, she moves out of the apartment and finds a job. However, she remains confused about her feelings for Yuichi; are they friends, or are they in love with each other? For all her growth she still needs a third party to tell her what everyone already knows: she is in love with Yuichi. Although the resolution is unclear, the reader does have reason to hope that they will unite and embark on a relationship.

Sotaro

Sotaro is Mikage's old boyfriend. He has always been very cheerful, and when they were together they made a "picture-perfect" couple, but they broke up when her grandmother became seriously ill. He tells her about Yuichi's former girlfriend confronting him in the school cafeteria. Reflecting on Sotaro, Mikage says, "I loved his hearty robustness, I thirsted after it, but in spite of that I couldn't keep pace with it, and it made me hate myself." She realizes, though, that she just is not attracted to Sotaro, and when they part, they part as friends.

Eriko Tanabe

Eriko is Yuichi's mother—actually, she is his biological father, but she had a sex-change operation after her young wife's death, and she lives as a woman. She is the owner of a gay nightclub.

When Eriko was young, she was taken in to live with a family and became very attached to the daughter of the family. They eloped when she was young. After her death, Eriko knew she would never love again, and that was when she decided to change over to the female sex. As a woman, Eriko is strong-willed, active, impulsive, and incredibly beautiful. It is her idea to have Mikage move in with Yuichi and her—in light of her past history, she probably recognized the possibility that they could have a romance like she and her dead wife once had. Her life is not easy, but, as she explains to Mikage, she accepts the difficulties that she encounters as a necessary part of the growth process: "But if a person hasn't ever experienced true despair, she grows old never knowing how to evaluate where she is in life; never understanding what joy really is. I'm grateful for it."

Eriko suffers a sudden, violent death. A stalker follows her on the street and becomes fascinated with her. He finds out that she was once a man and, in a rage, stabs her with a knife. Eriko beats him to death before she dies herself. The letter that she leaves behind for Yuichi is full of humor and self-satisfaction with the accomplishments of her life. After her death, Mikage remembers a story that Eriko told her about her wife's death, of how Eriko had brought a pineapple plant to her hospital room to cheer her up but the dying woman, when her time was near, asked that the plant be taken away. Eriko realized from this that the world was unyielding, that nothing could change the unpleasantness we face: "It was clear that the best thing to do was to adopt a sort of muddled cheerfulness. So I became a woman, and here I am."

Yuichi Tanabe

When Yuichi first comes to Mikage to invite her to live with the Tanabes, she remembers him from her grandmother's funeral; initially, she wonders if he was the old woman's lover, because the funeral upset him so much. Then she remembers that he worked at the flower shop that her grandmother had gone to every day.

Yuichi's mother died when he was a child, and Eriko was both mother and father to him. He attaches himself to Mikage, as he had to her grandmother, with total devotion, although he seems incapable of romantic love; the girl that he went out with for a year and then dropped suddenly "said that Yuichi was incapable of caring more for a girl than he did for a fountain pen." Yuichi does not contact Mikage about Eriko's death until a long time after the event because he is so distraught. He does not specifically blame himself for what happened to Eriko, but he does note the fact that there has been a lot of death in his family, as in Mikage's, and he suggests that they go into business as carriers of death—"destruction workers."

Even when he realizes that their relationship is not just friendship, or the brother-and-sister bond that it was when Eriko was alive, he does not change his aloof demeanor. Nor does she. But in the end, when he arranges to pick her up at Tokyo station, it is clear to see that they are in love, even though nothing to that effect is explicitly said.

Yuji Tanabe

See Eriko Tanabe

Themes

Sex Roles

One of the most notable facets of the story *Kitchen* is the calm and subtle treatment that it gives to Eriko's gender. When Mikage first meets Eriko, she is smitten with the beauty that she sees. Her fascination indicates a sexual attraction, but as she explains that she came to understand the word "charm" for the first time, it becomes clear that her attraction is not physical, that it is more like magic. When Yuichi tells her that Eriko is actually his biological father, that she has changed her sex, Mikage expresses some surprise—"I just stared at him in wide-eyed silence. I didn't know what to say"— but she is not overwhelmed, and her surprise soon fades as she becomes involved in a conversation about Yuichi's family history.

Raised by Eriko, Yuichi is kind; this can be seen in the way that he treats Mikage and her grandmother. He is a special case, though, and there are only two other males in the book to compare him to: Mikage's old boyfriend Sotaro, who is sensitive to the beauty of plants but ignorant of Mikage (his parting words to her are "Chin up, kid!"), and the anonymous stalker who murders Eriko, "screaming that he has been made a fool of." If Yuichi is shown to have a good balance of male and female characteristics, it is because Eriko went before him and blazed a path; if Mikage is also well-balanced, it is because her suffering and loneliness have introduced her to the harsher elements of masculinity.

Death

To say that death is a catalyst for change in this story would be an understatement. This point

Topics for Further Study

- What do you think Eriko's transsexuality adds to this story? Explain how you think Mikage's and Yuichi's love affair would have been different if Eriko had just been a mother who worked at a nightclub.

- Make a list of foods that you think would be comforting in a time of grief, and why. Try to determine if there is any physiological basis for your hunch.

- This book has been made into a movie twice in Japan. What problems do you think the scriptwriters would have encountered while adapting it? What scenes would be most effective on the screen? What key scenes would not translate well to movies?

- Write a short story explaining what life is like for Mikage and Yuichi one year, five years, or fifteen years into the future. You can write it from Mikage's point of view, as the book is, or from Yuichi's.

is made most obvious in the fact that Yuji/Eriko Tanabe, distraught over the death of his wife after a lingering illness, decided to become a woman, to flee what he had been when she was alive. By becoming a woman he feels closer to her.

Mikage's way of dealing with the loss of her grandmother is similar, if not so extreme; instead, she slides into a state of inertia, unable to respond to the world or deal with the simplest decisions. When Yuichi arrives on her doorstep offering a chance to live in a new place—to in effect become somebody different—it does not take much to convince her to go along.

The first effect of Eriko's death is that Mikage and Yuichi see themselves marked by death, surrounded by bad luck: "So I've become an orphan," Yuichi says, and Mikage responds with, "That goes double for me." Their grief brings them together, as Mikage, who suffered through similar circumstances with the recent loss of her grandmother, takes up the job of nursing Yuichi. She does that by cooking for him but also, less noticeably, just with her loving presence. It is this nurturing relationship that obscures their true romantic love from both of them until the end, when their separation from one another makes their feelings clearer.

Friendship

The issue at the center of this story, from the beginning to the end, is whether Mikage and Yuichi will become lovers, or if the special bond between them is limited to friendship. This question is raised in the story's first real scene, with Yuichi arriving at Mikage's doorstep and asking her to come and live in his home. In the absence of any preexisting friendship between them, she is confused as to the source of the bond she feels for him. "I saw a straight road leading from me to him," she says of their first encounter. "He seemed to glow with white light. That was the effect he had on me."

She later feels a similar attraction to Eriko, his mother/father, and the delight that all three of them find in each other makes their relationship seem like a very strong friendship. Mikage deflects her old boyfriend's suspicion that she and Yuichi are having an affair by pointing out that his mother lives with them, as proof that their living arrangement is nonsexual. Still, the supernatural aspect of their relationship indicates that they are more than friends, except that Mikage does not allow herself to see it as supernatural at all. After they both have the same dream at the same time, she acknowledges its implausibility at the same time that she denies that there is anything magical about it: "While what had happened was utterly amazing," she says, "it didn't seem so out of the ordinary, really. It was at once a miracle and the most natural thing in the world." For the purposes of this novel, the same miraculous quality can be ascribed to love, while friendship is "the most natural thing in the world."

When Mikage returns to Yuichi after Eriko's death, he asks her to move back into the apartment, and she wonders openly about their relationship for once, questioning whether they would be lovers or friends. He has no answer, though: "You mean, should we sell the sofa and buy a double bed?," he asks. "I myself don't even know." Mikage needs to be told by the transvestite Chika that she is in love with Yuichi, and he with her, before she is able to understand their relationship.

Style

Symbolism

In the opening pages of the novella the significance of the kitchen is explained. Mikage introduces herself and explains that she has been sleeping in the kitchen after her grandmother's death, indicating that the association with warmth and food was what she needed to comfort her worried soul. There is even a reference to Linus, the character in the *Peanuts* cartoon who carries a "security blanket" that provides him with psychological support against the furies of the world. The symbol of the kitchen makes sporadic, but significant, appearances throughout this novella.

Mikage establishes herself at the Tanabe residence by forming a special bond with their kitchen; her love of the kitchen, or perhaps her love of Eriko and Yuichi, prompts her to understand cooking. This understanding leads her to find her place in the outside world, among the likes of Nori and Kuri and their *Sensei,* or teacher. Most of the other major symbols in the story have to do with the kitchen too. At Mikage's moment of lowest despair in the first half, after she has been watching a dirigible float away with all her hope, she is brought back to happiness by the sight of a kitchen outside of the bus window. Later in the story the *katsudon* that breaks down the emotional barriers is only vaguely reminiscent of kitchens, capturing the sense of nurturing that food has without bringing in the kitchen's various physical qualities.

Narrator

Much of the drama in this story is due to the narration of this particular first-person narrator, Mikage. Another narrator would have emphasized different events—the strangeness of the dream that Mikage and Yuichi have simultaneously, for instance, or even the fact of Eriko's sex change. To Mikage, these events are no more or less mystifying than the juicer that Eriko brings home or the great taste of the *katsudon* at the late-night diner. She is young enough to be delighted with small, unexpected treats, yet old enough, having lived with her old grandmother, to recognize the joys of traditional, home-based values. She is urbane, both in the sense that she is a product of city life and because she accepts different cultural practices easily, having moved among all of the different sorts of people that compose a metropolis like Tokyo.

Mikage undergoes a huge change from the first part of the novella to the second. In Part 1,

Compare
&
Contrast

- **1988:** Hirohito, who had been Emperor of Japan since 1926, fell violently ill. He died the next year at the age of 87.

  Today: In part because of Hirohito's participation in World War II (1939–1945), the Emperor of Japan, Akihito, has mostly symbolic powers, with the real governing done by an elected democracy.

- **1988:** George Bush, who was vice-president for eight years during the administration of Ronald Reagan, was elected President of the United States.

  Today: Bush's one-term administration is remembered as a time of economic weakness, due

  in large part to the economic troubles that were inherited from the Reagan administration.

- **1988:** Polish workers went out on strike to demand the return of the labor union Solidarity, which had been outlawed since 1981. After three weeks their demand was met.

  1990: A new government was elected in Poland, with Lech Walesa, a leader of the Solidarity movement, as president.

  1991: Following Poland's lead, a number of countries in the Soviet Union demanded independence. The Soviet Union was dissolved on December 31, 1991.

"Kitchen," she is consumed by grief, and so is a more passive narrator, observing the things around her without taking a hand in her fate. The Tanabe household is clearly a happier place than before her arrival—both Eriko and Yuichi say so—but life goes on pretty much as it had before. Something, probably the fading of her grief, happens to Mikage between the first part and the second part, called "Full Moon": When she reappears after Eriko's death she is more in charge of her surroundings. She has an apartment and a job. The Mikage of Part 1 may have admired kitchens for their comforting emotional associations, but she would not have trained herself to work in the kitchen the way that the Mikage who appears in the second part has done.

Resolution

Kitchen does not come to a definitive resolution. The main character's problem is not solved by the end of the story, at least not in any way that gives readers confidence that she will not wake up tomorrow faced with the same problems that she felt free of today. She does come to an implied realization regarding Yuichi.

Historical Context

The Economic Boom

In 1988 the Japanese economy was in the middle of the longest financial boom it had experienced since World War II. After Japan lost the war, the American army occupied the defeated country, taking control of the government and steering it toward a new political and economic structure. The Emperor remained on the throne because the Americans wanted to use his presence to oppose the rise of Communism in southern Asia, but political control was shifted into the hands of elected officials. A new Japanese constitution came into effect in 1946, renouncing war forever and adapting a parliamentary democracy. Sovereignty was restored to the Japanese in 1952, in exchange for Japan's withdrawing from countries it had invaded during the war and paying reparations.

After that, Japan grew in economic stature. The first big boost was the Korean War (1950 to 1953) during which Japan provided the U.S. Army with many of its vehicles, from jeeps to tanks. Japan established itself as a leader in electronics in the late 1950s and early 1960s, becoming almost synonymous with transistor technology. By the time that Tokyo hosted the Olympic Games in 1964, the year of Banana Yoshimoto's birth, Japan led the world in economic growth.

Much of its growth was due to foreign trade; in fact, by 1971 Japan was the world's third-leading exporting nation in the world. The Japanese automobile industry expanded even as the rest of the economy suffered in 1973, when a cartel of Arab oil-producing countries raised gasoline prices around the world dramatically. Almost overnight, American-made "gas-guzzlers" went out of fashion and smaller, fuel-efficient models by Nissan, Toyota, and Honda were in demand. Prime Minister Yasuhiro Makasome, who held office from 1982 to 1987, oversaw an economic surge that made Japan a feared economic rival to many Americans.

As the world converted to a global economy in the 1980s, many industrial companies left America in search of a cheaper labor base. Most of these jobs did not go to Japan. American resentment at this situation often focused on Japan and its success in the international economy. In the 1990s, after Nakasome was out of office, the economic expansion in Japan was over. The government was unable to help, suffering through a series of scandals, with the Prime Ministers resigning in 1989 and 1994. For most of the decade, the country was in recession, and in 1998, when the Japanese economy was beginning to stabilize, the collapse of several economies around southeast Asia negatively impacted the recovering Japanese economy.

Critical Overview

In Japan, Yoshimoto's books have earned critical and popular success since her first one, *Kitchen,* was published in 1988. Western reviewers have attempted to explain her immense popularity when they consider her works. "Like comic books for businessmen and green-tea ice cream," David Galef wrote in *The New York Times Book Review,* "Banana Yoshimoto is a Japanese phenomenon that Americans find difficult to understand."

As much as Yoshimoto's writing may leave many American reviewers unimpressed, she has made a deep impression on millions of readers around the world. Reviewers trying to account for the fact that Yoshimoto is hugely popular both in Japan and with the book-buying public have frequently adjusted their critical standards to compensate for their understanding of her audience. Some have been able to appreciate Yoshimoto by

looking at her from someone else's perspective, while other critics simply have not been able to see what all the noise around this author is all about.

Nick Hornsby, reviewing *Kitchen* for *The Times Literary Supplement,* appreciated the subtlety of Yoshimoto's work while allowing that it would be easy to misunderstand the true craft involved. "Her stories possess a clarity and simplicity that can seem lightweight," he wrote, going on to speculate that the difficulty of translating Japanese might account for some of the book's lack of artistry. Scott Shibuya Brown, writing for *Book World,* also saw "a delicacy" in the novella that remained "*Kitchen*'s most beguiling charm." He put the book in the context of the past 120 years of Japanese literature, finding it to be, in contrast to the ultra-modern look at contemporary Japan that many reviewers saw in it, a book that instead was "shaped by the most traditional of aesthetics." To Brown, the Japanese tradition of "beauty as an ever-transitory, perpetually fading bittersweet phenomenon" is something that makes Westerners' experience of this novella incomplete.

While some reviewers have adjusted their expectations of the book to account for its Japanese roots, others have emphasized the youthfulness of the audience that it is aimed for. A review in the *New York Times Book Review* identified Mikage as the novella's "kooky young woman protagonist," while Deborah Garrison, writing in *The New Yorker,* appreciated the book as "a tangy, imperfect little snack" that was released in America with "a small but irresistible fanfare of cuteness." Her review goes on to describe Mikage's bright personality: "She keeps telling you she's depressed, listless, and tearful, but she can't hide her essentially sunny nature."

The duality that is noticeable in Garrison's tone—mocking but also fond of the story's harmless pleasantness—can be found in quite a few reviews by writers who like the story but cannot approve of it as art. There have also been reviews by writers who could see the book's appeal but were not willing to let themselves be drawn in by it. Todd Grimson held to the hard line in his 1983 review for the *Los Angeles Times Book Review:* "*Kitchen* is light as an invisible pancake," he wrote, "charming and forgettable, showing every sign of having been written when the author was only 23." Grimson described himself as a fan of recent Japanese literature, but he was clearly no fan of Banana Yoshimoto after reading the novella: "The release of information to the reader seems unskilled, or immature, weak in narrative or plot."

Throughout the years, as Yoshimoto's fame has grown, attention has shifted from her works to her celebrity status. In a December 1998 *Christian Science Monitor* review of *Honeymoon,* a book not yet available in America, Nichile Gaouette discussed the author, her worldview, and the chronology of her "reader-friendly books" that are "chatty, breezy affairs." It was only after the celebrity profile was done that the book was mentioned. Yoshimoto's detractors depict her as a kind of fiction machine, churning out one novel after another by combining and recombining a few standard elements in a mostly meaningless way. Her fans tend to characterize her detractors as the sort of spoil-sports who would find fault with any popular work just because it is popular, regardless of its true merit.

Criticism

David J. Kelly

Kelly is a literature and creative writing instructor at Oakton Community College and College of Lake County in Illinois. In this essay, he considers whether Kitchen's *happy resolutions constitute shallowness or a legitimate representation of this story's vision.*

I think that a lot of the critics who dismiss *Kitchen* as "lightweight" do so because its characters are just too happy, just as a lot of the novella's devoted fans dismiss the critics as grouches who disliked the story because they have a thing against happiness. The truth, as it always does, must lie somewhere in between.

There is no denying that there is a tendency throughout the story to break up moments of sober reflection with a cheerful shake of the head, an uncaused burst of enthusiasm for whatever life has to offer next. It is also pretty well established that, for reasons I will get into later, writers cannot have their characters just turn on a pin, go from one mood to another with the start of a new sentence— they *can* do it, that is, just as they can toss in singing toasters and invisible spaceships and anything else they can imagine that does not exist in the common world, but just because they can think it up does not mean it is good artistry. The suspicious thing about a book that always turns happy like this is that happiness is such a crowd-pleaser. If Yoshimoto had turned to misery at the end of every up-

beat scene, we might worry about her mental hygiene, but we would be less likely to think she does it for popularity's sake than we are when she gives the public what it wants time and again.

On the other hand, this is not a book that takes place in the reality that anybody lives in, even after we adjust for the cultural differences. This is a fantasy land, where people dream concurrently and the dying go down heroically swinging barbells and cab drivers say "Okay, then, let's get going" when they find out that the hundred-mile trip in the middle of the night is for love. Why should this novella be responsible for maintaining its characters' emotional consistency when it breaks almost all other rules of behavior without blushing? Isn't it allowed to set its own rules, as long as it sticks to them?

"Yuichi went to the refrigerator and got out a couple of grapefruits, then happily took the juicer from its box." That "happily," among all the other happy actions in the book, gets me most. First, because it seems so superfluous there, thrown into the middle of an action that isn't, itself, the sort of thing that makes one happy unless one really likes juice and has a really powerful thirst. A lot of what goes on in the story is like this, spiked with a little burst of enthusiasm. I imagine being able to watch from my window as Yuichi or Mikage comes up the street, and I'm certain that neither one of them could walk for half a block without sneaking in a little skip or a shuffle, forgetting for one step that they are not dancing through life. These people are full of joy. But look at the context in which Yuichi happily takes the juicer from its box, and you have to wonder if there's *nothing* that can quiet his joy for a few minutes. It is the middle of the night; he has just woken up from a weird dream; he is hungry; and he has just found out that Mikage was experiencing the same dream that he was, at the same time. I think it is fair to say that most of us would be curious about this. I'm not saying that there is an appropriate emotion, such as, oh, terror, required by this paranormal turn of events.

Mikage and Yuichi are so well-suited for each other that they are probably right in being happy to find that they can spend those nighttime, sleeping hours together, eating well and singing, as well as the day. But if there is ever a time when being just "happy" seems like a weak, insensitive reaction, this is it. What is the point of putting something astounding in a novella, if the characters are incapable of reacting to it? When they start to realize that they actually have been experiencing the same dream, Mikage says, "I ... I don't believe this."

What Do I Read Next?

- Many readers have found that Yoshimoto's novels remind them of Mexican writer Laura Esquivel's best-selling novel *Like Water for Chocolate,* published by Doubleday in 1992. As in *Kitchen,* food is the primary cure for love and loss in this book, which is structured like a cookbook.

- At the same time that Banana Yoshimoto's writing was capturing international attention for its portrayals of women in modern Tokyo, Tama Janowitz was establishing the same sort of reputation for her characters in New York City. Her 1986 collection of short stories, *Slaves of New York,* offers a vastly different look at the other side of the world.

- One of the most famous Japanese novelists to be printed in English is Tanizaki Junichiro, whose novels mainly explored the struggle between traditional values and modern culture. His most famous novel, *Some Prefer Nettles,* concerns an unhappy marriage in which a westernized wife and a traditional husband try to stay together despite their differences. Published in Japan in 1929, it became an international suc-

cess when the translation was published by Alfred A. Knopf in 1955.

- Kenzaburo Oe is a Japanese author who was the recipient of the 1994 Nobel Prize for Literature. Like Yoshimoto, he became famous while still quite young. He received national attention when he was twenty-three, with the publication in 1958 of the novella *Shiiku,* which translates to English as "The Catch." It is available in the collection *The Shadow of Sunrise,* published in 1966 by Palo Alto Press.

- The dust jacket of *Kitchen* compares the work to the early writings of French novelist Marguerite Duras, which also create an eerie mood from their tight prose. Her best works can be found in *Four Novels by Marguerite Duras,* published in 1965.

- The differences between eastern and western cultures have been explored recently in the work of Japanese-American author Ruth Ozeki. Her 1998 novel *My Year of Meats,* concerns a Japanese couple trying to have a child and contrasts contemporary trends like agribusiness and food additives with Japanese tradition.

When it is confirmed, she tells the reader, "That was strange," and Yuichi changes the subject. Who is unable to think of the words to address what has happened—the characters, or the author?

The other happy event that stands out is the episode on the bus, with the little girl, her grandmother, and the dirigible. This comes right before the coincidental dream in the story, but it has the opposite structure to it: While Yuichi's happiness when he is reaching for the juicer seemed like an afterthought, like something Yoshimoto felt she should throw in just in case we were distracted by the possibility of a more complex emotion, the whole *point* of the dirigible scene is that it dissolves into happiness. This scene is slathered with symbolism: The little girl and her grandmother reflect, of course, Mikage and her recently deceased grand-

mother; the dirigible is happiness, which Mikage vows to keep in sight just moments before she starts crying. It is the last time that she is leaving the apartment that she and her grandmother shared, and Mikage is torn between grief and that big airborne puff of happiness, and just as grief starts winning, and the tears start falling on her blouse, happiness rallies and presents itself to her in the form of good cooking in the kitchen that the bus is passing at that moment.

Although this scene is sort of adrift in the novella because it could have been wedged in at practically any place in the story, it has a few things going for it that make it more central than the dream. It has a sequence of events—the dirigible causes happiness, the granddaughter causes reminiscence, reminiscence causes sorrow, and food

---

smells cause happiness again—that reflects the general rhythm of cause and effect in this piece. Also, it allows the kitchen to have an integral, active role, while the fact that they ended up in the kitchen within the dream and then after it shows the hand of the author forcing the issue. In the one case, we are led step-by-step to Mikage's happiness, and we have to take it seriously, while in the other case Yuichi's happiness is thrown at us, and it doesn't stick.

In real life, emotions *do* seem to pop up out of nowhere, although psychiatry is the science of denying this. I'm sure that this would be used as a sort of defense for the incomplete emotional exchanges that take place in this story, usually leading to a hollow happiness. A reader feeling blue doesn't have to worry, happiness will pop up regularly, regardless of what is going on in the story. It announces itself as the replacement for the ignored, unfinished dream; in Mikage's exclamation, upon getting her special glass—"'Wow,' I said on the verge of tears. 'I'm so happy!'"; in the sight of Nori and Kuri giggling in their white aprons that makes Mikage happy ("Working side by side with them was a pleasure that put me at peace with the world"); or in its earliest case, where the narrator drags readers to the brink of despair ("Steeped in a sadness so great I could barely cry, shuffling softly in a gentle drowsiness, I pulled my futon into the deathly silent, gleaming kitchen") and then pops a champagne cork of delight ("However, I couldn't exist like that. Reality is wonderful.") Maybe happiness does show up like this—sometimes.

The unpredictability of life, though, is no excuse for unpredictability in fiction. I often wonder why anyone uses "That's the way it is in life!" as a defense of something that happens in fiction. Fiction isn't life. It certainly would be great to turn from any of life's low points with a feeling that reality is wonderful, the way Mikage does, although to tell you the truth, if I met anyone this happy this often I would bet that they are suppressing something in a most unhealthy way.

I do not think that the constant turns toward happiness in *Kitchen* reflect life as we live it, nor do I mind that they don't: Fiction's job is to reflect the world in an unreal, fictitious way. The problem is that they draw attention to the teller of the tale, making me wonder why Banana Yoshimoto wants so desperately, even when circumstances do not warrant it, for everything to come out okay. If there is anything worse than fiction that announces to its reader that "The world presented here is unlikely,"

it's fiction that seems to have some reason, other than basic, unmanageable truth, for wanting you to think one way or another. I sort of like the idea that *Kitchen* is promoting happiness—or, rather, I would like the idea if I thought there was nothing else needing to be examined, if I thought that happiness in itself was a good thing. The way that potentially grim situations resolve in this novella, though, leaves me with the uneasy feeling that the author is playing with loaded dice.

Source: David J. Kelly, in an essay for *Novels for Students,* Gale, 1999.

Albert Howard Carter III

In the following review, Carter offers a brief introduction to Kitchen.

This small volume contains two stories, *Kitchen,* a novella of about 100 pages and "Moonlight Shadows," a short story of 40. The latter won a prize upon its original publication in 1986, and the former won a magazine prize in 1987 before book publication in 1988. *Kitchen* has been wildly popular in Japan, selling millions of copies in some 57 printings.

Why is this author popular and why are these tales printed together? Yoshimoto is a young author (b. 1964) with an ear for young people's issues, conflicts, and yearnings. She also writes in a jazzy and often surprising style. The two stories work well as different ways of talking about love, both romantic and familial.

Kitchen begins: "The place I like best in this world is the kitchen." Our narrator, one Mikage Sakurai, is a young woman, an orphan. Symbolically, she is an abandoned child of modern Tokyo, that massive and complex city; a novice, she tries to find her own way, yearning for sustenance of food and love. Fortuitously, Mikage is taken in by a family, who are delighted that she loves to shop, cook, and "make the house a home," we might say. But what on the surface seems an attractive mother and son soon evolves into yet another urban oddity: Mikage learns that the mother is a transsexual—formerly the father. This unusual parent runs a nightclub, largely staffed by transsexuals, until she is murdered by a deranged admirer.

In this difficult world, young Mikage feels loneliness, anomie, even despair. Overcome by grief for her recently dead grandmother, she cries on a public street, but suddenly hears "the sound of a happy voice at work, soup boiling, knives and pots and pans clanging." Yes, it is a kitchen, that symbol of hope, order, and sustenance. She even gets a job as an assistant to a cooking teacher.

Meanwhile Mikage and the young man circle each other, neither declaring love nor even romantic interest. They attempt to fabricate their lives in the modern mixtures of Japanese and international culture, a world of takeout food, backpacks, warmup suits, *Bewitched* on TV, computer games, and an international range of cooking. It is the old standard, *katsudon* (a fried pork dish), however, that our young heroine takes on a taxi ride of some 100 miles to her mourning friend and, later (we assume), lover.

The style is breezy, whimsical, lyric, maybe even a bit goofy, but it is an appropriate style for a young person dealing with disruptions of family, culture, and love. The first-person narration is reminiscent of Salinger's *The Catcher in the Rye,* but without the trenchant satire.

The other story, "Moonlight Shadow," also deals with young love and death; this time the female narrator's boyfriend has been killed in a traffic accident. Through a mysterious woman figure—something like a good fairy—the narrator has a vision of her dead boyfriend, a vision that allows her to say a proper goodbye and continue on with her life. She concludes:

> One caravan has stopped, another starts up. There are people I have yet to meet, others I'll never see again. People who are gone before you know it, people who are just passing through. Even as we exchange hellos, they seem to grow transparent. I must keep living with the flowing river before my eyes.

Even this brief quotation suggests the mixtures of realism and fantasy, simple diction and poetic image that give Yoshimoto's writing freshness and novelty.

Source: Albert Howard Carter III, a review of *Kitchen,* in *Studies in Short Fiction,* Vol. 30, No. 4, Fall, 1993, pp. 614-15.

Deborah Garrison

In the following review, Garrison introduces Banana Yoshimoto to American readers and describes Kitchen *as a "tangy, imperfect little snack."*

Banana Yoshimoto's *Kitchen* is a tangy, imperfect little snack. The book, though it appears to be a short novel, is really a pair of stories—the first, called *Kitchen,* is just long enough, at a hundred and three pages, to be classed as a novella. A literary prize-winner and long-running best-seller in Japan a few years ago, it arrives here translated,

somewhat doggedly, by Megan Backus and attended by a small but irresistible fanfare of cuteness. There's a photograph on the mint-and-dark-peach jacket of a bright-eyed Japanese girl in a white eyelet dress, her hair stylishly longer on one side than the other—someone it might be fun to know. She's not Banana, but the packaging doesn't entirely lie. The author was only twenty-four when *Kitchen* was first published, and reading it, along with its less ambitious companion, "Moonlight Shadow," gives you the sense that you're meeting a real young woman, who is, among other things, cute. Both stories are told by a naïve, occasionally goofy first-person narrator, whose bursts of energetic resolve are as girlish as her cries of passionate despair.

What makes this girlishness palatable—what counterbalances it—is the author's preoccupation with grief. "When my grandmother died the other day, I was taken by surprise," Mikage, the twenty-ish heroine of *Kitchen,* explains at the start of her strange tale. "The fact that time continued to pass in the usual way in this apartment where I grew up, even though now I was here all alone, amazed me. It was total science fiction. The blackness of the cosmos." An only child whose parents died when she was little, Mikage was brought up by her grandmother. But her musings on her plight are mostly uplifting and practical in nature. She acknowledges, for example, the relief: "To live alone with an old person is terribly nerve-racking, and the healthier he or she is, the more one worries." She confesses the battier aspects of her search for comfort: "Steeped in a sadness so great I could barely cry... I pulled my futon into the deathly silent, gleaming kitchen"—and she sleeps there, curled like a forlorn family pet at the base of the refrigerator.

"However!" she continues. "I couldn't exist like that. Reality is wonderful." She's the opposite of the depressive who masks pain under a noisy (and transparent) cheerfulness; she keeps telling you she's depressed, listless, and tearful, but she can't hide her essentially sunny nature.

Yoshimoto's writing isn't itself very complex; it skips lightly over the surface of even Mikage's darkest hours. But what she's trying to describe—happiness—*is* complex, and is much trickier to evoke convincingly than misery, maybe because the sources of true contentment are more obscure. Obviously, reality isn't as wonderful as Mikage claims: she is utterly without family, and she has to find a way to manage on her skimpy inheritance. But she is graced with the stubborn happiness of the survivor, which can crop up out of nowhere after a death in the family and thrive like a weed.

What also crops up out of nowhere for Mikage is an invitation to live, rent-free, at the Tanabe residence. Yuichi Tanabe, a reserved young man about Mikage's age, visits her after her grandmother's funeral and proposes that she come to live with him and his mother. (Yoshimoto's way of effecting this and all transitions is so matter-of-fact you can't decide whether it's charming or dopey. "*Dingdong.* Suddenly the doorbell rang," she writes.) Mikage's reaction to Yuichi's polite appearance on her threshold—"I couldn't take my eyes off him. I think I heard a spirit call my name"—is a bizarre blend of teeny-bopper and Zen: love at first sight, non-Western style. Mikage also takes an instant liking to Yuichi's stunningly pretty mother, who turns out, to the reader's baffled delight, to be a man. Yuichi delicately introduces the subject to Mikage with "Guess what else…" His mother was his father—before plastic surgery. This is a wonderful touch, not because it's played for laughs (it isn't) or because it's a big surprise (strangely, it's not that, either) but because it's a piece of superfluous inventiveness on the author's part; it lends everything around it an air of cheerful unreality that mirrors Mikage's state of mind.

Yoshimoto, for all her narrative exuberance, understands the one-step-forward, two-steps-back emotional indirectness of a young person in crisis. The death of Mikage's grandmother is only the prelude to the more shocking, untimely death of Yuichi's mother, and the news of it causes Mikage, who has since moved into her own place, to appreciate the powerful solace of her days at the Tanabes': of sleeping on their couch and hearing Yuichi's mom clatter in on her heels, humming a tune; of perfecting her cooking skills in their underutilized kitchen; of waking up in the middle of the night at the same time as Yuichi and comparing dreams with him. The reader learns of these moments only in retrospect because it is only in retrospect that Mikage comes into full possession of their significance. Most of *Kitchen* occurs not in real time but in mental hyperspace—the virtual rather than chronological aftermath in which events are digested and understanding is gained.

But the story finally seizes on a down-to-earth matter: whether Mikage and Yuichi, in their shared orphanhood, should become lovers or remain fast, sibling-like friends. Yoshimoto can't render it a very compelling question: the intimate rapport between Mikage and Yuichi simply fails to be as interesting as the lively, perfectly achieved completeness of Mikage taken by herself. Her outburst following a good long cry over her grandmother ("I implored the gods: Please, let me live"); her remark at the sight of clouds blowing around in a strong wind ("In this world there is no place for sadness")—these rarities will stay with the reader.

Mikage is, throughout, a little bit weird, and so are the other characters. Yoshimoto's attraction to weirdness and her unpretentious approach to it—she's not trying to be hip, just faithful to her sense of people as they are—are what might make Western readers want more of her. (Two novels and two collections of essays have come out in Japan since *Kitchen.*) And Banana Yoshimoto herself seems an odd one; it's hard to know what genus to put her in. She can't be called a Japanese counterpart of members of the American literary brat pack. She's not jaded enough—she's too adorably nerdy, and she's way too friendly. She's not a brat. In fact, she makes you wonder if bounce-and-shine is still a standard feature in the artistic youth of other nations; you just don't see too much of it around here. Yoshimoto even includes an afterword to the American edition of *Kitchen,* in which she expresses the hope that the book will be a balm to those who have known setbacks in their lives; there's a generous, therapeutic impulse somewhere inside this fiction writer. "Surely we will meet someday," she closes her message to the reader, "and until that day, I pray that you will live happily." Such graciousness feels weird, too—it's foreign, anyway. But why be wary of a kind wish?

Source: Deborah Garrison, "Dayo!," in *The New Yorker,* Vol. LXVIII, No. 49, January 25, 1993, pp. 109-110.

Elizabeth Hanson

In the following review, Hanson offers a mixed assessment of Kitchen.

A Japanese maxim warns that "A gentleman does not go near a kitchen." Traditionally a cramped, dingy place—even in an otherwise well-appointed home—the old-fashioned kitchen revealed the low status of the women who spent much of their time there. Yet today, though still small by American standards and still largely the domain of women, kitchens are the showcases of Japanese consumer affluence.

Banana Yoshimoto's first novel evokes this modern opulence even in its title, which uses the trendy English loan-word *kitchin* rather than the Japanese term, *daidokoro.* Ms. Yoshimoto was all of 24 years old when *Kitchen* was published in Japan in 1988; with its kooky young woman protagonist, Mikage Sakurai, the novel—a best-seller that is now in its 57th printing—clearly has spoken to the author's contemporaries.

"The place I like best in this world is the kitchen," Mikage announces in the very first line. "I love even incredibly dirty kitchens to distraction —vegetable droppings all over the floor, so dirty your slippers turn black on the bottom." Left alone in the world when her grandmother dies, Mikage finds that her saddest moods are dispelled by the chance to scrub a refrigerator or even glimpse a busy kitchen from the window of a bus. She is befriended by a young man, Yuichi Tanabe, and his glamorous transsexual "mother," Eriko, and in this household finds some peace—at least for a time.

"Moonlight Shadow," the less satisfying story that fills out this volume, tells of a mysterious stranger who leads the young woman narrator— her voice sounds exactly like that of Mikage Sakurai—to a reunion with her deceased boyfriend.

Unfortunately, the endearing characters and amusing scenes in Ms. Yoshimoto's work do not compensate for frequent bouts of sentimentality. The English text feels choppy—this may be due to the author's style rather than the translation—and the translator, Megan Backus, uses Americanisms that sometimes sound odd coming from the mouths of Japanese characters.

For English-language readers, the appeal of *Kitchen* lies in its portrayal of the lives of young Japanese. Here are characters who disdain traditional meals made of tofu and pickled vegetables and instead tuck into doughnuts, sandwiches from Kentucky Fried Chicken and pudding cups from the local mini-mart. Yuichi and Eriko offer Mikage a huge sofa to sleep on, not a futon, and gleefully fill their apartment with electronic gadgets. And Mikage herself typifies the confusion of young Japanese women, attracted as she is to kitchens and cooking as symbols of comfort and womanliness, yet trying to live independently.

Observing the women pupils at a cooking school, Mikage feels how different she is: "Those women lived their lives happily. They had been taught, probably by caring parents, not to exceed the boundaries of their happiness regardless of what they were doing.... What I mean by 'their happiness' is living a life untouched as much as possible by the knowledge that we are really, all of us, alone."

Source: Elizabeth Hanson, "Hold the Tofu," in *The New York Times,* January 17, 1993.

Sources

Scott Shibuya Brown, "Adrift in the New Japan," in *Book World–The Washington Post,* January 10, 1993, p. 10.

David Galef, "Jinxed," in *The New York Times Book Review,* February 27, 1994, p. 23.

Nicole Gaouette, "Hip Novelist Combines Old and New Japan," in *The Christian Science Monitor,* December 10, 1998, p. 13.

Deborah Garrison, "Day-O!," in *The New Yorker,* January 25, 1993, pp. 109–10.

Todd Grimson, "The Catcher in the Rice," in *Los Angeles Times Book Review,* January 10, 1993, pp. 3, 7.

Elizabeth Hanson, "Hold the Tofu," in *The New York Times Book Review,* January 17, 1993, p. 18.

Nick Hornby, "Mystical Mundane," in *The Times Literary Supplement,* January 8, 1983, p. 18.

For Further Study

Anne Allison, *Nightwork: Sexuality, Pleasure and Corporate Masculinity in a Tokyo Hostess Club,* The University of Chicago Press, 1994.

> This sociological study provides a wonderful understanding of Eriko's character.

Donald Keene, *The Pleasures of Japanese Literature,* Columbia University Press, 1988.

> Keene is considered by some to be the leading interpreter of Japanese literature to the West, a frequent translator of criticism and literature. This recent, short book gives a good background on the culture that produced *Kitchen.*

Jonathan Rauch, *The Outnation: A Search for the Soul of Japan,* Harvard Business School Press, 1992.

> The author of this book was young, still in his twenties, when he traveled to Japan in 1990. His insights into the culture provide wonderful, intelligent background.

Edward Seidensticker, *Tokyo Rising: The City since the Great Earthquake,* Alfred A. Knopf, 1990.

> The earthquake of the title is the one that destroyed most of the city in 1923. His research is thorough, but academic.

Rex Shelley, *Culture Shock: Japan,* Graphic Arts Center Publishing Co., 1993.

> This book, part of a series of guidebooks aimed mainly at business travelers, gives a good sense of contemporary Japanese lifestyles, customs, and expectations.

A Lesson Before Dying

Ernest J. Gaines

1993

Published by Knopf in 1993, *A Lesson Before Dying* is set in Louisiana. Considered a success by readers and critics alike, the appeal for most readers is derived from the intense emotions the story evokes. The author, Ernest Gaines, wants the reader to feel compassion for the young black man, Jefferson, whom jurors convict for a murder he did not commit. Nor can readers ignore the personal struggles of Grant Wiggins as he teaches Jefferson to be a man.

Gaines credits his boyhood experiences for his ability to develop lifelike characters. In an interview with Paul Desruisseaux for the *New York Times Book Review,* Gaines says he learned by "working in the fields, going fishing in the swamps with the older people, and, especially, listening to the people who came to my aunt's house, the aunt who raised me." His attention to the people he loves results in characters that are believable. Alice Walker, in the *New York Times Book Review,* acknowledges Gaines's success with characterization in saying that Gaines "claims and revels in the rich heritage of Southern Black people and their customs; the community he feels with them is unmistakable and goes deeper even than pride.... Gaines is mellow with historical reflection, supple with wit, relaxed and expansive because he does not equate his people with failure."

Gaines's themes reveal universal truths. He demonstrates that racism destroys people; relationships suffer from people's choices; and pride, honor, and manhood can prevail in trying times. While

some critics denounce Gaines for his failure to address blacks' difficulties in today's society, his defense is that he writes for all times and all people.

Author Biography

Ernest J. Gaines, EJ for short, was born in the slave area of a Louisiana plantation on January 15, 1933. His father, Manuel, and mother, Adrienne J. (Colar) Gaines, worked as plantation laborers. Gaines's Aunt Augusteen cared for Gaines and his siblings as they grew up in "the Quarters." Gaines's earliest memories reflect times spent on his aunt's front porch listening to her friends' stories. After Gaines learned to read and write, he enjoyed writing letters for his aunt and her elderly friends. Through listening and writing, Gaines grew to understand himself and his people.

Gaines moved to San Francisco, California, with his mother and stepfather when he was fifteen years old. San Francisco offered Gaines a world of new experiences far removed from his aunt's front porch. Most importantly, he discovered libraries in San Francisco and quickly became an avid reader. Homesick for family, friends, and the Southern plantation lifestyle he had known, Gaines read any fiction he could find that was set in his homeland. He discovered that writers often gave the wrong impression of Southern blacks and the lives they led. These writers were white and had no personal experience with the kind of life Gaines knew existed for Southern blacks. He decided then to write those missing stories. He read other authors whose works he admired: Faulkner, Hemingway, Flaubert, and de Maupassant. The Russian writers, though, inspired him the most. Their stories about Russian peasants offered him a model for writing about the people he knew best.

In the meantime, Gaines graduated with a bachelor of arts degree from San Francisco State College in 1957 and completed graduate work at Stanford University in 1959. In 1962, a young black man named James Meredith tried to enter the University of Mississippi Law School, prompting civil rights demonstrations and violence. Gaines admired Meredith for his determination and courage. As a result, Gaines vowed to dedicate himself to writing about the Southern black experience. After returning to Louisiana, Gaines completed his first novel, *Catherine Carmier.* This 1964 success marked the beginning of his writing career.

Drawing from the stories he heard at his aunt's knee, Gaines writes about the people, places, and

Ernest J. Gaines

daily events of the rural South. Critics have always admired his work. They praise his portrayal of realistic characters and his capable handling of emotional themes: racism, personal relationships, social pressures, social change, and others. Jerry H. Bryant summarizes his talent in a comment in the *Iowa Review.* He asserts that his fiction "contains the austere dignity and simplicity of ancient epic, a concern with man's most powerful emotions and the actions that arise from those emotions, and an artistic intuition that carefully keeps such passions and behavior under fictive control. Gaines may be one of our most naturally gifted storytellers."

Plot Summary

Before the Jail Visits

A Lesson Before Dying examines the relationship established between two men in a rural Louisiana parish in the 1940s. One man, Jefferson, is convicted of murder and sentenced to die in the electric chair. The other man, Grant Wiggins, is the local schoolteacher.

The book is told from the point of view of Grant. Although he does not attend Jefferson's trial, he is able to give details from it because everybody in their small community has been talking about it.

He explains that Jefferson ended up in trouble because he had received a ride from some friends: they stopped at a liquor store before taking him home, and when the friends tried to rob the store a shoot out occurred, leaving both of his friends and the owner of the store, who was white, dead. Panicking, Jefferson took money from the open cash register before fleeing, and the all-white jury found him guilty of both robbery and murder.

His lawyer, in trying to convince the jury to not impose the death penalty, portrayed Jefferson as being subhuman, presenting him as being too stupid to knowingly be guilty of a crime: "What justice would there be to take this life?" he asked them. "Why, I would just as soon put a hog in the electric chair as this." The afternoon that he is sentenced to die, Jefferson's godmother, who raised him, comes to see Grant, to ask him to visit Jefferson in jail before his execution and to educate him. "I don't want them to kill no hog," she explains. "I want a man to go to that chair, on his own two feet."

Grant is hesitant about getting involved, unsure of what he can do to make Jefferson's life any better in the few weeks that he has left, but Jefferson's godmother, Miss Emma Glenn, is close friends with Grant's aunt, Tante Lou, whom he lives with, and she convinces him to do as Miss Emma asks. Before visits can be arranged, Grant is forced to go through the humiliating process of beseeching the sheriff's cousin for the sheriff's permission, and then being interviewed by the sheriff himself, to make sure that he will not cause any "aggravation."

With permission to proceed with regular visits to the prisoner, Grant has two experiences at the school where he works that bring some perspective to his own life. The superintendent of the schools visits, and Grant finds himself acting servile to him, the way a black man is expected to behave toward a white man, in order to assure that his little one-room school will be kept open. Also, he observes the old men who deliver his wood, and then the school children that he sends out to chop the wood: "And I thought to myself, What am I doing? Am I reaching them at all? They are acting exactly as the old men did earlier. They are fifty years younger, maybe more, but doing the same things those old men did who never attended a day of school in their lives. Is this just a vicious circle? Am I doing anything?"

Visits to Jefferson

Grant is reluctant to become involved with Jefferson from the start, and Jefferson is just as reluctant about receiving visitors. The first few visits, Grant comes with Miss Emma, and then he comes alone. Jefferson does not talk when Miss Emma, whom he calls his nannan, is around, but alone with Grant he bitterly asks about the electric chair and says that he is just a hog, while Grant insists that he is a man.

At the same time, Reverend Ambrose starts visiting Jefferson. Tante Lou, Miss Emma and the Reverend all wish that Grant would try to get Jefferson to be more concerned about his soul and getting into heaven, but Grant, though he believes in God, is not willing to promote their religious beliefs. When he talks with his girlfriend, Vivian, Grant expresses his fondest wish would be for them to leave the parish, to leave the South, as almost everyone who grew up in the area and gotten an education has done before, but he feels stuck there because Vivian's divorce is not final (actually, she points out, he left once, to live with his parents in California, but he came back on his own). At the school Christmas pageant, there is only one package under the tree, with a pair of warm socks and a wool sweater for Jefferson, indicating how much the community is thinking about his imminent execution.

After the date for the execution is set at April 8th, the second Friday after Easter, Jefferson becomes a little less bitter, and he becomes even more at ease with his situation when Grant brings him a radio, although the Reverend and the women are upset that he is listening to music when he should be thinking about God. Jefferson agrees to accept a pencil and a pad of paper to write down things that he might want to talk about during their visits. In the meantime, Grant loses some of the detached cool that he has maintained throughout the ordeal, starting a bar fight with a few mulattos who make racist remarks and say that Jefferson should die. Vivian reminds Grant of the danger that he puts her, and all of the people who depend on him, in when he acts recklessly. At their last visit together, Jefferson is still angry about his fate, but he promises to face it with as much calm as he can, for the sake of his nannan.

The Execution and After

Chapter 29 consists of excerpts from Jefferson's diary, written in his uneducated grammar. He describes his fears and his doubts, but also his relief that he has been able to comfort Miss Emma a little, and that she was able to kiss him for the first time. Chapter 30 describes the day of the execution from the points of view of different citizens in the town: those who saw the truck with the electric chair arrive, those who saw it taken into the courthouse, the deputies who were responsible for having Jefferson's head, arm and leg shaved, the people shopping two blocks away who can hear the generator that powers the electric chair, etc.

At his school out in the country, Grant has his children kneel in prayer from twelve o'clock until they receive word that the execution is over, just as Vivian earlier said she planned do with her students. The sheriff's deputy, Paul, who had been the only white man to treat him with respect during his visits to the jail, drives out to the school after it is over, bringing Jefferson's diary to him. "I don't know what you're going to say when you go back in there," Paul tells him. "But tell them he was the bravest man in that room today. I'm a witness, Grant Wiggins. Tell them so." Grant suggests that Paul might come back one day and tell them himself, and he responds, "It would be an honor." When he returns to the classroom, Grant, who has been a stern schoolmaster and a reluctant participant in Jefferson's final days, is crying.

Characters

Reverend Mose Ambrose

As the plantation church's pastor, Reverend Ambrose ministers to the laborers and their families. Even though he has no formal education, he serves his people with a true dedication to his vocation. He baptizes, marries, and buries them and offers words of hope and encouragement through his preaching and caring. He and Grant Wiggins share the privilege of visits to Jefferson. Devoted to God, Reverend Ambrose worries about not only Jefferson's soul, but also Grant's. He continually tries to talk to Grant about God and encourages Grant to discuss God with Jefferson. He wants to know if Grant has determined Jefferson's deepest feelings about death and what it will mean for his soul. Grant, however, feels that Reverend Ambrose is responsible for preparing Jefferson's soul for death. Reverend Ambrose accuses Grant of being selfish and uneducated because Grant will not accept that heaven exists and will not use his relationship with Jefferson to get Jefferson to accept salvation. Reverend Ambrose believes Grant is a lost soul.

Vivian Baptiste

Vivian is Grant Wiggins's girlfriend, even though she is still married. A beautiful woman, she draws attention to herself wherever she goes. She has light skin, long black hair, high cheekbones, and greenish-brown eyes. She stands tall—about five foot seven—and dresses well. When Tante Lou and Miss Emma first meet her, they resent her light skin and the fact that Vivian seldom visits her parents. They change their minds about her, however, when they learn that she regularly attends church. They call her a "lady of quality." Grant knows that Vivian is a lady. Also a teacher, Vivian understands Grant and his desire to move elsewhere to teach and to see more of the world. Grant turns to Vivian for solace during the trying months of his relationship with Jefferson.

Bear

Bear is one of the two boys who pick Jefferson up on their way to Mr. Grope's store. Bear does all the talking. Not only does he ask and plead for the liquor, he also takes the first steps around the counter toward Mr. Grope. Bear and his friend, Brother, die in the altercation, along with Mr. Grope.

Paul Bonin

Paul is the young deputy at the jail. When Miss Emma asks the older deputy how Jefferson is, and the older deputy says, "Quiet," Miss Emma mistakes the response for a command that she be quiet. Paul quickly sees what has happened and answers her question with "Jefferson's been quiet," which relieves the tension. Paul speaks civilly to both Miss Emma and Grant, not ordering them to do something, but asking them politely. For example, after checking Grant's pockets to make sure they are empty, Paul tells Grant that he can put his things back into his pockets. Paul is a white man with brown hair and gray-blue eyes and is a little younger than Grant. Paul takes Grant to Jefferson's cell each time Grant visits. As they see more of one another, Paul and Grant establish a sort of friendship, with Paul showing his sincere concern for Jefferson's fate. Paul hates having to search Grant when he visits and lets Grant know that he only does it because it is a matter of policy. Paul witnesses Jefferson's death and tries to tell Grant that he has done a good job as a teacher. Even though Paul and Grant do not agree on matters of faith, Paul tells Grant that he wants to be his friend.

Men working on a sugar cane plantation.

Brother

Brother is one of the two boys who pick Jefferson up on their way to Mr. Grope's store. When a fight breaks out among Mr. Grope, Bear, and Brother, all three die.

Joe Claiborne

Joe Claiborne runs the Rainbow Club bar and is married to Thelma. He drives a new white Cadillac and allows customers to buy on credit when they need to. Friends gather at the Club to talk and drink. Grant visits the club often because he feels wanted there, and it is a place where he and Vivian can dance and be together.

Thelma Claiborne

Thelma Claiborne runs the Rainbow Club cafe and is married to Joe. She has a smile full of gold teeth and wears strong perfume. People can depend on Thelma for good food and friendly conversation.

Irene Cole

Irene Cole serves as Grant's student teacher and assists him with the younger students. Even though Grant can not see it, Irene harbors a secret love for him.

Emma Glenn

See Emma Nannan

Alcee Grope

Grope is the white storeowner whom Jefferson is accused of killing. Grope likes Jefferson and asks about his nannan. When the two boys Jefferson is with ask for liquor, Grope refuses to give it to them because they do not have enough money to pay for it. The two boys are already drunk. A fight ensues, and Grope and the two boys are all dead when it is over.

Sam Guidry

Sam Guidry, the sheriff, always tries to put Grant Wiggins in his place. He expects Grant to behave like a subordinate, telling Grant when Grant uses proper grammar and speaks intelligently that he's too smart for his own good. As the sheriff, Guidry runs the jail, but he is seldom present when Grant visits. When he is on duty, Guidry looks like a cowboy; he wears a Stetson hat and cowboy boots. His appearance can intimidate people, though. Guidry has a strong face and large hands, and is tall and tanned. Guidry thinks that Grant's teaching Jefferson is a joke; he believes Jefferson is not only guilty of the crime, but stupid as well.

Mr. Henri

See Henri Pichot

Jefferson

A twenty-one-year-old slightly retarded black man, Jefferson has always lived on the Pichot plantation with his godmother, Miss Emma, or "Nannan," as he calls her. On his way to a bar one October day, Jefferson accepts a ride from two other young black men, Bear and Brother. Bear and Brother decide to stop to buy liquor but have no money between them. The two think the store owner, Mr. Grope, will allow them to get the liquor on credit. When they ask him, he disagrees, and they begin to argue. Already drunk, Bear starts around the counter. Mr. Grope gets his gun and begins to shoot. Before Jefferson knows what has happened, all three men are dead. Confused, he is still in the store when two white men find him. He gets blamed for robbing and killing the storeowner.

Jefferson's attorney tries to use Jefferson's mental disability as a defense, claiming he has no more intelligence than a hog. The white jury, however, finds Jefferson guilty, and the judge sentences him to the electric chair. Miss Emma resents Jefferson's being labeled a hog, and implores Grant Wiggins to teach him enough that he can walk to the electric chair with some pride.

Media Adaptations

- An unabridged audio version of *A Lesson Before Dying,* read by Jay Long, is a 1997 Random House production (ISBN: 0375402586).

- Juneteenth Audio Books offers an abridged edition of *A Lesson Before Dying* produced by Time Warner Audio Books (ISBN: 1570422230).

When Wiggins begins his visits, Jefferson greets him with silence, the whites of his eyes bloodshot. Jefferson later replaces his silence with talk full of self-disgust and a sense of hopelessness. After months of visits, though, Jefferson begins to question Wiggins about God and heaven, his nannan, and life. Wiggins brings Jefferson a radio; they share a favorite announcer. He also gives Jefferson a notebook. Jefferson writes in the notebook until his death on Good Friday in April. From their conversations during Jefferson's last days and the journal Jefferson has kept, Wiggins learns that to be a teacher, one has to believe. He concludes that Jefferson is the true teacher.

Inez Lane

The current cook at the plantation's big house, Inez greets Miss Emma, Tante Lou, and Grant each time they visit Henri Pichot. She wears the white dress and shoes of a cook, with a blue gingham apron and kerchief on her head. Inez suffers for her friends when Mr. Pichot and his friends keep them waiting. She says little but continues her duties serving the head of the household and his white visitors.

Tante Lou

Tante Lou, Grant Wiggins's aunt, raised him. She is also Miss Emma's best friend, having worked with her in the big Pichot house as a washerwoman. A large person like Miss Emma, Tante Lou keeps Grant in line with her stern nature and her devout faith. She hates that Grant does not attend church or admit to believing in God. She avoids him entirely on Sundays. She expects Grant to visit and teach Jefferson because it is what she and Miss Emma want him to do. Tante Lou is the one who sent Wiggins to the university to make a better life for himself and the people around him. As a result, Tante Lou believes that Wiggins is obligated to do what he can for Jefferson.

Miss Emma Nannan

To Jefferson, Miss Emma is "Nannan," his godmother and the person who loves and has raised him. Although in her seventies, Miss Emma strikes a formidable appearance. She weighs nearly two hundred pounds and commands respect from everyone she knows. Even her late husband called her Miss Emma. Miss Emma used to cook for the plantation owner, Henri Pichot. She pins her gray hair to the top of her head and often sports a wellworn brown felt hat and overcoat with rabbit fur trimming the collar and sleeves. She knows that Jefferson has limited intelligence but wants him to learn to read and write before he dies. More importantly, she wants him to understand that he is a man and not the "hog" the court says he is. A religious woman, Miss Emma prays for Jefferson's soul and relies on Reverend Ambrose for spiritual guidance for her and Jefferson.

Henri Pichot

A medium-sized man with long white hair, Henri Pichot owns the plantation on which Grant's school is located and where Miss Emma, Jefferson, Tante Lou, and Grant live. As the plantation owner, Mr. Pichot lives in its main house, a large structure containing modern amenities available to the wealthy. Mr. Pichot begrudgingly meets with Miss Emma, Tante Lou, and Grant to hear Miss Emma's request to allow Grant to visit Jefferson in his jail cell. Pichot only allows the visit because Miss Emma used to work for him. Mr. Pichot is the sheriff's brother-in-law, so Miss Emma thinks that Mr. Pichot might be able to convince the sheriff to permit Wiggins's visits to the jail. Although Pichot quickly dismisses Miss Emma and her friends on their first visit, he appears to become more sympathetic to their cause as time goes on.

Louis Rougon

Henri Pichot's cohort, Louis Rougon owns the bank close to the plantation. He is present each time Grant visits the plantation house and wears the clothes of a successful businessman: gray suit, white shirt, and gray-and-white-striped tie. Rougon

thinks it is amusing that Miss Emma wants Grant to teach Jefferson and smirks his thoughts in Grant's presence.

Mr. Sam
See Sam Guidry

Grant Wiggins

Grant Wiggins, the teacher, grew up on the Pichot plantation. Tante Lou, Grant's aunt and the plantation's washerwoman, raised him. Even though Tante Lou earned a living in the plantation's main house, she did not want Grant to have to enter the house ever again through the back door, the servant's entrance. Thus, she sacrificed to send him to the university to become a teacher, a respected member of society.

At the opening of the story, Grant has taught at the plantation school for six years. The school has not changed much since he left it ten years earlier, nor have the children changed. He knows the children and their families well. He knows which children will fail and which will succeed. He understands their family situations. He encourages the children to do the best they can and to help one another. The community, in turn, appreciates Grant's returning to the plantation to teach reading and writing. It is because Grant remains one of them, yet has the education no one else has, that Miss Emma chooses him to visit and teach Jefferson. Jefferson has just been convicted of killing the white storeowner and awaits his death. Grant is to try to teach Jefferson to be a man—to try to instill in him a sense of self-worth and pride.

Grant doubts first, his ability to reach Jefferson, and later, his ability to teach him anything of value. He feels frustrated with himself and angry with the system. Grant sees the injustice around him and realizes that he can do nothing to change it. For example, when Grant faces the sheriff or Henri Pichot, he knows that they expect him to act the part of a slave, bowing to their demands. This disturbs him so much that at one point, he fights a man for the hateful comments the man makes about Jefferson. When Grant needs understanding, he turns to Vivian Baptiste, his girlfriend. While Miss Emma, Reverend Ambrose, and Tante Lou would like for Grant to help Jefferson find God, Grant knows that he is the wrong one to help Jefferson with this. Grant questions his own beliefs and is unable to assure Jefferson of heaven. In the end, Grant believes that Reverend Ambrose and Jefferson are the real teachers. Grant takes no credit for having prepared Jefferson to face death and feels a great sadness for the realization and for the loss of Jefferson's life.

Themes

Justice and Injustice

From the beginning until the very end of *A Lesson Before Dying* a sense of injustice prevails. While this theme derives from the larger theme of racism, Gaines uses specific incidents to demonstrate how underlying racist beliefs can result in miscarriage of justice. Jefferson innocently accepts a ride with two conniving young men who are planning to take advantage of a white businessman. When the three other men die in the resulting struggle, Jefferson, who is slightly retarded, does not really understand what has happened or even remember how he got there. Unfairly accused by two white men who come into the store and find Jefferson leaving with money and whiskey in his pockets, Jefferson is later tried and convicted for the crime and sentenced to die in the electric chair. The injustice continues after Jefferson is jailed, and it extends to the people he loves. Tante Lou, the Reverend, and Grant Wiggins suffer ill treatment when they try to arrange visitation and each time that they visit Jefferson thereafter. The intolerance shown by the white accusers, jurors, judge, and jailers results from their racist belief that they are superior to black people.

Civil Rights and Racism

The story takes place in the late 1940s when the country's Civil Rights movement was moving towards integration. Integration enables equal rights to all people, allowing them to live together in harmony regardless of their race or skin color. In the South, however, during the time this novel is set, segregation still reigns. Segregation, the opposite of integration, separates races. Racism results when one race views itself as superior over another and determines that it should have more rights than the other. This view held true in the South, particularly on the large plantations where many blacks labored for white landowners. Whites considered blacks inferior human beings. Whites did not want to associate with blacks in any way. Gaines provides clear examples of racist behavior and the varying effects racist behaviors have on people's lives.

In *A Lesson Before Dying* whites treat Jefferson unfairly through their actions, their words, and

Topics for Further Study

- Define capital punishment. Trace its history since ancient times. Discuss the reforms introduced throughout the ages to eliminate the use of capital punishment.

- Research capital punishment. Take a position for or against it. Prepare to defend your position in a classroom debate.

- Critics refer to Gaines as a master storyteller. He, himself, credits others for the stories they told when he was growing up and that he has borrowed. In other words, the "oral tradition" greatly influences his writing. Describe the relative importance of the tradition in various cultures and explain the purposes the tradition serves for different peoples.

- Even though is set in the late 1940s, racism still exists in the small town of Bayonne. Trace the history of the Civil Rights movement. Relate your findings to the fictional events that occur in the story.

their attitudes. Not only are people inconsiderate of Jefferson, they also disenfranchise Jefferson's friends and family. For example, when his nannan, Miss Emma, Tante Lou, and Grant Wiggins visit Mr. Pichot, they must enter through the kitchen. They are expected to remain there until Mr. Pichot and his associates summon them, which was, in one case, two hours later. Mr. Pichot and his companions also expect Grant Wiggins to act a certain way because he is black. Even though they know Wiggins is an educated man, they make it clear to him that he should mumble, use improper grammar, and not meet them eye-to-eye.

Not only did racism exist between the blacks and whites, but also between the blacks and mulattos. The mulattos were of mixed black and European heritage. They refused to work side-by-side on the plantations with "niggers" and became bricklayers instead. Grant Wiggins fights two of them at the Rainbow Club one night when he hears them making derogatory comments about Jefferson and making light of Jefferson's impending death.

While racism abounds in the story, destroying people's lives along the way, one equitable relationship between a black man and a white man blossoms to serve as a beacon of hope for the future. Grant Wiggins and Paul Bonin forge the beginnings of a friendship. Paul, the young white deputy at the jail, sees beyond the color of Jefferson's skin and feels compassion for his situation. He appreciates, too, the part Grant Wiggins plays in trying to make the rest of Jefferson's life, and the thought of his upcoming death, more bearable. Paul tries to treat Wiggins with respect. He shows a deference for his education as well as his consideration for Jefferson and his nannan. When he speaks to Wiggins, he looks him in the eye and encourages Wiggins to do the same. He completes the required weapons searches on Wiggins less thoroughly than he might on someone he does not know or trust. Wiggins feels the same way about Paul. Wiggins understands that he and Paul have an appreciation for one another, although Wiggins does not feel worthy of Paul's. In the end, Paul compliments Wiggins on his teaching talent, even though Wiggins does not agree that he deserves the compliment. Paul tells Wiggins that he would like to be his friend.

God and Religion

Jefferson's relationship with God, and his understanding of faith, heaven, and salvation concern Miss Emma, Tante Lou, and Reverend Ambrose. Miss Emma and Tante Lou think that Wiggins's visits to Jefferson will prepare Jefferson to die with some dignity. They think that Wiggins, with his education, knows what it will take to instill in Jefferson some sense of self-worth. They believe that Wiggins can tell what Jefferson's deepest thoughts are about life and his upcoming death. When Wiggins gives Jefferson a radio, Reverend Ambrose, Tante Lou, and Miss Emma are appalled, calling it a box of sin and telling Wiggins that Jefferson needs God in his cell rather than a disembodied radio announcer. Wiggins tells them that he himself is not the one to provide Jefferson with spiritual guidance, admitting that he questions heaven's existence and God's love.

Jefferson, too, struggles with faith issues until his dying day, wondering if God loves only white people. Yet, he walks to the chair a man rather than an unsure, beaten-down slave. Paul credits Wiggins's teaching for the transformation. Wiggins sarcastically attributes it to God's work.

Style

Setting

Gaines sets *A Lesson Before Dying* in and around the fictitious Bayonne, a small town in Louisiana. It is 1948. Some events occur on the plantation, either in the school where Grant Wiggins teaches or in the homes of Henri Pichot, Tante Lou, or Miss Emma. Other events occur at the jail or at the Rainbow Club.

The church serves as the school for the black children whose parents labor on the plantation. There are no desks; the children write on their laps or kneel in front of the benches that are pews on Sundays. Grant Wiggins's desk is the collection table during church services. A woodburning stove for which there is never enough fuel heats the classroom. The same sparseness exists in the homes of both Tante Lou and Miss Emma. Tante Lou shares her small home with Wiggins. The furniture is old, and the wallpaper peels away from the walls. While Tante Lou has added her own homey touches, the house has a tired feeling to it. Wiggins refers to it as "rustic." Miss Emma's home is even smaller, with the bed in the living room. Henri Pichot's house, however, is a huge house with modern appliances. Instead of a woodburning stove, the cook uses a gas range for cooking. The same black iron pots that Wiggins remembers from childhood hang on the wall, but the old icebox he had known has been replaced by a sparkling white refrigerator.

The important events of the story take place in the jail. The jail is located in the old red-brick courthouse that resembles a castle. Housing both black and white prisoners in different areas, the cells themselves are located on the second floor of the courthouse, at the top of a set of steel stairs. The cells of the other African-American prisoners have two metal bunks each. Jefferson's, however, has only one bunk, equipped with a mattress and wool blanket. A toilet, a washbowl, and a small metal shelf take up the rest of the six-foot by ten-foot cell. For light, there is only a single light bulb hanging from the center of the ceiling and a small, high, barred window.

Wiggins goes to the Rainbow Club for company and comfort. Green, yellow, and red neon lights advertise the combination bar and cafe. In the bar, Wiggins can choose to sit on a barstool at the counter or at one of the white-clothed tables in the dimly lit room. The cafe boasts both a lunch counter and tables with cheery red-and-white-checkered tablecloths.

Point of View

Gaines uses the first person point of view to tell the story of Grant Wiggins. That is, Wiggins tells the story himself as the events affect him. By using his voice, Gaines can easily portray the intense emotions that Wiggins feels in relationship to the other characters and the struggles they endure. The resulting narrative enables Gaines to connect his fiction with historical reality. Gaines shares his own life experiences and perceptions with his readers through the lives and emotions of his characters. He aptly weaves fact and fiction to present his reflections on the Southern world that he knows existed. A twist to the typical personal narrative, though, is Jefferson's journal. Reading the entries, Wiggins knows Jefferson's innermost thoughts. By definition, a first-person narrator does not know what another character is thinking.

Style

Critics often compare Gaines's stories to epics. Although epics are usually in the form of long narrative poems, there are similarities between the two: both describe extraordinary achievements or events; and both have epic characters that stand heroic in the face of large-scale deeds. In the case of Wiggins, there is no hope that he can save Jefferson from the death that he will suffer as a result of a society's large-scale racist beliefs. Yet, Wiggins does help Jefferson gain self respect before he dies, in spite of the efforts of those who would persecute Jefferson for his skin color. Paul Bonin views Wiggins as a hero even if Wiggins, himself, does not.

Historical Context

Black Civil Rights in the Late 19th Century

With the Emancipation Proclamation of 1863, President Lincoln freed the slaves. Congressional Acts after that date granted blacks various civil rights. In 1866 and 1870, blacks received the rights to sue, be sued, and own property. With these rights, blacks gained the "privileges" of white citizens. The Fourteenth Amendment to the Constitution, in 1868, further extended black privileges, making former slaves eligible for citizenship. The Fifteenth Amendment gave blacks the right to vote and prevented state or federal governments from denying any citizen of this right on the basis of race. Blacks received further acceptance through the Civil Rights Act of 1871, which made it a crime to deny citizens of equal protection under the law, and the Civil Rights Act of 1875, which guaranteed blacks the right to use public accommodations.

The political climate in the United States shifted in the mid-1880s, however, to an attitude of indifference towards social justice. The Civil Rights Act of 1875 (right to public accommodations) was declared unconstitutional. Then, the Supreme Court legally instituted segregation through its decision in the case of Plessy v. Ferguson in 1896. Homer Plessy had been arrested and convicted for refusing to sit in a railroad car that was designated for African Americans. When he appealed his conviction on the grounds that it denied him his rights under the Thirteenth and Fourteenth Amendments, the Supreme Court overruled him. The Court upheld the principle of "separate but equal" facilities for blacks and whites. Even into the 1930s when Ernest Gaines was born, this principle and attitude towards blacks prevailed. Gaines set *A Lesson Before Dying* in the late 1940s, but the remnants of segregation still existed. The jail where Jefferson was incarcerated had a separate block of cells for African-American inmates, in addition to separate restroom facilities for African-American visitors to the jail.

Segregation in the South

Taking a step backwards after the Supreme Court's decision in the Plessy case, integration seemed impossible. Segregation was well established in the Northern states through custom rather than law. This was known as "de facto" segregation. Following the Plessy case, however, the South decreed laws that legalized racial segregation. This legal segregation is called "de jure" segregation. The laws that accomplished de jure segregation in the South are known as the Jim Crow laws, named after a pre-Civil War minstrel show character. These laws created a racial caste system in the South that held strong until 1954, when the Supreme Court declared public-school segregation unconstitutional in the Brown v. Board of Education case in Topeka, Kansas.

Early Steps Towards Integration in the 20th Century

The early 1900s saw steps being taken towards integration through two movements. One group worked towards equal treatment through integration; the other group wanted to establish a separate black state. In 1909, W. E. B. Du Bois founded the National Association for the Advancement of Col-

After the Emancipation Proclamation of 1863, Jim Crow laws legally enforced racial segregation until 1954.

ored People (NAACP). The NAACP still exists today and works for equality through integration. Another leader in the integration movement was Marcus Garvey, who founded the Universal Negro Improvement Association (UNIA) in 1914 to work towards a separate black state through black nationalism. While the UNIA no longer exists, the black nationalist movement continues.

Efforts to integrate continued to progress through the 1930s and 1940s. Black leaders found powerful support in black unions such as the Brotherhood of Sleeping Car Porters who helped apply economic pressure to pass such acts as the 1947 Fair Employment Practices Act. This legislation prevented discrimination in hiring on the basis of race or national origin. In 1948, Harry Truman ordered the integration of the armed forces. These early efforts to end segregation culminated in the Supreme Court ruling in the 1954 Brown v. Board of Education case. The ruling declared separate schools for blacks and whites unconstitutional.

Critical Overview

Gaines' sixth novel, *A Lesson Before Dying*, provides more support for his reputation as a tal-

ented writer. Since the 1964 publication of *Catherine Carmier,* his writing has served to present African-American culture in the same authentic light as the stories shared orally by the people who have lived them. Reading the stories of Ernest Gaines nearly equals having the experiences.

Critics agree that Gaines has a true sense of characterization. He asserts that his characters appear realistic because he has shaped them from people he knew while growing up on a Louisiana plantation. He cites the influence of Russian writers on his characterization. Russian writers relate stories about their peasant countrymen in a way that is caring, yet not cloying. These writers present truths without being harsh or disapproving. Gaines presents his people, his characters, in this same manner. He describes Southern blacks as he knows they truly are, not as they are represented in stories he read as a young man. The characters he encountered in those books were foreign to him. After failing to find accurate stories about his people, he decided to write them himself. Gaines told Joseph McLellan in the *Washington Post,* "If the book you want doesn't exist, you try to make it exist." The strength of his characters complements his exceptional writing. Just as "a swimmer cannot influence the flow of a river ..." says Larry McMurtry in the

New York Times Book Review, "the characters of Ernest Gaines ... are propelled by a prose that is serene, considered and unexcited."

Gaines's "serene" prose belies the serious nature of his writing. Part of the appeal of his work lies in the way that he handles life's intense themes in his stories. In fact, his stories do not always have happy endings. Gaines presents truths in his novels; critics applaud this. They commend him, for example, for confronting the tough issues that destroy relationships among people, yet build character and strength. His characters often struggle with questions that test their belief systems and pit friends or family members against one another. To illustrate, in one story, a young woman must choose between her father and her lover, a choice forced by the racial and social differences between them. In others, characters search for human dignity and pride. They face alienation and loneliness as well. As an example, both Jefferson and Wiggins experience isolation and desolation in *A Lesson Before Dying.* Yet the story really honors man's natural instinct to persevere in the face of adversity. This is demonstrated in Jefferson's learning the lessons that enable him to walk to his death with a sense of who he really is.

Reviewers often compare his writing to William Faulkner's. The story for example, takes place on a plantation near the small, imaginary town of Bayonne, Louisiana. This region compares to Faulkner's Yoknapatawpha County, a fictional county in rural Mississippi. Like Faulkner, Gaines created the place and its people from experiences and relationships he actually had as a child. Another comparison made between Gaines's and Faulkner's writing has to do with the characters the two writers portray. Faulkner writes about two families. One, the Sartoris family, boasts years of wealthy prominence in the community. The other, the newly rich Snopes family, lacks the social graces of people born into the area's aristocracy. Gaines aristocracy and "lesser quality" people are the southern white plantation owners and the Cajuns, respectively. The plantation owners, although French descendants themselves, consider themselves a higher class than the Cajuns, who are direct descendants of Canadian French. Of even lesser nobility, according to the southern class structure, are the blacks and the Creoles. The Creoles are often of mixed black and European heritage and referred to as mulattos. As do Faulkner's works, his stories reveal the complex socioeconomic interactions among his characters but even more explicitly point out the relationships between the blacks and whites.

Critics agree that his African-American heritage lends a uniquely original perspective to his stories. According to Alvin Aubert in his essay in *Contemporary Novelists,* "Gaines's peculiar point of view generates a more complex social vision than Faulkner's, an advantage Gaines has sustained with dramatic force and artistic integrity."

Criticism

David J. Kelly

David J. Kelly is a literature and creative writing instructor at College of Lake County and Oakton Community College in Illinois. In this essay he examines how the inaction of Grant Wiggins, the book's narrator, might make readers uncomfortable.

Readers who do not want to take the time to learn from fiction, who want a novel to have a straightforward, simple message, might find Ernest J. Gaines's *A Lesson Before Dying* a frustrating experience. This is definitely a moral book, with a distinct sense of right and wrong, but it is also too wise about the ways of the world to oversimplify the morals of its characters. For instance, if Jefferson were merely a witness to the liquor store shootings, then readers could easily agree that he is victimized by the legal system, but Gaines, rather than leaving him one hundred percent innocent, has him empty out the store's cash register. His lawyer certainly commits an offense against humanity by comparing Jefferson to a hog, but he does so for a good cause, to save the boy's life. Tante Lou and Miss Emma are too abrupt and narrow-minded to be thought of as saints, but they are too compassionate to be dismissed as comic types. It is not easy for a reader to interact with well-rounded characters: by their very nature, they challenge our assumptions. The more difficult they are, the more we can learn about the complexity of life.

For me, Grant Wiggins was a difficult character. I admired him at times, but more often I found myself annoyed with him. This annoyance was tiny, more like an itch than a headache, so that at first I could not be sure that I was feeling it at all. Once I accepted the fact that I was not comfortable with Grant, I had to question what it was about him, and, more importantly, about me, that was causing

What Do I Read Next?

- Gaines's 1964 novel, *Catherine Carmier* shows how characters deal with decisions based on their beliefs. Catherine, the daughter of a rich Creole, falls in love with Jackson Bradley, a black man caught between his love for Catherine and his understanding of the world beyond the community in which they live.

- Also a story of disallowed love, *Of Love and Dust* continues Gaines's search for human dignity. Published by Dial in 1967, Gaines's second novel portrays the doomed relationship between a black man and his white boss's wife.

- Many critics consider Gaines's third novel, *The Autobiography of Miss Jane Pittman,* his best work. The narrative recounts events in Miss Jane Pittman's background that originate during the Civil War and continue through the 1960s. The 1971 novel takes the reader on a trip back through time.

- Knopf published Gaines's fifth novel, *A Gathering of Old Men,* in 1983. Someone kills a white Cajun boss on a Louisiana plantation. When the lynch mob arrives to hang the black man they have decided is guilty, a group of elderly black men and a young white woman surround the accused and claim individual responsibility for the murder.

- Harper Lee wrote *To Kill a Mockingbird* in 1960. Combining the themes of racial prejudice and a child's perception of southern smalltown life, the story is about a reticent black man who is accused of rape, the man who defends him, and a nine-year-old girl who narrates the tale.

- Written by Albert French in 1993, *Billy* chronicles the tragic tale of two black boys growing up in the 1930s who fight back when they are attacked and accidentally commit murder. Ten-year-old Billy is charged, tried as an adult, sentenced to death row, and electrocuted.

---

the problem. As much as I liked the book, why couldn't I get along with its narrator? It wasn't that he had bad circumstances, because seeing characters overcome bad circumstances is what reading is all about: we can detest a character's circumstances and still admire the character. It wasn't that he had too much misery for me to bear, because his life really wasn't that bad. The good things he *did* have, he didn't appreciate, but that should not have bothered me—there is no reason a reader should have to agree with the values of the narrator in order for the book to be a meaningful experience.

I kept waiting for him to choose what he wanted to be, to be what he chose to be. I was kept in an uneasy middle ground, watching him do the wrong things, bickering and storming out in the middle of conversations. I waited for him to quit blaming and hating the people who cared about him. For a while I thought that my complaint might be a charge against the author's artistry: Grant seems to be more passive than a protagonist ought to be, observing and complaining but avoiding in-

teraction with his surroundings when he can, and writers and critics generally agree that passive protagonists are the cause of weak novels. But he *has* to be reserved in order for the novel to work—its whole point is to lead us to the last two words, when Grant shows emotion that he kept bottled up throughout. Then I considered whether my impatience with him was cultural: I am a white man from the North, born a few generations after the time of the book, and I checked and rechecked my values to see if I was turning against the oppressed, using that "Why don't these people quit complaining?" nonsense that we have all used to filter out other people's problems throughout history. It's a lot easier to believe in self-determination when mainstream society welcomes you. Still, even accounting for my own distance from the situation, it seemed that Grant knew himself well enough to have more control over his destiny than he exercised here.

Thinking it over, I am convinced now that there is no other way Grant can be but frustrating.

The story would be more pleasant to read if he would either do something heroic or something that readers can clearly disagree with, but a novel like that would make a different point than the one Gaines makes here.

There is a parallel here that is obvious but nicely left unstated, between the cell that Jefferson is held in and the fact that Grant, free as he is, feels locked into a position he never asked for. He sees himself as being penned in, circumscribed, as having his options cut off at all sides. To begin with, being a black man in the South limits his options drastically, narrowing his life to such a degree that any encounter with white people is bound to end in an insult to his intelligence, his compassion and his humanity. And if it wasn't bad enough that the cultural mainstream works to keep out Grant and people like him, he feels his life narrowed further still by the people within his own society. He feels trapped by his aunt Lou and those of her generation (note that the book begins with Grant feeling hemmed in between the hugeness of Tante Lou and Miss Emma at an event he did not even attend); by Vivian, who he blames for holding him back, keeping him from wandering the world; and by the responsibilities that come of being a teacher, of having to care for the problems of students and their parents and having to uphold a certain position of respect in a community where education is rare and valuable.

The beauty of Gaines's achievement here is that he does not feel that he has to make Grant Wiggins suffer like a saint in order to make readers sympathetic. There is undeniably some reference to the suffering of Christ surrounding the way Jefferson is treated, but that is not presented as any sort of hidden meaning: even Jefferson, uneducated as he is, recognizes the unavoidable symbolism. Grant himself is too sophisticated to be seen as a martyr. He is too well-educated to entirely hold our sympathies: we expect him to come up with a reason for putting up with being involved in this, but he keeps saying that he is only there to please others. He alternates between blaming Vivian for tethering him to this small parish and moaning that he loves her, but he cannot answer her when she asks what he means by love. He lives in his aunt's home while trying to avoid contact with her friends and her beliefs. He seems to never be in the classroom with his students, and finds himself distracted whenever he starts to grade their papers, all the while complaining that they never seem to learn. The white deputy, Paul, tries to reach out to him at the end, to span the gulch that divides the races,

and Grant stays mum. As Reverend Ambrose explains, he is trying to keep himself above the complication of hypocrisy, to avoid telling the lie that is necessary to save someone's feelings. Is it *really* circumstances that have penned him in? Or has he jailed himself? He's just likable enough as a narrator for me to want to see the world as he sees it, but I also have learned through years of reading to not fully trust a narrator who feels that his problems are caused by bad luck, that things just have not been going his way.

Grant himself would deny that he is claiming bad luck for the problems that make him unhappy with the world around him. He has his own view of the universe that explains, in very sensible and objective terms, why he does not belong, and why those around him need to feel that he does belong with them and therefore fool themselves into thinking that they love him. Social forces drive black men from the South, he tells Vivian, and those who stay are broken by the system. Having not left, though he would like to, Grant feels that his education, and the social position that comes with it, make him the most high-profile unbroken figure around. He feels like a conspicuous target for Irene, his aunt, Miss Emma, or any other woman who feels the absence of a strong man. To him, then, it makes sense that the world that he does not want to be part of does not want to let him go. He doesn't take their love personally, nor does he feel any responsibility for it.

To his credit, he sees the strength to be a part of society *and* to be strong as something that Jefferson can achieve better than he can. I think the reason I am unconvinced by his case, though, is that I don't understand why being part of society has to equate with "being broken," even if it is an oppressed society like a black community in the rural mid-century South. Obviously, this might be the cultural difference between me and Jefferson showing—I am certainly not broken by being a part of my society, but then, for me, social success is not tied to keeping my eyes down and my mouth shut, waiting, or calling people I do not respect "Sir" and "Ma'm." I can understand why Grant would consider a black man accepted by white society to be "broken."

But what about within his own society? Every society has its outcasts, who like to believe that they are not a part of the group that they actually do belong to. I have known too many people in social situations that are nothing like Grant's, but who fear becoming a part of the world around them.

They think of themselves as radicals, as free spirits who don't want their own uniqueness to be ruined by rubbing up against the commonness of the people around them. Grant calls it being broken; others call "selling out"; still others have no name for it, they just aren't content with where they are and they wish that people would leave them alone. These are the passive protagonists in life. Their stories don't usually make pleasurable reading.

That uneasiness I mentioned before has to be there. It is the sign that Ernest Gaines did not make Grant too comfortably sympathetic, which a lesser writer would do without thinking, and that he also did not make Grant so obnoxious that a reader would stop before traveling 256 pages with him. I wanted Grant to choose what he wanted to be and to be what he'd chosen—imagine, if the story had been tailored to my comfort, how little I would have learned about the world he lives in. Grant Wiggins is a complex character, neither saintly nor profoundly flawed, just smart enough to paint over his personal quirks to make them look like the consequences of the world around him. I don't know if I would like to know him. but I'm a much better person for having seen his world, and having seen it through his eyes.

Source: David J. Kelly, in an essay for *Novels for Students,* Gale, 1999.

Carl Senna

In the following review of A Lesson Before Dying, *Senna emphasizes Gaines's ability to evoke the social climate of the South in the 1940s and its foreshadowing of the 1960s Civil Rights movement.*

Near the end of Ernest J. Gaines's novel *A Lesson Before Dying,* set in the fictional town of Bayonne, Louisiana, in 1948, a white sheriff tells a condemned black man to write in his diary that he has been fairly treated. Although the prisoner assents, nothing could be farther from the truth in that squalid segregated jail, which is an extension of the oppressive Jim Crow world outside.

A black primary school teacher, Grant Wiggins, narrates the story of Jefferson, the prisoner, whose resignation to his execution lends credence to the lesson of Grant's own teacher, Matthew Antoine: the system of Jim Crow will break down educated men like Grant and prisoners like Jefferson to "the nigger you were born to be."

Grant struggles, at first without success, to restore a sense of human dignity to Jefferson, a semi-literate, cynical and bitter twenty-one-year-old

man, who accepts his own lawyer's depiction of him as "a hog" not worthy of the court's expense. The social distance between the college-educated Grant and Jefferson appears as great as that between the races, and class differences often frustrate their ability to communicate. It does not help that Grant has intervened only reluctantly, prompted by his aunt, a moralizing scold and a nag, and by Jefferson's godmother, Miss Emma.

Mr. Gaines, whose previous novels include *A Gathering of Old Men* and *The Autobiography of Miss Jane Pittman,* admirably manages to sustain the somber tone of the issues confronting the black citizens of Bayonne. What is at stake becomes clear. We find Grant vicariously sharing in the triumphs of Joe Louis and Jackie Robinson. The larger-than-life achievements of these black heroes make it intolerable to the black folks that Jefferson die ignobly. For that reason, Grant, who makes no secret of his disdain for Jefferson, reluctantly becomes their instrument in trying to save him from disgrace. Justice, or Jefferson's innocence, becomes secondary to the cause of racial image building—no trifling matter.

With the day of Jefferson's execution approaching, Grant begins to despair. Jefferson himself dismisses appeals from Grant and the blacks of Bayonne that he die with dignity—like a man, not like a hog.

To complicate the plot further, Grant must overcome another racial divide, crossing the color line to love a divorced Creole woman, Vivian Baptiste. She becomes yet another reason why Grant must save Jefferson's dignity, if not save him from execution. By rejecting Creole prejudice against blacks, Vivian must accept that she too has a stake in how Jefferson confronts the electric chair. She crosses the black-brown line, to the horror of other Creoles and the subtle animosity of Grant's black relatives.

It is a tribute to Mr. Gaines's skill that he makes the conflicts convincing. Jefferson, chained and securely behind bars, still has one freedom left, and that is the freedom to choose how he accepts death.

Despite the novel's gallows humor and an atmosphere of pervasively harsh racism, the characters, black and white, are humanly complex and have some redeeming quality. At the end, Jefferson's white jailer, in a moving epiphany, is so changed that he suggests the white-black alliance that will emerge a generation later to smash Jim Crow to bits.

The New England abolitionist preacher William Ellery Channing observed just before the Civil War that "there are seasons, in human affairs, of inward and outward revolution, when new depths seem to be broken up in the soul, when new wants are unfolded in multitudes, and a new and undefined good is thirsted for." *A Lesson Before Dying,* though it suffers an occasional stylistic lapse, powerfully evokes in its understated tone the "new wants" in the 1940s that created the revolution of the 1960s. Ernest J. Gaines has written a moving and truthful work of fiction.

Source: Carl Senna, "Dying like a Man: A Novel about Race and Dignity in the South," in *The New York Times Book Review,* August 8, 1993, p. 21.

Charles R. Larson

In the following review, Larson focuses on Gaines's treatment of human dignity and the "morality of connectedness" in A Lesson Before Dying.

The incident that propels the narrative of Ernest J. Gaines's rich new novel is deceptively simple. Shortly after World War II, in a Cajun Louisiana town, a twenty-one-year-old black man who is barely literate finds himself in the wrong place at the wrong time, an innocent bystander during the robbery of a liquor store. The white store owner is killed, as are the two black men who attempt to rob the store; Jefferson—who is just standing there—panics. He grabs a bottle of liquor and starts drinking it. Then he looks at the phone, knowing he should call someone, but he's never used a dial phone in his life. Flight seems the only option, but as he leaves the store, two white customers enter.

That event takes place at the beginning of *A Lesson Before Dying,* Gaines' most rewarding novel to date, and it's followed by a brief summary of Jefferson's trial. The twelve white jurors find him guilty, assuming he's an accomplice of the two other black men, and the judge sentences Jefferson to death by electrocution. Much of what follows in this often mesmerizing story focuses on Jefferson's slow rise to dignity and manhood.

The obstacle to be overcome is a derogatory remark made by the defense during the trial, supposedly to save Jefferson from the death sentence. The lawyer asks the jurors, "Do you see a man sitting here? Look at the shape of this skull, this face as flat as the palm of my hand.... Do you see a modicum of intelligence? Do you see anyone here who could plan a murder, a robbery ... can plan anything? A cornered animal to strike quickly out of fear, a trait inherited from his ancestors in the deepest jungle of blackest Africa—yes, yes, that he can do—but to plan?... No, gentlemen, this skull here holds no plans. What you see here is a thing that acts on command."

Finally, wrapping up his plea, the lawyer concludes, "What justice would there be to take his life? Justice, gentlemen. Why, I would just as soon put a hog in the electric chair as this."

The fallout from the lawyer's defense is devastating. In his cell, after receiving the death sentence, Jefferson is close to catatonic. As his aged godmother, Emma, and her friends try to make contact with him, he withdraws further into himself. In one wrenching scene when they bring him home-cooked food, he gets down on all fours and ruts around in the food without using his hands.

The complexity of this painful story is richly enhanced by Gaines's ironic narrator, Grant Wiggins. Only a few years older than Jefferson, Grant is college educated and a parish school teacher. Bitter in his own way and aloof from the community he has come to loathe, Grant is initially uninvolved, until his aunt (Miss Emma's friend) asks that he try to make Jefferson into a man. This quest for manhood becomes the emotional center of the story and a challenge for Grant himself to become reconnected to his people.

Assuming he will fail, Grant articulates his feelings to his mistress:

> "We black men have failed to protect our women since the time of slavery. We stay here in the South and are broken, or we run away and leave them alone to look after the children and themselves. So each time a male child is born, they hope he will be the one to change this vicious circle—which he never does. Because even though he wants to change it, and maybe even tries to change it, it is too heavy a burden because of all the others who have run away and left their burdens behind. So he, too, must run away if he is to hold on to his sanity and have a life of his own.... What she wants is for him, Jefferson, and me to change everything that has been going on for three hundred years."

Grant's task is further complicated by the local minister, who believes that saving Jefferson's soul is more important than making him into a man. The tensions between the teacher and the preacher add still another complex dimension to Gaines's formidable narrative.

Nowhere is the story more moving than in the scenes in which Grant and Jefferson are together in Jefferson's cell, agonizing over his horrific past—for Jefferson has been shaped not only by the animalistic designation thrust upon him in his twenty-first year but also by the deprivations of the previous twenty.

When Grant can finally mention the unspeakable—the last day of Jefferson's life—Jefferson tells him, "I never got nothing I wanted in my whole life." When asked what he wants to eat that last day, Jefferson responds, "I want me a whole gallon of ice cream.... Ain't never had enough ice cream. Never had more than a nickel cone. Used to ... hand the ice cream man my nickel, and he give me a little scoop on a cone. But now I'm go'n get me a whole gallon. That's what I want—a whole gallon. Eat it with a pot spoon."

More than any other novel about African-American life in the United States, *A Lesson Before Dying* is about standing tall and being a man in the face of overwhelming adversity. And, equally important, Gaines's masterpiece is about what Ralph Ellison and William Faulkner would call the morality of connectedness, of each individual's responsibility to his community, to the brotherhood beyond his self. This majestic, moving novel is an instant classic, a book that will be read, discussed and taught beyond the rest of our lives.

Source: Charles R. Larson, "End as a Man," in *Chicago Tribune Books,* May 9, 1993, p. 5.

Sources

Alvin Aubert, "Ernest J. Gaines: Overview," in *Contemporary Novelists, 6th ed.,* edited by Susan Windisch Brown, St. James Press, 1996.

Jerry H. Bryant, *Iowa Review,* Winter, 1972.

Paul Desruisseaux, in *New York Times Book Review,* May 23, 1971.

Joseph McLellan, in *Washington Post,* January 13, 1976.

Larry McMurtry, in *New York Times Book Review,* November 19, 1967.

Alice Walker, in *New York Times Book Review,* October 30, 1983.

For Further Study

Alvin Aubert, "Ernest J. Gaines: Overview," in *Contemporary Novelists, 6th ed.,* edited by Susan Windisch Brown, St. James Press, 1996.

The author provides not only points of comparison between the work of Gaines and Faulkner, but also an overview of how black-white relationships become the basic element in each of Gaines's novels.

H. A. Baker, and P. Redmond, P, editors, *AfroAmerican Literary Study in the 1990's (Black Literature and Culture),* University of Chicago Press, 1989.

This is first in a series of volumes dedicated to the scholarly study of African-American literature and culture.

B. Bell, "African American Literature," in *Grolier Multimedia Encyclopedia [CD-ROM],* Grolier Interactive, Inc., 1998.

An explanation of the tradition of African-American literature and its attributes. The author explains the effects of race, ethnicity, class, gender, and nationality on literature and discusses African-American literature in terms of genres and their contributing writers.

J. Dizard, "Racial Integration," in *Grolier Multimedia Encyclopedia [CD-ROM],* Grolier Interactive, Inc., 1998.

The author defines and gives the history of racial integration in the United States and provides references to Civil Rights acts of particular importance.

D. C. Estes, *Critical Reflections on the Fiction of Ernest J. Gaines,* University of Georgia Press (Athens), 1994.

This series of essays provides a comprehensive look at Gaines's work, including the themes he addresses, the techniques he uses, and his use of humor. The author also presents comparisons to other writers' works.

R. Laney, *Ernest J. Gaines: Louisiana Stories,* Video Production by Louisiana Public Broadcasting, Louisiana Educational Television Authority. [Online] Available http://oscar.lpb.org/programs/gaines/, 1998.

This video production provides viewers with an overview of the life of Ernest Gaines. Through interviews with Gaines, his lifetime acquaintances, and prominent writers and scholars, the viewer will come to an appreciation of Gaines and the influences on his writing.

V. Smith, and A. Walton, editors, *African American Writer,* Charles Scribner Sons, 1991.

A compilation of essays that are a combination of biography and literary criticism. They focus on the unique experiences of African Americans and their culture and tradition in the context of American history.

Mama Day

Gloria Naylor
1988

Gloria Naylor's first novel, *The Women of Brewster Place* (1982), made her an overnight success, but her third novel, *Mama Day* (1988), solidified her reputation as one of the foremost authors of the African-American women's fiction renaissance, along with Toni Morrison, Alice Walker, Toni Cade Bambara, and others. Although reviewers were initially confused by the novel's mixture of realism and the supernatural, most readers consider *Mama Day* a powerful and richly-layered depiction of how the past and the present, the real and the unreal, the living and the dead, the natural and the supernatural converge in the lives of African-Americans.

The novel juxtaposes the story of a successful African-American businessman, George, who has grown up in New York City, cut off from any sense of where he or his people came from, with that of a young African-American woman, Cocoa, who must come to terms with her powerful ancestral legacy. Their clash and uneasy union is brought to a head when they visit Cocoa's home, Willow Springs, a magical place that holds the secrets of Cocoa's past and the key to her future.

Author Biography

Born in 1950, Gloria Naylor was raised in New York by working-class parents. Her mother encouraged her to write when she began to exhibit

Gloria Naylor

creative ability at the age of seven. But when she graduated from high school, instead of attending college, as her parents wished, she became a Jehovah's Witness, traveling through New York and the South from 1968 to 1975. After she returned to New York, she earned her degree in English from Brooklyn College of the City University of New York in 1981.

It was in college that she first learned about the rich tradition of African-American literature. She told Allison Gloch in 1993, "I was 27 years old before I knew Black women even wrote books." Her reading of Zora Neale Hurston, Alice Walker, and others, inspired her to begin writing herself. Her first novel, *The Women of Brewster Place*, chronicled the lives of seven very different women living in an African-American community. The success of the novel immediately made her a prominent figure in the renaissance of African-American women writers. The following year, the novel won an American Book Award, and she received her M.A. in African-American Studies from Yale University. Her master's thesis became her second novel, *Linden Hills* (1985), which used Dante's *Inferno* as a thematic and structural guide for her explication of the moral downfall of well-to-do blacks who lose touch with their racial heritage.

Naylor's third novel, *Mama Day,* was her first to explore the experiences of African-Americans in the South. To write the novel, she drew on her parents' stories about living there and her own experiences as a Jehovah's Witness traveling the region. This novel was a culmination of her concern with the loss of identity and heritage suffered by contemporary urban African-Americans. The novel emanated, she told Michelle C. Loris in 1996, from her "belief in love and magic…. I know that love can heal."

Naylor connects her writings by having the same characters appear in more than one novel. Mama Day first appeared in *Linden Hills,* and George's mother became a central character in *Bailey's Cafe* (1992). The Day family will reappear in a future novel, *Sapphira Wade,* she told Loris. In this book, "Cocoa comes back as an old woman. It's 2023." Naylor will also tell the stories of Bascombe and Sapphira Wade from 1817 to 1823. "Always in my head Sapphira Wade would be the cornerstone because she has been the guiding spirit for now close to twenty years, and now it's time to grapple with her," Naylor said. For Naylor, writing about the present and future African-American community means grappling with its past as well as the rich folklore, language, and tradition that have sustained it.

Plot Summary

Part I

Though *Mama Day* is told from three perspectives, the story itself is a simple one; it presents the courtship and marriage of Cocoa and George, and finally George's death in Cocoa's ancestral home, Willow Springs. Cocoa first sees George in New York, where they both live, and then meets him formally at a job interview, which does not go well because Cocoa must spend August in Willow Springs with her grandmother, Abigail, and her great aunt Miranda, known as Mama Day. Cocoa does not get the job with George's engineering firm, but on her return from Willow Springs, she sends George a note. He in turn sends her application to a client, and asks her to dinner. Their first date is disastrous, but George decides to show Cocoa what he loves about New York City. Meanwhile, in Willow Springs, Mama Day helps Bernice to conceive a child, and Junior Lee leaves his common-law wife, Frances, for another woman, Ruby.

Cocoa loves seeing New York with George, although their regular outings don't seem romantic to her. After George tells her about his girlfriend Shawn, Cocoa tells him she doesn't have to see him again. Later he comes to Cocoa's apartment and they make love for the first time. The two have fallen in love, but there are still conflicts between them. Cocoa feels that George doesn't open up about his feelings. When she sees his old girlfriend in his building, she fights with him, calling him a "son of a bitch," then accepts a date with an old boyfriend. George waits outside the old boyfriend's apartment all night, then tells her he doesn't like being called a son of a bitch because his mother was a prostitute and his father a john. Then he asks Cocoa to marry him, and they elope.

George and Cocoa settle into their married life, but Cocoa returns to Willow Springs without him in their first August together. While there she experiences Ruby's jealousy when she makes plans to see a concert with Junior Lee and some other friends. Cocoa fights with Miranda, but she continues to visit Willow Springs each August. George does not come to visit Willow Springs until their fourth year of marriage, after Cocoa has graduated from college and they have made plans to start a family.

Part II

Mama Day is preparing for George's visit when she realizes that Ruby is trying to use magic against Cocoa. In a foreshadowing of George's death, George and Cocoa both have dreams about him drowning. George explores the island, meeting many of the inhabitants, including Dr. Buzzard. He beats him at cards, earning the respect of the other men. George talks about moving to Willow Springs, but Cocoa is undecided. Miranda realizes that a hurricane is coming, and George and Cocoa have a terrible fight when George sees that she's wearing makeup foundation that is too dark for her. At the party in their honor, George rebuffs Cocoa's attempt to speak to him. Junior Lee makes a pass at Cocoa, and Ruby witnesses it. When Cocoa comes to see Ruby, she braids nightshade into Cocoa's hair. George and Cocoa do not reconcile until the hurricane comes, when he brings her back into their bed.

The hurricane destroys the bridge to the mainland and kills Bernice and Ambush's son, Little Caesar. Cocoa is very ill, and George is frustrated by his inability to leave Willow Springs and get medical help for her. Mama Day realizes that Ruby has poisoned Cocoa and cuts off Cocoa's braids.

George gathers with the people of Willow Springs to "stand forth" for Little Caesar, and everyone says what Little Caesar was doing when they first saw him and what he'll be doing when they see him again. Miranda uses magic to make lightning strike Ruby's house, burning it to the ground, but Cocoa gets sicker and sicker, and begins to hallucinate, while George is frantic and frustrated by his inability to help her. When Miranda remembers the broken-hearted men of her past, she realizes that she needs George's help to rescue Cocoa.

George's plan to row across the Sound is thwarted by the townspeople, who know he won't be able to make it across. Abigail tells George to meet Mama Day at the "other place," the family homestead, and Dr. Buzzard tells George to work with the islanders, who also want Cocoa to recover. George does not believe in Miranda's magic, but he sees how ill Cocoa is, and he tries to obey Miranda, who has told him to go to the chicken house and bring back whatever he finds there. But George does not realize that Mama Day means his own two hands, and after tearing apart the chicken house, George's weak heart gives out, and he dies.

Cocoa feels that her life is over, and she spends three months on Willow Springs recovering from her illness and grieving. Cocoa decides not to return to New York. Eventually Cocoa remarries and moves to Charleston, where she names her second son after George. Abigail has died, and the story ends with Miranda eating her "last August 21st honeydew," foreshadowing the death of Mama Day as well.

Characters

George Andrews

George is an engineer from New York who marries Cocoa. His first-person narration makes up about a third of the text, as he explains to Cocoa his perspective on their courtship, marriage, and visit to Willow Springs. Near the end of the novel the reader learns that George has died and that he speaks from beyond the grave.

Shortly after his birth, George was abandoned by his mother, who was a prostitute, and raised by whites in an orphanage. There he learned that "only the present has potential" and only "facts" are relevant. He had no use for emotions, beliefs, myths, or superstitions. Once he was on his own, he said, "I may have knocked my head against the walls,

The mythical island of Willow Springs was settled in the early 1900s, around the same time this family photograph was taken.

figuring out how to buy food, supplies, and books, but I never knocked on wood. No rabbit's foot, no crucifixes—not even a lottery ticket." George has a bad heart and controls his condition with a pill twice a day with strict regularity. His only passion is football, a game that fascinates him by its mathematical possibilities.

When George meets Cocoa his world is turned upside down. She represents to him a world of great emotions and mysteries. He is especially intrigued by Cocoa's family and her past in Willow Springs. He envies her sense of belonging and tradition. But after their marriage, he continues to spend his vacations traveling to the NFL play-off games rather than going home with Cocoa. After four years of marriage, he finally makes the trip with her. While he at first romanticizes the island and its inhabitants, he is gradually confronted with phenomena that subvert his understanding of how the world works.

George represents contemporary urban African-Americans who have adopted white customs and beliefs and have lost touch with their roots. Having adopted Western rationalism, George sees Mama Day as a "crazy old woman" rather than a powerful conjurer who can save Cocoa from her mysterious illness. The only solution he can see is

to travel to the mainland and get a real doctor. Because the bridge has been destroyed by a storm, he half-heartedly helps Mama Day, but he loses control and has a heart attack in his rage. His dying rescues Cocoa from death's door, and he is buried on the island, where Cocoa frequently returns to visit him.

Baby Girl

See Cocoa Day

Dr. Buzzard

Dr. Buzzard pretends to be a hoodoo/medicine man, but his powers are trickery, and his remedies are largely made from alcohol from his still. He incurs Mama Day's disrespect for his deception.

Abigail Day

Abigail Day is Cocoa's grandmother and Mama Day's sister. She helped raise Cocoa and is a central nurturing figure. She does not possess the knowledge of the natural and supernatural worlds that Mama Day does, and when Cocoa is deathly ill, she can only sing and hope and try to feed her. Abigail has also cut herself off from her past by refusing to ever visit the other place, the home where she grew up.

Cocoa Day

Cocoa, as the grandniece of Mama Day and the wife of George Andrews, acts as a bridge between their two worlds—African-American mysticism and Western rationalism. Her first-person narration explaining her point of view to George makes up about one-third of the text. As a young person who has left Willow Springs and taken up residence in New York, she is in danger of losing touch with her heritage. Although she visits Willow Springs for two weeks every August, she becomes more and more a part of George's world. He introduces her to the "real" New York, and she earns a degree in history, which reminds the reader of Reema's boy, who goes to the mainland and earns an advanced degree only to return to the island a stranger.

When George agrees to visit Willow Springs with her, Cocoa is anxious to show him off to the townspeople, who always viewed her as a kind of freak because of her lighter skin. (Her family had nicknamed her Cocoa to "put some color on her.") But George does not understand her insecurities, and they get in a fight that threatens to tear them apart. While Cocoa is preoccupied with mending her relationship with George, she falls prey to Ruby. Not suspecting the jealous feelings Ruby has towards her, she lets Ruby braid her hair. But this time, the ritual which has helped bond her to the community since she was a child threatens to destroy her as Ruby poisons her.

During her ensuing illness, Cocoa has horrific hallucinations and pushes George away from her. She begins to believe that worms have invaded her body and are eating her alive from the inside out. Only the soothing strokes of her grandmother's hands can keep the parasites from devouring her. After George saves her by sacrificing his life, and Mama Day nurses her back to health, Cocoa leaves her life in New York and settles in Charleston, a Southern city that keeps her near her home but not fully a part of it. She later remarries and has two sons, one of whom she names George, and she visits Willow Springs often to talk to her first husband about what happened. As Mama Day notes, Cocoa is the only Day woman who has finally "been given the meaning of peace."

Grace Day

Grace, Cocoa's mother, died of grief after her husband was unfaithful to her, leaving Cocoa motherless.

Media Adaptations

- *Mama Day* was recorded on audiotape in 1989 by Brilliance.

- Naylor has written a screenplay for the film adaptation of *Mama Day* to be produced by her company, One Way Productions, Inc. The film has not yet been made.

John-Paul Day

John-Paul was Mama Day's and Abigail's father. He was a talented artist who could carve lifelike images of flowers, and he taught Mama Day to be at home in the woods.

Mama Day

The title character, Mama Day, has acquired her name because as a midwife she has helped to bring into the world nearly ever other inhabitant of the island, although she never married or had children of her own. She also serves as the community's doctor, possessing a vast knowledge of herbal remedies and how to treat most illnesses. She has gained the utmost respect of all of Willow Springs' inhabitants, who revere her as the descendant of Sapphira Wade and the inheritor of her foremother's conjuring powers.

In the first half of the novel, Mama Day helps Bernice become pregnant, performing a mysterious ritual with the help of her chickens. Her true "gift," she believes, is to help things grow. "Can't nothing be wrong in bringing on life, knowing how to get under, around, and beside nature to give it a slight push," she tells herself." "But she ain't never, Lord, she ain't never tried to get *over* nature."

In the second half of the novel, Mama Day must help save her grandniece Cocoa. Although she has tried to protect Cocoa from Ruby's murderous jealousy, she can only enact revenge on Ruby for poisoning Cocoa by sprinkling a metallic powder around her house, causing lightning to strike twice and kill her. She retreats to the other place, which she visits often, to learn from her Day ancestors how she can save Cocoa. While there, she finds a ledger with the bill of sale for a slave woman, her great-great-grandmother, whose name she has never known. But time has washed away most of the words, leaving only the letters Sa. In a dream, she learns the name Sapphira and that she must listen past the pain of her mothers. She realizes that Cocoa has placed part of herself in George's hands, so she must enlist his help. But because George does not trust her, he cannot bring back the symbol of life from the chickens' nests. Instead, he attacks the chickens and destroys them and himself, saving Cocoa in his own way by sacrificing himself. At the end of the novel, Mama Day is still alive at the age of 104, and she anticipates peeking into the next century before she finally dies.

Miranda Day

See Mama Day

Ophelia Day

Ophelia was Abigail's and Mama Day's mother. She went mad after her baby, Peace, died, and drowned herself in the sound between the island and the mainland.

Peace Day

Peace was Abigail's and Mama Day's younger sister who drowned in the well when she was still a baby. Abigail also named her first daughter Peace, and that child also did not live past infancy.

Ambush Duvall

Ambush is a resident of Willow Springs and is married to Bernice.

Bernice Duvall

Bernice, Ambush's wife, is desperate to have a baby. She enlists Mama Day's aid and undergoes a fertility ritual that allows her to finally get pregnant. Once she has her baby, she proves to be an overprotective and overindulgent mother. Bernice is also Cocoa's best friend from Willow Springs.

Charles Duvall

Charles is Bernice and Ambush's son. The townspeople call him Little Caesar because his mother treats him like a king. He dies in the hurricane.

Mrs. Jackson

Mrs. Jackson was George's teacher at the Wallace P. Andrews Shelter for Boys. She taught him that "only the present has potential, sir."

Junior Lee

Junior Lee is a no-good, lazy fool who cheats on his wife, Ruby.

Little Caesar

See Charles Duvall

Reema's Boy

Reema's boy is from Willow Springs, but once he goes to the mainland and gets an education, he becomes an outsider. He tries to collect research on the island's residents, but they thwart his efforts, and he misunderstands them.

Ruby

Ruby possesses great powers, but she uses them to hurt other women, in particular those to whom Junior Lee is attracted. She first puts a hex on his long-time girlfriend, who goes mad. Ruby makes Junior Lee marry her. She keeps a watchful eye over him. When Ruby catches Junior Lee making advances towards Cocoa, she lures Cocoa to her house and braids her hair, as she has done since Cocoa was a girl, combing poison into her hair and scalp. Mama Day uses her superior powers to kill Ruby with lightning as a result.

Brian Smithfield

Dr. Brian Smithfield, the medical doctor from the mainland, has held a grudging respect for Mama Day ever since she performed a Caesarean section birth with great expertise despite her lack of sophisticated implements or training.

Bascombe Wade

Bascombe Wade was a Norwegian slave owner whose family originally owned the island of Willow Springs. He fell in love with his slave Sapphira, and his grief over his inability to completely possess her initiated the tragic history of the Day family.

Sapphira Wade

Sapphira Wade was the great-grandmother of Mama Day. Although her name is no longer known to the residents of Willow Springs, she is remembered as a powerful conjurer and slave woman who convinced her master, Bascombe Wade, to deed all of the island to his slaves. She gave birth to seven sons and then flew back to Africa, the legend goes. "God rested on the seventh day and so would she," hence her family's last name, Day.

Themes

Supernatural

Mama Day is imbued with supernatural occurrences. As part of the hoodoo religion they have inherited from their slave ancestors, the inhabitants of Willow Springs believe in the supernatural. Near the end of the novel, readers learn that George, one of the narrators, has been dead for fourteen years, and that Cocoa speaks to him regularly.

But it is Mama Day who embodies the supernatural. She possesses a "gift" that she inherited from her great-grandmother, the slave Sapphira Wade. According to Willow Springs legend, Sapphira was a "conjure woman" who "could walk through a lightning storm without being touched; grab a bolt of lightning in the palm of her hand; use the heat of the lightning to start the kindling going under the medicine pot.... She turned the moon into salve, the stars into swaddling cloth, and healed the wounds of every creature walking up on two or down on four." According to the bill of sale for Sapphira that prefaces the novel, she "has served on occasion in the capacity of midwife and nurse, not without extreme mischief and suspicions of delving in witchcraft."

This language expresses the white world's view of Sapphira's power, but the novel goes to great lengths to demystify and present in a positive light the powers Mama Day possesses. In the world of Willow Springs, where all the inhabitants are descendants of slaves, magic and the supernatural are everyday parts of life, and Mama Day's gift is something to be respected and occasionally feared.

The novel makes a clear distinction between the kind of conjuring or hoodoo that Mama Day practices and two other kinds: the trickery of Dr. Buzzard and the evil practices of Ruby. Mama Day uses her powers for benevolent purposes, healing the sick, helping women to give birth, and helping Bernice get pregnant. As she says, she gets "joy" "from any kind of life." Her job is "bringing on life, knowing how to get under, around, and beside nature to give it a slight push." She works in concert with nature to help things grow, while Ruby uses spells, poisons, and herbal mixtures with graveyard dust to kill and drive insane the women whom she fears are after her man. The only time Mama Day kills is when she attracts lightning to Ruby's house in revenge for Ruby's poisoning of Cocoa. And while Dr. Buzzard also claims to heal, his remedies are fake, consisting mostly of alcohol and nothing of any real medicinal value. He also

Topics for Further Study

- Research the history and practices of African-American folk medicine and hoodoo and write a paper comparing them to Western medicine, using Mama Day and Dr. Smithfield as examples.

- Research your own family history, making a family tree like that at the beginning of *Mama Day*. Then write a paper about how your family's legacy continues to influence you and other family members.

- Explore historical and fictional accounts that describe the relations between slave women and their masters in early America (like those between Thomas Jefferson and Sally Hemmings) and write first-person narratives of Sapphira and Bascombe Wade's experiences. You can make them talk to each other the way George and Cocoa do in *Mama Day*.

- Compare Zora Neale Hurston's practices, methodology, and results in her *Mules and Men* (1935) to the efforts of the student, Reema's boy, who returns to Willow Springs at the beginning of *Mama Day*. You may also expand your research to include a historical survey of how anthropologists have approached and interpreted southern black folk culture.

exploits the villagers' fears and beliefs in ghosts to hawk his charms and talismans.

Mama Day's practices are described in great detail to emphasize that what she possesses most of all is a vast knowledge of effective herbal remedies. She also uses her understanding of psychology, such as when she helps Bernice by giving her black and gold seeds, which, rather than possessing supernatural powers, represent her negative feelings about her mother-in-law and her hopes for her baby. Naylor therefore demystifies some of Mama Day's practices and shows the reader that her supernatural powers are natural extensions of her understanding of the "real" world.

Cultural Heritage

The lesson that Cocoa must learn in *Mama Day* is that she cannot escape her past. Even though she has spent the last several years in New York, in the last half of the book she must come to terms with Willow Springs and her heritage, which means the loss of "peace" that the women in her family have suffered.

George cannot help her with this because he has no past and no understanding of the rich heritage of the Day family. He does not understand why they have to put moss in their shoes when they walk in the west woods where her ancestors are buried. She can only say, "it is a tradition" and "it shows respect." He is intrigued by the "other place," the Day ancestral home, and wants to become a part of it without knowing its sad history. While Cocoa hears voices telling her *"you'll break his heart,"* George hears nothing and tells her "we could defy history."

When Cocoa becomes ill from Ruby's poisoning, Mama Day goes to the other place to find out what she has to do to save Cocoa. She realizes that Cocoa has put a significant part of herself in George's hands, and that he must help her. When he is unable to join hands with Mama Day and make the "bridge for Baby Girl to walk over," he must sacrifice his life to save Cocoa. Only with his death and his letting go of Cocoa can Mama Day's remedies return Cocoa to health and her cultural heritage, making her the first Day to learn "the meaning of peace." And only in death can George become a part of the island and its heritage. He is buried on the island, and Cocoa names one of her sons from a subsequent marriage after him.

Style

Narrator

One of the most striking aspects of *Mama Day* is its use of multiples narrators, because, as Cocoa tells George at the end, "There are just too many sides to the whole story." Between one-half and two-thirds of the book is taken up with the conversation of George and Cocoa, expressed in alternating first-person narratives. These sections are separated from the rest of the text by three diamonds.

The narrator of the rest of the novel is hard to pinpoint. Most critics describe it as the communal voice of Willow Springs. But sometimes it sounds like an omniscient narrator, who oversees every-thing without being a part of the story, and sometimes it comes from Mama Day's consciousness. In the novel's preface, the voice of Willow Springs explains to the reader, "Think about it: ain't no-body really talking to you. We're sitting here in Willow Springs, and you're God-knows-where.... Really listen this time: the only voice is your own." Given the importance the novel places on multiple points of view, it is fitting that this unidentified narrator takes on different perspectives, even including the reader in its magic circle.

Setting

For the first half of the novel, George and Cocoa live in New York, and their experiences there alternate with the goings-on in Willow Springs. The second half of the novel takes place entirely in Willow Springs, an imaginary place. The two communities provide a stark contrast. While New York is a large city, Willow Springs is a small rural island. And while New York is one of the most famous cities in the world, Willow Springs does not even exist on maps, and the inhabitants like it that way. "Part of Willow Springs's problems was that it got put on some maps right after the War Between the States."

The island is located off the coast, near the border between South Carolina and Georgia, and neither state claims it. Therefore, Willow Springs is an independent, self-governing community that votes only in presidential elections. Although phone lines run over the sound and television signals are received on the island, its ties to the mainland are very tenuous: "We done learned that anything coming from beyond the bridge gotta be viewed real, real careful." The bridge is even destroyed by a storm every sixty-nine years or so, severing its connection with the mainland, as happens during the hurricane. Willow Springs doesn't really feel like part of the United States. Its beliefs and customs more closely resemble those its ancestors brought over from Africa than the ones George has learned in New York.

Symbols

Mama Day utilizes many symbols, beginning with the island of Willow Springs itself. More than simply a rural, isolated community, Willow Springs represents another world that is neither American nor African, neither real nor imaginary. It is a place where the past is still alive and boundaries have dissolved between the living and the dead.

On the island, many other things possess symbolic importance, such as the chickens, which are associated with Mama Day, fertility, and female-ness. When George battles the chickens, he is con-fronting all of the mysterious forces of Cocoa, the Day family, and Willow Springs. The quilt Abigail and Mama Day make for Cocoa is a weaving to-gether of the Day family that is to remind her of her cultural heritage. The bridge forms not only a real but also a symbolic link between Willow Springs (the imaginary and the past) and the main-land (the real and the present). When the storm, with a symbolic significance emanating from Africa, destroys the bridge, George fears not only that he cannot get a "real" doctor for Cocoa, but that they are trapped in this supernatural world.

Lastly, hands play a prominent role in the way Mama Day envisions her connection to her ances-tors and what must be done to save Cocoa. George must "hand" over his belief in himself to Mama Day: "She needs his hand in hers—his very hand—so she can connect it up with all the believing that had gone before.... So together they could build the bridge for Baby Girl to walk over." By joining hands, symbolically, they could heal her together.

Magical Realism

The best way to describe *Mama Day* is as mag-ical realism, in which the everyday and the super-natural coexist and are intertwined in one text. In effect, the magical becomes as "real" as the ordi-nary parts of the narrative. In *Mama Day*, the world of Willow Springs contains elements that can be associated with realism, such as when Mama Day watches "The Phil Donahue Show" and Bernice be-comes ill from taking a fertility drug. Magical el-ements exist too, such as when Mama Day helps Bernice get pregnant with a mystical fertility ritual involving chicken eggs and when Cocoa hears the voices of her ancestors at the other place. Further-more, the "real" aspects of the text are associated with the rational, white world of the United States mainland, while the magical aspects are derived from African folk medicine and beliefs and are cen-tered on the island of Willow Springs. Willow Springs, then, is a place where the "real" and mag-ical meet and peacefully coexist.

Historical Context

Rise of the Black Middle Class

In the 1980s, some African-Americans began to achieve a kind of material success that had been impossible for them before. Despite the Civil Rights Movement of the 1950s and 1960s, which allowed for much greater social equality, blacks still suffered great economic inequality in Amer-ica. In major cities, neighborhoods became strictly segregated in the 1970s with poor blacks living in the inner city, often in ghettoes of subsidized hous-ing, while whites moved to the suburbs where they established affluent communities. But in the 1980s, some blacks, reaping the effects of affirmative ac-tion (set in place in 1965) and benefiting from the booming economy and declining unemployment, were able to secure high-paying jobs. For the first time, a significant number of black Americans be-came part of the middle class. Some moved into prosperous white neighborhoods, while others es-tablished their own communities, like those Nay-lor describes in *Linden Hills* (1985). With these new developments, many blacks, including Naylor, feared that middle-class blacks were becoming dis-connected from their roots and were adopting white values and beliefs.

In *Linden Hills* and in *Mama Day*, Naylor ex-plores the negative impact such a transformation has on African-Americans. George, in *Mama Day*, represents the affluent black who was "dark on the outside and white on the inside," as the epithet "Oreo," used in the 1980s, signified.

African-American Women's Renaissance

With the emergence of Toni Morrison and Alice Walker as nationally recognized authors in the 1970s, it appeared that a renaissance of sorts for African-American women writers had begun. Walker's *The Color Purple* (1982) was translated to the screen by Steven Spielberg. Morrison's works, including *The Song of Solomon* (1977) and *Beloved* (1987), were widely admired; she won the Nobel Prize for Literature in 1993. Other writers, such as Toni Cade Bambara, Maya Angelou, Gayl Jones, and Ntozake Shange, among others, made names for themselves and solidified the idea that a flourishing of creative talent among black women was being realized. As Morrison said in conversa-tion with Naylor, published in the *Southern Review* in 1985, referring to the large number of important works by black women, "It's a real renaissance. You know, we have spoken of renaissance before. But this one is ours, not somebody else's."

So important have African-American women writers been in American letters that some critics believe they have created the most challenging and powerful fiction in late-twentieth-century America. When Naylor went to college in the late 1970s and

After the Civil War, southern agricultural crops were not doing well, and many African-Americans, like the freed slaves pictured here, were out of work. Large numbers of African-Americans left the South for jobs in growing northern industries.

early 1980s, she discovered these writers and their foremothers (most notably Zora Neale Hurston) for the first time. Their explorations of slavery, racism, black pride, and the double prejudice suffered by black women (as a woman and as an African-American) inspired Naylor and made her feel that she had something to say as a writer. Morrison's work was an especially important influence on her. As she wrote in the preface to her conversation with Morrison in 1985, Morrison's *The Bluest Eye* (1971) was the "beginning" for her because it "said to a young poet, struggling to break into prose, that the barriers were flexible; at the core of it all is language, and if you're skilled enough with that, you can create your own genre. And it said to a young black woman, struggling to find a mirror of her worth in this society, not only is your story worth telling but it can be told in words so painstakingly eloquent that it becomes a song."

Critical Overview

When *Mama Day* first appeared in 1988, the novel was met with mixed reviews. Some reviewers had a great respect for Naylor's ambitious book

and its accomplishments, while others were simply confused. Those who liked the book commented on its power to absorb the reader in its magical world. As Rachel Hass wrote in *The Boston Review,* "The rhythm of the prose pulls you inside the story like a magnet." And in the *Los Angeles Times,* Rita Mae Brown urged, "Don't worry about finding the plot. Let the plot find you." But she also admitted, "Naylor's technique can be a confusing one to read." While Brown found this difficulty to be surmountable, leaving readers with rich rewards for their efforts, others did not.

What seemed to bother reviewers most were the novel's diversity of speakers and its mixture of realism and fantasy. Linda Simon, in the *Women's Review of Books,* criticized Naylor for not "opt[ing] for character development in a more realistic setting." In the end, Simon felt that too many questions were left unanswered because of the novel's reliance on magic to resolve the situation. But for Bharati Mukherjee in *The New York Times Books Review,* it was the sections about the magical world of Willow Springs that carried the novel. Naylor "is less proficient in making the familiar wondrous than she is making the wondrous familiar," she concluded. Overall, although some reviewers found the novel confusing, many believed that Naylor had established herself as an important author with *Mama Day.*

In the 1990s, the novel has received substantial attention from critics and scholars who have found it a rich and multi-layered text deserving serious analysis. Some specifically deride earlier reviewers for misunderstanding the novel. Missy Dehn Kubitschek wrote in a *Melus* essay, for example, that "The major reviews of Naylor's 1988 novel, *Mama Day,* refuse in crucial ways to grant the novel's donnée, even when they are generally positive." They do so, she argues, because they oversimplify the novel's message, seeing it as belonging to "one or another overly exclusive tradition." The wide variety of analyses of the novel, which focus on many equally important aspects of the novel, attest to Kubitschek's claim that *Mama Day* is a much richer text than reviewers first realized.

Some of the most prominent interpretations of the novel focus on the use of quilting imagery, the importance of magic and hoodoo traditions, and allusions to *The Tempest.* Scholars such as Susan Meisenhelder, in the *African-American Review,* and Margot Anne Kelley, in *Quilt Culture,* have emphasized the importance of quilting to both the form and substance of *Mama Day.* As Meisenhelder argued, "Naylor repeatedly stitches past, present, and future together," and "*Mama Day* is ... a complex narrative quilt of distinct voices." This structure of the novel as quilt helps reinforce the novel's message for Meisenhelder, which she interpreted as the "failure to see 'the whole picture,' to see history, community, and relationships between men and women as quilts, dooms black people to the madness and suicide characterizing white tragedies."

Others have seen the use of magic as the defining aspect of the novel, including Elizabeth T. Hayes, who argued in *The Critical Response to Gloria Naylor* that "the magical is as quotidian in *Mama Day* as peach pie," making the novel a prime example of "magic realism." Hayes also linked this approach to African-American culture, as do other critics like Lindsey Tucker, who explicated in her article for the *African-American Review* the importance of conjure women such as Mama Day to Southern black folk culture, and Helen Fiddyment Levy, who in her book *Fiction of the Home* saw Naylor's use of magic and myth as powerful themes linking her characters to the African-American community.

Finally, many scholars have seen many direct connections between *Mama Day* and works by Shakespeare. Peter Erickson argued in his book *Rewriting Shakespeare, Rewriting Ourselves* that Naylor revises Shakespeare, questioning the importance of the white literary tradition he represents and elevating the black folk tradition represented by the community of Willow Springs. As he and other critics, including Kubitschek, have pointed out, Naylor specifically engages *The Tempest* by making Willow Springs an island community that appears on no map, naming her protagonist Miranda, and having a hurricane descend upon the island at the novel's climax. But Naylor revises Shakespeare's play, as Erickson argued, by "rewrit[ing] the exchange between Prospero and Caliban concerning ownership," giving the slave descendants ownership of the island, and by making Miranda (Mama Day) a wise old woman with divine gifts and matriarchal power as opposed to the innocent daughter of *The Tempest.* Miranda, in effect, becomes the Prospero figure, with a significant difference: she does not abuse her power.

Some critics also point to links between *Mama Day* and *Hamlet* and *King Lear.* In addition to these main interpretive approaches to *Mama Day,* there are still many others, most notably emphasizing black sisterhood, motherhood, and generational heritage in the novel. Overall, the criticism of *Mama Day* exhibits the text's many interpretive possibilities.

Criticism

Jane Elizabeth Dougherty

Dougherty is a Ph.D candidate at Tufts University. In the following essay, she explores issues of culture and history in Mama Day.

Mama Day is set on two islands, the island of Manhattan and the island of Willow Springs, which lies off the coasts of Georgia and South Carolina but is proudly independent of both. Manhattan represents a place where cultures collide, while Willow Springs is culturally homogenous, home to a group of African-American residents who claim a conjure woman as their ancestor. The three differing perspectives of the novel, those of George, Cocoa, and what Vincent Odamtten identifies as the voice "of the island of Willow Springs, an ancestral choral voice," reflect the differences in each voice's cultural background and history as well as

What Do I Read Next?

- In *American Voudou: Journey into a Hidden World* (1998), Rod Davis gives a personal account of his journey through America, primarily the South, to discover how African voodoo has been preserved and transformed in America. He describes his encounters with the practitioners of and believers in the many forms of African voodoo, such as hoodoo, root medicine, spiritual healing, and black magic.

- Zora Neale Hurston's *Mules and Men* (1935) records the folk tales, songs, and voodoo customs and beliefs of southern blacks that Hurston collected on her many travels through the South.

- Bruce Jackson's essay "The Other Kind of Doctor: Conjure and Magic in Black American Folk Medicine," in the book *African American Religion: Interpretive Essays in History and Culture* (1997), edited by Timothy E. Fulop and Albert J. Raboteau, pays serious attention to the long-ignored practice of hoodoo or conjure as a healing art in African-American folk culture.

- Paule Marshall's *Praisesong for the Widow* (1983) is about a black family's upward mobility in New York, its subsequent struggle with materialism, and the return of the widow Avey Johnson to her cultural roots on an island in the Caribbean.

- Nobel-prize winner Toni Morrison's *Beloved* (1987) tells the story of a mother's desperation to protect her children from slavery. The novel blurs the boundaries between the real and the unreal, the living and the dead, and the past and the present.

- In *The Tempest* William Shakespeare tells the story of the magician Prospero and his efforts to retain control over his daughter, Miranda, and the other inhabitants of their secluded island. This play is often referred to by critics as an American allegory.

- Alice Walker's short story "Everyday Use" (1973) explores the importance of quilting to nurturing black sisterhood and keeping intergenerational ties intact.

---

the differences among the past, the present, and the future. The narrative trajectory of the novel is one that honors the shared African-American identity of the two characters and the "ancestral voice" and integrates their multiple perspectives through love, magic, and sacrifice.

Cocoa, who has lived in New York for seven years, has adapted to the city by learning not to trust men and isn't open to the diverse people of New York, to whom she refers in terms of ethnic foods, thus diminishing the people around her to ethnic stereotypes. George, who has grown up in New York, takes it upon himself to teach Cocoa that.

> My city was a network of small towns, some even smaller than here in Willow Springs. It could be one apartment building, a handful of blocks, a single square mile hidden off with its own language, news-

papers and magazines—its own laws and codes of behavior, and sometimes even its own judges and juries. You'd never realize that because you went there and lived on our fringes. To live *in* New York you'd have to know about the florist on Jamaica Avenue who carried yellow roses even though they didn't move well, but it was his dead wife's favorite color. The candy store in Harlem that wouldn't sell cigarettes to twelve-year-olds without notes from their mothers. That they killed live chickens below Houston, prayed to Santa Barbara by the East River, and in Bensonhurst girls were still virgins when they married. Your crowd would never know about the sweetness that bit at the back of your throat from the baklava at those dark bakeries in Astoria or from walking past a synagogue on Fort Washington Avenue and hearing a cantor sing.

George respects the diversity of the cultures and histories of New York, and as a result of his openness towards others, which he teaches to Cocoa, they are able to fall in love. As Rachel Hass writes, "George and Cocoa are two nations learning to speak one another's language" and to respect one another's "laws and codes of behavior," even if it means that Cocoa must tolerate George's football obsession and he must learn that for a woman, "the shortest distance between two points is by way of China." Though George and Cocoa's marriage represents a kind of cross-cultural exchange, George, unlike Cocoa, is a man "without history." The orphaned son of a prostitute and one of her johns, George has been taught that "only the present has potential," and his outlook is that of a rationalist, someone who looks toward the future. George and Cocoa do not go to Willow Springs until their fourth year of marriage, and Cocoa speaks of this trip as a "crossing over" into the realm of magic, a place "where time stands still" because the past, present, and future are intertwined. Naylor notes that her book is magical in several different ways:

> I moved from the most universally accepted forms of magic into those things that we're more resistant to accepting. You're first made aware, in the first twelve or thirteen pages, that the act of reading, itself, is an act of magic. That's when the narrator turns to you and says, "Ain't nobody really talking to you." And yet, by that point you've laughed with these people, you've been moved by certain parts of their stories. And they say, "We're not real." And then the reader should go, "Oh, of course, the magic of the imagination!"

> I move from that into having a man like George and a woman like Cocoa, who are totally incongruent, meet and fall in love. We all have in our circles two individuals who we don't know what in the hell they're doing with each other. We do accept that; we accept the magic of love. And then, from there, I take you to the last frontier. That's where there are indeed women who can work with nature and create things which have not been documented by institutions of science, but which still do happen. So the book's an exploration of magic.

Willow Springs, unlike the island of Manhattan, is homogenous, a place with distinct and long-standing cultural traditions which unite the islanders. The inhabitants there trace their ownership of the land to a conjure woman whose body may have been enslaved, but who owned her own mind. The island reflects this legacy, of magic and independence, in its cultural traditions, including Candle Walk, which celebrates the events of 1823, when the conjure woman took title to the island, and the "standing forth," a funeral service in which the living imagine what the deceased will be doing the next time they see him or her. Willow Springs truly does have its "own laws and codes of behav-

ior," honoring no "mainside" laws, and maintaining a sense that the dead remain with the living and that the living must honor the connections with the dead and among themselves. In contrast to George's idea that only the present has potential, the past is always with the inhabitants of Willow Springs.

One example of this is the hurricane. All the islanders have heard stories about the last big hurricane, and the stories teach them how to prepare for and handle a big storm, including not building close to the water. On a metaphoric level, the hurricane represents the sorrowful history of African-Americans:

> The old walnut clock ticks on behind the soft murmuring of Abigail's voice, while far off and low the real winds come in. It starts on the shores of Africa, a simple breeze among the palms and cassavas, before it's carried off, tied up with thousands like it, on a strong wave heading due west. A world of water, heaving and rolling, weeks of water, and all them breezes die but one. *I cried unto God with my voice, even unto God with my voice.* Restless and disturbed, no land in front of it, no land in back, it draws up the ocean vapor and rains fall like tears. Constant rains. But it lives on to meet the curve of the equator, where it swallows up the heat waiting in the blackness of them nights. A roar goes up and it starts to spin: moving counterclockwise against the march of time, it rips through the sugar canes in Jamaica, stripping juices from their heart, shredding red buds from the royal poincianas as it spins up in the heat. Over the broken sugar cane fields—hot rains fall. But it's spinning wider, spinning higher, groaning as it bounces off the curve of the earth to head due north. *Thou boldest of mine eyes waking; I am so troubled that I cannot speak. I have considered the days of old, the years of ancient times.* A center grows within the fury of the spinning winds. A still eye. Warm. Calm. It dries a line of clothes in Alabama. It rocks a cradle in Georgia. *I call to remembrance my song in the night. I commune with my own heart—* A buried calm with the awesome power of its face turned to Willow Springs. It hits the southeast corner of the bluff, raising a fist of water to smash into them high rocks. It screams through Chevy's Pass. *And my spirit made diligent search*—the oak tree holds. *I will meditate also of all thy work, and talk of thy doings*—the tombstone of Bascombe Wade trembles but holds. The rest is destruction.

The storm begins in Africa, "tied up with thousands like it," enduring a "restless and disturbed" passage across the ocean in which the "rains fall like tears," then sweeps across the Caribbean and the Southern states. By personifying her descriptions of the storm, Naylor links it to the experience of slavery, which continues to haunt George and Cocoa as well as the Day ancestors. Cocoa is ashamed of her pale skin, which is the legacy of slaveholders' rapes, and George's emphasis on the present is, in part, a denial of this legacy. Likewise, some of the Day ancestors are "broken-hearted men" and women "who died without knowing peace." In order for Cocoa to get well, when she falls ill due to the treachery of Ruby and the aftermath of the hurricane, George must connect to Cocoa's past and to the larger history of African-Americans. Naylor writes of George:

> His heart gives out on him. He was meant to find nothing there, to just bring back his hand to Mama Day. That was it. And she would have just held his hand, which would have been a physical holding as well as a metaphysical holding of hands with him and with all the other parts of Cocoa's history, the other men whose hands had worked and who had broken hearts. But George could not see that because he was a practical individual. There was nothing there for him. But he still saves Cocoa through the powers of his own will.

Like the hurricane, Cocoa's illness is destructive and sorrowful, but George heals her through the power of a love that is stronger than any hatred, redeeming the past and its suffering. George does not believe in the magical worldview of the people of Willow Springs, but he creates his own magic, saving Cocoa by "the powers of his own will," doing what the other Day men have not been able to do. In redeeming the past Days, George becomes an ancestor, and his voice in the text is an ancestral voice. After his death, he stays on Willow Springs, and he lends his name to Cocoa's second son. By confronting the darker forces of Cocoa's past and of the island's history, through the magic of a sacrificing love, George unites the past, the present and the future and ensures that the Days will go on.

Source: Jane Elizabeth Dougherty, in an essay for *Novels for Students*, Gale, 1999.

Bharati Mukherjee

In the following review, Mukherjee suggests that literary excess is a blessing in Mama Day.

On a note card above my writing desk hang the words of the late American original, Liberace: "Too much of a good thing is simply wonderful."

Excess—of plots and subplots, of major characters and walk-ons, of political issues and literary allusions—is what Gloria Naylor's *Mama Day,* her third and most ambitious book, is blessed with. "There are just too many sides to the whole story," Cocoa, Mama Day's grandniece, explains at the end of this longish novel, and the story obviously feels urgent enough to both Cocoa and to Ms. Naylor that they present it to us whole.

If novels are viewed as having the power to save, then novelists are obliged, first, to relive the history of the errors of earlier chroniclers and fill in the missing parts. Recent novels like *Mama Day,* Toni Morrison's *Beloved* and Louise Erdrich's *Love Medicine* resonate with the genuine excitement of authors discovering ways, for the first time it seems, to write down what had only been intuited or heard. These are novelists with an old-fashioned "calling" (to bear witness, to affirm public virtues) in a post-modernist world; their books are scaled down for today's microwavable taste, but still linked to the great public voice of 19th-century storytelling.

Mama Day has its roots in *The Tempest.* The theme is reconciliation, the title character is Miranda (also the name of Prospero's daughter), and Willow Springs is an isolated island where, as on Prospero's isle, magical and mysterious events come to pass. As in *The Tempest,* one story line concerns the magician Miranda Day, nicknamed Mama Day, and her acquisition, exercise and relinquishment of magical powers. The other story line concerns a pair of "star-crossed" (Ms. Naylor's phrase, too) lovers: Ophelia Day, nicknamed Cocoa, and George Andrews.

Willow Springs is a wondrous island, wonderfully rendered. We learn its secrets only if we let ourselves listen to inaudible voices in boarded-up houses and hard-to-reach graveyards. We find out the way the locals do, "sitting on our porches and shelling June peas, quieting the midnight cough of a baby, taking apart the engine of a car—you done heard it without a single living soul really saying a word."

On this wondrous island, slavery and race relations, lover' quarrels, family scandals, professional jealousies all become the "stuff as dreams are made on." The island itself sits just out of the legal reaches of Georgia and South Carolina. "And the way we saw it," ghosts whisper, "America ain't entered the question at all when it come to our land.... We wasn't even Americans when we got it—[we] was slaves. And the laws about slaves not owning nothing in Georgia and South Carolina don't apply, 'cause the land wasn't then—and isn't now—in either of them places."

America, with all its greed and chicanery, exists beyond a bridge. The island was "settled" (if that word is ever appropriate in American history) in the first quarter of the 19th century by an Africa-born slave, a spirited woman named Sapphira who, according to legend, bore her master, a Norwegian immigrant named Bascombe Wade, and maybe person or persons unknown, a total of seven sons. She then persuaded Bascombe to deed the children every square inch of Willow Springs, after which she either poisoned or stabbed the poor man in bed and vanished ahead of a posse. We find out the conditions of Sapphira's bondage only at the end of the novel: love, and not a bill of sale, had kept Bascombe and Sapphira together. Bascombe had given up his land to her sons willingly. This disclosure may make for "incorrect" politics, but it is in keeping with the *Tempest*-like atmosphere of benevolence, light and harmony that Ms. Naylor wishes to have prevail on Willow Springs.

Mama Day, who made a brief appearance in Ms. Naylor's earlier novel, *Linden Hills,* as the toothless, illiterate aunt, the wearer of ugly, comfortable shoes, the hauler of cheap cardboard suitcases and leaky jars of homemade preserves, the caster of hoodoo spells, comes into her own in this novel....

Mama Day—over 100 years old if we are to believe what folks in Willow Springs say, unmarried, stern, wise, crotchety, comforting—is the true heir of Sapphira Wade. Sapphira and Bascombe's love nest, a yellow house set deep in the woods, yields secrets about the future as well as the past to the witch-prophet-matriarch Mama Day. She is the ur-Daughter to Sapphira's ur-Mother and, in turn, through a Leda-and-the-Swan kind of mysterious dead-of-night visitations, she peoples the land herself....

As long as the narrative confines itself to Mama Day and daily life on the bizarre island full of rogues, frauds, crazies, martyrs and clairvoyants, the novel moves quickly. Curiously, the slow sections are about the love story of 27-year-old Cocoa, who has relocated from Willow Springs to New York, and George Andrews, who is meant to be emblematic of the good-hearted, hard-driving but culturally orphaned Northern black man. The courtship occurs all over Manhattan—in greasy diners, in three-star restaurants, in midtown offices, on subways—giving Ms. Naylor a chance to accommodate several set pieces. But she is less proficient in making the familiar wondrous than she is in making the wondrous familiar. Discussions of black bigotry (Cocoa uses kumquats, tacos and bagels as race-related shorthand and has to be scolded into greater tolerance) or of the alienating effects of Barnard College on black women ("those

too bright, too jaded colored girls" is George's put-down) seem like arbitrary asides.

The love story suffers from a more serious flaw. Ms. Naylor, through strident parallels, wants us to compare Cocoa and George to Romeo and Juliet, and their courtship process to the taming of Katharina, the "shrew." The literary plan calls for George to sacrifice his life so that Cocoa might be saved, but the lovers never quite fill out their assigned mythic proportions. Cocoa just seems shallow and self-centered; and George is a priggish young man who wears dry-cleaned blue jeans for roughing it on weekends. For their love story to overwhelm us, with "all passion spent," the lovers' intensity should make whole paragraphs resonate. This, unfortunately, Ms. Naylor does not do. It seems the unchallenged domain of the 19th-century novel to link personal passion with the broader politics of an age. Cocoa is not Madame Bovary, Anna Karenina, Jane Eyre, Dorothea Brooke.

But I'd rather dwell on *Mama Day*'s strengths. Gloria Naylor has written a big, strong, dense, admirable novel; spacious, sometimes a little drafty like all public monuments, designed to last and intended for many levels of use.

Source: Bharati Mukherjee, "There Are Four Sides to Everything," in *The New York Times Book Review,* February 21, 1988, p. 7.

Michiko Kakutani

In the following excerpt, Kakutani gives a mixed review of Mama Day.

In her previous novel, *Linden Hills,* Gloria Naylor created an intimate portrait of a "perverted Eden," in which upper-middle-class blacks discover that they've achieved wealth and success at the expense of their own history and identity, that they've sold their souls and are now living in a kind of spiritual hell. *Mama Day,* her latest novel, similarly describes a hermetic black community, but this time, it's a pastoral world named Willow Springs—a small, paradisal island, situated off the southeast coast of the United States, somewhere off South Carolina and Georgia, but utterly sovereign in its history and traditions.

Legend has it that the island initially belonged to a Norwegian landowner named Bascombe Wade, and that one of his slaves—"a true conjure woman" by the name of Sapphira, who "could walk through a lightning storm without being touched"—married him, persuaded him to leave all his holdings to his slaves, then "poisoned him for his trouble." Before killing him, she bore him seven sons. The youngest of that generation also had seven sons, and the last of them fathered Miranda, or Mama Day. The great-nieces of Mama Day are Willa Prescott Nedeed, who readers of *Linden Hills* will recall came to an ugly and untimely end; and Ophelia, the heroine of this novel, who is likewise threatened with early and disfiguring death....

To set up the fast-paced events that conclude *Mama Day,* Ms. Naylor spends much of the first portion of the book giving us menacing hints and planting time bombs set to detonate later. We're told that Ophelia's the namesake of another Day, an unhappy woman who never recovered from one of the misfortunes that befell the family, and that her own hot temper is liable to get her into trouble. We're told that George suffers from a bad heart and that he shouldn't over-exert himself. We're told that Miss Ruby, a neighbor in Willow Springs, plans to use her magical powers against any woman who comes near her husband, and that her husband happens to be attracted to Ophelia. We're also told that Mama Day herself possesses potent conjuring powers, which she will use to defend her family.

One of the problems with this information is that it's force-fed into the story line, at the expense of character development and narrative flow. The plot is made to pivot around melodramatically withheld secrets (concerning the history of Willow Springs, the nature of Mama Day's second sight, the mysterious "hoodoo" rites practiced on the island); and we are constantly being reminded of the novel's themes by trite observations that are meant to pass as folk wisdom: "Home. You can move away from it, but you never leave it"; "they say every blessing hides a curse, and every curse a blessing" or "nothing would be real until the end."

To make matters worse, the island's residents, who are given to uttering such lines, come across as pasteboard figures, devoid of the carefully observed individuality that distinguished their counterparts in *Linden Hills.* Mama Day is just the sort of matriarchal figure that her name indicates—strong, wise and resolute; her neighbor, a "hoodoo" man known as Dr. Buzzard, is a folksy con man, who plays a crooked game of poker and makes moonshine on the side, and Ruby is the manipulative devil woman, absurdly possessive of her man. As for the visitors to Willow Springs, they're initially just as two-dimensional: Ophelia is a bigoted, demanding woman, who seems lucky to have found a husband at all, given her large mouth and even larger ego, while George appears to be a conscientious yuppie, neatly dividing his time between work, his wife and his passion for football.

Fortunately, as *Mama Day* progresses, Ms. Naylor's considerable storytelling powers begin to take over, and her central characters slowly take on the heat of felt emotion. The bantering exchanges between George and Ophelia demonstrate their affection, as well as their knowledge of each other's weaknesses, and George's gradual immersion in the world of Willow Springs serves to reveal much about both him and his wife.

Still, for all the narrative energy of the novel's second half, there's something contrived and forced about the story. Whereas Toni Morrison's recent novel *Beloved,* which dealt with many of the same themes of familial love and guilt, had a beautiful organic quality to it, weaving together the ordinary and the mythic in a frightening tapestry of fate, *Mama Day* remains a readable, but lumpy, amalgam of styles and allusions. The reader eventually becomes absorbed in George and Ophelia's story, but is never persuaded that the events, which overtake them, are plausible, much less inevitable or real.

Source: Michiko Kakutani, in a review of *Mama Day,* in *The New York Times,* February 10, 1988, p. C25.

Sources

Rita Mae Brown, a review in *Gloria Naylor: Critical Perspectives Past and Present,* edited by Henry Louis Gates Jr. and K. A. Appiah, Amistad, 1993, pp. 13–15.

Peter Erickson, " 'Shakespeare's Black?': The Role of Shakespeare in Naylor's Novels," in *Gloria Naylor: Critical Perspectives Past and Present,* edited by Henry Louis Gates Jr. and K. A. Appiah, Amistad, 1993, pp. 231–48.

Allison Gloch, "A Woman to Be Reckoned With," in *Special Report,* January-February, 1993, pp. 22–25.

Rachel Hass, a review in *Gloria Naylor: Critical Perspectives Past and Present,* edited by Henry Louis Gates Jr. and K. A. Appiah, Amistad, 1993, pp. 22–23.

Elizabeth T. Hayes, "Gloria Naylor's *Mama Day* as Magic Realism," in *The Critical Response to Gloria Naylor,* edited by Sharon Felton and Michelle C. Loris, Greenwood Press, 1997, pp. 177–86.

Margot Anne Kelley, "Sister's Choices: Quilting Aesthetics in Contemporary African-American Women's Fiction," in *Quilt Culture: Tracing the Pattern,* edited by Cheryl B. Torsney and Judy Elsley, University of Missouri Press, 1994, pp. 49–67.

Missy Dehn Kubitschek, "Toward a New Order: Shakespeare, Morrison, and Gloria Naylor's *Mama Day,*" in *Melus,* Vol. 19, No. 3, Fall, 1994, pp. 75–90.

Helen Fiddyment Levy, "Lead on with Light," in *Gloria Naylor: Critical Perspectives Past and Present,* edited by Henry Louis Gates Jr. and K. A. Appiah, Amistad, 1993, pp. 263–84.

Michelle C. Loris, "Interview: 'The Human Spirit Is a Kick-Ass Thing," in *The Critical Response to Gloria Naylor,* edited by Sharon Felton and Michelle C. Loris, Greenwood Press, 1997, pp. 251–63.

Susan Meisenhelder, "'The Whole Picture' in Gloria Naylor's *Mama Day,*" in *African-American Review,* Vol. 27, No. 3, 1993, pp. 405–19.

Bharati Mukherjee, a review in *Gloria Naylor: Critical Perspectives Past and Present,* edited by Henry Louis Gates Jr. and K. A. Appiah, Amistad, 1993, pp. 19–21.

Gloria Naylor and Toni Morrison, "A Conversation," in *Southern Review,* Vol. 21, Summer, 1983, pp. 567–93.

Linda Simon, a review in *Gloria Naylor: Critical Perspectives Past and Present,* edited by Henry Louis Gates Jr. and K. A. Appiah, Amistad, 1993, pp. 15–18.

Lindsey Tucker, "Recovering the Conjure Woman: Texts and Contexts in Gloria Naylor's *Mama Day,*" in *African-American Review,* Vol. 28, No. 2, 1994, pp. 173–88.

For Further Study

Tamala Edwards, "A Conversation with Gloria Naylor," in *Essence,* June, 1998, p. 70.
    Edwards interviews Naylor on the occasion of the publication of her most recent book, *The Men of Brewster Place.*

Sharon Felton and Michelle C. Loris, editors, *The Critical Response to Gloria Naylor,* Greenwood Press, 1997.
    This collection of articles on Naylor's works provides a helpful sampling of the criticism on *Mama Day,* with discussions of the quilting motif, the importance of the conjure woman, the work's revision of *The*

Tempest, and the work's use of magical realism. An interview with Naylor is also included.

Virginia C. Fowler, *Gloria Naylor: In Search of Sanctuary,* Twayne, 1996.
    Fowler's book provides a biography of Naylor as well as a discussion of her novels through *Bailey's Cafe.* There is also an interview with Naylor.

Henry Louis Gates Jr. and K. A. Appiah, editors, *Gloria Naylor: Critical Perspectives Past and Present,* Amistad, 1993.
    Included in this book are many of the initial reviews of *Mama Day* as well as some criticism of Naylor's works.

Rhea Mandulo, "Georgia on My Mind," in *Essence,* March, 1993, p. 144.
    Recounts the author's trip to the Sea Islands of Georgia, a trip partially inspired by the island of Willow Springs in *Mama Day.*

Vincent Odamtten, "Reviewing Gloria Naylor: Toward a Neo-African Critique," in *Of Dreams Deferred, Dead or Alive: African Perspectives on African-American Writers,* edited by Femi Ojo-Ade, Greenwood Press, 1996, pp. 115–29.
    Reads Naylor's text as a reflection of African ideas about religion, family, and culture.

Donna Perry, an interview in *Backtalk: Women Writers Speak Out,* Rutgers University Press, 1993, pp. 218–42.
    In this interview, Perry focuses on Naylor's relationship to other female writers and asks Naylor questions about each of her first four novels.

V. R. Peterson, a review in *People Weekly,* April 18, 1988, p. 9.
    A mostly favorable review which praises Naylor's writing style but criticizes her characterizations.

Charles Rowell, "An Interview with Gloria Naylor," *Callaloo,* Winter, 1997, pp. 179–92.
    This interview focuses mostly on Naylor's process of becoming a writer and her ideas about literature.

Moby-Dick

Herman Melville
1851

Now admired as a masterpiece of American literature and considered one of the greatest novels of all time, *Moby-Dick* was published to unfavorable reviews, and its author, Herman Melville, was subsequently unable to make a living as a writer. He wrote just three more novels after *Moby-Dick* and then retired from literary life, working as a customs officer, writing poems, a novella, and a few short stories. Not until the 1920s were the multi-layered qualities of his epic novel fully appreciated.

Ostensibly the story of a whaling voyage as seen through the eyes of Ishmael, the book's narrator, and the account of the pursuit of a white whale, the novel is concerned with many of the issues which dominated nineteenth-century thought in America. The relationship between the land and the sea echoes the conflict between adventure and domesticity, between frontiersman and city-dweller. Captain Ahab's tragic monomania, as expressed in his obsessive pursuit of the whale, is an indirect commentary on the feelings of disillusionment in mid-nineteenth-century America and on the idea that the single-minded pursuit of an ideal is both vain and self-destructive.

Highly symbolic, tightly packed with philosophical musings, and interspersed with goading questions, the novel put off many of its early readers with what was seen as a rejection of basic storytelling principles. Each time some form of narrative tension is established, the author appears to launch off into obscure ramblings. They are only arcane, of course, when the reader does not per-

ceive the hidden meanings within these passages; modern audiences have the advantage of being more receptive to disjointed narrative techniques. As for the novel's subtexts, only a few of these require sophisticated knowledge of nineteenth-century thought; the majority concern the big and immutable questions of life.

Author Biography

Melville was born in New York City on August 1, 1819. He was the third of eight children born to Allan and Maria Melville. His father, an importer, died in 1832, having struggled in vain to establish a sense of financial security for his family. Although only thirteen years old, Herman immediately went to work as a bank clerk to help support his family. His older brother, Gansevoort, was always considered the most promising son, and for several years the family depended upon his business endeavors. But by 1837 Gansevoort was bankrupt and the Melvilles had to rely on wealthy relatives for financial assistance.

After a brief spell as a schoolteacher, Melville signed up to serve as a cabin boy on the *St. Lawrence.* Afterwards, he returned to teaching, but this early adventure had whetted his appetite for the sea. On January 3, 1841, he set sail aboard the *Acushnet,* a whaling vessel, sailing out of Buzzard Bay. At the Marquesas Islands in the South Pacific, he left his ship to live with a native tribe reputed to be cannibals. Melville later said that when he discovered their taste for human flesh (it was never proved they were cannibals), he escaped the island, finding passage on the *Lucy Ann,* a whaling ship from Australia. Melville then enlisted in the navy, spending a year on the frigate *United States.* He did not return to American soil until October of 1844, and then he almost immediately began writing about his adventures.

Melville's first novel, *Typee,* published in 1846, described his adventure and captivity in the South Seas. Melville began courting Elizabeth Shaw, the daughter of a Bostonian judge, and he wrote a second novel, *Omoo,* again based on his South Seas adventures. It was published in 1847 and, on the strength of its sales, Herman and Elizabeth decided to marry.

The writing of *Moby-Dick* coincided with Melville's move to the Berkshires in Massachusetts, and the establishment of his friendship with

Herman Melville

fellow author Nathaniel Hawthorne. During the period of *Moby-Dick*'s composition, Melville held Hawthorne in very high regard, both personally and professionally, and in his correspondence he spoke of their role together as being the forefront of American letters.

Moby-Dick was written by Melville with an eye to establishing himself as a leading literary figure, which made its failure all the more difficult for him to bear. His next book, *Pierre* (1852), was written in a mood of depression. *Israel Potter,* a strange biographical novel published in 1854, did nothing to reestablish Melville's name, and an attack of sciatica heralded an insidious decline in his physical and mental health. *The Confidence Man* (1857) is now considered to be one of Melville's best books, a funny and sardonic look at human nature. Commercially, however, it was another flop, and Melville was forced to consider alternative employment. He sold his home, Arrowhead, to his brother Allan and moved to New York City, where, in 1866, he took up duties as an Inspector of Customs.

Melville's literary output from then on consisted mainly of poetry. Several of his Civil War poems are among the best poems of their period. His huge epic poem, *Clarel,* about religious doubt, which preoccupied him for nearly a decade, had to be published using private funds. Toward the end of his life he wrote a prose novel, *Billy Budd,* completed in the year of his death, 1891.

Plot Summary

Call Me Ishmael

Moby-Dick; or, The Whale chronicles the strange journey of an ordinary seaman named Ishmael who signs on for a whaling voyage in 1840s Massachusetts. A thoughtful but gloomy young man, Ishmael begins his odyssey in New Bedford, Massachusetts, a prosperous whaling town and crossing point to the island of Nantucket. Arriving on a dark Saturday night in December, he finds cheap lodgings in a waterfront dive called The Spouter Inn. There he is forced to share a bed with a South Sea islander and "cannibal" named Queequeg, a fierce-looking harpooner covered with tattoos and carrying a tomahawk and a shrunken head. After some initial uncertainty, the two become close friends and decide to seek a berth together on a whaling ship. Before leaving for Nantucket, however, Ishmael decides to visit the local whaleman's chapel, where he sees memorial plaques to lost sailors and hears a disturbing sermon about the prophet Jonah and the terrors of the whale.

On Nantucket, the two sailors set out to find the best ship for their voyage. After consulting Queequeg's "black little god," a tiny totem named Yojo, they settle on the *Pequod,* a whaling vessel run by the notorious Captain Ahab. They sign the ship's papers, but on their way back to the inn to get their belongings, they meet Elijah, a shabbily dressed old man who haunts the docks. Elijah hints at the dangers to come and warns the two not to get involved with the vengeful captain.

The Quest

The *Pequod* leaves Nantucket on Christmas day headed for the whaling grounds in the Pacific. Captain Ahab remains in his cabin for several days, while the crew accustoms itself to life at sea. When Ahab does emerge, his appearance startles Ishmael. A long, white scar runs down Ahab's face, and he walks on an artificial leg made of whale bone. Soon he calls the entire crew together and informs them that their voyage will be no ordinary whaling cruise. Ahab has returned to sea with the sole purpose of finding and killing the whale that took his leg on the previous voyage. He offers a sixteen-dollar gold piece to the first man who spots the white whale, Moby-Dick, and then conducts a demonic ceremony in which the three "pagan" harpooners cross their lances and drink to the death of the whale.

When not under the influence of Ahab's obsessive search, Ishmael gathers information and meditates upon the business of whaling and the strange attractive power of the white whale. Among other possible explanations, he suggests that Ahab both fears and hates the whiteness of Moby-Dick because this blankness recalls the "colorless, all-color of atheism," a nothingness that lies behind all nature. He also describes the ship's first whale hunt and the subsequent butchering of the sperm whale. He discusses the whale as it is depicted in paintings and compares the images to his own experiences; and he observes the whale itself, pondering the meaning of its huge and mysterious body, its equally peaceful and violent behavior, and its often contradictory significance to the men who hunt it.

Despite several successful hunts, including one encounter with a herd of sperm whales near the coast of Java, they continue to search for Moby-Dick. Having revealed the presence of his "infidel" boat crew led by Fedallah, the Parsee (a member of the Zoroastrian religious sect from India), Ahab can no longer hide the true extent of his obsession. He orders the blacksmith to forge a special harpoon from the nail stubs of racing horses. He then tempers the barb in the blood of the three harpooners, baptizing the weapon "in nomine diaboli!" (in the name of the devil). Soon after, he throws his navigational quadrant overboard and, in a moment of defiance of nature and God, cries out at the corposants, a strange blue fire of static electricity (sometimes called "Saint Elmo's Fire") that covers the ship's masts. Not even Starbuck, the respected first mate, can convince the captain of his madness.

At this stage in the story, Ishmael becomes less prominent as a character. He reappears occasionally to offer his thoughts on the mythological history of whaling and the symbolic meanings of the story of Jonah from the Bible. While Ahab rages at the world, Ishmael describes the sensual pleasures of squeezing lumps of whale oil or spermaceti. He tells how he once measured a whale's skeleton on the (fictional) island of Tranque in the Arsacides and describes the illness of Queequeg, who is so near death at one point that he orders a coffin from the carpenter. Queequeg survives, however, and turns the coffin into a bed, carving its exterior with the same "hieroglyphic marks" that are tattooed on his body. When the ship later loses its standard life-buoy, the carpenter nails the lid on the coffin, caulks it, and hangs it from the back of the ship as a replacement.

The Chase

Torn between the good and evil influences of Starbuck and Fedallah, Ahab instinctively guides the ship back to the "very latitude and longitude" of his first encounter with Moby-Dick. Starbuck makes a final appeal to his captain to "fly these deadly waters!" and return to his wife and child, but Ahab rejects his pleas and turns to Fedallah. In his role as demonic advisor, Fedallah has prophesied that Ahab will know "neither hearse nor coffin" and that before he can die on this voyage he must first see two hearses on the sea, one "not made by mortal hands" and the other made of American wood. He also declares that only hemp or rope can kill the captain, which Ahab understands as a reference to hanging. Since he is unlikely to be hung on his own ship and even less likely to see two hearses in the middle of the Pacific, Ahab declares himself "immortal on land and sea!"

With any chance of relinquishing his obsession now lost, Ahab finally spots the white whale and the chase begins. For three days the crew of the *Pequod* fights Moby-Dick but fails to kill him. On the third day, with Ahab's harpoon in his hump, the white whale turns toward the ship itself and, with a powerful blow of his forehead, sinks the *Pequod* with all the crew still on board. Combined with the death of Fedallah, seen wrapped in the ropes that now encircle Moby-Dick, the ship's sinking fulfills the first prophecy. Soon after, the third prediction also comes true when Ahab, trying to clear a kink in the rope attached to Moby-Dick, gets caught in a loop and disappears, dragged under by the whale. Caught in the whirlpool created by the sinking ship, all remaining members of the crew except Ishmael go down with the ship.

Pitched overboard by the violent struggles of Moby-Dick, Ishmael floats on the edge of the action, witnessing the final moments of Ahab and his crew. As the ship sinks, the whirlpool draws him closer to the site of the wreck, but because of his distance from the ship, he is not pulled under. Instead, out of the center of the whirlpool, Queequeg's coffin rises to save him. Aided by the strange "life preserver," Ishmael floats for "almost one whole day and night" before the *Rachel,* a whaling ship searching for part of its crew, picks him up.

Characters

Captain Ahab

Introduced by Captain Peleg as "a grand, ungodly, godlike man," the reader learns two things about Ahab, captain of the *Pequod* in *Moby-Dick:* Ahab was orphaned when he was twelve months old, and one of his legs was lost as a result of his most recent whaling voyage. The wound is so fresh that the stump is still bleeding. However, it is some time before Ishmael is able to verify this. Ahab does not make a proper appearance in the book until Chapter 28. The reader finds him standing upon his quarter-deck, looking "like a man cut away from the stake," with his white bone leg (carved from a sperm whale's jaw) jammed into a specially drilled hole on deck. The reader is told that Ahab has gray hair and has a white scar or disfigurement down the side of his face. There are some aboard the ship who suspect the mark travels the entire length of Ahab's body, from head to toe. But Melville is more anxious to communicate an atmosphere, in sentences such as, "There was an infinity of firmest fortitude, a determinate, unsurrenderable wilfulness, in the fixed and fearless, forward dedication of that glance." The long delay in Ahab's involvement in the action of the novel helps to build him up as a grand figure, the major tragic character Melville wants his readers to see.

Although Ahab is awe-inspiring, Melville is at pains to establish the captain's dignity. In Chapter 34, "The Cabin Table," he is presented as a sultan dining with his emirs. "Over its ivory-laid table, Ahab presided like a mute, maned sea-lion on the white coral beach, surrounded by his warlike but still deferential cubs."

Goaded by Starbuck for wanting his revenge upon the dumb beast which struck out at him from "blindest instinct," Ahab sets out in Chapter 36 his belief that, on the contrary, the whale acted out of inscrutable malice and that every action has a motive or reason. "I'd strike the sun if it insulted me," he states. The following chapter, a short soliloquy, makes explicit Ahab's Shakespearian intensity. "I am madness maddened!" he cries out to himself, alone in his cabin.

Having had the desire for revenge quickened within him, Ahab's obsession is presented as a ravenous monster, rapidly assuming an existence independent of the mind on which it feeds. Chapter 44 ends: "God help thee, old man, thy thoughts have created a creature in thee; and he whose intense thinking thus makes him a Prometheus; a vul-

Gregory Peck as Captain Ahab in the 1954 film Moby Dick.

ture feeds upon that heart forever; that vulture the very creature he creates."

Ahab's artificial leg is damaged as the result of an encounter with an English vessel, the *Samuel Enderby.* Having pulled alongside and gone aboard to discover that he has something in common with the English Captain Bloomer—an amputated limb and an ivory substitute—Ahab takes offence at a comment made by the English ship's doctor. Jumping down into the *Pequod*'s landing-boat, his ivory leg receives a fracturing blow. Although the leg is not completely broken, he orders the ship's carpenter to make him a new one, a fact that symbolizes the new light in which the reader has come to view the captain—he is no longer the magisterial commander of the start of the voyage, but a possessed man at the mercy of his obsession.

In Chapter 119, "The Candles," Ahab prays aloud and defiantly to the white flame of St. Elmo's fire. Shortly before this, he hurled the quadrant to the deck and trampled on it, an act in which he symbolically parts company with reason. Becoming an isolated madman—and some critics have compared Ahab with Shakespeare's King Lear—Ahab battles his evil forces alone and is destroyed as a result.

Captain Bildad

Captain Bildad is a retired whaling captain, a staunch Quaker, and a hard taskmaster. With Peleg, he is co-proprietor of the *Pequod,* and a licensed pilot. Melville, wondering how such a captain squared up his belief in pacifism with the violence of his lifelong trade, once commented: "Probably he had long since come to the sage and sensible conclusion that a man's religion is one thing, and this practical world quite another."

Captain Boomer

A one-armed English whaling captain, Boomer is master of the *Samuel Enderby.* He lost his arm in an encounter with Moby-Dick, and has good reason to hate the whale, but he doesn't. His character helps emphasize how extreme Ahab's behavior is.

Bulkington

A mariner who is made the subject of the short, transitionary Chapter 23, "The Lee Shore," in *Moby-Dick.*

Dr. Bunger

Dr. Bunger is the ship's doctor aboard the *Samuel Enderby.* He is responsible for amputating Captain Boomer's arm.

Daggoo

The third harpooner on the *Pequod,* Daggoo works from Flask's boat. He is described as "a gigantic, coal-black negro-savage."

Elijah

Elijah is the name of the self-styled prophet in *Moby-Dick* who accosts Ishmael and Queequeg on the quayside before they set sail. He warns them about Ahab.

Fedallah

First seen on deck in Chapter 48, Fedallah dresses all in black, apart from a white turban. He is a member of the Zoroastrian Parsees, a sect that emphasizes the free choice of good or evil and the consequences for the afterlife. He is seen by Stubb as the devil incarnate. Fedallah is present with Ahab at key moments, such as the smashing of the quadrant and the burning of St. Elmo's fire.

Flask

The third mate of the *Pequod* in *Moby-Dick,* Flask is a native of Martha's Vineyard. Pugnacious

Media Adaptations

- The first film of *Moby-Dick* was a silent movie, released under the title *The Sea Beast* in 1926, and starring John Barrymore as Ahab, and distributed by Warner.

- Warner produced a sound version of the novel in 1930; it was directed by Lloyd Bacon and again starred John Barrymore as Ahab.

- The best-known movie version is the John Huston-directed 1956 color production with Gregory Peck as Ahab. This is a powerful and faithful rendering of the novel, though opinions have been divided concerning the central casting. Other actors in the cast were Orson Welles, Richard Basehart, Leo Genn, and Harry Andrews. The screenplay was written by Huston and Ray Bradbury.

- An educational film, *Moby Dick: The Great American Novel,* was shot by CBS news in 1969.

- An animated version, entitled *Moby Dick* and produced by API Television Productions in 1977, is available on video.

- A reading by George Kennedy released by "Listen for Pleasure Books on Cassette" dates from 1981.

- A radio dramatization presented on NBC Theater is available on one fifty-minute cassette in the Audio Library Classics series, distributed by Metacom, 1991.

- A sound recording of the novel, read by Norman Dietz on thirteen audiocassettes, was produced by Blackstone Audio Books in 1992.

- A musical titled *Moby Dick: A Whale of a Tale* was staged in 1993 by Cameron Mackenzie in London's West End; it was an unsuccessful adaptation and only ran for a few weeks.

---

and fearless by virtue of a mediocre intellect, he is nicknamed King Post because his short, stocky appearance resembles a squared-off section of timber called by that name.

Fleece

The *Pequod*'s cook, Fleece is an old black man who is often teased by Stubb.

Gabriel

Gabriel is a freckle-faced young man with ginger hair who visits the *Pequod* after the *Jeroboam,* a sister vessel out of Nantucket, draws alongside. A crazed exile from the Neskyeuna Shakers, Gabriel, or the archangel Gabriel as he chooses to call himself, has turned the majority of Captain Mayhew's crew into his disciples, holding a fanatic's sway over them. Melville is quite clear about his disapproval of this character.

Captain Gardiner

Captain Gardiner is the commander of the *Rachel,* one of the ships the *Pequod* meets at sea.

Moby-Dick, it turns out, is responsible for the death of Gardiner's son. However, Gardiner, unlike Ahab, recognizes that this loss was the act of a wild animal rather than an evil creature.

Mrs. Hussey

Mrs. Hussey is the proprietor of the Try Pots, the hotel and restaurant in which Ishmael and Queequeg stay in Nantucket.

Ishmael

Ishmael is the name assumed by the otherwise anonymous narrator of Melville's *Moby-Dick.* A rootless individual, brought up as a good Christian in "the bosom of the infallible Presbyterian Church," his way of "driving off the spleen, and regulating the circulation" is to periodically sign aboard a sailing vessel. At the beginning of the book, Ishmael is in Manhattan, packing an old carpetbag and setting off for New Bedford, Massachusetts, where he arrives on a Saturday night, having just missed the ferry to Nantucket. This circumstance forces him to spend the weekend at the Spouter Inn, reluctantly sharing a room and a bed with a freakish-looking, harpoon-carrying savage named Queequeg.

After visiting the Whaleman's Chapel and hearing Father Mapple's sermon, the two sail out to Nantucket together and, boarding with Mrs. Hussey at the Try Pots, they both sign up to sail aboard the *Pequod.*

Having set sail, the nature of the narrative shifts and Ishmael's perspective is lost, not to surface again until Chapter 41. In this long, crucial chapter, Ishmael, in contrast to Starbuck's rugged rationality, empathizes with Ahab and fully understands the development of the Captain's monomania. In addition to understanding Ahab, we discover that Ishmael has himself, to some degree, become infected by all the rumors and gossip surrounding the white whale and, in the subsequent chapter, "The Whiteness of the Whale," has been willing to consider the albino whale as a visible symbol for all that remains horribly unseen. "Though in many of its aspects this visible world seems formed in love," he says, "the invisible spheres were formed in fright."

Ishmael's friendship with Queequeg is given a fulsome, erotic gloss that has given some critics grounds for exploring homoerotic themes in the novel. Certainly the fraternity which Ishmael appears to enjoy with the rest of the crew is in stark contrast to the lonely isolation of Ahab. It is this contrast—involved camaraderie against aloof detachment—which is being set up in such scenes as the sperm-squeezing incident in which Ishmael, grabbing his co-laborers' hands among the globules of whale sperm, is overcome with "an abounding, affectionate, friendly, loving feeling."

At the end of the novel, when Ahab and his crew are all killed by Moby-Dick, Ishmael is the only one to survive. Finding a coffin that had been built for Queequeg when he had become gravely ill, Ishmael manages to survive the sea until he is rescued by another ship.

King Post

See Flask

Father Mapple

Father Mapple is the preacher at the Whaleman's Chapel in New Bedford. The sermon he delivers in Chapter 9 is a set piece, used by many critics as a gloss on what subsequently befalls the *Pequod* and its crew. Certainly the sermon covers important issues, such as the passive submission to the will of God. But this conventional Christian doctrine is counterpoised by the fierce crescendo of Mapple's sermon when he defines the true Christian hero as one who "gives no quarter in the truth, and kills, burns and destroys all sin though he pluck it out from under the robes of Senators and Judges." This is the role of a proud Puritan hero.

Captain Peleg

Peleg is one of the owners of the *Pequod,* and serves as a device to introduce the reader to Captain Ahab by describing him to Ishmael.

Perth

The *Pequod*'s blacksmith, Perth is nicknamed Prometheus. In Chapter 113 he forges the harpoon with which Ahab hopes to triumph over Moby-Dick. When completed the spear is "baptized" with the heathen blood of Tashtego, Queequeg, and Daggoo.

Pippin

One of the few named sailors on the *Pequod,* Pip is just a boy, a bright and cheerful African-American child. The duties of Pip do not normally require him to go in the boats. In Chapter 93, however, Pip stands in for Stubb's after-oarsman, who has sprained his hand. After the whale has been harpooned, Pip panics, jumps overboard, and becomes tangled in the line. The capture has to be sacrificed to save the young lad's life. Tashtego, the harpooner, and other members of the crew are furious. Stubb, perceived as acting fairly, warns Pip in a businesslike way never to jump overboard again. When this advice is ignored, Stubb's boat declines to rescue Pip a second time. The boy is eventually picked up by the *Pequod,* but he has been in the water so long that he has lost his mind.

Prometheus

See Perth

Queequeg

Queequeg is a highborn native of an uncharted south-seas island. His father was a High Chief, and his uncle a High Priest. Queequeg is covered in tattoos and worships pagan gods, including a small black idol, Yojo. In the first hundred pages of the novel, Queequeg is a major character. While he and Ishmael board together at the Spouter Inn, and then at Mrs. Hussy's in Nantucket, he is the source of a considerable level of amusement. But the real point about Queequeg is his friendliness. He and Ishmael strike up an instant comradeship.

Starbuck

Starbuck is the chief mate of the *Pequod* and a native of Nantucket. He is a Christian of an earnest Quaker disposition, a "staid, steadfast man." Although only about thirty, his appearance is pinched and wizened. He selects Queequeg as his harpooner. Melville depicts Starbuck as a man who becomes possessed and demonized by Ahab. In the soliloquy, "Dusk," Chapter 38, Starbuck explains to himself that Ahab has "drilled deep down, and blasted all my reason out of me! I think I see his impious end; but feel that I must help him to it." Essentially, he trusts to God to put in the "wedge" that will divert Ahab from his objective. But there are some key moments when he stands up to his captain. Starbuck confronts Ahab in Chapter 109 upon discovering that sperm oil is leaking from the hold. This means, he insists, that they must "up Burtons" (that is, hoist up the casks and see what barrels need repairing). Ahab furiously refuses, at one point ordering his first mate at gunpoint to go on deck and proceed as usual. But Starbuck's calm self-righteousness impresses the captain. "Thou art but too good a fellow, Starbuck," says Ahab, as he proceeds to order "up Burtons." Later, in Chapter 123, "The Musket," Starbuck is tempted to murder Ahab in his sleep, using the very weapon that was used to threaten him in the earlier chapter. He holds the musket and takes aim but, after wrestling with his angel, turns away and puts the gun back in its rack.

Stubb

Stubb is the *Pequod*'s second mate. He is the brother-in-law of Charity and a native of Cape Cod. A jovial, easygoing, pipe-smoking character, he serves as a contrast to the upright Starbuck. Stubb catches and kills a whale with cool efficiency in Chapter 61. His colorful exchanges with the ship's crew provide, in the middle section of the book, some of the humor and entertainment that Queequeg provides at the start. He is more sensitive than Flask, but not inclined to speculation. His philosophy, such as it is, is to laugh at life, as he explains in the brief soliloquy found in Chapter 39, "First Night-Watch."

Themes

Individual vs. Nature

The voyage of the *Pequod* is no straightforward, commercially inspired whaling voyage. The reader knows this as soon as Ishmael registers as a member of the crew and receives, at secondhand, warnings of the captain's state of mind. Ahab, intent on seeking revenge on the whale who has maimed him, is presented as a daring and creative individual, pitted against the full forces of nature. In developing the theme of the individual (Ahab) versus Nature (symbolized by Moby-Dick), Melville explores the attributes of natural forces. Are they ruled by chance, neutral occurrences that affect human characters arbitrarily? Or do they possess some form of elementary will that makes them capable of using whatever power is at their disposal?

God and Religion

The conflict between the individual and nature brings into play the theme of religion and God's role in the natural world. The critic Harold Bloom has named Ahab "one of the fictive founders of what should be called the American Religion," and although Melville wrote his novel while living in the civilized Berkshires, near the eastern U.S. seaboard, and set it on the open seas, the reader must not forget that America at that time had moved westward. To Ahab it does not matter if the white whale is "agent" or "principle." He will fight against fate, rather than resign himself to a divine providence. Father Mapple, who gives a sermon near the beginning of the novel, and, to a lesser extent, Starbuck both symbolize the conventional and contemporary religious attitudes of nineteenth-century Protestantism. Ahab's defiance of these is neither romantic nor atheistic but founded on a tragic sense of heroic and unavoidable duty.

Good and Evil, Female and Masculine

Ahab picks his fight with evil on its own terms, striking back aggressively. The good things in the book—the loyalty of members of the crew, such as young Pip; Ahab's domestic memories of his wife and child—remain peripheral and ineffective, a part of life that is never permitted to take center stage. Other dualities abound. The sky and air, home for the birds, is described as feminine, while the sea is masculine, a deep dungeon for murderous brutes. Also contrasted with the sea is the land, seen as green and mild, a tranquil haven. In Chapter 58 Melville writes: "As the appalling ocean surrounds the verdant land, so in the soul of man there lies one insular Tahiti, full of peace and joy, but encompassed by all the horrors of the half known life. God keep thee! Push not off from that isle, for thou canst never return!" Although Melville's exact

Topics for Further Study

- By investigating various movie adaptations and juvenile editions of *Moby-Dick* (including comic books), attempt to analyze the qualities of Melville's novel which do not transfer to other mediums.

- Basing your work on Chapter 32 of the novel, "Cetology," check Melville's facts about whales with what is known about them today. How much, if any, of this chapter would need revising?

- Explore the issues of physical disability and revenge from the perspective of modern psychology; apply what you learn to the character of Ahab to try to understand his motivations.

- Imagine a reader of *Moby-Dick* who is given a copy in which Chapter 9 (Father Mapple's sermon) has been torn out. The reader claims it made no difference to his or her appreciation of the book. Present an argument in favor of the chapter.

- Compare and contrast practices of the whaling industry in the 1850s with current practices followed by whaling ships from Japan and Norway; what were the different tools used to hunt and process whales compared to those used now, and how are the different parts of the whale used in commercial products today?

---

point of view is debatable, and the symbolism in the book is too rich to allow for neat comparisons, it can be said that qualities of goodness tend to be equated with the land, the feminine, and with mildness of temper. Viewing the *Pequod*'s voyage as a metaphor for life, the book seems to be saying that in following ambition or any far-off goal, an individual risks missing out on many of the good things in life, including home and domestic happiness.

The fact that there are no female participants in the novel has encouraged some critics to consider that this is a commentary on the masculine character—thrusting, combative, and vengeful. But it is because the other characters are all male, and they are not all like Ahab, that interpretations cannot be so straightforward. The very masculinity of Ahab is complicated somewhat by the possibility that he has been castrated, not by the initial encounter with the whale, but by the subsequent accidental piercing of his groin by his ivory leg. Critics as diverse as W. H. Auden and Camille Paglia have written about the sexual symbolism in the novel. It is a matter which invites debate, although any discussion on the subject needs to take into account that in the nineteenth century, it was an accepted convention to give certain characteristics a gender bias. Melville, like his contemporaries, was sophisticated enough to know that men and women could embrace a combination of traits deemed to be masculine and feminine.

Choices and Consequences

Ahab is both a hero and a villain. In making a choice and sticking by it, he can be seen as valiantly exercising free will. But the consequences of his decision transform him into a villain, responsible for the death of such innocents as Pip and good men like Starbuck. His monomania or obsession chains him to a fate worse than that which might have prevailed had he not so stubbornly pursued his goal. Contrasting readings of the novel are possible, and most turn upon the interpretation of the character of Ahab and the choices he makes—or, rather, towards the end of the book, the choices he refuses to make. "Not too late is it, even now," Starbuck cries out to him on the third day of the climactic chase. The question is, in depicting a number of situations in which Ahab is given the possibility of drawing back, is Melville establishing a flaw in the individual character, or is he emphasizing the predestined and inescapable quality of the novel's conclusion?

For much of the final encounter, the white whale behaves as any ordinary whale caught up in the chase, but in its last rush at the boat, "Retribution, swift vengeance, eternal malice were in his whole aspect...." These are exactly the qualities which Ahab himself has exhibited during the voyage. Ahab is finally seen as both defined and consumed by fate. When, at the end of the novel, Ishmael, the lone survivor, is finally picked up and rescued by the *Rachel,* we are reminded that he had become a member of the crew as the result of an act of free will rather than necessity, as a means of escaping thoughts of death.

Appearance and Reality

Underscoring all of these themes is an ongoing consideration of the meaning of appearances. A key chapter in this regard is "The Whiteness of the Whale," a meditation in Ishmael's voice on the mask-like ambiguities which affect our interpretation of the visible world. There are ambiguities in the chapter itself, for in one of two footnotes Melville gives a firsthand account of his first sighting of an albatross. "Through its inexpressible, strange eyes, methought I peeped to secrets which took hold of God." Is the reader supposed to think this is Ishmael or Melville speaking? (Ambiguity becomes a major theme in Melville's next novel, *Pierre*.) In this particular chapter, Ishmael meditates on the strange phenomenon of whiteness, which sometimes speaks of godly purity and at other times repels or terrorizes with its ghostly pallor. The meditation leaves color references behind to become a general meditation on the nature of fear and the existence of unseen evil: "Though in many of its aspects this visible world seems formed in love, the invisible spheres were formed in fright."

Style

Point of View

Melville's earlier novels are mainly first-person accounts of romanticized sailing voyages presented as actual experience. When, after the introductory Etymology and Extracts, he opens *Moby-Dick* with the words "Call me Ishmael," it is as if he is giving notice that the narrative voice in this novel is to be more obviously fictional. There are periods, particularly in the first quarter of the book, when Ishmael is an active character, telling the story as an involved first-person narrator. But often during the middle section of the voyage Ishmael's voice recedes and the reader is presented with a traditional, omniscient narrator's view of events, with the consequence that the author, Melville, and the character Ishmael become identified as one and the same in many readers' minds. Shakespearean soliloquies and learned discourses on whaling history and anatomy are used to break up the narrative thread.

At no point is Ishmael given the perspective of one who is relating the story from a flashback point of view in which the outcome of the voyage is known, but since he could not be relating the story if he had gone down with the ship, the reader

knows this must be a survivor's tale. Nevertheless, this does not mean that Ishmael's attitudes and beliefs as they are reflected at the novel's beginning still hold by its conclusion, for Ishmael's experiences clearly have an effect on him.

Symbolism

The passages providing reference information on whales and whaling, which sometimes seem clumsily inserted into the narrative, are a means of making it clear to the reader that the story is about much more than a simple hunting expedition. It is not always apparent who is supposed to be presenting the information—Ishmael? Melville?—but it is certainly not Ahab, who has lost whatever interest he had in whaling as a purely practical and commercial enterprise. Nevertheless, some of the factual, general material provides relevant commentary on the thematic implications of Ahab's quest for one individual whale, so that there is a multi-layered symbolism at work in the book. The crudest and most straightforward symbolism is that which occurs when clusters of chapters make direct analogies with allegorical qualities.

In Chapter 73, for example, the hoisting of a captured whale's head to the side of the boat makes it lean until it is counterbalanced by the head of a second kill. This, the reader is told, is like first being influenced by one philosopher and then being brought to some degree of even keel by a dose of another. "Throw all these thunderheads overboard, and then you will float light and right" is the final exhortation. But a later chapter takes the analogy into an entirely different realm, one that touches upon the much broader symbolism of the novel. Chapter 76, "The Battering-Ram," in which it is explained that the mouth of a sperm whale is positioned entirely underneath the head, and its eyes and ears are situated on the sides, describes the whale's frontal appearance as a "dead, blind wall," a featureless barrier of flesh and bone against which Ahab has pitted himself. The whale's head thus symbolizes the unsympathetic and irresistible forces of nature.

Structure

After the initial, episodic beginning to *Moby-Dick*, Melville takes liberties with the structure of the novel. He introduces very short chapters, some barely a page in length, and puts words into the mouths of his characters as if they are performing on the Elizabethan stage, rather than in a nineteenth-century novel. Comparing *Moby-Dick* with other stalwart nineteenth-century texts, such as those by Charles Dickens or Anthony Trollope, it is easy to exaggerate Melville's eccentricities. In fact, Melville's contemporaries were perfectly happy with the traditionally accepted structures of the novel at the time. Reading reviews of *Moby-Dick* from both sides of the Atlantic helps one to realize that its critical reception was not at all bad. Discerning reviewers of the time, especially in the English press, actually did appreciate the novel in relation to Melville's preceding works and considered it to be his finest achievement to date.

Unfortunately, the general public was not so appreciative of the novel's subtleties and innovations. The book sold fewer than five thousand copies in Melville's lifetime. Its structure was undoubtedly a factor. For some readers it remains a difficult book to complete on first encounter. On the other hand, once it has been read from beginning to end, it is relatively easy to return to its decisive moments and examine afresh their relationship to the whole. This makes it a very accessible book for study, the brevity of its chapters helping students to find their way about the text.

Epic Style

Newton Arvin was one of the first critics to identify the characteristics of what he called Melville's "verbal palette." These include his fondness for verbal nouns such as "regardings," "allurings" and "intercedings," which give passages of the novel the magisterial tone of an ancient classic text. One of the source books for *Moby-Dick* was *Os Lusiados* (*The Lusiads*) by the sixteenth-century Portuguese poet Luis de Camoens. In this poem, Camoens did for the Portuguese language what Geoffrey Chaucer had done for English and Dante for Italian. Melville was increasingly conscious that no one had yet achieved this in American literature. He read and reviewed Nathaniel Hawthorne's *Mosses from an Old Manse* in the course of working on *Moby-Dick*. In his review he commented on the need for heroic national literature of a truly independent kind.

Many of the epic references and posturings in *Moby-Dick* are humorous (mock-epic). The three-day battle with the whale at the end of the book is on a grand scale, and the association with Prometheus (the Greek Titan who gave fire to mankind and was later punished by Zeus for it) is self-consciously "heroic," but Melville mixes this with passages of ranting slang. As John McWilliams said in his essay "The Epic in the Nineteenth Century," "*Moby-Dick* represents a moment in literary history when generic terms retain

old meanings that must be wilfully, even gleefully, broken down."

Historical Context

America in the Mid-Nineteenth Century

America was in a tumultuous period, establishing its national and international identity at the time *Moby-Dick* was being written. It is noteworthy that the classic American novel of the period is not ostensibly about westward expansion. Instead it *is* about pursuit and capture, about following a dream. The American Dream, as it was envisaged by the Founding Fathers, is now considered by some as a dangerous preoccupation, a consuming national obsession. In a real sense, Melville's book is not about its time, but about ours. A possible reading would have the *Pequod* as modern corporate America, intent on control and subjection, and Ahab as a power-crazed executive, quick to seek vengeance for any received aggression.

Self-Reliance

When the novel was being written, Transcendentalism was becoming the predominant philosophical and religious viewpoint. This view—propounded most cogently by Ralph Waldo Emerson in his essay *Self-Reliance*—held that God was present in the world, as well as in every individual soul. In this way, the soul's intuitions were divine and should be followed regardless of authority, tradition, or public opinion. "Trust thyself," was the basic tenet, and hence the term "Self-Reliance." This view (it never developed into a rigorous system of thought) was essentially a reaction against New England Puritanism. Like English Romanticism, it was heavily influenced by German philosophers, principally Immanuel Kant. As propounded by Emerson, Henry David Thoreau, Bronson Alcott, Margaret Fuller, Jones Very, George Ripley, and a host of other New England poets, essayists, divines, and public speakers, Transcendentalism was idealistic, skirting around such basic religious notions as sin and evil.

Although Melville fits the descriptions of the self-reliant individual in Emerson's essay—"to be great is to be misunderstood," "who so would be a man must be a nonconformist"—he, like Hawthorne, remained acutely aware that by taking self-reliance to extremes, as in the case of the monomaniacal Ahab, virtue could quickly turn to vice. The Calvinist heritage could not so easily be

Compare
&
Contrast

- **1850s:** Whaling is a largely unregulated business. American whalers are free to sail the open seas, and to hunt for whales in any waters.

  Today: In 1986 member nations of the International Whaling Commission (IWC) vote to ban commercial whaling. Some nations, including Norway and Japan, continue to slaughter whales.

- **1850s:** Americans continue to move west. The population of the northern states exceeds the population of the south by one million. Slave-holding states seek to expand their influence in the new territories, such as California and Utah. A compromise reached in 1850 holds the peace for a decade, but slavery becomes a major and confrontational domestic issue dividing North and South.

  Today: Differences between northern and southern states remain, but not at constitutional levels. Slavery has long been abolished but many blacks suffer from racism. Foreign policy issues lead the political agenda as America seeks to maintain and extend its international influence.

- **1850s:** As a rejection of Calvinistic sobriety, many middle-class people dabble in hydropathy, hypnotism, and phrenology, but these are still seen as alternatives to mainstream religious belief and medical therapies.

  Today: Proponents of alternative medicines such as reflexology and aromatherapy present them as whole belief systems and substitutes for orthodox religion.

- **1850s:** Body painting or tattooing is suggestive of paganism. Queequeg's tattoos convince Ishmael "that he must be some abominable savage or other shipped aboard of a whaler in the South Seas, and so landed in this Christian country."

  Today: Tattoos and body piercing as a fashion have become widely accepted alongside traditional jewelry.

---

shrugged off. (Calvinists followed John Calvin's theological system that included the doctrine of predestination and the belief that mankind was depraved by nature.) And in his essay "Hawthorne and His Mosses," Melville, approving Hawthorne's "power of blackness," explained that it "derives its force from its appeals to that Calvinistic sense of Innate Depravity and Original Sin, from whose visitations, in some shape or other, no deeply thinking mind is always and wholly free." It is this recognition of and sense of sin which separates Melville from Transcendentalism, the predominant movement of his period.

The American Whaling Industry

The United States had been a whaling nation since the seventeenth century, when the early colonists launched expeditions from the island of Nantucket and from ports along the Massachusetts coast. The early whalers hunted whales in the seas fairly close to shore. In 1712 a chance storm blew a whale ship off course and into much deeper waters. This resulted in an encounter with a pod of sperm whales, one of which was captured. The superior quality of sperm oil was thus discovered and from that point on American whalers extended voyage distances and times in their hunt for the sperm whale. They traveled the whole world, often venturing into uncharted waters, and their journeys contributed to the development of maritime cartography. *Moby-Dick* was written at a time when the American whaling industry, propelled by home demand, was at its peak. The United States owned three-quarters of the world's whaling ships.

Historical Coincidence

In the year of *Moby-Dick*'s publication, a whaler was sunk by a sperm whale in circumstances which appeared to replicate the climax to Melville's novel. The *Ann Alexander* had two of its whaling boats destroyed by the whale they were pursuing. The whale then deliberately rammed the main ship, causing it to sink.

Critical Overview

The first edition of *Moby-Dick* received a mixed reception. It was condemned for its unusual narrative style and for its irreverent tone. The proportion of positive to negative reviews was highest in England, where the book had been published in three volumes under the title *The Whale.* There were other differences between the American and English editions. The English publisher, Bentley, positioned the Extracts section at the end of the book and did not include the Epilogue at all. The main body of the text had also been abridged to cut out much of the overt blasphemy and sexual suggestiveness. One of the earliest and most expansive reviews appeared in the *London Morning Advertiser,* on October 24, 1851. In that review the rich, multi-faceted texture of the book was considered a strength. The novel was praised for its "High philosophy, liberal feeling, abstruse metaphysics popularly phrased, soaring speculation, a style as many-coloured as the theme."

On the other hand, in America the book was enjoyed only in regard to those aspects in which it resembled Melville's earlier sailing narrative, *Typee.* Readers liked its graphic accounts of whaling and ignored its soaring religious and philosophical ruminations. Where the speculation and abstruse metaphysics were taken note of, they were roundly deplored, especially in religious journals.

A critic for the *Methodist Quarterly Review* wrote in January, 1952: "We are bound to say … that the book contains a number of flings at religion, and even of vulgar immoralities that render it unfit for general circulation." The most scathing review appeared in the *United States Magazine and Democratic Review* in January, 1952. It attacked Melville's vanity and assumed hunger for fame. "From this morbid self-esteem, coupled with a most unbounded love of notoriety," commented the reviewer, "spring all Mr. Melville's efforts, all his rhetorical contortions, all his declamatory abuse of society, all his inflated sentiment, and all his insinuating licentiousness."

Harper and Brothers, Melville's publisher and a Methodist firm, were affected by this response, and when the critical reception was matched by disappointing sales, they offered Melville unsatisfac-

tory terms in his next contract. He was never to recover from this setback and although his position as one of the major writers of his time is now unassailable, it was never so in his lifetime. When Van Wyck Brooks set about a reassessment of the nineteenth century in his essay "America's Coming of Age," published in 1915, Melville's name was not considered worthy of mention. In Vernon Parrington's influential three-volume *Main Currents in American Thought,* published in the late 1920s, Melville is portrayed as an irrelevant eccentric. However, this decade was also the point at which several key voices were heard in support of Melville's reputation. D. H. Lawrence wrote an essay in 1923 which praised Melville as a great poet of the sea.

But of more profound critical importance was the publication, two years earlier, of *Herman Melville: Mariner and Mystic* by Raymond Weaver, one of the first books to treat seriously the religious and philosophical themes in *Moby-Dick* and Melville's other books. Weaver's influence on students who later became academics, particularly while he was at Columbia University in the 1940s, was immense. The 1950s saw an enormous increase in the volume of critical comment about *Moby-Dick,* good examples of which include a long introductory essay to the novel by Alfred Kazin, for whom it "conveys a sense of abundance, of high creative power, that exhilarates and enlarges the imagination," and an essay by Richard Chase, "Melville and Moby-Dick," which enthused, "The symbols are manifold and suggestive; the epic scope is opulent; the rhetoric is full and various; the incidental actions and metaphors are richly absorbing."

However, there was still a reluctance to shower *Moby-Dick* with the highest accolades. Chase, in his essay, tempered his praise with a carping reservation about the novel's narrowness of meaning and simplification of issues when compared with great works such as Shakespeare's *King Lear* or Dante's *The Divine Comedy.* Another critic of the period, R. P. Blackmur, criticized Melville for not making use of the conventional dramatic strategies of novelistic characterization and for allowing his allegorical agenda to take precedence over narrative technique.

The criticism of recent decades has been inclined to explore the idiosyncratic structure of *Moby-Dick* in terms of potential, rather than weaknesses and deficiencies, and to treat the whale as the novel's central character. A. Robert Lee interpreted the book in anatomical terms, searching for layers of meaning under the skin, and Eric Mottram is one of several critics who have discussed the novel's erotic and sexual connotations in Freudian terms. Certainly there now seems to be some agreement that it is no use approaching the book as if it were written by Henry James.

As John McWilliams put it in his essay "The Epic in the Nineteenth Century," published in *The Columbia History of American Poetry,* "The armada of scholars and critics who have felt compelled to reach a judgment upon Ahab are by now revealed to have been collectively gazing into Melville's doubloon." Inevitably, not all of the latest criticism is helpful or perceptive, and readers approaching the novel for the first time are advised to consider it both as a work that realistically portrays life on a whaling vessel and as a literary investigation of the conflict between humanity and fate.

Criticism

Clark Davis

In the following essay, Davis, an associate professor of English at Northeast Louisiana University, describes how Moby-Dick *reflects its author's philosophical, religious, and social ideals.*

Since the revival of interest in Herman Melville in the early 1920s, *Moby-Dick,* the author's sixth novel, has come to be considered his masterpiece. Part romantic sea tale, part philosophical drama, the story of Ishmael, Ahab, and the white whale combines Melville's experiences aboard the whaler *Acushnet* with his later immersion in such classic authors as William Shakespeare, John Milton, François Rabelais, and Laurence Sterne. After several years as a sailor, both in the whale fleet and in the United States navy, Melville returned to his native New York in 1844 and soon began writing about his experiences. His earliest works, such as *Typee* (1846) and *Omoo* (1847), were loosely based upon his time in the Marquesas Islands and Tahiti. Melville's third novel, *Mardi* (1849), though a failure, showed evidence of a greater ambition to write enduring works of literature. Just two years later, that ambition would find its fullest expression in the pages of *Moby-Dick,* a symbolic tale that dramatizes the struggle to find meaning in a complex and hostile world.

Moby-Dick is narrated—or, more accurately, "written"—by a sailor who calls himself Ishmael, after the biblical outcast and son of Abraham. As a young man not fully initiated into the mysteries of life, he undergoes a type of spiritual and philosophical education during the course of the novel. Initially hostile and potentially suicidal, he heads for the whaling fleet, hoping to exorcise some of his anger at the world. Before he can find a ship, however, his poverty forces him to share a bed in a seedy inn with a bizarre and frightening "cannibal" named Queequeg. Carrying a shrunken head and a tomahawk that doubles as a peace pipe, Queequeg suggests both death and life. Indeed, after sharing a bed with this harpooner, Ishmael is a changed man. He has experienced the first of a series of encounters with the mysterious "otherness" or strangeness of nature. In symbolic terms, he has embraced death in the form of Queequeg, and when he wakes the following morning he sees the world from a different perspective. Ishmael understands the mixture of life and death that Queequeg's tomahawk/pipe suggests and realizes, at least at that moment, that experience can lead to renewal.

The other major influence on Ishmael's growth is certainly the captain of the *Pequod,* Ahab. Named for an evil king in the Old Testament, Ahab demonstrates the dangers of an excessive focus on ideas. The object of his obsession is of course the white whale, nicknamed Moby-Dick by the sailors. On the voyage previous to the one described in the novel, Ahab lost one of his legs to Moby-Dick, and by the time Ishmael's story begins, he has sworn to take his vengeance by hunting down and killing the great whale. It soon becomes clear, however, that Ahab's fixation has more to do with what the white whale represents than with Moby-Dick himself. As Ahab explains in a notable speech to the crew, for him "all visible objects" are like "pasteboard masks" that hide "some unknown but still reasoning thing." Ahab hates "that inscrutable thing" that hides behind the mask of appearance. The only way to fight against it, he explains, is to "strike through the mask!" Moby-Dick, as a mysterious force of nature, represents the most outrageous, malevolent aspect of nature's mask. To kill it, in Ahab's mind, is to reach for and seize the unknowable truth that is hidden from all people.

Ahab's attitude toward nature is often referred to as a "monomania," a tendency to see everything in terms of himself. This vision of the world con-

What Do I Read Next?

- *Pierre; or, The Ambiguities* (1852), the novel which followed *Moby-Dick,* is an interesting and bitter novel. Many of the character Pierre's own speculations, and Melville's narrative comments, illuminate the themes in the whaling book.

- *Billy Budd,* the novella completed at the end of Melville's life but not published until 1924, presents an interesting contrast in tone, compared with the earlier novel.

- *The House of the Seven Gables* (1851) by Nathaniel Hawthorne was published at a time when he and Melville were friends. It is the story of a curse on the Pyncheon family and how the curse is eventually broken.

- *Two Years before the Mast,* Richard Dana's 1840 account of life on the waves, was read by Melville while he was a young man.

- *V* by Thomas Pynchon, published in 1963, is a novel of pursuit, dealing in large themes, including romantic delusion.

- *Elephant Gold* by Eric Campbell, 1997, a young adult novel set in Africa, is about a monomaniacal elephant hunter clearly based on Ahab.

trasts markedly with that of Ishmael after his first encounter with Queequeg. Under the influence of the more naturalistic "savage," Ishmael learns to understand what he sees from more than one perspective. He also begins to realize that objects in the world can have more than one meaning because meaning originates with the observer rather than the object. In chapter 99, for instance, Ishmael describes how Ahab and several members of the crew interpret a gold doubloon that Ahab has nailed to one of the masts as a reward for the first person to spot Moby-Dick. Though the marks on the coin never change, each man's description is different, revealing more about his own thoughts and ideas than about the coin. Ahab, in the grip of his mono-

mania, declares that each symbol on the coin "means Ahab" and that the whole coin is a reflection of the world as he sees it. Ishmael, by contrast, refuses to insist upon a single meaning for the objects he encounters. He gathers as much information and as many opinions as he can, suggesting that all readings are both partially valid and yet always incomplete.

The central dramatic event of the novel, Ahab's hunt for the whale, thus describes the consequences of conceiving of the world as a mask that hides unknowable truth. Ahab's frustration with the limits of human knowledge leads him to reject both science and logic and embrace instead violence and the dark magic of Fedallah, his demonic advisor. Like Christopher Marlowe's Doctor Faustus, he has made a pact with the devil, selling his soul for the secrets of the universe, only to find himself caught in the snares of his prophet's deception. Thinking himself immortal, Ahab attacks Moby-Dick, striking at the mask of appearance that supposedly hides ultimate truth. What he fails to realize, however, is that such truth exists only beyond the limits of the physical world; only in death will Ahab be able to reach the "unknown but still reasoning thing" and learn what cannot be known in this world. Accordingly, his attempt to kill Moby-Dick brings about his own death. His devotion to the idea that truth exists behind or beyond the physical world forces him to destroy himself in the attempt to reach it.

Ishmael, on the other hand, escapes destruction in large part because of his different attitude toward the physical world. While Ahab sees nature as deceptive, Ishmael learns to concentrate on the complexities and beauties of what he sees. Rather than imagine a truer world beyond that of the senses, Ishmael revels in the details of the world around him, compiling information and observations on the business of whaling, on the *Pequod's* crew, and on the inexhaustible wonders of the whale itself. Indeed, for Ishmael the whale becomes the overwhelming symbol of life itself and of the search for knowledge represented by the book that bears its name. The book's encyclopedic breadth is meant to suggest the vastness of his subject and the wealth of all sensual life. "Since I have undertaken to manhandle this Leviathan," Ishmael tells us, "it behooves me to approve myself omnisciently exhaustive in the enterprise; not overlooking the minutest seminal germs of his blood, and spinning him out to the uttermost coil of his bowels."

Because of its tremendous scope, *Moby-Dick* offers information and comment on a wide variety of topics related to nineteenth-century life. For instance, critics have often described the *Pequod* as a microcosm, or "little world," that represents social and political life in pre-Civil War America. Understood this way, Ahab and Ishmael stand for opposing political and social theories. Autocratic Ahab, with his Shakespearean speeches and dependence on magic, suggests an aristocratic ruler who maintains power through threat and superstition. Ishmael, on the other hand, appears to represent the radical democracy of America itself. His concern for others, his tolerance of different religions and cultures, and his resilience in the face of social collapse all mark him as a distinctly American character who opposes the old-world values of Ahab.

Other readers have commented on Melville's use of eastern religions and mythology, as well as his reliance on the relatively recent discoveries of Egyptian archaeology. In this vein, some have compared Ishmael's vision of the circularity of life and death to similar conceptions in Hinduism and Buddhism. His friendship with Queequeg in particular is often cited as evidence of his adoption of non-Western religious or philosophical views. Likewise, his descriptions of the whale often rely upon references to Egyptian architecture and writing to suggest both the whale's great antiquity and its mysterious power. On the whale's skin Ishmael sees "hieroglyphic" marks that, like Queequeg's tattoos, seem "a mystical treatise on the art of attaining the truth." Moby-Dick's "high, pyramidical white hump" suggests a mixture of geometrical purity and ancient knowledge. And the ocean itself, source of both life and death, becomes in Ishmael's mind a place of miracle, a "live ground" that "swallows up ships and crews."

Moby-Dick also provides an unprecedented view of the whaling industry in mid-nineteenth-century America. Ishmael's detailed descriptions of the hunting, capture, slaughter, and butchering of sperm whales both celebrates and questions the violent energy of American commerce. In one respect, the whaling industry demonstrated heroic action and astonishing efficiency. American ships, manned by sailors of all nations, circled the globe to gather the oil that fed the lamps of homes throughout the country. Hunting whales in small boats launched from ships demanded enormous courage, skill, and strength. And it seems proper that the democratic Ishmael should praise the traits of character that made such an industry possible.

In other respects, however, the tremendous violence of whale hunting suggests a world deeply at odds with nature. Disturbing doubts arise as Ishmael discovers, for instance, that the *Pequod* is owned by pacifist Quakers and that the violence that is necessary to run the whaling industry may very well produce the madness that plagues Captain Ahab.

With the completion of *Moby-Dick* in 1851, Melville knew he had produced an extraordinary book. His friend and neighbor Nathaniel Hawthorne, to whom the work is dedicated, sent him a letter praising the accomplishment. Commercially, however, the book was at first a failure. Melville's reading public still considered him the author of entertaining sea tales, and people were not prepared to accept his ambition to write a masterpiece. Melville's subsequent work fared even worse, and by 1857 he had given up writing short stories and novels and had turned instead to poetry. Despite this change of format, however, the central concerns of *Moby-Dick* never disappear from Melville's writings. Throughout his poetry and even as late as his last known prose narrative, *Billy Budd,* Melville continues to explore the conflict between acceptance and aggression best represented by Ishmael and Ahab.

Raymond Weaver, one of the critics to rediscover Melville in the early twentieth century, has called *Moby-Dick* "an amazing masterpiece" that reads "like a great opium dream." Despite its difficult passages, complex philosophical content, and unusual and sometimes awkward form, the book has sustained continuous and often extreme attention from readers for the last eighty years. Like the meaningful world it creates and describes, *Moby-Dick* seems inexhaustible, reflecting that "image of the ungraspable phantom of life" that, according to Ishmael, "is the key to it all."

Source: Clark Davis, in an essay for *Novels for Students,* Gale, 1999.

William B. Dillingham

Dillingham, in the following excerpt, sees the novel's narrator, Ishmael, as a character who represents Melville's theme of the isolation of individuals from the rest of humanity.

Throughout *Moby-Dick,* the theme of human isolation is prevalent. Each character exists as an island. While they influence each others' lives, they can never fully understand each other or experience a merger of souls. This is one reason Ishmael admits to a "strange sort of insanity" when he tells how he felt when squeezing the sperm in Chapter 94. He wanted then to say to his companions: "Come; let us squeeze hands all round; nay, let us all squeeze ourselves . . . universally into the very milk and sperm of kindness." His was, indeed, a "strange sort of insanity", as he looks back on it, for Ishmael has come to realize the truth of man's unalterable isolation. This is a central theme not only in *Moby-Dick* but also in Melville's other work, both his fiction and poetry. He saw man living utterly alone in a world where overwhelming questions have no positive answers. [In *Studies in Classic American Literature* (1964)] D. H. Lawrence saw to the heart of Melville's concern with human isolation when he wrote that Melville "pined for ... a perfect relationship; perfect mating; perfect mutual understanding. A perfect friend," but knew in his heart that such communion cannot be because "each soul is alone, and the aloneness of each soul is a double barrier to perfect relationship between two beings."

The theme of loneliness is dominant in the reasons for Ishmael's survival. A great deal has been written on why only Ishmael is allowed to escape death. [Writing in his *The Trying-out of Moby-Dick* (1949)] Howard Vincent believes that Ishmael undergoes a "spiritual rebirth", symbolically portrayed in his being saved. Only Ishmael is saved, argues Vincent, because only he has "obtained the inner harmony unrealized by Ahab". James Dean Young [writing in *American Literature,* January, 1954] feels that it is Ishmael's "humanity" that saves him. And C. Hugh Holman argues [in *Studies in Classic American Literature* (1964)] that Ishmael survives because he alone "of those on the *Pequod* has faced with the courage of humility the facts of his universe."

These interpretations, which see Ishmael's survival as his reward for a lesson well learned, are not entirely satisfying. It may be possible to make a list of the characters in *Moby-Dick* and then find some flaw in each—except Ishmael—but such an approach surely does violence to the novel. By almost any standard Queequeg is noble, courageous, and humane to the last. Starbuck is characterized as sensitive, tender, and mature. They are both at least as worthy of being saved as Ishmael.

But the point is that it is not at all clear that physical survival is Melville's symbol for spiritual salvation or even for moral superiority. Ishmael is not saved because he is a deeper thinker, or because he is more humane, or because he is stoical. The others of the crew do not die because they are be-

ing punished for following Ahab or for other assorted shortcomings. They are simply victims of Ahab's destructive design. Man has, as Ishmael puts it in the "Monkey-Rope" chapter, a "Siamese connection with a plurality of other mortals. If your banker breaks, you snap; if your apothecary by mistake sends you poison in your pills, you die." Ahab is their banker and their apothecary.

Melville chose to save Ishmael for at least three reasons, all of which are closely related to the meaning of the book. The first is that Melville wished to objectify the idea of man's loneliness through Ishmael. In spite of the "Siamese connection", which men have, they are, paradoxically, incapable of sharing each others' deepest and most meaningful thoughts and intuitions. Having Ishmael die with the rest of the characters would have, in a sense, made him a part of the group. But he is Melville's representative of man, alone in the universe, and saving him—only him—projects this image brilliantly. Perhaps the book's most unforgettable image is of Ishmael, after the sinking of the *Pequod,* alone in the eternal sea, in "the great shroud of the sea [which] rolled on as it rolled five thousand years ago." Although "the Fates ordained" as Ishmael puts it, that he should be rescued, he feels merely like "another orphan".

Ishmael's feeling about the Fates pervades the book and offers a second explanation for his survival. From the early pages, one senses the inevitability of the events, what Ronald Mason calls [in *The Spirit Above the Dust* (1951)] "fatal compulsion". But precisely how to account for the strange workings of "the Fates"—this is the unanswerable question which haunted Melville throughout his life. He resented dogma of all sorts which claimed to solve the riddle of the universe. In *Moby-Dick* doctrines of many kinds abound. Father Mapple's sermon on Jonah has been offered by some as the key to the book, but this interpretation, I suggest, goes contrary to all Melville believed. While there may be partial truth in what Father Mapple says, it scarcely accounts for the existence of a man like Ahab or for what he has to do, drawn on by the necessity of his innermost being. The sermon which the cook Fleece preaches to the sharks is as relevant to Ahab as are Father Mapple's words. For Ahab is like the sharks; he can no more turn back from his search than they can become "civilized". From Father Mapple's Christianity to Queequeg's pagan idol worship, the doctrines so frequently mentioned in the book simply underscore the fact that life's deepest truths are unfathomable. By what appears to be sheer chance, Ishmael is thrown from his whale boat at a crucial moment and is thus saved from the fatal encounter with Moby Dick. Ishmael survives to illustrate the inexplicability of life, another of the book's important themes. He is not, to restate an earlier point, allowed to live because he is morally better than anyone else aboard the *Pequod.*

The third reason for Ishmael's survival is in one sense the most obvious. He must live because he, after all, is the teller of the story. A great deal more is involved here than the obvious technical necessity of keeping the first-person narrator alive. And here we return to a consideration of the book's strange, wild tone. Melville kept Ishmael alive to show the later effect of the *Pequod* experience upon his mind. Why does Ishmael tell his story? Because he has to. Since shipping on the *Pequod,* he has wandered the earth, but it is what happened on that first whaling voyage that preoccupies him. Everywhere he goes, he feels the necessity to tell of Ahab and Moby Dick, just as the seemingly mad Elijah does in an early chapter of the novel. For example, in Chapter 54, Ishmael relates how he told part of the narrative—the "Town-Ho's Story"—in Lima, "one Saint's eve". In a good many ways, Ishmael is similar to the Ancient Mariner of Coleridge. In Chapter 42, "The Whiteness of the Whale", Ishmael refers to Coleridge's poem and tells of the "clouds of spiritual wonderment and pale dread" suggested by the albatross.

The references in *Moby-Dick* to Coleridge's poem suggest an influence which is borne out by a comparison of the book with "the Rime of the Ancient Mariner." Although critics have referred in passing to certain similarities in *Moby-Dick* and Coleridge's poem, the subject has not received extensive treatment nor has one of the most important similarities—the states of mind of the two narrators—been clearly shown. W. Clark Russell made a provocative statement when he wrote in 1884 [a remark quoted in Jay Leyda's *The Melville Log* (1951)] that *Moby-Dick* "is of the 'Ancient Mariner' pattern, madly fantastic in places, full of extraordinary thoughts, yet gloriously coherent."

To give a brief synopsis, the poem is the narrative of a sailor, who begins upon a promising voyage only to fall under a curse because he wantonly kills an albatross. After days of thirst, the Mariner sees a strange ship, which comes alongside. On it are two spectres, Death and Life-in-Death. They gamble with dice for the Mariner and the crew, Life-in-Death winning the Mariner and Death the rest of the men. Soon all members of the crew perish, leaving only the Mariner. The loneliness overcomes him, and he suffers profoundly. Later he experiences a sense of love for the creatures he sees in the ocean and is partially redeemed for his earlier sin of killing the bird. But—and this is an extremely important point in the poem—he has seen and felt too much to remain completely sane. His ship is manned by spirits that use the bodies of the dead crew, and finally it arrives in the Mariner's home port, where it sinks, leaving the Mariner as the sole survivor. He is picked up from the sea by a pilot, the pilot's son, and an old hermit. They think him mad, and he does seem to be partially insane. This entire story he tells to a wedding guest, who is anxious to get to the ceremony but is retained in fascination by the wild eyes and manner of the narrator. The Mariner must tell his tale because it is the only way he can relieve himself of the terrible burden with which the experience has left him. Since he was picked up by the pilot, to whom he immediately related the incidents of the voyage, he has wandered the earth, frequently feeling the deep need to tell other human beings what he has been through.

This summary may suggest some ways in which the poem is different from Melville's novel, but many ways in which the two are fundamentally similar. The Mariner's sin is a wanton act of cruelty. Ishmael commits no such act. He does, to be sure, take a vow with the rest of the crew to join Ahab in his frantic search for revenge, but this vow is by no means the primary cause of a curse. Ahab, and not Ishmael, brings on the destruction of the *Pequod.* Other, but less essential differences are also apparent. But the similarities are, nevertheless, striking. While Ishmael's vow to follow Ahab is not of the magnitude of the Mariner's sin, he is sorry for it. He takes the oath in a frenzy born of Ahab, whose "quenchless feud" seemed his. Later when he sits with other members of the crew squeezing whale sperm in the tubs before them, he negates his earlier vow: 'I forgot all about our horrible oath; in that inexpressible sperm, I washed my hands and my heart of it."

In just such a moment the Ancient Mariner feels the weight of guilt leave him as he contemplates the colorful water snakes before him:

> O happy living things! no tongue
> Their beauty might declare:
> A spring of love gushed from my heart,
> And I blessed them unaware:
> Sure my kind saint took pity on me,
> And I blessed them unaware.
>
> The self-same moment I could pray;
> And from my neck so free

The Albatross fell off, and sank
Like lead into the sea.

Ishmael's survival is a result of the same kind of interplay of fate and chance represented in Coleridge's poem. But the most important similarity in the two works is the profound loneliness which both narrators feel, a loneliness which penetrates to their very souls and produces the wildness, the half-madness which is evident in their narratives. The effect of the Mariner's loneliness is apparent in the following passage, which comes after he explains how he was the sole survivor:

Alone, alone, all, all alone,
Alone on a wide wide sea!
And never a saint took pity on My soul in agony.

Then toward the end of the poem, he tells his listener:

O Wedding-Guest! this soul hath been
Alone on a wide wide sea:
So lonely 'twas, that God himself
Scarce seemed there to be.

The ordeal of the Ancient Mariner, his facing of almost unendurable loneliness, is basically the ordeal of Ishmael. In both works, the experience leaves the character with a burden, which at times makes him all but unstable. That Ishmael has been left this way by his having witnessed the events he retells and by his experiencing the most intense loneliness is indicated in Chapter 93, "The Castaway." This chapter ostensibly deals with the cabin boy Pip, but it clearly is concerned with Ishmael's fate, too. Both are castaways. Pip was taken into one of the whale boats because of the illness of one of the sailors. But he could not contain himself during the dangerous whale chases. Consequently, he jumped overboard. Stubb, master of that particular boat, warned him that if he jumped again, he would be left behind. Ishmael fully realizes what it means to be abandoned in the sea:

Now, in calm weather, to swim in the open ocean is as easy to the practised swimmer as to ride in a spring-carriage ashore. But the awful lonesomeness is intolerable. The intense concentration of self in the middle of such a heartless immensity, my God! who can tell it? Mark, how when sailors in a dead calm bathe in the open sea—mark how closely they hug their ship and only coast along her sides.

By "the merest chance", as Ishmael puts it, Pip is rescued, but he is maddened by the experience:

The sea had jeeringly kept his finite body up, but drowned the infinite of his soul. Not drowned entirely, though. Rather carried down alive to wondrous depths, where strange shapes of the unwarped primal world glided to and fro before his passive eyes; and

the miser-merman, Wisdom, revealed his hoarded heaps; and among the joyous, heartless, ever-juvenile eternities, Pip saw the multitudinous, God-omnipresent, coral insects, that out of the firmament of waters heaved the colossal orbs. He saw God's foot upon the treadle of the loom, and spoke it; and therefore his shipmates called him mad.

The words that end that chapter are highly significant, because they link Ishmael, who is also thrown into the sea and left behind, only to be rescued by merest chance, with the maddened Pip: "For the rest, blame not Stubb too hardly. The thing is common in that fishery; and in the sequel of the narrative, it will then be seen what like abandonment befell myself."

What I should like to suggest by this reading of *Moby-Dick* is that the narrator, a man highly sensitive by nature, has himself been "carried down alive to wondrous depths" of truth and that this collective experience, terminating with his isolation in the sea, a symbolic projection of man's frightening plight in life, has left him in the state of mind which characterizes the tone of the narrative. If there is a certain wildness about *Moby-Dick,* as the early reviewers felt, it is Ishmael's. Such a reading accounts for the so-called inconsistencies of point of view and gives Ishmael the stature and importance which a first-person narrator should have. But more importantly, to see the effect of the events on Ishmael's mind is to feel the impact of the book's theme with profound and dramatic force.

Source: William B. Dillingham, "The Narrator of *Moby-Dick*," in *English Studies*, Vol. 49, No. 1, February, 1968, pp. 20-29.

John Parke

In this excerpt, Parke discusses the novel as being Melville's examination of the nature of evil.

Moby-Dick ... is ultimately a study of evil. But what sort of evil? What is Melville's notion of evil? Evil's first apparent manifestation (or so it is interpreted by Ahab) is the White Whale's mutilation of his leg. But the *Pequod* meets an English whaler whose captain has had his arm torn off by the same whale; this man is not maddened, nor does he regard the event as more than a perfectly natural, though fearful, accident incurred in the routine business of whaling. His sensible conclusion is that, as far as he and his men are concerned, this particular whale is best let alone. Now, Ahab, a deeper man by far, is obsessed not only with what seems the injustice of the excruciating treatment accorded him (he was delirious for days after the accident, and convalescent for months); he is obsessed too, as we have seen, with the notion of hidden forces in the universe. More than this, he is a sinisterly marked man, with a long, livid, probably congenital scar (an emblem, surely, of original sin); with a record of blasphemy and certain peculiar, darkly violent deeds; with a series of evil prophecies hanging over him; and with the given name of an idolatrous and savage king.

All this is fittingly suggestive preparation for the complete deliverance of Ahab's soul to evil through obsession and revenge. But his motive for revenge is not simple, not merely wicked. His quest for Moby Dick is in part a metaphysical one, for he is *in revolt against the existence of evil itself.* His vindictiveness, blind as it is, and motivated by personal hurt, is nevertheless against the eternal fact of evil. He thinks "the invisible spheres were formed in fright," feels his burden is that of all mankind ("... as though I were Adam, staggering beneath the piled centuries since Paradise"), thinks the White Whale either the "principal" or the agent of all evil. He, Ahab, is evil, Melville seems to say (through Starbuck and Ahab both), because he seeks to overthrow the established order of dualistic human creation; and yet he is admirable, for he has gone over to evil not merely, like Faustus, for purposes of self-gratification, but in angry and misguided protest against its existence and its ravages in him.

What inevitably happens is that, in casting himself as the race-hero opposing the existence of the principle of evil, he but projects his own evil outward ("deliriously transferring its idea to the abhorred white whale") and so becomes all the more its avatar and its prey. He would "strike through the mask" of the visible object (the agent of evil), hoping there to find the key to the riddle. His occasional suspicion ("Sometimes I think there's naught beyond") that this will not result in any discovery whatsoever, and so not in an effective revenge, deters him not at all, though it drives him ever in upon himself as his fatal hour approaches, till, near the end, he does see the working of evil in himself—and yet dies its avowed agent. For he is mad; he is "madness maddened," quite conscious of his own derangement, and obsessed with it. The final, terrifying chaos, then, is that which he discovers within himself as his vestigial sanity contemplates his madness and its futility, as he admits his incomprehension of the thing that has driven him to irreparable folly and has lost him his very identity ("Is Ahab, Ahab?"):

"What is it, what nameless, inscrutable, unearthly thing is it [the very language used earlier to describe evil]; what cozening, hidden lord and master, and cruel, remorseless emperor commands me; that against all natural lovings and longings, I so keep pushing, and crowding, and jamming myself on all the time?..."

Here is raised even the question of whether man, this proud and splendid aristocrat of the spirit, is indeed a free agent; Ahab, having at other times defied all the gods and called them cricket players, having assumed and never doubted that he could have made himself lord of creation, now turns (in "The Symphony") from Edmund's flouting, free-will cynicism to Gloucester's craven determinism: "By heaven, man, we are turned round and round in this world, like yonder windlass, and Fate is the handspike." He is not captain of his soul after all.

Ahab knows, then, everything about his predicament except its cause in himself—and so its solution. He feels the cause to be an immemorial curse visited upon all men. An exile from Christendom, he yet perceives and abhors the existence of evil. Worse still, he resists it; he will not come to terms with it. He wishes it could simply be swept away, or covered over: "Man, in the ideal, is so noble and so sparkling, such a grand and glowing creature, that over any ignominious blemish in him all his fellows should run to throw their costliest robes." But the dark side (which cannot be concealed) cannot be explained or avoided, either. And the most maddening thing of all about it—this is a constant refrain throughout the book—is the deceptive way it lurks beneath a smiling and lovely exterior. ("These temporary apprehensions, so vague but so awful, derived a wondrous potency from the contrasting serenity of the weather...." "... Fate is the handspike. And all the time, lo! that smiling sky, and this unsounded sea!" And on the very morning of the last terrible day of The Chase—

"What a lovely day again! were it a new-made world, and made for a summer-house to the angels, and this morning the first of its throwing open to them, a fairer day could not dawn upon that world.")

Ahab's tragedy (and, on this final level, the book's theme) is, then, his inability to locate and objectify evil in himself, or to accept it and deal with it prudently as part of the entire created world, and so to *grow* despite it and because of it; it is his own fated indenture to evil while he seeks to destroy it, and his more and more precise knowledge of what is happening to him. It is the magnificence and yet the futility of his attempt. "I know that of me, which thou knowest not of thyself, oh, thou omnipotent," he cries to the great impersonal spirit of fire which he acknowledges as his maker and which, as its individualized creation, he defies. He defies his paternal maker, light, because, discovering his own dual nature (he says he never knew his mother), he has revolted and leagued himself now with darkness (the unrecognized mother-symbol, standing here for a regressive identification, which is of course what supplies the destructive energy). Then, "I am darkness leaping out of light," and "cursed be all the things that cast man's eyes aloft to that heaven, whose live vividness but scorches him...." "So far gone am I in the dark side of earth, that its other side, the theoretic bright one, seems but uncertain twilight to me." And at his death, the magnificent line—as great and moving in its utter verbal simplicity, and yet as fraught with complex resignation as Edgar's "Ripeness is all": "I turn my body from the sun"—a line whose full and exact significance has been specifically constellated in advance by his own apostrophe to the dying whale in Chapter CXVI.

Ahab is no Faustus. He always has a choice. Many are the times he backslides; the tension between humanity and will is constantly active. Pip, the piteous embodiment of warmly instinctive human nature, of all that Ahab must tread on in himself, acts several times as the unwitting touchstone of that humanity. "Hands off from that holiness!" But, "There is that in thee, poor lad, which I feel too curing to my malady ... and for this hunt, my malady becomes my most desired health." Starbuck too again and again is the foil and the polar opposite; and once Ahab even finds it good to feel dependence on human aid, for when the White Whale has crushed his ivory leg in the "Second Day," he exclaims while half hanging on the shoulder of his chief mate, "Aye aye, Starbuck, 'tis sweet to lean sometimes ... and would old Ahab had leaned oftener than he has." And just once, in "The Symphony," "Ahab dropped a tear into the sea; nor did all the Pacific contain such wealth as that one wee drop."

He must remain, for the brooding Melville apparently and for us, a symbol of that independent spirit and will which, scorning all "lovely leewardings," pushes off from the haven of all creeds to confront an ultimate chaos in the human soul; admirable, perhaps, beyond all flawed heroes (Bulkington was too simple an embodiment—pure essence, he was fit only for deification) in his energy and his courage, but condemned to split at last on the rock of evil, the very thing he willed out of

existence; fated—and magnificently, agonizingly willing—to become the pawn (no, the prince, the king) of evil in consequence of his misguided revolt, to lose his identity in the end because he sought to exalt it against the immutable principles of its creation.

Source: John Parke, "Seven Moby-Dicks," in *The New England Quarterly*, Vol. 28, No. 3, September, 1955, pp. 319-38.

Sources

Richard Chase, "Melville and *Moby-Dick*," in *Melville: A Collection of Critical Essays,* edited by Richard Chase, Prentice-Hall, 1962.

Alfred Kazin, "Introduction to *Moby-Dick*," in *Melville, A Collection of Critical Essays,* edited by Richard Chase, Prentice-Hall, 1962.

A. Robert Lee, "*Moby-Dick* as Anatomy," in *Herman Melville: Reassessments,* edited by A. Robert Lee, Barnes & Noble, 1984.

John McWilliams, "The Epic in the Nineteenth Century," in *The Columbia History of American Poetry,* Columbia University Press, 1993.

Raymond Weaver, *Herman Melville: Mariner and Mystic,* Oxford University Press, 1921.

For Further Study

Gay Wilson Allen, *Melville and His World,* Thames & Hudson, 1971.
    An introduction to Melville's life and times.

Newton Arvin, *Herman Melville,* Methuen, 1950.
    A psychological, Freudian study of Melville that makes much of his relationship with his mother.

James Barbour, "The Composition of *Moby-Dick*," in *On Melville: The Best from American Literature,* edited by Louis J. Budd and Edwin Cady, Duke University Press, 1988, pp. 203-20.
    An up-to-date critical approach to Melville's technique as a novelist.

Harold Bloom, introduction to *Herman Melville's Moby-Dick,* Chelsea House, 1986.
    An overview of the novel and introduction to excerpts from important critical essays.

Harold Bloom, editor, *Ahab,* Chelsea House, 1991.
    A collection of essays and critical extracts.

Paul Brodtkorb Jr., "Ishmael: The Nature and Forms of Deception," in *Herman Melville,* edited by Harold Bloom, Chelsea House, 1986, pp. 91-103.
    Brodtkorb discusses the complexity of Ishmael's voice and position as narrator.

Albert Camus, "Melville: Un Createur de mythes," in *Moby-Dick as Doubloon: Essays and Extracts (1851-1970),* edited by Hershel Parker and Harrison Hayford, Norton, 1970.

Melville has appealed more than any other nineteenth-century American novelist to French writers and critics, including Camus.

Critical Essays on Herman Melville's Moby-Dick, edited by Brian Higgins and Hershel Parker, G. K. Hall, 1992.

An updated collection of valuable critical essays from the 1970s, 1980s, and 1990s.

Leslie A. Fiedler, "*Moby-Dick:* The Baptism of Fire and the Baptism of Sperm," in *Love and Death in the American Novel,* Meridian, 1962, pp. 520-52.

Fiedler reads the novel as a "love story" of "innocent homosexuality."

Andrew Fieldsend, "The Sweet Tongues of Cannibals: The Grotesque Pacific in *Moby-Dick,*" in *Deep South,* Vol. 1, No. 3, Spring, 1995.

An article which explores the development of Ishmael's character and the significance of the Pacific.

John Freeman, *Herman Melville,* Macmillan, 1926.

Freeman's book contributed to the reinstatement of Melville's reputation during the 1920s.

Robert L. Gale, *A Herman Melville Encyclopedia,* Greenwood Press, 1995.

A comprehensive guide to characters, plots, and biographical and historical facts related to Melville and his works.

Michael T. Gilmore, editor, *Moby-Dick: A Collection of Critical Essays,* Prentice-Hall, 1977.

A selection of classic essays and excerpts from important critics.

Harrison Hayford, Hershel Parker, and G. Thomas Tanselle, "Historical Note" to *Moby-Dick; or, The Whale,* Vol. 6 of *The Writings of Herman Melville,* Northwestern University Press and the Newberry Library, 1988.

Valuable overview of Melville's life, the composition of the novel, and the critical reaction over the years.

Brian Higgins and Hershel Parker, editors, *Herman Melville: The Contemporary Reviews,* Cambridge University Press, 1995.

Includes a reprinting of the October 24, 1851, *London Morning Advertiser* article, which is an expansive and complimentary review of the three-volume English edition of Melville's book.

John T. Irwin, "Melville: The Indeterminate Ground," in *American Hieroglyphics: The Symbol of the Egyptian Hieroglyphics in the American Renaissance,* Yale University Press, 1980, pp. 285-349.

Irwin examines the "inherently undecipherable character of the hieroglyph" as it appears in the novel.

R. W. B. Lewis, "Melville: The Apotheosis of Adam," in *The American Adam: Innocence, Tragedy, and Tradition in the Nineteenth Century,* University of Chicago Press, 1955, pp. 127-55.

Lewis considers Melville's role as "myth-maker" in the history of American ideas of innocence.

Kerry McSweeney, *Moby-Dick—Ishmael's Mighty Book,* Twayne, 1986.

McSweeney uses his focus on Ishmael to explore Melville's interest in psychology and metaphysics.

James Edwin Miller, "*Moby-Dick:* The Grand Hooded Phantom," in *A Reader's Guide to Herman Melville,* Farrar, Strauss, and Cudahy, 1962, pp. 75-117.

An introduction to and breakdown of the novel's major themes.

Charles Olson, *Call Me Ishmael,* City Lights, 1947.

In a fascinatingly energetic and poetic study, Olson interprets *Moby-Dick* as "mythic odyssey."

Hershel Parker and Harrison Hayford, editors, *Moby-Dick as Doubloon: Essays and Extracts (1851-1970),* Norton, 1970.

A broad collection of reviews and reactions to the novel from its publication to 1970.

Hershel Parker, *Herman Melville: A Biography, Vol. 1: 1819–1851,* John Hopkins University Press, 1996.

A detailed biographical study, this is the first volume of a planned two-volume set that provides exhaustive information on Melville's early life up to the publication of *Moby-Dick.*

Merton Sealts Jr., *Pursuing Melville,* Wisconsin University Press, 1982.

Contains illuminating correspondence between Sealts and Charles Olson in which they discuss Melville's philosophy.

William Ellery Sedgwick, *Herman Melville: The Tragedy of Mind,* Harvard University Press, 1945.

Sedgwick sees parallels between Melville and Shakespeare's development.

Nathalia Wright, *Melville's Use of the Bible,* Duke University Press, 1949.

Wright traces Melville's fascination with truth and signification back to Biblical influences.

Native Son

Richard Wright
1940

Richard Wright's 1940 novel, *Native Son,* was the first book by an African-American writer to enjoy widespread success. In fact, Wright's novel generated much popular and critical interest before it was even published. Three hours after the book hit the shelves, the first print run sold out. Soon a school of black American writers—the "Wright School"— began modeling itself after the author in the belief that candid art about the black American would lead to positive political change. Wright suddenly became the most recognized black author in America. Today, the novel is essential to an understanding of twentieth-century American literature.

Native Son introduces a figure familiar to mid-twentieth-century America, the lone man backed into a corner by discrimination and misunderstanding. Frustrated by racism and the limited opportunities afforded black men in society, Bigger strikes out in a futile attempt to transgress the boundaries and limits of his position. He murders Mary Dalton, the only child of a wealthy real estate magnate, by accident. Yet the act of murder gives his life meaning, and the consequent trial and execution are incidental. Bigger Thomas remains a seminal figure in American literature.

Author Biography

Richard Nathaniel Wright came from a family of slaves still living at Rucker's Plantation in

Richard Wright

Roxie, Mississippi. His father, Nathan Wright, was a sharecropper and his mother, Ella Wilson, had left the teaching profession to farm with him. Richard was born on September 4, 1908, the first of two boys. Three years later, the family moved to Ella's parents' house in Natchez.

The family moved to the city of Memphis, Tennessee, in 1913 but were soon deserted by Richard's father. For the next few years, Ella did her best to feed and clothe the boys, but her first of a series of paralytic strokes ended their independence. They moved a number of times. First, Ella and her boys went to the prosperous home of her sister Maggie and brother-in-law Silas Hoskins in Elaine, Arkansas. Unfortunately, Hoskins was murdered by a white mob, and Maggie, Ella, and the boys fled to West Helena.

Over the next few years, Ella's illness forced the extended family to care for Richard while she lay abed at her mother's. Richard eventually went there to be near her. In 1920, Richard attended the Seventh-Day Adventist school taught by his Aunt Addie. He later transferred to the Jim Hill School where he skipped the fifth grade. His last stint of formal schooling was at Smith-Robertson Junior High. While there, he published his first short story, "The Voodoo of Hell's Half-Acre," in the *Jackson Southern Register.*

After finishing junior high, Wright moved several times until, in 1928, he settled in Chicago. Over the next decade, he wrote poetry, published various stories in magazines, supervised a youth program, and wrote for Communist newspapers. Wright started his first novel in 1935, but "Cesspool" (posthumously published as *Lawd Today*) was not successful. By 1938, with a $500 prize for *Fire and Cloud,* Wright had embarked on a career as an author. That year, *Uncle Tom's Children* appeared to good reviews.

In 1940 Wright became a best-selling author when *Native Son* was carried by the Book-of-the-Month Club. Personally, however, reconciliation with his father failed, and his first marriage, to Dhima Rose Meadman, ended. Almost immediately, he married Ellen Poplar and had two daughters—Julia in 1942 and Rachel in 1949.

After *Native Son,* Wright published some articles and left the Communist party. In 1945, *Black Boy* was published and received excellent reviews while topping best-seller charts. In 1947, Wright expatriated to France.

Wright refused to return to America, partly because the FBI had been attempting to charge him with sedition since 1942. He published the first American existentialist novel, *The Outsider,* in 1952. He continued to write until he died of a heart attack in Paris, France, on November 28, 1960. *Native Son* gained new importance as the "Black Power" movement of the 1960s adopted Wright as a source of their inspiration. Wright's work continues to be controversial, widely read, and heavily examined.

Plot Summary

Book I: Fear

Bigger Thomas lives in a one room ghetto apartment with his brother, Buddy, his sister, Vera, and their mother. One morning, a rat appears. After a violent chase, Bigger kills the animal with an iron skillet and terrorizes Vera with the dark body. Vera faints and his mother scolds Bigger, who hates his family because they suffer, and he cannot do anything about it.

That same morning, Bigger has an appointment to see Mr. Dalton for a new job. Feeling trapped, he walks to the poolroom and meets his friend Gus. Bigger tells him that every time he thinks about whites, he feels something terrible will happen to him. They meet other friends, G. H. and Doc, and plan a robbery. They are afraid of attacking a white man, but none of them wants to say so. Before the robbery, Bigger and Jack, another friend, go to the movies. They are attracted to the world of wealthy whites in the newsreel and feel strangely moved by the tom-toms and the primitive black people in the film. But they feel they do not belong to either of those worlds. After the cinema, Bigger attacks Gus violently. The fight ends any chance of the robbery occurring. Bigger realizes that he has done this on purpose, hoping to get out of the robbery scheme.

When he finally goes to see Mr. Dalton at his home. Bigger is intimidated and angry. He does not know how to behave in front of Mr. Dalton. Mr. Dalton and his blind wife use strange words. They try to be kind to Bigger but they make him very uncomfortable because Bigger does not know what they expect of him. They hire him as a chauffeur. Then their daughter, Mary, enters the room, asks Bigger why he does not belong to a union and calls her father a "capitalist." Bigger does not know that word and is even more confused. After the conversation, Peggy, the cook, takes Bigger to his room and tells him that the Daltons are a nice family but that he must avoid Mary's communist friends. Bigger has never had a room for himself before.

That night, he drives Mary to meet her boyfriend, Jan. Jan and Mary infuriate Bigger because they try to be friends with him, ask him to take them to the poolroom where his friends are, invite him to sit at their table, and tell him to call them by their first names. Then Jan and Mary part, but Mary is so drunk that Bigger has to carry her to her bedroom when they arrive home. He is terrified someone will see him with her in his arms, but he cannot resist the temptation of the forbidden, and he kisses her.

Just then, the bedroom door opens. It is Mrs. Dalton. Bigger knows she is blind but is terrified she will sense him there. He tries to make Mary still by putting the pillow over her head. Mrs. Dalton approaches the bed, smells whiskey in the air, scolds her daughter, and leaves. Just then, Bigger notices that Mary is not breathing anymore. She has suffocated. Bigger starts thinking frantically. He decides he will tell everyone that Jan took Mary into the house. Then he thinks it will be better if Mary disappears and everyone thinks she has gone for a visit. In desperation, he decides to burn her body in the house's big stove. He has to cut her head off but finally manages to put the body inside. He leaves it there to burn and goes home.

Book Two: Flight

After the murder and disposal of the body, Bigger has irrevocably changed. The crime gives meaning to his life. When he goes back to the Daltons, Mr. Dalton notices her daughter's disappearance and asks Bigger about the night before. Bigger blames Jan. Mr. Dalton sends Bigger home for the day, and Bigger decides to visit his girlfriend, Bessie. Bessie mentions a famous case in which the kidnappers of a child first killed him and then asked for ransom money. Bigger decides to do the same. He tells Bessie that he knows Mary has disappeared and will use that knowledge to get money from the Daltons, but in the conversation he realizes Bessie suspects him of having done something to Mary. Bigger goes back to work. Mr. Dalton has called a private detective, Mr. Britten. Sensing Britten's racism, Bigger accuses Jan on the grounds of his race (he is Jewish), his political beliefs (communist), and his friendly attitude towards black people. When Britten finds Jan, he puts the boy and Bigger in the same room and confronts them with their conflicting stories. Jan is surprised by Bigger's story but offers him help.

Bigger storms away from the Dalton's house. He decides to write the false ransom note when he discovers that the owner of the rat-infested flat his family rents is Mr. Dalton. Bigger slips the note under the Dalton's front door, then returns to his room. When the Daltons receive the note, they contact the police, who take over the investigation from Britten, and journalists soon arrive at the house. Bigger is afraid, but he does not want to leave. In the afternoon, he is ordered to take the ashes out of the stove and make a new fire. He is so terrified that he starts poking the ashes with the shovel until the whole room is full of smoke. Furious, one of the journalists takes the shovel and pushes Bigger aside. He immediately finds the remains of Mary's bones and an earring in the stove. Bigger flees.

Bigger goes directly to Bessie and tells her the whole story. Bessie realizes that everyone will think he raped the girl before killing her. They leave together, but Bigger has to drag Bessie around because she is paralyzed by fear. When they lie down together in an abandoned building, Bigger rapes her, and he realizes he will have to kill her. He hits Bessie with a brick and then throws her through a window, but he forgets that the only money he had was in her pocket, a symbol of her value to him.

Bigger runs through the city. He sees newspaper headlines concerning the crime and overhears different conversations about it. Whites call him "ape." Blacks hate him because he has given the whites an excuse for racism. But now he is someone; he feels he has an identity. He will not say the crime was an accident. After a wild chase over the rooftops of the city, the police catch him.

Book Three: Fate

During his first few days in prison, Bigger does not eat, drink, or talk to anyone. Then Jan comes to see him. He says Bigger has taught him a lot about black-white relationships and offers him the help of a communist lawyer, Max. In the long hours Max and Bigger pass together, Max learns about the sufferings and feelings of black people and Bigger learns about himself. He starts understanding his relationships with his family and with the world. He acknowledges his fury, his need for a future, and his wish for a meaningful life. He reconsiders his attitudes about white people, whether they are prejudiced, like Britten, or liberal, like Jan.

At Bigger's trial, Max tells the jury that Bigger killed because he was cornered by society from the moment he was born. He tells them that a way to stop the evil sequence of abuse and murder is to sentence Bigger to life in prison and not

to death. But the jury does not listen to him. In the last scene, while he waits for death, Bigger tells Max, "I didn't know I was really alive in this world until I felt things hard enough to kill for 'em." Bigger then tells him to say "hello" to Jan. For the first time, he calls him "Jan," not "Mister," just as Jan had wanted. Then Max leaves, and Bigger is alone.

Characters

Mary Dalton

An only child, Mary is a wealthy girl who has far leftist leanings. She is filmed frolicking with Jan, a known communist party organizer. Consequently, she is trying to abide, for a time, by her parents' wishes and go to Detroit. She is to leave the morning after Bigger is hired as the family chauffeur. Under the ruse of a University meeting, she has Bigger take her to meet Jan. When they return to the house, she is too drunk to make it to her room unassisted, and Bigger thus helps her. Mrs. Dalton comes upon them in the room, and Bigger smothers Mary for fear that Mrs. Dalton will discover him. Mary, as a symbol of white America, is destroyed by Bigger, who symbolizes what America hates and fears.

Mr. Dalton

Father of Mary, Mr. Dalton owns a controlling amount of stock in a real estate firm. This firm manages the black ghetto in town. Blacks in the ghetto pay too much for rat-infested flats. As Max points out at the inquest, Mr. Dalton refuses to rent flats to black people outside of the designated ghetto area. He does this while donating money to the NAACP and buying ping-pong tables for the local black youth outreach program. Mr. Dalton's philanthropy, however, only assuages his guilt but does not change his shady and oppressive business practices.

Mrs. Dalton

Mary Dalton's mother is blind, and this condition accentuates the motif of racial blindness throughout the story. Both Bigger and Max comment on how people are blind to the reality of race in America. Mrs. Dalton betrays her metaphorical blindness when she meets Mrs. Thomas. Mrs. Dalton hides behind her philanthropy and claims there is nothing she can do for Bigger. She cannot prevent his death nor can she admit to her family's

Victor Love (left) and David Rasche in the 1986 film Native Son.

direct involvement in the creation of the ghetto that created him.

Jan Erlone

A communist, Jan is the boyfriend of the very rich Mary Dalton. Bigger attempts to frame him for the murder of Mary. Jan sees the murder as an opportunity to examine the issue of racism. Jan had already been seeking a way to understand the 'negroes' so as to organize them along communist lines against bourgeois people like Mr. Dalton. He is able to put aside his personal trauma and persuade Max to help Bigger. He represents the idealistic young Marxist who hopes to save the world through revolution.

Gus

Gus is a member of Bigger's gang, but he has an uneasy relationship with Bigger.

Jack Harding

Jack is Bigger's friend. Bigger views him as a true friend.

Mr. Boris Max

A lawyer from the Communist Party, Mr. Max represents Bigger after the murders. As a Jewish American, he is in a better position to understand Bigger. It is through his speech during the trial that Wright reveals the greater moral and political implications of Bigger Thomas's life. Even though Mr. Max is the only one who understands Bigger, Bigger still horrifies him by displaying just how damaged white society has made him. When Mr. Max finally leaves Bigger, he is aghast at the extent of the brutality of racism in America.

Bessie Mears

Bessie is Bigger's girlfriend. He murders her because he fears she might speak against him. She is representative of all the women in the ghetto, like Bigger's mother and sister. All these women have the same tired look about their eyes and the same dreary occupations of washing clothes or working in kitchens. Bessie is so tired and depressed by the drudgery of her life that she only wants to drink when not working. Bigger provides drink, and she has sex with him, yet there seems to be no love between them. Still, as oppressed as she is, she cannot acquiesce to the murder of Mary. Fearing her inability to sanction the crime, Bigger brings her out with him to hide. He rapes her, bashes her head, and tosses her body into an airshaft.

Peggy

Peggy is the Irish-American housekeeper for the Daltons and, like Max, can empathize with Bigger's status as an "outsider." However, she is more typical of poor whites who are sure to invest in racism if only to keep someone below themselves. Like everyone in the Dalton family, Peggy hides her dislike for blacks and treats Bigger nicely.

Bigger Thomas

The protagonist of the story, Bigger commits two ghastly murders and is put on trial for his life. He is convicted and sentenced to the electric chair. His act gives the novel action, but the real plot involves Bigger's reactions to his environment and his crime. Bigger struggles to discuss his feelings, but he cannot find the words or the time to fully express himself. The voice of the narrator relates that Bigger—typical of the "outsider" archetype—has finally discovered the only important and real thing: his life. His realization that he is alive—and able to choose to befriend Mr. Max—creates some hope that men like him might be reached earlier.

Even though Bigger seems to be developing as a person, Bigger is never anything but a failed human. He represents the black man who feels he has few options in life and, as a result, turns to crime. As he says to Gus, "They don't let us do nothing … [and] I can't get used to it." He even admits to wanting to be an aviator and later, to Max, he admits to wanting to be a great number of things. He can do nothing but be one of many blacks in the ghetto and maybe get a job serving whites; crime seems preferable. Not surprisingly, then, he already has a criminal history, and he has even been to reform school. Ultimately, the greatest thing he can do is transgress the boundary the white world has set for him.

Buddy Thomas

Buddy, Bigger's younger brother, idolizes Bigger as a male role model. He defends him to the rest of the family and consistently asks if he can help Bigger.

Mrs. Thomas

Mrs. Thomas is Bigger's mother. She struggles to keep her family alive on the meager wages she earns by taking in other people's laundry. She is a religious woman who believes she will be rewarded in an "afterlife," but as a black woman accepts that nothing can be done to improve her people's situation. Moreover, she knows that Bigger will end up hanging from the "gallows" for his crime, but this is just another fact of life.

Media Adaptations

- Richard Wright himself starred in a low budget film adaptation of *Native Son* in 1950. The film, directed by Pierre Chenal, is available on video from Classic Pictures Incorporated.

- *Native Son* was adapted to film in 1987. The film, directed by Jerrold Freedmand, starred Victor Love as Bigger Thomas, Elizabeth McGovern as Mary Dalton, Oprah Winfrey as Mrs. Thomas, and Matt Dillon as Jan Erlone. The film was produced by Diane Silver for Cinecom Pictures.

- Several recordings have been made of the novel. The most recent one was done in 1991 by Caedmon Productions.

- Richard Wright gave a talk on March 12, 1940, at Columbia University which explained his ideas about Bigger Thomas in *Native Son.* This talk has since been published as "How 'Bigger' Was Born" and is included in most recent editions of the novel.

Vera Thomas

Vera is Bigger's sister, and in her, Bigger sees his mother. Bigger knows that Vera will inevitably have the same tired look in her eyes and bear the continual strain of a family. The other option for Vera is to become a drunkard like Bessie.

Themes

Race and Racism

The central event in the novel is the murder of Mary Dalton, a white woman. Ironically, whites are more infuriated by the idea that Bigger presumably raped her than the fact that he killed her. But he did not rape her. The woman he did rape and murder—his girlfriend Bessie Mears—is forgotten by white courts and white society. With this stark contrast, Wright suggests the great racial chasm that

Topics for Further Study

- Read Ann Petry's *The Street*. Compare the climactic death in that novel to the crimes of Bigger Thomas. Does Lutie Johnson's escape from the street justify her crime and the abandonment of her child? Is she an innocent victim of circumstances or did she take advantage of circumstances?

- Consider the following list of questions compiled by Robert Butler as the essential list critics have long struggled with: "Is the novel an artistic success, or is it crude propaganda that is deeply flawed by the melodramatic action and stereotyped characterization required by the advancement of a political thesis? Does the book supply a believable vision of race relations in America? Does it provide an accurate image of Afro-American life? Is the central character a boldly conceived new hero, or is he an overdrawn, heavily exaggerated, symbolic monster?"

- Do some research on living conditions in Chicago in 1940. How realistic is depiction of the city in the novel compared to your research? (Start with the article "*Native Son:* The Personal, Social, and Political Background," by Kenneth Kinnamon.)

exists between blacks and whites. It is the image of Mary in a newsreel that inspired Bigger to take the job so that he might be closer to whites. He decides that by proximity he might learn how they make all their money. The film encourages him to pursue the American dream even though he is already excluded from it.

Naturalism

The theme of naturalism—how a character's environment influences the character and his or her actions—allowed Wright to create an explanation for the economic and social condition of African Americans. In other words, Wright sought to

demonstrate the "making" of Bigger. In doing so, he unveiled how a black individual's choice to pursue the ideals of freedom within American society (represented in the newsreel featuring Mary Dalton) leads him to destruction. Wright's theory of naturalism is often seen as an early form of existentialism, but it had this important difference—existentialism presents a character who realizes that only his choices give his life meaning. Naturalism posits that a character is formed and makes choices in response to the environment in which he lives.

The theme of naturalism is further strengthened by Wright's use of irony throughout the novel. An example is in the very title of the work, *Native Son*. Bigger longs to live the American dream. Yet when he admits his desires, someone is always on hand, like Gus, to remind him of the impossibility of doing so. Bigger cannot possibly reconcile his exclusion from the dream and his longing to be a "native son."

Violence and Cruelty

Native Son is a violent novel that includes a rape, two murders, fights, and a manhunt. There are also allusions to Bigger's thoughts of violence: "He felt suddenly that he wanted something in his hand, something solid and heavy: his gun, a knife, a brick." Such pervasive violence has disturbed many readers. Wright conveyed, in "How Bigger was Born," his belief that placing a group of oppressed people in a savage environment, like the ghetto, is an invitation for more Bigger Thomases. Wright prophesied that if society and government fail to address the horrendous living conditions of black Americans, then society would be responsible for the resulting violence.

Style

Point of View

An important technique employed in *Native Son* is a third-person-limited narrative structure. This technique reveals all the action in the novel but limits it to the perspective of the central character. The narrative voice, then, takes on the vantage point of—but does not become—Bigger Thomas. Consequently, other characters appear flat because they are visible only through this limiting filter.

One advantage of this technique is that the reader becomes close to the protagonist. In other words, since the point of the novel is to reveal the

Compare
&
Contrast

- **1940s:** Workers during the Great Depression are faced with unemployment rates as high as 25% and relief comes through socialistic government programs. The U.S. also increases defense spending as officials realize the nation will become involved in World War II.

  Today: Unemployment stands around 6%, but corporate downsizing has many workers concerned about their future. The government must reduce a multibillion dollar deficit, yet the stock market continues its strong performance.

- **1940s:** Blacks are excluded from the suburban housing boom of the era. The Federal Housing Authority practices "redlining": on city maps it draws red lines around predominantly black inner-city areas and refuses to insure loans for houses in those areas. This practice contributes to the demise of the inner city.

- **Today:** Though many upper- and middle-class blacks live and work in the suburbs, poor blacks are often confined to substandard housing in decaying urban areas, or ghettos.

- **1940s:** Race relations are tense as blacks grow frustrated with segregation and discrimination. In southern states, poll taxes and literacy tests are used to prevent blacks from voting. Tempers explode during race riots in Detroit and Harlem in the summer of 1943.

  Today: Though civil rights legislation enacted during the 1960s has improved the conditions of minorities, particularly African Americans, the nation was polarized along racial lines in the debates over the Rodney King and O. J. Simpson trials.

mind of a dehumanized black man cornered in the ghetto, the reader must identify with Bigger. Wright wanted readers to understand how hostile the American environment is to those who have already been excluded based on skin color.

Setting

In *Native Son,* Wright suggests that environmental conditions play a role in Bigger's psychodrama. Bigger sees the Dalton's neighborhood as "a cold and distant world." He learns that Mr. Dalton owns the South Side Real Estate Company, which in turn owns the decrepit house in which his family lives. During the trial, Max confronts Mr. Dalton, charging that the inadequate housing he rents to blacks contributes to their oppression.

A sense of claustrophobia pervades the work. Bigger's family is crowded into a rat-infested room. His hangouts include the street, where he feels like a rat. At one point, Bigger admits to feeling "bottled up" in the city like a "wild animal." He also feels that the "white world sprawled and towered" above him. The murder occurs when Bigger is trapped in Mary's room. As Bigger flees the police

manhunt, a record-breaking snowfall hits, blocking all roads in and out of Chicago and trapping Bigger in the city. The novel ends with Bigger alone in a small prison cell.

Symbolism

The drama of Bigger Thomas plays out in much the same way as the opening drama of the rat's death. Both Bigger and the rat find themselves trapped, leaving them little choice but to fight for survival. The rat is closely associated with the decrepit environment that constitutes ghetto life. The novel consistently reveals the psychology of Bigger as being similar to the rat, caught in the confines of a "narrow circle, looking for a place to hide...." Conversely, the white cat at the Dalton house symbolizes the justice system of the whites. Bigger does not like this cat because of the attention it draws to him when it lands on his shoulder. When the cat will not easily go away, the reader senses Bigger's eventual capture.

Bigger himself reflects on the degree to which those around him see the predicament of blacks and whites. Mrs. Dalton is blind, literally and metaphor-

Unemployed men standing in line outside a Chicago soup kitchen during the Great Depression (1931).

ically. She cannot see that her desire for Bigger to further his education is not what he wants from life. The rest of the family is blind to its own biases. The family's claim of having liberal politics is undercut by Max's charge that Mr. Dalton perpetuates the "black belt." The name Dalton ironically recalls daltonism—color blindness.

Historical Context

The Great Migration

Blacks had been leaving the South since the Emancipation Proclamation, but the numbers coming north increased dramatically over time. In 1910, blacks in America were overwhelmingly rural, with nine out of ten living in former Confederate states. From 1915 to 1930, one million blacks moved north. Richard Wright was part of this exodus from poverty and racism. By 1960, 75% of blacks in America lived in northern cities. This incredible alteration in the demographics of the United States had a profound effect on blacks as well as the political makeup of the nation as a whole. There are many reasons for this, the most important being the tremendous disappointment that met the individual migrants when they reached the North. The rapid

infusion of people into the northern cities produced the ghettos described in *Native Son.* In addition, little effort was made to integrate the new arrivals with the rest of society. Instead, as Max argues with Mr. Dalton in *Native Son,* concerted efforts were made to keep them in the ghetto.

The Great Depression

The stock market crash of 1929 and the following years of high unemployment hit blacks even harder than whites. Nationwide, the unemployment rate jumped from 15% in 1929 to 25% in 1933. Between 25 and 40% of all blacks in major cities of the country were on public assistance. By 1934, 38% of blacks could not find wage earnings higher than the subsistence provided by public relief. As with Bigger Thomas, most blacks—if they could find employment—worked menial, low-paying jobs. In response to these conditions, artists and intellectuals took on radical politics and openly questioned American political institutions and values.

Political Freedom

Although the country had still not entered World War II, the United States Congress passed the Smith Act. This extended the prohibitions of the Espionage Act of 1917. The Smith Act made it a crime to advocate the overthrow of the government. Whether in publication or in membership of a political group—such as the Communist Party—it was illegal to challenge the legitimacy of the United States government. The act indicated an increased atmosphere of intolerance for alternative political ideas, which would eventually culminate in the McCarthy witch-hunts of the 1950s.

Critical Overview

In *Native Son,* Richard Wright aimed to present the complex and disturbing status of racial politics in America. The great quantity of criticism that the work has generated and its popularity over more than fifty years indicate that Wright succeeded. The work has undergone several periods of critical assessment. Early reviewers, especially African American critics, recognized the book's significance. In the decade that followed its publication, the novel's stature was diminished by harsh criticism from James Baldwin and Ralph Ellison. Later critics, examining the ability of art to wage battle in the social war for greater equality, once again praised the novel. This phase coincided with the "black power" movement of the 1960s and 1970s. In the 1980s, the novel was faulted by feminist critics for its misogynist tone.

Early reviewers of the novel acknowledged its significance. Charles Poore, in the *New York Times,* declared that "few other recent novels have been preceded by more advance critical acclamation." *Native Son* was seen as a novel of social protest, typical of works from the 1930s, when writers who lived through the Great Depression created works critical of the American dream. Thus, Wright was easily subsumed in the category of "protest novelist" along with John Steinbeck, Theodore Dreiser, and others.

After World War II, writers like James Baldwin, in the *Partisan Review,* and Ralph Ellison, in the *New Leader,* soundly criticized Wright for being too harsh and impatient. They felt that his picture of the black man in America was too negative. Baldwin went further to say that the protest novel did not advance the cause of equality but instead worsened relations between the races. Ellison, meanwhile, declared the novel artistically crude and its perspective excessively committed to Marxism.

In his 1963 article, "Black Boys and Native Sons," Irving Howe defended Wright as a representative of the protest tradition in black literature.

The "black power" movement took inspiration from *Native Son* with many of its members declaring an emphatic identification with Bigger. Theodore Solotaroff stated in his *The Red Hot Vacuum & Other Pieces on the Writings of the Sixties:* "we came to our own yearly confrontation with the algebra of hatred and guilt, alienation and violence, freedom and self-integration and in the struggle for what is called today 'civil rights' the meaning of Bigger Thomas and of Richard Wright continue to reveal itself."

By the 1980s Wright's reputation was firmly established in American literature, and *Native Son* became required reading in high schools and colleges. New questions were being posed about his work. For example, an aspect of the novel previously unexamined was Wright's attitude towards women. Marie Mootry discussed this in her 1984 article, "Bitches, Whores, and Woman Haters: Archetypes and Typologies in the Art of Richard Wright." She was not alone in taking to task Wright's novel for its view of women, although she was more direct than some. She found that Bigger's inability to see women as human beings, with the same rights to expression that he claimed for himself, restricted his view of humankind and made his self-destruction a foregone conclusion.

David Bradley, a *New York Times* critic, admitted to hating the novel on his first reading, finding Bigger to be sociopathic. However, when reading it for the fourth time years later, he believed the book to be "a valuable document—not of sociology but of history. It reminds us of a time in this land when a man of freedom could have this bleak and frightening vision of his people."

In *Native Son: The Emergence of a New Black Hero,* Robert Butler offered a contemporary interpretation of Wright's work: "The novel is ... much more than the 'powerful' but artistically flawed piece of crude naturalism that many early reviewers and some later critics mistakenly saw. It is a masterwork because its formal artistry and its revolutionary new content are solidly integrated to produce a complex and resonant vision of modern American reality."

Criticism

Margara Averbach

In the following essay, Averbach, a writer and translator with a doctorate from the University of Buenos Aires, illuminates Wright's motivations for

What Do I Read Next?

- *Black Boy: A Record of Childhood and Youth,* published in 1945 by Harper, was a semi-autobiographical version of Richard Wright's life.

- The 1963 novel entitled *Lawd Today!,* published by Walker, is in many ways Wright's best work, although it was never as successful as *Black Boy* or *Native Son.*

- A member of the "Wright School," Ann Petry wrote about the trials of life on 116th Street in Harlem in *The Street.* In that 1946 novel, published by Houghton, Petry explores the relationship of environment to a black woman's effort to live with self-respect in the ghetto.

- The 1952 Random House novel, *Invisible Man,* by Ralph Ellison has become a classic portrayal of black experience in America.

- The most authoritative biography of Richard Wright to date is Michel J. Fabre's *The Unfinished Quest of Richard Wright,* Morrow, 1973.

---

writing the novel and discusses the strategies the author uses to express his themes.

In 1940, when *Native Son* was published, African Americans already had an impressive tradition of poetry and essay writing, but Richard Wright's work was the first critically significant novel by a black author in the United States. The subject of *Native Son* was quite a shock for many critics and writers. Some black critics protested because, according to them, the book was doing exactly what should not be done: showing white people that their prejudices against black men were true. Those critics believed black writers should only write about cultured, refined black people, so as to show the white world that blacks could be trusted, that they were capable of achieving the same things white middle class people could achieve. Wright wanted to do just the opposite: he wanted to show white America what black life was about, and that most black persons in America were not middle class. As he wrote in "How 'Bigger' Was Born," Wright was interested in the lives of people who told him: "I wish I didn't have to live this way, I feel like I want to burst."

Now, if we say *Native Son* was written to prove or show something, we are talking about a very special class of literature: "literature engage" or "politically committed literature." Literature has many definitions. To consider literature as a means to change the world around us is one way to define it. Richard Wright defined literature this way; therefore he wanted his ideas to be clear to his audience. He devised a form that would allow him to explain himself. The reader should try to understand that form before he or she passes on to the details of the novel.

The novel is divided into three sections: "Fear," "Flight," and "Fate." The first two sections tell the story of Bigger Thomas's crime and his arrest. If the novel were a thriller (and it has some elements of a thriller: the crime and the investigation are only two of them), this would be the end of the story. But for Richard Wright's purpose, the most important part of the novel is still missing. In "Fate" Wright introduces a lawyer named Max. Max's role is to explain the meaning of "Fear" and "Flight," not only to the reader but also to Bigger himself. A critic who despises politically committed literature would say that such explanations should be left to the mind of the reader. But if one wants to transmit certain ideas to the world in a novel, sometimes it is necessary to put those ideas into words.

The presentation of ideas makes this part of the novel very essay-like, but Wright manages to make it fiction through two devices. The first one is the use of the trial itself. Trials are important in American fiction: they impose a form of narration. They can be used as a means of manipulating the reader's emotions. One goes on reading because one wants to know whether the jury will say "guilty" or "not guilty." A writer can also use a lawyer as his spokesman. In the story the lawyer explains and analyzes his client's actions. He is required to do so within what we call a "realistic" presentation of fiction (that is, a narrative in which the writer tries to convince the reader that the actions taking place could really happen). The lawyer's analysis and explanations are, as we say, "justified." Richard Wright wanted to explain Bigger Thomas' actions from his point of view, and a lawyer was a good device to voice those explanations.

The second device has to do with the "psychological" presentation of fiction. In "Fate," Wright is interested in the mental changes undergone by Bigger. Max's explanations help Bigger understand himself. In the first two parts of the novel, Bigger does not know who he is. At the end of "Fate," he still does not know, but he has begun to think deeply about it. He is beginning to understand himself, and the explanations are part of this change; they are "justified" also in that sense.

When he wrote the novel, Wright was a communist. He thus analyzes Bigger's case and the role of society in it from a Marxist point of view. Yet he adds an ethnical dimension to Marxist ideas; that is why the Communist Party did not like the book, in spite of the fact that the communists (Jan and Max) play a very positive role in the novel.

Before leaving aside the general form of the novel, the character of Max should be looked at once more. In general, important characters are at least *mentioned* in the first pages of a novel. Yet Wright introduces Max only in the last third of his book. Max's character is what the Greeks called a *deus ex machina.* In Greek comedy, if situations became complicated, the author introduced a magical character who could solve everything at the end. The device of the *deus ex machina* has been rejected by the novel as genre, especially in the twentieth century. That is why Max's role in the novel may seem awkward to contemporary readers.

In "Fear" and "Flight," the story is told by an omniscient narrator. That is essential here because if Bigger Thomas does not understand himself, he cannot tell his story. Bigger is dominated by two forces: one is fear and the other is flight, the impulse to avoid problems. Before he kills, Bigger is a cornered animal, and as a cornered animal, he is violent and cruel. That is why the novel's opening scene (Bigger killing a rat in his apartment) is so important. As Wright himself says in "How 'Bigger' Was Born", he wrote that first scene after he had finished the rest of the novel because he felt he needed a strong, powerful introduction to the story. The scene is a symbolic summary of the rest of the novel: the rat is a cornered animal, as Bigger and his family are. The rat and Bigger are violent with each other, as white and black people are. Psychologically, the scene shows Bigger's tendency toward violence.

Bigger kills out of fear. After putting a drunken Mary Dalton to bed, he is about to be discovered in a very bad situation: alone with a helpless white girl in her bedroom. One of the stereotypes applied to black men is that they are attracted to white women and want to rape them. Bigger is so afraid of this image and its consequences that he kills Mary. But after the murder, he discovers he has finally accomplished something. He is in a way proud of the murder. This is an important point: society has forbidden Bigger to do almost everything. Now the horrid thing he has done gives meaning to his life because it is the only thing he could do. As he tells Max in the last book: "For a little while I was free. I was doing something. It was wrong, but I was feeling all right … I killed 'em 'cause I was scared and mad but I been scared and mad all my life and after I killed that first woman, I wasn't scared no more for a little while."

Wright shows the reaction of several black characters to the pressure of white society. Like Bigger, these characters do not know what they want out of life. The most dramatic expression of this lack of dreams appears in "Fate." When Max asks Bigger what happiness would have been for him, Bigger answers: "I don't know. It wouldn't be like this." Bigger, his family, Bessie, and the men at the poolroom want something different from life, but they cannot imagine what it would be. Society does not even allow them to dream. They deal with this situation in different ways: Bigger, Gus, and Doc through violence; Bigger's mother through religion; Bessie through alcohol. There seem to be no good choices for black people (religion is not shown as a positive force in this book). This is what makes Max cry in the last scene. Before he is sentenced, Bigger does not have time to learn how to dream something for himself. In that sense, the novel is deeply pessimistic.

If Wright wanted to show the conditions of blacks in the United States, he also had to describe whites' ideas and attitudes towards the blacks. He presents a whole catalog of white people's reactions to black reality. Britten, the racist, is the most predictable character, but the most interesting are the liberals, the Daltons and Jan.

There is one important metaphor of the condition of white people in *Native Son:* blindness. Whites are blind, literally (Mrs. Dalton) and symbolically (Mr. Dalton and Jan are blind because they do not understand blacks, much less their own reactions to them). Blindness here means not seeing another person, or seeing only what you yourself want to see in another. Mrs. Dalton wants Bigger to go to school. School is not Bigger's goal; it is Mrs. Dalton's goal for Bigger. Mr. Dalton thinks he helps blacks, but he charges outrageous rents for rat-infested rooms. Mary and Jan believe they are kind to Bigger, but in "Fate," when Max tells Bigger that Mary was being kind to him, Bigger answers: "What you say is kind ain't kind at all…. Maybe she was trying to be kind but she didn't act like it." For black people like Bigger, whites are like the blind wall Bigger sees in his future: something that crushes them. Kindness does not change that.

Now, what is Wright's diagnosis of this situation? As I said before, the ending seems pessimistic: "He (Bigger) heard the ring of steel against steel as a far door clanged shut." The sound symbolizes Bigger's lost life. He will not have the opportunity to finish the process of self-understanding he has started. Yet there is a ray of hope, an indication of the difference between the early Bigger, the one who kills the rat, and the later one. In the last scene, Bigger says something important to Max: "Tell…. Tell Mister…. Tell Jan hello…." Jan has tried to make Bigger call him by his first name from Bigger's first day at the Dalton's. Bigger hated him for that. The fact that now he can call a white man "Jan" is a big step, from Wright's point of view. That does not mean society recognizes this change and profits from it. On the contrary, society sentences Bigger to death. When one reads *Native Son*, one must reflect on these contradictions: they are part of the depth of a great novel about the black experience in America.

Source: Margara Averbach, in an essay for *Novels for Students*, Gale, 1999.

Joseph Hynes

In the following excerpt, Hynes discusses how Bigger could have no dreams of his own, only unobtainable aspirations fed to him by white America.

Richard Wright's novel appeared in 1940, just over half a century ago. One of his greatest problems at that time was akin to that of the other more recent black writers [Ralph Ellison and James Baldwin] I have mentioned: how to address both black and white readers while remaining true to his vision and hoping to effect a moral and social change. The faith of any serious writer (or teacher) must be that the emotional-intellectual wallop that follows upon *seeing* will shove readers out of ignorance and complacency, a little closer to union with other human beings.

Any artist in any medium wants to communicate with some audience, of course. My point at the moment is that black writers have had special difficulty in this regard. In order to touch on the enormity of an audience problem that was much graver in 1940 than it is today, one has only to imagine Wright's straining for a way to attack and appeal to white America, through a white publishing house, even as he sought to attract a potentially much smaller black readership. My own conviction is that his success has contributed a great deal to the gradual evolution of an American readership that now takes minority writers both seriously and in relative stride. He has made his mark, moreover, despite the fact that his reading of American culture was communist. In short, he could hardly have found a tougher task. How did he set about doing it?

For one thing, he focused on Bigger Thomas as his point-of-view character. As a comparatively uneducated eighteen-year-old black on Chicago's South Side in the late nineteen-thirties, Bigger is not up to narrating the story Wright wants to tell. Wright can, however, tell us what Bigger sees, feels, and wants, even if Bigger cannot, and Wright can thereby enable us to see Bigger as emblematic of the racial situation. In short, Bigger's name implies his extension to cover black status in this nation in 1940. We must eventually decide whether things have changed today.

Narrative point of view is not resolved, however, by Wright's showing and telling us Bigger's thoughts and feelings. Wright obviously wanted to put into his book, in addition, a white spokesman for Wright's own views. To this end he created Max, a Jewish communist lawyer affected by the viciousness of Bigger's behavior even as he believes his own communist reading of our society explains such behavior and ought to induce us to overhaul that society. In other words, Wright strives to make this a novel of and for both races by rooting it in a moral, economic, and political ground that the eloquent white, Jewish, communist lawyer—another outsider—tries to explain to an enraged judge and jury as well as to his friend, Bigger Thomas.

Max's effort is not to deny Bigger has killed a white woman and then a black woman, and that he has dismembered the white woman's body to stuff it into a furnace and be rid of it, but is instead to elucidate his own vision of how Bigger became who he is and of how he therefore did what he did. Max is Bigger's white lawyer and Wright's as well. Max tries to explain to whites—judge, jury, readers—what Wright's narrator has tried to show us in the character of Bigger. Max gives intellectual shape to what Bigger has experienced and what we know to be the truth of Bigger's life. We buy Max's rationale because we co-readers know he reads Bigger accurately.

Inevitably, in this heavily naturalistic fiction, the jury will have no part of Max's argument and decides to execute Bigger rather than imprison him. This sentence is virtually anticlimactic in its predictability. Indeed, it serves merely to reinforce Bigger's awareness of the black-white split and Max's explanation of that split. Neither the book nor the reader's experience ends with Bigger's being sentenced to death. However, before discussing the ending, I think it profitable to detail something of Bigger's history, to rehearse the experience Max summarizes in vain for the jury. Some such particularizing seems essential if we hope to convey an idea of Richard Wright's America, as well as to reflect on our own national situation more than fifty years later.

Early on, Bigger and his friend Gus speak:

"You know where the white folks live?"

"Yeah," Gus said, pointing eastward. "Over across the 'line' over there on Cottage Grove Avenue."

"Naw; they don't," Bigger said.

"What you mean?" Gus asked, puzzled. "Then, where do they live?"

Bigger doubled his fist and struck his Solar plexus.

"Right down here in my stomach," he said.

While it is true that Cottage Grove Avenue separates black and white neighborhoods in this novel, Bigger's point is Wright's larger one. Bigger—who represents frustrated, aspiring American blacks in Wright's view—feels white values and expectations right were he lives. He would like to fly an airplane, go to college, have a good job, but is conditioned to see things literally in black and white. In fact the book's symbols reinforce Bigger's view. In the Thomas tenement rooms, Bigger corners an enormous black rat and crushes it to death—a useful sign not only of the way Bigger himself sees a black maniac, but also of the way black turns against black, and of the fate that lies in store for the eventually cornered Bigger.

Fighting breaks out among the black youths. They are afraid to rob a white merchant but not necessarily a black one. Night and coal and darkness figure prominently, especially in contrast to the prosperous white Dalton family "across the 'line,'" who are associated with sun, snow, white hair and clothing, and even a white cat. Nearly everyone is unable to see the world they live in, and Mrs. Dalton, for all her philanthropic spirit, is literally blind. Max, Jan Erlone (another communist), and Bigger feel and know accurately. The rest operate in the dark and *foster* the refusal to perceive.

As I have mentioned, the terms of this book are basically naturalistic, meaning that any struggle to change things by appealing to people's freedom to choose must conquer what comes across as a decidedly deterministic culture. The whites own the property and know how to keep and augment it. They rent slums to blacks at absurd rates and resist making such dwellings livable. To ease their consciences, in those instances where consciences act up, the whites behave philanthropically by being kind to their black domestics and contributing generously to beneficent societies or scholarship funds for aspiring blacks they regard as deserving of a boost.

But no basic change is contemplated, and any suggestion of genuine human proximity between the races is shunned and feared. The city-wide search for Bigger is presented as a struggle between this escaped "nigger" and "ape" who has dared to violate a white woman and the collectively outraged white social forces—police, courts, press—determined to blot out this intruder and preserve white territorial claims. The hunters care about white values, not about the value of human life. The press plays up Bigger's fatal encounter with Mary Dalton, which we know to have been accidental homicide, but never expresses interest in Bigger's having murdered Bessie, his black girlfriend. Obviously, Bessie does not interest the whites. As long as blacks stay in their psychological place, carry out their chores, and go back across Cottage Grove Avenue after a day's work, all is well. But any alteration of this pattern is threatening.

As for the blacks, they are acutely conscious of the need to maintain an undeclared *apartheid*. Bigger's mother prays for heavenly consolation in the next life and pleads with her children to show respect to the whites, who own everything, and for whom blacks work. Her son Bigger's psychology, the basis for Wright's novel, shows him torn between hatred and envy felt for whites, on one hand, and contempt for himself for being the black man whom he sees the whites judging and putting in his place. When Jan and Mary attempt to befriend him and enter into his world by asking him to join them in a restaurant on *his* side of Cottage Grove Avenue, Bigger knows the humiliation of being laughed at by his friends for presuming to bring these white folks on a slumming tour. As a result he hates both himself and these whites even more intensely. He is conditioned to want what whites have, but because he is acutely aware of how he is evaluated by them, he is ashamed of wanting a "white" life and loathes himself even more profoundly.

This psychology emerges with an almost wrenching irony when Bigger and his friend Jack attend a neighborhood double feature. The first movie, called *The Gay Woman,* portrays a rich young white woman abandoning a career of adventurous infidelity with her lover in order to return contritely to her business-driven, mill-owning husband when she realizes his life is threatened by a bomb-throwing communist. Bigger is so smitten with the woman's beauty, with the glamour and ornate trappings of her existence, that he is thoroughly sympathetic to what he supposes her life to offer and is accordingly opposed to the young communist. All he sees is that if he takes the Dalton job he may meet some such beautiful white woman and come in for sexual adventure and economic opportunity. He is swayed completely by this Hollywood version of good white capitalism and bad "red" communism.

So involved is he in his daydreaming, in fact, that he misses out on *Trader Horn,* the second feature, which of course is at least marginally about black African "roots," as distinct from black history, the development of the slave trade. The narrator of the novel describes men and women freely and happily dancing in Africa, and the movie shows Horn's belatedly coming to love Africa and its people. What happened after that we know because we are reading Wright's novel—even if we somehow failed to notice the American black's condition before we read this book.

The point is that Bigger misses this second film completely because he is so blinded by the Hollywood propaganda of the first movie. Instinctively, he accepts the white producer's simple-minded political and social reading of good and evil, a version imbibed as automatically by this black man as by the mass audience of whites. Wright is obviously interested in having us think about *why* the communist might want to kill the capitalist, but all Bigger sees is the silk-and-satin erotic fantasy conjured by capitalistic white society.

When Bigger subsequently picks a fight with Gus, he does so because he is afraid of failing if the black group goes through with their plan to rob a white merchant, but also because he feels robbery and other violence are just that behavior of which whites always accuse blacks, and because he doesn't want to ruin his chances of winning the Dalton job now that *The Gay Woman* has infatuated him with the possibilities that might flow from his involvement with whites. Thus, Wright does a grimly beautiful job of showing that the only values to be seen as worthwhile and good are white values.

Not to want what whites have renders one unworthy and subhuman (a "gorilla" is Jack's word). Yet to dare to reach across that "line" is tantamount to suicide. This is the psychological bind Bigger experiences. It is demonstrated vividly by his surrealistic dream, in which he sees himself trapped by his pursuers. To repel them he decapitates himself and throws his head at them. Bigger has no words for this nightmare, but Wright is making manifest Bigger's impossible simultaneous needs to fight off the whites and to express his self-loathing death wish.

Let us return to the courtroom at this point, to Max's appeal before the jury, now that we have briefly examined Bigger's psychology. What this white lawyer tells the white jury is that Bigger is the creature of white America, that he represented a whole category of human beings nurtured from literal slavery to virtual slavery, that he is one of us, the native son of Wright's title. Max works to persuade the courtroom that Bigger and his fellow blacks cannot be expected to live by the code now being broadcast, printed, and ambiguously touted as virtuous, civilized, decent American. Rather, Max asserts, Bigger has been so conditioned to regard himself and his race as inferior and subservient that it took his acts of violence to instill in him a feeling of life, creativity, and freedom—as if for the first time he had taken control of his actions and done something on his own, irrespective of what the dominant whites might expect or condone.

Max's argument we know to be true, for we are privy to that feeling of exhilaration he is talking about. Bigger does experience a sense of release and personal worthiness after taking Mary's life—however unintentionally—and disposing of her body. Max is perfectly ready to agree that according to white values such an attitude is perverse, but he wants his listeners (and Wright's readers) to understand that such an attitude is quite understandable in the kind of native son white society has shaped. Max emphasizes that a careful reading of black and white psychologies will clarify Bigger's behavior and should lead to a sentence of imprisonment rather that execution.

In developing his argument Max hangs psychology on the terms of guilt, fear, and hate. He points out that the Daltons, for all their good-heartedness, and indeed because of it, typify white guilt at the way whites keep blacks down and build fortunes by employing blacks and shunting them off to white-owned slums at the end of the working day. By corollary, his thesis holds that whites therefore hate themselves for this behavior and likewise hate and fear the oppressed persons whose existence sustains white guilt and who may sometime rebel against such treatment and thereby overturn the social arrangement that both supports and punishes whites.

Looking to the blacks, Max then argues that guilt fills them because they are trained to see themselves as inherently less than white, which means less than human. Guilt intensifies, then, when they contemplate improving their lot by approaching whiteness. Yet they are simultaneously conditioned to believe whiteness holds all worth, at least on earth. Blacks are accordingly filled with hatred for their unworthy selves and for their white enemy. Finally, blacks fear whites but also fear their own potential for turning violent.

Such are the American scene and psyche as Max reads things. As readers, we must accept his argument as valid for Bigger, whom we have lived with throughout the narrative. The very condition Max describes obviously assures a white jury's refusal to attend to his words, and guarantees Bigger's execution. He cannot be imprisoned as a permanent reminder of white involvement in creating him and the racial *schema* Max outlines. Bigger must be obliterated to prove Max is wrong and white authority is right and good.

However, the book does not end in the courtroom. Rather, it ends with discussion between Max and Bigger in a jail cell on the eve of Bigger's execution. Bigger, who has not understood Max's public presentation, asks him to put the matter more clearly. Bigger wants to know himself before he dies. Max at first dodges this appeal, seeing it as futile, and would prefer simply to carry any last messages Bigger may want to convey. But when Bigger persists, Max takes him to the window and points to the buildings in the Loop. Max explains that the people who own the buildings may have doubts about the rightness of the dream that impelled them to build those properties, but they will do whatever is necessary to retain their property and acquire more. Max's meaning is that the capitalistic system created Bigger and will kill him for threatening it.

Bigger, however, thinks Max is assuring him that whites kill to get and create what they want, just as he killed to protect himself and create for himself the only experience of freedom he had ever known. For Bigger, then, his communist friend's parting lesson has the effect of making Bigger think he is just like the whites, at least in possessing an acquisitive drive and the determination to protect his gains from all competition. Thus Max fails to reach the jury and likewise fails to reach his client and friend. Bigger dies with a smile having felt that in the end he, too, is in some sense white and that all humans are one in following the capitalistic spirit. Max is crushed; Bigger is as happy as such a situation enables him to be....

My modest advice is to read *Native Son,* make political decisions based not exclusively on the "me" principle, think about what makes for a good life, as distinct from a fat one, for all people.... Readers who derive sane conclusions from a study of Richard Wright will have taken a large human stride and will indirectly honor a powerful book after half a century and millions of lifetimes.

Source: Joseph Hynes, "*Native Son* Fifty Years Later," in *Cimarron Review,* January, 1993, pp. 91-97.

Hilary Holladay

In the following excerpt, Holladay dissects the motivations behind Max and his faulty defense of Bigger Thomas.

Boris Max's speech defending Bigger Thomas in *Native Son* has been called [by James Baldwin in "Many Thousands Gone," *Notes of a Native Son,* Dial, 1963] "one of the most desperate performances in American fiction." By the time Max arrives on the scene late in Richard Wright's novel, Bigger has already been sentenced to death by the white mobs who hate and fear him for killing Mary Dalton. We have little reason to expect that Max's oratory will reverse Bigger's apparent fate. Max, however, seems to feel otherwise. Brought into the case by Jan Erlone, Mary's fantastically forgiving boyfriend, Max sees Bigger not as the brutal, ape-like murderer portrayed by the prosecutor but as a living symbol of black oppression. His closing speech is a long, impassioned appeal to the judge. But it is not a sound argument. Not only is the speech "desperate"; it is riddled with flaws. Max, in effect, is verbally propelling Bigger toward the electric chair.

Though critics [such as John Reilly in his "Afterword" to *Native Son,* 1966] often see Max as Wright's two-dimensional attempt to "assimilate the dogma" of the Communist Party into his novel, I view him differently. He is not simply, as Keneth Kinnamon believes [in his book *The Emergence of Richard Wright,* 1972] an "authorial mouthpiece" espousing communist ideology. Nor can we say definitively [as Dorothy Redden does in her essay "Richard Wright and *Native Son:* Not Guilty," *Bigger Thomas,* edited by Harold Bloom, 1990] that he is "clearly intended to be the most intelligent and humane person in the book." On close inspection, Max emerges as a troubling character, more complex than a cardboard communist but much less heroic than the exalted tone of his speech suggests.

Max is suspect from the beginning. Wright describes him in almost the same terms he uses to describe Mary Dalton's father, who is "a tall, lean, white-haired man." Similarly, Max has "a head strange and white, with silver hair and a lean white face," and he, too, is tall. Max's whiteness does not bode well: White-haired white men, blind white women in white clothes, white cats, white buildings, and white snow invariably presage discomfiture and desperation for Bigger. Max's name, furthermore, implies that he may not be Bigger's best advocate. His last name is one letter removed from "Marx," and, as Max tells the prosecutor, Buckley, "If you had not dragged the name of the Communist Party into this murder, I'd not be here." He comes to the case, then, as an ideologue. He embodies a doctrine disliked and rejected by most of his courtroom audience, and he is Jewish. The prejudices the audience feels toward Max will not aid Bigger's cause.

Max's first name provides another clue to his personality:"Boris Max" may be recast as "Bore is Max." He is almost always referred to as Max or Mr. Max, but his full name, with its punning revelation, often seems more apt during his seventeen-page speech, which is part secular sermon and part filibuster. If the pun seems unlikely, consider the wordplay in the other characters' names. "Bigger Thomas" harks back to Harriet Beecher Stowe's Uncle Tom and Wright's own Big Boy in "Big Boy Leaves Home"; it also [remarks Kinnamon] evokes "nigger" and "big nigger." And when Bigger says he is not worth the effort being put into his trial.

Max brings him up short: "Well, this thing's bigger than you, son." Max himself is "bigger" or more powerful than his client if his name is read as an abbreviation for "maximum." "Dalton" also has ironic resonance; Daltonism is a form of color blindness [as noted by Kinnamon]. Suffice it to say that Wright probably did not select the name "Boris" at random.

The prosecutor, however, far from boring his audience, knows just how to fuel the fires of outrage. He has rounded up sixty witnesses, including fifteen newspaper reporters and virtually all of Bigger's acquaintances. Because the Dalton murder case centers around the ghastly fate of a beautiful young woman, the trial cannot be drawn out long enough for the perversely fascinated spectators and newspaper readers. Buckley gives the people exactly what they crave: all the key players in a horrifying spectacle. Max, for his part, would do well to bolster his defense by bringing in psychiatrists, social workers, and character witnesses. But he complains that the time he had to prepare his case was "pitifully brief" and declines to call any witnesses. Without reliable authorities to back him up, he must depend on his own rhetorical skills to carry his argument. These skills are not good enough.

Max's speech is often evasive. He spends an inordinate amount of time talking about himself, perhaps because he feels the need to justify the guilty plea he has entered on Bigger's behalf. Sometimes his argument sounds like a sleepless man's late-night soliloquy. After stating that he is "not insensible" to the burden the guilty plea places on the judge, Max pontificates:

> But, under the circumstances, what else could I have done? Night after night, I have lain without sleep, trying to think of a way to picture to you and to the world the causes and reasons why this Negro boy sits here a self-confessed murderer. How can I, I asked myself, make the picture of what has happened to this boy show plain and powerful upon a screen of sober reason, when a thousand newspaper and magazine artists have already drawn it in lurid ink upon a million sheets of public print? Dare I, deeply mindful of this boy's background and race, put his fate in the hands of a jury (not of his peers, but of an alien and hostile race!) whose minds are already conditioned by the press of the nation; a press which has already reached a decision as to his guilt, and in countless editorials suggested the measure of his punishment?

Far from garnering sympathy for Bigger or Max, this aside suggests, first of all, that Max has deep-seated doubts about his ability to defend

Bigger. He feels that the odds are against him, and he does not expect to win the case. This excerpt also reveals Max's condescending attitude toward his audience. The judge, a member of the "alien and hostile race," may not take kindly to Max's characterization. Since Max, too, is white, the slur on white people implies that Max believes he alone is a superior specimen, capable of rising above racial prejudice. But his own repeated references to the twenty-year-old Bigger as a "boy" contain a hint of racism: While the word might portray Bigger as a youth incapable of comprehending murder, the rest of Max's defense hinges on Bigger's adult reactions to a life and heritage of racial oppression. Finally, the excerpt is one of many examples of Max's overblown rhetoric. He says in many words what could be said in a few; he says things that probably should not be said at all. Whatever else he is, Max is a ham who enjoys being in the spotlight.

Furthermore, Max is so intent on generalizing about black oppression that he barely mentions the most convincing—and accurate—defense available to him. Instead of arguing that Bigger smothered Mary solely by accident, he portrays his client as "a self-confessed murderer" and the perpetrator of "one of the darkest crimes in our memory." As if these descriptions were not damning enough, he later rages nonsensically: "The truth is, this boy did *not* kill! Oh, yes; Mary Dalton is dead. Bigger Thomas smothered her to death. Bessie Mears is dead. Bigger Thomas battered her with a brick in an abandoned building. But did he murder? Did he kill?" It seems as if Max is inciting his opposition to riot, but he appears oblivious to the incendiary possibilities of his rhetoric. He reminds the judge and everyone else that Bigger not only killed Mary but savagely murdered Bessie as well. And then he expects his appalled audience to agree that Bigger's behavior "was an act of *creation!*" Furthermore, "[h]e was impelled toward murder as much through the thirst for excitement, exultation, and elation as he was through fear! It was his way of *living!*" If Max is indeed "one of the best lawyers" working for the Communist Party in Chicago, as Jan Erlone has said, then the party is in trouble. Buckley's outraged response is inevitable: "And the defense would have us believe that this was an act of *creation!* It is a wonder that God in heaven did not drown out his lying voice with a thunderous 'NO!'" Max, however, seems blind to the ways in which he is destroying his own case. Although he puts on a show of passionate commitment to Bigger, his faulty argument undercuts his purpose.

Although Max appears to believe that philosophizing is his strong suit, he does not flesh out his philosophical claims well enough to make them convincing. For example, his assertion that Bigger's crimes were creative acts reflects a Nietzschean ideology. In Nietzsche's essay "'Good and Evil,' 'Good and Bad,'" in *On the Genealogy of Morals,* the discussion of the relationship between oppressors and oppressed supports Max's seemingly outlandish claim. The powerless members of society, Nietzsche writes, define themselves by striking out against those who wield power. Their defining, or "creative," acts enable them to label themselves "good" in contrast to their oppressors, whom they perceive as an omnipotent "evil." This kind of creation is reactionary, springing from a deeply ingrained hatred of the ruling class. Such a paradigm may apply to Bigger and his situation, but Max does not prepare his audience for a Nietzschean revelation. Out of context, his claim that Bigger murdered others to create himself hardly inspires sympathy. The judge, unless he has a Nietzschean bent of his own, is unlikely to fill in the gaps Max leaves in his argument. Whatever logic underpins his claim, it does little good if it remains unarticulated.

Max's argument is further weakened by a series of logical fallacies. Several examples will illustrate the point. First, in assuming that Bigger's crimes followed naturally from his perceptions of a hostile world ("This is the case of a man's mistaking a whole race of men as a part of the natural structure of the universe and of his acting toward them accordingly."), Max is guilty of a *post hoc,* or "doubtful cause," fallacy. He is unable to prove that coming of age in a racist society caused Bigger to act as he did. Without defense witnesses or testimony from Bigger himself, the judge has nothing to go on but Max's word in this instance. And, as in his allusions to Nietzsche, Max omits the crucial connections in his argument. He admits that he speaks "in general terms"—but these terms do not substantiate his claim.

Max also uses the fallacy known as "two wrongs make a right." Instead of focusing his discussion on Bigger, he lashes out at other people whom he considers wrongdoers. This, of course, does not lessen Bigger's crimes. Having rhetorically asked who is responsible for the mob raging outside, he answers:

> The State's Attorney knows, for he promised the Loop bankers that if he were re-elected demonstrations for relief would be stopped! The Governor of the state knows, for he has pledged the Manufactur-

ers' Association that he would use troops against workers who went out on strike! The Mayor knows, for he told the merchants of the city that the budget would be cut down, that no new taxes would be imposed to satisfy the clamor of the masses of the needy!

The prosecutor, the governor, and the mayor may well be scheming—even crooked—politicians, but they are not on trial. Since he is speaking in a court of law, Max's unsubstantiated accusations are dangerously disrespectful as well as illogical. The attack, which occurs early in his speech, does not strengthen his defense of Bigger, nor is it likely to endear him to the judge, who also holds political office.

But Max makes an even greater mistake in lashing out at the Daltons, the object of sympathy in the courtroom and throughout the city. He does not seem to realize that his attack on Mary's parents is obtuse to the point of being cruel:

> The Thomas family got poor and the Dalton family got rich. And Mr. Dalton, a decent man, tried to salve his feelings by giving money. But, my friend, gold was not enough! Corpses cannot be bribed! Say to yourself, Mr. Dalton, "I offered my daughter as a burnt sacrifice and it was not enough to push back into its grave this thing that haunts me."

> And to Mrs. Dalton, I say: "Your philanthropy was as tragically blind as your sightless eyes!"

These comments are another example of the "two-wrongs-make-a-right" fallacy. Max does not stand to gain anything by accusing the Daltons of complicity in Bigger's crimes. While they may not be as well-intentioned toward blacks as they say they are, Mr. and Mrs. Dalton are no more on trial than the mayor of Chicago is. Further, they are in mourning, and it is unrealistic of Max to expect the judge or any of his listeners to see the aging couple as guilt-ridden schemers.

The "slippery slope" fallacy is at the crux of Max's argument. He insists that sentencing Bigger to death is tantamount to starting an open war between the races:

> The surest way to make certain that there will be more such murders is to kill this boy. In your rage and guilt, make thousands of other black men and women feel that the barriers are tighter and higher! Kill him and swell the tide of pent-up lava that will some day break loose, not in a single, blundering, accidental, individual crime, but in a wild cataract of emotion that will brook no control.

But Bigger's death will not necessarily lead to more violence in Chicago's Black Belt or elsewhere. In fact, Bigger's death in the electric chair may come as something of a relief, even to those who don't despise him. Bessie Mears's friends and family, though they do not appear in the novel, would probably be glad to see Bigger die. He has murdered one of his own race, after all. Blacks have as much reason as whites do to fear him.

At the close of his speech, Max declares: "With every atom of my being, I beg this in order that not only may this black boy live, but that we ourselves may not die!" The statement implies that all of American society will collapse if Bigger is put to death. Though personally convinced that Bigger's fate is momentous enough to rock civilization, Max has no sound basis for this claim. In Max's eyes, Bigger is a symbol of all the oppression blacks have suffered since they first arrived in America, but in most other people's eyes, Bigger is a self-confessed murderer, an object of terror. And it is the judge's responsibility to decide the man's fate, not a symbol's. Max's illogical hyperbole does not effectively further his case. His inability—or refusal—to make sound connections between his generalizations and Bigger's own experience ultimately undermines his argument

In spite of his generalizations, self-doubts, long-winded tangents, and logical fallacies, Max might still win his case if he could characterize Bigger Thomas as a flesh-and-blood man, not a symbol to be inflated like a balloon and floated over white people's heads. He makes a start on this late in his speech when he suggests that life in prison "would be the first recognition of his personality [Bigger] has ever had." But overall, Max's defense amounts to little more than an extended exercise in convoluted philosophizing and moralistic finger-pointing. His patronizing air does not help his case, either. We can imagine the judge gritting his teeth as Max informs him: "There are times, Your Honor, when reality bears features of such an impellingly moral complexion that it is impossible to follow the hewn path of expediency." Max is so caught up in his own windy rhetoric, in fact, that he ignores two glaringly obvious means of winning the case: pleading not guilty or pleading insane. The former plea would place the burden of proof on the prosecution, and the latter would at least give him the opportunity to recast Bigger's crimes in a different light.

By making Bigger plead guilty, Max puts himself center-stage, and his own hubris takes over. The length of his speech and its rambling content suggest that Max has wanted to tell off the world for a long time. He picks the wrong occasion to do so. The judge cannot be faulted for sentencing Bigger to death: One man's diatribe does not blot out two dead women, sixty witnesses for the prosecution, and a city full of outraged citizens.

Buckley, despite being an almost absurdly abrasive, racist figure, knows how to play the legal game much better than his opponent does. In his opening statement, Buckley announces, long before Max's speech, "There is no room here for evasive, theoretical, or fanciful interpretations of the law." He is right. And Max, [as Dorothy Redden suggests] hardly "the author's spokesman for the truth," is wrong to assume the role of an angry prophet when his client desperately needs a level-headed lawyer.

The question remains: How does this interpretation of Max alter our reading of *Native Son?* Put briefly, when we view Max as a subversive presence destroying whatever slim chance Bigger has to survive, book three becomes an even darker denouement to the action in books one and two. Max, like the Daltons, attempts to assuage his own conscience by championing Bigger. In the end, he fails himself as well as his client. Perhaps in Bigger's final facial expression, "a faint, wry, bitter smile," we see his recognition of this failure. Max, too, is guilty, but only Bigger will die.

Source: Hilary Holladay, "*Native Son*'s Guilty Man," in *The CEA Critic*, Winter, 1992, pp. 30-36.

Sources

James Baldwin, "Many Thousands Gone," in *Partisan Review,* Vol. XVIII, 1955, pp. 665-80.

David Bradley, "On Rereading *Native Son,*" in *The New York Times,* December 7, 1986, pp. 68-79.

Robert Butler, *Native Son: The Emergence of a New Black Hero,* Twayne Publishers, 1991, 132 p.

Ralph Ellison, "The World and the Jug," in *New Leader,* Vol. XLVI, December 9, 1963, pp. 22-6.

Hilary Holladay, "*Native Son*'s Guilty Man," in *The CEA Critic,* Winter, 1992, pp. 30-6.

Irving Howe, "Black Boys and Native Sons," in *A World More Attractive,* Horizon Press, 1963, pp. 98-110.

Joseph Hynes, "*Native Son* Fifty Years Later," in *Cimarron Review,* January, 1993, pp. 91-97.

Maria K. Mootry, "Bitches, Whores, and Woman Haters: Archetypes and Typologies in the Art of Richard Wright," in *Richard Wright: A Collection of Critical Essays,* edited by Richard Macksey and Frank E. Moorer, Prentice Hall, 1984.

Charles Poore, review in the *New York Times,* March 1, 1940, p. 19.

Theodore Solotaroff, "The Integration of Bigger Thomas" (1964), in his *The Red Hot Vacuum & Other Pieces on the Writings of the Sixties,* Atheneum, 1970, pp. 122-32.

For Further Study

Richard Abcarian, *Negro American Literature,* Wadworth, California, 1970.
A fundamental commentary on African American literature, its roots, and importance in the canon. There is a significant discussion of Richard Wright's novel.

Gordon W. Allport, *The Nature of Prejudice,* Cambridge, 1954.
A fundamental source to understand the problem of prejudice and racism in general and concepts such as visibility and difference.

James Baldwin, "Many Thousands Gone," in *Partisan Review,* Vol. XVIII, 1955, pp. 665-80.
Baldwin argues that "protest" novels, like *Native Son,* do little to advance the cause of racial justice in America.

James Baldwin, *Nobody Knows My Name,* Dell, 1961.
Baldwin's essays about African Americans and Black literature. Some of them include references to his mentor, Richard Wright, whom he later rejected.

Russel Carl Brignans, *"Richard Wright: An Introduction to The Man and His Works,"* University of Pittsburgh Press, 1970, p. 147.
Brignans posits that Bigger Thomas was a precursor of the existentialist hero more closely associated with French literature.

Arthur Davis and Michael W. Peplow, *Anthology of Negro American Literature,* Holt, New York, 1975.
A collection of critical essays on African American literature, including Richard Wright's texts, plus a very clear and interesting introduction.

Ralph Ellison, "The World and the Jug," in *New Leader,* Vol. XLVI, December 9, 1963, pp. 22-6.
Ellison believes *Native Son* has an aesthetically narrow view of the black experience in America because it is filtered through a sociopath, Bigger Thomas.

Leslie Fiedler, "Negro and Jew: Encounter in America," in *No! In Thunder,* Stein and Day, New York, 1972.
This article investigates the relationships between Jews and African Americans in the United States. Useful to understand the relationship between Bigger and Jan.

Katherine Fishburn, *Richard Wright's Hero: The Faces of a Rebel-Victim,* Scarecrow Press, 1977.
Fishburn declares that Bigger is an anti-hero whose quest for freedom leads to his ultimate alienation from the world.

Irving Howe, "Black Boys and Native Sons," in *A World More Attractive,* Horizon Press, 1963, pp. 98-110.
Defending Wright against Ellison and Baldwin, Howe asserts that *Native Son* continues the tradition of black protest through literature and takes that protest to a higher level.

Dale McLemore, *Racial and Ethnic Relations in America,* Boston, 1980.

> An advanced study of the subject of ethnic relations in the United States with a large section devoted to African Americans and a discussion of cultural versus racial differences.

Maria K. Mootry, "Bitches, Whores, and Woman Haters: Archetypes and Typologies in the Art of Richard Wright," in *Richard Wright: A Collection of Critical Essays,* edited by Richard Macksey and Frank E. Moorer, Prentice Hall, 1984.

> Mootry asserts that Bigger is unable to see women as human beings who have the same rights to expression as he does. Consequently, this restricted view makes his self-destruction a foregone conclusion.

Toni Morrison, *Playing in the Dark, Whiteness and the Literary Imagination,* Picador, 1992.

> This work contains the ideas of the Noble Prize winner about African American literature: its roots, purposes, and future.

Charles Poore, review in the *New York Times,* March 1, 1940, p. 19.

> Poore sums up the excitement surrounding the release of *Native Son.*

Louis Tremaine, "The Dissociated Sensibility of Bigger Thomas in *Native Son*" in *Studies in American Fiction,* Vol. 14, No. 1, Spring, 1986, pp. 63-76.

> Tremaine views Bigger as a man hungering for self-expression even though he knows that expression is denied him.

1984

George Orwell
1949

Published in 1948 and set thirty-six years in the future, *1984* is George Orwell's dark vision of the future. Written while Orwell was dying and based on the work of the Russian author Yevgeny Zamyatin, it is a chilling depiction of how the power of the state could come to dominate the lives of individuals through cultural conditioning. Perhaps the most powerful science fiction novel of the twentieth century, this apocalyptic satire shows with grim conviction how Winston Smith's individual personality is wiped out and how he is recreated in the Party's image until he does not just obey but even loves Big Brother. Some critics have related Winston Smith's sufferings to those Orwell underwent at preparatory school, experiences he wrote about just before *1984*. Orwell maintained that the book was written with the explicit intention "to alter other people's idea of the kind of society they should strive after."

Author Biography

George Orwell was born Eric Arthur Blair in Bengal, India, in 1903, into a middle-class family. The son of a British civil servant, Orwell was brought to England as a toddler. The boy became aware of class distinctions while attending St. Cyprian's preparatory school in Sussex, where he received a fine education but felt out of place. He was teased and looked down upon because he was

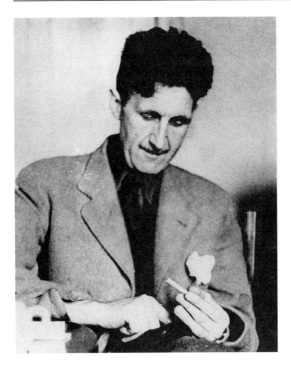

George Orwell

not from a wealthy family. This experience made him sensitive to the cruelty of social snobbery.

As a partial-scholarship student whose parents could not afford to pay his entire tuition, Orwell was also regularly reminded of his lowly economic status by school administrators. Conditions improved at Eton, where he studied next, but instead of continuing with university classes, in 1922 he joined the Indian Imperial Police. Stationed in Burma, his class-consciousness intensified as he served as one of the hated policemen enforcing British control of the native population. Sickened by his role as imperialist, he returned to England in 1927 and resigned his position. He planned to become a writer, a profession in which he had not before shown much interest.

In 1928, perhaps to erase guilt from his colonial experiences, he chose to live amongst the poor of London, and later, Paris. In Paris, he published articles in local newspapers, but his fiction was rejected. His own life finally provided the material for his first book, published in 1933. *Down and Out in Paris and London,* which combined fictional narrative based on his time spent in those two cities with social criticism, was his first work published as George Orwell. The pseudonym was used so his parents would not be shocked by the brutal living conditions described in the book. The next year, Orwell published *Burmese Days,* a novel based on his stay in Burma. Subsequent novels contain autobiographical references and served as vehicles for Orwell to explore his growing political convictions.

In 1936, Orwell traveled to Barcelona, Spain, to write about the Spanish Civil War and ended up joining the battle, fighting against Spanish leader Francisco Franco on the side of the Republicans. Wounded, he returned to England. Two nonfiction books, *The Road to Wigan Pier,* a report on deplorable conditions in the mining communities of northern England, and *Homage to Catalonia,* the story of his participation in the Spanish Civil War, allowed Orwell to explicitly defend his political ideas. Dozens of pointed essays also revealed his political viewpoint.

By that time, Orwell clearly saw himself as a political performer whose tool was writing. He wrote in a 1946 essay, "Why I Write," that "every line of serious work that I have written since 1936 has been written, directly or indirectly, *against* totalitarianism and *for* democratic socialism, as I understand it."

Orwell's next book, *Animal Farm,* a fable about the events during and following the Russian Revolution, was well liked by critics and the public. He had had trouble finding a publisher during World War II because the work was a disguised criticism of Russia, England's ally at the time. When it was finally published, just after the war, however, it was a smashing success.

The money Orwell made from *Animal Farm* allowed him, in 1947, to rent a house on Jura, an island off the coast of Scotland, where he began to work on *1984.* His work was interrupted by treatment for tuberculosis, which he had contracted in the 1930s, and upon his release from the hospital in 1948 Orwell returned to Jura to complete the book. Under doctor's orders to work no more than one hour a day, but unable to find a typist to travel to his home, he typed the manuscript himself and collapsed upon completion of the book. For the next two years he was bedridden. Many critics claim that Orwell's failing health may have influenced the tone and outcome of the novel, and Orwell admitted that they were probably right.

Orwell did plan to write other books, according to his friends, and married while in the hospital, but three months later in 1950 he finally died of tuberculosis.

Plot Summary

Part One

In George Orwell's *1984* Winston Smith, a member of the Outer Party from Oceania (a fictional state representing both England and America), lives in all visible ways as a good party member, in complete conformance with the wishes of Big Brother—the leader of the Inner Party (Ingsa). He keeps his loathing for the workings of the Party—for the vile food and drink, the terrible housing, the conversion of children into spies, the orchestrated histrionics of the Two Minutes' Hate—deep inside, hidden, for he knows that such feelings are an offense punishable by death, or worse. But, as the year 1984 begins, he has decided, against his better judgment, to keep a diary in which his true feelings are laid bare. He sits back in an alcove in his dingy apartment, just out of view of the telescreen (two-way television screens that are in all buildings and homes, which broadcast propaganda and transmit back the activities of anyone passing in front of the screen) and writes of his hatred for Big Brother.

Winston works at the Ministry of Truth (Minitrue, in Newspeak), the branch of the government responsible for the production and dissemination of all information. Winston's job is to alter or "rectify" all past news articles which have since been "proven" to be false. Only once has he ever held in his hands absolute proof that the Ministry was lying. It concerned three revolutionaries, Jones, Aaronson, and Rutherford, who were executed for planning a revolt against the state. Winston found evidence that their confessions were falsified and out of fear he destroyed that evidence.

One day during a Two Minutes' Hate session, Winston catches the eye of O'Brien, a member of the Inner Party who seems to carry the same disillusionment about the Party that Winston harbors. Winston realizes that all the stories told by the Party about Emmanuel Goldstein—the head of an underground conspiracy to overthrow the Party—and the traitorous Brotherhood are at least partly true. Perhaps there is another way, and he begins to see hope in the proletariat. They are the 85% of the population of Oceania that exists outside the Party, kept in a perpetual state of slovenly poverty but mostly unregulated, unobserved.

Winston's wanderings among the proles, desperately searching for that little bit of hope, take him one evening to the junk shop where he purchased his diary. The proprietor, Mr. Charrington, shows him a back room outfitted with a bed, where he and his wife used to live before the Revolution. And there is no telescreen—the proles aren't required to have them.

As he leaves the shop, Winston notices that he is being watched. A dark-haired woman from the fiction department at Minitrue was spying on him. Fearing the worst, Winston contemplates killing her, but instead he quickly heads home.

Part Two

Winston sees the dark-haired girl at the Ministry of Truth. She stumbles, and as he helps her up, she passes a slip of paper into his hand. Winston reads it in secret and discovers that it is a note saying that she loves him. Lonely and intrigued by her, he manages to eat lunch one day with her. They make plans for another such accidental meeting that evening. In the midst of a crowd, she gives him a complex set of directions to a place where they will meet on Sunday afternoon.

Winston and the girl—Julia—meet in the woods, far out in the country, away from the telescreens. There they are actually able to talk and make love. Julia reveals that she is not what she appears; she despises the Party, but pretends to be a good party member.

The couple meets at irregular intervals, and never in the same place, until Winston suggests the idea of renting Mr. Charrington's room. The two meet, sharing the delicacies that Julia gets on the black market (delicacies like sugar, milk, and real coffee) and relishing their moments of freedom. Their bliss is interrupted only once by the presence of a rat. Julia chases it off and prevents it from coming back.

O'Brien, under the guise of having a copy of the newest Newspeak dictionary, approaches Winston at the ministry and invites him to his apartment. Winston believes he has a friend and agrees to go with Julia. When Winston and Julia finally do appear, O'Brien assures them that Goldstein and the conspiracy to overthrow the Party do indeed exist, that he is part of that conspiracy, and he wants them to work for it. O'Brien sends Winston a copy of Goldstein's forbidden book on the secret history of Oceania which Winston and Julia read in the privacy of Mr. Charrington's room.

Shortly after waking up from a long nap, Winston and Julia hear a voice from a hidden telescreen which suddenly commands them to stand in the middle of the room. Mr. Charrington enters with a crew of stormtroopers who beat Winston and Julia, then hurry them separately away.

Part Three

Winston is tortured in jail—known as the Ministry of Love—for an interminable length of time. O'Brien is in charge of the torture. Winston confesses to various crimes, including his years of conspiracy with the ruler of Eastasia—one of the three superpowers that are often at war with Oceania. O'Brien explains to Winston that, among other things, Goldstein's book was in fact a Party creation.

It becomes clear, however, that the purpose of Miniluv is not to produce forced confessions and then kill its victims, but to "cure" the confessors, to enable them to see the truth of their confessions and the correctness of the Party's doublethink, in which "War is Peace," "Freedom is Slavery," and "Ignorance is Strength." The Party is not content with negative obedience, but must have the complete and true belief of all members. No one is executed before coming to love Big Brother.

Winston is at length able to persuade himself that the Party is right about everything—that two and two, in fact, make five—but he has not betrayed Julia, whom he still loves. At last the time comes for that step, and O'Brien sends Winston to Room 101, where each individual's darkest fear is catalogued. In Winston's case it is rats. When they threaten him with rats, he betrays Julia.

One last hurdle remains: Winston must come to love Big Brother, for the Party wanted no martyrs, no opposition at all. Winston is released a shell of a man, his hair and teeth gone, his body destroyed. He is given a small job on a committee that requires no real work. He spends most of his time in a bar, drinking oily victory gin. He sees and even speaks to Julia one day, who admits matter-of-factly that she betrayed him just as he betrayed her. They have nothing more to say to one another.

At last, it is announced over the telescreen in the bar that Oceania has won an important victory in the war. Suddenly Winston feels himself purged, no longer running with the crowd in the street but instead walking to his execution in the Ministry of Love. He can be shot now, for he at last believes. He loves Big Brother.

Characters

Big Brother

Big Brother, the mysterious all-seeing, all-knowing leader of the totalitarian society is a god-like icon to the citizens he rules. He is never seen in person, just staring out of posters and telescreens, looking stern as the caption beneath his image warns "Big Brother Is Watching You." Big Brother demands obedience and devotion of Oceania's citizens; in fact, he insists that they love him more than they love anyone else, even their own families. At the same time, he inspires fear and paranoia. His loyal followers are quick to betray anyone who seems to be disloyal to him. Through technology, Big Brother is even able to monitor the activities of people who are alone in their homes or offices.

Of course, Big Brother doesn't really exist, as is clear from the way O'Brien dodges Winston's questions about him. His image is just used by the people in power to intimidate the citizens of Oceania. Orwell meant for Big Brother to be representative of dictators everywhere, and the character was undoubtedly inspired by Adolf Hitler, Francisco Franco, Joseph Stalin, and Mao Tse-tung, all of whom were fanatically worshipped by many of their followers.

Mr. Charrington

Mr. Charrington is an acquaintance of Winston's who runs a small antique/junk shop and rents Winston a small room above it. Winston and Julia do not realize he is actually a cold, devious man and a member of the Thought Police. Charrington is responsible for Winston and Julia's eventual arrest.

Emmanuel Goldstein

Emmanuel Goldstein is the great enemy of Big Brother. An older Jewish man with white hair and a goatee, Goldstein is a former Party leader but now the head of an underground conspiracy to overthrow the Party. When his face is flashed on telescreens, people react to him as if he were the devil himself, frightening and evil. He personifies the enemy. Winston fears him yet is fascinated by him as well. He thinks Goldstein's speeches, which are broadcast as a warning against anti-Party thoughts, are transparent and shakes his head at the thought of people less intelligent and more easily led than him being taken in by such revolutionary talk. Yet Winston changes his mind later, and as he reads Goldstein's revolutionary tract, "The Theory and

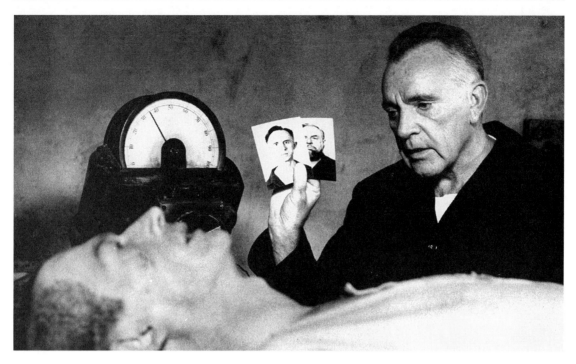

John Hurt and Richard Burton in the film Nineteen Eighty-Four, *released, appropriately enough, in 1984.*

Practice of Oligarchical Collectivism," he is more impressed than ever by Goldstein's ideas.

Goldstein is reminiscent of Leon Trotsky, the great enemy of Soviet leader Joseph Stalin who led an unsuccessful revolt and was later brutally murdered by Stalin's men. It is no accident that he is a Jewish intellectual because dictators Stalin and Adolf Hitler deeply feared and hated the Jewish intelligentsia.

Julia

At first Winston doesn't like Julia because she seems like a zealous pro-Party advocate. Moreover, she is also a member of the Anti-Sex League, and deep down Winston resents that he will never be able to have sex with her. However, when he takes her up on her request that they meet privately, Winston discovers that Julia is smart and funny and loves sex, and she doesn't care at all about Big Brother. As for her membership in the Anti-Sex League, she is simply doing what is expected of her in society. A pretty woman with dark hair and freckles, she is basically a simple woman who doesn't worry about the revolutionary implications of her actions; she does what she does because it feels good and right. She cares little about revolution and even falls asleep when Winston is reading

from Emmanuel Goldstein's revolutionary tract. Julia is practical as well. For instance, she is discreet in arranging her meetings with Winston and warns him that they will eventually get caught.

When they are caught, it is Julia who insists that her love for Winston cannot be destroyed, but she betrays Winston more quickly than he betrays her (at least, according to O'Brien), and when they finally meet again she is indifferent to him.

Katharine

Winston's wife. She was a tall, fair-haired girl, and, according to Winston, remarkably vulgar and stupid. Technically, he is still married to her, though they've lost track of each other. They parted ways about ten or eleven years before, after only fifteen months of marriage, when they realized that she could not get pregnant by him. The Party has declared that the only reason for marriage is procreation, and in fact it is illegal to have sex simply for pleasure. Therefore, there was no reason for Winston and Katharine to stay together. The Party does not believe in divorce, just separation, so Winston and Katharine just sort of drifted apart.

Readers only see Katharine through Winston's memory of her, and her main purpose in the novel

Media Adaptation

- *1984* (1984), a very fine adaptation of George Orwell's infamous novel, *1984,* by director Michael Kadford, features John Hurt and Richard Burton in his final screen performance.

is to show how the Party destroys love, sex, and loyalty between husband and wife.

O'Brien

O'Brien is a member of the Inner Party. He is a large, burly, and brutal-looking man, and yet Winston thinks he has a certain charm and civility. Winston suspects he is very intelligent and may share his subversive views of society. When O'Brien reveals that he does have revolutionary thoughts, Winston is excited to go with him to a secret underground meeting led by Emmanuel Goldstein. The group aims to overthrow the Party. Winston does not realize that O'Brien is secretly loyal to the Inner Party and that the secret underground group is simply a set-up by the Party to detect potential subversives. O'Brien betrays Winston and becomes his interrogator and torturer. It is he who reveals to Winston that the true, ugly purpose of the Party is to stay in power for power's sake. Like the Party, O'Brien cares for one thing only: power. He has no personal ambition, however. He only needs and wants to be a part of the Party's power structure.

As a torturer, O'Brien reveals himself to be extremely intelligent and sophisticated. His relationship with Winston is complicated and twisted. O'Brien seems to respect Winston, and he enjoys their conversations because Winston is a challenge. O'Brien and Winston ought to hate each other; after all, it's O'Brien's job to brainwash Winston and thereby destroy him. Still, they are drawn to each other out of respect and mutual understanding.

Old Man

Old man is a prole who lives near Winston. He remembers a lot about the past, but only insignifi-

cant snippets of his own life, so he can't answer Winston's pressing questions, such as, "Was life better then than it is now?" Winston describes him as an ant who can't see the bigger picture.

Tom Parson

Winston's neighbor, Tom Parson, is a representative of the proletariat, or working class. His children, like children in Nazi Germany, belong to scout-like organizations sponsored by the government. They wear uniforms and are encouraged to betray their parents to the authorities should they see any signs of disloyalty. His wife, Mrs. Parsons, is about thirty but looks much older because she lives in constant fear of her own children. Tom Parsons, age 35, is sweaty, fat, pink-faced and fair-haired. He is also not very bright, a zealous man who worships the Party. Eventually, his daughter turns him in for Thought crime because he says "Down with the Party" in his sleep. He tells Winston he is grateful he was turned in before his terrible thoughts became conscious.

Prole Woman

A heavyset neighbor of Winston's, he watches her singing to herself as she hangs out the laundry. She is a symbol of the future, representing the spirit of the proletariat that cannot be crushed.

Winston Smith

Orwell named his central character Winston Smith after Winston Churchill, the Prime Minister of England during World War II; he also gave him the most common British last name, Smith. A thirty-nine-year-old man who works in the Ministry of Truth, Winston Smith is fairly ordinary. His heroism is heartfelt, not out of false notions of rebellion for the sake of power and glory. Because of the visceral nature of his actions, he acts in a foolhardy manner. For example, he keeps a diary in order to record events as he experiences them, even though he is very likely to get caught by the Thought Police. Similarly, he rents the room above a junk shop to use as a love nest with Julia despite the obvious risks. Finally, Winston trusts O'Brien, not suspecting that he is a loyal member of the Inner Party who is trying to entrap him.

When he is captured and tortured, Winston continues his defiance as long as possible. He has a strange respect for his torturer, O'Brien, and seems to enjoy their battle of intellect, ideas, and wills. Indeed, he has been thinking about and fascinated by O'Brien for years, even dreaming about him. In a way, he seems happy to be confronting him at last.

Syme

Syme, who works in the Research Department of the Ministry of Truth, is a small man with dark hair and large eyes. He is helping prepare a new dictionary of Newspeak which will eliminate even more words from the language. He is so smart and straightforward that Winston knows Syme is destined to be purged. Syme's lack of savvy and self-protectiveness irritates Winston because he knows he is loyal to Big Brother.

Winston's Mother

Dead for thirty years, Winston's mother appears only in his dreams of the past. He recalls her as a fair-haired and self-possessed woman. He's not certain what happened to her, but he thinks she was probably murdered in the purges of the 1950s (reminiscent of Joseph Stalin's infamous purges in Russia, in which large numbers of people simply disappeared overnight and were murdered). Winston misses his mother greatly and feels guilty that he survived and she did not. In fact, he has the feeling that somehow she gave her life for his.

Themes

Freedom and Enslavement/Free Will

Orwell's *1984* is set in Oceania, a totalitarian state ruled by a god-like leader named Big Brother who completely controls the citizens down to their very thoughts. Anyone who thinks subversive thoughts can be turned in by spies or by Big Brother, who monitors them through highly sensitive telescreens. If someone does not have the proper facial expression, they are considered guilty of Facecrime, so all emotions must be extremely carefully guarded. It is even possible to commit Thoughtcrime by being overheard talking in one's sleep, which Winston Smith fears will happen to him; it actually happens to his neighbor Tom Parson. Freedom exists only in the proletarian ghetto, where crime and hunger are commonplace. Winston feels he could not live in this ghetto, even though his life is almost as grim as that of the ghetto dwellers.

The punishment for even minor crimes is severe, yet people occasionally choose to break the law. The Party knows that people instinctively want to have sex, form loving bonds, and think for them-

selves instead of accepting unquestioningly whatever the totalitarian government tells them. As long as people choose to exercise free will, the Party must be ever-vigilant against crime and make their punishments severe in order to remain in control.

Appearances and Reality

In totalitarian Oceania, it seems as if everyone is slavishly devoted to Big Brother and believes everything the government tells them. However, as we can understand from Winston's thoughts, all is not as it seems. Some people secretly feel and believe differently from how they behave; of course, they are extremely careful not to betray themselves. Moreover, the Party is in control of all information and revises history, even yesterday's history, to reflect their current version of events. Winston is very much aware of this, because it is his job in the inaccurately named Ministry of Truth to change the records of history. He cannot ignore what he remembers: Oceania was at war with Eurasia and allied with Eastasia yesterday, and not vice versa. If anyone else remembers differently, they certainly won't say so.

Only the old man, a powerless prole who lives on the street, speaks about what really happened in the past, but in short and irrelevant snippets about his personal experiences. It is Winston's need to reconcile what he knows with the Party's version of reality that leads to his downfall. The Party cannot allow people to have a perception of reality that is different from theirs. As Winston writes in his diary, "Freedom is the freedom to say that two plus two make four. If that is granted, all else follows."

Loyalty and Betrayal

In order to remain all-powerful, the Party destroys loyalty between people: co-workers, friends, even family members. Children are encouraged to betray their parents to the state if they suspect them of Thoughtcrimes (thinking something that goes against the Party line).

The Party has outlawed sex for pleasure and reduced marriage to an arrangement between a man and woman that exists only for procreation. Sexual urges must be repressed for fear they will lead to love, human connection, and personal loyalty, all of which threaten the Party. Winston believes that love like the love he and Julia share will eventually destroy the Party, but he underestimates the Party's ability to destroy that love and loyalty. Winston and Julia both give in to torture and betray each other. When they are released, their love and loyalty to each other has been destroyed.

Topics for Further Study

- Explain how history is distorted and hidden from the citizens of Oceania. What is the result?

- Discuss how Newspeak works to alter the expression of thoughts in *1984*. Give examples from today's society of institutions and leaders that have used language to distort reality.

- Explain Winston's feelings about the proletariat, its past, present, and future.

Because the Party can easily detect Thoughtcrimes, people always act as if they are completely loyal to the Party. No one trusts anyone else completely. Winston makes fatal mistakes when he trusts O'Brien and Charrington, both of whom betray him. His misjudgment is almost understandable, given the subtle cues both give him to indicate that they are fellow subversives. But as it turns out, they are deliberately setting a trap for him and Julia. In the end, no one can be trusted.

Utopia and Anti-Utopia

1984 is clearly an anti-utopian book. As O'Brien tells Winston, the world he and his comrades have created is "the exact opposite of the stupid hedonistic Utopias that the old reformers imagined." Instead of being a society that is a triumph of human spirit and creativity, the society the Party has created is full of fear, torment, and treachery that will worsen over time. O'Brien gives Winston an image of the future: a boot stomping on a human face, forever and ever.

Such a pessimistic vision of the future serves a purpose, as Orwell knew. He wrote *1984* as a warning in order to make people aware that this type of society could exist if trends such as jingoism, oppression of the working class, and the erosion of language that expresses the vastness of human experience continued. Readers are supposed to see that this is only one possible future, one they must work to avoid. Orwell's anti-utopian vision captured the horrors of World War II and the fears

of the cold war in the same way that earlier utopian novels, from British author Thomas More's *Utopia* to Edward Bellamy's *Looking Backward,* captured the hope and self-confidence after the end of the medieval era.

Patriotism

The blind patriotism that fueled the dictatorships of German leader Adolf Hitler and Soviet leader Joseph Stalin in the 1930s and 1940s inspired Orwell to write of Oceania and its leader, Big Brother. Just as the Germans fanatically cheered and revered Hitler, treating him as a beloved father, the citizens of Oceania look up to Big Brother as their protector, who will watch over them just as a real brother would. The huge pictures of Big Brother that can be found everywhere in Oceania are reminiscent of those of Communist leader Mao Tse-tung displayed by the Chinese.

As in real totalitarian regimes, the children of Oceania play a large part in maintaining the loyalty and patriotism of the citizens. Just as German children joined the scout-like and militaristic Hitler Youth organization, the children of Oceania enjoy wearing their Junior Spies costumes, marching around, and singing patriotic songs. Orwell depicts how sinister it is for a government to use children to promote their policies when he portrays the Parsons' children as holy terrors, threatening to denounce their parents to the authorities if they don't give in to their childish demands. In the 1960s, the Chinese under Mao would indoctrinate an entire generation of children to be loyal to the state by taking them away from their parents for long periods in order to insure that the government's message could not be contradicted by the children's parents.

Style

Point of View

Orwell's *1984* is told in the third person, but the point of view is clearly Winston Smith's. Through his eyes, readers are able to see how the totalitarian society functions, in particular how an individual deals with having illegal thoughts that can be detected easily by spies and telescreens that monitor one's every movement. Because readers are in Winston's head, they make the mistakes he makes in judging people. At one point he looks around a room at work and tells himself he knows just who will be vaporized within the next few years and who will be allowed to live. His perceptions of who is a loyal party member and who is not turn out to be inaccurate, however. In this way, Orwell shows that in a paranoid society, where personal relationships with others are at best only tolerated and at worst illegal, no one can really know his fellow man.

Winston is a well-drawn character with clear opinions (clear to the reader, that is; he cannot reveal his opinions to anyone in his society). Often, critics have claimed that these opinions echo George Orwell's. For example, Winston admires the spirit of the proletariat, but looks down on them because they will never have the means or intelligence to change their lives and their government. On the other hand, he admires the sophistication of the wealthy, cultured O'Brien, even though he is an evil character. This may reflect Orwell's own class prejudices, as someone who was far more educated and worldly than most of the people from the economic class in England (the lower middle class).

Setting

Written between 1947 and 1948, *1984*'s original title was 1948, but Orwell changed it so that it would be set in the future, but still be close enough to the present to be frightening. The action takes place in London, which is now part of a country called Oceania. Oceania is one of three world superpowers, and it is continually at war with one of the other two superpowers, Eastasia and Eurasia. Enemies can change overnight and become an ally, although the Party automatically rewrites history when this happens so that no one will remember that circumstances were ever any different. This perpetual state of war consumes most of the state's resources, so city buildings are in a constant state of disrepair. All consumer goods, from food to clothing, are rationed, just as they were in England during World War II. Winston lives in what was once London, now a drab, gray, and decaying urban area.

Language and Meaning

Orwell was very aware of the power of language, so he has the totalitarian government of the future create a new language called Newspeak. Newspeak is used throughout the book by the citizens of Oceania and explained in detail in an appendix. The language is derived from Standard English and will go through many versions over the years until it reaches its final version in the year 2050. The 1984 version, however, still bears a strong resemblance to English.

The basic idea behind Newspeak is to take all words that refer to ideas the Party disagrees with and strip them of their original meaning or eliminate them entirely. The purpose of Newspeak is to narrow the range of ideas that can be expressed, so as the language develops it contains fewer and fewer words. Word forms and grammar are simplified, as is pronunciation, so that eventually the number of readers can be kept to a minimum. Newspeak also contains words to express new ideas, such as *oldthink,* which means the way people thought before the revolution. Naturally, it has a wicked and decadent connotation.

When Newspeak appeared citizens were unable to read about old ideas and express new ones that were counter to what the Party wanted them to think. An entire passage from the Declaration of Independence, "We hold these truths to be self-evident ...," can be reduced to one word: crimethink. Simplistic slogans replace more complicated ideas. The Party's most famous slogans are "War Is Peace," "Freedom Is Slavery," and "Ignorance Is Strength."

Through the device of a fictional language, Orwell is able to point out that language can be misused to mislead people. In creating Newspeak, Orwell was influenced both by political rhetoric that takes the place of substantive communication and advertising lingo that makes ridiculous and vague promises.

Structure

1984 is divided into three parts plus an appendix. Part one sets up Winston's world, which readers see through his eyes and his thoughts. They understand his loneliness and why this leads him to take risks that will lead to his downfall.

In part two, the lengthiest part of the narrative, Winston becomes connected with people he believes are rebels like himself. He has an affair with Julia and follows O'Brien to an underground meeting of dissidents. Also in part two, Orwell includes lengthy sections from the fictional Emmanuel Goldstein's political tract. It is interesting to note that his publishers originally wanted Orwell to delete this material, because it stops the action of the narrative.

In part three, Winston and Julia have been caught by the Inner Party and separated. Winston undergoes severe torture and brainwashing at the hands of O'Brien. His dialogue and interaction with O'Brien has much dramatic tension because underlying their battle is mutual respect. Unfortunately for Winston, this respect does not translate into O'Brien freeing him. O'Brien successfully brainwashes Winston into loving Big Brother.

The book ends with an appendix on the development and structure of the language called "Newspeak." The appendix is written as if it were a scholarly article, and while it serves to clarify the use of Newspeak in the novel it is interesting to note that the publisher originally wanted to cut it, thinking it unnecessary.

Historical Context

Totalitarianism

In 1948, when Orwell's *1984* was published, World War II had just ended. One of England's allies had been Russia, which was ruled by a despotic dictator named Joseph Stalin. Stalin ruled with an iron fist, and was famous for his midnight purges: he would round up hundreds of citizens at a time and murder them in deserted areas, much as Oceania citizens are "vaporized." Stalin's victims were his imagined enemies, such as political dissidents, artists, or Jews. Meanwhile, Adolf Hitler, in Germany, had slaughtered his enemies as well, in the end killing six million Jews plus nine million Slavs, gypsies, political dissidents, homosexuals, and mentally challenged people. Mao Tse-tung in China was fighting for communism against Chinese nationalist forces under Chiang Kai-shek. Mao would finally defeat the nationalists in 1949 and begin a long, oppressive totalitarian regime.

Other dictators of the time included Francisco Franco in Spain and Benito Mussolini in Italy. These oppressive rulers controlled citizens through propaganda and violence. This state of affairs prompted Orwell to create Big Brother, the ultimate totalitarian leader who dominates all political, social, and economic activities.

Socialism and Communism

Orwell fought against Franco in the Spanish Civil War in the mid-1930s, supporting the socialist left. He was not a communist, but a dedicated Democratic socialist who believed that the government, not private enterprise, should control the production and distribution of goods, and as such he was greatly concerned about the lives of the poor and working class.

All over the world, throughout the twentieth century, working class people had been fighting for better lives. In America, workers fought a long and hard battle for labor reforms that would eventually include such benefits as job security, safety regulation, overtime and hazardous duty pay, vacation and sick days, health insurance, pensions, disability, and child labor laws, which modern workers sometimes take for granted. Some U.S. and British workers turned to socialism and communism, thinking that perhaps these alternate forms of economic and social structure would solve their problems. In the late nineteenth century, Karl Marx of Germany proposed that to resolve the gross inequality between the workers and the bosses, the working class, or proletariat, would have to revolt and establish a new communist regime in which one authoritarian party would control the political and economic systems. He believed workers ought to own their farms and factories and distribute the profits evenly among workers.

Here in America, the capitalist factory and mine owners eventually conceded to labor's demands and the socialists and communists were marginalized. This act deferred American workers from revolting against their government. Communist revolutions did occur in Russia and in China, but eventually those countries modified their economic systems.

America's response to communism was extreme during the Cold War era of the 1950s; in fact, many people believed the U.S. government was acting just as oppressively as communist governments were. Under the leadership of Senator Joe McCarthy, the House (of Representatives) Committee on Un-American Activities aggressively attacked public figures who were suspected communists, demanding that they name other communists or be blackballed in their industries. Hollywood writers and filmmakers were especially hard hit by the mania and many careers were destroyed before President Truman and public opinion turned against McCarthy and the witch hunt ended. The paranoia that characterized the McCarthy era was similar to the paranoia in *1984,* as people were pressured to betray their friends, co-workers, and even parents in order to save themselves. Today, communism still has some followers in the United States and England, as does Democratic socialism, which Orwell embraced wholeheartedly.

Television

Aside from being concerned about labor and government, Orwell was very aware of an important invention that was just becoming popular after World War II and would eventually be a dominant force in Western culture: the television. The first

Compare
&
Contrast

- **1948:** West Berlin, Germany, is blockaded by the Soviets. The Americans begin an airlift to help the stranded Berliners.

  1984: The Berlin wall, built in 1961 to keep East Germans from defecting to the West, remains in place.

  Today: East and West Germany are reunified, after the Berlin wall was taken down in 1990.

- **1948/49:** Mao Tse-tung battles Chiang Kai-shek and his nationalist forces, finally defeating them in 1949 and establishing a totalitarian communist regime.

  1984: China has survived the severe cultural purging of the Great Proletarian Cultural Revolution in the 1960s. Opened to the West in the 1970s because of President Nixon's visit in 1972, China is now trading with the West and incorporating some small democratic and economic reforms.

  Today: In 1989, students demanding greater economic and civil rights reforms protested in Tiananmen Square in Beijing and were gunned down by Chinese troops. China continues to trade with the West, but its democratic movement has been slowed considerably.

- **1948/49:** In September, 1949, President Truman announces that Russia, too, has the atom bomb, having developed the technology on its own.

  1984: In 1991 the Cold War continues as the arms race between the Soviet Union and the United States escalates.

  Today: On December 8, 1987, President Ronald Reagan and Soviet leader Mikhail Gorbachev sign an agreement to dismantle all 1,752 U.S. and 859 Soviet nuclear missiles within a 300 to 3,400-mile range. In 1991 the former Soviet Republic breaks up. American investors are helping the Soviets establish new businesses as the Soviets concentrate their attention on revamping their economy.

- **1949:** There are one million television sets in the United States and two dozen TV stations. There will be ten million TV sets by 1951, fifty million by 1959.

  1984: Eighty-five million U.S. households own a television set. Cable television reaches almost half of those households. Computers start to become a household product in the United States with approximately 13% or 516,750 computers owned by consumers.

  Today: Ninety-eight percent of U.S. households (95 million homes) own a color television set, 28 percent own three or more televisions, 65 percent have cable access. New TV technology on the horizon includes high-definition television. In 1995, over three million people owned a personal computer. Use of a vast computer network, called the Internet, which originated in the 1960s and connects users from over 160 countries to each other via electronic mail, exploded during the 1990s with an estimated count of 20 to 30 million users in mid-1995.

BBC broadcast in Britain occurred in 1937, and TV was first demonstrated to the American public in 1939 at the New York World's Fair. Television's popularity grew enormously throughout the 1950s, and today 98% of American households own at least one color television set. Orwell recognized the enormous potential of this communication tool, which would soon be in every home. He imagined that the television could one day not only broadcast propaganda nonstop but that it could transmit back images of action in front of the screen, allowing the broadcaster to spy on its viewers.

Critical Overview

When *1984* was published, critics were impressed by the sheer power of George Orwell's grim and horrifying vision of the future. They

In the late 1940s, Orwell used many aspects of existing totalitarian and communist governments to construct the fictional government of Nineteen Eighty-Four. *Pictured here are Chinese army tanks bearing down on a man during the Tiananmen Square uprising of 1989.*

praised Orwell's gripping prose, which captured so well the details of life under an oppressive regime, from the tasteless, sodden public meals Winston eats to the gritty dust of the gray streets. In 1949, critic Mark Shorer wrote in his *New York Times Book Review* essay that "No real reader can neglect this experience with impunity.... He will be asked to read through pages of sustained physical and psychological pain that have seldom been equaled and never in such quiet, sober prose." In the same year, British novelist V. S. Pritchett wrote his reaction to the novel in *New Statesman and Nation.*

"I do not think," the critic concluded, "I have ever read a novel more frightening and depressing; and yet, such are the originality, the suspense, the speed of writing and withering indignation that it is impossible to put the book down."

Critics also praised Orwell's ability to provoke moral outrage at Oceania, a society that so completely destroys the human values many people hold dear, from love to art.

Because *1984* was published during the reign of Russian leader Joseph Stalin, a former ally of England and the United States who was proving to be a cruel and violent dictator, critics of the time believed that the novel was about the events in the Soviet Union. Some mistakenly believed that by setting the story in England, Orwell meant to criticize British socialism, particularly since he names the Inner Party Ingsoc ("ENGlish SOCialism"). Orwell strongly denied this. Then again, some critics saw the novel as a satire of the contemporary social and political scene. Certainly, many of Orwell's details bear a resemblance to life in London post-World War II. However, over time critics came to realize that Orwell meant the story to be a universal warning about the dangers of any totalitarian dictatorship.

Criticism

Kathleen Fitzpatrick

In the following essay, Fitzpatrick, an author and doctoral candidate at New York University, maintains that although Orwell's dystopian vision has not been borne out by Soviet-style communism, the author's fears about the ability of the state to control people is still a danger in modern society.

George Orwell's dystopian (a fictional place where people lead dehumanized and fearful lives) vision of the year 1984, as depicted in what many consider to be his greatest novel, has entered the collective consciousness of the English-speaking world more completely than perhaps any other political text, whether fiction or nonfiction. No matter how far our contemporary world may seem from *1984*'s Oceania, any suggestion of government surveillance of its citizens—from the threatened "clipper chip," which would have allowed government officials to monitor all computer activity, to New York Mayor Rudy Giuliani's decision to place security cameras in Central Park—produces cries of "Big Brother is watching." Big Brother, the all-seeing manifestation in *1984* of the Party's drive for power for its own sake, has come to stand as a warning of the insidious nature of government-centralized power, and the way that personal freedoms, once encroached upon, are easily destroyed altogether.

Critics generally agree that the hero of the novel, Winston Smith, may be recognized by his name as related to both the great British statesman and World War II leader Winston Churchill and a non-descript Everyman. However, the point is not that Winston is a great man, or even that he is one man among many; rather, O'Brien, while torturing Winston, says that if Winston is "a man," as he claims to think of himself, then he is the last man. In fact this echo of the novel's original title, *The Last Man in Europe,* reveals Winston as symbolic of what critic Ian Watt has described as Orwell's conception of a dying humanism. Whether Winston Smith is truly a humanist, in the classical sense of the term, is of no matter; in comparison to the totalitarian regime which destroys him, Winston is, in fact, the last embodiment of the human. In converting Winston to the love of Big Brother, the last man in Europe is destroyed.

Winston maintains, throughout the novel, two avenues of hope for a life outside the confines of the Party and the watchful eyes of Big Brother, a life which may undermine or even overthrow the Party's hold on Oceania. One of these possibilities is conscious, spoken: the proles. Just as Marx foresaw, in the nineteenth century, that the Revolution would come from a spontaneous uprising of the proletariat as they shook off the chains of their oppressors, so Winston writes in his diary that if there is hope, it lies in this 85 percent of Oceania's population that exists outside the confines of the Party. And yet, the impossibility of a proletarian uprising presents itself to him at every turn. Echoing Marx, Winston writes: "Until they become conscious they will never rebel, and until after they have rebelled they cannot become conscious." And, unfortunately, he is right; as O'Brien admonishes Winston in the Ministry of Love, "The proletarians will never revolt, not in a thousand years or a million. They cannot." Thus this small bit of hope is crushed.

The second possibility remains mostly unspoken and unconscious: desire. It is this possibility, the momentary destruction of the Party through intimate union with another person, which solidifies Winston's relationship with Julia. Though they are drawn together at first by what seem to be basic animal urges, it is precisely the baseness and the animality of those urges that gives them their liberatory potential. As Winston relates earlier, in contemplating the sterility of his relationship with his wife: "The sexual act, successfully performed, was rebellion. Desire was thoughtcrime." Desire is thoughtcrime in Oceania because it elevates the human, the individual, above the powers of the state to control him. In fact, as Winston and Julia begin to make love for the first time, this piece of repressed knowledge becomes conscious; "the animal instinct," he thinks, "the simple undifferenti-

What Do I Read Next?

- *Animal Farm* (1945) was George Orwell's 1945 fable about the inevitable course of all revolutions. In it, a group of animals revolt against the farmer who is their master and set up their own form of government. The most intelligent animals, the pigs, are in charge, and hopes are high when the animals write their own bill of animal rights. However, over time, these rights are eroded as the pigs begin changing the rules.

- *Brave New World* by Aldous Huxley (1931) influenced Orwell's own futuristic novel, *1984.* Huxley's totalitarian state, which exists in London six hundred years in the future, is less grim than Orwell's, but its inhabitants are as powerless and oppressed as the citizens of Oceania. Huxley's characterization and prose is less sophisticated than Orwell's, but his novel is funny and fascinating. The inhabitants of his society are controlled from before birth by a handful of elite rulers with sophisticated technology. When a primitive person, the Savage, from outside the society is introduced, he confronts the shallow values of the citizens.

- *This Perfect Day* by Ira Levin (1970) is another futuristic novel about a totalitarian society with very different values from that of contemporary society. As in *Brave New World,* citizens dull their pain and fears through drugs and are genetically very similar. Those who have genetic differences have a greater tendency to be dissatisfied with the pacified society, which is controlled by a huge computer that dispenses the mood-altering drugs.

- *The Handmaid's Tale* by Margaret Atwood (1985) is the story of a woman named Offred, who lives in the Republic of Gilead, an oppressive society of the future in which women's roles are severely limited.

- *Harrison Bergeron,* a satirical story by Kurt Vonnegut, was inspired by Orwell's *1984* and Huxley's *Brave New World.* Harrison lives in a totalitarian state in the future. He is very intelligent—not an advantage in this society—so to "correct" this "defect" and allow Harrison to be as mediocre and middle-of-the-road as his fellow citizens, doctors plan to perform brain surgery. However, Harrison is whisked away by an elite group that secretly controls all of society and given a choice: join the rulers and disappear from society for good or be lobotomized.

- *We* by Russian writer Yevgeny Zamyatin (1924) influenced George Orwell's *1984.* It, too, is a dystopian novel set in the future, in this case the twenty-sixth century, and features a totalitarian state. This society, called OneState, is ruled by a Big Brother-type dictator called simply Benefactor, who has scheduled the day of every citizen down to the very minute. The narrator, D-503 (all the citizens have numbers, not names), is the designer and builder of a space probe called INTEGRAL and is waiting for the day when he finally has the Great Operation: the lobotomy the government performs to erase the last vestige of each individual's humanity: the imagination.

ated desire: that was the force that could tear the Party to pieces."

The threat to the Party of the thoughtcrime that desire represents is sufficiently serious that the state must exert formidable control over any such human, instinctual reactions. In his essay "1984: Enigmas of Power," Irving Howe writes, "There can be no 'free space' in the lives of the Outer Party faithful, nothing that remains beyond the command of the state. Sexual energy is to be transformed into political violence and personal hysteria." It is this recognition by the Party that there may be no element of "human nature" which can remain the province of the individual without endangering the Party's hold on its members that represents the great "advance" of Ingsoc (English Socialism, in Oldspeak) over previous totalitarian regimes. There was always room, notes Howe, in these previous regimes, for "'free space,' that margin of personal autonomy which even in the worst moments of Stalinism and Hitlerism some people wanted to protect."

The "advance" represented by Ingsoc, according to Emmanuel Goldstein's *The Theory and Practice of Oligarchal Collectivism,* the book written by a collective of Inner Party members including O'Brien, is the realization by the Party that all previous oppressive regimes were nonetheless "infected" with liberal ideas about the individual:

> Part of the reason for this was that in the past no government had the power to keep its citizens under constant surveillance. The invention of print, however, made it easier to manipulate public opinion, and the film and the radio carried the process further. With the development of television, and the technical advance which made it possible to receive and transmit simultaneously on the same instrument, private life came to an end. Every citizen, or at least every citizen important enough to be worth watching, could be kept for twenty-four hours a day under the eyes of the police and in the sound of official propaganda, with all other channels of communication closed. The possibility of enforcing not only complete obedience to the will of the State, but complete uniformity of opinion on all subjects, now existed for the first time.

With that development, the totalization of surveillance of Party members, not only does private life come to an end, but so does the possibility of sexual desire as truly liberating. Julia and Winston do manage to steal their moments together away from the Party. But the Party's enforcers, the Thought Police, are watching even when the lovers are convinced they are safe, and the revenge they exact for this transgression of Party control is enormous.

It is significant that the instrument of this totalized surveillance is the "telescreen," Orwell's projection of the future of television. As Orwell was writing *1984* in 1948, television was just emerging from the developmental hiatus forced upon the broadcasting industry by World War II. Many people were worried, in the late 1940s and early 1950s, about what this new medium would be, how it would function, how much control over its watchers it would create. Orwell's own concerns about the future development of television are reflected in *1984*'s telescreens, which on the one hand, broadcast an endless barrage of Party propaganda, and on the other hand, act as transmitters as well, enabling the Party to exercise the total surveillance it required.

Martin Esslin has claimed in his essay "Television and Telescreen," however, that Orwell's

fears about television missed the mark on two counts. First, Orwell was evidently more concerned about the potential for televisions to become cameras, a technological development which has not taken place, overlooking the importance of "what they have actually become, the omnipresent, constant providers of highly colorful visual entertainment for the broad masses." Secondly, Orwell's notion of what these telescreens did transmit was the crudest possible sort of propaganda—martial music and endless lists of production figures—which overlooks the utility of entertainment as a form of mass manipulation. In Esslin's words:

> There is, after all, not that much difference between a society that floods the masses with cheap, novelettish romance, raucous and sentimental pop music, and pornography to keep them amused and politically inert and one that does the same thing for commercial gain—but with the identical ultimate political result: apathy, ignorance of real issues, and acquiescence in whatever the politicians are doing. And does not commercial television do just that?

Furthermore, both Esslin and Irving Howe point out another weakness in Orwell's depiction of the telescreen when compared to the development that television has actually taken in the latter half of the twentieth century: the proles—fully 85 percent of the population of Oceania—are not required to have telescreens. If the machine-made novels and songs are being put onto the market in order to keep the masses complacent, wouldn't the telescreen prove much more effective? Moreover, the proles, kept free of the telescreen's powers of surveillance, retain the ability to have a private life which Party members have lost. The Party clearly regards the proletariat as not being worth watching, as being unable to develop the "humanity" which must be guarded against in Party members. As it is stated in *The Theory and Practice of Oligarchal Collectivism,* "What opinions the masses hold, or do not hold, is looked on as a matter of indifference. They can be granted intellectual liberty because they have no intellect."

This division of society into Party members and proles in *1984* was clearly modeled on the division which was coming into focus in the Soviet Union in 1948, in which Party members were closely monitored while proles were less controlled. Both Esslin and Howe, however, point out that Orwell's vision of the powerlessness and inertia of the proles did not bear out, given the evidence of history. In fact, numerous uprisings against the Soviet machine, from the Hungarian Revolution to the student uprisings in France, from the Prague Spring to the rise of Solidarity in Poland, to the eventual fall of the Berlin Wall, demonstrate that the proletariat, and even party intellectuals, were not completely crushed by Party ideology, and that, in Esslin's words, "the totalitarian manipulation of popular feelings and ideas by the mass media is far less effective than Orwell had imagined."

Nonetheless, by the novel's end, Big Brother is ultimately victorious, having won over the last man in Europe. In today's world, Big Brother is still a force, especially to those who worry about the continued possibility of the rise of totalitarianism today. However, there is another face to Big Brother, which is precisely that "manipulation of popular feelings and ideas by the mass media" about which Orwell warned. If people find in government endless new reasons to be vigilant about the incursions into personal liberties which *1984* depicts, they would do well to remember, as Neil Postman claims in the introduction to *Amusing Ourselves to Death,* that there is a very different version of the dystopian universe presented in Aldous Huxley's *Brave New World,* in which "no Big Brother is required to deprive people of their autonomy, maturity and history. As he saw it, people will come to love their oppression, to adore the technologies that undo their capacities to think." Big Brother may not be watching; he might be broadcasting.

Source: Kathleen Fitzpatrick, in an essay for *Novels for Students,* Gale, 1999.

James E. Davis

In the following essay, Davis argues that, in addition to its literary merits, 1984 *should be kept in the high school curriculum for its look at totalitarianism.*

George Orwell's *Nineteen Eighty-four* has been challenged on such grounds as profanity, immorality, and obscenity. It has been charged with being Communistic, containing sex references, and being depressing. Some of these charges are absurd, and though some have a grain of truth when items are taken out of context, on the whole the book stands up well and though frequently challenged has a history of rarely being removed from classrooms and libraries. Critics, as well as readers in general, have recognized the book as significant and valuable since its appearance at the end of the 1940s. Some examples: On the dust jacket of the first American edition of *Nineteen Eighty-four* Bertrand Russell and Alfred Kazin are quoted. Russell states, "*Nineteen Eighty-four* depicts the hor-

rors of a well-established totalitarian regime of whatever type with great power and skill and force of imagination." He adds that it is important that we should be aware of these dangers. Alfred Kazin characterizes the book as "an extraordinary experience ... overwhelming in its keenness and prophetic power." He further comments: "I hardly know which to praise more—Orwell's insight into the fate of man under totalitarianism, or his compassion for him." Reasons for reading and teaching *Nineteen Eighty-four* continue today to be much the same as these critics gave four decades ago.

The book does express a mood of near but not complete despair. The mood is despair only if readers do not heed the warning of what will happen if we continue on some of our present courses. But we do not have to become soulless automatons. It is not foreordained. The scenario of *Nineteen Eighty-four* is that atomic wars had started in the 1940s, accelerated ten years later in Russia, Western Europe, and North America. This atomic war led the governments (Eurasia, Oceania, and Eastasia) to conclude that unless atomic wars stopped, organized society would be doomed. Of course, this would also mean the end of governmental power. Thus atomic war stopped, but bombs continued to be stockpiled awaiting the right time to kill a large segment of the world's population without warning in a few seconds. Orwell portrays this continued military preparedness as essential also for the continuation of the economic system and shows the consequences of a society in a constant state of war readiness, always afraid of being attacked.

As Erich Fromm says in the Afterword to the 1961 New American Library paperback, "Orwell's picture is so pertinent because it offers a telling argument against the popular idea that we can save freedom and democracy by continuing the arms race and finding a 'stable' deterrent." With technical progress geometrically progressing, the caves will never be deep enough to protect us.

The novel begins on a bright cold day in April, "and the clocks were striking thirteen." From there on a world is presented that is permeated by fear and hate with such slogans as HATE WEEK, WAR IS PEACE, FREEDOM IS SLAVERY, IGNORANCE IS STRENGTH. The society has nothing like our first amendment. Everything is censored by the MINISTRY OF TRUTH. It is even a crime to keep a diary and Winston Smith's life is endangered by doing so. Ironically Winston is employed by the MINISTRY OF TRUTH, and his job is to constantly rewrite history. Government predictions which do not come true (and they never do) are made to disappear. And, of course, people have to be made to disappear too (to become nonpersons) if they commit THOUGHT CRIME, which the THOUGHT POLICE are to control. BIG BROTHER affirms that: "Who controls the past controls the future: Who controls the present controls the past." The following extended quotation from the book demonstrates in some detail how this control of the past was accomplished:

> As soon as all the corrections which happened to be necessary in any particular number of the *Times* had been assembled and collated, that number would be reprinted, the original copy destroyed, and the corrected copy placed in the files in its stead. This process of continuous alteration was applied not only to newspapers, but to books, periodicals, pamphlets, posters, leaflets, films, sound tracks, cartoons, photographs—to every kind of literature or documentation which might conceivably hold any political or ideological significance. Day by day and almost minute by minute the past was brought up to date. In this way every prediction made by the Party could be shown by documentary evidence to have been correct; nor was any item of news, or any expression of opinion, which conflicted with the needs of the moment, ever allowed to remain on record. All history was a palimpsest, scraped clean and reinscribed exactly as often as was necessary. In no case would it have been possible, once the deed was done, to prove that any falsification had taken place. The largest section of the Records Department, far larger than the one in which Winston worked, consisted simply of persons whose duty it was to track down and collect all copies of books, newspapers, and other documents which had been superseded and were due for destruction.

A few cubicles away from Winston is Ampleforth, who juggles rhymes and meters, producing garbled versions of poems which have become ideologically offensive but for one reason or another are to be retained in anthologies. There is also a whole army of reference clerks who spend all of their time preparing lists of books and magazines to be recalled. There are also huge warehouses where corrected documents are stored and furnaces where original copies are burned.

By controlling all information BIG BROTHER controls responses of citizens, primarily through the giant two-way TV screens in every living space. These permit THOUGHT POLICE to observe all citizens to see that they are responding in a desirable manner—hating enemies and loving BIG BROTHER. Reality control, DOUBLETHINK in NEWSPEAK, means an "unending series of victories over our memory."

In *Nineteen Eighty-four* orthodoxy means not thinking or even needing to think. It is unconsciousness. Orthodoxy is to close the book. One of the U.S. Supreme Court justices in the Island Trees case talks about censorship resulting in a "pall of orthodoxy." One of the functions of literature in a free society is to help protect us from this "pall of orthodoxy." This book is one of the best examples of a work of considerable literary merit worth reading and studying in the classroom as part of a protection program against the orthodoxy pall. It is also a very interesting study of the effects of an orthodoxy that finally convinces Winston Smith, a party member who opposes the system, that four is five. It takes brain-washing and torture by the MINISTRY OF LOVE to accomplish this convincing. Winston's final orthodoxy is: "Whatever the Party holds to be true is truth. It is impossible to see reality except by looking through the eyes of the Party."

In answer to the question of why this particular novel to study the relationship between totalitarianism, technology, psychology, and language instead of a social studies, science, or language text, Roy Orgren, writing in the Fall 1983 *Connecticut English Journal,* says:

> Simply because, set forth in a work of fiction, the ideas are more accessible, more interrelated, and more engaging; the sheer horror of totalitarianism is more real. We flinch when the truncheon-wielding guards in the MINISTRY OF LOVE crack Winston's fingers and shatter his elbow; we writhe in our armchairs as O'Brien virtually disembodies Winston with electric shocks; we shudder as moist pads are applied to Winston's temples; and we, like Winston, are dazed by the "devastating explosion," "the blinding flash of light" which so numbs his mind that he consents to seeing—no, actually sees—five fingers when only four are held to him.

We are jolted out of our complacency so that it is likely that we will never slacken our vigil against oppression and human rights violations.

Orwell, with his presiding interest in language, shows how BIG BROTHER manipulates society and controls reality by corrupting language. NEWSPEAK is calculated to get rid of individuality by limiting the range of thought through cutting the choice of words to a minimum. As Syme, the NEWSPEAK expert, says, "You think, I dare say, that our chief job is inventing new words. But not a bit of it! We're destroying words—scores of them, hundreds of them, every day. We're cutting the language down to the bone. The Eleventh Edition won't contain a single word that will become obsolete before the year 2050."

Studying the effects of NEWSPEAK can only help us in cherishing our language with all of its rich diversity and ambiguities. Valuable, exciting classroom discussion and writing projects can grow from this, and surely the lesson of the importance of using language that is not vague and misleading but clear and precise can be learned.

Another major emphasis of the novel is the use of technology combined with advertising techniques (especially by the government) that are deeply psychological to eliminate individuality and privacy. Many of the same techniques used in *Nineteen Eighty-four* are in use today in our world, and many of them have become much more sophisticated. We surely have full-wall TV screens and the two-way television. Closed circuit security systems are not just for banks anymore. In fact, they are practically everywhere. Heartbeat, respiration, surface tension of the skin, stiffness of hair, and temperatures can be measured remotely by voltage sensors and ultrasensitive microphones. Our government puts out a glut of newspeak. It is significant that National Council of Teachers of English Doublespeak Award has twice been awarded to Ronald Reagan. The number of records, many kept without our knowledge, on each of us stored in computers, retrievable in seconds by almost any person or organization with the knowhow, is frightening. Behavior modification and drug therapy are widely used. Studying about these technologies and techniques, discussing them, exposing them, can make students aware in a way that may serve to make them less vulnerable to these techniques.

Perhaps the most interesting and discussable feature of Orwell's novel is its description of the nature of truth. Is there an objective truth, or is "reality" not external? Does it exist only subjectively and internally? Is it reality that what the Party holds to be truth *is* truth? The Party believes that truth is only in the mind and that by controlling the mind truth is controlled. Controlling minds and truth is ultimate power. Truth is subordinated to the Party. As Erich Fromm says, "It is one of the most characteristic and destructive developments of our own society that man, becoming more and more of an instrument, transforms reality more and more into something relative to his own interests and functions. Truth is proven by the consensus of millions; to the slogan 'how can millions be wrong' is added 'and how can a minority of one be right.'" The "one" must be insane. The "consensus truth" concept can serve as the basis for much valuable discussion about many things such as individuality,

minority rights, majority rule, and, of course, values.

It is hard to imagine a modern novel that has more reasons to be read and taught. In addition to its literary merit, it has special implications for our times and the society toward which we may be heading. Its depiction of a well-established totalitarian regime, a nuclear stand-off with a world in constant fear, total censorship, NEWSPEAK, DOUBLETHINK, orthodoxy, and consensus truth offer almost sure-fire topics for discussion and writing in classes—discussions that can serve to foster sincere thinking and maturity. Yes, the book is depressing, but readers can react to that by trying to do positive things to influence the future rather than becoming more depressed and pessimistic. *Nineteen Eighty-four* teaches us, as Erich Fromm says at the end of his essay, "the danger with which all men are confronted today, the danger of a society of automatons who will have lost every trace of individuality, of love, of critical thought, and yet who will not be aware of it because of 'doublethink'. Books like Orwell's are powerful warnings."

Critical language involving reading, thought, and discussion of books like *Nineteen Eighty-four* may help us to avoid Winston's fate of total loss of self, of humanity, as presented in the last paragraph of the novel:

> He gazed up at the enormous face. Forty years it had taken him to learn what kind of smile was hidden beneath the dark mustache. O cruel, needless misunderstanding! O stubborn, self-willed exile from the loving breast! Two gin-scented tears trickled down the sides of his nose. But it was all right, everything was all right, the struggle was finished. He had won the victory over himself. He loved Big Brother.

Source: James E. Davis, "Why *Nineteen Eighty-Four* Should Be Read and Taught," in *Censored Books*, Scarecrow Press, 1993, pp. 382-87.

Ralph A. Ranald

In the following essay, Ranald discusses Orwell's presentation of controlled madness and of a reversed society in his novel.

"I shall save you, Winston, I shall make you perfect." So O'Brien, the Grand Inquisitor of *1984*, has said to the antihero Winston Smith, in one of the dream sequences which strangely go almost unnoticed in that inverted Platonic dialogue which is Orwell's monument. It is as if the lives of the Platonic philosopher-kings were viewed from the point of view of one of the Auxiliaries. But it is not the old style of dialogue, in which there is a certain amount of free interchange of ideas, even between master and disciple. Rather, in this new style of dialogue, one party has the ability to inflict pain on the other party in any degree desired, even while the two proceed to discuss the most abstruse political questions. Dialogue implies the ability to have one's mind changed, but in the condition of "controlled insanity" which is *1984,* communication consists in the imposition of an insane view of reality by the strong few upon the weak many, through overwhelming force. O'Brien must "save" Winston, but this is religious salvation turned backward, and its purpose is to prevent even one "just man" from existing anywhere in the world, by convincing that man that he is insane. "Is it possible that a whole society can be insane?" asked Orwell in one of his essays, speaking of Hitler's Germany.

Orwell's *1984* is about religion reversed, law and government reversed, and above all, language reversed: not simply corrupted, but reversed. In the world of *1984,* the mad world which Orwell sought by his writing to lead men to *avoid*—for he was a political activist not interested in simple prediction—in this world, which I call Orwell's "anti-universe," because of his conversion of all the positives of Western civilization into their negatives, all of the channels of communication are systematically being closed down, restricted to just the minimums necessary for the technical functioning of society. For Orwell, as for his master, Swift, language and politics are equivalents, and political corruption is always preceded by linguistic corruption, of which the phrases "two plus two equals five" and "black is white" are only the ultimate logical (and mad) projections. Communication will become, if the political tendencies which Orwell saw in the forties continue, not the transmission of meaning, but the attempt to *avoid* meaning in furtherance of a political end which we feel must be mad but are unable to prove, even as Winston Smith cannot prove to his tormentor the madness of the Party's doctrines.

Instead of the Electric Age resulting in a quantum jump in communication, as Professor McLuhan asserts in *Understanding Media: The Extensions of Man,* when he says that "as electrically contracted, the globe is no more than a village," what McLuhan calls both "cool" and "hot" media have been, in the Orwellian view, dampened down as between individual and individual, and distorted terribly as between the individual and the State. I mention McLuhan not only because his book is current but also for what I think is his place in the direct line of descent from Orwell on the general sub-

ject of communication, and Orwell would have understood what McLuhan was driving at while not agreeing with most of his doctrine. At any rate, the deliberate, managed breakdown in communication—not extension but breakdown—at the linguistic level and indeed in all media is one of Orwell's master themes, as it is such a theme in the Theater of the Absurd, the Beat Generation, the use of the lunatic in literature to convey truth, as in Faulkner's *The Sound and the Fury* or the recent hit play, *Marat-Sade,* and, it may be, in the language of current underground cultures, such as that of drug addiction or crime.

If meaningful communication has less and less chance of conveying impressions in the usual communications media, how does Orwell envision communication as taking place in his nightmare world? He does so primarily at the level of the infliction of pain. Torture is communication. Worse, to be tortured is not the worst thing in the world, if only the victim is *understood* by his torturer, as Winston feels he is understood by O'Brien.

In the mad world of *1984,* all human relationships are based on pain, either its infliction or its avoidance. "We are the dead," says Winston of himself and his mistress, Julia, but just as the Platonic dialogue form has been adapted in *1984* in the torture scenes for satiric purposes, so Orwell has modified the Cartesian *cogito* to "'I suffer pain, therefore I am.'" No communication, nor self-definition, nor relation can occur in the Orwellian anti-universe without pain, and in this Orwell follows an important trend in modern literature. If one suffers pain, he is at least certain of being alive.

One is reminded, in the relationship between O'Brien and Winston which is the only human relationship in *1984*—the Winston-Julia relationship being hollow and merely physical by comparison—of relationships between pairs of characters such as Raskolnikov and Svidrigailov, and while we think of *Crime and Punishment ,* one of the prime progenitors of this theme, also Raskolnikov and Porfiry Petrovitch. "Suffering, Rodion Romanovitch, is a great thing," observes Porfiry, as he invites him to confess. There is the climactic, though brief, relationship between Joe Christmas and Percy Grimm—their entire lives having been preparation for this confrontation—in *Light in August,* when the only way in which Grimm can become a man communicating with another is via an automatic pistol, emptying its magazine through a tabletop into his victim and then castrating him and defining him as the hated *Other.* There is the relation-

ship between the former *agent provocateur,*
Rubashov, and the commissar Gletkin in Koestler's
Darkness at Noon which, written a decade before
1984, shows some of the same but is on a cruder
level, especially in terms of the dynamics of the
power-pain relationship between O'Brien and Winston Smith. And in Brecht's haunting 1927 play,
Im Dickicht der Städte, occurs the very sophisticated perception of the ambivalent relationship between Shlink, the Malay lumber dealer residing in
the Chicago of 1912, and George Garga. "You observe the inexplicable boxing match between two
men …," says Brecht, and he explains it in sexual
terms. Shlink explicitly dies the death of Socrates,
by poison, sitting upright, even as Winston Smith
dies the death of Socrates reversed: spiritually, not
physically, by the mastering of his will by that of
the Party incarnated in O'Brien. Orwell explains
the relationship in ostensibly non-sexual, political
dynamics. Brecht uses such communication
through pain in many of his plays, especially, I
should say, in that between P. Mauler and Joan in
St. Joan of the Stockyards, and in the enforced
metamorphosis of Galy Gay in *A Man's a Man.*
This kind of communication only between political or sexual aggressors and victims is that which
Orwell was to dwell on. The Brechtian distinction
between sexuality and politics is blurred by Orwell,
because he saw the two drives as convertible, each
an aspect of the other, in that sexual frustration or
hysteria was one of the primary causes of political
fanaticism.

That human beings can communicate only by
inflicting pain on each other, or at any rate that this
will be the state of things soon, is a desperate thesis. Orwell's life was a consistent development toward this frightening perception. But Orwell was,
as has been said of Browning, "an ardent and head-
strong conventionalist," who was defining a norm
by its opposite, a moral universe by an antiuniverse.

Orwell saw human life under the primary
philosophical category of *relation,* and this may be
why he was never able to create a "round" character, even those characters which in the terms of
what we know about Orwell's experience were
clearly his own personae, aspects of himself at different stages of his life. He is the "I" as a schoolboy and the "I" as a Paris *plongeur* and English
tramp in "*Such, Such were the Joys …* " and *Down
and Out In Paris and London,* respectively. Incidentally, neither of these purportedly autobiographical documents is really the objective truth,
as those who knew Orwell have testified; he took
his artist's liberty of arranging the time sequence

in *Down and Out* in the same way as Thoreau did
in *Walden,* compressing two years of clock time
into a single seasonal year, for increased concentration of effect. There is the civil servant, Flory,
in *Burmese Days:* Orwell, or rather his portrait of
the artist as a young imperialist. Flory shoots himself, as one imagines Orwell about to do in Burma
before he resigned from the Indian Imperial Police.
There is Winston Smith as middle middle-class
man of the future, whom I have called a member
of the Auxiliaries, the Outer Party, in the inverted
Platonic Republic which is *1984.* There is S. Bowl-
ing, the very important member of the English
lower-middle class who has sharp perceptions
about his society as the result of native wit and his
educating himself beyond his class because of absurd circumstances in World War I. There is Gordon Comstock, the literary intellectual of the English lower-middle class, who refuses to climb out
of his impoverished and unsatisfactory life at first
when he has the opportunity; he leads the life of
The Loneliness of the Long-Distance Runner, refusing the shackles of his society, until he is
brought to bay by that most fundamental drive: the
procreation of the race. Least believable of his characters is the antiheroine of *A Clergyman's Daughter*—a novel in which we again have the impoverished middle class, seen through the eyes of a
neurotic and repressed woman, and in this portrait
we see more than a hint of Orwellian antifeminism.
For while Orwell deplored what he saw as the modern denigration of love in favor of sheer power, he
recognized power as the greater reality.

In each of these characters, essentially the
same story—the conflict of an individual with an
unsatisfactory, if not mad, society—is told from a
somewhat different perspective. But all of them are
two-dimensional, and the central focus is not even
on society, but on power, the central question of
which, as Orwell himself said, was "how to prevent it from being abused." Orwell's basic motivation was to communicate with other social
classes, especially with the working class which is
as near to a true hero, albeit a collective hero, as
he ever developed. And he emphasized the difficulties of such communication: for him, bred to an
extreme class-consciousness despite himself, the
simple step of walking into a working-class pub,
incognito, was as hazardous as visiting a tribe of
isolated Australian aborigines, and his equivalent
of obtaining First Class Honours in P.P.E. at Oxford, which he never attended, was his being accepted by English coal miners and Spanish revolutionaries in *The Road to Wigan Pier* and *Homage*

to Catalonia. This effort at interclass communication on Orwell's part was to succeed beyond the achievements of any of his English contemporaries. But it led him to pessimistic conclusions. "If there is hope," writes Winston Smith in *1984,* "it lies in the Proles." But the Proles will never become rebellious against their insane surroundings until they become self-aware first, and, as O'Brien assures Winston, they will never become self-aware until they rebel, a rebellion which is impossible.

Lately, one still reads Orwell, and his books are available in most paperback stores, but few write about him. Perhaps this is a blessing, or the highest form of praise of him. One wonders why there is such a lack of interest in the man. Or is it that everything which can be said about him and his portrayal of the Mad World has been said? I doubt it. The biographical and critical studies, such as they are, leave one absolutely unsatisfied. Lionel Trilling expressed best a belief about Orwell, in his introduction to *Homage to Catalonia* fifteen years ago, that Orwell was a very unusual kind of man, almost a saint, and not a genius; one who, uncharacterized by really superior intelligence, *lived* his vision as well as *wrote* it. He is in this view a Mark Twain, Thoreau, Whitman, or possibly Henry James. "He is not a genius—what a relief!" observed Trilling. "He was a virtuous man."

Yet Orwell lived a life of allegory on which his works are the commentary, unobtrusively passing through the very worst phase to date of European and British civilization, noting everything about the actual power realities, successfully communicating in his personal life with a wide range of nationalities and classes both inside and outside of his own country. He told us something very significant about his works when, in his will, he specified that no biography of him was ever to be written. Perhaps his mystery is that he made no mysteries in his writings, though his life I would call mysterious; he may have concluded early that the rarest of all sophisticated literary devices is clarity. As he wrote of a mad antiuniverse in his work, and expressed his despair at the breakdown of valid communication, so his style was exceptionally clear, as though he would prove his point in terms of technique by its opposite, just as he wished to establish a norm by a portrait of its opposite. For him, the only valid communication is nondestructive communication.

In considering *1984* it is well to proceed by way of *Animal Farm,* for it is substantive: the first work, as he himself said later, "In which I tried,

with full consciousness of what I was doing, to fuse political purpose and artistic purpose into one whole." This avowed political purpose accounts for the absence of real characters in Orwell's writing, other than himself moving through an absurd world. It is, in fact, to his political interest to show non-characters, such as Winston Smith who, passive as he is in the grip of overwhelming force against which he briefly rebels, is the only one in *1984* who is even given a complete name: the most ordinary English family name, and the first name of the most extraordinary Englishman of the century. Winston is passive and not self-aware, though we see something of his stream-of-consciousness through his dreams, his diary, and his reactions to various tortures in the Ministry of Love. He does not act; he is acted upon, even in his revolt against Big Brother. Winston, from the first moment we meet him, never makes a free decision.

We can document the completeness of Winston's slavery by reference to the series of dreams which he has, involving his mother, his sister, O'Brien, Julia, "The place where there is no darkness"—i.e., the torture cellars of the Thought Police—and The Golden Country. This last is the Orwellian archetypal dream, to be set against the nightmare of the Mad World, which perhaps ultimately stems from some boyhood experience. Whatever it was, it is his pre-Adamic state, and it appears again in *Coming Up for Air,* in the hidden fishing pool with the huge trout. The dreams are a key to the deeper meaning of *1984,* and to the lunacy of this projected world which is even more sinister than has been perceived. The truth is that Winston Smith has been designed as a victim of his society and his Party from childhood; he is marked down years before we meet him at the beginning of the book, on that day when he sets his will against that of the Party and, on April 4, 1984, writes in his diary: DOWN WITH BIG BROTHER!

Seven years prior to that date, Winston had dreamed that he was in a dark room and that someone had said to him: "We shall meet again in the place where there is no darkness." And that someone was O'Brien. It is clear that Orwell intended his readers to perceive that Winston has been under surveillance for at least that long. It may be, in the highly efficient madness of 1984, that O'Brien, one of the society's most important men, has had no other job than to be a sort of "project officer" in charge of Winston's entrapment, torture, and repentance. To be the project officer of Socrates would have been a full-time job in ancient Athens.

It is O'Brien himself who explains to Winston in the torture chamber why such pains are being taken with him. And there is a deep psychological tie between Winston and O'Brien, with sexual overtones transposed into power fantasies. Winston has a guilt neurosis implanted in his subconscious; his parents and his sister have "disappeared," and as he tells Julia, he believes that he was partly responsible for this, though he had been only a child at the time. In defiance of his surroundings, he comes to the intuitive belief that everything about his society is mad. *They* foresaw this, too. Finally, when Winston is arrested by the Thought Police, and O'Brien appears to him in prison, he, Winston, realizes that he has always known that O'Brien was an agent of the State. "You knew this, Winston," said O'Brien. "Don't deceive yourself. You did know it—you have always known it." And Winston reflects, even as the guard moves toward him with a rubber truncheon: "Yes, he saw now, he had always known it."

This, too, follows the classic criminological theory that the criminal commits his crime *because* he is seeking to be caught and punished: seeking, in other words, structure and order, and in Winston's case seeking simply communication. The most ingenious tortures are used on Winston; some of them, for example, based on his fear of rats, could only have been known if he had been the object of minute study. This he has been—a textbook case.

As for Winston's job—the rewriting of history in a minor office of the Ministry of Truth—it is absolute madness by any rational norm, that is, if there were rational norms in 1984 instead of antinorms. History is bunk, and Winston's creation of a Party hero, a Comrade Ogilvy, has its exact, almost uncanny parallel in the published diary of the Chinese Communist soldier, Lei Feng, passages of which were reprinted in the New York *Times* of April 7, 1963. Lei Feng is "a model for the youth of New China." He exists on the same evidence as Comrade Ogilvy and is more likely than not a fictional creation.

As for law, this instrument for the structuring of society is reversed in 1984. In that antiworld, there is no written law, and everything is, or can be, considered a crime at the pleasure of the State. The legal maxim *nulla poena sine lege* is completely reversed. All crimes are comprehended in one crime: thoughtcrime, which involves the religious offense (converted into political terms) of setting up one's will against that of Big Brother, in

"an instant of rebellious pride." Thoughtcrime involves, not forbidden *acts,* but forbidden *thoughts.* The common law, or the civil law, takes no account of thoughts, other than tangentially in the doctrine of *mens rea* in the specific instance of the establishment of degrees of homicide or manslaughter. These regard only acts, while for the Party in a universe whose values are transposed, the act is unimportant; it is the prohibited thought which is the cardinal danger. When Winston confesses to all of the crimes it is possible to commit, including treason and murder, it makes no difference that the confession is objectively false. By willing these acts, he has done them.

If, finally, in *1984,* Orwell was presenting a satiric antiuniverse, with the expressed political intention of alerting democracy to the perils of its only and coming alternative, totalitarianism, what is his norm? It is expressed most straightforwardly in three works: *Down and Out ... , The Road to Wigan Pier,* and a little-known short history which he wrote in haste right after World War II and before *1984,* a *History* of the English people. This last is particularly valuable because it was not colored by the wartime propaganda from which even Orwell was not immune (proving his point about the Two Minutes' Hate and its all-enfolding nature in *1984,* if proof were needed). What is the special thing, he asks, which the English can contribute to the Western world? Simply their outstanding and— "by contemporary standards—highly original quality ... their habit of *not killing one another.*" In other words, he holds up the possibility of communication not by the infliction of pain but by rational discourse.

Orwell's thought, in this same *History,* about the English language adds to what he was to say in *Politics and the English Language* and in the linguistic satire of *1984.* English, he said, is peculiarly subject to jargons. And, as he always did, he made the jump from the quality of language to the morality of politics, concluding that "the temporary decadence of the English language is due, like so much else, to our anachronistic class system." This is, he adds, one of the chief evils resulting "when the educated classes lose touch with the manual workers." And we can foresee, at this juncture, where he will end, for these statements about language touch on his own deep desire to immerse himself in a class other than that "lower upper-middle class" into which he was born. One must have human contact, and the world, if one can no longer communicate through language but only through the infliction of suffering or the enduring of pain, is mad, because embraced pain is madness—or sainthood. For Orwell, it is madness. Orwell desired to communicate without smashing in faces with monkey wrenches, or goosestepping over the prostrate, in a world which he saw as that of an increasing, though at the same time a controlled, madness. It is easy to decry his vision, and, after all, he was desperately ill while writing *1984,* which may have darkened his outlook. But there he is, an honest man at noonday with a candle, searching for his like, seeking rational discourse, and not finding it.

Source: Ralph A. Ranald, "George Orwell and the Mad World: The Anti-Universe of *'1984,'" South Atlantic Quarterly*, Autumn, 1967, pp. 544-53.

Sources

Elaine Hoffman Baruch, "The Golden Country: Sex and Love in *1984,"* in *"1984" Revisited: Totalitarianism in Our Century,* Harper & Row, 1983, pp. 47-56.

Robert Christgau, "Writing for the People," in *The Village Voice,* February 1, 1983, pp. 54–5.

Martin Esslin, "Television and Telescreen," in *On Nineteen Eighty-Four,* edited by Peter Stansky, W. H. Freeman & Co., 1983, pp. 126-38.

Irving Howe, "*1984:* Enigmas of Power," in *1984 Revisited: Totalitarianism in Our Century,* edited by Irving Howe, Harper & Row, 1983, pp. 3-18.

Marcus Smith, "The Wall of Blackness: A Psychological Approach to *1984,"* in *Modern Fiction Studies,* Winter, 1968-69, pp. 42-33.

Ian Watt, "Winston Smith: The Last Humanist," in *On Nineteen Eighty-Four,* W. H. Freeman, 1983, pp. 103-13.

For Further Study

Paul Chilton and Aubrey Crispin, editors, *Nineteen Eighty-Four in 1984,* Comedia Publishing Group, 1983.
  Collection of essays focusing on the relevance of Orwell's novel in contemporary political and social life.

College Literature, Vol. XI, No. 1, 1984, pp. 1-113.
  Issue devoted to studies of *1984.*

Miriam Gross, editor, *The World of George Orwell,* Simon & Schuster, 1972.
  Collection of critical and biographical essays.

Alfred Kazin, "Not One of Us," in *The New York Review of Books,* Vol. XXXI, no. 10, June 14, 1984, pp. 13-4, 16, 18.
  Kazin discusses the political nature of Orwell's novel.

Modern Fiction Studies, Vol. 21, No. 1, Spring 1975, pp. 3-136.
  Issue devoted to Orwell criticism.

Erica Munk, "Love Is Hate: Women and Sex in *1984,"* in *Village Voice,* Vol. XXVIII, No. 5, February 1, 1983, pp. 50-2.
  Munk criticizes Orwell novel for its inattention to the roles (or lack thereof) of women in Oceania.

Norman Podhoretz, "If Orwell Were Alive Today," in *Harper's,* Vol. 266, No. 1592, January, 1983, pp. 30-2, 34-7.
  Podhoretz, using the text of *1984* as evidence, claims Orwell for the neo-conservatives.

Ian Watt, "Winston Smith: The Last Humanist," in *On Nineteen Eighty-Four,* edited by Peter Stansky, W. H. Freeman & Co. 1983, pp. 103-13.
  Watt describes Winston Smith as a humanist and his destruction at the hands of the Party as the destruction of the values of humanism.

George Woodcock, *Remembering Orwell,* edited by Stephen Wadhams, Penguin, 1984.
  Woodcock disagrees with writers such as Podhoretz who claim Orwell for the neo-conservatives, placing him instead in a line of English literary radicals including Jonathan Swift and Charles Dickens.

A Portrait of the Artist as a Young Man

James Joyce

1916

Published in 1916, *A Portrait of the Artist as a Young Man* established its then thirty-two-year-old author, James Joyce, as a leading figure in the international movement known as literary modernism. The title describes the book's subject quite accurately. On one level, *A Portrait of the Artist as a Young Man* can be read as what the Germans call a *Bildungsroman,* or coming-of-age novel.

Set in Ireland in the late nineteenth century, *Portrait* is a semi-autobiographical novel about the education of a young Irishman, Stephen Dedalus, whose background has much in common with Joyce's. Stephen's education includes not only his formal schooling but also his moral, emotional, and intellectual development as he observes and reacts to the world around him. At the center of the story is Stephen's rejection of his Roman Catholic upbringing and his growing confidence as a writer. But the book's significance does not lie only in its portrayal of a sensitive and complex young man or in its use of autobiographical detail. More than this, *Portrait* is Joyce's deliberate attempt to create a new kind of novel that does not rely on conventional narrative techniques.

Rather than telling a story with a coherent plot and a traditional beginning, middle, and end, Joyce presents selected decisive moments in the life of his hero without the kind of transitional material that marked most novels written up to that time. The "portrait" of the title is actually a series of portraits, each showing Stephen at a different stage of development. And, although this story is told in a

third-person narrative, it is filtered through Stephen's consciousness. Finally, the book can be read as Joyce's artistic manifesto and a declaration of independence—independence from what Joyce considered the restrictive social background of Catholic Ireland and from the conventions that had previously governed the novel as a literary genre. More than eighty years after its publication, *A Portrait of the Artist as a Young Man* continues to be regarded as a central text of early twentieth-century modernism.

Author Biography

Joyce was born on February 2, 1882, in Dublin, Ireland. He was the eldest child of John Stanislaus and Mary Jane Murray Joyce, who had, according to Joyce's father, "sixteen or seventeen children." Joyce's upbringing and education had much in common with that of the fictional Stephen Dedalus in *A Portrait of the Artist as a Young Man.* Joyce's parents were devout Catholics, and they sent him to Clongowes Wood College, a Catholic boarding school in County Kildare, south of Dublin. Run by the Jesuit order, this was considered the best Catholic school in Ireland. However, Joyce was taken out of Clongowes Wood a few years later when his father suffered some financial losses and the family's standard of living declined. After his family moved to Dublin, Joyce enrolled at Belvedere College, a Jesuit day school, where he was especially interested in poetry and languages.

By the time he entered University College, Dublin (also a Catholic institution), Joyce had become estranged from the Catholic Church and from Irish society in general. However, Joyce gained the attention of the Irish literary establishment with an undergraduate essay that he wrote on the Norwegian playwright Henrik Ibsen. Joyce was soon introduced to W. B. Yeats, Ireland's greatest poet, but he rejected Yeats's offer of help.

After graduating from University College in 1902, Joyce went to Paris for a year. He was supposed to be studying medicine but spent most of his time reading and writing, and decided to pursue a literary career. He returned to Ireland briefly when his mother became terminally ill. In 1904 he met Nora Barnacle, a young woman from the west of Ireland who worked as a chambermaid at a Dublin hotel. The two became lovers, and in October of that year they left Ireland for good. They first settled in Trieste, Italy, where the multilingual

James Joyce

Joyce taught English at the local Berlitz school and worked on an autobiographical novel titled *Stephen Hero.* Although he did not finish this novel, he later used some of the material from it in *A Portrait of the Artist as a Young Man.*

At the outbreak of World War I in 1914, Joyce and Nora moved to Zurich in Switzerland. (Joyce's most famous comment about the war was that it interfered with the public reception of his first two books.) His collection of short stories, *Dubliners,* was published in London in 1914 after a long dispute with the publisher, Richards. With the help of the American poet Ezra Pound, *A Portrait* was serialized in *The Egoist* magazine in London. It appeared in twenty-five installments from February 1914 to September 1915. Published as a complete book in 1916, the novel established Joyce's reputation as one of the most original authors of his time.

Despite his growing fame, Joyce continued to live in relative poverty. He was also troubled by eye problems—a theme that he touched on in *A Portrait*—and by his daughter Lucia's mental illness. Although he spent most of the rest of his life in Paris and never again lived in Ireland, his subsequent books were all set in Ireland and their characters were Irish. Joyce refined the stream-of-consciousness technique in *Ulysses* (1922), generally considered his most important novel. In *Finnegans Wake* (1939), an extended mythic dream sequence filled with obscure multilingual wordplay, private jokes, and arcane references, the stream-of-consciousness technique completely obliterated any trace of traditional narrative.

Joyce regarded himself as a genius and refused to make any compromises in his writing to achieve commercial success. His difficult personality alienated many people who came into contact with him, but he enjoyed the devotion of Nora, his brother Stanislaus, and a number of close friends and patrons who recognized and helped to nurture his exceptional talent. Since his death in Zurich in 1941, readers, critics, and scholars have continued to study his works. He is regarded today as one of the most important authors of the twentieth century and as a giant of literary modernism.

Plot Summary

The young man eventually becoming an artist in James Joyce's first novel, *A Portrait of the Artist as a Young Man,* is the Irish-born Stephen Dedalus. Set at the turn of the twentieth century, the novel charts Stephen's preschool experience to his university years, from an individual at the mercy of events to a person in control of them and himself.

Childhood and School Years

A Portrait devotes the equivalent of only one page to Stephen's pre-school years. The passage contains simple, childlike sentences skipping from subject to subject like a child's attention diverted from object to object. In this short passage, Joyce alludes on one level to Stephen's cultural, political, and familial influences, on another to Stephen's primal joys and fears, and finally to figures of theme and image recurring throughout the book.

From here, the reader is catapulted several years into the future, to the time when Stephen is a young man away at Clongowes, a Jesuit boarding school. The bulk of this first chapter is devoted to Stephen's development from a fearful and confused boy—twice knocked down by other boys—into a brave, confident student successfully protesting to the rector that he, Stephen, has been unfairly beaten on his palms by a prefect.

The school year is only broken up by Stephen's visit home for Christmas. A sole event from the vacation is imparted: a religious dispute at the family's lavish Christmas dinner. All participants are Catholics who favor Ireland's independence from Britain. But while three men object to the Church's participation in politics, one woman, Dante, believes religious involvement is righteous and that the Church must be followed and respected in all matters. By the end of Chapter One, the reader gleans an early version of Stephen's portrait. He is an Irish-Catholic boy confused about language, politics, and religion. He stumbles and falls through childhood, then picks himself up and stands tall before authority, his peers, and himself.

The Girl with the Shawl

Home in Blackrock for the summer, playing, reading, and daydreaming, Stephen increasingly views himself as different from others. That his family fortunes plummet only worsens matters. Forced to pack up and move with his family to Dublin, Stephen walks around the city—young, foolish, and no longer rich.

After a party he walks with an unnamed girl wearing a shawl to the streetcar. The event passes by without even a kiss, yet the memory remains with Stephen throughout the book. In Stephen's second year at the Dublin Jesuit school Belvedere, he performs in a school production as the girl with the shawl watches. His post-performance euphoria is overwhelming and only after running into town and to the stables can the smell of urine and rotting hay bring him back to earth.

Later, Stephen rides with his father to Cork for an auction of his father's family property. Listening to his father's advice and recalling childhood memories and things old acquaintances say about his father, Stephen is struck dumb at the distance between himself and his father, between himself and his surroundings, and between his present self and his childhood. Stephen feels that he never had what his father did, neither a boyhood of "rude male health nor filial piety." He views himself as cold, detached from life, and lustful, drifting "like the barren shell of the moon."

In the final segment of Chapter Two, Stephen wins money from an essay contest and tries—through gifts and loans—to reconnect himself with loved ones. The scheme fails, however, and Stephen feels even more morosely detached and lustful. One night, looking for connection, he wanders the more "hellish" and grimy streets of Dublin and has sex with a prostitute.

Stephen Sins

Stephen's whoring lies uncomfortably on his mind. At the beginning of Chapter Three, he feels guilty. While remaining convinced of his apartness from others, Stephen is not yet ready to detach himself from the Church, especially from the Virgin Mary, a figure he sees as compassionate. At a Catholic retreat for St. Francis Xavier, students are asked to dwell on "last things": death, judgment, heaven, and hell. After attending sermons on the physical and mental torments of hell, Stephen emerges physically shaken. That evening he awakens from a nightmare and vomits. Finally convinced of the enormity of his sin, Stephen confesses, is relieved, and feels himself joyfully connected with all life, from the muddy Dublin streets to a plateful of sausages. The next morning, fully confessed and kneeling at mass, Stephen readies himself to be reborn.

Chapter Four opens with Stephen's immersion in the rituals of devotion and flesh mortification. He begins to doubt his devotion and humility and is only able to keep his doubts at bay by telling himself that at least he has amended his life. Stephen's display of piety is not lost on the director of Belvedere, who asks Stephen to become a Jesuit priest. Realizing he cannot lead a cloistered life, Stephen arrives home to find that his family will once again be moving, presumably because they are unable to pay the rent.

Next, Stephen is shown agitatedly waiting outside the university while his father likely attends to business connected with Stephen's admission. No longer able to wait, Stephen walks to the beach and reflects that, within him, art, nature, and sensuality are gradually overshadowing religion. There is a sense now of Stephen's increasing isolation amid a sea of humanity.

The Final Chapter

Leaving family and religion behind him, Stephen thinks about his courses, classmates, and his increasing poverty. At the university he casually discusses beauty with a dean, attends physics class, and finally meets friends for a political gathering. At the meeting he refuses to sign a declaration for world peace, perhaps because he suspects the emptiness of the gesture and disrespects the classmates who support it, and further, because over the declaration there is a framed picture of the Russian Czar, a figure Stephen dislikes. Stephen's political independence is driven home in a conversation in which he expresses his distaste for Irish

nationalism. Walking out on politics and into another discussion about beauty and art, Stephen later writes a poem to the shawled girl of ten years ago. One evening he stands watching migrating birds over the library, foretelling of his eventual departure from Ireland. Finally, walking and talking with a friend, Stephen declares his distance from family, nationality.

Characters

Father Arnall

Father Arnall is a Jesuit priest who teaches at Clongowes Wood College, the first school that Stephen Dedalus attends.

Mr. John Casey

Mr. Casey is a friend of Stephen Dedalus's father, Simon Dedalus, in Chapter One. When Mr. Casey visits, young Stephen likes to sit near him and look at "his dark fierce face." Stephen notices that "his dark eyes were never fierce and his slow voice was good to listen to." He gets into the argument with Dante on Christmas, asserting that the Church should stay out of politics and leave Charles Stuart Parnell alone.

Uncle Charles

Charles is Stephen Dedalus's great-uncle. He is present at the family's Christmas dinner in Chapter One but does not take part in the argument. Indeed, he seems somewhat bewildered and only mutters a few vague comments to try to calm things down. Uncle Charles is kindly but slightly eccentric and ineffectual. Later in the chapter readers learn that he has died.

Father Conmee

A Jesuit priest who is the rector (principal) of Clongowes Wood College, the first school that Stephen Dedalus attends. In Chapter One, after Father Dolan pandies Stephen (punishes him by hitting his hands with a stick known as a pandybat), Stephen's friends urge him to go to Father Conmee and report Father Dolan. Although he is afraid to do so, Stephen works up the necessary courage and goes to Father Conmee's room. Although Stephen (and the reader) expects that Father Conmee will react angrily, he in fact receives Stephen in a kindly manner and listens to his complaint sympathetically. Stephen's visit to the rector is his first act of independence and self-determination. Stephen's fa-

Challenging conventions is as much a part of growing up today as it was in the early 1900s.

ther later reveals that Father Conmee has told him about this incident, and that the rector and Father Dolan had a good laugh over it.

Cranly

A friend of Stephen Dedalus at University College, Dublin, Cranly appears in Chapter Five and is one of the four friends who tries to tempt Stephen. The opposite of Davin in many respects, Cranly is sophisticated and irreverent. Stephen finds Cranly's accent and use of language dull; it reminds him of "an echo of the quays of Dublin given back by a bleak decaying seaport" and its energy "an echo of the sacred eloquence of Dublin given back flatly by a Wicklow pulpit." He represents expedience, compromise, and hypocrisy. Beneath his bluster, Stephen also perceives a form of despair in him.

Davin

Davin is a friend of Stephen Dedalus and a student at University College, Dublin. Davin appears in Chapter Five and is one of the four friends who tries to tempt Stephen. He is from the Irish countryside and is described as a peasant. His speech has both "rare phrases of Elizabethan English" and

"quaintly turned versions of Irish idioms." Strong and athletic, Davin is honest, straightforward, and without guile. He calls Stephen "Stevie." In the book, he represents Irish nationalism, a viewpoint that Stephen rejects. Davin is a member of the Gaelic League, an organization that advocates a return to the Irish language and traditional Irish sports.

Dean of Studies

Stephen Dedalus discusses his ideas of art and beauty with the unnamed Dean of Studies at University College, Dublin. The Dean, a Jesuit priest and an Englishman, is kindly and approachable. He also displays a dry sense of humor, remarking that "We have the liberal arts and we have the useful arts." The Dean acknowledges that Stephen is an artist. He tells Stephen that "the object of the artist is the creation of the beautiful. What the beautiful is is another question."

Mrs. Dedalus

Stephen's mother's first name is never given, and although she appears on several occasions she remains a more shadowy character than her husband, Simon Dedalus, Stephen's father. Like most of the other characters, she seems to exist only in relation to Stephen. The character is based largely on Joyce's mother, Mary Jane Murray.

Mr. Simon Dedalus

Simon is Stephen's father. Based on Joyce's own father, John, Mr. Dedalus appears in only a few scenes, but his presence is omnipresent. He is generally portrayed as an amiable man, but there is also a sense of failure about him. He is known as a storyteller. During the novel, Mr. Dedalus suffers some financial misfortune; to save money he has to take Stephen out of Clongowes Wood College and move the family to a smaller house. When he takes Stephen to visit his hometown, Cork, in southwest Ireland, he regales Stephen with tales that Stephen has heard before. In an attempt at a heart-to-heart talk, he advises Stephen to "mix with gentlemen."

As Stephen grows older, he regards his father with some embarrassment and distances himself from the older man. In Chapter Five, while talking to his friend Cranly, Stephen "glibly" describes his father as "a medical student, an oarsman, a tenor, an amateur actor, a shouting politician, a small landlord, a small investor, a drinker, a good fellow, a storyteller, somebody's secretary, something in a distillery, a taxgatherer, a bankrupt, and at present a praiser of his own past." There is the implication that in rejecting Ireland and deciding to pursue a course of creative independence, Stephen is also rejecting his father and his father's failure.

Stephen Dedalus

Stephen Dedalus is the "artist" and "young man" of the title. It is impossible to consider him in the way that a reader would consider most characters in fiction, for his roles goes far beyond that merely of central character. He is the sole focus of the book, and the events of the novel are filtered through his consciousness. His presence is felt on every page.

The character is based largely on Joyce himself. The name "Stephen Dedalus" itself has symbolic significance. Saint Stephen was the first Christian martyr, put to death for professing his beliefs. In Greek mythology, Dedalus was an inventor who escaped from the island of Crete using wings that he had made; however, his son Icarus flew too near the sun, melting the waxen wings and crashing into the sea. From the novel's opening page, it is clear that Stephen is sensitive, perceptive, intelligent, and curious. He also proves to be aloof and at times arrogant and self-important. Moreover, despite his intelligence, he is often the victim of his own self-deception.

Joyce's narrative is not continuous, and there is no "plot" as such. Rather, the book is a series of "portraits" of Stephen at various important moments in his young life, from his introduction as an infant ("baby tuckoo") through selected schoolboy experiences to his declaration of artistic independence as a student at University College, Dublin. The process of Stephen's maturation is registered in his expanding awareness of the world and in the novel's increasingly sophisticated use of language. His relationship to his family, schoolmates, teachers, friends, religion, and country as well as to his own language form the essence of this novel.

In a series of epiphanies and corresponding anti-epiphanies, Stephen alternately affirms and rejects different aspects of his existence. In so doing, he makes difficult moral and aesthetic choices that help to define his character. Perhaps the most telling characterization of him occurs during the episode set in Cork. Here, Joyce describes Stephen as "proud and sensitive and suspicious, battling against the squalor of his life and against the riot of his mind." In the final chapter Stephen confides to his friend Cranly that he will henceforth rely on "the only arms I allow myself to use—silence, ex-

Media Adaptations

- *A Portrait of the Artist as a Young Man* was adapted as a feature film by Judith Rascoe, directed by Joseph Strick, and starring Bosco Hogan, T. P. McKenna, Rosaleen Linehan, John Gielgud, Maureen Potter, Brian Murray, and Luke Johnson, Ulysse, 1979. Available from Howard Mahler. Distributed by Instructional Video.

- The book was also recorded, unabridged, in a series of eight sound cassettes, read by Donal Donnelly. Available from Recorded Books, Prince Frederick, MD, 1991. The publisher's catalogue number is 91106.

ile, and cunning." Given the originality of James Joyce's conception of this character, it is significant to note that the book ends not with Stephen himself but with excerpts from his diary that indicate his intention to "go to encounter for the millionth time the reality of experience and to forge in the smithy of my soul the uncreated conscience of my race."

Father Dolan

Father Dolan is a Jesuit priest who is the prefect of studies at Clongowes Wood College, the first school that Stephen Dedalus attends. He punishes Stephen. Believing he has been punished unfairly, Stephen later goes to see the rector, Father Conmee, and reports this injustice. Father Conmee listens sympathetically and promises that he will speak to Father Dolan. Stephen's defiance of Father Dolan earns him the acclaim of his schoolmates and is seen as his first assertion of his independence. Later in the book, Stephen's father reveals that Father Conmee and Father Dolan had a good laugh over this incident.

Vincent Heron

Heron is a boy who is a friend of Stephen Dedalus and a fellow student at Belvedere College.

The relationship between the boys is uneasy: as two of the top boys at the school, they are as much rivals as friends. There is a disturbing edge to Heron's mockery of Stephen. Heron criticizes Stephen for saying that Byron is the greatest poet of all. Heron and his friends verbally and physically abuse Stephen, but Stephen refuses to give in to Heron's insistence that Tennyson is the best poet. Heron also strikes Stephen twice on the leg with his cane to make him admit that he is interested in a particular girl. Stephen notices that Heron's face is "beaked like a bird's. He had often thought it strange that Vincent Heron had a bird's face as well as a bird's name."

Lynch

Lynch is a friend of Stephen Dedalus and a fellow student at University College, Dublin. Described by Joyce as appearing reptilian, he argues with Stephen about art and aesthetics. In this respect, he represents a foil for Stephen, allowing him (and, by extension, Joyce himself) to expound his own theory of art and beauty. Although he seems to be interested in Stephen's long intellectual talk, Lynch is really unable to appreciate Stephen's ideas or to contribute to the conversation on Stephen's level. Whereas Stephen has high artistic aspirations, Lynch's personal goals are much narrower. He will be satisfied with a job and a conventional life.

Mrs. Dante Riordan

Dante is introduced on the first page of the novel, when she and Uncle Charles applaud young Stephen's dancing. Dante introduces the theme of the Church and politics. Stephen is conscious of the fact that Dante has two brushes: "The brush with the maroon velvet back was for Michael Davitt and the brush with the green velvet back was for Parnell." (The two brushes have symbolic significance.)

Dante later appears at Christmas dinner at the Dedaluses, where she has a furious argument with Mr. Casey. The argument centers around the Church's denunciation of the Irish nationalist politician Charles Stuart Parnell, who had an affair with a married woman, Kitty O'Shea. Dante, a devout Catholic, argues that it was right for the Church to denounce the sinful Parnell, who she calls "a traitor, an adulterer!" She says that the Irish people should submit to the authority of the bishops and priests, even if this means losing a chance for independence. Mr. Casey, who is also a Catholic, bitterly resents the Church's actions in the Parnell case. He argues that the clergy should stay out of politics. The argument escalates, and the chapter ends as Dante flies out of the room in a rage, slamming the door behind her. Stephen does not understand why Dante is against Parnell, but he has heard his father say that she was "a spoiled nun."

Temple

Temple is a friend of Stephen Dedalus at University College, Dublin. Temple appears in Chapter Five and is one of the four friends who tries to tempt Stephen. Described by Joyce as a "gypsy student … with olive skin and lank black hair," he professes to be a socialist and to believe in universal brotherhood, but he does not present a strong intellectual argument for his beliefs. Temple admits that he is "an emotional man…. And I'm proud that I'm an emotionalist."

Eileen Vance

Eileen is the first girl Stephen knows. In his early childhood, Stephen imagines that "when they were grown up he was going to marry Eileen." He particularly notices her "long white hands," which feel cool to his touch and which he likens to ivory. Dante does not want Stephen to play with Eileen because she is a Protestant.

Themes

Consciousness

In literary terms, one of the revolutionary aspects of *A Portrait of the Artist as a Young Man* is the fact that there is no actual plot to the book. Instead, the progress of the novel is organized around the growing consciousness of the central character, Stephen Dedalus. His consciousness of the world around him is an ongoing theme and is developed differently in each of the book's five chapters. He experiences many types and levels of consciousness. Moreover, Joyce uses a highly original "stream-of-consciousness" technique to render Stephen's thoughts and experiences.

Stephen's initial consciousness comes through his five senses, a theme that is introduced on the first page. Here Joyce reports Stephen's awareness of how his father's face looks, how the wet bed feels, the "queer smell" of the oilsheet and the nice smell of his mother. He sings a song and listens to his mother's piano playing.

From the beginning, Stephen is conscious of words as things in themselves. When he goes to Clongowes Wood College, he becomes conscious of what words *mean*—and of the fact that a word can have more than one meaning. Stephen's consciousness of trouble is at first vague—he is not sure what Dante and Mr. Casey are arguing about at the Christmas dinner, but he knows that the situation is unpleasant. He is conscious of impending trouble when Father Dolan enters the classroom and threatens to "pandy" any "idle, lazy" boys. A little later he is also conscious that his father is in trouble of some sort, but he does not know the cause of this trouble.

Stephen develops a consciousness of the opposite sex early in his life, though that consciousness does not translate into conscious action until the end of Chapter Two, when he encounters a prostitute. Subsequently he is troubled by his consciousness of sin. Foremost, however, is his creative consciousness. As the novel progresses, Joyce's language becomes more sophisticated, matching Stephen's growing maturity and understanding. Simultaneously Stephen becomes increasingly conscious of his artistic vocation, until in the last chapter he decides to devote himself entirely to his art, regardless of the consequences to his life.

Artists and Society

As the title indicates, a central theme of the book is the development of the young artist and his relationship to the society in which he lives. The opening sentences of the book show baby Stephen's awareness of language and of the power of the senses. Because the novel is to a large degree autobiographical, it is not only about Stephen's development as a literary artist but also about Joyce's own development. Joyce believed in "art for art's sake," and *A Portrait* reflects this belief. That is, Joyce did not feel that art was supposed to have a practical purpose. It was not the function of the artist to express a political or religious opinion in his or her work, or even to teach the reader about the society in which he or she lived. To the contrary, the artist was to remain aloof from society and devote himself to his art.

For Stephen, as for Joyce, the ability to use the language to create a work of art is its own reward. Stephen is especially sensitive to words and to sensuous phrases, such as "a day of dappled seaborne clouds" and "Madam, I never eat muscatel grapes." He is not so much concerned with what sentences mean as with how they sound and what they sug-

gest. This musical, suggestive quality of his art comes through in the villanelle ("Are you not weary of ardent ways …") that Stephen writes near the end of the book. Because of his artistic temperament, Stephen feels increasingly estranged from society. He considers the vocation of the artist a sort of independent priesthood "of eternal imagination" that ultimately prevents him from serving the Catholic Church, from taking part in politics, and even from participating in ordinary Irish life.

Throughout the book, Stephen records his feelings of being different and distant from his classmates, his siblings, and even his friends. At the end of the novel, Stephen records his artistic manifesto in his diary: "I go to encounter for the millionth time the reality of experience and to forge in the smithy of my soul the uncreated conscience of my race."

Coming of Age

A Portrait of the Artist as a Young Man is not generally considered a "coming of age" novel as such. Joyce intended the book to have a wider scope, and the novel encompasses more than the brief time-scale—often just a single school year or a summer—that usually marks the "coming of age" genre. In Joyce's novel, the chronology spans approximately twenty years, as we follow the central character, Stephen Dedalus, from his very early childhood to his college years. Nonetheless, there are a number of typical "coming of age" elements here. Among them are young Stephen's growing consciousness of self-identity and of family problems, his increasing understanding of the rules that govern the adult world, and, later, his keen awareness of and preoccupation with the mysteries of sex.

God and Religion

Religion—in the form of the teachings of the Roman Catholic Church—forms a major theme of the novel. Indeed, religion was a pervasive force in late nineteenth-century Irish life, the time in which this novel is set. Stephen's first consideration of God occurs early in Chapter One. While looking at his name and address on his geography book, Stephen ponders his place in the world. This stream of consciousness leads him to wonder about the infinity of the universe and about God: "It was very big to think about everything and everywhere. Only God could do that…." He goes on to consider God's name in other languages and the fact that God can understand all languages: "But though there were different names for God in all the dif-

Topics for Further Study

- The Order of Catholic priests that figures in Joyce's novel, the Society of Jesus, is known historically for its schools and colleges. Research the order and its educational philosophy. What is the approach of the Jesuits to teaching and study? In what ways would the Jesuit education that Stephen Dedalus received have differed from a public school education in America today?

- Research the Irish Literary Revival of the late nineteenth and early twentieth centuries. Who were some of the writers in this movement and how did their ideas differ from the literary ideas that Stephen Dedalus expresses?

- Research the Irish Home Rule movement and the role that Charles Stuart Parnell played in that movement. How do Dante's and Mr. Casey's differing attitudes toward Parnell reflect Irish public opinion of the time?

- James Joyce once said that if Dublin was destroyed, people could reconstruct the city from his books. Research the city of Dublin. What are some its famous buildings, sights, and landmarks, and how does Joyce use these places as settings in *A Portrait of the Artist as a Young Man*?

ferent languages in the world and God understood what all the people who prayed said in their different languages, still God remained always the same God and God's real name was God."

The place of religion in Ireland, and the conflict between clerical and secular authority, is the subject of the argument between Dante Riordan and John Casey at Christmas dinner in Chapter One. The argument centers on the Church's treatment of the Irish nationalist politician Charles Stuart Parnell. Parnell, a member of the British Parliament, had led the fight for Home Rule, a form of limited independence for Ireland. However, just as he seemed on the verge of success, he had been named

in a divorce case. (Parnell had been having an affair with a married woman, Kitty O'Shea.) Because of this, the Catholic Church in Ireland denounced Parnell, who was disgraced and who died shortly thereafter. Dante argues that it was right for the Church to denounce the sinful Parnell, saying that the Irish people should submit to the authority of the bishops and priests even if this means losing a chance for independence. Mr. Casey, who is also a Catholic, bitterly resents the Church's actions in the Parnell case. He argues that the clergy should stay out of politics, and says that "We have had too much God in Ireland." Simon Dedalus echoes this argument, calling the Irish "an unfortunate priestridden race…. A priestridden Godforsaken race!"

Stephen is a silent witness to this argument, but he soon becomes embroiled in questions of religion himself. Much of the novel concerns Stephen's relation to his religion, and his ultimate rejection of that religion. Although he finally rejects church authority, Stephen is nonetheless shaped by his Jesuit education and by a powerfully Roman Catholic outlook on life.

In Chapter Four, the unnamed dean asks Stephen to consider becoming a priest. Stephen is tempted by the invitation and imagines himself leading a religious life. He decides not to join the priesthood. He wishes to maintain his independence and does not feel that he can be a part of any organization. His power, he realizes, will come not from his initiation into the priesthood but from devoting himself to his solitary art, even at the cost of losing his family, friends, nation, and God.

Sin

Sin—particularly Stephen's sense of sin, as defined by the Catholic Church—is a major aspect of his awareness of God and religion. Deeply disturbed by the consciousness of his own sin (including masturbation and encounters with prostitutes), Stephen goes to confession. Afterward, absolved of his sins, he is "conscious of an invisible grace pervading and making light his limbs…. He had confessed and God had pardoned him. His soul was made fair and holy once more, holy and happy." He feels that life is simple and beautiful, and that life is spread out before him. For all his efforts, however, Stephen is unable to maintain this kind of life, and he lapses once again.

Style

Narrative

Like many of the novels that precede it, *A Portrait of the Artist as a Young Man* is written in the third person point of view. However, this novel is anything but a traditional third-person narrative. Joyce's narrative voice is utterly unlike the omniscient (all-knowing) narrative voice found in traditional nineteenth-century novels. Earlier novelists such as Charles Dickens and George Eliot concentrated on exterior detail and attempted to give a broad overview both of the action that they were depicting and the society in which it took place. Joyce had no interest in writing this sort of novel. His narrative is narrow and tightly focused; he does not *tell* what is happening but rather tries to *show* what is happening without explaining the events that he is showing.

There is no plot as such in the novel; the narrative is not continuous but fragmented, with gaps in the chronology. The focus is exclusively on the central character, Stephen Dedalus, who is present on virtually every page. Every narrative detail is filtered through Stephen's consciousness. Joyce uses the experimental techniques stream-of-consciousness and interior monologue to let the reader see, hear, and feel what Stephen is experiencing as the action unfolds. One result of this focus on Stephen is that most of the other characters are seen only in relation to him.

In the earlier sections of the novel, Stephen is very young and is not fully aware of the significance of the situations in which he finds himself. Here the narrative mirrors the level of Stephen's intellectual development. For example, at the very beginning of the book, Stephen is a baby or, at the most, a toddler. Thus, Joyce begins the book using a simple vocabulary and imitates the style of a children's story: "Once upon a time and a very good time it was there was a moocow coming down along the road…." A little later in the novel, young Stephen witnesses a political argument during a Christmas dinner. The dialogue of the argument, between Mr. Casey (a friend of Stephen's father) and Stephen's Aunt Dante, is reported without comment. Stephen is not aware of what the argument is about, but he knows that it is disturbing and that it disrupts the harmony of the Christmas dinner. However, Joyce the author knows that readers of his day certainly would have recognized the significance of the argument, which concerns the late Irish nationalist leader Charles Stuart Parnell. *A Portrait of the Artist as a Young Man* is full of this sort of narrative duality: Joyce the author knows what is happening, the reader might know what is happening, but the central character through whom the action unfolds is not always aware of its full significance.

The narrative becomes increasingly sophisticated as Stephen matures. By the last chapter, Chapter Five, Stephen is a student at University College, Dublin. Much of the chapter is taken up with philosophical discussions of art and aesthetics. In several conversations, Stephen explains his ideas, which are based on the ideas of Aristotle and of Thomas Aquinas. Critics have remarked that Stephen's dialogue in this section reads more like a nonfiction philosophy work than like fiction.

Setting

The action of the book takes place in Ireland at the end of the nineteenth century and at the turn of the twentieth century, a span of about twenty years. Although Joyce gives specific settings for the incidents in the book, he does not give dates for the events that he is reporting. However, critics know that the events of Stephen Dedalus's life mirror events in Joyce's own childhood and young adulthood.

Specific settings include various Dedalus homes (the first outside Dublin and later ones in the city), the schools that Stephen attends (Clongowes Wood College in County Kildare and Belvedere School in Dublin), the chapel where Father Arnall delivers his fiery sermon, and, later in the book, University College, Dublin. Stephen also visits the city of Cork in southwest Ireland with his father. Both indoor and outdoor settings are used.

Regardless of the specific setting of any scene in *A Portrait of the Artist as a Young Man,* Joyce gives a minimum of external description. He is more concerned with the state of mind of his main character, Stephen Dedalus, than with the external circumstances of Stephen's situation. Yet without giving lengthy descriptions of a classroom, for example, Joyce is able to create the atmosphere of a school.

Joyce himself was a Dubliner by birth and upbringing. He does not evoke the city of Dublin in as much detail here as in his earlier short story collection *Dubliners* or in his later novels *Ulysses* and *Finnegans Wake.* Nonetheless, in *A Portrait,* Dublin is prominent both as a physical city and as a symbol of the center of Irish consciousness. In any case, whether he is writing about Stephen's life at school, at home, or at large in Dublin or in particular neighborhoods elsewhere in Ireland, Joyce's larger subject is always Ireland—a subject that he renders in an ambivalent stance.

Structure

A Portrait of the Artist is divided into five chapters. Each chapter deals with a different period in the first twenty years of the central character, Stephen Dedalus. Each also addresses a specific theme related to Stephen's development as an artist.

Chapter One takes Stephen from his infancy into his first years at school. In this chapter, Stephen becomes aware of the five senses and of language itself, and he takes the first steps to assert his independence. Chapter Two includes his awareness of his family's declining fortunes and his move from Clongowes Wood School to Belvedere School in Dublin. It ends with his sexual initiation in the arms of a prostitute. In the third chapter, Stephen is preoccupied with his sin and the possible consequences of his sin. The fourth chapter takes place at Belvedere School. Stephen attempts to understand the precepts of his religion and to lead a life in accordance with those precepts. However, he recognizes that his independent nature will not allow him to serve as a priest of the Church. Instead, he will become an artist, a "priest of eternal imagination." In Chapter Four, Stephen takes further steps to formulate his aesthetic theory. He also makes a final declaration of independence from his friends, his family, his religion, and his country.

Within each chapter there are several distinct, self-contained scenes or episodes. These episodes are, in effect, "portraits." Each episode centers around or culminates in an epiphany—a moment of euphoric insight and understanding that significantly contributes to Stephen's personal education. The epiphany often occurs during an otherwise trivial incident, and is the central organizing feature in Joyce's work. However, these epiphanies are undercut by "anti-epiphanies"—moments of disillusion or disappointment that bring Stephen back to earth. Each shift between epiphany and anti-epiphany is accompanied by a shift in the tone of Joyce's language. The epiphany scenes are generally written in a poetic and lofty language. By contrast, the language in the anti-epiphany scenes emphasizes less noble aspects of life. Taken together, Joyce uses the give-and-take shift between epiphany and anti-epiphany to show the paradoxes of life.

Punctuation

The author's punctuation is not normally an issue in a discussion of a work of fiction. Up until Joyce, most English-language novelists used standard punctuation. As part of his effort to create an entirely new type of novel, however, Joyce employed unusual punctuation. Immediately noticeable in *Portrait* is the fact that there are no quotation marks. Instead, Joyce uses a long dash at the beginning of a paragraph where he wishes to indicate speech by a character. (One effect of this technique is that the reader is not immediately able to tell what portions of a paragraph might be part of the narrative apparatus rather than the speaking voice of a particular character.) Joyce is also sparing in his use of commas. Many of his longer sentences appear to be "run-on" sentences. He does this deliberately to show the "run-on" nature of a character's thoughts—a technique known as the "stream of consciousness."

Symbolism

Critics have remarked on Joyce's unique combination of realism and naturalism on the one hand and symbolism on the other. Joyce's realistic and naturalistic approaches are evident in his pretense that he is presenting things as they are. At the same time, he uses symbolism extensively to suggest what things mean.

The five senses—sight, sound, taste, smell, touch—are recurrent symbols throughout *A Portrait of the Artist as a Young Man.* Stephen's reliance on the five senses is signaled in the book's first few pages. Here we are made aware of the way his father looks to Stephen (sight), the songs that are sung to him and the clapping of Uncle Charles and Dante (sound), the feeling when he wets the bed (touch), and the reward of a "cachou" (cashew—taste) from Dante. Joyce considered the five senses to be indispensible tools for the literary artist. Of these, the sense of sight is most prominent. The importance of sight—and its fragility—is a recurring motif throughout the novel. This reliance on, and fear for, sight is embodied in the phrase "the eagles will come and pull out his eyes," which Dante says to Stephen after his mother tells him to apologize for something. Stephen makes a rhyme, "pull out his eyes / Apologise." (Significantly, Joyce suffered from eye problems later in his life, and was to undergo several eye operations.) At various points in the novel, Stephen refuses to apologize for his actions and decisions, even at the risk of perhaps losing his vision, metaphorically. For example, in Chapter One he listens to Mr.

Casey's anecdote about spitting in a woman's eye. At Clongowes school, Father Dolan punishes Stephen for having broken his glasses. In Chapter Four, Stephen attempts a mortification of the senses to repent for his earlier sins.

Religious symbols abound. There are numerous references to various elements and rites of Roman Catholicism: the priest's soutane, the censor, and the sacraments of communion and confession. Bird symbolism is prominent too. In addition to the eagles mentioned above, there is Stephen's school friend and rival Heron, who is associated with the "birds of prey." Stephen later thinks of himself as a "hawklike man," a patient and solitary bird who can view society from a great height but who remains aloof from the world that he views.

Historical Context

Joyce's Ireland: The Historical and Political Context

A Portrait of the Artist as a Young Man is set in Ireland in the late nineteenth century and at the very beginning of the twentieth century. Joyce does not give precise dates in the narrative, but there is a reference to at least one historical event (the fall of Parnell) that helps to date the action. Moreover, critics agree that the incidents in the life of Stephen Dedalus, the "young man" of the title, closely parallel incidents in the life of Joyce himself. (In 1904, Joyce wrote an autobiographical essay titled "A Portrait of the Artist.") Joyce was born in 1882 and graduated from University College, Dublin, in 1902. These years approximately form the parameters of the novel.

Joyce grew up in an Ireland that constitutionally was a part of a nation formally known as the United Kingdom of Great Britain and Ireland. Located just to the west of the island of Great Britain, Ireland had its own distinctive customs and culture. Most significantly, while Protestantism was the predominant religion in Great Britain, most native Irish people were Roman Catholics. However, both politically and economically, Ireland had long been dominated by Britain.

This dominant British presence in Ireland went back to the middle ages, when Norman knights from England first arrived in Ireland at the invitation of local Irish chieftains. The British presence in Ireland grew over the next few hundred years, for a variety of reasons. During the reign in Eng-

land of Queen Elizabeth I (1558-1603), British settlers (mainly from Scotland) went to Ireland and suppressed local Irish resistance. In the mid-1600s, British rule of Ireland was further consolidated by the English Parliamentary leader Oliver Cromwell, whose army scoured the Irish countryside. Cromwell drove many thousands of native Irish from their land and persecuted Irish Catholics. The Roman Catholic Church was outlawed in 1695, but Catholic priests continued to practice underground.

Periodically, Irish factions rebelled against British rule, but these rebellions (notably one in 1798) were easily put down. (Ironically, many of the leaders of these Irish nationalist movements were Irish Protestants who were descended from earlier British settlers.) In 1800 the Irish parliament in Dublin was dissolved, and the two countries were joined under a single government headquartered in London. Nonetheless, despite British persecution of the native Irish, a distinctive Irish identity remained strong. By the late nineteenth century many Irish people aspired to a form of limited Irish independence known as Home Rule.

The Great Famine of the 1840s saw the deaths or emigration of some several million Irish men, women, and children—more than half the total population of Ireland at the time. However, this period proved a turning point in the Irish struggle for self-determination. In 1879 a Catholic nationalist named Michael Davitt formed the Irish National Land League, which agitated for rights for the Irish Catholic tenants of Protestant-owned land. Davitt is mentioned in *A Portrait of the Artist as a Young Man,* along with Charles Stuart Parnell.

The action of *A Portrait* occurs some time after the activities of Davitt and the downfall of Parnell. However, in the novel the memory of Parnell is still strong. Joyce, an individualist, was disturbed both by Ireland's nationalist politics and the strict doctrine of the Catholic Church. He regarded himself as a cosmopolitan, a citizen of Europe if not of the world. This is made very clear in the final chapter of *A Portrait,* in which Stephen Dedalus declares his intention to fly past the nets of "nationality, religion, language." Nonetheless, like Stephen himself, Joyce was very much shaped by the history and religion of his country. Ironically, the Irish nationalist uprising that eventually led to Irish independence occurred in 1916, the very year in which *A Portrait* was published in England. By this time, Joyce was living in Zurich.

Compare
&
Contrast

- **1880s-1910s:** The entire island of Ireland is part of the United Kingdom of Great Britain and Ireland. Ireland does not have its own government, but Irish representatives are elected to the British Parliament in London.

  Today: The independent Republic Ireland, comprised of 26 Irish counties, has its own government in Dublin. The six counties of Northern Ireland remain affiliated with the United Kingdom and send representatives to the Parliament in London.

- **1880s-1910s:** The majority of Irish people belong to the Roman Catholic Church, which has a strong influence on most of the population. However, most of the leading writers, landowners, and political figures in Ireland belong to the Church of Ireland, a Protestant denomination related to the Church of England.

  Today: Roman Catholicism is the predominant religion in the Republic of Ireland, with ninety-five percent of the population considered Catholic. Virtually all Irish political leaders are Catholics. However, the Church's influence on Irish society is less strong than in the past.

- **1880s-1910s:** A large number of educated people, including James Joyce himself, emigrate abroad in search of greater economic and cultural opportunities.

  Today: Irish emigration rates remained high for most of the twentieth century. However, by the 1990s, authorities report that many young educated Irish who had moved abroad are returning to Ireland, attracted by a vibrant economy and an interesting cultural life.

- **1916:** A small group of Irish nationalists seizes the main post office in Dublin and proclaims Ireland an independent republic. British troops quickly crush the revolt and fifteen revolutionary leaders are executed. However, support for independence grows; in 1922 the twenty-six southern counties of Ireland gain self-government as the Irish Free State. The majority of voters in the six northern counties—Northern Ireland—vote to remain part of the United Kingdom.

  Today: Members of the outlawed IRA (Irish Republican Army) carry out intermittent attacks against British troops and pro-British Protestant citizens in Northern Ireland, as well as terrorist bombings in England. However, the majority of Irish people, both Catholics and Protestants, favor a peaceful solution to the problems in Northern Ireland.

Joyce's Ireland: The Literary Context

By the time Joyce made his mark as a writer, Ireland already had a long and distinguished literary history. During the so-called Dark Ages, Irish monks helped preserve classical learning, copying classical texts in beautiful manuscripts. Poets were greatly esteemed and held high positions in the courts of Irish kings. During the long period of British domination, some of the finest writers in the English language were Anglo-Irish (that is, Irish of British descent). Among these were the poet and satirist Jonathan Swift (1667-1745), who served as dean of St. Patrick's Cathedral in Dublin; the poet and prose writer Oliver Goldsmith (1730?-1774); the statesman and political philosopher Edmund Burke (1729-1797); the lyricist Thomas Moore (1779-1852); the novelist Maria Edgeworth (1768-1849); and the comic writers Somerville and Ross (pen name of Edith Somerville, 1858-1949, and Violet Martin, 1862-1915), whose stories chronicled the chaotic lives of Anglo-Irish landlords and their servants and tenants in the "big houses" of rural Ireland.

By the mid-1800s, however, sentimental stories and ballads of no great literary merit were the norm. The late 1800s and early 1900s—the time frame during which *A Portrait* is set—saw a movement known as the Irish Literary Revival. Leading writers in this movement were Douglas Hyde (1860-1949, founder of the Gaelic League), Lady Augusta Gregory (1852-1932), and the playwright John Millington Synge (1871-1909). Unquestionably the central figure in this group was the poet and dramatist William Butler Yeats (1865-1939). Almost single-handedly Yeats created a new Irish literature. By the time Joyce was an undergraduate student at University College, Dublin, Yeats was the most famous living Irish writer. However, the work of Yeats and his associates made much use of Irish themes and subjects drawn from Irish folklore and mythology.

Joyce, on the other hand, had discovered the work of French writers and of the Norwegian playwright Henrik Ibsen. Stephen Dedalus's statements in Chapter Five of *A Portrait* suggest that Joyce had already decided to reject the celebration of Irish nationalism as a literary theme. When the young Joyce was introduced to Yeats, he told Yeats that the poet was already too old to help him. Rather than write about ancient heroes and legends, Joyce wanted to chronicle the lives of ordinary people in his early fiction.

There is another notable difference between Joyce and his best-known predecessors. At a time when Protestants dominated the cultural institutions of Ireland, Joyce was the first major Irish Catholic writer. Even though he himself rejected Roman Catholicism—a process that is detailed in *A Portrait of the Artist as a Young Man*—he made his religious background an integral aspect of this novel. And although he wrote brilliantly in the English language, Joyce was keenly aware that he wrote in the language of Ireland's conquerors.

Critical Overview

A Portrait of the Artist as a Young Man attracted much attention when it was published, and also caused controversy. The book was widely reviewed in Europe and the United States. The most enthusiastic reactions came from other leading novelists and intellectuals of the period, who acclaimed it as a work of genius. However, not all early critics agreed on the book's merits. Rather than praising its originality, some critics denounced the work as formless or as blasphemous and obscene.

The English novelist H. G. Wells reviewed the book in 1917, the year after its publication. Writing in the *New Republic,* Wells called it "by far the

A young artist painting postcards, 1917.

most living and convincing picture that exists of an Irish Catholic upbringing. It is a mosaic of jagged fragments that ... [renders] with extreme completeness the growth of a rather secretive, imaginative boy in Dublin." Wells went on to remark that "one believes in Stephen Dedalus as one believes in few characters in literature." However, Wells was also disturbed by Joyce's references to sex and bodily functions. Like many critics of the time, Wells felt that these subjects were best left out of a serious work of literature. Joyce, he said, "would bring back into the general picture of life aspects which modern drainage and modern decorum have taken out of ordinary intercourse and conversation."

Other critics were more blunt and more scathing in their attacks on the novel. An anonymous reviewer in *Everyman* called the book "garbage" and said that "we feel that Mr. Joyce would be at his best in a treatise on drains." Some of the reviews in Ireland were particularly harsh. A reviewer for the *Irish Book Lover* warned that "no clean-minded person could possibly allow it to remain within reach of his wife, his sons or daughters." The reviewer for the British newspaper the *Manchester Guardian* was more receptive, saying that "When one recognizes genius in a book one had perhaps best leave criticism alone."

The distinguished British novelist Ford Madox Ford admired the book for its stylistic excellence. In a 1922 review of Joyce's next novel, *Ulysses,* he paid tribute to *A Portrait of the Artist as a Young Man.* He called it "a book of such beauty of writing, such clarity of perception, such a serene love of and interest in life, and such charity...."

The book's impact continued to be felt in Ireland long after Joyce's death. Although the Catholic Church disapproved, important Irish writers saw it as the first great Irish novel of the twentieth century. In 1955, the short-story writer Sean O'Faolain remarked that "this autobiographical-imaginative record [is] so mesmeric, so hypnotic a book that I can never speak of it to young readers without murmuring, *Enter these enchanted woods ye who dare....*"

In the decades since its publication, *A Portrait of a Artist as a Young Man* has continued to receive the attention of many scholars and critics. It has perhaps suffered in comparison with *Ulysses,* which critics generally regard as a much richer, more ambitious, and more complex novel. For example, Joyce's biographer Richard Ellmann devoted an entire book (*Ulysses on the Liffey*) to *Ulysses* but had noticeably less to say about *A Portrait.*

The Oxford don J. I. M. Stewart (better known as the author of detective novels under the pseudonym Michael Innes) appreciated Joyce's command of language and imaginative brilliance in *A Portrait,* but felt that the result was uneven. According to Stewart, "Stephen Dedalus is presented to us with a hitherto unexampled intimacy and immediacy." However, Stewart found that this was "achieved at some cost to the vitality of the book as a whole." Because the narrative focuses exclusively on Stephen's thoughts, the reader is "locked up firmly inside Stephen's head." As a result, Stewart says, "There are times when when we feel like shouting to be let out." Also, because the central character "is aware of other people only as they affect his own interior chemistry, there is often something rather shadowy about the remaining personages in the book."

Hugh Kenner has pointed out that the opening pages of the novel attempt to do something that has never been done before. The author does not guide the reader in understanding the narrative, but leaves the reader to work things out for himself or herself. Kenner sums up the book's impact on literary history, saying that after this novel, "Fiction in English would never be the same."

Criticism

Jhan Hochman

Hochman, who teaches at Portland Community College, analyzes whether Joyce's hero should be viewed as either serious or absurd, and he discusses references to Greek mythology in the book.

James Joyce's first published novel, *A Portrait of the Artist as a Young Man* (1916), recounts Stephen Dedalus's struggle to understand and then break free of family, church, and country. The journey of this representative young artist is a growing apart or wrenching away from increasingly imprisoning influences, in Stephen's case, from an economically impoverished home, a theologically impoverished Catholic Church, and the politically impoverished nationalism of Irish independence. Crucial here is that familial, religious, and national "railings" that first fascinate and guide the child increasingly become "bars" that imprison the adult. The task of the artist, then, is to break free of these constraints and from their bars forge new and better formations. The artist will create not only the guideposts and protective railings of the future, but in the process will likely have to sacrifice his well-being and perhaps a bit of his sanity as well. For Joyce, the image of the artist apart conjures up ambivalence, specifically, excitement alternating with dread.

At the beginning of *A Portrait of the Artist,* Stephen is not only a very young child, an "object" protected and guided, but an object in a story, a character (baby tuckoo) "written" in by his father's narration. Stephen is the near-opposite of a man apart—he is the very young child whose story is being created by another. Stephen is at once both a child shaped by his parents and a character embedded in a story he didn't create, a combination producing an object who is anything but apart. Later, at home and in Catholic school, Stephen is either speechless (at Christmas dinner) or victimized (knocked down by schoolmates and beaten on the palms by a prefect). Stephen's only independence revolves around his sensitivities to words ("belt," "iss," "suck") and stimuli, especially temperature, moisture, and smell.

By the end of Chapter One, however, Stephen commits his first real act of independence: he protests his palm-whipping. At the end of Chapter Two, the increasing apartness Stephen feels as the result of his family's sudden poverty and his sensibilities—which separate him from his father and his surroundings—culminates in his "French kiss"

What Do I Read Next?

- *Dubliners* is James Joyce's first published book of fiction. It is a collection of fifteen short stories about ordinary characters in Dublin in the late-nineteenth and early-twentieth centuries. The themes are childhood, adolescence, maturity, and old age. Some of the stories first appeared in an Irish magazine in 1904, under the pseudonym "Stephen Dedalus." The last and most famous story, "The Dead," was finished in 1907, but publication of the book was delayed until 1914.

- The character Stephen Dedalus also appears in Joyce's 1922 novel, *Ulysses,* a classic of literary modernism. The action is set in a single day, June 16, 1904 (the date on which Joyce met his future wife, Nora Barnacle). The story follows Stephen, a newspaper advertising salesman named Leopold Bloom, and Bloom's wife Molly as they go about their business in Dublin. This elaborately structured novel parallels Homer's classic epic *The Odyssey.* Each chapter is written in a different prose style, and Joyce makes much use of the stream-of-consciousness technique.

- *The Country Girls,* published in 1960, is the first novel by Edna O'Brien, Ireland's most famous female writer. Two girls leave their homes in the Irish countryside and go to Dublin to escape their strict Catholic upbringing and seek excitement. Because of its feminist viewpoint and frank treatment of adolescent female sexuality, this book caused much controversy when it was published.

- *Fools of Fortune* (1983), by William Trevor, is about a doomed love affair during the Irish civil war as seen through the eyes of a young boy. Born in Ireland in 1928, Trevor is considered one of the finest Irish writers of his time and is particularly known for his poignant short stories.

- Christopher Nolan's *Under the Eye of the Clock* (1987) is a remarkable autobiography by a young Dubliner who is severely physically disabled and unable to speak. Nolan overcame great obstacles to write a book that critics have compared to the work of Joyce.

- Richard Ellmann's *James Joyce* (1959, revised 1982) is the definitive biography of this author.

- For a different view of Joyce's life in Europe, read *Nora: The Real Life of Molly Bloom,* by Brenda Maddox. Published in 1988, this book shows how Nora Barnacle helped Joyce as he struggled to create great literature in the face of economic and personal hardship.

- *The Oxford Illustrated History of Ireland,* edited by R. F. Foster and published in 1989, is a good introduction to Irish history. Chapter Six, "Irish Literature and Irish History," by Declan Kiberd, provides a useful survey of Irish writers and their relationship to the culture from which they sprung. Among the many interesting pictures is a photograph of James Joyce at the piano.

---

with a prostitute, the prelude to a period of whoring that would seem to break his ties to Catholicism. The social apartness created by Stephen's whoring is less a creative, artistic separation than a destructive, uncreative separation, a mere rebellion. Therefore, in Chapter Three, Stephen gradually regrets his falling away from the Church until, at the end, he not only confesses but readies himself for the Host. In this chapter, Joyce creates, after a gradual slope toward the heights of separation, a fall: this physically central chapter of the book is a loss of Stephen's momentum toward apartness, a reversal, a device to create audience conflict and make final victory more sweet: the reader, cheering Stephen on toward separation, wonders, "Can he do it, can he really break free?"

Joyce keeps reader conflict alive as Stephen decides to mortify his flesh and devote himself to prayer. But Stephen's movement toward separateness cannot, of course, be stopped: interior apartness is manifested when Stephen declines an offer to join the Jesuits; exterior apartness is forced on him when his family must move because they cannot pay the rent. Later, Stephen wanders alone on the beach meditating on his apartness from immature peers and staring at multiple figurings of his solitude: little islands of sand amidst the sea; the moon as a body detached from earth, solitary in the evening sky; a hawklike man confused for a god.

Chapter Five cuts once and for all Stephen's ties to family, religion, and nation. Leaving the house, Stephen figuratively leaves behind the economic and spiritual poverty that make him feel apart. Then he asserts his interior solitude. Arriving at the Catholic university, he scorns a dean for his cloistered lifelessness, attends a boring physics class with cobwebbed windows and a droning professor, and denounces a political gathering for its unthinking worship of hero and nation. In conversations with friends, and in a poem he writes to the shawled girl, E. C., or Emma Clery (fully named in *Stephen Hero,* Joyce's first and only unpublished novel from which *A Portrait of the Artist* was taken), Stephen asserts aesthetic independence. Finally, Stephen asserts his independence from nation when he tells Cranly he will leave Ireland. Here then, is a heroic odyssey into apartness, one ending far from its beginning: from a character (baby tuckoo) in someone else's story and real life drama (his family's) to, at the end of the book, Stephen's diary entries, those solitary, mini-narratives, where others become, for Stephen, characters in *his* story. Stephen traverses the distance from a character inextricably interconnected to a creator apart.

A recurring debate in Joyce criticism concerns this issue of Stephen's heroism. The question is whether Stephen's journey from character in a story to the creator of stories is heroic. Joyce's brother, Stanislaus, regarded the title he invented, *Stephen Hero,* as deliberately ridiculous. Wayne Booth states and asks, "The young man takes himself and his flight with deadly solemnity. Should we?" F. Parvin Sharpless answers, "Joyce's classicism sees all aspects of human life as meaningful and absurd at the same time. This is true even of things which he might be expected to value most: the creative process of the literary artist." While Sharpless's answer is a good one, it might be better if Booth's question were broken into two more specific questions. First, Is Stephen an exciting victor or a tragic loser? Second, Is Stephen a serious or absurd figure?

Searching for an answer to the winner/loser question, readers can look back to the last name Stanislaus Joyce invented for Stephen, "Dedalus."

Daedalus, "Old father, old artificer" as Stephen calls him in the last line of the book, was a mythical Greek figure whose name means "cunning craftsman." Recall here Stephen's declaration: "I will try to express myself in some mode of life or art as freely as I can and as wholly as I can, using for my defence the only arms I allow myself to use—silence, exile, and *cunning.*" Daedulus is an ambivalent figure. A renowned sculptor and engineer, he apprenticed his nephew, Talos, but pushed him off a cliff when Talos proved a greater genius than Daedulus and when it was discovered Talos was having incestuous relations with his own mother, Daedulus's sister. Daedulus also built several ambivalent devices. First, a hollow wooden cow so King Minos's wife Pasiphae could have sex with a magnificent white bull. Second, the labyrinth, which kept in the half-man/half-bull minotaur (the monstrous product of the coupling mentioned above) but also kept his food—humans—from getting out. Finally, Daedulus created the famous wax wings that melted and caused Icarus's fall.

In summary, Daedulus, the mythic character on which Joyce builds his novel's character, is not just skillful but deceitful or *cunning.* Further his devices are ambivalent, both good and bad. The depiction of Daedulus, and other artificers in mythology, points to the idea that human creation and creations have their price, their *down* side, just as valued knowledge of good and evil produced its price: the Fall from the Garden of Eden.

The reader should also recall the Latin epigraph (opening quotation) from *Portrait of the Artist* that Joyce borrowed from Ovid's *Metamorphoses.* Here is a translation: "And [Daedulus] altered/improved the laws of nature," written in the context of constructing the waxy wings. The figure of the great artist and grand artificer are myths still having purchase on the present, on the role of the artist, but especially for our own times, on the ambivalent state of technology: that all creations are ambivalent, not only in their effects upon their creators, but upon nature and humanity. The artist, then, is both hero and, like Daedulus, Icarus and Talos, victims who when approaching too close to the gods or the "laws" of nature, must either be punished or sacrificed. This is key to understanding Stephen's friends calling him "Bous Stephanomenos" and "Bous Stephanoforos." As Ernest Bernhardt-Kabisch explains, *Bous* is Greek for bull. *Foros* is the bull as powerful victor and *menos* is the bull as sacrificed animal. Stephen, as artist, is this bull, an ambivalent symbol of powerful victor and tragic victim.

While the bull symbol still has application to the pagan bullfight, it has largely been replaced by the Christian symbol of a meek sacrificial lamb. The lamb may have less magical ambivalence because it is not both strong and weak, but it does have greater application to the more common defeat of the weaker by the stronger. Armed with all of this classical mythology, it should be clearer why Stephen has been represented as a bull rather than a lamb: he is strong, or resolved, and un-Christian; further he is becoming a pagan, a lover of nature, the senses, and experience.

Now to the question of whether Stephen is absurd or serious, which may, in turn, be broken down into multiple specific questions. Here are just three of many that could have been asked. Is the recently self-excommunicated Stephen absurdly selfish or uncompromisingly principled when he refuses to do his "easter duty" for his mother? Is Stephen's villanelle to be taken by readers as an adolescent poem or a serious work of art? Is Stephen's own association with Daedulus, including the line, "I go to encounter for the millionth time the reality of experience and to forge in the smithy of my soul the uncreated conscience of my race," to be looked on as the product of foolish youth, or as an inspiring declaration. There is little doubt that Stephen views his principles, artistic output, and philosophy as serious. But, echoing Booth, should we? This is a far more difficult question than whether Stephen is a winner or loser for this answer depends far more on taste. While Joyce, as I hope I have shown, furnishes ample and hard hints that Stephen is both winner *and* loser, Joyce does not tell the reader what his—Joyce's—tastes are.

Some might sympathize with Stephen's principled rejection of his "easter duty" feeling that his mother will get over it. And some of us might like Stephen's anti-love poem which combines images of mother, Virgin, and Emma Clery; womb and mind; gestation and artistic creation; the child, the poem, the art object; religious devotion, sexual attraction, and self-sacrifice. But others might view the poem and its creation as elementary. But there is still the question of whether we readers should regard Stephen's most famous declaration above as absurd or serious. In other words, should we understand this line as an example of childish megalomania, hubris, and youthful pride bound for an adult fall? Or is this serious stuff, the artist as smith

of a new conscience, new ethics, a new way of seeing and understanding the world?

Perhaps this question can have no answer, since we cannot know what Joyce meant here (unless it is stated somewhere clearly in his letters). Without evidence we must decide for ourselves. Perhaps it is just as well. Even if we interpret Stephen as a selfish and foolish youth, it is less the rightness or wrongness of his struggle that is at issue than depicting the struggle itself. And, after all, if Stephen is selfish and foolish, this is, after all, a portrait of a *young* man, not a mature one. Had Stephen's principles, poems, and aesthetic philosophy been mature and fully formed, these would not have belonged to the realist portrait of a *young* man.

Whether or not one likes the way Stephen handles his struggle, it does show the effects of the battle fought by anyone refusing to act on certain received ideas or act out particular received practices: ostracism, loneliness, self-doubt, and conversely, intolerance, selfishness, hubris. In many ways, Joyce knew these problems as his own. Should readers fault either Joyce or Stephen—or both—if they deem Stephen's principles selfish, his poem adolescent, and his declaration overblown? Or should they credit Joyce for a realistic portrait of youth? As answering involves knowing the thoughts of Joyce, perhaps it is better to shift focus from mere evaluation of talent toward his work's effect on the world. Perhaps we might say the following: If Stephen and Joyce can be faulted for anything, it is far less for what they said and did than what they didn't say or do. That is, in *Portrait of the Artist* both concentrated almost exclusively on how the artist, him or herself, must suffer and be sacrificed for freedom. On the other hand, precious little in *Portrait of the Artist* indicated how the artist's "alteration or improvement of nature," as Ovid put it in Joyce's epigraph, impacts upon the world.

Source: Jhan Hochman, in an essay for *Novels for Students*, Gale, 1999.

William O'Neill

In the excerpt below, O'Neill illustrates how Joyce's understanding, appreciation, and use of myth in forming one's identity is revealed in A Portrait of the Artist as a Young Man.

The Literary Revival of turn-of-the-century Dublin was much concerned with expressing Irish aspirations through heroes. Finn and Cuchullain supplied imaginatively what Ireland had not been able to achieve in reality: an Irish hero who vanquished all foes. Joyce's contempt for this form of self-consolation is well documented. In his broadside "The Holy Office" he parodies Yeats as he declares that he, Joyce, "must not accounted be / One of that mumming company." Stephen of *Stephen Hero* devotes much energy to debunking the Revival. What is perhaps less well known is that Joyce's initial contempt gave way to a profound understanding of the psychology of the Revival and of the uses of myth in the creation of identity....

The English, having been their own masters for centuries, have created many models of the successful life; the Irish, being colonials, have been unable to do so. As with American blacks and Indians, subjection to a foreign culture has destroyed all authority figures in the society.

This latter point is, I think, the theme of the first episode of *A Portrait*. The novel begins with the beginning of a children's story, a moocow coming down along the road and meeting a nicens little boy, Stephen. The little boy, who will grow up to become the "bullock befriending bard," learns as he grows older to associate cows with mothers and with mother Ireland. And what comes down along the road and meets Stephen in the early part of the novel is his nationality. He goes off to Clongowes to find that his father is not as important as the other fathers.

—What is your father?

Stephen had answered:

—A gentleman.

Then Nasty Roche had asked:

—Is he a magistrate?

Lesson: the civil officers of the English government are the important people in Ireland. He learns the Story of Hamilton Rowan, who used the only strategy available to him, silence, exile, and cunning, to escape English captivity. Lesson: Irish heroes are not conquerors, but people who cope cleverly with being conquered. He gets shouldered into the square ditch. Lesson: the small and the weak must develop cunning or must suffer.

He summarizes the lessons he has learned on the flyleaf of his geography book:

Stephen Dedalus

Class of Elements
Clongowes Wood College
Sallins
County Kildare
Ireland

Europe
The World
The Universe

For now, at least, he is defined by his place. His mind will be formed by the experience of this place. And the process of formation is what we are reading: the narrative style of this section is that of a young boy's internal voice explaining the salient features to himself:

That was the way a rat felt, slimy and damp and cold. Every rat had two eyes to look out of. Sleek slimy coats, little little feet tucked up to jump, black shiny eyes to look out of. They could understand how to jump. But the minds of rats could not understand trigonometry. When they were dead they lay on their sides. Their coats dried then. They were only dead things.

Unlike the internal voice of Maria in the story "Clay," which helps her exclude anything which might endanger her rather fragile idea of who she is, Stephen's voice, like Leopold Bloom's, actively explores his world and comes to conclusions about world and self that are scrupulously tentative. It is this scientific approach which will eventually enable him to see his personal myths and those of his culture for what they are: an imaginative accommodation of subject status to the creation of a significant self.

Stephen's education in the effects of colonial status is also the theme of the Christmas dinner episode which follows. The real tragedy of the fight between Dante and the two men, Mr. Casey and Simon Dedalus, is not that the family does not get along, but that their ideas of themselves have been formed entirely by the institutions that govern them. Their powerless rage succeeds only in spoiling the dinner, and is capped by Mr. Casey's tale of spitting in a woman's eye, and Dante's boast of the church's role in killing Parnell. Injustice of the conqueror begets the meaner injustice of the conquered. This Christmas dinner is Stephen's first with the adults; the children eat in a separate room. It is his initiation into the adult world, and what he learns is that, in Ireland at least, there is no adult world. Stephen writes his complete address as citizen of the universe, but Simon, Mr. Casey, Dante show him that Ireland will be his farthest boundary if he stays there.

Stephen encounters his nationality just as David Copperfield encounters Murdstone and Grinby's warehouse or as Pip gets temporarily lost in the feckless Finches of the Grove men's club, but his is the greater hurdle. The nationality dilemma is particularly insidious because one's identity is derived from the very thing that is the impediment to one's development.

Young Stephen comes to awareness of his situation only gradually, by intuiting from small signs. There is something about the adult males around him that affects his feeling about himself. For example, he thinks how pleasurable it would be to deliver milk for a living

> if he had warm gloves and a fat bag of gingernuts in his pocket to eat from. But the same foreknowledge which had sickened his heart and made his legs sag suddenly as he raced round the park, the same intuition which had made him glance with mistrust at his trainer's flabby stubblecovered face as it bent heavily over his long stained fingers, dissipated any vision of the future. In a vague way he understood that his father was in trouble and that this was the reason why he himself had not been sent back to Clongowes.

The father's descent has apparently been precipitated, as John Joyce's was, by the demise of Parnell and the victory of anti-Parnell forces within the Irish Party. Stephen's fantasies of himself as the Count of Monte Cristo indicate that something of this has come through to his youthful consciousness. The Monte Cristo fantasy is formed on the same pattern as the Celtic Revival fantasy. Edmond Dantès (read heroic Ireland) languishes in prison while Mercedes (read Kathleen ni Houlihan) is forced to marry the rich enemy; Dantès escapes, becomes rich Count, gets revenge. It is, of course, the usual fantasy of the powerless. Later Stephen will figure himself as artist spurned by a materialist woman, and, in *Ulysses,* as Hamlet: characters wrongfully cast out by philistines. The mythic formula of his life has been determined by the story of Parnell and its aftermath in his own family. The Celtic Revivalists had resurrected Parnell as Cuchullain, but Stephen, as he did under the table, chiasmically changes the form of the story. Parnell rises from obscurity to heroic status, then falls; Dantès falls from heroic status to obscurity, then rises. In progressing from the Count to Hamlet, one essential change has taken place: his youthful belief in ultimate victory has been defeated.

This habit of savoring one's position as victim of injustice is a species of mental sin discussed by Aquinas under the name "morose delectation." "He chronicled with patience what he saw, detaching himself from it and testing its mortifying flavour in secret." It is a solitary sin, dependent for its continuance upon continued mortification. This helps to explain why Stephen is not interested in joining societies for the improvement of things in general:

> [W]hen the movement towards national revival had begun to be felt in the college yet another voice had bidden him be true to his country and help to raise up her fallen language and tradition.… [But] he was happy only when he was far from [such voices], beyond their call, alone or in the company of phantasmal comrades.

As an alternative to his private myths the Celtic Revival is emotionally unsatisfactory: the springdayish optimism of the civic improver lacks the kind of interesting complexity he seeks.

In choosing Edmond Dantès over Cuchullain, Stephen has chosen, with Gabriel Conroy, the Continent in preference to Ireland. He has also chosen a literary form: he has chosen to be a novelistic hero in preference to an epic hero. As M. M. Bakhtin has pointed out, epic heroes do not develop and they have no secrets:

> The individual in the high distanced genres is an individual of the absolute past and of the distanced image as such, he is a fully finished and completed being. This has been accomplished on a lofty heroic level, but what is complete is also something hopelessly ready-made.… He is, furthermore, completely externalized. There is not the slightest gap between his authentic essence and his external manifestation. All his potential, all his possibilities are realized utterly in his external social position.… Everything in him is exposed and loudly expressed.

Clearly, Stephen Dedalus, he who hides under the table and composes the chiasmic word-charm, he who will understand trigonometry and politics, cannot be a never-changing Cuchullain. Similarly, the world that he inhabits cannot be the easily interpreted good-or-bad world of the epic and of the Celtic Revival; it must be the difficult to interpret world of the novel. Cuchullain always knows who his enemies are. Even if they are his son or his foster brother, there is no doubt about their enmity, and his course of action is clear. Edmond Dantès, on the other hand, does not know who his enemies are, is not aware of all the machinations and secret self-interests that determine his fate.

The peasant theme in *A Portrait* offers an example of the shifting and tentative, the novelistic nature of Stephen's personal mythopoeia. Stephen's thoughts on the subject begin with a struggle between the romantic view of peasants as picturesque and the view that associates them with darkness and bats, and, unlike the peasant theme in *Stephen Hero,* undergoes a progression. Stephen, going to sleep at Clongowes, thinks,

> It would be lovely to sleep for one night in that cottage before the fire of smoking turf, in the dark lit by the fire, in the warm dark, breathing the smell of the

peasants, air and rain and turf and corduroy. But, O, the road there between the trees was dark! You would be lost in the dark. It made him afraid to think of how it was.

Romantic notions based on the repetition of the word *fire* give way as the word *dark* repeats in his mind. Living with peasants would destroy his boundary line, the embryonic identity he has been constructing; the "you" he has created, a person who, in contrast with rats, will someday understand trigonometry and politics, would disappear in the darkness.

But his attitude is not one of simple revulsion. He likes the way peasants smell, and from the beginning he has associated the sense of smell with his mother, who put the queer-smelling oilsheet on his bed. Mothers are frightening too because they embody the dark womb that precedes the "once upon a time" of consciousness. He sees the peasant seductress of Davin's story as "a type of her race and his own, a batlike soul waking to the consciousness of itself in darkness and secrecy and loneliness and, through the eyes and voice and gesture of a woman without guile, calling the stranger to her bed." The guileless Kathleen calls the stranger, a common Irish term for the English, to her bed. The political joining of Ireland with England which took place in 1800 was called the Act of Union. Out of this union is born the "disorder, the misrule and confusion of his father's house and the stagnation of vegetable life, which was to win the day in his soul."

Later the girl he is in love with flirts with a priest who is of the Celtic Revival persuasion. The priest, Father Moran, has a brother who is a potboy in Moycullen, so Stephen imagines her as giving herself to the peasantry and associates her with Davin's seductress. Again: feminity—peasantry—preconsciousness. Stephen contrasts himself to this peasant priest: he himself is the "priest of eternal imagination, transmuting the daily bread of experience into the radiant body of everliving life." In the logic of this metaphor the Celtic Revival is journeying into dark chaos looking for the "radiant image of the eucharist." And the priest is perfectly willing to encourage the journey toward the Celtic past and toward the peasant life, knowing that it leads to Catholic Ireland.

The peasant theme of the novel concludes with the diary entry—a condensation of a section of *Stephen Hero*—about John Alphonsus Mulrennan, a Celtic Revival folklorist who has just returned with a new hoard of material he got from an old man with red eyes; material about terrible queer creatures at the latter end of the world. Stephen, as he did at Clongowes, expresses fear:

> I fear him. I fear his redrimmed horny eyes. It is with him I must struggle all through this night till day come, till he or I lie dead, gripping him by the sinewy throat till … Till what? Till he yield to me? No. I mean him no harm.

It is here that the peasant theme reveals itself for what it has been from the start: a personal myth which has changed gradually in its meaning. At Clongowes Stephen longed for some ideal life away from home and school, a Lake Isle of Innisfree, and the peasant cottage appeared briefly in this form. Then he needed a creation myth to explain his condition, and Davin's Kathleen ni Houlihan seductress filled the part. Later, as he began to see his life as a struggle for intellectual survival the peasant became the force of primordial darkness. In Mulrennan's account, however, he is too much the real peasant, with pipe and comic carryings on, to sustain any of these myths. The peasant myth collapses. And with the collapse Stephen takes a step toward achieving the classical temper he has been striving for.

> The first step in the direction of truth is to understand the frame and scope of the intellect itself, to comprehend the act itself of intellection. Aristotle's entire system of philosophy rests upon his book of psychology and that, I think, rests on his statement that the same attribute cannot at the same time and in the same connection belong to and not belong to the same subject.

Stephen's peasant, like the Celtic Revival peasant, has been formed by the fears and desires of the beholder. In this final passage, before he catches himself at it, he has nearly turned the peasant into the jailer of Edmond Dantès. Stephen, like his countrymen, has been actively repairing the damage of colonial status with elaborate mental constructions. Having begun to realize this, he rejects the Yeatsian reconstruction of the Celtic past as the proper goal of his art: "Michael Robartes remembers forgotten beauty … Not this. Not this at all." According to his own esthetic doctrine he will have to learn to see through his own mental nimbus and discover a consistent view of his subject based upon its perceivable attributes.

And *A Portrait* itself, when compared to *Stephen Hero,* illustrates this point. In *Stephen Hero* Stephen's objection to the Celtic Revival is the subject; in *A Portrait* the mythopoeic process itself—the human need which results in Celtic Revivals—is the subject. "Once upon a time" signals the beginning of Stephen's conscious life as the beginning of a made-up story. "He was baby tuckoo." All human identity is myth-created. We know ourselves by a story we tell, or are told. Joyce has "disentangle[d] the subtle soul of the image from its nest of defining circumstances." "The image," that which will be his artistic subject in all of his major work, is identity and mythopoeia.

The theme is a treacherous one; to deal with it the writer must first undergo a stripping of his own self-myth. The high-flying images of the final diary entry show that Stephen, although he has taken the first steps, is not yet ready. In *Ulysses,* under the tutelage of the clear-eyed Leopold Bloom, he will complete the lesson begun here.

Source: William O'Neill, "Myth and Identity in Joyce's Fiction: Disentangling the Image," in *Twentieth Century Literature*, Vol. 40, No. 3, Fall, 1994, pp. 379-91.

William T. Noon

Noon is an American educator and literary scholar who has written frequently on Joyce's work. He is the author of Joyce and Aquinas. *In the following excerpt, he offers a general study of* A Portrait of the Artist as a Young Man, *focusing upon it as a novel of personal rebellion.*

James Joyce's *A Portrait of the Artist as a Young Man* was first published forty-seven years ago, not in Ireland but in New York, 1916. This was a year in the First World War; in Dublin the year of the Easter Week rebellion. Joyce, then at Zurich in neutral Switzerland, was thirty-three, fifteen years younger than [Samuel] Butler had been when he gave up his rewriting of *The Way of All Flesh.* The haze was not so dense for Joyce, and he had not so far to look backward. The *Portrait* is also a most carefully rewritten or restyled novel, in fact an entirely recast one. He had begun it in its original form as *Stephen Hero* even before he went away from Ireland in 1904. He had carried this first form of the book forward to double the final, present length of the *Portrait,* and then gave it up still incomplete so as to start his story all over. Looking back, he himself called *Stephen Hero* "rubbish." But even as it stands, the *Portrait* might be justly styled in part an autobiographical revenge, for like Butler Joyce voices through his story the grievances that he still held against his home, his mother country and most of her people. His recollections of the System, if that is the right word here, are rather bitter ones, though the bitter tone is notably muted by comparison of the *Portrait* with what survives of the earlier *Stephen Hero* draft. The real life prototypes are at times so thinly veiled that

any reader with even the most casual knowledge of James Joyce and his city is obliged to recognize some of them and to sense that the *Portrait* as a whole is the actual life story of a gifted young man's Catholic upbringing in Ireland at the turn of the century. The great danger is to read it as straight third person, the entire story comes filtered to us through the consciousness of a persona, here the young man whose artistic dilemmas and moral strictures it re-presents. Stylistically it is the most subtle of the three novels in the interaction of its own images and the verbal miming of its own thought. It is a literary classic of our times. Already it shows us Joyce busy as a beaver working hard to rechannel the tradition of the novel and to dam up the deep and dark waters of the subconscious, or unconscious. Quite explicitly he proclaims a revolution of the word.

Rebellion, revolt, and resistance have for centuries found in Ireland a fertile soil in which to flourish. "The Croppy Boy," "Kelly the Boy from Killanne," "The Rising of the Moon," "Seaghan O'Duibhir an Gleanna," are a few only of the defiant rebel songs, set to traditional airs, that Joyce, a gifted singer as a young man, heard in the air all about him in his own Irish days:

> And though we part in sorrow
> Still Seaghan O'Duibhir a cara
> Our prayer is "God, save Ireland"
> And pour blessings on her name.
> May her sons be true when needed,
> May they never fail as we did,
> For Seaghan O'Duibhir an Gleanna
> We're worsted in the game.

Most of these are political rallying songs. James Joyce's disenchantment with Ireland extended so far as to make him despair of the turn taken by most of Ireland's revolutionary politics, of her better-left-unspoken Gaelic speech, and, as he saw it, of the fatal paralysis that left her prostrate at the portals to the realm of the spirit, "the realms of gold" that he himself most of all respected: art, the way of the artist, and in particular the power that the word of the artist, or literature, has to help a people know itself, judge itself truthfully, and face the chaos and possibilities that the contemplation of its own image might disclose. Thus the *Portrait* becomes an artist's, not a social reformer's story as is Butler's *Way.* Stephen Dedalus leaves Ireland at the end of the story, but he is defiantly hopeful: "I go to encounter for the millionth time the reality of experience and to forge in the smithy of my soul the uncreated conscience of my race." "Silence, exile, and cunning" are the "only arms" that he now finds at hand to defend himself in the unjust warfare that has been pro-voked, as he sees it, by his home, his fatherland, and his church. No one would dream from this end-ing that Dublin was then a city of classical song and the center of the Irish Renascence, Lady Gre-gory, the Abbey Theater, W. B. Yeats; nor might one infer readily, nor indeed at all that some few years earlier, 1886, Dom Columba Marmion, the distinguished Benedictine, a curate in Dundrum on the outskirts of Dublin, also left Ireland to enter a European cloister at Maredsous. Still one wonders sometimes: If those whose job it was to educate James Joyce had been themselves more creative spirits, would his Catholic faith have become so much unhinged? They might have opened their minds and hearts perhaps wider to what was going on in his.

Stephen Dedalus is as deeply convinced that the Church is to blame for the paralysis he finds all around him as had been Butler's Ernest Pontifex. Whereas Ernest blames mostly the Church of Eng-land, Stephen blames instead the Church of Rome. For the English Establishment, for Crown and Cas-tle, for the Anglican Ascendancy in Ireland, Stephen has as much contempt as Ernest has for Victorian piety, but Stephen's own spiritual reac-tion has been conditioned by the Catholicism that as he sees it had made Ireland a land neither of scholars, artists, nor of saints.

The Stephen Dedalus story, at least as we have it in the *Portrait,* is that of a young man's growing up in Holy Ireland, his discovery of himself and of his vocation, his loss of innocence and his growth in experience, his flight to the continent of Europe. "You talk to me," he says, "of nationality, lan-guage, and religion. I shall try to fly by those nets." *The Adventures of Huckleberry Finn,* another sub-versive book, is the American novel with which the *Portrait* has been persistently compared. Huck's territory and Stephen's, the wilderness and the ur-ban diaspora, are, however, different kinds of soli-tude for retreat. Hemingway's Nick Adams, "the town's full of bright boys," and Scott Fitzgerald's Nick Carraway, in *The Great Gatsby,* are Ameri-can cousins of Stephen Dedalus as well as is Huck Finn. This quest is age-old, as old as Homer. It sent the son of Odysseus on his travels. Joyce calls the three opening Stephen Dedalus chapters of *Ulysses* his Telemachia.

The *Portrait* tells the Stephen story mainly in terms of the three Jesuit schools that Stephen, and Joyce himself, attended in Ireland: Clongowes Wood, an exclusive elementary boarding-school;

Belvedere College, or high school, as we might say, Dublin; and, finally, University College, Dublin, the Catholic University that John Henry Newman founded for Ireland in the early 1850s, which had been rescued by the Jesuits from extinction in 1883 and carried on under their administration for the next troubled quarter-century until 1909. Although it might look at first sight as though Stephen is as hard on his Irish Jesuits as Ernest Pontifex is on his Anglican schoolteacher divines, this judgment would go beyond the evidence of the *Portrait* it-self. Father Dolan, "Baldyhead Dolan," the prefect of studies, a priest of the Dr. Skinner type, beats Stephen at Clongowes for having broken his glasses, but Father Arnall, Stephen's own class teacher, is remembered as "very gentle," and Fa-ther Conmee, the Clongowes Rector, as a "kind-looking" man, who treats Stephen's protest de-cently. Long after this, in *Finnegans Wake,* Joyce alludes to *The Way of All Flesh* as "a butler's life … strabismal [or, wall-eyed, cross-eyed, and abysmal] apologia." Jesuit readers of the *Portrait,* more likely than others, are apt to take note of Stephen's appraisal of those Irish Jesuits who in the fiction at least show themselves eager at Belvedere to welcome the sixteen-year-old Stephen as a novice into their own priestly ranks: "Whatever he had heard or read of the craft of Jesuits," writes Joyce, "he [Stephen] had put aside as not borne out by his own experience. His masters, even when they had not attracted him, had seemed to him al-ways intelligent and serious priests."

The central conflict that the *Portrait* drama-tizes is that of Stephen's vocation: Shall he be an artist or shall he be a priest? This conflict is actu-ally resolved in the fourth, or Belvedere, section of the novel, after the crisis of Stephen's high school retreat. Stephen is intellectually tempted by the prospect of a priestly vocation. His imagination, however, is powerless to view this otherwise than as "the pale service of the altar," "cerements shaken from the body of death," and in the half-vision, half-actuality of seeing the bird-like girl "in mid-stream, alone and still, gazing out to sea," he makes up his mind not to be a priest but an artist, and to follow this vision of "mortal beauty," "profane joy," wherever it might lead him, even unto "the gates of all the ways of error and glory." Unlike Ernest Pontifex, Stephen never commits himself to a priestly service in which he has no heart: "I will not serve that in which I no longer believe, whether it call itself my home, my fatherland, or my church." Still the *Portrait* nowhere inveighs against the family system that brings down in retrospect

Ernest's strictures. In fact, tried as it is, Stephen's sense of solidarity with his family is very strong. Stephen's father, Simon Dedalus, is a drunkard, but on the whole he is shown as an amiable drunkard, who flirts with the barmaids and knows how to sing. Stephen's mother is a rather ineffectual lady, but always a lady, a gentle lady, even when she and her impoverished brood of children are obliged, after many auctions and house-movings, to live on the wrong side of the tracks as the novel comes to a close.

For the most part its tone is serene; at times it is very comic. It would not be easy to find in modern fiction a more amusing and still realistic scene than the famous Christmas-dinner in the first section, when Stephen comes home from Clongowes Wood during his family's affluent days to celebrate with them the birthday of the Prince of Peace. The Dedalus family and their invited guests quarrel violently about the rights and wrongs of Kitty O'Shea's divorce and the consequent repudiation of Charles Stewart Parnell, "uncrowned king of Ireland": the dinner breaks up with door-slammings, shouts, curses, clenched fists and crashes, upturned chairs and rolling napkin-rings—a first-class Irish brawl. The much frightened little boy Stephen "sobbed loudly and bitterly." As Joyce closes the incident, "Stephen, raising his terror stricken face saw that his father's eyes were full of tears." Whereas the wealthy, leisured aristocrat Towneley is Ernest's hero in *The Way of All Flesh,* so an idealized Parnell, blameless and broken, is Stephen's hero in the *Portrait.* Neither Stephen nor James Joyce ever forgave Ireland for throwing Parnell to the wolves. Stephen cannot follow Parnell in person, and he cannot serve God as priest at the altar. He has no call to the drawing-room. What can he do? He can be, he thinks, an artist. In this way he will be saving Parnell and all his people, "race of clodhoppers" that he calls them, for the world of art: "I tried to love God, he [Stephen] said at length. It seems now that I failed."

Fortunately it is not any man's business to judge of Stephen's, or Joyce's, failure before God. Joyce himself succeeded admirably as artist; as he grew older, he edged far away from his symbolic identification with Stephen Dedalus. In *Ulysses,* the good man is Leopold Bloom: as Joyce told his friend Frank Budgen while *Ulysses* was still in the making, "As the day wears on Bloom should overshadow them all." And in *Finnegans Wake,* he is Everyman, Humphrey Chimpden Earwicker, H.C.E., "Here Comes Everybody," in a story where Everybody is Somebody Else. Stephen Dedalus did not become a priest at the altar, and neither did Joyce. When Stephen says in the *Portrait* that he will become instead "a priest of the eternal imagination," his metaphor is meaningful, but he is talking about something else than the rite of priestly consecration. This metaphor should not be pushed too far in Stephen's case, and in Joyce's own it is one that has tended to obscure the two vocations between which he made an election; he himself chose not altar but art. It is a choice that haunted him most of his life.

Source: William T. Noon, "Three Young Men in Rebellion," in *Thought,* Vol. XXXVIII, No. 151, Winter, 1963, pp. 559-77.

Sources

Ford Madox Ford, "A Haughty and Proud Generation," in *YR,* No. 9, 1922, p. 717.

Hugh Kenner, *A Colder Eye: The Modern Irish Writers,* Alfred A. Knopf, 1983.

J. I. M. Stewart, "James Joyce," in *British Writers,* Vol. VII, edited by Ian Scott-Kilvert, The British Council/ Charles Scribner's Sons, 1984, pp. 41-58.

For Further Study

Chester G. Anderson, editor, *James Joyce: A Portrait of the Artist as a Young Man; Text, Criticism, and Notes,* Viking Press, 1968.
    Considered the definitive critical edition of Joyce's novel, the work includes excerpts from a number of early reviews.

Bernard Benstock, "James Joyce," in *Dictionary of Literary Biography, Volume 36: British Novelists, 1890-1929: Modernists,* edited by Thomas F. Staley, Gale, 1985, pp. 80-104.
    An essay by a leading Joyce scholar. Benstock surveys Joyce's literary accomplishment and discusses the narrative technique and symbolism of *A Portrait of the Artist as a Young Man.*

Ernest Bernhardt-Kabisch, "View Points," in *Twentieth Century Interpretations of A Portrait of the Artist as a Young Man,* edited by William M. Schutte, Prentice Hall, 1968, pp. 114-15.
    A discussion of "Bous Stephanomenos" and "Bous Stephanoforos."

Wayne Booth, "The Problem of Distance in *A Portrait of the Artist as a Young Man,*" in *Twentieth Century Interpretations of A Portrait of the Artist as a Young Man,* edited by William M. Schutte, Prentice Hall, 1968, pp. 85-95.
    Booth discusses irony in *Portrait.*

Joseph A. Buttigieg, *A Portrait of the Artist in Different Perspective,* Ohio University Press, 1987.

This work attempts to come to terms with the effect of Joyce's modernism in a postmodern age.

Richard Ellmann, *James Joyce,* Oxford University Press, 1959; second edition, 1982.
   The definitive biography of James Joyce by one of the leading scholars of modern Irish literature.

A Nicholas Fargnoli and Michael Patrick Gillespie, *James Joyce A to Z,* Facts on File/Oxford University Press, 1995.
   A handy reference source to the life and work of James Joyce.

William E. Morris and Clifford A. Nault, Jr., editors, *Portraits of an Artist,* Odyssey, 1962.
   This anthology collects publisher's comments, essays, reviews, and pedagogical questions.

W. M. Schutte, editor, *Twentieth Century Interpretations of A Portrait of the Artist as a Young Man,* Prentice-Hall, 1968.
   Includes useful essays by a number of scholars including Wayne Booth and Hugh Kenner.

David Seed, *James Joyce's A Portrait of the Artist as a Young Man,* St. Martin's, 1992.
   This is a study of many aspects—language, women, diary, etc.—of Joyce's novel.

Weldon Thornton, *The Antimodernism of Joyce's A Portrait of the Artist as a Young Man,* Syracuse University Press, 1994.
   Thornton discusses Joyce's novel alongside the question of whether Western society can live with the modernism it has long wished for.

The Trial

Franz Kafka
1925

Franz Kafka is one of the greatest influences on Western literature in the twentieth century. He has inspired a whole range of artists from the creators of the detective story to writers of the television series *Twilight Zone*. He began work on *The Trial* in 1914 after a horrendous encounter with his fiancé, Felice Bauer, her sister, Erna Bauer, and Grete Bloch (a short-term lover). According to Kafka's friend Max Brod, he never finished the work and gave the manuscript to Brod in 1920. After his death, Brod edited *The Trial* into what he felt was a coherent novel and had it published, despite the German ban on Jewish literature, in 1925. The manuscript eventually passed from Brod's heirs to the German national literary archives in the late 1980s for several million dollars. Since then, new editions have been published and some textual integrity restored to the English version of the story.

Author Biography

The first of six children, Franz Kafka was born in 1883. His father, Hermann Kafka, was an industrious man; he owned a dry-goods store in the Jewish ghetto in the city of Prague. Hermann was ashamed of his Jewish heritage and tried, as much as possible, to appear German. He married into a higher social class when he married Julie Loewy, Franz's mother.

A bright child, Kafka was an excellent student at a prestigious German high school. When he grad-

Franz Kafka

he wrote in his *Diaries* that he viewed "coitus as the punishment for the happiness of being together." Kafka sabotaged his long engagement with Felice Bauer in 1917. Two years later he was engaged to the daughter of a janitor. Kafka's father said that the shame of such a match would be so disastrous that he would have to sell his business and emigrate. In response, Kafka wrote the angry and self-lacerating *Letter to His Father* and gave it to his mother. She decided against giving it to her husband. Kafka broke off the relationship just after they had found an apartment together.

Not surprisingly, work and family strains began to take their toll and Kafka took restorative vacations for his health. Finally, in 1923, he retired from business in order to devote himself to writing. He also moved to Berlin. Missing the activity and tensions of home, he returned. His health problems persisted, however, and he traveled to find a kinder climate for his fragile condition. Kafka died of tuberculosis on June 3, 1924, in Kierling (near Vienna, Austria).

uated his parents rewarded him with a trip to the North Sea. Afterwards, instead of entering the family business, Kafka decided to go to university. As a student, his rebelliousness led to reckless living and deteriorating health. In 1902 Kafka met the writer Max Brod, and the two men became close friends. Kafka published his first work, *Description of a Struggle*, in 1904. In 1906, Kafka received his doctorate in law from the German university, Karls-Ferdinand, in Prague.

Armed with his law degree, Kafka entered the insurance business. Through a family contact, he began a successful sixteen-year career as one of a handful of Jews working in the semi-public German Workers' Accident Insurance in 1908. There he produced technical writings with a masterful lucid prose. He worked long hours and then managed his brother's factory. Seeing the obvious strain on his friend, Brod begged for help from Kafka's mother. She secretly hired a manager to take her son's place. During this time, Kafka lived at home, in a room between the living room and his parents' noisy bedroom. He gained some recognition as a writer when he was awarded the Theodor Fontane Prize in 1915.

Kafka never married. He had several long-term relationships but companionship troubled him and

Plot Summary

The Arrest

At the start of *The Trial,* Joseph K. awakes on the morning of his thirtieth birthday. He is greeted by two warders, Franz and Willem, who tell him he's under arrest, and introduce him to the Inspector. He refuses to tell K. why he has been arrested. Confused, K. is surprised when they let him go with orders to come back for his trial. After work that evening, K. talks with his landlady, Frau Grubach, who is sympathetic to his plight. K. likes Fraülein Bürstner, whose room the Inspector had commandeered. When she returns late at night, K. insists on talking to her about his day, and then makes a grab for her.

First Interrogation

K. is told to present himself for a brief inquiry into his case. He goes to the address, only to find that it's a tenement house. A woman doing laundry directs him to the Court of Inquiry. The Court is sitting in a stuffy room, packed with bearded men in black. K. addresses the audience about the stupidity of the court. He is cut off by a man grabbing the laundry woman and shrieking.

The Offices

K. returns to the offices the following Sunday, but no one is there except the laundry woman. She is the wife of the Usher, and explains that the man who had grabbed her was a law student, Bertold, who has been chasing her. K. examines the books left on the table, only to find that they are pornography. The Usher's wife tells him about the Examining Magistrate, but Bertold enters and carries her off. The Usher returns and complains about Bertold, and he leads K. into the labyrinthine law offices in the attic to look for him. They pass through a hallway filled with accused men. K. feels faint and has to sit down. He makes his way out, carried along by a man and young woman, badly shaken.

Fraülein Bürstner's Friend

K. wants to talk to Bürstner again, but cannot find her. A commotion in the hall reveals that Fraülein Montag, a sickly teacher, is moving in with her. Joseph is upset, and goes to Fraülein Montag. She won't tell him why she's moving in, and says that Bürstner doesn't want to talk to him.

The Whipper

K. is walking to his office in the Bank when he hears a horrible scream. He finds the warders, Franz and Willem, being whipped in a storeroom. They plead with him to help them, but the whipper is adamant about doing his duty. K. tries to buy him off, and fails. The next week, still troubled, he goes back to look at the room, only to find the whipper and the two warders there again.

K.'s Uncle

K.'s Uncle Karl, upset over the case, comes in from the country. They go to see one of his uncle's friends, Dr. Huld, who is very sick but knows all about K.'s predicament. K. is distracted by the Lawyer's nurse, Leni, and sneaks off to visit her in the middle of the conversation. Leni shows him her webbed fingers, and tries to seduce him, giving him a key so he can return at any time. He returns, and his uncle berates him for fooling around when he should be resolving his case.

The Painter

K. obsesses over the case, which has dragged on for six months. One of his work clients, a manufacturer, knows about his situation and tells him that a painter, Titorelli, might be able to help. K. goes to see Titorelli. The painter explains that things are never as they seem and elaborates on the nature of the plea system. K., disheartened, leaves after buying three identical pictures from the painter, only to find that this building too has law offices in its attic.

Block

When K. decides to dismiss Dr. Huld, he finds a half-naked man, Block, with Leni. Block describes his own case, which has been going on for five years. Block tells him that it is widely believed that K. will lose his case. K. consults Huld, who tells him that Leni sleeps with all of the accused men. Dr. Huld, to illustrate the nature of the law to K., makes Block abase himself.

The Cathedral

K. is asked to escort a client around the cathedral. While there he meets a priest who tells him he is the prison chaplain, and that his case is going badly. The priest relates a parable called *Before the Law*. A man from the country comes to the door seeking admittance to the Law, but the guard says he can't enter. The man sits and waits by the door for years, trying to find a way to make the guard let him in. Finally, when he is about to die, he asks why nobody else ever came to the door. The guard says that the door was only ever meant for him, and now it will be closed. K. and the priest discuss the parable. Is the doorkeeper subservient to the man or vice versa? Did the man come of his own free will? Is he deluded? The priest says that it is not necessary to accept everything as true, only to accept it as necessary. K. counters that the world must then be based on lies.

The End

On the evening before his thirty-first birthday, two men come to Joseph's apartment and take him away. At an abandoned quarry they take off his coat and shirt and lay him down. Taking out a butcher knife, they pass it to each other over him. He is supposed to take it and plunge it into his own chest, but he doesn't, instead looking over at a house across the way. Someone is standing at the window on the top floor. Joseph wonders who it is, and where the Judge is, and the High Court. He holds out his hands and spreads his fingers. One of the men takes the knife and stabs him, twisting the knife twice. K.'s last words are, "Like a dog!"

Characters

Uncle Albert

K.'s Uncle Albert rushes into town after hearing from his daughter, Erna, that K. is on trial. He is extremely annoyed that K. is unconcerned with

Kyle MacLachlan and Anthony Hopkins in a scene from the 1993 version of The Trial.

his predicament, "Josef, you've undergone a total metamorphosis; you've always had such a keen grasp of things, has it deserted you now?" K.'s uncle impresses upon him that the honor of the family is at stake. Albert represents the accomplished man and exposes the collective nature of K.'s actions.

Bertold

The "first student of the unknown system of jurisprudence" that K. meets is Bertold. "This horrible man" with bandy legs and a scraggly red beard, is in pursuit of the Usher's wife. At first it appears that he is pursuing her for himself but he carries her off to the Examining Magistrate.

Rudi Block

"Block, Block the merchant" is a little man. Before he divested all his holdings, he tells K., so as to focus himself entirely on his case, he was a successful grain merchant. When he meets K., he has illegally employed five petty lawyers, called hucksters, to his cause. His crime is unknown too. His relationship with Dr. Huld, however, is strange and masochistic. Mr. Block, from K.'s viewpoint is a dog with no self-respect.

Fraülein Bürstner

Bürstner is K.'s neighbor. She is a single, independent woman making her way in the world.

As such, she is K.'s ideal of femininity but the traditional Frau Grubach is suspicious of her morals for the same reason. When K. stops by to apologize for an event she was never aware of, he learns that she too is "fascinated with court matters. The court has a strange attraction … " She also tells K. that she will "start next month as a secretary in a law firm." With a possible intelligent female ally before him, K. launches into a noisy summary of that morning's events that ends with a strange declaration of love in the form of an unwanted sexual advance. This assault is a symbolic arrest of Bürstner's equanimity with the world, which she acknowledges by carrying her head bent at the neck back into her room.

K.'s failed attempt to create a positive relationship with a decent woman is indicative of his actions at large. He believes himself to be good with details and negotiating, but he is boorish and heavy-footed in his approach. As a final reproach to K., she is the last person—other than his wardens—that he sees on the way to his execution.

The Chief Clerk

When the Chief Clerk emerges from the corner of Dr. Huld's room, he represents the obscurity of the Law.

Elsa

K. pays a weekly visit to Elsa, a waitress in a wine house who receives daytime "visitors only in bed." Leni says she is too tightly corseted in her photo. K. chooses, on one occasion, to see her instead of going to court. This preference for a distraction doesn't help K.'s standing with the court.

The Examining Magistrate

Although he writes all night in a school exercise book and sits in court all day, The Examining Magistrate never reveals the charges against K. The one time The Examining Magistrate has a role, he says, "You're a house painter?" This apparent mistake sets K. off on a defiant speech. The Examining Magistrate appears to seek solace in his notebook while K. talks. Throughout the rest of the novel, The Examining Magistrate is referred to in hushed tones though he is "so small he's almost tiny." He chases the Ushers wife and reads pornography.

Franz

The first guard K. sees, after he rings his bell for Anna, is Franz. He is a young man with a wife who pleads with K. to save him from the whipping.

Media Adaptations

- "Say what you like, but *The Trial* is the best film I ever made!" So says Orson Welles, director of a 1963 adaptation of the novel to black and white film. Welles played the advocate opposite Anthony Perkins as Josef K.

- Using a script by Harold Pinter, David Hugh Jones directed a 1993 remake of the film. Josef K. is portrayed by Kyle MacLachlan and Anthony Hopkins plays The Priest.

- Throughout the 1990s, *The Trial* has been adapted to the stage several times. Most recently, Ivan Rajmont used Evald Schorm's adaptation at the Theatre of Estates in 1998.

Along with Willem, Franz asks K. for a bribe and for his clothes. To K.'s protestations, Franz says, "You see, Willem, he admits that he doesn't know the Law and yet he claims he's innocent." The two guards eat his breakfast; K.'s complaints about their actions lead to their punishment.

Frau Grubach

"The only person I can discuss [my case with] is an old woman," K. says to himself while looking at Frau Grubach. To her the trial "seems like something scholarly." Frau Grubach is K.'s landlady and she is very fond of him, though, like most everyone else, she avoids shaking his hand. Grubach also owes K. a large sum of money. She suspects K. is guilty.

Hasterer

See Prosecuting Counsel

Dr. Huld

The ailing Dr. Huld is a famous lawyer although he is not a great lawyer. K.'s uncle introduces him to Dr. Huld. Huld is important enough that court officials pay him visits and, in fact, when K. and his Uncle enter, the Chief Clerk is sitting, unseen, in the corner. K. is frustrated by Dr. Huld's style as it does not match with his own financial sense of efficiency. He bemoans the fact that Dr. Huld takes forever with the first petition.

The Inspector

The sole purpose of the Inspector is to inform K. that he is under arrest. His very presence, however, as a high functionary of the Law, causes K. to talk in a guilty manner. Having performed his duty, he departs from the house unseen.

The Italian Colleague

K. is volunteered by the President to show an important client from Italy around the city. The Italian's presence reminds him that there is a whole world out there. The labyrinths of the trial are reflected in the convoluted Italian that this man speaks. K. can not follow him but the President can. Even in this instance, K. is left out of the information loop and, therefore, simply accepts the President's directions as to the place and time for the tour.

Josef K.

The novel begins with the protagonist, Chief Financial Officer Josef K., asleep in bed on his thirtieth birthday. "Someone must have slandered Josef K., for one morning, without having done anything truly wrong, he was arrested." K., however, is incapable of accepting his new situation because, as he admits to his guards, "I don't know the Law ... it probably exists only in your heads." Eventually, the court renders its verdict and sentences K. to death on his thirty-first birthday.

K.'s plight is that of every person who attempts to understand the intricacies of life. Each person, like the man in the Priest's parable, has his or her own gate to enter. K. wants, very much, to enter with success. A very detail-oriented person, he tries to ferret out the rules of his trial so that he may best deal with them in a dignified manner. Against his will he shows signs of resistance, "the pressure of the crowd behind him was so great that he had to actively resist." Doing so, however, lends him an air of resistance that is interpreted by others as a potential source of salvation, "Do you think you'll be able to improve things?" asks the Usher's Wife. But K.'s appearance as a Christ-like figure is a stretch. In fact, he is unable to deal with real life with the same brilliance with which he handles financial transactions. He is unable to go with the flow because he needs to understand his situation. Therefore, much like the truthseeker in Plato's parable of the Cave, he is executed.

Kaminer

Kaminer always wears a smile due to a muscle twist and is repulsively modest. He is a witness to K.'s arrest and hands K. his hat when they finally set off for the bank.

Kullych

Kullych is one of the three low-level bank assistants present at K.'s apartment when he is brought before the Inspector. Later, when K. is leaving the bank in order to visit his mother, Kullych pursues him. This assistant is a "dull-witted ... big-headed blond fellow" who doesn't seem to understand that K. is asserting his right as a high-powered bank official to wave off his responsibilities. Kullych wants to consult K. about a letter but K. tears it into pieces, though he wishes—in an obvious allusion to spanking—to give the Aryan "two loud slaps on his pale round cheeks."

Captain Lanz

Captain Lanz is the nephew of Frau Grubach who happens to be sleeping in the living room while K. is talking to Bürstner. When Montag moves in with Bürstner, he moves into her room. He stands nearby when Montag confronts K.

Leni

Dr. Huld's maid and nurse is a young woman named Leni who is sexually attracted to men involved in trials. She promises to help K. but only introduces him to Block. Leni has a webbed hand and this deformity attracts K. In the only instance of affectionate display in the novel, K. tenderly kisses Leni's "claw."

The Manufacturer

A businessman with whom K. has done business with in the past seeks K.'s help again. The Manufacturer also offers K. some information, which he hopes will be useful in his trial. He gives K. a letter of introduction to the court painter.

Fraülein Montag

Fraülein Montag moves in with Bürstner soon after K. assaults her. It is Montag who answers K.'s protestations and tells him to stay away from Bürstner.

The Priest

Instead of finding the Italian in the cathedral, K. meets a Priest who turns out to be the court's chaplain. It is the clearest exchange in the work and the Priest reveals that K.'s case is going very badly.

The Priest puts K.'s position into perspective with the parable of the Gatekeeper. The Priest represents religion in the novel and his presence, and his speech, leads to an easy interpretation of the novel as a theological commentary.

Prosecuting Counsel

K. strikes up a wonderful friendship with a well-regarded prosecuting counsel named Hasterer. They have long conversations and hold court in a tavern. Due to the high regard in which Hasterer holds K., many lesser figures seek audiences with Hasterer through K. Despite Hasterer's standing in the court, he is no help to K. Hasterer and K. become so inseparable that Hasterer's girlfriend, Helene, becomes jealous and eventually she leaves.

Rabensteiner

"Wooden, arm-swinging" Rabensteiner is the first of the three lowly clerks that K. recognizes. To K., Rabensteiner is the epitome of lethargy.

Titorelli

Titorelli is the painter of the court. K. is introduced to him by The Manufacturer. In one of the fragments, the encounter between K. and the painter is wrought with sexual tension. Titorelli is more informative about the practical workings of the court than Dr. Huld. Titorelli represents the art world and reveals the way in which the law spills over into all other aspects of life. In the same way that only a man versed in the law can be an advocate, only a man who knows all the rules of art can be a painter. Titorelli is fortunate enough to have grown up learning the rules of painting.

The Usher

The Usher takes K. on a tour of the Law offices while asking him to bring his wife back. Though in the service of the court, he is not unaware of its brutality. He answers K.'s comment about stumbling over a step, saying, "they show no consideration of any kind."

The Usher's Wife

The Usher's Wife cleans the courtroom. K. believes that she is offering herself to him. But when Bertold takes her away, K. realizes "he had suffered defeat only because he had sought to do battle." From the Usher's Wife, K. gains an insight into the industrious character of the Examining Magistrate. He doubts the image as soon as she allows him to see the Examining Magistrate's books—a pornographic book and a novel.

The Vice President

K.'s trial occurs when it is essential for him to be at his professional best. The President is in decline and his subordinates are jockeying for position. The Vice President views K. as his rival. Consequently, he takes advantage of K.'s distraction to siphon off K.'s clients.

Willem

Willem is the other lowly employee paid to watch K. for ten hours a day. He is older than Franz and has seniority. He reminds K. that, in comparison to K., he and Franz are free men.

Themes

Religion

A central element of Judeo-Christian theology is the belief that humans are guilty of original sin. There are various ways to deal with this situation but in many theological doctrines, redemption and entry to heaven depend upon people leading moral lives. For Protestants, salvation is gained when the individual confesses to God. Assistance in this task comes from the Bible as well as through the teachings of those who spend their lives studying the Bible. In Judaism, the book of God is the Torah, and literally speaking, God is the Law.

K.'s story takes place in a world familiar with this theology; yet this theology is changing. For example, the Calvinists' theory of predestination, which is the belief that what you do in life does not matter since people have already been selected by God (before birth) for salvation, is evoked by K.'s situation. K. has been predestined for a judgment. In religious terms, this means he should accept his guilty nature and seek redemption in whatever form the court decides. Block has done so and has avoided death but has paid a humiliating price: he must forever run on all fours before a representative of the law.

K. resembles a character from the Old Testament named Job. Job is a wealthy man who steadfastly believes in God. One day, the devil makes a bet with God that, if allowed to do so, he can put Job's faith on trial so that he curses God. The bet is on but despite all the pranks and hardships of a trial by faith, Job doesn't curse God. Instead, it is Job's faith that sees him through. K., who has been similarly slandered by someone, undergoes a trial but he has no faith in the Law to see him through.

Topics for Further Study

- Compare the several editions of *The Trial* (Brod's—if possible, Muir's and Breon Mitchell's—based on Pasley's German edition). How do interpretations of single words affect the story? What is the importance of the chapter order?

- Whether in literary forms, science fiction, movies, or television shows, Kafka has proved to be an infinite source of inspiration. Select a work which you feel is Kafkaesque and defend your choice.

- What do you think Kafka would think of the Internet? Or, more narrowly, how would Josef K. handle himself inside a Multi-User-Domain?

- Kafka's novel has often been interpreted as a religious commentary. How far do you think such a critique is supported by the text? Pick one creed—Calvinism, Catholicism or Judaism—and discuss the possible textual evidence for its influence in *The Trial*.

- Does the knowledge that *The Trial* was written by a Jewish author in pre-WWII Europe add an extra dimension to our understanding of the legal nightmare K. is dragged into? Discuss the novel as what George Steiner has called a "prophetic statement" about the holocaust.

K.'s predicament is neatly summed up, "I don't know the law."

Calvinism, Protestantism, and Judaism are not the only theologies under assault. The descriptions of the court's personnel evoke the cosmology of Catholicism with its levels of angels, its history of Inquisitions, and its secret tribunal of Cardinals. Also, Catholic degrees of grace are transformed into degrees of guilt. There is, of course, innocence and guilt, the discussion of which always involves a statement that K. must know some law. With Bürstner, he discusses being guiltless and "not as guilty as they thought." Much later, Titorelli describes the states of permanent guilt: actual acquittal (heaven), apparent acquittal (purgatory), and protraction (hell). Catholics believe that sins can be dealt with through the sacrament of confession. In this sacrament, the guilty person discusses his or her sins with a priest and he gives counsel, as well as a set number of prayers to be recited. That is how the person may cleanse his or herself of the sin. This practice was abused during the time of the Inquisitions when torturers forced people to confess to all sorts of crimes—like witchcraft. In Catholic fashion, K. is constantly told that "all you can do is confess. Confess the first chance you get."

Language and Meaning

K. views his trial as "no different than a major business deal" in which he must pay close attention to details such as how people exit or how people use words. The Inspector notices this obsession with details and cautions him. K. disregards the advice and berates himself whenever he loses focus. The scene that exemplifies K.'s failure to understand what is happening to him, despite his best efforts, is the conversation with the bank president and the Italian client. Despite his knowledge of Italian, K. cannot understand the client's dialect and he is bothered by the client's lips being obscured behind a mustache. To K., the client's words "literally poured from his lips" and all K. can see are "various difficulties."

Another example is when K., who knows something about art, thinks he will understand a portrait but does not. He misreads a portrait as that of a great judge, but Leni tells him that the subject of the painting is actually a small man and an examining magistrate. When confronted by Titorelli's work in progress, K. needs guidance immediately, "It's the figure of Justice," says the painter. "Now I recognize it," says K., as he traces out what he knows as the allegorical image of law. His assessment is incorrect and the painter reveals that the court allows only those paintings done according to a code that only Titorelli knows. In other words, art, like the Law, can only be known by its priests. Finally, K. enters the cathedral where he intends to show the client the famous religious artworks. The lighting inside, however, makes it impossible and he is unable to tell a column from a statue. Clearly, outside of financial numbers—and even the trial ruins his ability to help the manufacturer—K. is lost.

Justice

Block reveals to K. that "a suspect is better off moving than at rest, for one at rest may be on the scales without knowing it, being weighed with all his sins." Unfortunately, K. later sees a painting at Titorelli's wherein the allegorical figure of Justice is also the winged and mobile figure of Victory.

Sex Roles

Women, for K., perform the impossible and mysterious acts which keep life functioning. "A woman's hand indeed works quiet wonders, he thought he might have smashed the dishes on the spot, but he certainly couldn't have carried them out." Women are also capable of great influence on the unknowable court: "Women have great power. If I could get a few of the women I know to join forces and work for me, I could surely make it through." However, this dream is as unlikely as the idea of flogging a judge. The reason is that women, in the novel, have their particular doors to guard. They are somewhat like Gatekeepers. They also have a defect. For example, Leni has a claw and Elsa is confined to a corset. The exception to this rule is Bürstner. She is not a Gatekeeper but someone who works and learns. She will not help K. because he is incapable of respecting her or the Law.

The Universe vs. The Individual

K., except for a brief friendship with Hasterer, prefers his own company. In the matter of his trial, "he didn't want to enlist anyone's aid and thus initiate them in the matter even distantly." To do so would be to initiate another person into himself. This is an act he cannot even do in the form of a petition. This is as it should be since the trial is his own, it is his guilt, and no matter what he does or where he goes, that is where the inquiry will be located: "he is certainly being treated with strange carelessness."

As much as K. desires it, he is not alone. Everyone who knows him also knows about his trial. From his point of view, the entire universe finds him guilty from the casual observer to the men who kill him like a dog.

Style

Parable

Parables are familiar teaching devices that reveal moral lessons through short and simple stories. A parable's simplicity lends it a timeless quality. For this reason, parables thousands of years old hold relevance today. Parables can also be enigmatic sayings or tales, which obviously contain a message though the precise meaning is anyone's guess.

Kafka intentionally set out to write parables, not just novels, about the human condition. *The Trial* is a parable that includes the smaller parable of the Gatekeeper. There is clearly a relationship between the two but the exact meaning of either parable is left up to the individual reader. K. and the Priest discuss the many possible readings. Both the short parable and their discussion seem to indicate that the reader is much like the man at the gate; there is a meaning in the story for everyone just as there is one gate to the Law for each person.

Defamiliarization

The Russian formalist, Viktor Shklovski, formulated the term *ostranenie* in his 1917 article, "Art as device." This term has been variously adopted in the West as defamiliarization or, more popularly, by way of Bertold Brecht, as "the alienation effect." Quite independent of both, Kafka employs defamiliarization with unrivaled mastery. This process works by making the reader/audience perceive familiar, everyday reality in a new and unsettling way, hence the term "defamiliarization." The result, the artist hopes, is a newfound sense of appreciation or reconsideration by the perceiver of the norm.

The world is presented in a strange way so that the viewer sees things as if for the first time. Shklovski conceives of the device as operating in an artwork on three levels. First, at the level of language, words, or linguistic rhythms, not normally associated with each other can be brought together to expose new meanings (examples can be found in the poetry of the Dadaists or the work of John Cage). Second, at the level of content, accepted concepts and ideas are distorted to reveal new perspectives on the human condition. Finally, at the level of literary forms, the canon is departed from and subliterary genres (like detective and crime stories) are elevated to high art.

Kafka accomplishes defamiliarization on all three levels with a crime story whose suspect's reality becomes so distorted as to approach the absurd. The story's language is precise even at the moment where it is circumventing the key to understanding. As a result the basic concept of law is newly perceived. At the linguistic level, Kafka uses words like "assault," "guilt," and "trial" in different contexts but in such a way that the meaning of the term is just as useful (and is interchangeable) with another.

An explicit example of Kafka using everyday understandings to defamiliarize the reader occurs in the form of the tools employed by the Inspector. The Inspector takes great pains to make the announcement of K.'s arrest look official by rearranging a bedroom to look like a court in the way a child arranges furniture to play house. Instead of a gavel and a law book, the Inspector has a random book, a pincushion, and matches. Finally, by simple and almost legalistic attention to wording, Kafka causes a constant air of doubt to cover anything said or thought. Phrases like, "could he really rely so little on his own judgment already?" are always double entendres where K. refers both to his slip of the tongue with the Manufacturer as well as the greater judgment he awaits.

Symbolism

Every element of the story is pregnant with allegorical significance. The position of bodies and their size symbolize a person's value before the Law. The men of the court sit with their heads bent up against the ceiling of an attic because they are so close to heaven. An arrested person, however, hangs their head. A strong and free person stands tall and straight. Furniture exaggerates this body language. K. points out whether there are chairs for him to sit on and how this strips him of power.

K. awakens, like Adam, from sleep to the customary comfort of his bedroom where he waits for Anna. Instead of Anna, he finds himself under arrest by guards from a department which does not seek the guilty, rather, "as the law states, is attracted by guilt and has to send us guards out." After wandering about the room, he returns to his bed and eats an apple—the allegorical fruit from the tree of knowledge—and, thereby, becomes aware of his being on trial. The Apple signifies original sin and eating the apple ends innocence.

Tone

One of the keys to Kafka's success is his consistent employment of atmosphere. He uses a clear prose style at all times. Even when Dr. Huld is imparting the intricacies of law, the sentence structure is not complex. The rooms are fastidiously described in terms of where the air may enter and the risk of soot and dust this entrance holds for the human lung. His use of shadows and obscurity cause both K. and the reader to redouble their efforts to pay attention. Shadows are attributed with intelligence as they seem to intentionally obscure the object of K.'s vision.

Historical Context

Bohemia

The earliest known inhabitants of the mountain-rimmed nucleus of the Czech Republic were the "Boii" people. Not much remains of them but the name, Bohemia, or, "home of the Boii." They integrated completely with a Slavic tribe called Czechs around the fifth century AD. By the fourteenth century, Bohemia was the most prosperous kingdom in Europe. In the next century, Jan Hus made Bohemia the center of Protestantism.

In 1526, Ferdinand I's marriage transferred Bohemia to the Roman Catholic Austrian House of Hapsburg. Despite Protestant grumbling, Ferdinand kept the peace and the Austro-Hungarian Empire thrives. The situation is fine until discontent with Roman Catholic rule boils over. The Protestant uprising that led to the disastrous Thirty Years' War involving all of Europe began in Bohemia. The Protestants are finally defeated at White Mountain in 1620 and Bohemia again came under Austrian rule. This situation lasted until a Serbian terrorist named Gavrilo Pincip assassinated Archduke Francis Ferdinand on June 28, 1914, in Sarajevo. Austria decided the assassination was a good excuse to declare war on Serbia.

World War I

There was no singular event that caused World War I. Several factors contributed to the conflict. It started when Austria-Hungary bungled relations with the Balkan States and, together with Germany, antagonized Russia. In addition, Britain was anxious about losing control of its empire and eager to cement an alliance with France.

In 1908 Austria-Hungary's annexation of Bosnia-Herzegovina exacerbated the situation and angered Serbia. Austria-Hungary could have dueled with Serbia in 1909, when that nation was weak. Instead, Serbia emerged, in 1913, prepared to attain its dream of a greater Serbia. Austria-Hungary responded with the creation of Albania in the path of Serbia. Germany, meanwhile, declared itself a friend of Turkey and threatened Russia's use of the Straits of Constantinople over its grain exports—from which Russia derives 40% of its income. Consequently, the nations of Europe mobilized their armies for an inevitable war. The assassination of the Archduke provided the final act.

Austria-Hungary's declaration of war on July 28th, 1914, activated the two alliances that existed in Europe. Germany, Italy, and Austria-Hungary comprised the Triple alliance, or Central Powers. England, France, and Russia made up the Triple Entente Powers, or Allies. Russia, now in the mood to protect Serbia and the Balkan States, sided with Serbia. France and Britain followed. It was a gruesome war.

Hoping to win early, each side went on the offensive. The death toll was huge: of the sixty million men mobilized for war, 8.5 million died, and twenty-one million were wounded. Every city and town in Europe has its memorial to World War I. When the offensives failed, Europe hunkered down into a deadly trench warfare; disease killed more men than bullets. Finally, the Americans were drawn into the conflict on the side of the Allies in 1917 and the simple introduction of new energy turned the tide. The Allies won in 1918 and the Austria-Hungarian Empire was dismantled. Bohemia became the central province of the Republic of Czechoslovakia.

Anti-Semitism

The ghetto was an invention of Pope Paul IV, who, in 1555, decreed that all the Jews in Rome would live in a particular area of the city. Such decrees spread throughout Europe as anti-Semitic fervor waxed and waned. Many ghettos were abolished in the late nineteenth century.

Although the Nazi program of genocide is several decades away, anti-Semitism was as natural in Eastern Europe as Jim Crow laws in the American South. Jews, by economic social circumstance, were forced to remain in the ghettos. Such a concentration of Jews in one place made them vulnerable to violence and discrimination. Early in the twentieth century, anti-Semitism flared up in the form of the Russian and Romanian pogroms. In 1903 and 1905, thousands of civilians—mostly Jews—were tortured or murdered. At the time, Germany was appalled and offered refuge to many. One million Jews fled the pogroms to New York City.

Kafka's Works

Although written against a backdrop of war, Kafka's writings do not depend on the events of the time. The reason is that Kafka's aesthetic intent was to create timeless parables about the human condition. Gas jets being the exception, there are few details that allow the novel to be dated. Clothes, for example, are nondescript and described in terms of function and wear rather than style. In fact, the condition of a man who deals with money being under investigation by a court could happen

Anthony Perkins and Akim Tamiroff in a scene from the 1963 version of The Trial, *directed by Orson Welles.*

at any time. Due to this timeless quality, innumerable artists have borrowed Kafka's technique. Many see a prophecy of totalitarianism in Kafka's novels. Kafka, they say, foresaw the era of hidden courts and death squads.

Critical Overview

Kafka has inspired many of the great novelists of the twentieth century. Consequently, there is an incredible amount of literary criticism devoted to his work. The critical material discussing *The Trial* falls between two poles. On the one hand, Kafka is viewed through a psychological or religious lens that sees the tensions of his work as derived from an Oedipal complex or the heritage of the Judaic law. At the other extreme, where few tread, are the positivist approaches of Walter Benjamin, Gilles Deleuze, and Felix Guattari. This latter approach finds a new philosophy, a new politics, in Kafka that is as yet unexplored. Whatever the approach, there is general agreement that Kafka should be praised for his deft depiction of twentieth-century alienation and bureaucracy at the universal level.

"*The Trial:* What a strange, exciting, original, and delightful book this is … a web of gossamer, the construct of a dream world," wrote Herman Hesse after reading Max Brod's version in 1925. "In short," Hesse continues, "this "trial" is none other than the guilt of life itself." So Hesse begins the predominant theme of critical approaches to Kafka; he is responding to Judaic and Calvinist philosophers (especially Soren Kierkegaard and Karl Barth). Hesse was not far from Brod's own opinion of his friend's writing. In *Frank Kafka: A Biography,* after relating the joy Kafka derived from reading chapter one of the novel aloud, Brod asserted that *The Trial* should be viewed as the old parable of Job. In general, continued Brod, "Kafka's fundamental principle: pity for mankind that finds it so hard a task to do what is right."

The religious interpretations were not always so exact. Instead, critics compare Kafka to the Calvinists indirectly and couch their critique in terms of absolutism or, as Albert Camus put it, "[his] work is probably not absurd … His work is universal." R.O.C. Winkler, in "The Novels," stands as an example of the religious approach:

> In Kafka's view, there is a way of life for any individual that is the right one, and which is divinely sanctioned. So much is perhaps admitted by most of our moral novelists; but to Kafka this fact itself constitutes a problem of tremendous difficulty, because he believes the dichotomy between the divine and the human, the religious and the ethical, to be absolute. Thus, though it is imperative for us to attempt to follow the true way, it is impossible for us to succeed in doing so. This is the fundamental dilemma that Kafka believes to lie at the basis of all human effort.

Philip Rahr, in "Franz Kafka: The Hero as Lonely Man," echoes Winkler with a comparison to Gide, "in Kafka's catastrophic world there is no escape for the protagonist … Kafka never assumes an unmotivated act on the part of his heroes, as Gide does in some of his novels, but invariably an unmotivated situation." Thomas Mann, in "Homage," summed up this religious approach by labeling Kafka a "religious humorist."

The autobiographical approach characterizes Kafka's work as merely the enactment of a struggle with his father. This approach is based on Kafka's *Letter to His Father.* Ernst Pawel takes this approach in his *The Nightmare of Reason: A Biography of Franz Kafka,* and Ronald Hayman in *Franz Kafka.* Yet even from a biographical viewpoint, Kafka is a very contradictory persona who appears personally incompetent yet wrote professional pieces of high sophistication and technical accuracy. As a result, autobiographical approaches have lost popularity through time.

In addition to that, says Ralph Freedman in "Kafka's Obscurity: The Illusion of Logic in Narrative," "an exclusively psychological explanation leaves vast areas of Kafka's obscurity unexplained. We need not dwell on the obvious psychoanalytic motif which recurs in his fiction [where, for example] *The Trial* … can be diagnosed as an enactment of his relationship with his father and with the authoritarian society he found so intolerable." Freedman prefers richer veins, "for, as we shall see, the shadowy characters who appear to his heroes are independent entities, through which manifold relations are explored."

Edwin Muir, in "A Note on Franz Kafka," also prefers to enjoy Kafka's literary genius. He writes that, "the logic of Kafka's narrative is so close that it builds up a whole particularized system of spiritual relations with such an autonomous life of its own that it illumines the symbol rather than is illumined by it. It is almost certain, moreover, that Kafka put together this world without having his eye very much on the symbol; his allegory is not a mere re-creation of conceptions already settled; and the entities he describes seem therefore newly discovered, and as if they had never existed before. They are like additions to the intellectual world."

With Benjamin, who strongly identified with Kafka at a personal level, analysis of Kafka enters a whole new realm. In *Illuminations* Benjamin writes, "there are two ways to miss the point of Kafka's works. One is to interpret them naturally, the other is the supernatural interpretation. Both the psychoanalytic and the theological interpretations equally miss the essential points." However, Benjamin could only go so far due to his own ideological position. Deleuze and Guattari, however, in *Kafka: Toward a Minor Literature,* took up where he left off. "We believe only in a Kafka *politics* that is neither imaginary nor symbolic. We believe in one or more Kafka *machines* [and in] Kafka *experimentation* [resting] on tests of experience." In other words, instead of locking Kafka into an Oedipal complex, or a show of technical mastery, Deleuze and Guattari explore Kafka at his prophetic word. "By making triangles transform until they become unlimited, by proliferating doubles until they become indefinite, Kafka opens up a field of immanence that will function as a dismantling, an analysis, a prognostics of social forces and currents, of the forces that in his epoch are only beginning to knock on the door."

Criticism

Tabitha McIntosh-Byrd

McIntosh-Byrd is a doctoral candidate at the University of Pennsylvania. In the following essay she examines the extent to which Kafka's The Trial *can be read as a parable about the history of European Christianity.*

The body of critical commentary on the works of Franz Kafka is huge enough to have warranted the description, "fortress Kafka," and the extant criticism on *The Trial* is no exception. Readings of the novel have spanned the range from Calvinist to postmodernist, by way of Marxism, feminism and post-structuralism. In many ways, the seemingly endless series of commentaries and perspectives is highly appropriate to the subject matter of *The Trial.* Both within the novel and by nature of the body of critique which surrounds it, *The Trial* raises insistent questions about the nature of meaning, interpretation and reality which ultimately remain unanswered and unanswerable. Joseph K.'s inability to find or understand the High Courts and the Highest Judges is directly analogous with a basic inability to pin the book down to simple interpretations.

Like the parable that Joseph hears at the cathedral, *The Trial* is capable of withstanding extended and divergent exegetical commentary without ever offering up a clear or essential lesson. In doing so it serves as a meta-commentary—a critique of the shortfalls of critique itself, which has much in common with Medieval Christian mystic writing. In both Kafka's novel and the work of such mystics as Julian of Norwich and Hildegard of Bingen, 'Truth' and supreme authority are unknowable—capable only of being grasped at by metaphor, diffusion and analogy. Indeed, Kafka's text perhaps works best as a commentary upon religious commentary—a critical analysis told through fable and analogy of the impossible psychological burden imposed on humanity by western Christianity. The fact that the essence of *The Trial* remains unknowable thus becomes a structural reinforcement of the central theme. Just as God's ways are all important but forever mysterious to the 'Everyman' of Christian Europe, so the reading experience pulls 'Everyreader' into textual authority, only to refuse access to essential textual meaning.

The perfect paradigm of the text's machinations can be found in the first page of the novel. From the opening line of *The Trial,* we are thrown into a bewildering profusion of textual meaning that is as puzzling to us as it is to Joseph K. We begin *in media res,* thrust into a confusing lack of narrative explanation in the same way that Joseph is thrust into his case without understanding what the facts of it are:

> Someone must have been telling lies about Joseph K., for without having done anything wrong he was arrested one fine morning.

Neither K. nor we will ever receive satisfactory answers to the causes of his arrest, and we are even more at a loss than he since his essential identity will remain hidden from us throughout the novel. He will always be a linguistic cipher to us, his last name known only 'through a glass, darkly' with the single letter, 'K.' The period marks it as an abbreviation instead of a generic signifier, both creating and undermining our ability to read it as a parable. In other words, Joseph K. is both Everyman and a specific character—his namelessness makes him a cipher, even as the period implies specificity and invites guesswork. Such guesswork will, of course, remain unconfirmable, just like every other aspect of *The Trial.*

The essential similarities of Joseph K.'s initial plight and the basic premises of Judeo-Christian theology are obvious and have been frequently commented upon. In the former, Joseph awakes to find himself guilty of a crime he is sure he has not personally committed, but for which he will suffer and eventually die. In the latter, man 'wakes up' guilty—born with the burden of an original sin which he has not committed, but for which his days will be a trial to him. Essentially, both K. and the Judeo-Christian subject are forced into a world where existence consists of awaiting judgment for sins that they cannot comprehend. The "fine apple" that K. eats as a replacement for his stolen breakfast underscores the parallel. The essential symbol of the Fall of Man that the apple serves here—as it does in *Metamorphosis* to signify the existentially guilty fate of the protagonist.

From this initial re-staging of the Fall of Man, the actions contained in *The Trial* can be plotted onto a trajectory that describes the development of Christian theology in the West. The first stage is Catholic—a system of religious signification that is firmly based on a top-down hierarchy of power in which intercession and removal from the sources of authority are essential aspects of the power infrastructure. Like the Church officials who enforce a Papal Bull, the Warders who come to arrest K. are serving a remote 'Law' to which they are un-

What Do I Read Next?

- Kafka's 1915 story, *The Metamorphosis,* begins: "As Gregor Samsa awoke one morning from uneasy dreams he found himself transformed in his bed into a giant insect."

- Published in German in 1919, Kafka wrote *The Penal Colony* in 1914. Some see a reflection of trench warfare in this story about law and punishment told by a traveling anthropologist.

- Kafka wrote the *The Blue Octavo Notebooks* while spending a happy vacation with his favorite sister, Ottla. This work is a book of proverbs, reflections, and literary sketches.

- Written in 1922 but not published until 1926, *The Castle* tells the tale of a surveyor (K.) who answers a work summons. He arrives at the town below the Castle but the town officials do not know what he is talking about. K. tries to catch the attention of a Castle official named Klamm but fails.

- Kafka agreed to the publication of the *The Hunger Artist* in 1924 as he was dying. The story is about a circus entertainer whose trick is to not eat. He sits in a cage and fasts alongside the other attractions.

- There are some striking echoes of Samuel Taylor Coleridge's poem, "Rime of the Ancient Mariner." The poem is the tale of a sailor who unthinkingly shoots down an Albatross–an omen of good luck—and suffers cosmic punishment as a result.

- Kafka learned how to write about courts and the law from reading *Bleak House* by Charles Dickens, published in book form in 1853. The book criticizes the English court system through an account of those involved with the never ending suit of Jarndyce vs. Jarndyce.

- The greatest criminal psychology thriller is Fyodor Dostoyevsky's *Crime and Punishment.* This 1866 novel concerns the tale of Raskolnikov's crime of murder. This work is another influence on *The Trial.*

---

thinkingly obedient, but whose workings they do not understand. Further, this very 'unknowability' is taken as proof positive of its untouchable, almost sacred nature. In this way, neither the warders nor the Inspector are privy to the actual facts of the legal system which they represent, and since K. cannot learn which law he has broken, he is *de facto* incapable of proving that he hasn't broken it. As Franz says, "See, Willem, he admits that he doesn't know the Law and yet he claims he's innocent."

In this cosmology, power and meaning are continually deferred and removed. The Warders are following the orders of the Inspector, who is following the orders of the Court, who in turn are following the orders of a higher Court. Above it all is the Law—the Papal Bull that is yet another step removed from the source of power, since the Pope too receives meaning from an unknowable higher Authority.

The intercessionary motif is elaborated throughout the first half of the novel, and its association with Catholicism is strengthened by K.'s relationship to women. Just as Catholic tradition draws heavily on the intercessionary role of woman in the guise of the Virgin Mary, so K. is drawn to a series of women from whom he seeks reassurance and aid with his Case. As he says to the Priest:

> Women have great influence. If I could move some women I know to join forces in working for me, I couldn't help winning through.

The first is his landlady, Frau Grubach, who is present at his arrest and to whom K. looks for comfort and explanation. His next impulse after he has realized the implications of the situation is to go to another woman—Fraulein Burstner—and explain his woes. Neatly, K.'s need to 'make a confession' about the horrors of his situation is tied to the symbolic role of women in Catholic theology. The fact that Fraulein Burstner is of dubious sexual morality points to the other Mary, the Magdalene, and K.'s sexual reaction to her is perhaps a commentary on the deeply conflicted role of the Goddess/Whore binary in the history of European thought.

The next intercessionary women to whom K. turns are again sexually active ones—the Usher's wife and Leni, the Lawyer's nurse. With each woman that K. turns to, he gets closer and closer to the authority of the court, and the women would seem to be more and more capable of playing an active role in the mitigation of his circumstances. Leni especially seems to be able and willing to help him, both in her ability to give him valuable information about the legal system, and in her role as the first port of entry to the Lawyer's services. In this reality of deferred meaning, the Lawyer is, of course, a stand-in for Priesthood—the church's first representative.

K. comes to realize that the power of the Lawyer is limited after the painter describes for him the Byzantine complexity of the legal hierarchy, of which the lawyer and his friends are but the smallest cogs. In the style of the Protestant Reformation, K. revolts against the hierarchy—deciding to represent his own case. Just as Protestantism rejected the intercessionary authority structure of the Catholic Church and placed its emphasis instead on personal salvation, so K. rejects his lawyer—the established means of communicating with 'the Law'—and attempts to take his fate into his own hands. With his rejection of this 'priesthood' comes a rejection of the intercessionary female. K.'s realization that the Lawyer can do nothing for him occurs simultaneously with his realization that Leni has no real power to help him; that her relationship with him is not special, but instead symptomatic of her fetish for condemned men. Again, this is in direct parallel with the massive drop in the power status of the Virgin Mary—and women in general—in Protestant Christianity.

Following his decision, however, the essence of K.'s situation remains unchanged. He is still incapable of understanding the crime he has committed, and—most importantly—equally incapable of escaping the looming judgment. His nature still condemns him, as Block suggests when he informs K. that:

> you're supposed to tell from a man's face, especially the line of his lips, how his case is going to turn out. Well, people declared that judging from the expression of your lips you would be found guilty, and in the near future too.

Here K. is 'guilty by nature.' His physiology marks an essential condemnation that is as inescapable as Augustinian original sin even while he is switching to a 'theology' that would seem to promise hope for the individual soul. Again, this hopelessness directly parallels the history of European Christianity. This time it is the bleak doctrine of Calvinism that is at play. In this theology the doctrine of predispensation decrees that individual souls have been judged guilty or not guilty before they are born, and are as powerless to alter their fate as they are to know which sentence has been passed upon them. As the parable in the Cathedral shows, the issues surrounding free will and determinism are as opaque and unknowable as those surrounding direct intercession. In the final line of the novel, K. dies—an end that has proved to be inescapable no matter which style of theological maneuvering he has chosen. If the Law is God, this would suggest, then, the very fact of God condemns man to misery, condemnation and guilt. By accepting and believing in the power of the Law, K.'s society has allowed itself to be structured by nothing more or less than guilt.

Of course, this reading is reductive. To draw a coherent system of meaning from Kafka's text, more must be excluded than is included. To create a meaningful narrative to describe this most elusive of texts is to be reminded again and again that *The Trial* is a novel about the failures of narrative—a text about extra-textuality, as it were, that cannot be reduced to a simple trajectory. The acts of reading and analysis thus become part of the text itself—another part of the ongoing meditation on the nature of language, reality and meaning which the novel represents. In the final analysis, the most intelligent—and intelligible—thing that can be said about *The Trial* is that it is intelligently unintelligible.

Source: Tabitha McIntosh-Byrd, in an essay for *Novels for Students*, Gale, 1999.

Louis Kronenberger

In the following essay, Kronenberger reexamines The Trial *almost fifty years after its initial publication.*

When the late Franz Kafka's *The Castle* was published in this country some years ago, it created no general stir, but it was immediately seized upon by a few people as a very distinguished book. Time has passed, and other people—though still not many—have concurred in that conclusion. I must confess that I have not read *The Castle,* but I mean to, for I have read *The Trial,* and not in a long time have I come upon a novel which, without being in any vulgar sense spectacular, is more astonishing.

The Trial is not for everybody, and its peculiar air of excitement will seem flat enough to those who habitually feed on "exciting" books. It belongs not with the many novels that horrify, but with the many fewer novels which terrify. It does not trick out the world we know in grotesque and fantastic shapes; it is at once wholly of our world and wholly outside it. It keeps one foot so solidly on the ground that you can think of few books which stay there more firmly with both feet. But its other foot swings far out into space, conferring upon the literal action of the story a depth of meaning—or if meaning is often elusive, a power of suggestion—which can best be called visionary.

Something of the book's quality may be guessed from a brief mention of its plot. Joseph K., a young bank official, gets up one morning to find that he has been arrested. He knows he has committed no crime, and he is never then or later told what his crime is supposed to be. He is permitted his freedom, except that periodically he must go to court. Court is a weird place, full of other accused people and innumerable petty officials. There K. is allowed to assert his eloquence, but the business of his trial never makes any progress.

There is more to the story than an account of K.'s "trial." We are told much about his life at the bank, about his relations with his landlady and with the young woman who has the room next to his. In all these things K. is made to feel just as uncertain and frustrated as in the matter of his trial and this frustration contributes most of all to the dream character of the book. It is exactly the sensation we have during a lingering nightmare.

No summary can convey the atmosphere which Kafka cunningly distills—the atmosphere of some idiotic and hellish labyrinth where Joseph K. is forced to wander. The more he tries to control the situation, the more stranded he becomes. On psychological grounds alone the story has a peculiar force and distinction. But the impact of *The Trial* is much more moral than psychological. Kafka is at bottom a religious writer, with a powerful sense of right and wrong and an unquenchable yearning toward the unrevealed source of things. His story then is a great general parable. It is a proof of Kafka's other talents as a novelist, a humorist, a psychologist and a satirist that he does not leave his parable a bald one, but works into it every kind of human gesture and lifelike detail. The

man who can, while writing symbolically, make a hilarious stuffed shirt out of K.'s advocate, and then —in a later scene—express his religious feeling in the richest organ tones, was a writer in whose death literature suffered a real loss.

Source: Louis Kronenberger, "Special K," in *The New York Times Book Review,* October 6, 1996, p. 44.

Sources

Walter Benjamin, "Franz Kafka: on the Tenth Anniversary of His Death," in his *Illuminations: Essays and Reflections,* edited by Hannah Arendt, Schocken, 1968, pp. 111–45.

Max Brod, *Franz Kafka: A Biography,* translated by G. Humphreys Roberts, Schocken, 1947.

Albert Camus, "Appendix: Hope and the Absurd in the Work of Franz Kafka," in his *The Myth of Sisyphus and Other Essays,* translated by Justin O'Brien, Knopf, 1955, pp. 124–38.

Gilles Deleuze, and Félix Guattari, in *Kafka: Toward a Minor Literature,* translated by Dana Polan, Theory and History of Literature series, Volume 30, University of Minnesota Press, 1986.

Ralph Freedman, "Kafka's Obscurity: The Illusion of Logic in Narrative," in *Modern Fiction Studies,* Vol. VIII, No. 1, Spring, 1962, pp. 61–74.

Herman Hesse, "Eine Literatur in Rezensionen un Aufsatzen," in his *Gesammelte Werke* Vol. 12, Suhrkamp Verlag, 1970, p. 482.

Thomas Mann, "Homage" in *The Castle* by Franz Kafka, translated by Willa Muir and Edwin Muir, Alfred A. Knopf, Inc., 1940, pp. ix–xvii.

Edwin Muir, "A Note on Franz Kafka," in *The Bookman,* Vol. LXXII, No. 3, November, 1930, pp. 235–41.

Philip Rahr, "Franz Kafka: The Hero as Lonely Man," in *The Kenyon Review,* Winter, 1939, pp. 60–74.

R. O. C. Winkler, "The Novels" in *Kafka: A Collection of Critical Essays,* edited by Ronald Gray, Prentice Hall, Inc. 1982, pp. 45–52.

For Further Study

Margaret Atwood, *The Handmaid's Tale,* Anchor Books, 1998.

> Using Kafkaesque devices, Atwood satirizes society's obsession with reproductive rights. In a strange future, women are valued only if their ovaries function.

Terry Gilliam, *Brazil,* Universal Studios, 1985.

> Named as the best film of the year by the Los Angeles Film Critics Association, *Brazil* is the story of a bureaucratic cog named Sam Lowry and is often compared to Kafka's *The Trial.* Lowry's life is destroyed when an insect bug causes a typo on a print-

out. Due to this accident, he is labeled a miscreant by the bureaucracy he works for.

Ernst Pawel, *The Nightmare of Reason: A Life of Franz Kafka,* Noonday Press, 1992.

This book is held to be the best biography of Franz Kafka.

Ayn Rand, *The Fountainhead,* Bobbs-Merrill Co., 1979.

Ayn Rand presents a different view of the individual than Kafka in this story from 1949. Her individual is an architect who successfully meets the challenges of the world and his rival. In Rand's work, good wins and the individual is triumphant.

Glossary of Literary Terms

A

Abstract: As an adjective applied to writing or literary works, abstract refers to words or phrases that name things not knowable through the five senses.

Aestheticism: A literary and artistic movement of the nineteenth century. Followers of the movement believed that art should not be mixed with social, political, or moral teaching. The statement "art for art's sake" is a good summary of aestheticism. The movement had its roots in France, but it gained widespread importance in England in the last half of the nineteenth century, where it helped change the Victorian practice of including moral lessons in literature.

Allegory: A narrative technique in which characters representing things or abstract ideas are used to convey a message or teach a lesson. Allegory is typically used to teach moral, ethical, or religious lessons but is sometimes used for satiric or political purposes.

Allusion: A reference to a familiar literary or historical person or event, used to make an idea more easily understood.

Analogy: A comparison of two things made to explain something unfamiliar through its similarities to something familiar, or to prove one point based on the acceptedness of another. Similes and metaphors are types of analogies.

Antagonist: The major character in a narrative or drama who works against the hero or protagonist.

Anthropomorphism: The presentation of animals or objects in human shape or with human characteristics. The term is derived from the Greek word for "human form."

Antihero: A central character in a work of literature who lacks traditional heroic qualities such as courage, physical prowess, and fortitude. Antiheroes typically distrust conventional values and are unable to commit themselves to any ideals. They generally feel helpless in a world over which they have no control. Antiheroes usually accept, and often celebrate, their positions as social outcasts.

Apprenticeship Novel: See *Bildungsroman*

Archetype: The word archetype is commonly used to describe an original pattern or model from which all other things of the same kind are made. This term was introduced to literary criticism from the psychology of Carl Jung. It expresses Jung's theory that behind every person's "unconscious," or repressed memories of the past, lies the "collective unconscious" of the human race: memories of the countless typical experiences of our ancestors. These memories are said to prompt illogical associations that trigger powerful emotions in the reader. Often, the emotional process is primitive, even primordial. Archetypes are the literary images that grow out of the "collective unconscious." They appear in literature as incidents and plots that repeat basic patterns of life. They may also appear as stereotyped characters.

Avant-garde: French term meaning "vanguard." It is used in literary criticism to describe new writing that rejects traditional approaches to literature in favor of innovations in style or content.

B

Beat Movement: A period featuring a group of American poets and novelists of the 1950s and 1960s—including Jack Kerouac, Allen Ginsberg, Gregory Corso, William S. Burroughs, and Lawrence Ferlinghetti—who rejected established social and literary values. Using such techniques as stream of consciousness writing and jazz-influenced free verse and focusing on unusual or abnormal states of mind—generated by religious ecstasy or the use of drugs—the Beat writers aimed to create works that were unconventional in both form and subject matter.

Bildungsroman: A German word meaning "novel of development." The *bildungsroman* is a study of the maturation of a youthful character, typically brought about through a series of social or sexual encounters that lead to self-awareness. *Bildungsroman* is used interchangeably with *erziehungsroman,* a novel of initiation and education. When a *bildungsroman* is concerned with the development of an artist (as in James Joyce's *A Portrait of the Artist as a Young Man*), it is often termed a *kunstlerroman.* Also known as Apprenticeship Novel, Coming of Age Novel, *Erziehungsroman,* or *Kunstlerroman.*

Black Aesthetic Movement: A period of artistic and literary development among African Americans in the 1960s and early 1970s. This was the first major African-American artistic movement since the Harlem Renaissance and was closely paralleled by the civil rights and black power movements. The black aesthetic writers attempted to produce works of art that would be meaningful to the black masses. Key figures in black aesthetics included one of its founders, poet and playwright Amiri Baraka, formerly known as LeRoi Jones; poet and essayist Haki R. Madhubuti, formerly Don L. Lee; poet and playwright Sonia Sanchez; and dramatist Ed Bullins. Also known as Black Arts Movement.

Black Humor: Writing that places grotesque elements side by side with humorous ones in an attempt to shock the reader, forcing him or her to laugh at the horrifying reality of a disordered world. Also known as Black Comedy.

Burlesque: Any literary work that uses exaggeration to make its subject appear ridiculous, either by treating a trivial subject with profound seriousness or by treating a dignified subject frivolously. The word "burlesque" may also be used as an adjective, as in "burlesque show," to mean "striptease act."

C

Character: Broadly speaking, a person in a literary work. The actions of characters are what constitute the plot of a story, novel, or poem. There are numerous types of characters, ranging from simple, stereotypical figures to intricate, multifaceted ones. In the techniques of anthropomorphism and personification, animals—and even places or things—can assume aspects of character. "Characterization" is the process by which an author creates vivid, believable characters in a work of art. This may be done in a variety of ways, including (1) direct description of the character by the narrator; (2) the direct presentation of the speech, thoughts, or actions of the character; and (3) the responses of other characters to the character. The term "character" also refers to a form originated by the ancient Greek writer Theophrastus that later became popular in the seventeenth and eighteenth centuries. It is a short essay or sketch of a person who prominently displays a specific attribute or quality, such as miserliness or ambition.

Climax: The turning point in a narrative, the moment when the conflict is at its most intense. Typically, the structure of stories, novels, and plays is one of rising action, in which tension builds to the climax, followed by falling action, in which tension lessens as the story moves to its conclusion.

Colloquialism: A word, phrase, or form of pronunciation that is acceptable in casual conversation but not in formal, written communication. It is considered more acceptable than slang.

Coming of Age Novel: See *Bildungsroman*

Concrete: Concrete is the opposite of abstract, and refers to a thing that actually exists or a description that allows the reader to experience an object or concept with the senses.

Connotation: The impression that a word gives beyond its defined meaning. Connotations may be universally understood or may be significant only to a certain group.

Convention: Any widely accepted literary device, style, or form.

D

Denotation: The definition of a word, apart from the impressions or feelings it creates (connotations) in the reader.

Denouement: A French word meaning "the unknotting." In literary criticism, it denotes the resolution of conflict in fiction or drama. The *denouement* follows the climax and provides an outcome to the primary plot situation as well as an explanation of secondary plot complications. The *denouement* often involves a character's recognition of his or her state of mind or moral condition. Also known as Falling Action.

Description: Descriptive writing is intended to allow a reader to picture the scene or setting in which the action of a story takes place. The form this description takes often evokes an intended emotional response—a dark, spooky graveyard will evoke fear, and a peaceful, sunny meadow will evoke calmness.

Dialogue: In its widest sense, dialogue is simply conversation between people in a literary work; in its most restricted sense, it refers specifically to the speech of characters in a drama. As a specific literary genre, a "dialogue" is a composition in which characters debate an issue or idea.

Diction: The selection and arrangement of words in a literary work. Either or both may vary depending on the desired effect. There are four general types of diction: "formal," used in scholarly or lofty writing; "informal," used in relaxed but educated conversation; "colloquial," used in everyday speech; and "slang," containing newly coined words and other terms not accepted in formal usage.

Didactic: A term used to describe works of literature that aim to teach some moral, religious, political, or practical lesson. Although didactic elements are often found in artistically pleasing works, the term "didactic" usually refers to literature in which the message is more important than the form. The term may also be used to criticize a work that the critic finds "overly didactic," that is, heavy-handed in its delivery of a lesson.

Doppelganger: A literary technique by which a character is duplicated (usually in the form of an alter ego, though sometimes as a ghostly counterpart) or divided into two distinct, usually opposite personalities. The use of this character device is widespread in nineteenth- and twentieth-century literature, and indicates a growing awareness among authors that the "self" is really a composite of many "selves." Also known as The Double.

Double Entendre: A corruption of a French phrase meaning "double meaning." The term is used to indicate a word or phrase that is deliberately ambiguous, especially when one of the meanings is risqué or improper.

Dramatic Irony: Occurs when the audience of a play or the reader of a work of literature knows something that a character in the work itself does not know. The irony is in the contrast between the intended meaning of the statements or actions of a character and the additional information understood by the audience.

Dystopia: An imaginary place in a work of fiction where the characters lead dehumanized, fearful lives.

E

Edwardian: Describes cultural conventions identified with the period of the reign of Edward VII of England (1901-1910). Writers of the Edwardian Age typically displayed a strong reaction against the propriety and conservatism of the Victorian Age. Their work often exhibits distrust of authority in religion, politics, and art and expresses strong doubts about the soundness of conventional values.

Empathy: A sense of shared experience, including emotional and physical feelings, with someone or something other than oneself. Empathy is often used to describe the response of a reader to a literary character.

Enlightenment, The: An eighteenth-century philosophical movement. It began in France but had a wide impact throughout Europe and America. Thinkers of the Enlightenment valued reason and believed that both the individual and society could achieve a state of perfection. Corresponding to this essentially humanist vision was a resistance to religious authority.

Epigram: A saying that makes the speaker's point quickly and concisely. Often used to preface a novel.

Epilogue: A concluding statement or section of a literary work. In dramas, particularly those of the seventeenth and eighteenth centuries, the epilogue is a closing speech, often in verse, delivered by an actor at the end of a play and spoken directly to the audience.

Epiphany: A sudden revelation of truth inspired by a seemingly trivial incident.

Episode: An incident that forms part of a story and is significantly related to it. Episodes may be either self-contained narratives or events that depend on a larger context for their sense and importance.

Epistolary Novel: A novel in the form of letters. The form was particularly popular in the eighteenth century.

Epithet: A word or phrase, often disparaging or abusive, that expresses a character trait of someone or something.

Existentialism: A predominantly twentieth-century philosophy concerned with the nature and perception of human existence. There are two major strains of existentialist thought: atheistic and Christian. Followers of atheistic existentialism believe that the individual is alone in a godless universe and that the basic human condition is one of suffering and loneliness. Nevertheless, because there are no fixed values, individuals can create their own characters—indeed, they can shape themselves—through the exercise of free will. The atheistic strain culminates in and is popularly associated with the works of Jean-Paul Sartre. The Christian existentialists, on the other hand, believe that only in God may people find freedom from life's anguish. The two strains hold certain beliefs in common: that existence cannot be fully understood or described through empirical effort; that anguish is a universal element of life; that individuals must bear responsibility for their actions; and that there is no common standard of behavior or perception for religious and ethical matters.

Expatriates: See *Expatriatism*

Expatriatism: The practice of leaving one's country to live for an extended period in another country.

Exposition: Writing intended to explain the nature of an idea, thing, or theme. Expository writing is often combined with description, narration, or argument. In dramatic writing, the exposition is the introductory material which presents the characters, setting, and tone of the play.

Expressionism: An indistinct literary term, originally used to describe an early twentieth-century school of German painting. The term applies to almost any mode of unconventional, highly subjective writing that distorts reality in some way.

F

Fable: A prose or verse narrative intended to convey a moral. Animals or inanimate objects with human characteristics often serve as characters in fables.

Falling Action: See *Denouement*

Fantasy: A literary form related to mythology and folklore. Fantasy literature is typically set in non-existent realms and features supernatural beings.

Farce: A type of comedy characterized by broad humor, outlandish incidents, and often vulgar subject matter.

***Femme fatale*:** A French phrase with the literal translation "fatal woman." A *femme fatale* is a sensuous, alluring woman who often leads men into danger or trouble.

Fiction: Any story that is the product of imagination rather than a documentation of fact. Characters and events in such narratives may be based in real life but their ultimate form and configuration is a creation of the author.

Figurative Language: A technique in writing in which the author temporarily interrupts the order, construction, or meaning of the writing for a particular effect. This interruption takes the form of one or more figures of speech such as hyperbole, irony, or simile. Figurative language is the opposite of literal language, in which every word is truthful, accurate, and free of exaggeration or embellishment.

Figures of Speech: Writing that differs from customary conventions for construction, meaning, order, or significance for the purpose of a special meaning or effect. There are two major types of figures of speech: rhetorical figures, which do not make changes in the meaning of the words, and tropes, which do.

***Fin de siecle*:** A French term meaning "end of the century." The term is used to denote the last decade of the nineteenth century, a transition period when writers and other artists abandoned old conventions and looked for new techniques and objectives.

First Person: See *Point of View*

Flashback: A device used in literature to present action that occurred before the beginning of the story. Flashbacks are often introduced as the dreams or recollections of one or more characters.

Foil: A character in a work of literature whose physical or psychological qualities contrast strongly with, and therefore highlight, the corresponding qualities of another character.

Folklore: Traditions and myths preserved in a culture or group of people. Typically, these are passed on by word of mouth in various forms—such as legends, songs, and proverbs—or preserved in customs and ceremonies. This term was first used by W. J. Thoms in 1846.

Folktale: A story originating in oral tradition. Folktales fall into a variety of categories, including legends, ghost stories, fairy tales, fables, and anecdotes based on historical figures and events.

Foreshadowing: A device used in literature to create expectation or to set up an explanation of later developments.

Form: The pattern or construction of a work which identifies its genre and distinguishes it from other genres.

G

Genre: A category of literary work. In critical theory, genre may refer to both the content of a given work—tragedy, comedy, pastoral—and to its form, such as poetry, novel, or drama.

Gilded Age: A period in American history during the 1870s characterized by political corruption and materialism. A number of important novels of social and political criticism were written during this time.

Gothicism: In literary criticism, works characterized by a taste for the medieval or morbidly attractive. A gothic novel prominently features elements of horror, the supernatural, gloom, and violence: clanking chains, terror, charnel houses, ghosts, medieval castles, and mysteriously slamming doors. The term "gothic novel" is also applied to novels that lack elements of the traditional Gothic setting but that create a similar atmosphere of terror or dread.

Grotesque: In literary criticism, the subject matter of a work or a style of expression characterized by exaggeration, deformity, freakishness, and disorder. The grotesque often includes an element of comic absurdity.

H

Harlem Renaissance: The Harlem Renaissance of the 1920s is generally considered the first significant movement of black writers and artists in the United States. During this period, new and established black writers published more fiction and poetry than ever before, the first influential black literary journals were established, and black authors and artists received their first widespread recognition and serious critical appraisal. Among the major writers associated with this period are Claude McKay, Jean Toomer, Countee Cullen, Langston Hughes, Arna Bontemps, Nella Larsen, and Zora Neale Hurston. Also known as Negro Renaissance and New Negro Movement.

Hero/Heroine: The principal sympathetic character (male or female) in a literary work. Heroes and heroines typically exhibit admirable traits: idealism, courage, and integrity, for example.

Holocaust Literature: Literature influenced by or written about the Holocaust of World War II. Such literature includes true stories of survival in concentration camps, escape, and life after the war, as well as fictional works and poetry.

Humanism: A philosophy that places faith in the dignity of humankind and rejects the medieval perception of the individual as a weak, fallen creature. "Humanists" typically believe in the perfectibility of human nature and view reason and education as the means to that end.

Hyperbole: In literary criticism, deliberate exaggeration used to achieve an effect.

I

Idiom: A word construction or verbal expression closely associated with a given language.

Image: A concrete representation of an object or sensory experience. Typically, such a representation helps evoke the feelings associated with the object or experience itself. Images are either "literal" or "figurative." Literal images are especially concrete and involve little or no extension of the obvious meaning of the words used to express them. Figurative images do not follow the literal meaning of the words exactly. Images in literature are usually visual, but the term "image" can also refer to the representation of any sensory experience.

Imagery: The array of images in a literary work. Also, figurative language.

In medias res: A Latin term meaning "in the middle of things." It refers to the technique of beginning a story at its midpoint and then using various flashback devices to reveal previous action.

Interior Monologue: A narrative technique in which characters' thoughts are revealed in a way that appears to be uncontrolled by the author. The interior monologue typically aims to reveal the inner self of a character. It portrays emotional experiences as they occur at both a conscious and unconscious level. Images are often used to represent sensations or emotions.

Irony: In literary criticism, the effect of language in which the intended meaning is the opposite of what is stated.

J

Jargon: Language that is used or understood only by a select group of people. Jargon may refer to terminology used in a certain profession, such as computer jargon, or it may refer to any nonsensical language that is not understood by most people.

L

Leitmotiv: See *Motif*

Literal Language: An author uses literal language when he or she writes without exaggerating or embellishing the subject matter and without any tools of figurative language.

Lost Generation: A term first used by Gertrude Stein to describe the post-World War I generation of American writers: men and women haunted by a sense of betrayal and emptiness brought about by the destructiveness of the war.

M

Mannerism: Exaggerated, artificial adherence to a literary manner or style. Also, a popular style of the visual arts of late sixteenth-century Europe that was marked by elongation of the human form and by intentional spatial distortion. Literary works that are self-consciously high-toned and artistic are often said to be "mannered."

Metaphor: A figure of speech that expresses an idea through the image of another object. Metaphors suggest the essence of the first object by identifying it with certain qualities of the second object.

Modernism: Modern literary practices. Also, the principles of a literary school that lasted from roughly the beginning of the twentieth century until the end of World War II. Modernism is defined by its rejection of the literary conventions of the nineteenth century and by its opposition to conventional morality, taste, traditions, and economic values.

Mood: The prevailing emotions of a work or of the author in his or her creation of the work. The mood of a work is not always what might be expected based on its subject matter.

Motif: A theme, character type, image, metaphor, or other verbal element that recurs throughout a single work of literature or occurs in a number of different works over a period of time. Also known as *Motiv* or *Leitmotiv.*

Myth: An anonymous tale emerging from the traditional beliefs of a culture or social unit. Myths use supernatural explanations for natural phenomena. They may also explain cosmic issues like creation and death. Collections of myths, known as mythologies, are common to all cultures and nations, but the best-known myths belong to the Norse, Roman, and Greek mythologies.

N

Narration: The telling of a series of events, real or invented. A narration may be either a simple narrative, in which the events are recounted chronologically, or a narrative with a plot, in which the account is given in a style reflecting the author's artistic concept of the story. Narration is sometimes used as a synonym for "storyline."

Narrative: A verse or prose accounting of an event or sequence of events, real or invented. The term is also used as an adjective in the sense "method of narration." For example, in literary criticism, the expression "narrative technique" usually refers to the way the author structures and presents his or her story.

Narrator: The teller of a story. The narrator may be the author or a character in the story through whom the author speaks.

Naturalism: A literary movement of the late nineteenth and early twentieth centuries. The movement's major theorist, French novelist Emile Zola, envisioned a type of fiction that would examine human life with the objectivity of scientific inquiry. The Naturalists typically viewed human beings as either the products of "biological determinism," ruled by hereditary instincts and engaged in an endless struggle for survival, or as the products of "socioeconomic determinism," ruled by social and economic forces beyond their control. In their works, the Naturalists generally ignored the highest levels of society and focused on degradation: poverty, alcoholism, prostitution, insanity, and disease.

Noble Savage: The idea that primitive man is noble and good but becomes evil and corrupted as he becomes civilized. The concept of the noble savage originated in the Renaissance period but is more closely identified with such later writers as

Jean-Jacques Rousseau and Aphra Behn. See also Primitivism.

Novel of Ideas: A novel in which the examination of intellectual issues and concepts takes precedence over characterization or a traditional storyline.

Novel of Manners: A novel that examines the customs and mores of a cultural group.

Novel: A long fictional narrative written in prose, which developed from the novella and other early forms of narrative. A novel is usually organized under a plot or theme with a focus on character development and action.

Novella: An Italian term meaning "story." This term has been especially used to describe fourteenth-century Italian tales, but it also refers to modern short novels.

O

Objective Correlative: An outward set of objects, a situation, or a chain of events corresponding to an inward experience and evoking this experience in the reader. The term frequently appears in modern criticism in discussions of authors' intended effects on the emotional responses of readers.

Objectivity: A quality in writing characterized by the absence of the author's opinion or feeling about the subject matter. Objectivity is an important factor in criticism.

Oedipus Complex: A son's amorous obsession with his mother. The phrase is derived from the story of the ancient Theban hero Oedipus, who unknowingly killed his father and married his mother.

Omniscience: See *Point of View*

Onomatopoeia: The use of words whose sounds express or suggest their meaning. In its simplest sense, onomatopoeia may be represented by words that mimic the sounds they denote such as "hiss" or "meow." At a more subtle level, the pattern and rhythm of sounds and rhymes of a line or poem may be onomatopoeic.

Oxymoron: A phrase combining two contradictory terms. Oxymorons may be intentional or unintentional.

P

Parable: A story intended to teach a moral lesson or answer an ethical question.

Paradox: A statement that appears illogical or contradictory at first, but may actually point to an underlying truth.

Parallelism: A method of comparison of two ideas in which each is developed in the same grammatical structure.

Parody: In literary criticism, this term refers to an imitation of a serious literary work or the signature style of a particular author in a ridiculous manner. A typical parody adopts the style of the original and applies it to an inappropriate subject for humorous effect. Parody is a form of satire and could be considered the literary equivalent of a caricature or cartoon.

Pastoral: A term derived from the Latin word "pastor," meaning shepherd. A pastoral is a literary composition on a rural theme. The conventions of the pastoral were originated by the third-century Greek poet Theocritus, who wrote about the experiences, love affairs, and pastimes of Sicilian shepherds. In a pastoral, characters and language of a courtly nature are often placed in a simple setting. The term pastoral is also used to classify dramas, elegies, and lyrics that exhibit the use of country settings and shepherd characters.

Pen Name: See *Pseudonym*

Persona: A Latin term meaning "mask." *Personae* are the characters in a fictional work of literature. The *persona* generally functions as a mask through which the author tells a story in a voice other than his or her own. A *persona* is usually either a character in a story who acts as a narrator or an "implied author," a voice created by the author to act as the narrator for himself or herself.

Personification: A figure of speech that gives human qualities to abstract ideas, animals, and inanimate objects. Also known as *Prosopopoeia.*

Picaresque Novel: Episodic fiction depicting the adventures of a roguish central character ("picaro" is Spanish for "rogue"). The picaresque hero is commonly a low-born but clever individual who wanders into and out of various affairs of love, danger, and farcical intrigue. These involvements may take place at all social levels and typically present a humorous and wide-ranging satire of a given society.

Plagiarism: Claiming another person's written material as one's own. Plagiarism can take the form of direct, word-for-word copying or the theft of the substance or idea of the work.

Plot: In literary criticism, this term refers to the pattern of events in a narrative or drama. In its simplest sense, the plot guides the author in composing the work and helps the reader follow the work. Typically, plots exhibit causality and unity and have a beginning, a middle, and an end. Sometimes, however, a plot may consist of a series of disconnected events, in which case it is known as an "episodic plot."

Poetic Justice: An outcome in a literary work, not necessarily a poem, in which the good are rewarded and the evil are punished, especially in ways that particularly fit their virtues or crimes.

Poetic License: Distortions of fact and literary convention made by a writer—not always a poet—for the sake of the effect gained. Poetic license is closely related to the concept of "artistic freedom."

Poetics: This term has two closely related meanings. It denotes (1) an aesthetic theory in literary criticism about the essence of poetry or (2) rules prescribing the proper methods, content, style, or diction of poetry. The term poetics may also refer to theories about literature in general, not just poetry.

Point of View: The narrative perspective from which a literary work is presented to the reader. There are four traditional points of view. The "third person omniscient" gives the reader a "godlike" perspective, unrestricted by time or place, from which to see actions and look into the minds of characters. This allows the author to comment openly on characters and events in the work. The "third person" point of view presents the events of the story from outside of any single character's perception, much like the omniscient point of view, but the reader must understand the action as it takes place and without any special insight into characters' minds or motivations. The "first person" or "personal" point of view relates events as they are perceived by a single character. The main character "tells" the story and may offer opinions about the action and characters which differ from those of the author. Much less common than omniscient, third person, and first person is the "second person" point of view, wherein the author tells the story as if it is happening to the reader.

Polemic: A work in which the author takes a stand on a controversial subject, such as abortion or religion. Such works are often extremely argumentative or provocative.

Pornography: Writing intended to provoke feelings of lust in the reader. Such works are often condemned by critics and teachers, but those which can be shown to have literary value are viewed less harshly.

Post-Aesthetic Movement: An artistic response made by African Americans to the black aesthetic

movement of the 1960s and early '70s. Writers since that time have adopted a somewhat different tone in their work, with less emphasis placed on the disparity between black and white in the United States. In the words of post-aesthetic authors such as Toni Morrison, John Edgar Wideman, and Kristin Hunter, African Americans are portrayed as looking inward for answers to their own questions, rather than always looking to the outside world.

Postmodernism: Writing from the 1960s forward characterized by experimentation and continuing to apply some of the fundamentals of modernism, which included existentialism and alienation. Postmodernists have gone a step further in the rejection of tradition begun with the modernists by also rejecting traditional forms, preferring the anti-novel over the novel and the antihero over the hero.

Primitivism: The belief that primitive peoples were nobler and less flawed than civilized peoples because they had not been subjected to the tainting influence of society. See also Noble Savage.

Prologue: An introductory section of a literary work. It often contains information establishing the situation of the characters or presents information about the setting, time period, or action. In drama, the prologue is spoken by a chorus or by one of the principal characters.

Prose: A literary medium that attempts to mirror the language of everyday speech. It is distinguished from poetry by its use of unmetered, unrhymed language consisting of logically related sentences. Prose is usually grouped into paragraphs that form a cohesive whole such as an essay or a novel.

Prosopopoeia: See *Personification*

Protagonist: The central character of a story who serves as a focus for its themes and incidents and as the principal rationale for its development. The protagonist is sometimes referred to in discussions of modern literature as the hero or antihero.

Protest Fiction: Protest fiction has as its primary purpose the protesting of some social injustice, such as racism or discrimination.

Proverb: A brief, sage saying that expresses a truth about life in a striking manner.

Pseudonym: A name assumed by a writer, most often intended to prevent his or her identification as the author of a work. Two or more authors may work together under one pseudonym, or an author may use a different name for each genre he or she publishes in. Some publishing companies maintain "house pseudonyms," under which any number of authors may write installations in a series. Some authors also choose a pseudonym over their real names the way an actor may use a stage name.

Pun: A play on words that have similar sounds but different meanings.

R

Realism: A nineteenth-century European literary movement that sought to portray familiar characters, situations, and settings in a realistic manner. This was done primarily by using an objective narrative point of view and through the buildup of accurate detail. The standard for success of any realistic work depends on how faithfully it transfers common experience into fictional forms. The realistic method may be altered or extended, as in stream of consciousness writing, to record highly subjective experience.

Repartee: Conversation featuring snappy retorts and witticisms.

Resolution: The portion of a story following the climax, in which the conflict is resolved. See also *Denouement.*

Rhetoric: In literary criticism, this term denotes the art of ethical persuasion. In its strictest sense, rhetoric adheres to various principles developed since classical times for arranging facts and ideas in a clear, persuasive, appealing manner. The term is also used to refer to effective prose in general and theories of or methods for composing effective prose.

Rhetorical Question: A question intended to provoke thought, but not an expressed answer, in the reader. It is most commonly used in oratory and other persuasive genres.

Rising Action: The part of a drama where the plot becomes increasingly complicated. Rising action leads up to the climax, or turning point, of a drama.

Roman a clef: A French phrase meaning "novel with a key." It refers to a narrative in which real persons are portrayed under fictitious names.

Romance: A broad term, usually denoting a narrative with exotic, exaggerated, often idealized characters, scenes, and themes.

Romanticism: This term has two widely accepted meanings. In historical criticism, it refers to a European intellectual and artistic movement of the late eighteenth and early nineteenth centuries that sought greater freedom of personal expression than that allowed by the strict rules of literary form and logic of the eighteenth-century neoclassicists. The Romantics preferred emotional and imaginative ex-

pression to rational analysis. They considered the individual to be at the center of all experience and so placed him or her at the center of their art. The Romantics believed that the creative imagination reveals nobler truths—unique feelings and attitudes—than those that could be discovered by logic or by scientific examination. Both the natural world and the state of childhood were important sources for revelations of "eternal truths." "Romanticism" is also used as a general term to refer to a type of sensibility found in all periods of literary history and usually considered to be in opposition to the principles of classicism. In this sense, Romanticism signifies any work or philosophy in which the exotic or dreamlike figure strongly, or that is devoted to individualistic expression, self-analysis, or a pursuit of a higher realm of knowledge than can be discovered by human reason.

Romantics: See *Romanticism*

S

Satire: A work that uses ridicule, humor, and wit to criticize and provoke change in human nature and institutions. There are two major types of satire: "formal" or "direct" satire speaks directly to the reader or to a character in the work; "indirect" satire relies upon the ridiculous behavior of its characters to make its point. Formal satire is further divided into two manners: the "Horatian," which ridicules gently, and the "Juvenalian," which derides its subjects harshly and bitterly.

Science Fiction: A type of narrative about or based upon real or imagined scientific theories and technology. Science fiction is often peopled with alien creatures and set on other planets or in different dimensions.

Second Person: See *Point of View*

Setting: The time, place, and culture in which the action of a narrative takes place. The elements of setting may include geographic location, characters' physical and mental environments, prevailing cultural attitudes, or the historical time in which the action takes place.

Simile: A comparison, usually using "like" or "as", of two essentially dissimilar things, as in "coffee as cold as ice" or "He sounded like a broken record."

Slang: A type of informal verbal communication that is generally unacceptable for formal writing. Slang words and phrases are often colorful exaggerations used to emphasize the speaker's point; they may also be shortened versions of an often-used word or phrase.

Slave Narrative: Autobiographical accounts of American slave life as told by escaped slaves. These works first appeared during the abolition movement of the 1830s through the 1850s.

Socialist Realism: The Socialist Realism school of literary theory was proposed by Maxim Gorky and established as a dogma by the first Soviet Congress of Writers. It demanded adherence to a communist worldview in works of literature. Its doctrines required an objective viewpoint comprehensible to the working classes and themes of social struggle featuring strong proletarian heroes. Also known as Social Realism.

Stereotype: A stereotype was originally the name for a duplication made during the printing process; this led to its modern definition as a person or thing that is (or is assumed to be) the same as all others of its type.

Stream of Consciousness: A narrative technique for rendering the inward experience of a character. This technique is designed to give the impression of an ever-changing series of thoughts, emotions, images, and memories in the spontaneous and seemingly illogical order that they occur in life.

Structure: The form taken by a piece of literature. The structure may be made obvious for ease of understanding, as in nonfiction works, or may obscured for artistic purposes, as in some poetry or seemingly "unstructured" prose.

Sturm und Drang: A German term meaning "storm and stress." It refers to a German literary movement of the 1770s and 1780s that reacted against the order and rationalism of the enlightenment, focusing instead on the intense experience of extraordinary individuals.

Style: A writer's distinctive manner of arranging words to suit his or her ideas and purpose in writing. The unique imprint of the author's personality upon his or her writing, style is the product of an author's way of arranging ideas and his or her use of diction, different sentence structures, rhythm, figures of speech, rhetorical principles, and other elements of composition.

Subjectivity: Writing that expresses the author's personal feelings about his subject, and which may or may not include factual information about the subject.

Subplot: A secondary story in a narrative. A subplot may serve as a motivating or complicating force for the main plot of the work, or it may provide emphasis for, or relief from, the main plot.

Surrealism: A term introduced to criticism by Guillaume Apollinaire and later adopted by Andre Breton. It refers to a French literary and artistic movement founded in the 1920s. The Surrealists sought to express unconscious thoughts and feelings in their works. The best-known technique used for achieving this aim was automatic writing—transcriptions of spontaneous outpourings from the unconscious. The Surrealists proposed to unify the contrary levels of conscious and unconscious, dream and reality, objectivity and subjectivity into a new level of "super-realism."

Suspense: A literary device in which the author maintains the audience's attention through the buildup of events, the outcome of which will soon be revealed.

Symbol: Something that suggests or stands for something else without losing its original identity. In literature, symbols combine their literal meaning with the suggestion of an abstract concept. Literary symbols are of two types: those that carry complex associations of meaning no matter what their contexts, and those that derive their suggestive meaning from their functions in specific literary works.

Symbolism: This term has two widely accepted meanings. In historical criticism, it denotes an early modernist literary movement initiated in France during the nineteenth century that reacted against the prevailing standards of realism. Writers in this movement aimed to evoke, indirectly and symbolically, an order of being beyond the material world of the five senses. Poetic expression of personal emotion figured strongly in the movement, typically by means of a private set of symbols uniquely identifiable with the individual poet. The principal aim of the Symbolists was to express in words the highly complex feelings that grew out of everyday contact with the world. In a broader sense, the term "symbolism" refers to the use of one object to represent another.

T

Tall Tale: A humorous tale told in a straightforward, credible tone but relating absolutely impossible events or feats of the characters. Such tales were commonly told of frontier adventures during the settlement of the west in the United States.

Theme: The main point of a work of literature. The term is used interchangeably with thesis.

Thesis: A thesis is both an essay and the point argued in the essay. Thesis novels and thesis plays share the quality of containing a thesis which is supported through the action of the story.

Third Person: See *Point of View*

Tone: The author's attitude toward his or her audience may be deduced from the tone of the work. A formal tone may create distance or convey politeness, while an informal tone may encourage a friendly, intimate, or intrusive feeling in the reader. The author's attitude toward his or her subject matter may also be deduced from the tone of the words he or she uses in discussing it.

Transcendentalism: An American philosophical and religious movement, based in New England from around 1835 until the Civil War. Transcendentalism was a form of American romanticism that had its roots abroad in the works of Thomas Carlyle, Samuel Coleridge, and Johann Wolfgang von Goethe. The Transcendentalists stressed the importance of intuition and subjective experience in communication with God. They rejected religious dogma and texts in favor of mysticism and scientific naturalism. They pursued truths that lie beyond the "colorless" realms perceived by reason and the senses and were active social reformers in public education, women's rights, and the abolition of slavery.

U

Urban Realism: A branch of realist writing that attempts to accurately reflect the often harsh facts of modern urban existence.

Utopia: A fictional perfect place, such as "paradise" or "heaven."

V

Verisimilitude: Literally, the appearance of truth. In literary criticism, the term refers to aspects of a work of literature that seem true to the reader.

Victorian: Refers broadly to the reign of Queen Victoria of England (1837-1901) and to anything with qualities typical of that era. For example, the qualities of smug narrowmindedness, bourgeois materialism, faith in social progress, and priggish morality are often considered Victorian. This stereotype is contradicted by such dramatic intellectual developments as the theories of Charles Darwin, Karl Marx, and Sigmund Freud (which stirred strong debates in England) and the critical attitudes of serious Victorian writers like Charles Dickens and George Eliot. In literature, the Victorian Period was the great age of the English novel, and the latter part of the era saw the rise of movements such as decadence and symbolism. Also known as Victorian Age and Victorian Period.

W

Weltanschauung: A German term referring to a person's worldview or philosophy.

Weltschmerz: A German term meaning "world pain." It describes a sense of anguish about the nature of existence, usually associated with a melancholy, pessimistic attitude.

Z

Zeitgeist: A German term meaning "spirit of the time." It refers to the moral and intellectual trends of a given era.

Cumulative
Author/Title Index

Cumulative
Nationality/Ethnicity Index

Wiesel, Eliezer
  Night: V4

Mexican

Esquivel, Laura
  Like Water for Chocolate: V5

Native American

Dorris, Michael
  A Yellow Raft in Blue Water: V3
Erdrich, Louise
  Love Medicine: V5
Marmon Silko, Leslie
  Ceremony: V4

Nigerian

Achebe, Chinua
  Things Fall Apart: V3

Norwegian

Rölvaag, O. E.
  Giants in the Earth: V5

Romanian

Wiesel, Eliezer
  Night: V4

Russian

Dostoyevsky, Fyodor
  Crime and Punishment: V3

Solzhenitsyn, Aleksandr
  *One Day in the Life of Ivan
    Denisovich:* V6

South African

Gordimer, Nadine
  July's People: V4
Paton, Alan
  Cry, the Beloved Country: V3

West Indian

Kincaid, Jamaica
  Annie John: V3

Subject/Theme Index

Native Son: 227–231
The Trial: 287–290, 292–293, 295

H

Happiness
Candide: 73
Happiness and Gaiety
*Fried Green Tomatoes at the
Whistle Stop Café:* 87, 92, 95
Kitchen: 150–152
Hatred
1984: 235, 242, 251, 254
Candide: 69, 74
*Fried Green Tomatoes at the
Whistle Stop Café:* 87, 91,
94–95
Native Son: 225–229
*A Portrait of the Artist as a
Young Man:* 274–276
Heaven
The Trial: 287–288, 290
Heritage and Ancestry
Mama Day: 173–174, 179–181,
183–186
Heroism
1984: 252, 254
*The Caine Mutiny: A Novel of
World War II:* 41, 43, 50–51,
62–63
Candide: 73
*A Portrait of the Artist as a
Young Man:* 272–275
The Trial: 292
History
1984: 235, 239, 241
Candide: 66, 75
The Grapes of Wrath: 106,
112–113
Mama Day: 180, 183
Moby-Dick: 192, 199–200
Native Son: 221
The Trial: 288
Honor
*The Caine Mutiny: A Novel of
World War II:* 51, 62
Hope
Candide: 66, 68–69, 72–73,
75–83
The Grapes of Wrath: 110, 113, 116
Human Condition
Candide: 71
Humor
The Accidental Tourist: 8–9
*Alice's Adventures in
Wonderland:* 29–30, 32,
35–37
Candide: 73, 76
*Fried Green Tomatoes at the
Whistle Stop Café:* 85,
92–93,97
*The Hitchhiker's Guide to the
Galaxy:* 132–133, 135–138

I

Identity
*Alice's Adventures in
Wonderland:* 27
Imagery and Symbolism
The Accidental Tourist: 8–9
*The Caine Mutiny: A Novel of
World War II:* 52
The Grapes of Wrath: 106, 112,
114, 116, 118–120
Mama Day: 180–181, 183
Moby-Dick: 190, 192, 197–199,
202
Native Son: 223–224
*A Portrait of the Artist as a
Young Man:* 279
Individual vs. Nature
Moby-Dick: 197
Individual vs. Society
The Grapes of Wrath: 111
Insanity
1984: 251, 253–255
*Alice's Adventures in
Wonderland:* 37
Ireland
*A Portrait of the Artist as a
Young Man:* 273–279
Irony
The Grapes of Wrath: 119–120

J

Justice
The Trial: 288
Justice and Injustice
A Lesson Before Dying: 163

K

Killers and Killing
Candide: 66, 68, 72–74
*Fried Green Tomatoes at the
Whistle Stop Café:* 87, 91, 95
The Grapes of Wrath: 105–106,
112
A Lesson Before Dying: 158
Moby-Dick: 192–193, 199, 201
Native Son: 214–215, 217,
223–224, 226–227, 229–230
The Trial: 283, 289, 291

L

Landscape
Moby-Dick: 208
Language and Meaning
The Trial: 288
Law and Order
1984: 236, 239–242, 251–254
*The Caine Mutiny: A Novel of
World War II:* 43, 47–48, 50,
59–64

*Fried Green Tomatoes at the
Whistle Stop Café:* 86–87,
94–95
The Grapes of Wrath: 105–106,
112, 115
A Lesson Before Dying: 156,
158–159, 163–166, 171
Native Son: 215, 217, 219, 221,
224–231
The Trial: 282–283, 287–291,
293–295
Loneliness
Candide: 80–82
Moby-Dick: 205–208
*A Portrait of the Artist as a
Young Man:* 273
Love and Passion
1984: 235–236, 239–240, 242,
244–245, 247–250
*The Caine Mutiny: A Novel of
World War II:* 47
*Fried Green Tomatoes at the
Whistle Stop Café:* 85, 87, 92,
96, 100–101
Kitchen: 141, 143, 146–147,
152–153
Mama Day: 184–187
Native Son: 226
Lower Class
1984: 235, 239–243, 245,
247–248
*A Portrait of the Artist as a
Young Man:* 275–276
Loyalty
1984: 239–240
*The Caine Mutiny: A Novel of
World War II:* 41, 47
*A Portrait of the Artist as a
Young Man:* 259
Loyalty and Betrayal
1984: 239

M

Magic
*The Caine Mutiny: A Novel of
World War II:* 55
Mama Day: 175, 179, 182–186,
188
Magic Realism
Mama Day: 181
Marriage
The Accidental Tourist: 4, 6
Middle Class
1984: 252, 254
Monarchy
*Alice's Adventures in
Wonderland:* 30
Candide: 75
Money and Economics
1984: 241–243
Candide: 74
The Grapes of Wrath: 103,
110–111, 113–114